Subjects and Sojourners

The publisher and the University of California Press Foundation gratefully acknowledge the generous support of the Constance and William Withey Endowment Fund in History and Music.

Subjects and Sojourners

A HISTORY OF INDOCHINESE IN FRANCE

Charles Keith

UNIVERSITY OF CALIFORNIA PRESS

University of California Press
Oakland, California

© 2024 by Charles Keith

Library of Congress Cataloging-in-Publication Data
Names: Keith, Charles, author.
Title: Subjects and sojourners : a history of Indochinese in France /
    Charles Keith.
Other titles: History of Indochinese in France
Description: [Oakland, California] : University of California Press,
    [2024] | Includes bibliographical references and index.
Identifiers: LCCN 2023022682 (print) | LCCN 2023022683 (ebook) |
    ISBN 9780520396845 (hardcover) | ISBN 9780520396852 (paperback) |
    ISBN 9780520396869 (ebook)
Subjects: LCSH: Indochinese—France—History.
Classification: LCC DC34.5.I54 K45 2024 (print) | LCC DC34.5.I54
    (ebook) | DDC 305.800944—dc23/eng/20230530
LC record available at https://lccn.loc.gov/2023022682
LC ebook record available at https://lccn.loc.gov/2023022683

32 31 30 29 28 27 26 25 24
10 9 8 7 6 5 4 3 2 1

For Helen

Beyond India, towards Europe, the climate changes
One sees only new flowers and curious plants
Thus is one surprised to find, in this land of glacial wind
   and intense cold
Our bamboo growing green and tall

NGUYỄN TRỌNG HIỆP,
"Paris: capital de la France" (1897)

CONTENTS

ILLUSTRATIONS

ACKNOWLEDGMENTS

I am grateful for the access and support I received at the many places where I conducted research for this book. In Vietnam, they include the National Archives Centers I-III, the National Library in Hà Nội, and the General Sciences Library in Hồ Chí Minh City. In France, they include the Archives nationales d'outre-mer in Aix-en-Provence, the Centres des archives diplomatiques in La Courneuve and in Nantes, the Archives nationales, the Archives de la préfecture de police de Paris, the Archives de la chambre de commerce et d'industrie de Marseille-Provence, the Archives départementales de l'Indre, the Archives de la Société des missions étrangères de Paris, and the Bibliothèque nationale.

Many scholars have supported this book with materials, feedback, and encouragement. My deepest thanks to Emmanuelle Affidi, Jennifer Boittin, Pascal Bourdeaux, Karl Britto, Patrick Buck, Bruno Cabanes, Joshua Cole, Alice Conklin, Naomi Davidson, Bradley Davis, Olga Dror, George Dutton, Claire Edington, Kathryn Edwards, Penny Edwards, Julia Emerson, Charles Fawell, Christina Firpo, Elizabeth Foster, Wynn Gadkar-Wilcox, François Gauthier, David Glovsky, Martin Grossheim, François Guillemot, Caroline Herbelin, Alec Holcombe, Eric Jennings, Ben Kiernan, Andy Knight, Anh Sy Huy Le, Lê Nguyên Long, Victor Lieberman, Liêm-Khê Luguern, Shawn McHale, Michael Montesano, Cindy Nguyen, Duy Lap Nguyen, Nguyễn Nguyệt Cầm, Nguyễn Phương Ngọc, Uyen Nguyen, Emmanuel Poisson, Johanna Ransmeier, Brett Reilly, Christophe Robert, Gerard Sasges, Sacha Sher, Leonard Smith, Hue-Tam Ho Tai, Chau Tran, Claire Lien Thi Tran, Nhung Tuyet Tran, George R. Trumbull IV, Jack Yeager, and Peter Zinoman.

Haydon Cherry, Christopher Goscha, and Martina Nguyen read and commented on the entire manuscript. This book is immeasurably better thanks to their insights and advice. I am fortunate to have such brilliant and generous colleagues.

Several individuals and organizations graciously allowed me to reproduce photographs for this book. My thanks to the Archives nationales d'outre-mer, the Archives de la préfecture de police de Paris, the Centre des archives diplomatiques in Nantes, the Chambre de commerce et d'industrie de Marseille-Provence, the Bibliothèque la contemporaine, Philippe Ramona, Hoàng Xuân Mai, Joël Pham, Véronique Baverstock, Brett Reilly (who first discovered many of the precious photographs of Indochinese held in the Paris police archives) and especially François Trieu, whose collection of family photographs was particularly invaluable.

While researching and writing this book, I received financial support from the American Philosophical Society, as well as from Michigan State University's College of Social Science and Asian Studies Center. My thanks to my wonderful colleagues in MSU's Department of History, particularly Leslie Moch and Lewis Siegelbaum, who read much of the manuscript and are much missed in their retirement.

It has again been a pleasure to work with the University of California Press. I am particularly grateful to Enrique Ochoa-Kaup for taking on this book and guiding it so well through development and production.

John Merriman passed away during this book's final stages, and his influence is on every page. As an historian and a human being, he was *hors pair*. I will always miss him.

Clara, Gretchen, and Molly, you have spent much of your childhoods with this book lurking in the background of our family life. You're my three best reasons for having absolutely no regrets that it's finally in our rearview mirror. And Helen, you're my sun in the morning and my moon at night. Thank you for doing all of this with me. This book is for you.

Introduction

"AT 4 PM THE SHIP PULLED in the gangplank and weighed anchor. White handkerchiefs fluttered in the breeze."[1] As Nguyễn Tường Tam stood on Hải Phòng's docks in 1927, awaiting a steamship to France, the aspiring writer may have thought of his life to that point as the early chapters of a colonial *bildungsroman*. Nguyễn Tường Tam was a provincial, born in 1906 in a poor village in Hải Dương province, near enough to the capital city of Hà Nội to know how far away it was. Very bright, he overcame his humble origins and the sudden death of his father (a low-level bureaucrat) to earn a scholarship to Hà Nội's elite Lycée du Protectorat, after which he found work as a clerk in the capital's Bureau of Finance. But the young man was restless. Bored and demeaned by his career like his father had been, Nguyễn Tường Tam quit his job and began writing, drawing, painting, and dabbling in the colony's percolating political life.

In 1927, Nguyễn Tường Tam wrote a short story, "A Dream of Từ Lâm." Its narrator Trần Lưu, stuck in the drudgery of work for the colonial bureaucracy, meets an old friend whose parents' death had led him to abandon his career in law for a life of wandering. "I am now a lonely shadow returning home to visit my parents' tomb," the friend says; "after that, I'll be a wanderer. I'll roam all over the country, traversing the mountains and rivers. I'll no longer have a home. . . . I intend to find work as I mix with people along the way. That will give me the opportunity both to study and to teach and to examine human nature."[2] While his narrator finds Utopia in a small village, Nguyễn Tường Tam himself saw France as his best chance of leaving the *cul de sac* of colonial society. Shortly after his story was published, thanks to a scholarship from the Society for the Encouragement of Western Studies (An

Nam Như Tây Du Học Bảo Trợ Hội), Nguyễn Tường Tam was on his way to the capital of the empire.

In some ways, France was just what he had imagined. He ended up in Montpellier, where he earned a science degree for the marketable qualification and because, as he told a friend, "in underdeveloped nations like ours, science is crucial for the work of social reform."[3] But his passion, like many of his generation, was journalism. He briefly enrolled in journalism school but soon realized that "all the necessary things to learn about it were best studied outside the classroom."[4] He learned everything he could about how journalists worked, how newspapers were organized and printed, and how publishing houses were managed and financed. He inhaled France's newspapers and novels, "pondering their craft and how to incorporate it into and transform Vietnamese literature."[5] He took in plays, concerts, and museums. "He should have studied literature," his brother would later write, "but the most important thing was that he had graduated from the university of French society, he had seen the face of a progressive and democratic civilization, and he now knew what freedom and equality was."[6]

But empire's harsh realities soon intruded on Nguyễn Tường Tam's journey of self-transformation in France. His scholarship covered only half of his expenses, so he was always broke despite periodic infusions of "a little money to buy books, clothing and food"; his wife (left behind) sold areca nuts to help support his mother while he was away.[7] New arrivals from Indochina kept him immersed in colonial goings-on. During his first months in Montpellier, rival Indochinese political activists came to speak: Bùi Quang Chiêu, an advocate of moderate colonial reform, and Nguyễn Thế Truyền, the leader of a French network of more radical anti-colonial activists. By 1930, politics bitterly divided the city's once-staid Indochinese student association, whose members now "opened each others' mail" and "destroyed newspapers or posters that displeased them." Its February 1930 meeting, raw with news of a failed mutiny of Indochinese soldiers in Yên Báy, was "tempestuous and menacing."[8] Three months later, a friend of his was deported for protesting in front of the Elysée Palace.[9] By Nguyễn Tường Tam's return to Indochina in late 1930, he knew very well how porous, even nonexistent, the boundaries between "colony" and "metropole" really were.

As he had before he left, Nguyễn Tường Tam wrote a semi-autobiographical short story after returning to Indochina. The principal literary device of "Going to France" (*Đi Tây*) is "the ironic and, often, absurdist interplay of notions of universal 'civilisation' (*văn minh*) and local 'backwardness' (*lạc hậu*)" that he experienced in France.[10] In France, the narrator Lãng Du often feels genuine liberation from colonial society. People speak to and treat him politely, he dodges his status as a colonial subject when he is mistaken for Chinese or Japanese, he drinks too much in cafés, and he enjoys train rides and weekend jaunts in the countryside. But "Going to France" ultimately mocks the conceit of leaving Indochina behind in France. Shortly after his arrival, Lãng Du (which can be translated as "aimless wandering")[11] is harrassed by "a colonial" on the street and meets a woman whose son is an official in Hà Nội. He spends his days with other "Annamese" preparing recipes from home (using bouillon cubes instead of fish sauce) and scheming how to pay their bills. Letters, telegrams, and newspapers bring news and needed financial lifelines from home. When he moves outside of these networks from what he ironically describes as his "former life," Lãng Du is less a flâneur than a voyeur, his freedom laced with anomie: he rides the metro aimlessly for hours, ogles women, loiters in parks, and eats alone in the university cafeteria (despite never managing to make it to class). At the story's end, Lãng Du and a friend have been deported after being mistaken for "members of a group from X Province who had come to Paris to cause trouble."[12] For Nguyễn Tường Tam and his narrator alike, France—as distant and different as it was—was part of colonial society after all.

Nguyễn Tường Tam wrote "Going to France" in 1935, five years after returning to Indochina. The story's irony and ambivalence are thus inseparable not only from his French sojourn, but also from how it affected his life after his return. "Many people studied in France then came home," his brother wrote, "but few of them with such aspiration and determination. It is no surprise that thereafter, Nguyễn Tường Tam became Nhất Linh."[13] His *nom de plume,* meaning "One Spirit," reveals how France had broadened his professional and literary horizons. His French degree got him a teaching job at Hà Nội's prestigious Thăng Long school. With friends, he formed a publishing house and refashioned a moribund journal on the model of the satirical journals he read in France. The new literary collective, the Self-Reliant Literary Group (Tự Lực Văn Đoàn), published two journals (*Phong Hóa* and *Ngày Nay*) that became among the most important publications of late colonial literary and cultural life. Nguyễn Tường Tam also began pursuing a reformist political program that synthesized "classical French republican values of democracy and freedom with the moderate socialist objectives of decreasing social inequalities and promoting social cohesion through participation in the state."[14] But the same "France" that had broadened his horizons soon shuttered his journals and squashed his reformist campaigns. By the late 1930s, he had "abandoned journalism and reform for political agitation," turning to clandestine anti-colonial activism.[15] Nguyễn Tường Tam's experience of colonialism, in short, was of a series of unpredictable, often countervailing forces that brought him from colony to metropole and back again, and in doing so transformed his education, his literary work, his journalism, his politics, and how he thought about himself and his world.

Subjects and Sojourners is a history of the roughly two hundred thousand people from Indochina who, like Nguyễn Tường Tam, sojourned in France during the colonial era (from the 1850s until the 1950s). People from the region had traveled to France well before colonial rule: Catholic priests and novices, local families of French adventurers, and officials of the region's imperial states. Beginning in the 1860s, French military interventions and land grabs brought diplomatic envoys seeking to stave off or shape the growing ties between their empires and France. After the consolidation of French rule around the turn of the century, Indochinese officials of the colonial and protectorate regimes came for practicums in public administration and economic development, and members of the region's royal families came as human spectacles of the Franco-Indochinese partnership. Thousands of Indochinese came to French secondary schools or universities in search of broader horizons or marketable credentials. Others came for the experience and imprimatur of literary, journalistic, and artistic circles, or as tourists seeking their own kind of colonial exoticism. Sojourners were not just elites. Servants and soldiers came to France as part of the region's first diplomatic embassies. After them came cooks and domestics working for French families; artisans, masons, carpenters, and other laborers at French expositions; and sailors on steamships that linked Europe and Asia. Nearly one hundred and twenty thousand came during the world wars to fight and to work. Political activists from Indochina went to France to pursue their causes and agendas. And as French rule began to collapse, thousands of Indochinese came to France through the networks of the region's new postcolonial states or as refugees of a devastating war of decolonization.

Nearly all Indochinese who went to France returned home, and their time abroad profoundly marked colonial and postcolonial societies in Indochina after their returns. The Indochinese imperial officials who witnessed the economic and cultural dynamism of fin-de-siècle France became influential proponents of Western-style reform after their returns (some in far-reaching reform movements that the French repressed). French educations shaped hundreds of Indochinese intellectuals, many of whom assumed leading roles in the region's professional and scholarly worlds after empire. In France, some Indochinese journalists first learned their vocation, and some artists and writers explored new forms and found markets for their work. Laborers acquired new competencies and found opportunities that transformed their fortunes. Colonial Indochina's major political movements all extended into the metropole; some Indochinese first discovered politics there, and metropolitan political culture influenced—even transformed—the existing political commitments of others. During Indochina's war of decolonization from 1946 until 1954, the region's new postcolonial states extended their political and cultural networks into France as part of their quests for legitimacy and authority. And sojourns in France, finally, shaped Indochinese friendships, relationships, selves, and subjectivities.

Subjects and Sojourners uses Indochina as a case study of the circulation of colonial subjects through what Gary Wilder calls the French imperial nation-state, a "disjointed political form" in which "republicanism, bureaucratic authoritarianism, and colonialism were internal elements of an expanded French state" that was "simultaneously rationalizing and racializing, modernizing and primitivizing, universalizing and particularizing."[16] In French colonies, this produced "novel sociopolitical formations that were irreducibly different from those in the West yet were incontestably modern and inseparable from their European counterparts," in which "subject-citizens confronted the emancipatory and oppressive aspects of both the universalizing and particularizing dimensions of French colonial politics."[17] The French imperial nation-state, Wilder also argues, "generated corresponding networks of social circulation" in which "colonial soldiers, workers, professionals, and subjects were not simple immigrants" but "a social network that facilitated movement *back and forth* between the metropole and its colonies as well as between France's colonial federations."[18] Wilder thus rejects a conceptual topography of the French empire grounded in an "antithesis between metropolitan republicanism (defined by democracy and civil society) and overseas colonialism (defined by tyranny and racism)," arguing instead that "if colonial government must be understood as continuous with the French state, the metropole must also be understood as the very center of an empire of which it and the colonies were integral parts."[19]

Many scholars have explored how the French imperial nation-state's "constitutive contradiction between political universality and particularity" shaped Indochina as a colonial society: what Pierre Brocheux and Daniel

Hémery, in their seminal general history of Indochina, describe as "an ambiguous colonization."[20] But most, Brocheux and Hémery included, confine "colonial society" to Indochina's borders. *Subjects and Sojourners* argues that the extension of the French imperial nation-state into Indochina, in turn, extended Indochina's colonial society into France. Indochinese sojourns in France were both a form of colonial power and one of its most significant unintended effects. They spanned the entire colonial era, and they included the most elite to the most marginal members of colonial society. Moreover, France was by far the most common destination for Indochinese leaving the colony during the colonial era. As such, sojourns in France were a more significant force in the making and remaking of colonial society than those in other places outside of the colony, which were all limited to specific groups of people, in smaller numbers, and for limited periods of time.[21] *Subjects and Sojourners* argues, in short, that Indochinese sojourns in France were not a departure from colonial society, but one of colonial society's core structural features: they are best conceived of and studied as a form of human circulation *within* colonial society, rather than outside of it. It thus echoes Sukanya Banerjee's argument that "the terrain of empire, where the 'nation' itself is in various stages of making, unmaking, and nonmaking," is "a more apt lens for studying beneath, above, and beyond the nation" than either nationalist approaches to the history of Indochina or the transnational and global approaches that have followed them.[22]

Subjects and Sojourners challenges how other discrete but intersecting historiographies approach the sojourns of colonial subjects in metropoles. Historians of Europe have long cast imperial metropoles as, in Antoinette Burton's words, "a site productive not just of imperial policy or attitudes directed outward, but of colonial encounters within." Her rich portrait of three elite Indians in colonial Britain in *At the Heart of Empire* (1998) advances two arguments. First, she argues that "empire was and is not just a phenomenon 'out there' but a fundamental and constitutive part of English culture and national identity at home, where 'the fact of empire was registered not only in political debate . . . but entered the social fabric, the intellectual discourse and the life of the imagination.'" Second, she argues that the "colonial peoples moving through the United Kingdom" made "Britain at home a multiethnic nation and a site of diasporic movement." Her ultimate concern is European society, not colonial society: she evokes but does not explore the influence of her subjects' European sojourns "on regional Indian politics and with it, on 'national' Indian history as well."[23] Historians of France generally follow this approach. Some scholars superficially subsume the histories of colonial subjects in France into the metropole's "colonial culture" of advertising, education, and entertainment: an inadvertent scholarly recapitulation of "native village" exhibits at French colonial expositions.[24] Others, meanwhile, consider colonial-era circulations only as origin points for contemporary French society's postcolonial dimensions and divisions.[25]

In the field of Southeast Asian history, early studies of colonial subjects in metropoles—deeply shaped by that region's nationalist historiographies— conceptually confine "empire" to the colony. For example, Rudolf Mrazek saw the Indonesian revolutionary Tan Malaka's time in the Netherlands as the source of a politically-formative dialectic between "the motherland" and "the outside world."[26] These studies also focus almost exclusively on the political movements that took power after empire. *Leftward Journey* (1989), an early study of Vietnamese student sorjourns in France, betrays its teleology in its title: it casts these sojourns as "a springboard for Vietnamese communists to win a hegemonic position in the movement for Vietnamese national self-determination."[27] Even Benedict Anderson's peripatetic, incandescent *Under Three Flags* (2005), though deeply attuned to imperial networks and transimperial exchanges, remains focused largely on a single iconic political figure.[28] Historians of Southeast Asia have long been interested in the role of human movements in the making of the region (sojourners and migrants from China in particular), and recent studies of the labor circulations of the British Indian Ocean, the "cosmopolitanism" of the region's colonial-era port cities, and the experience of exile and diaspora (among others) are further deepening a portrait of what Takashi Shiraishi called "An Age in Motion."[29] But scholars have still not fully considered how the sojourns of Southeast Asians in colonial-era Europe transformed the region itself. In Michel Espagne's words, "former colonies reappropriate their own histories, but they rarely if ever go so far as to consider the histories of the metropoles of which they were dependent."[30]

Global and transnational histories of colonial subjects in Europe have, at their best, helped explain political projects, like black internationalism or right-wing authoritarian anti-colonialism, that crossed imperial borders.[31] But they have often overemphasized—and at times fetishized—contact and exchange between future citizens of the Global South, despite this being neither specific to European networks of anti-colonial politics nor their most important structural feature. Michael Goebel's *Anti-Imperial Metropolis* (2015), an influential example of the genre, explores interwar Paris as a crucible of exchanges between (in his regrettable framing) "non-Europeans" from around Asia, Africa, and Latin America. In Paris, he argues, "through contact, networks, and connectivity . . . later Third World nationalists dreamed up a post-imperial world order" by "the creation of a common anti-imperialist language" that then "prepared the ground for the posterior simultaneity of decolonization" by imbuing postcolonial nationalisms of the Global South with universalist "assertions of ethno-cultural particularity" and "the claim for citizenship."[32] Like many other global and transnational historians, Goebel has critically weak area knowledge of most of his case studies; he overstates connections and commonalities between discrete political cultures; he inadequately contends with their pluralisms and divisions; and he instrumentalizes a superficial socio-cultural history of migration in service of a political analysis. The flaws of his study, like others like it, stem from a methodology that largely neglects both archival collections outside of Europe as well as sources in "non-European" languages.

Subjects and Sojourners, in contrast to such approaches, is part of an ongoing "respatialization of area studies" that uses "developed competencies such as the linguistic skills, the deep understanding of cultural features as a result of long field-work experience, and the close connection to local academia" to better understand the networks and mobilities that extended colonial societies into other imperial arenas.[33] It holds that the history of Indochinese sojourns in France must be studied first and foremost in the context of Indochina's history itself. This demands a temporality that spans the entire colonial era, and a commitment to looking beyond well-known individuals to consider how sojourns came from and changed all parts of colonial society. Moreover, in rejecting the idea that the metropole was "a self-contained entity that can be considered apart from the imperial nation," it also demands a spatially and temporally rigorous conception of "France."[34] *Subjects and Sojourners* moves beyond the analytical seductions of Paris into the campuses of Montpellier and Aix-en-Provence, the chic vacation spots of the Côte d'Azur, the gritty docks of Marseille and Le Havre, French Algeria, other parts of Europe, and the steamships and port cities that linked France and Indochina to one other. It focuses closely on more explicitly "metropolitan" contexts and transformations that affected Indochinese in France more than in the colony: the fin-de-siècle rise of the republican state and economy; the upheavals and aftermaths of the Great War; the interwar political culture of republicanism and its seething discontents; and occupation and liberation during the Second World War, among others. In sum, *Subjects and Sojourners* seeks to answer—for all of Indochina—Michel Espagne's call for "a Vietnamese history of France."[35]

Subjects and Sojourners employs "Indochinese" as an analytical version of what Gayatri Spivak calls a "strategic essentialism": an ethno-racial category employed not ontologically but tactically.[36] "Indochinese," as Christopher Goscha has shown, became a meaningful identity both because of and beyond the French empire's legal and racial categories, much as "Indian" or "West African" did in other imperial contexts.[37] But my use of this term is emphatically not to claim its primacy over the colonial era's other ethno-racial categories and identities (such as "Cochinchinese," "Annamese," "Tonkinese," "Vietnamese," "Khmer," "Lao," "métis," or other). I use it instead almost grammatically: to explore sojourns that, because they spanned all colonial society, benefit—even demand—being studied together. For example, it helps explore how the "Annamese" emperor Bảo Đại and the "Khmer" king Sisowath both sojourned in France as "monarques Indochinois," or how "Tonkinese," "Cochinchinese," and "Khmer" served in the Great War as "tirailleurs Indochinois." Similarly, despite their many differences, each "Indochinese" whose history this book explores was a "sojourner": "an individual who spends an unspecified period of time in a new, different or unfamiliar environment" for a "moderate length of time . . . with the intention of returning 'home' . . . whose motives are specific and goal-oriented."[38] The genealogy of "sojourner" as an analytical category for specifically Asian forms of circulation, particularly its stress on choice and agency, makes it preferable to "temporary migrants," "circular migrants," or other such concepts in migration studies.[39]

Colonial society's diversity and complexity, however, did not disappear on the steamship journey to France. *Subjects and Sojourners* employs a range of other analytical categories to move beyond the flattening effects of both the status of "colonial subject" and the era's ethno-racial categories and identities. It employs "non-Indochinese" ethno-racial categories when analytically helpful, such as when exploring the presence of "Tonkinese" in student sojourns assumed to have been wholly "Cochinchinese," or when tracing the rise of the region's national toponyms as lived realities. But more importantly, the people who fill the pages of *Subjects and Sojourners* do so as monarchs, imperial officials, students, journalists, writers, actors, painters, musicians, entrepreneurs, sailors, soldiers, domestics, artisans, factory workers, and others. Social categories like these are not only more analytically precise, they also often best reflect how the people explored in this book thought of themselves. As demographically and socially broad as Indochinese sojourns in

France were, they remained deeply uneven in two critical ways: they emerged from and shaped Indochina's Vietnamese regions far more than its Khmer or Lao regions, and they were overwhelmingly male. Those Khmer, Lao, and women who did sojourn in France are part of this book, but their small number means that they inevitably have a smaller place in its pages. Further, except for a small handful of people from powerful families, Indochina's upland communities were not a part of these colonial-era sojourns. Like most forms of colonial power and socio-cultural transformation in Indochina, French sojourns both reflected and reinforced a disparate, differentiated colonial society.

Subjects and Sojourners is in part a synthesis and interpretation of a body of literature on the history of Indochinese in France that has grown steadily in scope and sophistication. It owes much to seminal early studies of Indochinese political movements in France by Daniel Hémery, Thu-Trang Gaspard, Scott McConnell, Đặng Văn Long, and Sacha Sher; to more recent works of social, cultural, and literary history by Mireille Le Van Ho, Liêm-Khê Luguern, Solène Granier, Kimloan Vu-Hill, Giang-Huong Nguyen, and Nguyễn Hữu Sơn; and to a growing body of memoirs and memory projects.[40] However, *Subjects and Sojourners*—the first comprehensive history of Indochinese in France—engages with a much broader range of Vietnamese-language sources than existing studies: these include travelogues (*du ký*), memoirs (*hồi ký*), newspapers (published in France and in Indochina), fiction, and secondary literature. Although I do not read Khmer or Lao, many of the (few) primary sources from those regions of Indochina that are relevant to this book are in French, whether originally or in translation; for a small number of crucial sources in Khmer or Lao, I rely on studies by other scholars. *Subjects and Sojourners* also makes greater use of colonial-era materials in archives in the former Indochina (Vietnam National Archives centers I–III) than do other related studies.

Subjects and Sojourners also draws heavily from a remarkable documentary collection for the study of Indochinese in France essentially untouched by other scholars. The catalogued portions of the archives of the Service de liaison avec les originaires des territoires français d'outre mer (SLOTFOM), the final bureaucratic incarnation of the surveillance apparatus that oversaw colonial subjects in France, contain mostly police documentation on "subversive" incidents, organizations, and movements. Many scholars have used these materials to write the histories of anti-colonial movements. However, section XV of SLOTFOM, still uncatalogued and unexplored at the publication of this book, contains nearly three hundred boxes of biographical dossiers (*dossiers nominatifs*) on Indochinese who sojourned in France between 1916 and 1954. These dossiers, to begin with, organize copies of police documents by person, which makes it easier to trace individual political activities and trajectories. But far more importantly, these dossiers also contain a wealth of more quotidian documentation rarely found in the rest of the SLOTFOM materials: biographical notices, passports, personal letters, employment contracts, records of life events (marriage, divorce, naturalization, death, financial hardship, repatriation, etc.), and others. SLOTFOM XV dossiers also nearly always include the diacritical markings for Vietnamese names (I omit them when they are unknown, or when they are absent in a quoted passage or in the title of a document or publication). SLOTFOM XV thus not only gives more depth and nuance to well-known lives (for example, I found dozens of previously unknown personal letters by and to some of Indochina's most famous figures), it also allows for rare, at times extraordinary glimpses into the lives of ordinary people whose movement through the imperial nation-state's migration bureaucracy produced far deeper archival records of their lives than exist for ordinary people who never left Indochina. Moreover, reflecting the bureaucratic and legal moments and processes that rendered these lives partially visible, SLOTFOM XV contains documentation produced in both colony and metropole, at times outside of both.

SLOTFOM XV is, perhaps, at once the most granular *and* the most global archive for the study of Indochina—it is a true example of what Durba Ghosh calls "a voluminous archive of the margins."[41] Though *Subjects and Sojourners* draws from many sources and archives, SLOTFOM XV's scope and precious anomalies have profoundly shaped its, in Claire Anderson's words, "life-writing approach" that blends episodes (often unknown or understudied) in the lives of well-known figures with "moments of individual lives that reach beyond the extraordinary."[42] But unlike her study of convicts in the Indian Ocean or Haydon Cherry's luminous portrait of six marginal lives in colonial Sài Gòn, *Subjects and Sojourners* is not a collection of what Anderson calls "biographies of colonialism."[43] My desire to write a history of all Indochinese sojourners in France, as well as the fragmentary nature and inescapable "disciplinary intent and partiality" of SLOTFOM XV, ultimately led me away from this approach.[44] But if *Subjects and Sojourners* is a collective biography composed of "ensembles of multiple fragments" (a method Anderson calls "subaltern prosopography"), it is a decidedly ambivalent one; it attempts a portrait of a group in order to illuminate, as much as is possible, the diversity and particularity of the individuals who composed it. In Anderson's words,

Subjects and Sojourners is "most centrally concerned with the articulations between individuals, identities and the contingencies of colonial power, rather than with a search for typicality or representativeness."[45]

Subjects and Sojourners is structured in a manner that hopes to capture both the human arc of Indochinese sojourns in France as well as their evolutions from the era of conquest until decolonization. The first chapter, "To the Docks," which spans the entire colonial era, traces the many political, economic, and social forces that brought Indochinese to a colonial port, waiting for passage to France. The second chapter, "Crossings," reconstructs the weeks-long steamship voyage to France, which augured the unpredictable mix of ruptures from and continuities with colonial society that Indochinese would experience in France. The third chapter, "From Contact to Conquest," explores how diplomatic embassies, exposition delegations, royal tours, students, and political exiles began extending Indochina's colonial society into France before the Great War. The following two chapters show how during the interwar era, regularized and intensified sojourns extended a highly stratified colonial society from Indochina into France. The fourth chapter, "Cultural Sojourners," focuses on students, writers, intellectuals, journalists, artists, and others whose French sojourns reveal how "humans in motion carry culture to and find culture at their journeys' temporary or permanent end."[46] The fifth chapter, "Labor Sojourners," studies Indochinese who came to France to work, both through official state initiatives and new colonial-era economic networks. The sixth chapter, "Daily Life," explores the everyday socio-cultural realms of Indochinese society in France—food and clothing, leisure, relationships, and ties to home. The seventh and eighth chapters ("Political Sojourners from Peace to War," and "Political Sojourners from War to Decolonization") explore how sojourners transformed Indochinese political life in France from a small group of émigré activists into a critical arena of late colonial political movements, and then into a site of postcolonial state-building projects. The ninth chapter, "Returns," returns to Indochina and explores how French sojourns shaped the region both during and after empire. Finally, a brief coda considers the few sojourners who never left, thus becoming the first members of the Indochinese diasporic communities in France that would grow with the ravages of decolonization and war.

ONE

To the Docks

WAITING ON THE DOCKS IN INDOCHINA for a steamship to France, surrounded by porters loading crates, customs officers checking documents, and vendors hustling for one last sale, was—if only for a fleeting moment—to be part of a whole. "When a ship has arrived, especially a ship going to France, the crowds on the docks are like an anthill," wrote Lê Văn Đức in 1923. "Whether French or Vietnamese, Khmer, or Chinese, traveling alone or with their families, all hope for smooth seas and calm winds. A small ensemble sends off two military officers about to board, and the happy sound of their music lets all present forget, for a moment, the bustle and the melancholy of the moment of departure. Gradually, as night falls, people begin to shake hands and wish each other well, and when all is said and done, some return home while others go to their cabins."[1] In their berths, awaiting the ship's whistle and the rumble of its engines, all on board contemplated a future, often months or years in the making, that was about to become real. "Tonight is our last night on our native soil, before we set foot in strange, faraway lands," wrote Phạm Quỳnh in 1922. "Traveling from Hải Phòng to Sài Gòn may mean drifting far from home, but it did not mean leaving the waters of our country; from this point until our return, however, is truly to enter a strange new world. . . . All of us now are moved in our souls by the solicitude of our fellow travelers and by thoughts of our native country and foreign lands."[2] As the ship's horn blew, all on board—alone or with others, missed or forgotten—often left to a final goodbye. "On the docks," wrote Đặng Văn Long, "thousands of people of all ages . . . wave handkerchiefs or shake their arms to say goodbye to those they don't even know."[3]

The unity of the moment, however, belied the complexity of an entire colonial society on the move. "On board," wrote Phan Văn Hùm in 1929, "are

FIGURE 1. The steamship *Athos II* entering Sài Gòn harbor, c. 1906. Source: Philippe Ramona personal collection.

men, women, and children. There are people going to study and to have fun. There are those who have never been, and those who have been many times before." In his first few hours on board, he met an electrical engineer, a clerk, a former teacher "seeking a new path," a wealthy woman tourist, a communist activist recently released from jail, and a gaggle of students. He soon also met the ship's less visible Indochinese passengers—domestics traveling with French families, as well as shiphands who served food, cleaned the decks and cabins, and operated the machines in the ship's infernal underbelly, who unlike most passengers rarely disembarked when the ship docked. One told him that seeing the flower gardens on shore, feeling the wind on his face, and seeing the moon above helped him "forget life for a moment and feel like part of the world."[4] Phan Văn Hùm traveled to France in peacetime, but in wartime tens of thousands of Indochinese soldiers and laborers also waited on the docks, wearing shabby uniforms, surrounded by war materials, and barked at by officers.

This chapter explores the forces that brought people from all parts of Indochina's society to its docks, from the conquest of Cochinchina in the 1850s until the war of decolonization in the 1950s, awaiting a steamship to the heart of the empire. Though people from what would become Indochina had sojourned to France since the seventeenth century, the extension of the

French imperial nation-state into the region—and the economic, cultural, and political transformations that colonial rule set into motion—radically intensified these circulations. During the century of French rule, the imperial nation-state moved Indochinese to and from the metropole as part of its project of political, economic, and cultural control. French officials used royal tours, practicums, and courses of study in France in hopes of cultivating monarchs, literati, and talented youth as partners in colonial rule, and they also sent some of colonial society's most marginal members to France to work or wage war. Colonial rule, however, also created conditions and opportunities for Indochinese to sojourn to France beyond and below the imperial nation-state's structures and authority, seeking everything from a literary vision to a living wage. Just as, in Gary Wilder's words, "republican France was never not an empire," metropolitan France was never not a site of Indochina's colonial society.[5] Nhất Linh's narrator Lãng Du perhaps put it best: "When I landed on French soil and looked around at the scenery," he says, "I didn't see anything strange at all. The vegetation, houses, objects, people: it was as if I had seen them all before in a former life."[6]

FROM CONTACT TO CONQUEST

Seductive origin myths aside, the first people to go to France from what would one day become Indochina were not harbingers of a colonialism to come, but part of networks and communities that linked Europe and Southeast Asia for centuries before the French conquest. They came to the docks through the Catholic Church's global networks, alliances in Southeast Asian imperial politics, or familial and personal relationships. It will probably never be clear who first made the journey. It may have been the two Catholic catechists Mighê Văn Phụng and Diny Lý Thành, whose sojourns Nhung Tuyet Tran has discovered; as seminarians in Siam in 1687, they left Tonkin for France as part of a Jesuit mission appealing for support against rival Catholic orders.[7] Others followed in their footsteps. Some did so simply as part of their religious formations, but others were active agents in the Church's bitter internecine rivalries. In 1781, the Jesuit novices John Thiều and Paul Cuyến left Tonkin with their Italian superior to appeal to Pope Pius VI to limit the influence of Spanish Dominicans and the Société des missions étrangères de Paris in the northern Vietnamese kingdom of Đàng Ngoài. When they arrived in Rome, the Pope told them that authority in the matter rested with the king of Portugal. He denied their request to travel to Lisbon but allowed them to continue their seminary educations in Rome, where they were ordained. When the priests were finally allowed to leave Rome four years later, they were sent not to Lisbon but to Paris, where they arrived in 1785. Surely to their displeasure, the priests were lodged at 128 Rue du Bac, the seat of the Société des missions étrangères de Paris, whose influence they had hoped to challenge when they came to Europe in the first place.[8]

The priests may still have been in Paris, anxiously awaiting permission to leave, when a more famous figure arrived at the nearby palace of Versailles after a journey of nearly two years. Nguyễn Phúc Cảnh was the eldest son of Nguyễn Phúc Ánh, leader of the Nguyễn ruling house in the southern Vietnamese kingdom of Đàng Trong and the future Gia Long emperor. During the 1780s, the Tây Sơn rebellion had brought Đàng Trong to the brink of collapse and forged an unlikely alliance between Nguyễn Phúc Ánh and Pierre Pigneau de Béhaine, the French bishop of Cochinchina, who rallied to the Nguyễn in hopes of securing protection for the Church. In 1785, after failed appeals to the Siamese court and to the Spanish in Manila, Pigneau crossed the Indian Ocean to try his luck with the French governor in Pondicherry and Portuguese officials in Goa. With him was Nguyễn Phúc Cảnh, five years old, whose father had entrusted him to the bishop to signal his commitment to the alliance and to protect his son from the raging civil war. After failing in India, Pigneau set off for France with the little Nguyễn prince to appeal directly to King Louis XVI.[9]

Nguyễn Phúc Ánh won his war. In 1802, as the Gia Long emperor, he ruled over a territory that spanned the former kingdoms of Đàng Trong and Đàng Ngoài. Like many other Asian rulers of the time, Gia Long had European advisers. Jean-Baptiste Chaigneau (Nguyễn Văn Thắng in Vietnamese) and Philippe Vannier (Nguyễn Văn Chấn), had served Gia Long during the Tây Sơn wars, earned powerful positions in his administration, and married into influential Catholic families in the new royal capital of Huế. Chaigneau traveled to France in 1819 to become the first French consul to the Nguyễn empire. When he returned to Huế in 1821 with a proposal for a commercial treaty, he left five of his children in France. The Minh Mạng emperor, who had assumed the throne in Chaigneau's absence, rejected the treaty. With a new political order emerging in Huế, Chaigneau and Vannier chose to leave for France with their wives and some of their children.[10]

The Minh Mạng emperor sent the first formal mission from a Southeast Asian imperial state to France in 1840, after Qing policing of British opium smuggling erupted in a war in the troubled Chinese empire to the north that laid bare growing European interest and influence in Asia. The mission's two envoys, Tôn Thất Thường and Trần Viết Xương, traveled to "the region of the Great West, famous as a hub of commerce" to "thoroughly report on all they had seen and heard in Europe in order to better understand the nature of this distant region."[11] But by the Nguyễn dynasty's next embassy to France in 1863, European imperialism had arrived at its doorstep. In 1858, after fifteen years of French gunboat diplomacy, a Franco-Spanish invasion forced the Tự Đức emperor to cede the southern provinces of Biên Hòa, Gia Định and Định Tường to France in 1862. Over the next thirty years, the Nguyễn dynasty would attempt to counter French Cochinchina's belligerent cabal of naval officers, missionaries, and consular officials by direct diplomacy with officials in the French ministries of colonies and foreign affairs, who were often divided over Asia policy and distracted by other imperial pursuits and domestic political crises. Like Qing diplomats in Europe during the era of the Opium Wars, Nguyễn envoys and ambassadors sent to France "were responsible for a wide range of activities aimed at self-strengthening and minimizing the pernicious effects of foreign encroachment" and "researching, documenting and interpreting the West."[12] They were thus not simple avatars of a looming colonial conquest, but full participants in bilateral, if increasingly asymmetrical, international relations.

The goal of the embassy sent to France by the Tự Đức emperor in 1863, headed by the official Phan Thanh Giản, was to negotiate retrocession of the three lost provinces. Phan Thanh Giản's efforts initially seemed partially successful: in return for an indemnity, port concessions, and a loose protectorate, he secured a promise of retrocession from French officials preoccupied with an ill-fated imperial adventure in Mexico.[13] But French interests in Cochinchina and a growing colonial lobby in Paris ultimately scuttled the agreement and drove the annexation of three more Cochinchinese provinces in 1867. The next Nguyễn embassy to France, a delegation to the 1878 Universal Exposition in Paris, sought retrocession of the now-six provinces under French control. Its lead delegates, Nguyễn Tăng Doãn and Nguyễn Thành Ý, faced steep odds. A disastrous treaty after an 1873 French invasion of Tonkin had spread France's influence in the kingdom, and French official and popular support for imperialism had swelled after the nation's defeat by Prussia in 1870–71. Unlike Phan Thanh Giản had in 1863, the 1878 embassy returned home empty-handed. In 1883, the French Third Republic, now hell-bent on colonial expansion, rescued another adventurist French naval invasion in Tonkin and defeated Nguyễn and Qing armies in a war that resulted in French protectorates over the rest of the Nguyễn empire. Jean de Lanessan, an early governor general of the new "Indochina" (established in 1887), saw Nguyễn delegations to French expositions in 1889 and 1894 as "decisive manifestations of the successful pacification," but Nguyễn delegates saw them as last-ditch efforts to shape protectorate policy.[14] The viceroy of Tonkin (*kinh lược*) Nguyễn Trọng Hiệp sought to use a Nguyễn delegation to the 1889 universal exposition to pitch a plan to keep Annam independent in exchange for direct rule in Tonkin. "In 1886, such a project might have been seductive," wrote de Lanessan, but ambitious visions for the new French protectorate doomed Nguyễn Trọng Hiệp's plan.[15] French officials in Cochinchina forced his replacement with a more pliant official, Miên Triện. Nguyễn Trọng Hiệp, a less risky envoy as armed anti-French resistance waned, would head the next embassy in 1894.

Nguyễn officials also hoped to use embassies and delegations to France to strengthen the dynasty by engaging with Western ideas and techniques. Unlike Minh Mạng had in 1840, Tự Đức did not charge the 1863 embassy to collect technical and economic information. But in 1867, influenced by the admiring portrait of France in the 1863 embassy's official report, Tự Đức dispatched a mission to France to buy books and materials and to hire technical advisers. At its head was Nguyễn Trường Tộ, a Catholic whose missionary education and travels in Hong Kong, Penang, and elsewhere in Asia (some sources claim, with no evidence, that he had also been to France) made him a fervent advocate of reform. During the 1860s, Nguyễn Trường Tộ had submitted a series of petitions to the Nguyễn court calling for religious liberty and a range of Western-style judicial, economic, and fiscal reforms.[16] The leaders of the 1878 embassy were also reformists, thanks in part to their experiences overseas. Nguyễn Tăng Doãn had traveled with Nguyễn Tường Tộ to France in 1867; Nguyễn Thành Ý was the Nguyễn court's first ambassador to French Cochinchina, and he had participated in embassies to Guangzhou and Macao. Like Phạm Phú Thứ's account of the 1863 embassy, the 1878 embassy report (written by its secretary Nguyễn Hữu Thơ, also known as Nguyễn Hữu Cư, who had studied in a Catholic school in France in the 1860s) recommended adopting French ideas and techniques.[17] Nguyễn Trọng Hiệp, the driving force behind the 1889 and 1894 embassies, wrote to the Governor General Paul Doumer in 1899 that "thanks to reading European works translated into Chinese, as well as my trip to Paris," he had "come to understand France's morals and its administrative system. Indochina must imitate Europe."[18] Even after the consolidation of the protectorate, Nguyễn officials would continue to go to France in hopes of strengthening their own imperial state.

Khmer officials also made France a site for their campaigns for monarchical autonomy. Unlike the Nguyễn dynasty, the Khmer monarchy initially welcomed the French protectorate, formalized in a treaty in 1863, to counter the expansionist Nguyễn and Rattanakosin (Siamese) empires on its borders. But in 1884 the Governor of Cochinchina, Charles Thomson, forced the Khmer king Norodom—at gunpoint—to sign a treaty that radically expanded French control over the monarchy's economic and political affairs. This led to a rebellion throughout the kingdom and enflamed rivalries within the Khmer court. Prince Duong Chakr, one of Norodom's preferred sons, supported the revolt and fell afoul of his father. He was arrested in 1891 but escaped and fled to Siam. In 1893, Duong Chakr went to Paris to appeal to the Ministry of Colonies to limit the power of protectorate officials. Seven years later, with the Khmer monarchy further subordinated, Prince Yukanthor—the heir apparent to the throne and once an avid supporter of French influence—did the same. Their failures reflected the commitment of metropolitan officials and the French public to a new colonial project that linked France's Vietnamese, Khmer, and Lao colonies and protectorates into a single political formation: Indochina.

During the era of the French conquest, Nguyễn and Khmer embassies and delegations thus sojourned in France seeking to prevent Indochina from becoming, or to assert their own autonomy within it. But for some in their ranks, sojourns in France birthed or reinforced their commitment to French rule. Pétrus Trương Vĩnh Ký, the most famous of this group, was born in 1837 in Vĩnh Long and educated in Catholic schools: he knew more than ten languages. In 1860, after a recommendation from the bishop of Cochinchina, he became an interpreter for the French navy. Phan Thanh Giản, who knew Trương Vĩnh Ký's father, chose him as the lead interpreter for the 1863 embassy. Its other interpreter was Tôn Thọ Tường, who joined the naval administration in Cochinchina after failing the imperial exams.[19] Nguyễn Hữu Thơ, secretary of the 1878 embassy and author of its report to Tự Đức, had studied in a Catholic seminary in France; after returning, he directed the Service of the Interpreters at the Nguyễn court and served as an interpreter for the 1874 treaty negotiations in Sài Gòn.[20] Trương Minh Ký, an interpreter for the Nguyễn embassy in 1889, had studied with Trương Vĩnh Ký at the Collège des interprètes and at the prestigous Lycée d'Alger. He went to metropolitan

France in 1880, after accompanying some Indochinese students going to study at his Algerian alma mater. Theirs would be the first of many Indochinese sojourns in France that birthed or intensified a commitment to French rule.

When Indochina's delegation to the 1900 universal exposition reached Paris, the new colony's foundations were firmly in place. Its Cochinchinese delegates had studied at French schools before becoming administrators, teachers, or entrepreneurs; French officials chose them "to demonstrate in France how certain Annamites have associated themselves with our action in Indochina."[21] Delegates from Tonkin, Annam, and Cambodia (Laos, where the French presence in 1900 was still nascent, sent no delegates) were officials in the Nguyễn and Khmer imperial states, preserved under the protectorate's system of mixed rule. Their support for France was also unquestionable. Vũ Quang Nhạ and Trần Đình Lượng, both Catholic, had helped lead campaigns against the anti-French resistance in the Red River Delta. Đặng Văn Nhã had requested to go to France "to better grasp the sources of Western strength in cultural, scientific, technical, financial and military domains."[22] Son Diep, the Khmer delegate, had studied with missionaries and at the Collège d'Adran in Sài Gòn before working as a teacher and interpreter and assisting in pacification efforts, credentials that made him a powerful official in Sóc Trăng, a majority-Khmer province in Cochinchina.[23] They were, in short, France's chosen Indochinese partners: the delegation, if formally a diplomatic visit, "had more of the character of a study mission."[24]

Nothing more visibly underscored French control over Indochina than the French sojourns of its ruling monarchs. The first was the Khmer king Sisowath's visit to the colonial exposition in 1906. He firmly believed in the protectorate as a defense against his kingdom's rapacious imperial neighbors, and he wanted to go to France to establish his legitimacy in the eyes of his subjects: "By the visible and warm expressions of consideration he would receive from the representatives of the French Republic, the monarchy would affirm itself as the kingdom's institution that, under the French protectorate, would preserve Cambodia's political continuity." French officials, for their part, saw Sisowath's visit as a chance to perform respect for Khmer institutions in hopes that the Khmer "would more easily accept the reform of traditional structures that prevented the opening of these lands to world commerce if undertaken by local elites."[25] With the Khải Định emperor's visit to the colonial exposition in 1922, the French would accomplish the same symbolic authority over the more restive Nguyễn monarchy that they had achieved with Sisowath in 1906. Khải Định's son Bảo Đại, the last Nguyễn emperor, would spend formative years in France in preparation for a role as a symbol of the colonial partnership. In many ways, it was in France where colonial authority over Indochina's imperial states would reach its zenith.

For early opponents of the emerging colonial project in Indochina, French sojourns were a form of exile. In the 1860s, two of Phan Thanh Giản's sons had joined the resistance in Cochinchina in hopes of redeeming their father's dishonor. The French arrested them in Hà Nội in 1873. "For reasons of public security," wrote the governor of Cochinchina, "it is impossible for me to keep them in Cochinchina, where their presence could cause problems."[26] They were exiled to Toulon in January 1874. In 1888, French forces captured the young Hàm Nghi emperor—the titular, if unwilling, leader of the Cần Vương resistance—and exiled him to Algiers, where he would remain for the rest of his life. Two more emperors, Thành Thái and Duy Tân, father and son, were later exiled to Réunion. And Phan Châu Trinh, the most famous of all Indochinese political exiles in France, arrived in 1911, after his withering public criticisms of the Nguyễn court and the French protectorate earned him a death sentence forestalled only by his liberal French allies' intervention. His forced sojourn reflected the countervailing and often competing new political ideas remaking Indochinese politics: the colonial authoritarianism that sentenced him to death, and the colonial republicanism that shaped his political ideas and spared him execution. In France, he would become a symbol of colonial oppression and a leader in a vibrant French world of an Indochinese political culture wholly remade by colonial rule.

CULTURAL SOJOURNERS

In 1922, Phan Châu Trinh, broke and in poor health, moved from Paris to Marseille to work as a photo retoucher at the colonial exposition. But his prestige was undimmed a decade after his exile, and one day two of Indochina's most famous intellectuals knocked on his door. Phạm Quỳnh and Nguyễn Văn Vĩnh were in France to write laudatory accounts of Khải Định's visit and to tout the administration's reform agenda in speeches and meetings with politicians and journalists. "I see a great opportunity," wrote the governor general about Phạm Quỳnh, "to profit from the trip to France of this native journalist, who enjoys a reputation as the most celebrated Annamite literary figure of his day."[27] Although they dutifully wrote their articles and flattered their interlocutors, they had other motivations for their travels. "Though the official purpose of the trip was to go to the exposition," wrote Phạm Quỳnh, "the real reason was my desire to see France," a place that he still knew as irreducibly "vague and indistinct." Going to France, he felt, was the only way to see its "true face."[28] The men soon tired of their official responsibilities. Helped by the car Nguyễn Văn Vĩnh had bought, they embarked on a dizzying program of museums, libraries, historic sights, theaters, and restaurants spanning Paris's seedy back streets to Aix-en-Provence's chic Cours Mirabeau. Nguyễn Văn Vĩnh even went to Germany, where he bought a printing press and dyes for his newspaper *Trung Bắc Tân Văn*. The men also dabbled in politics. They attended a lecture by a French communist about her trip to the Soviet Union, for which Nguyễn Văn Vĩnh "dressed very simply, a worn felt cap on his head and a red scarf around his neck."[29] More concerning for colonial officials, they enjoyed several meals and festive evenings with Phan Châu Trinh's more radical associates: Phan Văn Trường, Nguyễn Thế Truyền, and Nguyễn Ái Quốc—the recently-adopted nom de guerre of Nguyễn Tất Thành, the future Hồ Chí Minh.[30]

Phạm Quỳnh and Nguyễn Văn Vĩnh's 1922 sojourns underscore how, as Penny Edwards argues, the "dynamic intersection of European and indigenous worldviews" driving cultural change in colonial Indochina became "dislodged from a specifically Southeast Asian location to a broader arena of trends and ideas reaching back and forth into the Métropole."[31] This cultural arena was inseparable from the imperial nation-state's power structures. Especially before the Great War, colonial officials believed that embassies, exposition delegations, administrative practicums, and sanctioned courses of study in France would transform the culture and worldviews of Indochinese elites. Such cultural sojourns reflected what Peter van der Veer calls "the cosmopolitanism of the colonial empire," reflecting a "desire to bring civilization and improvement, a cosmopolitanism with a moral mission"; they were, arguably, a cultural version of France's trans-imperial security and intelligence networks.[32] But as Phạm Quỳnh and Nguyễn Văn Vĩnh's unscripted wanderings and epiphanies in France suggest, even official cultural sojourns could have effects that were far from what colonial officials imagined. And especially in the interwar era, a time of percolating cultural experimentation in Indochina, thousands of Indochinese students, intellectuals, journalists, writers, and artists sojourned in France outside of official initiatives—and often against the wishes of French officials. This made France a site of the "search for multiple syntheses between past and present, native and outsider, East and the West" that characterized the culture of late colonial Indochina.[33]

In the earliest years of the conquest, French officials used diplomatic embassies and exposition delegations from the Nguyễn and Khmer empires to culturally and politically cultivate the elites they were trying to conquer. When the 1863 embassy docked in Marseille, the mayor and departmental prefect "made themselves available to the ambassadors to do the city honor."[34] In Paris, the naval official Gabriel Aubaret led the embassy's visits to factories, monuments, and public institutions. During the 1860s and 1870s, naval officials sent hundreds of Cochinchinese to study in Catholic schools in France in hopes that "after two or three years in the metropole, these young men will acquire sufficient skills to be usefully employed in the colony's public services."[35] In 1873, Trân Văn Của was named the first Indochinese assistant instructor (*répétiteur*) at the École spéciale des langues orientales in Paris (today known as Inalco), which would help train dozens of colonial officials. A French official enthused that Cochinchina's delegates to the colonial exposition in 1906 would "demonstrate in France the support of elite Annamites for our actions in Indochina. The delegates, who must speak French comfortably and correctly, will be tasked with receiving exposition visitors in the Cochinchinese pavilion and providing necessary and interesting information about everything on display."[36]

In 1886, as a faction of Khmer elites attempted to mobilize the population against the French protectorate, the explorer Auguste Pavie and the Governor of Cochinchina Charles Thomson founded the École cambodgienne in Paris, "the first school in France devoted to the education of the colonized ... to give the sons of leading mandarins a grounding in French language, to train auxiliaries devoted to [colonial] policies, and to cultivate Francophile sentiment among influential families."[37] In 1889 it became the École coloniale, meant mostly to train Frenchmen as colonial administrators but with some places reserved for colonial subjects; Etienne Aymonier, the school's first director and a former official in Cambodia, wondered if "given the current situation in Indochina, the presence of these ten children of mandarins give us some useful hostages."[38] From 1905 to 1908, the "Permanent Mission of Indochinese Mandarins" sent dozens of imperial officials from Tonkin, Annam, and Cambodia to France for practicums in administration and industry; its goal was to bring about the same transformations that a generation of French rule had produced in Cochinchinese elites. Pierre Pasquier, then Resident Superior in Annam, hoped that "in judging our institutions, our social life and the economic vitality of our country," its participants "will henceforth be more apt to grasp our reasoning and the finality of our actions.

They could be useful intermediaries between the thought of the popular masses and our guiding ideas."[39] "Apart from ideas they will acquire by listening to conferences or seeing our factories and workshops," another official wrote, "these mandarins will take home from their time in France something other than memories of our power ... their spirits will acquire a breadth of ideas that will make of them useful and devoted collaborators, for they will recognize that our project in Indochina is good, that it is based on what is done in other parts of the world, and that it is beneficent."[40]

But French officials eventually became ambivalent about Indochinese studying overseas. The Permanent Mission was, in fact, an effort to counter the Eastern Study movement (Đông Du) led by the anti-French militant Phan Bội Châu, which in 1905 had begun recruiting Vietnamese to travel to Japan to study and build an anti-colonial movement. In 1908, French officials ended the Permanent Mission after one of its delegates criticized the protectorate in a Parisian newspaper. Few such initiatives still existed after the Great War, when the colonial administration sent Indochinese to France less for cultural formation than as embodiments of colonial cultural goals supposedly already achieved. The 1931 colonial exposition featured dozens of Indochinese dancers, singers, painters, and performers, sent to the Bois de Vincennes to embody France's contributions to Indochina's cultural vitality. Also during the 1930s, a few Indochinese Francophone writers received French literary prizes for works that had helped shape images of the colony in French popular culture. In 1939, three of Indochina's most prominent Francophile intellectuals—Phạm Quỳnh, the novelist Trần Văn Tùng, and the scholar Nguyễn Tiến Lãng—represented the colony at celebrations of the French revolution's sesquicentennial.

But from the beginning of the colonial era, Indochinese cultural sojourns in France went far beyond official initiatives. By the late nineteenth century, some Cochinchinese elites yearned to visit a country that had profoundly shaped them. Đỗ Hữu Phương, the powerful viceroy, rich landowner, and noted gastronome, went to France four times between 1878 and 1894, leading the scholar Trương Minh Ký "to write a satirical poem ... which described Phương sitting in the café de la paix in Paris, chatting with leading colonial personages."[41] Trần Đại Học cited a "desire to see France, which I consider as my true mother country," in his request to serve as a delegate to the 1900 universal exposition.[42] That era also saw the rapid spread in Indochina, especially in the Nguyễn empire, of the so-called "new books" (Tân thư), a body of translation, commentary, and analysis that placed Western and Asian thought in dialogue.[43] Protectorate institutions like the Quốc Học (founded in Huế in 1896) or the École des stagiaires (Trường Hậu bổ, founded in Hà Nội in 1897), established to train imperial officials, became crucial mediums for the diffusion of these ideas. Many Indochinese who went to France for exposition delegations, imperial study missions, and other official initiatives had first studied in these institutions. The fruitful cross-fertilization of ideas and techniques they encountered in their study made them optimistic that studying in France would help them shape the direction of the French protectorate.

Desire for educations in France soon spilled into broader elite milieus in Tonkin and Annam. Đỗ Văn Tâm, a powerful imperial official, was a leading voice for intellectual reform not only within the Nguyễn administration, but in society.[44] In 1907, as governor (*Tổng đốc*) of Hải Dương province, he helped form the Société d'encouragement aux études occidentales (Pháp Học Bảo Trợ Hội), one of many such societies in the colony. The most prominent, the Société d'enseignement mutuel du Tonkin (Hội Trí Tri, founded in 1892) had a broad program of lectures and conferences, as well as courses and publications on scientific and humanistic disciplines. Its five hundred members included not only imperial officials and literati, but also protectorate officials, teachers, lawyers, and businessmen, many of whom now saw Confucian educations as outdated and protectorate schools as inadequate.[45] "In sending our compatriots to France," Đỗ Văn Tâm wrote in 1907, "we hope that they will acquire the qualities of initiative and energy that are often lacking in our students, a result of our overly formalist system. We want them to witness France's prosperity and grandeur, the result of its marvelous industry and important commerce, and for them to turn away from the bureaucratic careers that are the sole path to honor and dignity in Annamite society. We must transport them to another milieu to open their eyes."[46] Hundreds of young elites from Annam and Tonkin studied in France before the Great War. The powerful official Nguyễn Thân embodied the change: he had gone to France in 1902 as an imperial envoy, but in 1909 his four sons went there to study architecture, agriculture, commerce, and chemistry.[47]

Colonial officials soon sought to control growing Indochinese study in France. The Comité Paul Bert was founded in 1907 when the Pháp Học Bảo Trợ Hội requested French help to fund and place their students. The Comité, and the protectorate's program of scholarships (*bourses*), helped French officials choose candidates and keep an eye on their activities in France. The Groupe de l'enseignement indochinois en France, founded in 1908, established further oversight over Indochinese study associations, as well as individual families, now sending students to France. But it was soon clear that no supervision could fully control the unpredictable effects of metropolitan educations. One example of this was Nguyễn Thế Truyền, the son of an imperial official, who in 1911 won a scholarship from the Pháp Học Bảo Trợ Hội to study at the École Parangon outside of Paris, where dozens of colonial subjects studied technical and applied fields. He spent much of the next decade studying in France. By 1922 he had abandoned his advanced studies at the Sorbonne, married a French woman, and become a leading figure in Paris's anti-colonial circles.

By the interwar era, cases like Nguyễn Thế Truyền made French officials ambivalent about Indochinese studying in France. "The question," wrote the governor general in 1923, "is above all a political one, consisting of knowing if the government of Indochina should support or prevent distancing young natives from their natural centers of intellectual formation.... We must protect, in all ways, these young people who risk many dangers in expatriating themselves in a climate so different from their own, in a milieu where they will be exposed to innumerable *temptations*."[48] Some French officials felt that an expanded colonial educational system made overseas study unnecessary. Others saw Indochinese as unprepared for or incapable of success in French schools. Others opposed Indochinese studying "liberal" subjects like history or law in France, which they saw as politically riskier than technical subjects. Above all, officials worried that experiencing French society would leave Indochinese, in the words of the colony's director of public education, "unprepared to live in the social milieu that nature and birth have imposed on him; he will be poorly adapted to the role he must play in the human organism of which he is a part; he will be a *déclassé*, a *déraciné*, or, if one can express it as such, a *déracé*."[49]

But as colonial officials grew leery about study in France, more and more Indochinese wanted nothing but that. Many in the colony's educated classes, steeped in French culture from a young age, saw study in France as an opportunity to leave behind the colony's mediocre institutions and repressive norms. "I came to France not to be educated like everybody else," wrote Nguyễn Văn Sang, "but to immerse myself in important questions.... To become a functionary is the goal of bounded spirits.... In Indochina, I was like a fish in a vase, a bird in a cage; I could do nothing without encountering obstacles. My actions had no effect. It is this that led me to leave for France."[50] Trần Văn Hà wrote that France offered a "true education that has produced the prodigious material development of all of Europe," while education in Indochina "is shallow and functional."[51] "If I am continuing on to France for my studies," wrote Lưu Thực Tự, "it is not in order to parade around the pompous title of bachelier or to find a slave's work in the administration like so many of my compatriots, who think only of riches and honor but never of the misery of our race.... I am studying here to develop my spirit."[52] The many failures and disillusionments of students in France would never fully extinguish such optimism.

But educational sojourns also reflected more ordinary and superficial motivations. Many sought only credentials to help them advance in the growing colonial administration: public works needed engineers, schools needed teachers, hospitals and clinics needed doctors and medical assistants, plantations needed agronomists, and the state bureaucracy needed clerks, secretaries, and interpreters. And for colonial society's nouveaux riches, a French education—like a villa, a car, or a wardrobe of Western suits—signified status. As a French official scoffed, "they want above all for their children to have an education considered more aristocratic than the others.... They want their children to flaunt the family's wealth in the metropole, and to come back if possible with a diploma, but in any case with a varnish, with the manners and reputation of distinguished people."[53] "On the deck of the *Porthos* or the *Aramis*," the critic Đào Đăng Vỹ wrote in 1938, "they were already thinking of a triumphal return, of the elevated posts they would occupy.... They were already dreaming, on the waves of the Indian Ocean, of the luxurious cars, beautiful women, and comfortable villas they would have when they became doctors or lawyers at the court of appeals... dreaming of the immense, unbounded good fortune that would come spontaneously to them at the end of this marvelous voyage."[54]

Political pressure from Cochinchina's landed and professional classes made it easier to study in France in the 1920s, a time when the strength of the Indochinese piaster lowered the cost of school fees paid in the relatively weaker French franc.[55] But the cost remained high even for well-off families, who often sold land or property to finance an education in a French collège or lycée. This could be ruinous, especially when students failed to graduate or frittered away family funds in cafés and dance halls. Nevertheless, the greater affordability and bureaucratic ease of a French education produced a study-abroad boom from Cochinchina in the 1920s, most often for a year or two of pre-baccalauréat studies. The few who came from Annam and Tonkin at this time (almost none came from Cambodia or Laos until the 1940s) more often received a scholarship from the colonial administration or the study associations that continued to spread after the war, like the Association pour la formation intellectuelle et morale des annamites (Hội Khai Trí Tiến Đức, formed in Tonkin in 1919) and the Société d'encouragement aux études occidentales (An Nam Như Tây Du Học Bảo Trợ Hội, formed in Annam in 1925).

The Great Depression's sudden and brutal blow to Cochinchina's landed and professional classes led most of them to abandon the ambition, or frivolity, of a metropolitan education almost overnight. From an annual peak of roughly two thousand in the mid-1920s, the number of Indochinese in France classified as "students" dropped to 524 in 1930–31.[56] But the Depression did not change a long-standing pattern of migration of a small core of Indochinese elites to France's prestigious schools. In the 1930s, as had been true before the war, Indochinese studying in France came roughly equally from Tonkin, Annam, and Cochinchina (again, few came from Cambodia or Laos). But most were now the cream of a colonial educational system that had improved significantly during the interwar era. Many came from L'Université indochinoise in Hà Nội, founded in 1906, which by the 1930s was attracting elites from around Indochina to study administration, medicine, public works, law, agronomy, and the sciences.[57] When they arrived in France, these students were generally well-prepared for their studies at some of the world's best universities. Many would become enormously influential in the region's intellectual and scientific worlds after empire.

Like some students, Indochinese writers and artists who sojourned in France were often profoundly idealistic about a country and culture that had deeply marked their lives and work. In his novel *Rêves d'un campagnard annamite*, Trần Văn Tùng wrote, "this child of the countryside . . . is no longer. He has become a young man, full of worry and anxieties. He has spent long years in the city. He has read many books from France. Life keeps him far from his village, far from his parents, far from his ancestors. Now he contemplates a pilgrimage to the gentle land of France."[58] Although few were so saccharine, many shared Trần Văn Tùng's belief that going to France was to enter a world they valued and desired. Nguyễn Mạnh Tường "dreamed of associating old Europe to the building of young Asia" and he felt "a mission to supply the oriental workshop with Western materials." He described his experiences, memories, and feelings of travel as "stones of France," to be carved out, carried home, and used to build a new culture.[59] In his novel *Les Cahiers intimes de Heou-Tam, étudiant d'Extrême-Orient* (1939), Hoàng Xuân Nhị tells the story of "a shy and solitary walker, a bohemian covered with dust and poverty," yearning to break away from the stultifying weight of family and tradition. "It was after reading Baudelaire's *Voyage*," he wrote, "that I had the idea of also taking a voyage. But instead of seeking, as he did, to discover the perversity of the human race, I hoped to discover a small piece of humanity . . . to glean a few of the flowers that men cultivate . . . the best, the most tender, the freshest, the most exquisite—in order to build a paradise on earth for me alone."[60] Vũ Cao Đàm's trip to exhibit his paintings at the 1931 colonial exposition was the culmination of a lifelong immersion in French art that began under his passionately Francophile father (a scholar and delegate to the 1889 exposition), and continued during his studies at the École des Beaux-Arts de l'Indochine.[61] Nguyễn Ngọc Cương, a leading figure in Indochina's reformed theater (*cải lương*), returned to France often seeking inspiration in the popular songs that he had first heard there as a student.[62]

But also like students, many Indochinese writers and artists who sojourned in France had more mundane reasons for doing so. Many journalists went because French society and politics, and the growing Indochinese community there, warranted direct engagement and reporting. Hoàng Tích Chu and Đỗ Tắt Văn, journalists at *Khai Hóa,* went to France to study journalism and printing in hopes of forming their own newspaper.[63] Diệp Văn Kỳ, the publisher of *Tribune indochinoise,* sent his reporter Trịnh Hưng Ngẫu to France in 1927 to study journalism.[64] Cao Văn Chánh traveled to France in 1929 as correspondent for *Phụ Nữ Tân Văn.*[65] Aspiring journalists also sojourned there. "I assure you and will wager that in ten years, I will be the king of journalism," wrote Nguyễn Văn Sang to a friend in 1928. He tried to start a newspaper in Sài Gòn but failed, so he went to Marseille "to get a broader understanding of journalism than journalists at home."[66] Nguyễn Công Tiểu, the first Indochinese member of the Conseil de recherches scientifiques de l'Indochine, went to France in 1937 for professional congresses and to visit institutions and scholarly societies relevant to his work.[67] And for painters, singers, dancers, artisans and other artists, to exhibit or perform in France could be remunerative. French officials recruited heavily in Indochina's art and artisanal worlds before an exposition, and to recruit top talent they dangled handsome contracts and the chance to perform or sell their work in a lucrative market. Displaying at an exposition also brought visibility in the colonial press for artists and artisans who, like anybody else, had to make a living.

LABOR SOJOURNERS

Sometime early in 1916, a visitor broke the daily routines of the village of Tả Quan in Kiến An province in Tonkin. The visitor, a local official, was a familiar face, but the purpose of his visit was not: France, the "protector" of the Nguyễn empire, was asking for volunteers to help fight a war raging on the other side of the world. Lê Hữu Xứng was one of several men from Tả Quan who, a few weeks later, went to Hải Phòng, underwent medical and physical exams, was assigned to the second battalion, first company of the Tirailleurs Tonkinois, and boarded a ship for France. In 1918, his brother Lê Hữu Thế joined the French merchant marine. When the war ended, Thế stayed in the service but Xứng returned home. But in 1923, perhaps now restless with village life, Xứng took a job with Messageries maritimes, whose steamships had made travel between Asia and Europe routine. In 1932, Thế left the French merchant marine "to provide for his and his family's needs by cultivating the earth." But after six years of grinding poverty, Thế again followed in his brother's footsteps and found work with Messageries maritimes. When the next war began, a generation after leaving Tonkin as young men, the brothers were still sailing the seas between Hải Phòng and Marseille.[68]

Lê Hữu Xứng and Lê Hữu Thế, in Andrew Hardy's words, "were imperial subjects and they were labouring subjects. . . . They made their journeys for work."[69] Much like cultural sojourns in France, labor sojourns reflected the agendas of the imperial nation-state as well as the new networks and horizons that empire brought into being. The imperial nation-state regularly used Indochinese labor in France. The brothers were two of tens of thousands from the colony to fight in French battlefields and work in factories; in peacetime, the imperial nation-state sent Indochinese to France to work at expositions or as agents of intelligence and surveillance services. But when the brothers went to work for Messageries maritimes, they became two of the thousands of Indochinese labor sojourners—white-collar professionals, businesspeople, skilled artisans, ship workers, domestic servants, and others—who went to France outside of the imperial nation-state's official structures, and sometimes even out of its reach. Their sojourns reflected "decisions to migrate that were often collective, familial or individual," even if they "remained embedded in a context that created the opportunities and conditions of their labor."[70]

The primary engine of Indochinese labor sojourns in France was war: about 120,000 came as soldiers or (more often) laborers during the two world wars. In the heady days of 1914, few French officials dreamed that this might be necessary, and many still opposed the use of colonial labor even as trenches lengthened and body counts rose. Many saw Indochinese as an effeminate and physically inferior race, unfit either for combat or for grueling wartime labor. A vocal pro-colonial political lobby led by Ernest Outrey, Cochinchina's delegate in the Chamber of Deputies, also argued that mobilization would hurt Indochina's agricultural and industrial enterprises. Other colonial officials worried that recruitment campaigns might be socially and politically disruptive. French labor unions also opposed the use of colonial labor in the war, which they saw as the latest salvo in their long war with the French state in defense of their rights.[71]

Ultimately, the war's catastrophic turn overwhelmed any opposition. The arguments for mobilization also dovetailed with the politics of Albert Sarraut, Governor General of Indochina from 1911–14 and 1917–19. Sarraut hoped that war service would make productive and loyal colonial subjects. "In calling these indigenous auxiliaries to the honor of defending the flag," he wrote, "France does not accept the 'inferiority' of some races as dogma. It simply notes their delayed evolution and sets out to counteract its effects and accelerate its progress."[72] This was the same logic behind sending Indochinese imperial officials to France a decade before. Many Indochinese elites supported Sarraut in hopes that contributing to the war effort would lead to colonial reform. Even the exiled Phan Châu Trinh, thrown in jail in Paris in 1915 on the spurious charge of inciting Germany to support anti-colonial movements, wrote after his release that Indochinese "must profit from the opportunity presented to them to mix their bodies to those of French people in Europe, to aid France in this circumstance, so that French people of good heart will have reason, for their part, to help our compatriots."[73]

The mobilization began slowly. First came a small number of naturalized Indochinese who answered the French government's call for a general mobilization. Hundreds of lacquer workers, machine operators, and mechanics followed as civil employees of French industrial enterprises. Next came four thousand auxiliaries from the colonial Garde indigène, followed by two thousand reservists and two thousand volunteers. A vast recruitment campaign beginning in late 1915 produced about fifty thousand recruits by the end of 1916, and another twenty thousand by the end of 1917. A final wave of several thousand went in 1918. Recruiters were particularly interested in the small core of skilled workers in factories, arsenals, railways, airfields, shipyards, technical schools, medical services, and (of course) military battalions. But virtually all who went were peasants who had never seen a factory or even a French person, and the war would transform their lives in ways they could never have imagined.[74]

Virtually all of these men were technically "volunteers," and many had real reasons for choosing to go. Indochina's few naturalized French citizens often felt the powerful nationalism that suffused France in 1914. François-Bertrand Can, a captain in the colonial army, volunteered just after the declaration of war; "the time has come," he wrote, "to be a man and to prove that France's métis children in Asia, too often decried, are worthy of being French."[75] Nguyễn Văn Thinh, later the first president of the Republic of Cochinchina, was one of dozens of Indochinese elites already in France (in his case, studying medicine) to volunteer in 1914. Some rank-and-file volunteers were moved by lofty appeals on posters and newsreels in Indochina's village halls, pagodas, schools, and train stations.[76] Contracts could seem attractive; apart from the salary that included room and board, many received a bonus for volunteering, their families received monthly allowances during their service, and they were promised pensions if disabled (which their families would receive if they died).[77] Some saw the war as chance to obtain new skills that could lead to better employment. Some desired the formal grades in the mandarinate they would receive as soldiers. Some were reportedly eager enough to go that they had a healthy person stand in for them in physicals that they risked failing themselves.[78] A few women even beseeched officials to let them volunteer too. "We, a group of Annamite women," read one petition from Hà Đông province, "request to go to France to fulfill our duty alongside our sisters in France, where the mère patrie will know how to make use of us, either in health clinics or in workshops." One traveled from Hưng Yên to Hà Nội to plead her case directly to the mayor.[79]

But many, probably most, "volunteered" reluctantly. Floods, famine, and cholera devastated many parts of Annam and Tonkin in the three years before the war: in these regions, many enlisted to provide desperately needed income, to fulfill a family quota in place in some areas (thereby allowing a primary breadwinner to remain at home), or due to the pressure of zealous local officials who saw robust recruitment as a path to promotion and as a way to get rid of local "undesirables" (even if they were willing to accept bribes from those trying to avoid enlisting). In Cochinchina and Cambodia (there was no recruitment in Laos), better economic conditions and weaker corporate village structures made the recruitment harder. Cambodia's skeletal protectorate administration produced meager results; in Cochinchina, local administrators often resorted to outright coercion to corral unwilling residents for whom the terms of engagement were not nearly as appealing as they were in poorer northern regions. "In some places," reported an official in Cochinchina, "it was a veritable manhunt."[80] More recruits deserted in Cochinchina than in any other region—as many as one in four in early 1916.

The region also saw more protests about recruitment efforts, which a French official attributed to "the liberalism of colonization" making its people "more aware of their rights and to whom they could appeal."[81] Some soldiers in the colonial army even deserted instead of going to France despite severe punishments for doing so.[82]

The empire's contributions to the war effort led Sarraut and his supporters to call for more colonial laborers in postwar France, "almost exclusively for the most poorly paid agricultural and factory work."[83] Labor unions staunchly opposed the idea, but military planners were now more receptive. Not only did the military lack manpower as it faced the daunting challenges of reconstruction and defense, but the war had challenged racial thinking in the army. Some officials believed that an integrated French military would benefit the empire. "The time that Annamite soldiers spend in France," one wrote, "will help realize the fusion of Indochina's races, creating the germ of an Indochinese nationality not yet in existence (like Siam's military realized the Siamese nation) and help reconcile and unify French and indigènes in our splendid Asian colony."[84] Nguyễn Văn Ký, son of an officer in Indochina's army, had entered a school in Sài Gòn for children of military officers at eleven. His father's death in the Great War did not deter him: in 1920, he joined the Tirailleurs annamites, performed well, and was sent to officers' school in Hà Nội, graduating second in his class. The promising young officer was sent to France in 1922.[85] He was one of as many as seven thousand Indochinese soldiers posted in France each year between 1922 and 1933, many from military families.[86]

As the specter of war loomed again, the governor general estimated in 1939 that Indochina could mobilize fifty thousand men.[87] But pressure from colonial industry led to exemptions for some sectors (Quảng Yên's mines, Nam Định's cotton fields, and the rubber provinces of the Mekong Delta), and the governor general refused to send skilled workers.[88] Seven thousand Indochinese soldiers and twenty thousand laborers reached France before the catastrophic defeat of June 1940 ended Indochina's mobilization. Wisps of patriotic enthusiasm still persisted even after a decade of political repression and economic crisis. "We went to France at the time to answer the call of the motherland," remembered one worker.[89] As in the last war, women tried to volunteer: Lê Hoàng Yến enlisted the newspaper *Tiếng Dân* in her own campaign.[90] But few were so enthusiastic. Phạm Duy Khiêm, recently returned from his brilliant studies at Paris's École normale supérieure, shocked Hà Nội's elite circles when he volunteered. "France, which recognizes you as its spiritual son," the governor general wrote, "receives your offering with gratitude and pride."[91] Phạm Duy Khiêm justified his decision to friends by saying "when your neighbor's house is burning you are obliged to bring him a bucket of water whether you like him or not." One, Ngô Đình Nhu, replied, "Our house has been burning for years. Have you brought even one bucket of water?"[92]

Quotas were stricter in 1939 than in the last war: two-thirds of those who went to France as unskilled workers (ouvriers non-spécialisés, or ONS) were conscripted. Nearly 90 percent again came from poor, densely populated Annam and Tonkin (58 percent from Annam).[93] Volunteers again often succumbed to desperate economic circumstances or pressure from village councils and local officials: as in the Great War, "traditional institutions were the armed hand of colonial requisition policies."[94] Tepid official propaganda campaigns and lower wages than in the last war made the mood even grayer. But in Annam and Tonkin, there was again little active resistance. Growing landlessness and high taxes meant harsh conditions in many areas, decades of work in distant plantations and mines had normalized colonial labor migration, and fresh memories of the brutal repression of the uprisings in 1930–31 weighed on thoughts of resistance. Cochinchina was again more restive, and reluctance to enlist was more explicitly political than in the last war. The region had seen widespread mass political action in 1936–37 under the Popular Front, and anti-colonial forces organized dozens of public protests at recruitment events. At one, in front of six hundred people, one man enjoined, "let us take back our democratic liberties—support the Indochinese soldiers who defend Indochina, and oppose sending them overseas!"[95]

But the imperial nation-state did not only bring Indochinese laborers to France during wartime. Perhaps the most visible markers of empire in France were the universal and colonial expositions, which, in Herman Lebovics's words, "unveiled a radiant vision of the colonial empires" in which the "beauty of the display transformed aesthetic appreciation into political ontology: the show became a token of the worth of the colonial effort and of a new grander vision of what it was to be French."[96] As French visitors streamed to expositions for entertainment and a taste of the exotic, Indochinese did so to work. But even as their labor and their very bodies undergirded these colonial spectacles, virtually all Indochinese exposition laborers came voluntarily to France, and at times even competed for work that could bring not only adventure, but also economic and personal enrichment.

The most indispensable and most sought-after exposition workers were woodworkers, stone carvers, painters, and other artisans responsible for building the pavilions and pagodas that recreated far-off Indochina for fairgoers. Many were highly skilled graduates of Indochina's art schools; exposition organizers recruited many of them personally. Exposition organizers also recruited well-known artisans to display their silks, ceramics, metalwork, embroidery, jewelry, lacquered wood, instruments, and paintings in France. Because seeing artisans at work was also part of the show, French officials had to offer compensation that surpassed what they would have earned at home. Artisans also kept the profits from their sales in France, and many welcomed the opportunity to access this lucrative market. To represent a craft or tradition at an exposition could also bring enormous prestige, and sales, in Indochina.[97] Some artisans hoped that working at an exposition might lead to further employment in France, as it did for one lacquer worker and painter at the 1900 exposition who found jobs thereafter in Parisian workshops.[98]

It is harder to speculate about why ordinary exposition workers went to France. Pressure, when it existed, came less from colonial officials than from the intermediaries working for them. Most artists who performed at expositions worked either for professional companies or for Indochina's royal courts. "Native restaurants" at expositions were contracted out to figures like the Sài Gòn hotel owners Frasseto and Sicè, who staffed the "Franco-Annamite restaurant" in Marseille in 1922 with their employees.[99] Most artisans brought assistants from their workshops with them. Although it may have been hard for them to decline to come to France, the experience could be appealing. Indochinese recruited to live and work in "native villages" (with recreated homes, workshops, markets, and temples) signed contracts that paid them some wages up front; provided food, lodging, and clothing in France; the chance to sell their crafts; and (at least at the 1906 exposition) French lessons, "made more interesting by regular strolls in Paris and occasional visits to factories."[100] Indochinese at the 1931 colonial exposition were limited by contract to eight-hour workdays, and actors or dancers had a fixed number of performances and rehearsals. Pay for overtime was 30 percent higher than their hourly wage, and all received a day off a week. Workers received 450 francs a month and artisans 600, about what skilled Indochinese lacquer workers in France earned at that time, and their families at home could receive part of this salary directly.[101] Although the working and living conditions certainly did not always live up to promises, many Indochinese who set off for an exposition were willing, even eager, to go.

In the shadows of official mobilizations for war or colonial spectacles, Indochinese also came to France through their work for private companies or families. As steamship companies like Messageries maritimes and Chargeurs réunis expanded into Asia, they drew laborers from near Indochina's ports, particularly Hải Phòng. As one shiphand recounted in 1936, "there are a hundred or so of us from the same village exercising the profession of ship worker in Marseille." In France, they rented rooms in groups of as many as fifteen to save money; "it often happens," he noted, "that twenty or thirty of us dine together, to better endure the nostalgia for our home."[102] His village was likely in Kiến An or Quảng Yên provinces; this was, a French official noted, where "many of these sailors are from . . . they belong often to a few villages." "They have," he added, "assured themselves of this professional specialty and guard it jealously" by leveraging inside information or personal connections to shipping company agents.[103] Some worked on ships to France for other reasons. Nguyễn Tất Thành, the future Hồ Chí Minh, was a kitchen worker on the *Latouche-Tréville* on his way to France in 1911, and he worked on other ships regularly for years afterwards. And there were dozens, perhaps hundreds of people like Nguyễn Văn Hiện, who in 1931 worked on a ship to pay his way back to Indochina after the Depression wiped out his tuition money and he lost a short-lived job as a chemist's assistant.[104]

Much like work on a steamship, domestic service brought thousands of Indochinese to France. For many French people returning from the colony, to bring an Indochinese cook, nanny, or gardener with them was a way to preserve their colonial social status and racial privileges. In 1929, there were over twelve hundred Indochinese domestics in Paris alone.[105] For domestics themselves, the choice to come to France could reflect satisfaction with the work and even real affection for their employers. The terms could be appealing; employers often offered high wages or salary advances to convince domestics to go, and contracts almost always included food, lodging, and clothing.[106] But just as often, Indochinese desperate for work entered into unfavorable contracts for years of work far from home and family, and they often faced terrible conditions upon arrival that made them perhaps the most isolated and vulnerable of all Indochinese labor sojourners in France.

POLITICAL SOJOURNERS

France was just one of many places outside of the colony where Indochina's modern political movements were imagined and forged. But unlike the more ideologically particular Indochinese political theaters of Japan, south China,

Siam, or the Soviet Union, the Indochinese political world in France encompassed the diverse, often opposed political identities and commitments of an entire colonial society extended into the metropole through the imperial nation-state's administrative, economic, and cultural networks. While undoubtedly shaped by both the particular structural features of metropolitan political life and by sojourners from many other parts of the world, Indochinese political sojourns in France remained less a departure from than an extension of, in Brocheux and Hémery's words, the "contradictory" and "differentiated" political dynamics, "simultaneously revolutionary and conservative," of colonial Indochina's variegated and complex political culture.[107] In France as in the colony, Indochinese, in Wilder's words, "confronted the emancipatory and oppressive aspects of both the universalizing and particularizing dimensions of French colonial politics."[108]

France first became a theater of Indochinese politics during the colonial political crisis of 1907–08, which saw the exile of the Thành Thái emperor, a failed plot to poison a French garrison in the Hà Nội citadel, the brutal repression of an anti-tax uprising in Annam, and the dissolution of the modernist Tonkin Free School. While Phan Châu Trinh languished in jail in Indochina, French officials pressured the Japanese government to expel the exiled anti-French Nguyễn prince Cường Để and his deputy Phan Bội Châu. Phan Bội Châu went to southern China, but Cường Để, after drifting around Asia for years, went to Europe seeking support. In 1913, he dispatched a journalist, Trương Duy Toản, from London to Paris to enlist Phan Châu Trinh's support in his dialogue with French officials. Also in England in 1913, likely as one of Cường Để's partisans, was Nguyễn Tất Thành, who had left for France months after Phan Châu Trinh (perhaps at his urging). After failing to gain admission the École coloniale, he worked on steamships, and perhaps briefly in New York, before going to England. The Great War squelched Cường Để's reformist gambit when the French jailed Phan Châu Trinh and his close collaborator, the Sorbonne-educated lawyer Phan Văn Trường (a French citizen). But the war also radicalized this nascent French network of Indochinese politics, which came to include the brilliant law student Nguyễn An Ninh; they soon turned to the Intercolonial Union, deeply influenced by newly-formed French Communist Party (PCF).

France remained a vibrant site of Indochinese politics in France even after this cluster of Indochinese radicals dissolved. The early 1920s was an optimistic moment in colonial politics, as Governor General Albert Sarraut's agenda of economic and political modernization seemed poised to achieve real reform. Supporters of the Constitutionalists, an influential reformist political party in Cochinchina, soon made France a theater of their activities. Trần Văn Khá came to France in 1911 to work for the Ministry of War, while Dương Văn Giáo came five years later as a war interpreter; in 1919, he began working at the École des langues orientales and studying law at the Sorbonne, writing a thesis about Indochina's contributions to the war. In the early 1920s, these two Constitutionalist activists began organizing events and recruiting supporters among French politicians and journalists. Their ranks grew as hundreds of bourgeois Cochinchinese flowed into French lycées after the war. Bùi Quang Chiêu, the leading Constitutionalist, came to France in 1925. He had been one of the first Indochinese to study there decades before—at the Lycée d'Alger, the École coloniale, and the Institut agronomique—before returning to Indochina for a career as an engineer and a journalist.[109] Now a powerful forced in colonial politics, he came—as Nguyễn officials had a generation before—to urge metropolitan officials to support political reform.

But thanks in no small part to Phan Văn Trường and Nguyễn An Ninh's activities after their returns from France, more radical strains in Indochinese politics percolating in the mid-1920s soon spread to France through the circulation of Indochinese newspapers, epistolary networks, and especially the sojourns of political activists who went to France to act on the deep feelings of frustration, and possibility, awakened in them by colonial political life. "At home," wrote Nguyễn Văn Sang in 1928, "I was like a fish in a vase, a bird in a cage; I could not move without hitting an obstacle. My actions had no effect. This is why I left for France."[110] Many were already politically active, including those expelled from colonial schools during student strikes in 1926–27. Hồ Hữu Tường's dismissal from the Collège de Cần Thơ in 1926 blocked him from study in a colonial school. "But," he later wrote, "I was able to present myself as a candidate for the metropolitan educational exams. The Third Republic's laws left us a small opening, through which we could slide to win our liberty."[111] Other activists who were not expelled went to France anyway: "after that," Trần Văn Giàu wrote of his choice to leave in 1928, "sitting and studying were no longer possible, because the lure of politics outside in society was urging us, the young."[112] Tạ Thu Thâu and Nguyễn Khánh Toàn left for France after losing their teaching positions for political activism; Phan Văn Hùm and Nguyễn An Ninh went after serving time in prison. Ninh's earlier sojourns in France had helped birth his political activism, but after leaving prison in 1927, he sought refuge in France from his political failures. "I am sad to see the sincere and admirable men of our country so miserable," he wrote; "it is to no longer have this spectacle before me that I left Cochinchina. Perhaps I will find forgetting in France."[113] Sojourns extended nearly all interwar Indochinese political networks and movements—reformist, radical, and revolutionary—into France in meaningful and consequential ways.

As the 1945 Vietnamese revolution gave way to a war of decolonization, the French theater of Indochinese politics would intersect with the region's postcolonial states as they extended into France in their search for independence and legitimacy. In December 1944, in the exhilarating aftermath of the liberation from the German occupation, Indochinese activists founded the Délégation générale des Indochinois en France, a fleeting but fertile alliance linking Gaullists, socialists, trade unionists, Stalinists, and Trotskyists. Its makeup reflected the distinctive qualities of a French world of Indochinese politics that had emerged over the previous decades. The doctor Nguyễn Tấn Di Trọng recognized this when he came to Paris in April 1946 as part of a "friendship delegation" from the Democratic Republic of Vietnam (DRV). After witnessing hundreds of fervent "overseas compatriots" (*kiều bào*) who greeted the delegation, he wrote, "we must persuade them, but carefully and without alarming them. . . . Though we are a friendly delegation, we are from outside and must not intervene too hastily in their affairs."[114]

The DRV's friendship delegation was indeed the first step of the revolutionary state's sustained effort to make France a site of communist diplomacy and public relations effort throughout the war. After the inconclusive Fontainebleau Agreement in summer 1946, DRV delegates, citing article 18 that gave "Vietnamese citizens in France . . . the same liberties of opinion, instruction, commerce, circulation, and democratic rights as French citizens," forced French authorities to authorize a DRV delegation in Paris.[115] Until its dissolution in 1949, the delegation would use associations, newspapers, and public events to rally support for the revolutionary regime. And Indochina's noncommunist Vietnamese, Cambodian, and Lao states also extended into France as they emerged during the war. Hundreds of Indochinese would sojourn in France via the structures of these French-aligned postcolonial states: delegations, political or military training initiatives, or diplomatic or intelligence missions. And as cultural and labor sojourns from the region to France revived after the Second World War, so too would France's vibrant Indochinese political milieus, which after 1945 would begin to mobilize in support not only of ideas or movements, but of independent nations.

Some Indochinese sojourns in France, finally, were irreducibly personal. Their traces—often poor fits with the broad categories of sojourns proposed here—underscore the need for what Julia Clancy-Smith has described as "a multisided historical ethnography, with its attention to fleeting facts, ostensibly trivial events, petty detail, the mundane, and experienced."[116] Some Indochinese went to France to sate the same kinds of romantic and exotic desires driving many French going in the opposite direction. "France is sincere, friend to all that is beautiful, sublime, and philosophical, not like England or America, slaves to the material and the frigidly positivist," wrote Bùi Quang Tấn."[117] When war came in 1939, Lê Hữu Thọ "ran to the recruitment bureau of my town, Vinh.... Full of joy, I was already imagining Marseille, Paris, Versailles. I had swum in this marvelous ambiance for a long time thanks to the letters of my brother-in law, a biologist at the Institut Pasteur in Paris.... I was twenty years old, and I was leaving more for an adventure than for war."[118] Many wanted to taste *la vie en rose*. "So, Mới, you're not coming to France," wrote Lý Bình Kiệt to a friend in 1927. "Why not? You see Hùng has left his little darling. Why don't you do like him? . . . In your first letter, you warned me not to drink too deeply of the pleasures I have tasted, but I can tell you now that I have become their apostle."[119] Wanderlust is also perceptible in itineraries like that of Trương Văn Vĩnh, who left a white-collar job with an export firm in Sài Gòn to work on a steamship.[120] Some indulged idealism or adventurism in other ways: French officials encouraged tourism from Indochina to France through official programs, long-term visas and even subventions that sent a small but steady stream of Indochinese tourists to France.[121] This ticked up during expositions, which many in the colonies wanted to see. The 1931 short story "Minh, I Want to See the Exposition in Paris!" opposes a white-collar husband, fretful of his family's finances, to his wanderlusting wife. He loses.[122] Before leaving, many of these bourgeois tourists armed themselves with guidebooks like Lê Văn Đức's 1931 *Cách đi Tây* (How to Go to France), which provided instructions on everything from passports and steamship tickets to finding apartments and tipping cleaning ladies.[123]

Other Indochinese saw France—attainable yet appealingly distant—as a refuge from intractable or intolerable personal circumstances. In 1916, Nguyễn Trọng Lộc volunteered to serve as an interpreter in the war. Despite having two wives and eight children, he stated to French officials that he was unmarried. In April 1919 he married Angèle Trioux; their daughter was born later that year. In 1920, Nguyễn Trọng Lộc was arrested for ignoring his repatriation order but sucessfully appealed on the grounds that his wife and their daughter would suffer. The family moved to Paris, where Nguyễn Trọng Lộc worked as an accountant and his wife in a department store. In 1922, his brother-in-law Nguyễn Văn Vĩnh, in France for the exposition, called on Nguyễn Trọng Lộc and beseeched him to return to his family in Indochina, but to no avail.[124] Nguyen Van Thanh volunteered for the war in 1939 to escape his stern and remote father, whose infidelity he could not stand, and his mother, whose sadness suffused his childhood: he described his choice as "a revolt without a name, a wandering in space, against nothing and nobody, to escape what I knew."[125] Phan Tấn Lựu, raised by an unwilling stepfather, left for France once he had "reached an age to understand certain aspects of life, especially the sadnesses of family life that ceaselessly tormented me."[126] Bùi Thị Trâm and her husband had spent two years in France for his studies; after he left her, she returned to France with their daughter "to give her a more liberal education and to efface the jealousy that plagued her."[127] And some went to France in hopes of rebuilding a lost family. In 1925, Nguyễn Văn Khuê stowed away in the hold of a ship to rejoin his father, who fought in the war and stayed after marrying a French woman.[128] And in 1915, Phan Minh volunteered "to serve France in hopes of obtaining amnesty for his father, a political prisoner at Poulo Condore."[129]

There were, finally, no shortage of banal or sordid motivations. Nguyễn Đào Thành, a cadastral official, fled to France in 1926 to avoid an inquiry into his professional negligence.[130] Phạm Hữu Điệc, an employee of Cambodia's Post, Telephone, and Telegraph administration, was convicted of embezzlement in 1935. With his sentence suspended but his reputation in tatters, he left for a job on a steamship; over the next four years, he would set foot in ports around the world before returning to Indochina as the secretary to the widow of a French peer.[131] And for Phạm Viết Cẩn, the motivation to leave was nothing more than the 10,000 francs he owed to Chettiar moneylenders.[132] Truly, all kinds found their ways to the docks.

TWO

Crossings

AS STEAMSHIPS LEFT INDOCHINA BEHIND, emotions were mixed.
Trần Lý "was filled with joy" as he reached "the open sea, with the evening
wind gently blowing and the sun about to set." "I contemplated the scenery
of the island of Poulo Condore," he continued, "which I found very beautiful.
The sea was calm. I cast my gaze toward the island's hills covered with green,
and the lighthouse throwing its rays upon them. How this calm scene stirred
my innermost thoughts!"[1] "Facing this immense journey, weeks on the sea, a
tiny ripple on the earth," wrote Trần Bá Vinh in 1931, "my thoughts were
everywhere . . . what would I think of what I saw? I have long sought to set
foot on the soil of a civilized nation, and soon I will. Will I be able to benefit
from the experience? Will I be able to describe it to my compatriots?"[2] Bùi
Ái was "overtaken by a strange and undefinable melancholy. It seemed to me
like I was in another world, even if the blue sea and serene sky were still those
of my country."[3] Lê Văn Đức had already been to France once when he left
in 1922. As his ship moved out of Sài Gòn's harbor, he heard the bell of the
Xóm Chiếu church that had greeted him when he last returned home. Filled
with sadness, he prayed to God to protect him during his time abroad.[4]

Nhất Linh satirized such maudlin expressions, widespread in Indochinese
traveler accounts. In "Going to France," when Lãng Du's ship set sail, he
"forgot all about my friends and fixed my eyes on my girlfriend who was
standing there gazing back at me. As the ship moved farther away, she became
smaller and smaller, until she looked no larger than a child, a vase, a cake, and
then completely vanished. When I could no longer see her, I began to feel
hungry."[5] Such insouciance was not limited to satirical fiction. "My heart is
as it always is," wrote Tùng Hương. "I don't feel worried at all, my worries
have gone to a strange and distant place so that I may go live my own life. . . .

All parts of my world are in flux but I don't feel at all unsettled."[6] Others, however, felt neither exhilaration nor nonchalance but profound dread: even adventurous soldiers and war laborers felt shock and despair as they descended into the depths of their steamships for what they knew would be a brutal journey. "The men, tears in their eyes, were swallowed by the ship's immense hold," wrote Lê Hữu Thọ in 1940; "they lay flat like condemned men, awaiting with anguish the moment of departure."[7] "In the hold," wrote Nguyen Van Thanh of his journey in 1940, "we lived from the first day as automatons, sad, without dreams, without purpose, without thought."[8]

This chapter explores the steamship journey from Indochina, which extended colonial society into the metropolitan heart of the imperial nation-state. "The steamship," Benedict Anderson writes, "safe, speedy, and cheap . . . made possible unprecedently massive migrations from state to state, empire to empire, and continent to continent."[9] In Indochina, the steamship followed the gunboat almost seamlessly. Messageries maritimes opened a Sài Gòn office in 1862 just after the peace treaty giving France its first foothold in Cochinchina; its Hải Phòng office opened in 1882, when Henri Rivière's invasion of Hà Nội set off the war that would make French Indochina. A line connecting Sài Gòn and Hải Phòng via Đà Nẵng also opened that year. Chargeurs réunis began its service in Indochina in 1901. Until the advent of commercial air travel in the 1930s, nearly all Indochinese who went to France did so on journeys of three to four weeks (pending itineraries and conditions) on these company's Far Eastern lines between Marseille and Yokohama.[10] The workhorses of these routes—*André Lebon, Athos II, Chantilly, Chenonceaux, D'Artagnan, Paul Lecat, Porthos*—were a familiar part of the landscape of Indochina's port cities.

The steamship journey from Indochina to France was, like the experience of waiting on the docks, only superficially democratic. Much like the myriad emotions evoked by departure, life on board not only mirrored colonial society's diversity and divisions, but the ship's structures, rules, and routines often magnified them. Charles Fawell argues that French steamships, conduits of colonial power, were also "mobile borderlands where social worlds collided and cohabited. . . . A moving environment in which social life, while liminal, carried on after departure and before arrival."[11] The Indochinese who traveled on them knew this very well. "For anyone who wants to understand how class works in society," wrote Cao Văn Chánh, "it is enough to look at the organization of a ship."[12] "Fate is ironic and humans are cruel," wrote Bùi Ái of the *Cap St. Jacques,* "for they often put the insolence of wealth and the darkness of misery in the clearest relief."[13] "Whatever class a passenger is in," wrote Nguyễn Văn Vĩnh, "all are aware of the other classes on board and have their own conceited ways of thinking about them. First-class passengers feel themselves to have far more dignity than those in second class, while those in second class look down on those in third class as their miserly neighbors."[14] The steamships that Indochinese boarded in Sài Gòn, Đà Nẵng, or Hải Phòng might have taken them to the other side of the world, but they did not take them outside of the empire or of the colonial society that had emerged in empire's wake.

A SOCIETY ON BOARD

The first Indochinese embassy to France, sent by the Minh Mạng emperor in 1840, sailed on a Nguyễn naval vessel, but most embassies and envoys in the nineteenth century did so on French ships. Their accounts contain few details about life on board, which fit uncomfortably in formal envoy reports. Conditions were often ruder than those on passenger ships later in the colonial era. In 1863, the three Nguyễn envoys lodged with French officers while their servants and guards slept with the rank-and-file French soldiers below. There were two meals daily: Phạm Phú Thứ and his fellow officials "ate bread, dried meat, butter, and fruit, and drank wine and strong, sweet spirits."[15] Unless the ship was in port, there was little to do to break the monotony but walk around the deck and spend hours staring at the ocean, the birds circling the ship, and the few landmarks they happened to pass by. Phạm Phú Thứ passed the time observing the ship's procedures and routines, paying attention to the division of labor between the ship's personnel and the punishments for carelessness or insubordination. As more Indochinese began going to France in the late nineteenth century, many did so on military or commercial ships hastily adapted for civilian passengers. Conditions could be rough: many on board were French soldiers being repatriated from the military campaigns in Tonkin (some badly wounded, some bedridden with disease, some corpses).

Passenger steamships transformed the journey. First-class berths were the realm of the wealthiest and best-connected Indochinese: tourists, monied students, or high-ranking Indochinese delegates to expositions, nearly always a minority relative to French travelers in the same class (some ships had a few extra-luxurious berths above first class for dignitaries or the very richest). When the landowner and writer Lê Văn Đức went to France in 1922, 7000 francs bought him a first-class berth on the *André Lebon*. This meant a private cabin, "clean and well-equipped," tidied daily by cabin boys, with a fan for hot nights and both hot and cold water. If the weather was pleasant, he could sit in a lounge chair on the first-class deck, reading a book from the well-stocked library. When it rained, he enjoyed the leather armchairs, wood-paneled walls, and oriental carpets of the first-class lounge. As evening fell, he could enjoy a brandy and cigar in the bar and smoking room before a dinner served on fine china. Having already lunched on marinated tuna, a beet and apple salad, gnocchi, Irish stew, roast pork loin, potatoes à la Bretonne, Dutch cheese, pineapple, and wine and coffee on demand, it is hard to imagine him having room for a twelve-course dinner including oxtail soup, veal cutlets from Navarre, artichokes from the Côte d'Azur, Indian rice, Nesselrode pudding, and (of course) more wine and coffee. After dinner, he might dance or (if he was too full) listen to a live orchestra in the *salon de musique* before returning to a freshly-cleaned cabin.[16] Cao Văn Chánh, one of many envious Indochinese on lower decks, saw first class as "very luxurious" (*xa xí lắm*).[17]

In second class, which on the *André Lebon* in 1922 cost 2000 francs less than the 7000 Lê Văn Đức paid, were the well-off but not wildly wealthy—students or tourists with ample but finite resources, *boursiers* of the colonial state, officials or skilled artisans on their way to an exposition, or domestic servants with an unusually generous employer in first class, along with with those French travelers who could not afford first class. The cabins had several beds but some might get lucky and have a room for themselves if the ship wasn't full. The second-class deck and common spaces were less luxurious than in first class—meals, though usually still with table service and linens, were simpler; the musical accompaniment was more often a gramophone or a radio. On many ships, one large and comfortable lounge was a more modest version of the first-class library, bar and smoking room, and salon de musique.

Third and especially (when ships had it) fourth class (2600 and 1350 francs on the *André Lebon* in 1922) were for cash-strapped students, laborers, and the poorest French travelers, which often included soldiers returning from a tour, a rough and scary lot for civilians. On return trips they included repatriated Indochinese who could not afford a ticket home, or at times Indochinese *boursiers* or officials demoted to a lower deck for poor behavior in France; "this downgrading of class," wrote one peeved French official, "will be a clear marker of our dissatisfaction."[18] "While they are ensconced in well-padded chairs and nonchalantly fondle their silver knives and forks, lapping up succulent and savory food," wrote Bùi Ái from third class, "we make do with a tasteless vegetable soup and an eternal lamb ragout a few trips old." He "would have preferred the peelings they throw to the rabbits. Add to that a hunk of stale bread and you have some sense of the lot of passengers in the lowest class. I forgot to mention that we were also allowed a quarter bottle of a rosé that was not even socialist but whose taste was more bitter than any of Kerensky's diatribes."[19] They stood in line for their food, sometimes ate on the deck when there was no dining room, and bussed their own dishes. Some servers held back wine or the better bits of meat for those willing to pay a little more. Apart from a common room with a bar to buy extra food and drink, third- and fourth-class passengers had no leisure spaces except for decks that were always crowded and usually lacked chairs. Bùi Ái noted that ship officials occasionally mobilized these passengers "for a few small chores here and there."[20]

Conditions were similar for third- and fourth-class passengers during the day, but nights reminded all involved why a third-class berth cost twice as much. Third-class cabins could have as many as eight passengers, there were no fans to fight the stifling heat, and they were rarely cleaned. But cabins of any sort were but a dream for fourth-class passengers, who spent their nights where they spent their days—on deck. "Imagine a small space of fifteen square meters or so with many people (men and women) stretched out lazily on planks and you will have an idea of my part of the boat," wrote Bùi Ái. "Next think of a bunch of Annamites lying down in the middle of it, with cigarette ashes and butts and dirt flying in their faces, with gallant little lovers giving each other kicks, then please tell me your honest opinion."[21] Fourth-class passengers used coats as blankets and suitcases as pillows, arms tangled in the straps to deter theft. They washed with salt water from the deck faucets—the same faucets used to clean where they slept, which on Bùi Ái's trip on the *Cap St. Jacques* happened at 4:30 in the morning. The only protection from the rain was a tent stretched nightly over the deck. There were four or five toilets for hundreds of passengers. "Those who emerge from there are never in a position to complain," noted a French observer; "when the cargo arrives in Marseille, they have but one desire, to escape from this Gehenna, to scatter like a bunch of rats escaping from a trap."[22]

Perhaps other than ship workers, discussed in chapter 5, stowaways experienced the most wretched travel conditions during peacetime. If they paid the right trafficker, stowaways could spend the journey dressed as a ship worker, living with them but not working; the luckiest might find themselves in an empty cabin with food squirreled away to them during the night. But most, especially those who bypassed a trafficker's services, spent the journey in the ship's darkest and dirtiest corners—a lifeboat, packed storerooms, behind the machines or, as in Nguyen Van Chu's case, rolled up in a spare tarp—trying to avoid discovery and paying off ship workers who came across them.[23] "During my twenty-nine days of travel," wrote Trần Văn Lâm, "I lived a life more miserable than those of buffalos and pigs in our country. I felt like my flesh and bones would soon be feeding fish in the ocean."[24] Many were caught before they arrived in France—a few were expelled from the ship at nearly every stop. Given the conditions, it may have been a relief.

But even clandestine travel was often better than wartime travel. Almost to a man, Indochinese soldiers and laborers in the world wars remembered journeys to France as uniquely horrible experiences. Most traveled on refashioned cargo ships whose few cabins went to French officers and, if space permitted, their Indochinese interpreter-overseers. The rank and file slept in the hold in cramped stacks of bunks, surrounded by machinery, crates of supplies, and even animals. Coal and oil, human and animal waste, vomit and sweat, all baked in the heat, made the atmosphere suffocating. The food—usually rice with dried fish or stew, served in trough-like vessels that forced ten people to share—was inadequate and often inedible. Pneumonia, bronchitis, dermatoses, lice, beri-beri, and other personal ailments were widespread, as were outbreaks of cholera and meningitis. Lack of medicine and the inability to properly quarantine made things worse. Hundreds of Indochinese soliders and laborers died on wartime journeys to France, their bodies thrown into the sea with a minimum of ceremony. In the Mediterranean, submarine attack was another concern: the worst disaster came on March 1, 1917, when thirty-seven Indochinese were among the over seven hundred who perished when a U-boat torpedoed the steamship *Athos*.[25] An outbreak of illness or threat of attack at times meant lengthy delays in a port, during which most Indochinese were confined to the hold. And French officers meted out severe punishment for small infractions, including weeks of solitary confinement in storerooms: one confined laborer stuck his head out of the storeroom's porthole for a glimpse of Djibouti and was decapitated by the anchor's cable.[26] Some, unable to tolerate the conditions, committed suicide.[27]

Ship workers and passengers alike policed the boundaries between different classes closely, and (in the eyes of lower-class passengers) often maliciously. On the *Amboise* in 1931, third-class passengers protested that the second-class deck was nearly empty while theirs was overcrowded. They asked the captain to grant each class on board access to the deck above their class, to no avail.[28] When Bùi Ái tried to sneak a nap in an empty chair on the third-class deck, some passengers informed the captain, who berated him, in his words, "like a little negro" and forced him back to fourth class. "Woe to those who do not follow the rules!," he wrote, "they will be quickly and brutally expelled from these places after being screamed at, and sometimes kicked."[29] When Trần Văn Thạch went to France in 1927, he bought a third-class ticket but was moved to first class, a happy result of the French military requisitioning the third class for soldiers returning from the colony. "It goes without saying," he wrote, "that this favor—which was a necessity—stopped there. We enjoyed— if one can describe it as such!—the third-class cuisine, and we were told that the first class deck was not . . . ours."[30] During wartime, soldiers and workers were rarely allowed on deck except for periodic salt-water hosings that served as their baths, and they chafed at the luxury enjoyed by French officers and Indochinese interpreters above them. "Up there, they lacked nothing" wrote Nguyen Van Thanh, who pined for their "well-stocked dining tables, fresh water showers, and an infirmary."[31] French officers cultivated strategic alliances with some down below, giving them easier jobs and extra rations in exchange for their efforts to diffuse ill will or tips about troublemakers, with ruinous consequences for relations in the hold. Although there were few episodes of mass resistance or violence on wartime steamships, they were often, in Nguyen Van Thanh's words, "like a munitions factory, threatened by the tiniest spark."[32]

LIFE ON BOARD

During the early days of his journey, Bùi Ái felt overwhelming solitude. "From the moment that the ship's workers lifted the gangplank," he wrote, "I was separate from all friends to whom I could turn in a time of need. My life changed enormously in the blink of an eye, and I seemed to make out through the veil of infinity all sorts of difficulties I would have to overcome. From that point on, I would only be able to count on my own abilities, I would have to make do on my own."[33] The soldier François-Bertrand Can felt it too. "Little by little," he wrote in 1915, "the shores of Annam are erased in the evening mist: there is nothing around me but the infinite sea, and I feel terribly alone."[34] But solitude usually faded quickly. Friends and families often traveled together from Indochina to France, and soldiers and workers in war-

FIGURE 2. Two unidentified Indochinese passengers on the steamship *Normandie,* c. 1940. Source: François Trieu personal collection.

time were often in units with others from their village or formed friendships and alliances in transit camps before departure. And even those who came on board alone soon mixed with others in cabins, decks, and dining rooms, and sought out others whether out of material necessity, affective or sexual attraction, or boredom. In short, all passengers soon became part of the ship's social world one way or another, whether they liked it or not. "While chatting with my traveling companions," wrote Bùi Ái, "I examined them discreetly one after another and tried to 'analyze' their words and gestures, to know and 'catalogue' them. This is, indeed, something one must take on when one is obliged by circumstances to live side to side, for a time, with people one has never met."[35]

Socio-cultural differences between Indochinese passengers, and the ship's many ways of reinforcing them, forged distinct social worlds on board. As Bùi Thanh Vân observed, during the early days of a journey "passengers get to know one another and form small groups as a function of their class and preferred distraction."[36] On upper decks, plentiful space and amenities made socializing far more comfortable than lower down. More privileged Indochinese travelers spent time together singing songs around a piano, playing bridge or whist, or discussing current events after reading the newspapers (picked up for their library at each ship's stop). Meals—relaxed, effortless, and enjoyable—provided regular opportunities to chat. And if they desired solitude, they could find it in their private cabins or the library. Phạm Quỳnh spent hours writing in the *Armand Béhic*'s comfortable first-class salon. Lê Hữu Thọ, who went to France in 1940 as a war interpreter, received permission to sleep in the ship's first-class library, where he curled up and "peacefully reread *Les Misérables, Les Mystères de Paris, Emile, Les Rêveries du promeneur solitaire, Le Comte de Monté Cristo* . . . in short, a studious journey," and a luxurious one compared to the suffering of soldiers and laborers in the hold.[37] Upper decks also hosted live concerts and dances: on his way to France in 1922, Lê Văn Đức attended a benefit for wives and children of sailors that raised 10,000 francs.[38]

Nguyễn Văn Vĩnh was enjoying one such evening in 1922 when he noticed third-class passengers two decks below, gawking up at "the madames with their beautiful clothes and expensive jewelry."[39] Indeed, while bourgeois amenities and conventions shaped social life on the ship's upper decks, very different things did so lower down. Bùi Ái's solitude in fourth class ended when some domestic servants invited him to sit beside them on the deck and share a large French sausage, "rolled in a spiral, as big as a medium cobra, that made my mouth water." It was not quite as good as they had hoped but they did their best to enjoy it, so as "to not overly regret the good things of Annam that we would be going without for a long time yet."[40] Passengers on lower decks found companions not only by sharing food, cigarettes, alcohol, or newspapers, but also to avoid annoyances or dangers. On-board acquaintances protected each other's belongings from theft, walked around the ship at night together for safety, played marathon games of cards, or talked to pass the time. In 1927, a charity ball in first class inspired Trịnh Hưng Ngẫu and some fellow third-class passengers to organize a gathering where guests exchanged travel tips, drank tea, and listened to live music not by an orchestra, but by a talented passenger playing a cheap guitar he had bought in Singapore.[41] At another gathering the following week with some Chinese students, political debate was the order of the day: "Chinese students have done their duty and everywhere now we speak of their nation. What is keeping us from doing our duty?," asked the budding Indochinese radical Tạ Thu Thâu in a fiery speech. The evening was so memorable that the guests took a group photo in Port Said.[42]

While it was unusual for passengers to truly feel that they were on the same boat as those in different classes, there were exceptions. On the *Chantilly* in 1930, "the anniversary of July 14 celebrated on the Mediterranean" was "an occasion for a pleasant gathering among all three classes brightened up with decorations and refreshments."[43] Bùi Thanh Vân attended a more solemn event in 1929 when all classes joined for the funeral of a two-year-old Japanese boy who had died on board.[44] But even when they did not mix, Indochinese sojourners of all backgrounds shared experiences and feelings on board. Perhaps the most ubiquitous was boredom. "If you want to know just how long a day can be," wrote Phạm Quỳnh, "you must spend a month on a ship; the sky above, the sea below, endless days without seeing the shore, every day seeming like a week. The ship sways, the passengers are slow-witted, there's nothing to do, you're tired of reading. . . . Days blend into each other, each like the last, eat and sleep, sleep then eat, anybody who endured this would get sick of it."[45] "We got so bored," wrote Bùi Ái, "that we had to invent things to do to kill the time."[46] Indochinese spent hours staring at the sea for unusual fauna (the thrill of seeing a school of flying fish comes up in many accounts), a glimpse of coastline or islands, or other steamships to wave to. Bùi Ái saw bored passengers ritualistically unpacking and repacking their suitcases, shining shoes that already glistened "like a copper plate in the sun," and plucking out unwanted facial hairs one by one. By the Indian Ocean crossing, he noted, some passengers were so bored that they tied a large hook to a rope and tried fishing for sharks.[47] Seasickness also knew no social boundaries. "At 4:00 a.m. on the fifteenth," wrote Phạm Quỳnh in 1922, "our ship left for Singapore. We hit rough seas after passing Vũng Tàu (Cap Saint Jacques), and I lost a full day to seasickness." Most got used to the ship's movements, but seasickness plagued a few unlucky travelers all the way to France. This included Phạm Quỳnh, who tried various positions and gaits to protect his weak stomach but to no avail. He was bedridden during the rough Indian Ocean crossing. "I had to lie down and any time I sat up I was immediately unsteady," he wrote, "so for days I could not hold a pen to write anything."[48]

The ship's close quarters could lead to unexpected encounters and connections. Vương Văn Mui was on deck one night, "contemplating the moon and singing a little poetry," when a woman approached him. "Because she had been expelled from school for striking," he wrote to a friend, "I thought she must see herself as a patriot, so I started harping on political affairs. That's how I caught her in my trap."[49] Bùi Huy Cường's serialized 1932 story "She and I from France to Home" follows a chance encounter on board a ship as it evolves into flirtation, longing, love, and finally heartbreak, as the two young lovers reach Indochina and are pulled back into family life.[50] The devout Catholic Lê Văn Đức befriended a missionary, and they set up an impromptu altar in the first-class salon to hold mass.[51] Cao Văn Chánh met some Chinese students who shared his anti-imperialism, and they spent the journey talking politics via the age-old medium of brush conversations, but now with a pen (nói chuyện bằng bút).[52] Phan Văn Hùm was less impressed with the Chinese students he met, whom he found loud, rude, and (for the women) immodestly dressed.[53] In Đào Trinh Nhất's fictional travelogue, an Indochinese and a Japanese woman share a cabin and bond over their inferior social status.[54] Finally, privileged and poor alike were thrilled by glimpses of famous figures whom fortune had placed on their ship—political luminaries like Bùi Quang Chiêu, cultural icons like Rabindranath Tagore, or sports stars like the tennis champions Chim and Giao, whom Cao Văn Chánh noticed, trailed by journalists, when he walked onto the *André Lebon*.[55]

Some noted a change in French attitudes and behavior as Indochina faded from view. The most famous passage in Nhất Linh's "Going to France" is when Lãng Du observes:

> The farther the ship sailed from Vietnam and the closer it got to France, my experience was that the more decent people on board were. In the China Sea, they did not want to look in my direction. In the Gulf of Siam, they looked at me with disdain, as though I were a mosquito carrying malaria germs to Europe. When we entered the Indian Ocean, their eyes started to become infected with gentleness and compassion, and they began to recognize that I was a human being with a few brains. Crossing the Mediterranean they suddenly regarded me as someone who was as civilised as them and began to have some respect for me. When I reached France itself, I had the impression that I could bully them.[56]

This was not a unique observation. Bùi Ái also saw Singapore as the "psychological point at which they shift their behavior toward Annamites." Once they reached the English port, French passengers who had barely acknowledged the Indochinese on board suddenly became friendly; on the return trip, however, Singapore was where "they distanced themselves from their yellow companions with whom they had been on good terms until then." He recalled a Cochinchinese student telling him how French and Indochinese often danced and sang together until Singapore, after which all such intimacy summarily ceased.[57] Such experiences carried with them a lesson: that, in Alexander Woodside's words, "the inequities and reciprocal social antagonisms of colonial Vietnam were associated with the idiosyncratic conventions and laws of one specific setting, not with any universal determinisms ... that could never be challenged."[58] For some, witnessing changes in French behavior on board presaged their later experiences of metropolitan France as a meaningful, often radical departure from the colony's profoundly racialized hierarchies and norms.

But for others, persistent invective and mistreatment by French passengers were the first of many reminders that going to France did not mean leaving empire beind. The few Indochinese in first class, who were usually in the minority, were often just ignored. Bùi Thanh Vân was the only Indochinese in first class on his trip to France in 1922 and also on his trip around the world in 1929; "I too have my group," he wrote, "which includes nobody but me."[59] But French passengers were often in the minority on lower decks, and mixed cabins—which steamship companies tried to avoid—could cause problems. In December 1928, French sailors protested sharing berths with "Annamites and Arabs," and convinced the ship's French personnel to strike until their demand for separate housing was met.[60] Verbal abuse and petty assertions of power were common, like when Phan Văn Gia briefly left his deck chair and came back to find it taken by a Frenchman, who refused to return it.[61] In Đào Trinh Nhất's fictional travel account, a French woman rudely *tutoies* the female narrator when asking what she is reading; "a book about French manners" is her response.[62] Such retorts could be risky; when Nguyễn Hiển parried "the unparalleled haughtiness" of a French passenger with a few choice comments of his own, the man (who happened to be a magistrate) telegraphed from Singapore to arrange for Nguyễn Hiển to be arrested in Sài Gòn.[63] The captain of the *Amboise* noted three instances of French passengers beating Indochinese cabin boys during one journey in 1927.[64] In 1926, a domestic servant named Nguyễn Thị Liên wrote the minister of colonies to report that her employer, one Monsieur Beau, had tried to rape her on the way to France. When she resisted, he beat her in front of other passengers, had the crew remove her from her third-class berth, refused to feed her, left her to fend for herself for the rest of the trip, and abandoned her in Marseille.[65] Empire truly did not fade out of sight with Indochina's shoreline.

SEEING THE WORLD

Indochinese did not have to wait weeks to experience life outside of the colony—they only had to disembark in the many ports where their ships stopped before reaching Marseille. Most steamships first stopped in Singapore, which they reached two days after departing from Sài Gòn. Except for some ships that passed through Penang, the next stop was Colombo, about five days later (some ships stopped in Madras and then Pondicherry instead of Colombo). Then there was a week-long haul across the Indian Ocean's rough seas, mercifully ended when the ship docked in Djibouti (some stopped first in Aden, across the mouth of the Red Sea). It took three to four days to cross the Red Sea and pass through the Suez Canal before Port Said. From there it was but a few more days across the Mediterranean to Marseille. Inclement weather, mechanical problems, illnesses requiring quarantine, or the threat of submarine attack in wartime could all lengthen stops at a port, but in normal circumstances the ship rarely docked for more than a day. There were always some who could not disembark—those without proper visas, stowaways, the sick, wartime soldiers and laborers (sometimes given permission), and others. Bùi Ái was stuck on board simply for lack of a reliable person to watch over his luggage, too bulky to take with him during a stroll on shore. Some *had* to get off: in 1929, Hoàng Khải, working as a ship's cook, was smuggling communist documents between Canton and Paris when he learned that the British police might try to arrest him in Colombo. He slipped off the ship, stayed on shore after it left, found work in a Chinese restaurant, and only left his room at night (dressed as a woman). He spent several months hiding there, but he was arrested when he tried to reenter Indochina.[66] But most who got off the ship were simply desperate for a change of scenery and eager for a glimpse of far-off places.

Much like on board, personal circumstances shaped how passengers experienced port cities: the more money they had to spare, the more they could see and do. In Singapore, Nguyễn Văn Vĩnh hired a car to take him to a quiet and secluded stretch of the coast lined with luxurious villas, to escape the ship's close quarters.[67] From Colombo, Indochinese who could afford to often drove to the famous Sri Dalada Maligawa shrine (reputed to house one of the Buddha's teeth) in the city of Kandy, the Royal Botanical Gardens at Peradeniya, or the Sri Pada mountain. "The pagoda's scale and artistry," wrote Đào Trinh Nhất of Sri Dalada Maligawa, "is beyond description. Only those who have seen Angkor can begin to imagine it. The beauty of the Creator is also the beauty of those who built it. It may be that the language of human-kind is lacking, but does this structure not express it all?"[68] Monks traveling with the Khmer king Sisowath in 1906 returned home after their pilgrimage to Sri Dalada Maligawa.[69] After Lê Văn Đức visited Peradeniya and Sri Pada, which some Christians believe was where Adam was expelled from the Garden of Eden, he had lunch at the famous Queen's Hotel before returning to Colombo in a private car.[70] Indochinese were less excited about stops on the other side of the Indian Ocean, which few felt had anything worth seeing: Bùi Thanh Vân wrote of Aden that "an Egyptian cigarette factory is the single thing of interest in the place."[71] Nguyễn Mạnh Tường saw Djibouti as "a flaming hell where nothing grows other than zinc-colored palm trees painted green placed along the streets to give an illusion of the absent greenery."[72]

Most Indochinese could not afford this kind of tourism, but there was still plenty to see and do on shore. In each port, divers (often children) performed tricks off the docks, in hopes of earning a few coins from passengers waiting to disembark. In Singapore, Nguyễn Công Tiểu saw a man dive with a ciga-rette and resurface with it still lit, having retracted it into his mouth while underwater.[73] On the docks, buskers and touts sold souvenirs, postcards, and lottery tickets, and offered rides, guide services, and money changing. In Colombo, Tùng Hương noted that "people here are quick witted, they see how we look, they know we're foreign, they pull us toward shops of all kinds, rickshaw pullers offer to take us around for very cheap, taxi drivers fight over us, but the truth is they're all overcharging us."[74] Tempting local fare beckoned: Chinese noodles in Singapore, curries in Colombo, crayfish in Djibouti, Turkish delight in Port Said. Even a rickshaw or taxi ride was enough to see much of a city. Trịnh Hưng Ngẫu and friends were happy to have splurged on a taxi in Colombo to see "Muslim, Buddhist, and Hindu temples; the market; the Colombo Club; the Oriental Club; the homes of princes and well-off Sinhalese; the native and European quarters; the theat-ers and cinemas."[75] Some ventured into markets for local color or wares to resell elsewhere. Phan Văn Hùm replenished his reading material in Singapore's Chinese bookstores.[76] Many simply strolled about, poking their heads into museums or temples, sitting in parks and gardens, and watching a new city unfold around them.

For most Indochinese, port cities were their first experience of British colonialism, and many compared it favorably to the French variant they knew. Bùi Thanh Vân saw Singapore as "a pearl"; as Cao Văn Chánh noted, "we could see its imposing sights, unlike Saigon."[77] "The buildings, the streets, and the scale of commerce are all far bigger than in our country," wrote Trần Bá Vinh; he praised the British choice to make Singapore free from any import duties, unlike protectionist Indochina.[78] He noted Singapore's many cars, which made the city hazardous to explore on foot. Penang, for Lê Văn Đức, was "as bustling and pleasant as any large city in any colony, with broad and clean streets."[79] In Colombo, Bùi Thanh Vân marveled at the architecture of the Post and Telegraph building, which allowed it to operate largely without electric light (he compared it to Sài Gòn's, where hallways and kiosks were so dank that employees wore sweaters despite the heat outside).[80] Trần Bá Vinh was also impressed with Colombo. "The British have paid close attention to the city's economic development," he noted; "there are trains to the furthest parts of the island's rural areas, and many schools." "The results of British colonial policy," he wrote, "have reached great heights."[81] The Suez Canal left François-Bertrand Can with an indelible memory. "From the outset," he wrote," it was as if we were crossing into a fortress. High sand banks had been transformed into ramparts covered with artillery. In the infinite plains were long rows of gray tents housing a multitude of English and Arab soldiers milling about. An unusual activity now animates this dreary and desolate place."[82] Others, however, saw in British ports familiar and borderless forms of oppression. One traveler crossed from Singapore into Johor, which exposed "the real situation of the natives" in British Malaya, a sight that "filled him with pity. Barely dressed, they work in plantations edging the road, hatless under a brutal sun. In all colonies, misery is the lot of the natives."[83] Two of Cao Văn Chánh's companions risked a short anti-colonial speech outside a restaurant just before getting back on board in Singapore, applauded by some Indochinese, Chinese, Indians, and Europeans who had stopped to listen.[84]

Indochinese observations of the people in port cities reflect a blend of exoticism and racism common at the time. In nearby Singapore, Phan Văn Hùm felt that "the street life and the scenery are vaguely like home. Trees and plants aren't at all strange. . . . Houses are also like ours. The people on the street are dressed normally."[85] The island's large Chinese population was certainly familiar, though many were impressed at the degree of their influence over the island's economy. Phạm Quỳnh wrote that to see Singapore "was enough to know the will of the Chinese, who lack nothing that the English have. The English have the skill to create enterprises, the Chinese have the strength to do the work, the English are the brains, while the Chinese are the hands, any place with both races is one where life is thriving."[86] But the Malay population was unfamiliar. Bùi Thanh Vân noted that in Singapore, Malay women "are invisible, whereas in Indochina native women show their face everywhere. The few I saw on the doorsteps of their homes do not have the facial beauty and the physical elegance of Annamite women and girls." He reported that they "must be cloistered until the moment of their marriage" and "can only go out in the evenings, accompanied by friends of their own sex, and walking apart from men and boys."[87]

The further the ship traveled from Indochina, the stranger—and often, less civilized –people came to seem. Bùi Thanh Vân wrote that the "Hindus" in Colombo "lacked cleanliness in their homes and public spaces" and their women "wear excessive jewelry. They wear it on their ears, their noses, their necks, on their chest, on their fingers and toes, and on their ankles."[88] Phạm Quỳnh did not hide his disgust at Colombo's Tamils, who he saw as "a truly hateful race. They are black as a waterlily root, their faces small and wrinkled, and all of the men look like swindlers hoping to pilfer the money of visitors."[89] Cao Văn Chánh, perhaps (?) more charitably, noted that "despite their dark skin," Sinhalese "can be pleasant to look at."[90] Bùi Ái waxed exotic about some sheep traders from Djibouti traveling with him. "It seemed like the deck of the ship was their native soil and the tent their paternal home. . . . They were always there, those four, sitting crosslegged, playing, snapping their fingers, drinking hot tea and babbling to no end."[91] But most had nothing but invective for the peoples of the Red Sea. Nguyễn Công Tiểu described "Arabs" he saw in Aden as "miserable people" in "tattered circumstances."[92] François-Bertrand Can left Djibouti with memories of "the repugnant filth of the homes and the people in them." "I will certainly not choose Djibouti to retire to," he wrote.[93] Veiled women, who many Indochinese first encountered in these ports, were another shock. "Arab women dress very strangely," wrote Phạm Quỳnh. "They use a black cloth to cover their head, face, and entire body, we only see their two eyes and their nose. . . . You don't know if they're old or young, ugly or beautiful."[94] For Bùi Thanh Vân, veils made women in Port Said seem like "ghosts in Annamese theater."[95]

Finally, the steamship journey ended. *"Et voila,"* wrote Bùi Ái, "one beautiful morning—the fourth of April, if memory serves—while chatting with a French sailor . . . the *Cap Saint Jacques* entered Marseille's harbor. What did I see? What did I think of it? It is hard for me to tell you now, for my impressions are no longer very clear. And believe me, they were not any clearer at the time, for I was a little unsettled."[96] The scenery was appropriately stunning as a finale—as they approached the port, ships passed the island of the famous Château d'If, where Edmond Dantès was jailed in Dumas's *Count of Monte Cristo* (a wildly popular book in colonial Indochina), and they glimpsed the basilica of Notre-Dame de la Garde towering over the bay from its perch on the foundations of an old fort, the city's highest point. As the shore came into view, anticipation grew. "All of us were eager to see this mythical port, this legendary city," wrote Lê Hữu Thọ. "We had talked about it for so long. We were astonished by the large dimensions of the docks, by the number of boats docked there, by the enormous volume of merchandise . . . by the rigorous organization of the operations of such an enormous port."[97] After weeks at sea, arrival felt like a second beginning to a journey that most, even those going to war, were eager to finally begin. "On all decks," wrote Bùi Ái, "it was an indescribable commotion. The boat hadn't even touched the wharf and people already wanted to get off. Finally we dropped anchor, and as people waited for the gangplank, they pushed and shoved in hopes of setting foot on the ground before the others."[98]

For some, setting foot on shore meant immediate incorporation into the structures of imperial power that had brought them to France. Royal delegations were met with requisite pomp and circumstance: when King Sisowath's boat docked in Marseille, a flock of journalists and photographers accompanied the politicians on hand to greet him.[99] French officials—often naval officers or former colonial administrators—came to meet exposition delegates and whisk them to the meetings, ceremonies, and informational tours that structured their stays. Although some soldiers and war laborers had a few days in Marseille before going on to their units or factories, most marched directly from the gangplank into the war machine. "We were met by soldiers who had served in Indochina," remembered Nguyễn Văn Liên. "Dozens of military trucks awaited us. A lieutenant jumped from his car, saluted his colonel, turned to us and yelled 'Hurry up you peasants, get into the trucks quickly now!' Since it was crowded, we could not move quickly. So the lieutenant yelled 'Hurry up you goddamn animals!'"[100] Trucks took them to transit camps, where they were clothed, received medical exams, and waited to be sent to military or work units. Barracks were overcrowded in both wars, so transit camps were often ad hoc: empty warehouses, tents on the grounds of the 1906 colonial exposition, or (during the Second World War) Marseille's new municipal prison, where the rude conditions foreshadowed the ordeals to follow. As Nguyen Van Thanh remembered, "The overall atmosphere of the camp was lugubrious. Tall buildings of several floors hemmed in by walls topped with barbed wire. An enormous gate opened into a courtyard without grass. . . . A familiar fetid odor of vomit and poorly-cleaned defecations assailed us. . . . The rooms were identical, uniformly cold and somber, barred windows, and frozen droplets hanging from the end of the faucets."[101]

Setting foot on land brought all Indochinese into the metropolitan structures of the imperial administration and surveillance apparatus that would shape their time in France. This varied greatly between individuals and over time. Before the Great War, such supervision was more personal than bureaucratic. As Indochinese students began to trickle into France in the nineteenth century, most met a retired official or missionary who had known their families in Indochina and agreed to help with their schooling and care in France. But as more Indochinese came to France to study, their surveillance became increasingly bureaucratic and political. Julien Fourès, a former lieutenant governor of Cochinchina, kept a close watch over the Permanent Mission of Indochinese Mandarins (1905–08) and reported on its activities. The intermediary between the Comité Paul Bert in France and Indochina was André Salles, a retired colonial official, whose petty and paranoid interventions made him roundly hated by the Indochinese under his watch. "I inferred that I must involuntarily have made him suffer," wrote Phan Văn Trường, whose 1914 arrest on the dubious grounds of conspiring with German agents was largely Salles's doing. "This always filled me with pity for the moral tortures that I inflicted upon him without knowing."[102]

The surveillance regime that oversaw Indochinese sojourners in interwar France had its roots in the Great War. As the fighting dragged on and rank-and-file attitudes darkened, French officials grew increasingly anxious that their experiences—from witnessing French defeat in battle to sexual relationships with French women—would gravely destablilize the colonial cultural and political order. By early 1917, a new bureaucratic organ, the Contrôle général des tirailleurs et travailleurs indochinois en France, was overseeing soldiers and laborers. In cooperation with representatives of industry and cultural organs like the Alliance française or the Mission laique, it created centers and libraries where Indochinese could read colonial newspapers, take courses in French or *quốc ngữ,* or enjoy concerts or plays—in the words of the minister of war, "healthy hobbies and useful occupations."[103] But the service's real purpose was policing, through monthly inspection tours of Indochinese military and labor units, and by inspecting and censoring letters. This required personnel with deep cultural and linguistic knowlege, for the task was enormous; in February 1918 alone, Indochinese sent two hundred thousand letters home.[104] The service soon ran out of former colonial officials and began regrouping Indochinese interpreters and importing current imperial officials to serve as its agents. After the war ended, the worrisome activities of Phan Châu Trinh, Phan Văn Trường, and Nguyễn Ái Quốc gave the service a new lease on life. In 1919, French officials transformed it into a civil agency to combat the growing specters of communism and anti-colonialism in liaison with the colonial Sûreté, the Ministry of Colonies, the French police, and European security services. In 1923, it became the Service de contrôle et d'assistance en France des indigènes des colonies françaises (CAI), a familiar institution to nearly all Indochinese sojourners in France.

The CAI's emergence and evolution was part of a broader transformation of the colonial security services under Albert Sarraut. By the early 1920s, before they left for France most Indochinese were officially required to obtain some form of permission (at least a passport, and often a work permit like a *livret de marin*), which meant providing a range of personal details and a photograph. Upon arrival in France, these materials entered into the CAI's dossiers on individual sojourners, which swelled with the CAI's communications with the Ministry of Colonies, the metropolitan and colonial Sûreté, municipal police departments, the French military, and other bureaucracies. The CAI also solicited, even hounded, steamship companies, schools and universities, employers, and friends and family for information. But the CAI was far from simply a recipient of intelligence from elsewhere; its dozens of agents produced reams of information critical to trans-imperial intelligence and surveillance. Yet as potent as this regime was, its officials perennially contended with spotty information, inaccurate or falsified personal details, confusion between people with the same or similar names, clandestine travel, and other realities that intruded on their quixotic quest for legibility.

The surveillance of Indochinese sojourners in France had some more paternalistic and pedagogical sides. These were largely the purview of the Service d'assistance morale et intellectuelle des indochinois en France (SAMI), founded in 1927 at the urging of Governor General Aléxandre Varenne, who felt that the "tutelage" of colonial subjects in France must be kept "separate from the nature and tendencies of policing."[105] Indochinese hectored by SAMI officials about improving their grades or writing home more often could be forgiven for not appreciating the distinction. But the SAMI offices did become a regular stop for Indochinese looking for work, in a dispute with an employer, in need of housing, or desperate to get home. There were many like the domestic servant Vu Van Hien, who—fifty-two years old, sick, broke, and homeless in Marseille—sought the SAMI's help in forcing his employer to pay for the return ticket stipulated in his contract. SAMI officials found him medical care and lodging, browbeat his employer, and put together funds for his ticket home.[106] The SAMI received hundreds of anguished letters from people looking for loved ones who had disappeared in France, and its efforts on their behalf could be quite humane. In 1930, one SAMI official wrote to a father in Indochina whose son had come to France to study but left school, married a French woman, had a child, and left them after his father refused to help the young family. His destitute French wife approached an SAMI official, who wrote this to her reluctant father in-law in Indochina:

> It must certainly be difficult when the child in whom one has invested so much hope and sent so far for his studies, instead of carrying them out seriously, does them halfheartedly or not at all, and even worse, gets married without his parents' consent. It is painful to contemplate such things, and it is surely out of grief that you have categorically refused your son's request for assistance. But the damage has been done, sir, and in hopes of not making it worse, allow me in all friendliness to say the following: good, charitable people have done their utmost to help those who you cannot prevent from being your son's wife and your grandson. I hope that after having shared these details, my role has ended. It is to you and you alone to decide what to do, but I do hope to receive a telegram from you with a response.[107]

This realm of the French surveillance regime undoubtedly had, as one French official said of the SAMI, "a familial and sentimental side."[108]

But sentimentality was rarely discernible in most of the CAI's activities, which saw political conspiracies everywhere and whose harassment and vindictiveness upended many Indochinese lives. Most Indochinese sojourners only engaged with the CAI in routine official interactions: customs, a marriage or divorce, a family death, naturalization, and the like. But all knew that its informants could be anywhere, and that saying the wrong thing in a meeting or appearing on a subscriber list for an illicit newspaper could result in an "invitation" to meet with local police or with Léon Josselme, the CAI's relentless and ruthless director for most of the interwar era. Popular restaurants and cafés were common places for CAI agents to pick up a little gossip, which meant being careful about conversation partners and subjects, or even reading material. Most knew that their letters home were not private. "Did you receive my letter?" wrote Ngô Quốc Quyển. "Did it arrive safely at its destination, or was it once again violated by these bastard spies and censors who rummage in our correspondence to once again discover no grand conspiracy or no revolutionary communist propaganda? May God forgive these people who abuse their own sense of honor with such cowardice and infamy."[109] Even the specter of the CAI led Indochinese to fear participating in organizations or events, to stifle their speech, and to make them suspicious of each other. And political activists of any kind could expect to be greeted in Marseille as the journalist Cao Văn Chánh was in 1929: with an interrogation about his past activities and the purpose of his trip to France.[110] Thereafter, any involvement in an illegal publication or subversive political organization—or even attending the wrong meeting—could result in harassment, searches of one's residence, arrest, or expulsion. And a fling with or even suspicion of activism could become a bureaucratic band, indelible no matter how specious or remote the charge, with lasting consequences for passport applications, naturalization applications, and repatriation requests.

As they stepped onto Marseille's docks, many Indochinese sojourners also entered into family, community, educational, and other social networks that linked metropole and colony. "I was on the deck with my old friend Lê Thái Ất," wrote Trương Mỹ Sáo in 1929, "scanning the chaotic docks for familiar faces. Two Annamites, young like us, stood amid a crowd of French people; as soon as they saw us, they began waving their hats and calling our names. One was Ất's nephew and the other was Trương Văn Minh, president of the comité Annamite, who was responsible for meeting me."[111] Students often gravitated to French schools where siblings or others from their community were already studying. "Out of the about fifty Annamite students in Montpellier," wrote Phan Văn Thiết in 1927, "twenty are from Sa Đéc.... It is a point of honor for us to succeed, not only to help those who come after us, but to uphold the prestige of the people of Sa Đéc, to show that they do not get discouraged in the face of a challenge."[112] Many were first taken in by family or friends: when Lê Văn Tiểu arrived in Montpellier to study, he lived with his father's cousin (a lawyer who had attended lycée and university there).[113] In 1930, Trần Văn Mại stayed with a former classmate from Hà Nội as he hunted for an affordable room in Paris.[114] Although most sojourners soon found their own ways, personal networks like these could become useful again during a financial or personal emergency. And epistolary networks—greatly facilitated by air mail, which linked France and Indochina by the 1920s—meant that news of friends and family at home would never be too far away.

FIRST IMPRESSIONS

Most Indochinese spent at least a few days in Marseille after their arrivals, and the bustling, seedy quarter around its docks was an exhilarating, if overwhelming place to first encounter France. Restaurant, hotel, and taxi touts crowded around the new arrivals; even after they had been fended off, disorientation persisted. "My first impressions were so vague and in flux that it's impossible for me to describe them to you," wrote Bùi Ái. "I felt crushed by the tall buildings and the streets full of people, and I felt more than a little apprehension."[115] "My first impressions," wrote Đào Trinh Nhất," were of an immense, never-ending place about which I knew nothing at all. The houses, cars and trains, boulevards, and people—everything seemed immense and beautiful, but I admittedly knew very little about what I was seeing."[116] Even Marseille, however, paled in the face of the quasi-mythical Paris, where the greatest numbers of sojourners soon ended up. When the intellectual Nguyễn Tiến Lãng first saw the capital in 1939, he wrote, "Ten years, fifteen years, I had carried Paris within me as a living presence. And here is Paris in its grandeur and its beauty, and all of it is both utterly expected and unexpected, matching my expectations, imagination, and desire, yet at the same time gloriously surpassing them, more absorbing, captivating, and bewitching than I could have imagined."[117] "An Asian can never imagine what it is," wrote Lê Văn Huê. "Entering through a revolving door, riding an escalator, etc. are childish for a Parisian but they make you tremble the first time. Having seen Paris and its many wonderous things, we become less provincial [nhà quê]."[118] "Excuse me uncle," wrote Phan Tư Nghĩa, "for saying in all honesty that in leaving our country and coming here, it seems to me as if I have left darkness behind for light."[119] "I crossed cities and the countryside," wrote Hoàng Văn Tấn, "and realized that despite the heavy taxes burdening the French people, they enjoy a liberty and equality that our oppressed populations do not know."[120] "Upon arriving in France," wrote Nguyễn Văn Chửng, "I immediately compared it to our country. It is only from here where we can fully appreciate the slavery and oppression that we endure."[121]

Such exuberance owed much to sojourners' first interactions with French people outside of the colony. "What do you think of France and French people?" Lý Bình Huệ asked a friend. "Are they different from the ones over here?"[122] For some, it was an immense relief just not to be immediately marked as a colonial subject. "They thought I was Chinese or Japanese," wrote Phạm Quỳnh, far from the only person this happened to.[123] And for many, at least at first, the humanity of French passengers in the later part of the steamship journey carried over onto the shore. "In France," wrote Phạm Thông Thảo, "people are *human,* polite; at home, we have *sharks, crocodiles.*"[124] "Once we arrived in France," wrote Trịnh Đình Thảo, "condescending looks were replaced with furtive, curious glances followed by sympathetic smiles. . . . We were no longer subject to the racial discrimination that shaped how settlers treated natives, our hearts opened at this warm ambiance, and this environment of liberty and equality infused our spirits."[125] "French politeness," wrote Hồ Hữu Tường,

> surpasses the Annamite manners that we so often vaunt. The feeling of hatred is nearly unknown here, and the sense of humanity (love of one another) is very cultivated. I would like France to serve as an example, a model, for Annamite youth, for after what I have seen and done here, I feel that we should not regard with distrust and disdain this honorable France whose reputation has been soiled by its capitalists and colonialists—who I regret being unable to properly curse here.[126]

After Trần Xuân Hồ and two friends enlisted in Toulon in August 1914, a crowd showered them with cries of "Vive la France! Vive l'Annam!" "These cheers were so moving that they still give us sustenance," he wrote years later. "Coachmen offered us free rides. . . . Others brought us from café to café to buy us drinks—everywhere, they hailed us."[127] "French people in France conduct themselves with dignity," wrote Đặng Văn Long. "Do you see the women selling fish on the docks? They are kind, they greet us warmly."[128] After a fight landed Nguyễn Văn Ngàn in a Montpellier police station, he exulted that "they were at fault, so we left freely. At home, hitting a Frenchman brings severe penalties. But here ... the commissioner received us respectfully. Annamites here fear neither God nor the Devil."[129] For Indochinese Catholics, however, it was precisely the fear of God—still powerful even in a secularizing age—that they were so happy to find in France. "Oh! How joyous I was to hear the chants and prayers, and to see the beautiful ceremonies and rich altars of French churches!" one war laborer exulted. "Never in Tonkin have we seen such beauty." He would make five pilgrimages to Lourdes during the Great War.[130]

Occasional encounters with French who had been to Indochina, and who behaved as if they were still there, reinforced these feelings. In 1927, Lieu Sanh Tran had just bought a copy of the communist daily *L'Humanité* when he heard an old man say, "The Annamites are now feeding on that? What a disgrace." "Ah, a colonial!" replied Lieu Sanh Tran, after he learned that the man had been a colonel in the Indochinese army. "Here, we are in a civilized country, where all are equal," he later wrote home. "It is sad to see such things happen here."[131] He wrote an article about the incident for *L'Humanité*. "They make the law when they are in our country," wrote Phạm Chí Phụng, "but on their own soil, they are just starving dogs. . . . I've met many recently repatriated French people, who tell me stories that make me suspicious; they introduce themselves as chief of the Sûreté, engineer, police commissioner, or other titles they think will intimidate me." He continued, "I terrified them during our conversations, for here we have a freedom of opinion that bears no resemblance to politics in our country."[132]

But more complex feelings soon set in. Lê Quang Ngọc was one of many to be gripped by a *mal de pays* upon arrival that, for some, never faded.

> I cannot recall without bitter disappointment, the moment when the arrival of the ship that brought me so far from home finally allowed me to touch the object of my dreams. It was at that moment that I felt myself gripped more than ever by the anguish and the anxiety of exile. The object of my dreams, this France, that my parents had taught me to love. . . . I had dreamed, with joy, that it would open its arms to receive its child; but today, a cold indifference shadows its door. I contemplated with sadness the waving hands and handkerchiefs, the smiles reserved for my traveling companions, as I, an isolated vagabond, in such need of a friendly smile, was excluded from this universal joy.[133]

Ngô Quốc Quyền wrote of

> a pain that, more than anything, can afflict even the greatest of travelers: homesickness. . . . The love of freedom and liberty are behind the great

migrations of all living things, but it is nostalgia that gives mankind its moral superiority, that noble sentiment that makes you miss your country even when you are better off elsewhere. . . . I left with the goal of becoming a man, but I cannot shake a sentiment of anguish when I realize that I might not see my country, my family and my friends for six years, or even eight.[134]

Other sojourners felt a powerful sense of inferiority and inadequacy that would linger in their studies, work, and relationships in France. Lê Văn Đắc (Phan Thanh Giản's grandson) wrote that "our compatriots, including myself, who in our country pass for elites, in France are awkward and gauche, made to amuse others with their exoticism and inappropriate behavior. How many among us know how to speak, eat, or behave properly?"[135] And as time passed, many came to feel that France and Indochina shared more than they had thought. This realization often came with the first encounter with French poverty. Bùi Thanh Vân was shocked when he saw "a beggar telling fortunes on the street to make a living from passersby, who slide money in his pocket from pity," "peddlers hawking their wares like Asians," and poor peasants in wooden shoes and tattered rags.[136] "I saw French people who worked hard in the fields like we do in Vietnam," noted one war laborer; "the French in Vietnam live like kings but here, they work hard like we do, there is no difference."[137] And few sojourners waited all that long for reminders of their status as colonial subjects: a rude remark (or worse) in the street, a censored letter that never reached its recipient, an encounter with a suspected provocateur, or an "invitation" to meet with the CAI or the police. In short, as they settled into their sojourns, more Indochinese would come to think of France not as a departure from the world they had left behind on the docks of the colony, but simply as another part of it.

THREE

From Contact to Conquest

PHẠM PHÚ THỨ WROTE THE POEM "A Few Notes, in France, on a Train" on November 9, 1863, as he prepared to leave France after months of diplomacy and ethnographic observation.

> This kingdom was established over eighteen hundred years ago
> It dominates in the West through its strong administration and ingenious machines
> From the window of the train, I see the countryside. . . .
> Telegraph lines run alongside the city streets and buildings
> The projects realized by their institutions are excellent
> It is a pity that they do not know the deep spirit of the four principles
> If the East had known to acquire techniques in good time
> Neither Paris nor London would be worthy of elegy.

Phạm Phú Thứ was writing for the Tự Đức emperor, and he was clearly mindful of his ruler's sensibilities. But he was clear about what he felt France's growing ambitions in Asia meant for the Nguyễn empire. "It is the custom of these nations," he added in a note, "not to prohibit the spread of knowledge and techniques. We must, in my opinion, acquire their techniques, create instruction manuals, and obtain results that speak for themselves before we express any pride."[1] Phạm Phú Thứ went to France in hopes that diplomacy would preserve the Nguyễn empire's autonomy, but what he experienced there left him convinced that more meaningful engagement with French ideas, knowledge, and techniques was necessary for it to survive.

In the second half of the nineteenth century, French statesmen, naval officials, merchants, explorers, and missionaries made choices and led campaigns that helped bring Indochina into being.[2] This chapter explores how the emergence of Indochina also began to bring the region's empires and peoples to

France. These circulations had deep roots in the religious and mercantile networks that had connected France and Southeast Asia for centuries before colonial conquest. But beginning in the 1840s, imperial officials and members of royal families from the Nguyễn and Khmer empires arrived in France in hopes of using direct diplomacy to first forestall, then limit, and then shape, France's growing Asian empire. They also hoped to study and learn from French economic, military, and political power. As French rule in Indochina solidified at the end of the century, colonial authorities began organizing sojourns in France for the region's elites and even its ruling monarchs, in hopes of inculcating their loyalty and cooperation. But by the early twentieth century, they would be joined by Indochinese who were both victims of France's increasingly repressive colonial apparatus and also converts to its radical political tradition. They would become the first Indochinese political sojourners—but far from the last—to seek solutions to the problem of empire in France itself.

FIRST ENCOUNTERS

The Catholic seminarians Mighê Văn Phụng and Diny Lý Thành, the first we know of to arrive in France from what would become Indochina, landed on the Atlantic coast sometime in 1688. In Rennes, they were greeted by a royal entourage that included King Louis XIV. After giving testimony in Paris in favor of the Jesuits, they crossed the Mediterranean to Rome, where, in an audience with Pope Innocent XI, they "genuflected to the Holy Father, allowing their heads to touch the ground three times. To each, the pontiff bestowed a rosary, a golden medallion, indulgences, and a coveted letter addressed to the 'Christian mandarins' of their country."[3] Others followed in their footsteps; one Tonkinese Catholic in France during the 1720s served as a translator for Hu, the Chinese convert whose French sojourn Jonathan Spence made famous.[4] Most likely spoke Latin or other European languages, which may have made France slightly less foreign. For John Thiều and Paul Cuyên, the four years they spent in Italy before arriving in Paris in 1785 likely also helped, although the roiling anticlericalism just outside the seminary gates may have been intimidating.

Prince Nguyễn Phúc Cảnh, who arrived in France in early 1787, made a splash with the French royal family. He sat for portraits at the request of Marie Antoinette's court—the queen's hairdresser invented a hairstyle in his honor, calling it "au prince de Cochinchine."[5] He also met Thomas

Jefferson, the American minister to France, who knew of Cochinchina's robust rice and hoped that it might be suited to his new nation's climate. He sought an audience with the prince to request that seeds be sent to him in America. Jefferson recorded that the prince agreed, but he never obtained the seeds.[6] But Nguyễn Phúc Cảnh spent most of his time not at Versailles but at the Rue du Bac in a room that was "quite simple and without any ornament." Pigneau visited his family several times during his stay in France but, as his brother wrote, "he could not leave the little prince for more than eight days, as the child could absolutely not be without him." He urged Pigneau to send the prince to the family's home in Origny "with a Cochinchinese student to keep him company, to allow the bishop to devote himself to his family."[7]

On November 2, 1840, the first Nguyễn delegation to France arrived in Locmariaquer, a small fishing village in Brittany. The humble destination was not a purposeful slight—a storm had blown their boat away from their intended port of Bordeaux—but it symbolized the minor role of Asian affairs in French politics at the time. Its envoys Tôn Thất Thường and Trần Việt Xương toured factories and arsenals and visited the Chamber of Peers and various ministries, but they never received an audience with King Louis-Philippe. This slight, and hostile receptions from some French officials, reflected missionary efforts to publicize the dire plight of Catholics in the Nguyễn kingdom. A letter from MEP officials to Louis-Philippe, received while the envoys were in France, told stories of Catholic faithful in the Nguyễn empire being imprisoned, forced into hiding, and subjected to a barbaric menu of tortures. In 1843, this pressure led Louis-Philippe to authorize his navy to protect French missionaries in the Nguyễn empire, the first salvo in a campaign that would culminate in a Franco-Spanish invasion in 1858. But despite these percolating tensions, some missionaries were present to see the Nguyễn officials off when they left Bordeaux for England in early 1841. A Nguyễn interpreter expressed "charm at the warm reception they had received" and said that his parents were Christian and that he hoped to convert after finishing his Confucian education. Whether this was true or a final effort at cultural diplomacy is impossible to say.[8]

ENVOYS AND EMBASSIES IN THE CONQUEST ERA

Before the consolidation of French political control in Indochina in the 1880s, Nguyễn embassies in France experienced the bilateral norms and conventions typical of Asian diplomacy in Europe during the nineteenth century. In 1863, delays due to French infighting on Cochinchina issues left time for "long exchanges on the protocol to be followed, French and Vietnamese, on how the Vietnamese emperor's letter would be presented, on who would receive it: the emperor or one of his ministers, on the composition of the Vietnamese delegation admitted to the audience, on the respective positioning of the three ambassadors, on the wearing of headdresses, etc."[9] The three ambassadors presented their letter to Napoleon III while bowing three times, their hands clasped in front; after passing the letter to the foreign minister, the emperor and his wife bowed their heads in turn. Patrice de MacMahon, president of the new Third Republic, welcomed the 1878 Nguyễn delegation at the Elysée Palace with full military honors.[10] In 1863 and 1878, Nguyễn embassies enjoyed equal status with many other nations in Paris's diplomatic world. At a banquet at the Ministry of Foreign Affairs in 1863, Nguyễn envoys met with diplomats from Brazil, Venezuela, Mexico, Sweden, Russia, and the United States, in the throes of its civil war. In 1878, the Nguyễn envoys sat with other foreign envoys at the opening ceremony of the universal exposition, after which they went to Spain to renegotiate the treaties signed after the Franco-Spanish war in Cochinchina. Envoys of both embassies were appropriately housed in *hôtels particuliers* (private mansions).

But such status and courtesies faded as France consolidated its control in Indochina. The 1889 and 1894 delegations only saw the French president from afar; they met with the minister of colonies. Some French officials maintained diplomatic niceties, but others pointedly ignored them. In 1894, a French official observed the "difficult and regrettable situation" of the Nguyễn delegation. Abandoned by their minders and awaiting an audience in "very modest lodgings" on the Rue de Grenelle, the delegation had been reduced to making cheap purchases at the nearby Bon Marché and calling for a private car when they wanted to go out, "a heavy expense." "As if it was so difficult to have them visit what interested them," wrote the indignant official. "This is not a negro tribe," he continued, "it is a mission sent from a country that counts."[11] "Free this morning, without any official responsibility," wrote the head delegate Nguyễn Trọng Hiệp, "I add another stick of incense to the stand."[12] The 1900 delegation obtained a brief audience with the French president, where its head delegate Vũ Quang Nhạ proclaimed that "Thanks to France's protection, Annam too has a place in this great exposition.... We desire that France will always rule over our kingdom and

FIGURE 3. The audience of three Nguyễn dynasty envoys with Emperor Napoleon III, November 11, 1863. Source: *Le Monde illustré,* November 21, 1863.

bring it great prosperity." "France and Annam," the French president responded, "are now tightly bound by an unbreakable tie of friendship."[13]

In France, Nguyễn officials also observed and reported on what they saw and learned. France's long-standing religious and commercial presence in the Nguyễn empire meant that in many ways, it was already familiar. But Nguyễn officials were stunned by the economic and commercial dynamism they witnessed, which only direct experience could fully convey. David Harvey describes the economy of Napoleon III's Second Empire (1852–70) as "the imposition of intense labor discipline and the liberation of capital circulation from its preceding constraints," which produced wide-ranging and often radical experiments in "the proper role of the state in relation to private interests and the circulation of capital; the degree of state intervention in labor markets, in industrial and commercial activity, in housing and social welfare provision; and the like." This was spectacularly evident in Paris, which "the Emperor and his advisers sought to liberate . . . from constraints that bound it so tightly to an ancient past" through Haussmann's revolutionary urbanism of "spacious boulevards, parks, gardens, and monuments of all sorts."[14] In the particular and often tightly-controlled contexts of their diplomatic visits, the "France" that Nguyễn embassies witnessed was one of, in Walter

Benjamin's words, "the institutions of the bourgeoisie's worldly and spiritual dominance."[15]

Most Nguyễn delegations came during a universal or colonial exposition, and they marveled at what Benjamin would famously call "places of pilgrimage to the fetish commodity," where they often wandered in between their official duties.[16] In 1878, the Seine's waters, pumped through thirty kilometers of pipes, powered elevators and burst from the ground in arcing jets. The 1889 exposition unveiled the Eiffel Tower, then the world's tallest structure; its largest building, the Galerie des Machines, featured the first gasoline-powered automobile and all of Thomas Edison's 493 inventions. Nguyễn Thành Ý dutifully described his own empire's mother-of-pearl crafts as "the finest of all" on display, but he focused more on the breadth and beauty of French goods. He returned, like most visitors, with souvenirs (in his case, navigational maps).[17] "The resplendent pavilions appear as palaces in the style of each nation," the Khmer envoy Son Diep wrote in 1900. "I contemplate them without fatigue. A multitude of people come to admire them. Some walk, some jump and others stand, listening to the music. The Trocadero, Eiffel Tower and Dumotte Tower are of an incomparable beauty." He was among the first to ride on the Paris metro's "electric cars, rolling under buildings and under the earth," inaugurated in 1900. "At the exposition," marveled Vũ Quang Nhạ in 1900, "nothing is missing."[18] And expositions were but one stop in broader programs of economic and industrial tourism. While awaiting an audience with Napoleon III in 1863, Nguyễn envoys visited factories that produced guns, iron, clocks, rugs, pottery, paper, tobacco, crystal, and plumbing parts. The 1889 delegation went to Lyon to see its famous silk industry. In 1894, Nguyễn Trọng Hiệp visited the Creusot ironworks. And industrial and technical dynamism was evident in Paris's streetlights, underground water and gas lines, streetcar tracks seamlessly woven into the paved roads, and elevated train lines, all of which prompted close description.

French dynamism was also evident to Indochinese envoys in more everyday contexts. One core feature of Haussmann's revolutionary urbanism was "a constructed concept of nature . . . fashioned according to very distinctive criteria" that "brought 'the spectacle of nature' into the city and thereby contributed to the luster of the imperial regime."[19] Colonial urbanism was still decades away, but Nguyễn envoys in 1863 understood Paris's parks and plazas as signs of French power. "We see woods and gardens everywhere . . . as often inside the city as outside of it," wrote Phạm Phú Thứ.[20] "On all sides, the circulation of carriages in the streets raises dust," wrote Nguyễn Trọng Hiệp.

"Thankfully, the gushing water from thousands of fountains refreshes the busy atmosphere."[21] At the Bois de Boulogne, Phạm Phú Thứ noted that its landscaped environment included guards "who come and go in military uniforms, a rifle and a saber in hand," and that that the layout of Versailles's grounds allowed for military drills. The 1878 and 1894 embassies visited Paris's Jardin d'acclimatation and Jardin des plantes, where, as Nguyễn Trọng Hiệp marveled, "is gathered from far-off countries all that is rare and beautiful in the animal and vegetable kingdoms."[22]

Indochina's envoys also experienced theaters, circuses, concerts, cabarets, and other new forms of leisure that, as Vanessa Schwartz writes, "produced a new crowd as individuals joined together to delight in the transformation of everyday life into spectacle while avidly consuming spectacles of a sensationalized everyday life."[23] On the Champ de Mars, the 1863 envoys were in a crowd that witnessed the ascension of "Le géant" (The Giant), at that point the largest-ever hot-air balloon. They took in a magic show in a gaslit theater decorated with landscapes and a map of world ports, including Đà Nẵng. They saw a panorama of the French navy's role in the siege of Sevastopol a few years earlier. "Things but a few steps from the spectator appear as if at a distance of one hundred *lý*," Phạm Phú Thứ wrote; "the faces of the soldiers and officers coming and going from the carnage, the color of the broken weapons or the smoke coming up from the ramparts, make one believe they are in front of reality, yet all is from the trick of the drawing."[24] The members of the 1863 embassy were also almost certainly the first Indochinese to be photographed. In 1889, Nguyễn envoys saw shows at the Garnier opera house, the Folies Bergère, and other hotspots. In 1900, Son Diep spent an evening at the théâtre de Châtelet, where he experienced the same kind of sexual exoticism that many French viewers would feel while watching Khmer dancers at Marseille's colonial exposition six years later. "The dancers are radiant," he enthused, "comparable to the goddesses who descend from the sky, young, slender, their hair in a chignon. Their breasts are firm . . . their beauty makes one dream of them constantly."[25]

"The waters are blue and the plants pink; the evening is sweet to look upon; one goes for a stroll. The great ladies are out for a stroll; behind them walk lesser ladies." Nguyễn Trọng Hiệp wrote this quatrain in his 1897 poem "Paris: the Capital of France," about his experiences as an envoy in 1894. In 1933, Walter Benjamin included it as an epigraph to his essay "Paris, Capital of the Nineteenth Century." Writing during the Depression and in exile from fascism, Benjamin looked back upon the marvels of nineteenth-century

Paris as "residues of a dream-world." "With the destabilizing of the market economy," he wrote, "we begin to recognize the monuments of the bourgeoisie as ruins even before they have crumbled."[26] But Indochinese envoys wrote about this era as it was becoming, and their sojourns in fin de siècle France—which offered extraordinary, often overwhelming glimpses of material and cultural power—evoked, above all, wonder and guarded optimism about a union with France. "Europe's political institutions are different from Asia's," wrote Nguyễn Trọng Hiệp, "but their basic preoccupation is the same. This is to seek to develop the people's material and moral prosperity. These two principles form the basis of conduct for all officials. As we develop and reflect on these two principles, we come to know that there are not two modes of reason in this world."[27]

But for all their optimism, it was difficult for them to ignore signs of their subjugation in the new political union of "Indochine." The 1878 envoys, for example, may well have known of the French fate of Phan Thanh Giản's two sons, who as punishment for their role in the anti-French resistance had been exiled in a village in the Aveyron and interned in a hospital in Toulon before being allowed to return home.[28] France's *mission civilisatrice* had played only a bit part in the 1867 and 1878 expositions—"Annam's" only presence in 1878 was an imperial-style facade stuck hastily on a structure depicting Muslim nations, "deemed 'of no importance and scarcely demanding notice.'"[29] But by 1889, Indochina had its own section in a colonial esplanade that spanned a hundred acres; it included the first of many large replicas of the spectacular Angkor Wat, and the "Pagoda of Great Tranquility," where nine Buddhist monks lived and carried out rituals under the gaze of curious onlookers. The historian of religion Jean Réville, who spoke with them at length, reported that "they had come to Europe in hopes of gaining followers." They "felt that white missionaries had been coming from Europe long enough for them to now have a right to come spread Buddhism among the people of Europe."[30] In 1900, Indochina accounted for a quarter of the universal exposition's colonial section, in which merchants, artisans, soldiers, musicians and "typical villagers" served as actors in a French colonial play. The Nguyễn envoys who visited these expositions were spectators, but by the turn of the century they had also become exhibits of sorts.

Nguyễn Trọng Hiệp seems to have felt this when he came to Paris in 1894. In the paean to the city he wrote three years later, he described the Bon Marché, where he had shopped, as "an immense house open on all sides, resonant with the murmurs of tides of shoppers and thousands of products whose incomparable splendor tricks the eye; one would think that the 'Sea Market' had come to the middle of the capital."[31] The "Sea Market" is a reference to P'u Sung-Ling's "The Rakshas and the Sea Market," a story about a shipwreck that strands a Chinese merchant in the kingdom of a hideous barbarian race. It is a metaphor for the Manchu conquest of the Ming dynasty, the defining event of P'u Sung-Ling's life, just as the French conquest of the Nguyễn dynasty was for Nguyễn Trọng Hiệp. In the story, the merchant learns to manipulate the Raksha court by donning different masks in their encounters; in one, he writes a poem in praise of the barbarian king. This pleases the Rakshas but makes the merchant uneasy. "Men must put on false, ugly faces to please their superiors," wrote P'u Sung-Ling. "Such is the hypocritical way of the world. Something of which you feel a little ashamed may win praise, and something of which you feel exceedingly ashamed may win much higher praise. But any man who dares to reveal his true self in public is almost certain to shock the multitude and make them shun him."[32]

Nguyễn Trọng Hiệp's grandson would come to France a generation later, but under very different circumstances. Nguyễn Sĩ Giác had passed the *tiến sĩ* examination like his grandfather, but the protectorate had rendered the Nguyễn imperial state a servile shadow of its former self. In 1907, he had joined the circles of the Tonkin Free School (Đông Kinh Nghĩa Thục), founded by intellectuals committed to modernization and reform, among them some Nguyễn officials who had studied in France. In 1908, French authorities blamed the school for contributing to the eruption of revolts in Annam and arrested many in its ranks, Nguyễn Sĩ Giác among them. He went to France after his travel ban had been lifted. Sûreté officials noted that "he is totally opposed to the French administration, which he accuses of being the cause of his disappointments and his missed career."[33]

COLONIAL ACOLYTES AND MODERNIZING MANDARINS

"Every epoch, in fact, not only dreams the one to follow," wrote Walter Benjamin, "but, in dreaming, precipitates its awakening."[34] On his way to France in 1863, Phan Thanh Giản wrote a poem redolent of reluctance and unease: "Because of my obligations, I must travel to France." "The French extend a welcoming hand to their visitors," he continued; "thinking of the country's destiny, I long to return home." Tôn Thọ Tường, an official in the

French naval administration and one of the embassy's interpreters, wrote a response (*họa thơ*) that instead evoked adventure and possibility: "The endless sky and water make the mountains seem small/As the ship takes us to distant regions."[35] During the French conquest, the defenders of Indochina's imperial states and colonial rule's first Indochinese advocates traveled to France on the same boats.

Trương Vĩnh Ký, the other interpreter in 1863, would become one of the most influential early Indochinese supporters of colonial rule after his return. But anything he may have written about his sole trip to France no longer exists.[36] The only known firsthand evidence of his time there is an 1864 account by Richard Cortambert, a geographer introduced to Trương Vĩnh Ký by Henri Bineteau, a scholar and naval attaché during the French war in Cochinchina. His portrait of Trương Vĩnh Ký, painted as they strolled Paris's streets, is of a man with a servile admiration for France and a dismissive view of his own government. "My compatriots," Cortambert notes him saying, "are a very docile people, very imitative, but completely inert.... I dare to hope that as of today they will no longer remain in this night of inactivity but will march like the Western world in the direction of progress."[37] It is unclear whether Cortambert faithfully recorded Trương Vĩnh Ký's ideas, but the young interpreter did have close contact with colonial circles in Paris. He attended meetings of the Société de géographie de Paris; at one, he presented his "Note sur le royaume Khmer ou le Kambodje," later published in the society's bulletin. Trương Vĩnh Ký met many men of letters in Paris. Many accounts claim that they included Paul Bert, a brilliant young scientist; the two would work together closely decades years later when Bert, then the resident general in Tonkin, enlisted Trương Vĩnh Ký's help in negotiations with the Nguyễn court.

Nguyễn Trường Tộ had written his first petition calling for reform in 1863 as the Nguyễn embassy prepared its departure for Paris. Four years later he arrived in France, sent by Tự Đức "to purchase modern machinery and books and hire French experts to come to Vietnam as instructors," all to prepare "to open a school for studying Western machinery" in the Nguyễn empire.[38] With him were the French bishop Gauthier, three priests, and two Nguyễn officials. The mission visited French ministries to ask for financial support, met industrial and business leaders, attended meetings of learned societies, and bought books and equipment (including microscopes, a telegraph, an air pump, a gas lamp, and an electric motor). But three months after their arrival, the French navy invaded the provinces of Vĩnh Long, Châu Đốc, and Hà

Tiên, prompting the Nguyễn court to restrict the mission's activities and then recall it altogether. The invasion only furthered Nguyễn Trường Tộ's belief in the need for far-reaching change. Before leaving France, he wrote a detailed and impassioned report calling for the adoption of modern military equipment and tactics, the standardization of imperial administration, fiscal and tax reforms, scientific agriculture, a comprehensive census, stronger border control, and institutions for social welfare.[39] Nguyễn Tăng Doãn, another member of that mission, would head the Nguyễn embassy in 1878. Nguyễn Hữu Thơ (also known as Nguyễn Hữu Cư), its interpreter, had also been to France as a young Catholic novice in 1864, where he was ordained a priest; his written account of his trip, like any Trương Vĩnh Ký may have written, has not survived.[40]

Two years after the 1878 embassy, Trương Minh Ký visited France after accompanying a group of students to the Lycée d'Alger. A good Catholic, he spent his first days in Paris visiting cathedrals and religious orders, whose martyrs moved him "with tender love for those who suffered and died so unjustly." But he was also a teacher and scholar, and he took in with equal reverence the Sorbonne, the École normale supérieure, the École des beaux-arts, and other prestigious schools where many Indochinese would later study. He also admired state institutions taking care of the blind, the deaf, the wounded, and other vulnerable members of society. His wanderings also took a lighter turn. He spent days at the Louvre ("over there lords and kings, over here exotic and ancient objects"), took in an array of concerts and cabarets, and idled in cafés, taking in "happy gatherings on all sides." On Bastille Day, he marveled at the "flags at every door and window," the crowds, the military parades, and the festivities stretching into the early hours.[41] It all left him enthused about the future: "Like a ship makes mountains and rivers move; France and the Great South become harmonious with one another. . . . Travel opens one's eyes to strange sights, and brings one to read, hear and experience new things."[42] A decade later, after seeing the 1889 exposition, he was further convinced that his nation's future lay with France:

> France is a great nation, pure, rich, and strong, respected and loved in the world.
> Its rulers, jurists and generals are fair and righteous.
> Our small nation has aligned with it, so as one day to be comparable to the West.
> We can no longer depend on our own feeble strength, talent, or wealth.
> Like a person in need, we must turn toward a wealthly and powerful nation.[43]

Trương Vĩnh Ký, Tôn Thọ Tường, and Trương Minh Ký would all become crucial cultural and political auxiliaries after returning to Indochina. But French initiatives before the Great War to reproduce their transformative French sojourns were mixed at best. By the early 1870s, the naval officials who had sent dozens of Cochinchinese to study in French schools since the conquest admitted that "the results have been far from favorable." Among the forty-two who returned to Cochinchina, few seemed to have potential; one student in Seyne had almost burned down his school when he hurriedly discarded a cigarette to hide it from an approaching teacher.[44] The experiment ended with the arrival of civilian rule in Cochinchina in 1879. The students at the École cambodgienne in Paris were all sons of royals and court officials.[45] They studied French language and literature, history, geography, math, physical sciences, drawing, music, and physical education; its director invited the Parisian press to the Bois de Boulogne to watch foot races, canoeing, and cricket in which "young Cambodians, flexible, skinny, and nervous, demonstrated remarkable agility." Their Wednesday afternoons were devoted to "visits to industrial establishments in and around Paris," and vacations to exhaustive tours around France and Switzerland.[46] Despite its grand visions, the school "rapidly gained a reputation as a finishing school for princes"; its mediocre instruction and casual atmosphere led many students to study elsewhere or go home.[47] In 1888, a French deputy in Cochinchina reported that "I knew two Cambodians: the first had spent eleven years in France, while the second hadn't left Cambodia and did his studies there. And it was the second who had to give instruction to the first."[48]

At least eighty-two Indochinese studied at the École coloniale between 1889 and 1911.[49] The first were close allies of France's in the region; they included figures like Hoàng Trọng Phu (son of Tonkin's viceroy), Thân Trọng Huế (scion of an elite Huế family whose granddaughter Trân Lệ Xuân, better known as Madame Nhu, would spend her last years as a recluse a stone's throw away from the school), the Lao princes Phetsarath Ratanavongsa and Sisavang Vong (soon to be the king), Pierre Somchine Nginn (whose father François was Auguste Pavie's translator in Laos), and the sons of the White Tai clan leader Đèo Văn Trị. Some students had French patrons; for Nguyễn Phú Khai, it was the famous writer Pierre Loti, who had first popularized Angkor with French audiences. Others got there on their own. Trần Trọng Kim had worked as an interpreter in Tonkin before enrolling in a commercial school in Lyon in 1905. He worked as a mosaicist at the colonial exposition in Marseille in 1906 to spend time there with Nguyễn

Văn Vĩnh, there as a delegate. Trần Trọng Kim secured a scholarship to the École coloniale shortly after.[50] But the most famous Indochinese associated with the École coloniale never attended: Nguyễn Tất Thành, the future Hồ Chí Minh, whose 1911 application was rejected.

The dozens of Nguyễn and Khmer imperial officials who came to France with the Permanent Mission of Indochinese Mandarins between 1905 and 1908 came out of fertile modernist milieus in protectorate administrations at the turn of the century. They included figures like Phạm Gia Thụy, from the village of Đông Ngạc near Hà Nội, which produced many modernist literati in the early twentieth century; Ưng Dự, grandson of the Minh Mạng emperor and a professor at the Quốc Học; and Nguyễn Doãn Thạc, whose grandfather Nguyễn Tư Giản had been an influential reformist figure during the Tự Đức era.[51] Khmer participants in 1906 included Oknya Keth, a product of the École cambodgienne. The Permanent Mission spent a few months each in Paris, Lyon, and Nancy. Participants visited factories and workshops; chambers of commerce and banks; political institutions; schools and universities; orphanages and hospitals; printing presses and publishing houses; and museums. At the Musée de Sèvres, participants excitedly noted a tea service from the famous Bát Tràng kilns, a gift from the 1863 embassy. In the evenings, French minders (former protectorate officials headed by Julien Fourès, a former Resident Superior in Tonkin) led discussions about what they had seen and done that day, and the officials listened to lectures about subjects from history to hygiene. The schedule was so intensive that some of the officials complained that they did not have enough time to write their required monthly reports.

The participants and their French overseers lived together; Indochinese domestics cooked and cleaned. Small stipends covered private purchases and outings, extra French lessons, warmer clothes, or more food. Life in France challenged many habits. Fourès noted that "some mandarins wanted a platter of fish day and night, along with the platter of meat and of vegetables. It is difficult to make them understand that fresh fish is hard to find every day."[52] A Khmer official reported that "we were very upset to see horse meat consumed, which caused us great horror since horses are never eaten in our country."[53] Nguyễn Huy Tưởng, "not used to circulating by means other than a palanquin, was quite opposed to all walks. He preferred staying in his room instead of going outside and participating in the scheduled events. He worked by himself on a memoir of his time in France."[54] But France also stimulated new habits. Hoàng Văn Cảnh and Võ Văn Chất both took up photography, taking as their subjects "the industrial, artistic and scientific riches of France."[55] Fourès reported that in Paris, the officials felt "a bit *dépaysé* . . . the public is not interested in them: they do not distinguish them from the other passersby."[56] But in Nancy and Lyon, a French official worried that the officials "mistook as signs of deference what was, on the part of our compatriots, simple politeness" and "assumed the importance that the courtesy of their hosts seemed to attribute to them, thereby developing a misleading sense of our mentality and of their merit."[57]

By the early twentieth century, the Third Republic had expanded education and social welfare, and its support of scientific and technological innovation through public finance had helped drive a "second industrial revolution" reviving the French economy after a crisis in the late nineteenth century. The Permanent Mission's members were impressed. "Oh human genius! Oh human intelligence! I would never have thought that you could be pushed to such a degree! Everywhere, in this land, I saw only signs of wealth and power," wrote Trần Tấn Bình.[58] For the Nguyễn empire, they saw the most potential in mechanized agriculture, artisanal production, and small-scale industry. They wrote about how fertilizers and water pumps could increase agricultural yields; how roads, canals, chambers of commerce, and standard weights and measures might link markets to one another; and how sewing machines, kilns, electrical saws, and chemicals could help fabric production, porcelain, woodworking, and tanning. They also wrote about the problem of capital. "Indochina's money is always hidden, unproductive and always shrinking without any knowledge of how to apply it productively to industry and commerce," wrote one.[59] Another bemoaned that "only Chinese control large commercial enterprises . . . and possess substantial capital" and argued that small savings banks modeled after the French *caisses d'épargnes,* as well as agricultural and artisanal cooperatives, could help capital to accumulate and circulate.[60]

The Nguyễn and Khmer officials who saw France ultimately imagined the Republican state more as a parallel to their own imperial states than as as a wholly different political model. In 1897, Nguyễn Trọng Hiệp described the Third Republic as grounded in ancient imperial traditions. "Today in this vast palace where affairs of state are treated," he wrote of the Chamber of Deputies and Senate, "I seem to see the perpetuation of antique institutions, but with glorious progress."[61] The Permanent Mission's members offered similar assessments of Republicanism's tumultuous history and revolutionary character. "The French are equal to one another and the people are sovereign," wrote Nguyễn Huy Tưởng, "but a great people cannot directly exercise its sovereignty. It must choose proxies to represent them."[62] He likened the Pantheon's luminaries to Asia's cults of ancestors and great men. These officials understood popular sovereignty as largely passive: the right to observe debates in the Chamber of Deputies or read about them in the press. They felt that the purpose of public education was to teach citizens how to choose talented, morally upright elites to serve as political authorities and technical experts who would assume responsibility for stability and prosperity. To them, the lesson of modern French politics was the need for a central state, the danger of autonomous local administration, and the use of military service, national education, and social welfare to shape loyal subjects.

When they left for Paris, most members of the Permanent Mission hoped that that the colonial fait accompli in Indochina would bring "progress" to their own imperial states. Some continued to believe it despite ominous signs, such as the eruption of political unrest across the colony in 1907–08. "France is here and intends to stay out of its own interest," wrote Trần Tấn Bình in 1907. "However, do we not know that the best actions are often self interested? . . . I have told you what France's interests are in Indochina; to preserve them, she asks but one thing: to instruct us, to develop our natural resources, to make us one day worthy of no longer being her protégés, but her allies, allied by common interest."[63] But for others, going to France intensified a nagging sense that they had become spectators in a project carried out for French glory alone. "If the purpose of our mission was to come to France to learn about industry in a brief period of time," wrote delegates from Annam in 1906, "we would ask that, before showing us something, to have us study it for several days to allow us to better understand its principles, and thereafter to bring us to where it is done to show us its practical implementation." Instead, "our visits to factories are hardly instructive, we only see the machines work and are not able to ask for the information we desire; at times, many among us retain almost nothing about what we have seen, especially when it is somewhat complex."[64]

Events in Indochina drove home the contradiction. On April 29, 1908, as anti-tax protests raged in Annam and the former imperial official Phan Châu Trinh languished in prison, what would be the last delegation of the Permanent Mission left for France. One of its delegates was Vũ Huy Quang, who had been raised by French missionaries, clerked for a French attorney, served on the Chambre Consultative du Tonkin, and received an honorary grade in the mandarinate that qualified him to become part of the Permanent

Mission.[65] His career reflected exactly the kind of nepotism and subservience for which Phan Châu Trinh pilloried the Nguyễn imperial state in his 1907 letter to Governor General Paul Beau. But recent upheavals had brought Vũ Huy Quang closer to Phan Châu Trinh's point of view. During the trip to France, he wrote a letter criticizing the forced abdication of the Thành Thái emperor, Phan Châu Trinh's arrest, and the hapless French response to a cholera epidemic in Hà Nội. Shortly after the mission's arrival, its stunned French minders learned that all of Tonkin's delegates had signed the letter and sent it to the governor general. "The French presented themselves to us as 'older brothers' and assured us that they would soon initiate us to the secret of their force and grandeur," it read. But "all of these troubles, all of these agitations, are obstacles hindering the progress of Annam and Tonkin. It is a disaster for all involved; the protesters and the protectors suffer equally. The best remedy for this would be to realize the reforms that intelligent and illuminated Annamites await impatiently."[66] These included much of what Phan Châu Trinh called for: an end to corruption, reforms to educational and judicial structures, less onerous tax policies, and the like.

The matter became even more urgent when the letter was published in *La presse coloniale*, followed by articles about it in other newspapers, including some by Albert de Pouvourville, a popular commentator on colonial affairs. An investigation revealed that in Paris, Vũ Huy Quang had frequented none other than Alfred-Ernest Babut, the muckraking colonial journalist and friend of Phan Châu Trinh. In his exculpatory scrambles, Vũ Huy Quang claimed that Babut wrote the letter and had the delegates sign it in hopes that officials would not dismiss it as agitations of a French rabble-rouser. Babut probably did play a role: he may have hoped that the letter would suggest that Phan Châu Trinh's ideas were widespread within the Nguyễn administration. But French officials believed Vũ Huy Quang quite capable of writing his own letters, and they sent him home. He had a first-class cabin on the trip over but was now demoted to third class.[67] Vũ Huy Quang's foray into journalism was the death blow for the Permanent Mission, which ended that year. The crisis of 1908 set colonial policy in a new direction: Albert Sarraut's "Franco-Annamese collaboration" (Pháp-Việt Đề Huề) in partnership with Indochina's urban and French-educated elites. Colonial officials had listened to Phan Châu Trinh after all, even if he remained too dangerous to set free. In 1915, four years after Phan Châu Trinh's exile, another mission of Indochinese imperial officials came to France to observe, interview, advocate for, and—above all—watch over the nearly one hundred thousand Indochinese fighting and laboring in the cataclysmic war engulfing France. After the war, a few would remain briefly to work for the new metropolitan branch of the colonial security services. In the 1860s, colonial officials had brought Indochinese imperial officials to France in hopes of making them partners in colonial rule; by the Great War, they did so to make them into French intelligence agents.

ROYAL SOJOURNS AND THE REMAKING OF INDOCHINESE MONARCHIES

The Permanent Mission, though brief, left a deep impression on one young colonial official. Pierre Pasquier's first encounters with Indochinese came at the École coloniale, where he and Thân Trọng Huế (both 1898 graduates) had become friends. Pasquier accepted a position in Indochina in 1900; he traveled with Tonkin's delegation to the Permanent Mission when he returned to France for the colonial exposition in 1906. In 1907, he enthused about the initiative. "On their way to France they kept to themselves," he wrote, "without bothering with the Europeans on board, but their time in France has given them points of contact with our *mentalité,* to become closer to us, to communicate with no restraint." "I truly feel," he concluded, "they have acquired our way of being."[68] After reentering the administration in Indochina, Pasquier set into motion an effort to "remodel kingship's symbolic significance and mobilize the sacred nature of sovereigns" to "create . . . colonial kings." He and his collaborator Albert Sarraut envisioned France as a stage, even a laboratory, to "colonize the royal body" and refashion it into a symbol of Franco-Indochinese cooperation.[69]

France first became a site of Indochinese monarchical politics years before Pasquier's project. Although the Khmer king Norodom had welcomed the 1863 protectorate treaty to hedge against Nguyễn and Siamese ambitions, the governor of Cochinchina's 1884 power grab stoked deep division and resistance at the court. Prince Duong Chakr, one of the king's favored sons, had escaped sanction for supporting an anti-French revolt in 1885, but years of political machinations (including a plot to assassinate the king) led his father to disown him and, finally, to his incarceration. Duong Chakr escaped from prison, fled to Siam, and in 1893 traveled to Paris with his wife to appeal for reforms and seek protection from protectorate officials (and his own father). But his profligate spending forced him to hock family jewels and borrow money, forcing French officials to muster up an allowance and set him up in a modest apartment. From there, with the help of a sympathetic former protectorate official, he waged a campaign that, though it attracted the attention of the Parisian press, ultimately came to naught. Seven years later, the king sent another of his sons to France to appeal to metropolitan officials to reverse new limits on the Khmer monarchy that even he found excessive. Prince Yukanthor, officially a royal envoy to the 1900 exposition, had greater access to French officials and to the press than Duong Chakr, and he attempted to appeal to the "generous, benevolent, and exquisite" French of the metropole to fend off the "arrogant, dominant, abusive" French agents of the protectorate.[70] The campaign garnered him attention and sympathy, and it boomeranged back to the colonial press. Bowing to pressure from the governor general, Norodom soon called for his son's return. But in a daring *contre-pied,* Yukanthor skipped his steamship home at the eleventh hour and fled first to Brussels and then Singapore, where he learned of his father's death and the ascension to the Khmer throne of Sisowath, France's chosen successor, in 1904.

Two years later, Sisowath arrived in France for the colonial exposition. His visit was a choreographed festival of empire; he was paraded from ministries to factories to public outings (racetracks, department stores, the opera). The king reveled in the pageantry, chatting with spectators, passing out medals, shopping, watching a silent film at the Elysée Palace, betting on horses, attending the circus (twice), and urging French officials to take back Battambang and Siem Reap, which he called "my Alsace-Lorraine," from Siam.[71] Although he cut an appealing figure, the real attraction in 1906 was the Royal Khmer Ballet, a troupe of dancers and musicians which "conquered the French public with the solemn grace of these strange dances, in poses and balances, oddly expressive in their lethargy," and the "fluidity of melodic lines bereft of modal markers or harmonics, the shivering of the xylophones, and timpani, and the heartrending cry of the sudden and dramatic acceleration of the drums preceding the singer's nasal incantations."[72] The dancers stoked the exotic and sensual fantasies of many French observers, among them Auguste Rodin, who sketched them for days. But Pasquier described the visit as "carnivalesque," a "lamentable and ridiculous exhibition" that trivialized royal rituals whose sacrality he hoped to mobilize in the symbolic service of the empire.[73]

Plans to bring the Nguyễn emperors to France, first imagined at the turn of the century, took two decades to come to fruition. In 1902, a delegation led by the regent Nguyễn Thân, who had been instrumental in crushing the Cần

FIGURE 4. King Sisowath at the revue de Longchamp, Paris, July 14, 1906. Source: Agence photographique Rol.

Vương resistance, went to France to prepare for the visit of the young Thành Thái emperor, part of a project to cultivate him as "an intermediary between an archaic court, whose grandiose but senile pomposity gave an impression more of representation than of action, and the modern and dynamic society that the protectorate intended to develop."[74] Thành Thái was keenly interested in Western ideas, objects, and styles, but French control over his life and activities likely contributed to the increasingly erratic behavior that first prevented him from traveling to France in 1902 and then led to his 1907 exile in Réunion. The French had no more luck with his successor, Duy Tân, whom they also planned to send to France to study.[75] But sensing an opening with France mired in the Great War, Duy Tân heeded the call of anti-French officials, fled the royal palace for the mountains, and called for revolt. The short-lived uprising ended with Duy Tân joining his father in exile in Réunion in 1916. Ironically, Duy Tân would in exile become a proud, even passionate believer in the Third Republic, waging a futile campaign to be allowed to relocate to France. He would only set foot there in 1944, after years of service in Free French forces.

In 1919, Sarraut and Pasquier began to plan for the visit of the Khải Định emperor, Duy Tân's successor, to the 1922 colonial exposition. Pasquier left no detail to chance, overseeing the emperor's retinue, his housing, his itinerary, his interlocutors, and even his clothes: Khải Định had ordered wardrobes of

European outfits for him and his retinue "to go out incognito to study the customs of the diverse classes of French society" but Pasquier killed the idea, leading the emperor to remark bitterly that he could not even get out of bed without Pasquier's approval.[76] Every aspect of Khải Định's visit was a curated spectacle of Franco-Indochinese collaboration cemented in the Great War's shared sacrifices. Indeed, although the emperor visited ministries, schools, and hospitals, his visit's symbolic centerpiece were ceremonies at the Souvenir Indochinois, a communal house (*đình*) moved to France for the 1906 exposition and repurposed as a memorial for Indochinese war dead, and at the Arc de Triomphe, where he laid a wreath and saluted the Tomb of the Unknown Soldier.[77] His very presence outside of the Nguyễn kingdom was momentous: as Phan Châu Trinh noted bitterly, "thanks to the influence of the protectorate government, the 'Son of Heaven' has decided finally to divorce with the ancestral custom that an emperor of Annam does not leave his realm."[78] His French sojourn was, in Nguyễn Thế Anh's words, "the definitive death of the Confucian order."[79]

Few observers of Khải Định's trip paid much attention to the real target of Sarraut's and Pasquier's efforts: the nine-year-old prince Vĩnh Thụy, the emperor's son and successor. Khải Định was ill and not long for this world, and Sarraut and Pasquier had brought him to France in part to convince him to entrust them with his son's education and upbringing. Their goal was to make Vĩnh Thụy into "a colonial monarch, allied to Republican France, who incarnated, quite literally, the colonial politics of 'Franco-Annamese collaboration.' . . . The Franco-Vietnamese alliance would reflect itself in the manners, the gestures, the movements, the language and the thought of the future sovereign." This task, in their minds, could only be accomplished in France. "Let him," Pasquier wrote, "be caressed by the elegant wind of the Isle of France but not have time to drink too deeply of the brisk air of liberty. . . . Make of Vinh Thuy a prince who is elegant, gracious, talented in the arts, understanding of the French soul, speaking clearly our language, able to understand our civilization but equally apt not to deny anything of his own past, while becoming a sovereign who will bring about, in the French sense, the evolution of his country."[80]

After Khải Định's death in 1925, Vĩnh Thụy took the throne under the name Bảo Đại (Great Defender) and was whisked again to France, where he spent his formative years in its haut-bourgeois and aristocratic circles. He lived with the family of Eugène Charles, a former Resident Superior of Annam, in their *hôtel particulier* on Paris's Avenue La Bourdonnais. He studied at the prestigious Cours Hattemer and the École libre des sciences politiques alongside Rothschilds, Taittingers, Bourbons, and other scions of finance, industry, and politics. He played football and rode horses. The mystique of royalty still held real sway in France, and the young emperor was a popular subject in newspapers and magazines. In photographs of Bảo Đại from the time, he is nearly indistinguishable from his French classmates: studying in his Parisian mansion, paying homage to the assassinated president Paul Doumer (a former governor general of Indochina) and enjoying a rest cure at the spa town of Vichy. But at the 1931 colonial exposition, he appeared in the traditional royal garb he had worn when he assumed the throne, "playing the exotic and indigenous role in this perfectly studied Republican ritual celebrating the French empire." Wedged between Pasquier and Sarraut, he did not speak—he was there to be seen and photographed.[81]

Dozens of members of Indochina's royal families came to France in the shadows of such spectacles. Some came for an education, sent to France by parents anxious to gain favor or simply to give their children what they hoped was a first-rate education. In 1902, Pierre Guesde brought the Khmer prince Sisowath Souphanouvong with him to Pau, a small city tucked in the Pyrenees. Souphanouvong struggled with the language, the climate, and the food, and he could not adapt to the local lycée—Guesde's parents educated him for years. He visited Paris just once, when the Guesdes took him sightseeing and to meet surprised officials at the Ministry of Colonies.[82] In 1927, Phan Tấn Quế wrote home from Montpellier about "one of my closest friends here in France (the heir to the Lao throne). . . . Several times a year, the President of the Republic invites him to Paris; but he is still simple and modest, which I appreciate about him."[83] Some of Indochina's royals excelled in their studies in France. King Monivong's son Monireth studied at the Saint-Cyr military school with the son of the exiled Hàm Nghi emperor, who had married the daughter of a French official. Hàm Nghi's daughter, Princess Như Mai, graduated first in her class at the Institut agronomique in 1929.

But in the political and cultural eclipse of Indochina's monarchies, many members of the region's royal families came to France not as parables of the civilizing mission, but as its flotsam and jetsam. Bửu Thập, a direct descendant of the Minh Mạng emperor, fled to France in 1921 to escape gambling debts and the charge of impersonating an imperial official. He found work as a secretary; "I earn 600 francs a month," he wrote home, "just enough to live and to frequent *les dancings*."[84] The Khmer prince Norodom Norindeth, in Paris to study, was "subjugated by the charms of a lovely dancer of Belgian origin" until "a crisis of Buddhist mysticism" led him to go home and join a monastery. She sued him (unsuccessfully) for damages.[85] Few embody the eclipse of Indochina's monarchies better than the Khmer prince Norodom Ritharasi. In 1922, after his father forbade him from continuing his studies in France, he made the journey in secret. After refusing his father's order to return from Paris, he was stripped of his royal lineage. He worked as an insurance agent before entering medical school. After graduating in 1929, he returned to Indochina as only the second Cambodian medical doctor with a French degree. He practiced there for most of the 1930s, but returned to France before the war. He saw few people in his final years, but when he died of tuberculosis in 1944, his friends felt it important "to appeal to Indochinese solidarity so that the burial did not give that heartbreaking sense of abandonment that one feels when one sees a funeral procession followed only by a few assistants." They managed to muster up a few old French Indochina hands to come pay their respects as Ritharasi's coffin, draped in the tricolor, was lowered into French soil.[86]

THE ORIGINS OF INDOCHINESE POLITICS IN FRANCE

When Khải Định visited the colonial exposition in 1922, Phan Châu Trinh was toiling there retouching photographs. Since being exiled to France in 1911, he had suffered isolation, poverty, his son's death, and imprisonment; the abject submission of the Nguyễn emperor on top of all this was too much to bear. That summer, he waged a scorched-earth campaign against Khải Định that culminated with a withering letter accusing the emperor of "arrogance, lustful excesses, immoral conduct, breaches of regulated practices, reckless promotion of autocratic monarchy, unfair rewards and penalties, the trampling of people under the heel of your tyranny, reckless extravagance, actions contrary to humanity and civilization, obstruction of the people's progress, the list goes on and on." "Your majesty has been to Paris," he wrote. "Along its long boulevards and in the large public squares, you must have seen the bronze statues commemorating the philosophers and the heroes who risked their lives in defense of freedom. You must have seen the pillar that reaches up into the clouds; atop it stands ... the goddess of Liberty, who illuminates the whole world and has no mercy for any tyrant monarch on earth. If you use your spare time to visit the Place de la Concorde and

Versailles, know that it was at Versailles that Louis XVI was captured and at the Place de la Concorde that he was executed. After you have witnessed these reminders of the final moments of a tyrant monarch, you may reflect upon yourself."[87] A young radical calling himself Nguyễn Ái Quốc seconded Phan Châu Trinh, writing newspaper articles and a stage play, "The Bamboo Dragon," which "ridiculed the emperor and derided the feudal regime and the monarchy."[88] As rumors swirled of a plot to assassinate Khải Định, the French police closely watched the two men and their associates.

This small but extraordinarily consequential French network of Indochinese anti-colonial activists had grown out of the political crisis of 1907–08. Phan Châu Trinh had received the *phó bảng* degree in 1901 and was working as a secretary in the Ministry of Rites when he began to read the "new books" (*Tân thư*) trickling into Indochina from China and Japan, which he spent hours discussing with the reformist official Thân Trọng Huề, recently returned from the École coloniale. Convinced that French rule had fatally corrupted the Nguyễn monarchy, he resigned in 1904 and began to meet and correspond with like-minded critics. He went to Japan, where he met with Cường Để, a Nguyễn prince exiled for his opposition to France, and Phan Bội Châu, his principal lieutenant. After returning in 1907, he published a public letter to Governor General Paul Beau which Christopher Goscha describes as "a colonial 'j'accuse.'" It offered a withering critique of the Nguyễn monarchy and a call for France to live up to its own republican values by "introducing freedom of the press, Western knowledge and a public education system, favoring the diffusion of French and *quoc ngu,* developing industry and commerce, and creating forms of representative government."[89] Phan Châu Trinh's vision of Indochinese republicanism was too extreme for French officials and especially for the Nguyễn monarchy. In 1908, he was accused of instigating the anti-tax movements that had erupted in Annam that spring, and the Imperial Privy Council (*cơ mật viện*) sentenced him to death. Only the intervention of his friend Alfred-Ernest Babut, the radical journalist, saved his life. His sentence was commuted to house arrest in Mỹ Thọ. He appealed to be sent instead to exile in France, where he and his son Phan Châu Dật arrived in April 1911.

Phan Châu Trinh's closest collaborator in France was also a casualty of the political crisis of 1907–08. Phan Văn Trường was a member of an illustrious literati family from Đông Ngạc, near Hà Nội. After a traditional education, he studied at the Collège des interprètes and worked briefly for the protectorate administration. He had met a few of the members of the Permanent

Mission in the Tonkin Free School's circles before it closed. In 1908, three of his brothers were implicated in the plot to poison French soldiers. Phan Văn Trường, worried that this would limit his prospects in the colony, left for France soon thereafter, where he found work teaching Vietnamese at the École des langues orientales.[90] He supposedly first met Phan Châu Trinh when he called on him at his apartment at 78 rue d'Assass, a quick walk from his own (later famous) apartment at 6 Villa des Gobelins. The two were regularly invited to events at the École pratique d'enseignement colonial in nearby Joinville-le-Pont, where dozens of Indochinese were studying. French officials began to worry when they formed the Đồng Bào Thân Ái (Fraternity) in early 1912. The mutual aid and study society, often miscast as "ethnic," explicitly appealed to Khmer and Lao (a few of whom were students in Joinville-le-Pont) as well as Vietnamese; its mission was to "allow people of our country who have come from afar to gather and frequent one another, to forge ties and to communicate" and "visit and comfort those who have fallen into hardship or sickness."[91] But Phan Văn Trường and Phan Châu Trinh also affirmed that the society would "endeavor to instruct Indochinese people by the popularization, through works in quốc ngữ, of useful ideas both scientific and literary," making the romanized Vietnamese language "a means for unification" of the colony's ethnicities.[92] French officials feared political conspiracy. "This is," one official fretted, "a program to unite ... all Indochinese students in France. There will be members in France and in Indochina; they will have patrons who will offer support for these young people in Paris, like what was done for those in Japan, but with the difference that the French colonial administration will be unable to object to an association that fully conforms with our laws."[93]

It remains unclear whether the Đồng Bào Thân Ái was just a student-initiated mutual aid society, as Phan Văn Trường claimed in his memoir, or, as French officials believed, an anti-colonial organization. Although the group likely "indulged in little more than exile talk," French paranoia blossomed.[94] In January 1912, some of its members attended a performance of *Les Sauterelles,* a play criticizing French rule in Indochina, which led French officials to seek to know when and why they applauded during the performance.[95] Phan Văn Trường's leadership of the Đồng Bào Thân Ái led to his dismissal from his position at the École des langues orientales, but it was another episode that brought down the full weight of the security apparatus on the two men. In October 1913, a man named Trương Duy Toản knocked at Phan Châu Trinh's door. He claimed to have come from Berlin to deliver a letter from Cường Để, whom Phan Châu Trinh had met in Japan years earlier, ultimately intended for Sarraut. The letter, a proposal for colonial reform, left Phan Châu Trinh suspicious of entrapment. He marched the letter and its messenger to the Ministry of Colonies to inform French officials and shield himself from blame.[96]

But the letter was authentic. Cường Để had come to Europe months earlier at the urging of German officials in China, seeking support in Berlin for his campaign against France—part of a broader German effort to mobilize support for the anti-French Vietnamese Restoration League (Quang Phục Hội). But Berlin produced no useful contacts, and Cường Để soon moved off to London. Phan Văn Trường went to England several times in 1913, probably to meet with Cường Để's agents.[97] Cường Để's proposals in his letter largely reflected Sarraut's own program of political and economic reform. But Cường Để suspected a trap when Sarraut invited him to return to Indochina, and he went to China instead. Dreams for the Quang Phục Hội were soon dashed; Phan Bội Châu, Cường Để's right-hand man, was jailed in January 1914 by anti-republican factions in China, and German financial support for anti-French uprisings produced only a few tentative border raids. But for French officials already deeply suspicious of Phan Châu Trinh and Phan Văn Trường, even the specter of an alliance with Germany was enough: they arrested the two men in September 1914.

Phan Châu Trinh and Phan Văn Trường languished in Paris's Santé prison until July 1915. In his memoir, Phan Văn Trường described the rude conditions of his incarceration—cramped cells, forced labor, lice and pruritus, and meager food. "Oriental sobriety," he wrote, "allowed me to suffer less than the European inmates."[98] By his own account, he awaited the end of his sentence with equanimity, informing only one friend, though news of his arrest had spread in the colony.[99] But Phan Châu Trinh fired off missives proclaiming his innocence to the military court and wrote two hundred poems about his experience of captivity. His French friends again came to his defense—the captain Jules Roux (who had helped him avoid his death sentence in Indochina) and the Socialist deputy Marius Moutet sent appeals to the French president—and his trial ended when the main Indochinese witness fell mute. Soon after his release in 1915, his son returned to Indochina with tuberculosis, where he died. Devastated and destitute, Phan Châu Trinh was forced to turn to photo retouching.[100] Phan Văn Trường worked for the rest of the war as an interpreter for Indochinese laborers in Toulouse, periodically harassed by military authorities.[101] When he returned to Paris in late 1918, he and Phan Châu Trinh shared the apartment at 6 Villa des Gobelins. Embittered by their experiences and emboldened by the political winds now sweeping through Paris, the friends set about reviving the Đồng Bào Thân Ái and collaborating on a plan to achieve colonial reform in Indochina. They did so with a young Indochinese activist whose path to France had taken a very different course.

Nguyễn Tất Thành, born Nguyễn Sinh Cung in Nghệ An, was the son of an imperial official who received his degree in 1901 in the same examination class as Phan Châu Trinh. In 1909, a scandal that cost his father his position upended Nguyễn Tất Thành's education and career prospects. The family's fall seems to have drawn it closer to reformist circles; Nguyễn Tất Thành's father may have met Phan Châu Trinh as early as 1901, and evidence exists of the literati's influence on the family, and possibly direct contact between them, as early as 1909. Nguyễn Tất Thành left Indochina in mid-1911, possibly at Phan Châu Trinh's urging, hoping to continue his studies in France. He worked as a kitchen boy during the journey. In September he requested admission to the École coloniale "to become useful to France in relation to my compatriots, and . . . to help them profit from the benefits of Instruction," a request "redolent of Phan Chu Trinh's tactics of critical collaboration, which called on Vietnamese to master the best of France's cultural and democratic traditions for their own ends."[102] Denied admission, he kept working on steamships to earn a living and help his father. By late 1913 or early 1914 he was in England, likely connected to Cường Để's small network of supporters there (again possibly at Phan Châu Trinh's urging). Nguyễn Tất Thành's experiences during the Great War are obscure and cloaked in myth: they include a possible 1916 trip to France to meet Phan Châu Trinh and Phan Văn Trường, and a possible sojourn in the United States in 1917–18, where he later claimed to have been inspired by Marcus Garvey and exiled Korean nationalists. But it is clear that when the Sûreté began to pay attention to the young man living with Phan Châu Trinh and Phan Văn Trường at 6 Villa des Gobelins, Nguyễn Tất Thành's political awakening was already years old.

In the summer of 1919, as Western diplomats redrew the map of the world, the three men waged a campaign for colonial reform in Indochina. Its heart was the "Revendications du peuple annamite," a petition sent to participants in the Peace Conference, just a few of whom (including the American representative) bothered to acknowledge its receipt; thousands more copies were soon printed and circulated in France and Indochina.[103] Phan Văn Trường probably wrote most of the petition, but it was signed "Nguyễn Ái Quốc"

("Nguyễn the Patriot"), Nguyễn Tất Thành's nom de guerre until his rebirth as Hồ Chí Minh. "While waiting for the principle of national self-determination to pass from ideal to reality through the effective recognition of the sacred right of all peoples to decide their own destiny," it read, "the inhabitants of the ancient Empire of Annam, at the present time French Indochina, present to the noble Governments of the entente in general and to the honorable French Government in particular the following humble claims." These included amnesty for political prisoners, judicial reform, freedom of the press and association, freedom of instruction and movement, and democratic representation.[104]

The "Revendications du peuple annamite" reflected the intersection of Indochinese politics with a global constellation of ideas about Atlantic liberalism, republicanism, nationalism, and constitutionalism.[105] The three men had first encountered these ideas in Indochina, through networks of textual circulation and exchange linking the colony to East Asian reformist thought. But their French sojourns had been essential to their political evolution. "Over the past twelve years," Phan Châu Trinh would soon write in his letter to Khải Định, "I have lived in the land of democracy, breathed the air of liberty. Thanks to that, I became familiar with the principles of universal justice, recognized the duties of progress and civilization in the modern world."[106] His claim was not rhetorical. Indeed, for all the surveillance and incarceration the men suffered in France, its milieu of leftist political meetings and organizing, its vibrant press, and its networks of global political activists had helped to forge their political visions. As Indochinese sojourns exploded after the war, hundreds more young political activists would have similar experiences in France, with equally crucial legacies for colonial and postcolonial politics.

But the "Revendications du peuple annamite" also laid bare a tension at the heart of these new "Indochinese" political ideas. Exposition delegations, pedagogical missions, and royal tours in France brought together officials, cultural elites, and monarchs from all parts of Indochina into imperial political structures and spaces that not only reflected French visions of Indochina but also helped bring them into being. The importance of "Annamese" as colonial auxiliaries in the new colony's Khmer and Lao regions had in many ways simply continued the Nguyễn empire's imperial projects in these places. For the "Annamite" authors of the petition, there was thus little tension in equating "the former Annamese Empire" with "French Indochina"; indeed, Phan Châu Trinh had conflated them in his writings for a decade, and he and

Phan Văn Trường had done so in the Đồng Bào Thân Ái. But not all "Indochinese" thought that way. "What," wrote a critic of the petition in *Courrier saïgonnais,* "are the Cambodians, the Laotians and the countless other nations occupying the summits of the Annamese Cordillera going to say? They are annexed by the stroke of a pen by our so-called Annamese patriots."[107] Because "Annamese" would continue to dominate growing circulations between colony and metropole after the war, this tension would persist as postwar sojourns made France an increasingly important theater of Indochinese politics.

FOUR

Cultural Sojourners

IN 1911, PHAN VĂN TRƯỜNG WAS TEACHING at the École des langues orientales when André Salles, the director of the Comité Paul Bert, asked him to teach a course in "morale Annamite" for the dozens of Indochinese studying under his watch at the École pratique d'enseignement colonial in the confines of Parangon castle in Joinville-le-Pont near Paris. Phan Văn Trường quickly discovered their percolating unhappiness with the situation. The Comité's goal was to educate useful colonial auxiliaries: as Salles wrote, students at Parangon would receive "an excellent family discipline" and "a practical and adapted course of study" to orient them to "agricultural, commercial and industrial careers."[1] But the students, as Phan Văn Trường wrote, "told all who would listen that they were learning almost nothing at this private primary school and that if they had known that in France, they would be interned in such a place, they would not have traveled so far from family and made so many unnecessary sacrifices."[2] In the Đồng Bào Thân Ái they organized with Phan Văn Trường, the students made for themselves the education they had hoped to find in France. During its meetings, they discussed subjects from medicine to philosophy, debated articles in *Le Temps* and *L'Humanité,* and read Montesquieu's *Spirit of Laws,* Rousseau's *Social Contract,* and Châteaubriand's historical essays. The contrast between the two forms of cultural sojourns the students experienced in France—one directed by colonial authorities, and one forged on their own—could not have been clearer. As a student wrote home, "if an elevated and well-conceived education represents a war of revolutionary ideas, it is also the embryo of modern civilization." This prompted Salles to intone darkly, "these students will soon come to desire not the *evolution* of their country, but a *revolution.*"[3]

Parangon and the Đồng Bào Thân Ái, inextricably linked but countervailing cultural forces on the Indochinese who experienced them, capture France's dual role as a site of cultural change in colonial Indochina. Before the Great War, embassies, delegations, study missions, and other official initiatives helped make France part of Indochina's "modernist moment," a juncture when "the reformist tradition of the imperial state, the modernizing colonial project, and the reformism of . . . social elites" largely overlapped.[4] But during the interwar era, as official cultural sojourns faded as a colonial strategy, students, intellectuals, writers, journalists, artists, and other Indochinese sojourned in France as part of an engagement with French cultural and intellectual life that was at the heart of their vocations and horizons. The novelist Vũ Trọng Phụng, Peter Zinoman argues, was a "provincial cosmopolitan" who "never traveled abroad and yet still pursued a passionate interest in the culture and politics of the wider world through dog-eared foreign novels and dated French newspapers."[5] For the many Indochinese who did make cultural sojourns to France, perhaps the reverse was true: some went in hopes of leaving colonial society behind, but most were "cosmopolitan provincials," who remained oriented toward Indochina's literary, intellectual, artistic, and journalistic worlds from the other side of the empire.

EDUCATION

Parangon, where hundreds of Indochinese studied during the decade before the Great War, reflected long-standing French efforts (from the École cambodgienne, the École coloniale, and the Permanent Mission of Indochinese Mandarins) to use educations in France to form Indochinese allies, a privilege reserved largely for members of royal and elite families or, as the Resident Superior in Tonkin put it, as "compensation for services rendered by their father in the course of his official duties."[6] It taught Indochinese students "to receive customers, sales, wrapping and shipping merchandise, as well as accounting, typing and stenography." Its agriculture students learned "practical skills like planting and maintaining flower or vegetable gardens" and animal husbandry.[7] The school reflected a French belief that Indochinese were, in its director's words, "practical, careful, and meticulous rather than original and inventive . . . more at ease in the domain of *familiar realities* than in that of *ideas* themselves."[8] Its location, an impregnable castle outside of Paris, reflected the Comité Paul Bert's vision for the Indochinese students it supervised there and at a smattering of other collèges or technical schools. "We keep our young people away from the big cities," Salles wrote; "the village or small city is far better for them than Marseille or Paris both morally and physically, and especially to help them come to know the France that works and not the France that idles."[9] Hosts (often retired colonial officials) supervised their studies, how they spent their time, and whose company they frequented.

But in the last years before the Great War, this vision grew increasingly remote from Indochinese expectations. Indeed, the colonial administration created the Comité Paul Bert to cope with growing demands for study in France, many by learned societies whose candidates for scholarships "were distinguished by their intelligence, aptitude, and good conduct" rather than their personal or political connections.[10] Even those students firmly committed to France's enterprise in Indochina had educational horizons far beyond the vocational training of schools like Parangon. The colonial administration's preference for technical subjects would never waver: about 70 percent of Indochinese recipients of state scholarships for study in France during the colonial era studied agriculture, commerce, or other applied fields.[11] But at the turn of the century, more began following paths like that of Bùi Quang Chiêu, who studied rice cultivation at the Institut agronomique in the 1890s, bypassing colonially-specific courses of study for rigorous French formations in fields from sericulture to distilling, silk production to veterinary science.

One important group of these were medical students. Most were graduates of the École de médecine de l'Indochine (founded in 1902) who had worked as auxiliaries in the colonial health services. One of the first was Lê Văn Chỉnh, who was in awe of the French surgeons he observed in 1910 and 1911: "The sight of these great masters of surgery," he wrote, "made me want to become one myself."[12] Before returning to France, he requested financial help to ship back three hundred kilos of medical books he had acquired in France. "In Tonkin," he wrote, "there is no library in this field; these books will help preserve the learned instruction and good advice of the masters of French medicine."[13] Lê Quang Trình, the first Indochinese *docteur de médecine* (1911) was one of several other Indochinese medical students in France (among them Nguyễn Văn Thinh, later the president of the Republic of Cochinchina) to volunteer for the Great War. Others from Indochina soon joined them for a formative professional experience in often horrendous conditions. Nguyễn Xuân Mai came in 1916 after six years as a military doctor in Indochina. He served with the 21st Indochinese battalion, which in 1918 endured chemical attacks and massive German offensives. His service created powerful bonds with his French fellow doctors and nurses. He remained in France to earn his doctorate, which he received in 1921: the first words of his dissertation are "the war that any book is able to accurately depict, leaves us with memories that are engraved there forever and reappear in the hours of daydream of our civilian life."[14]

"Purely bookish studies," Salles wrote in 1912, "dangerously excite young Indochinese minds. . . . Eventually, they lift their eyes from their books to look at their country, and it is not surprising that most of them become impatient to apply there the theories that they have learned in France, which they dream about without any sense of reality."[15] Beliefs like these made it less likely for Indochinese to receive official scholarships to study non-technical fields in France (roughly 15 percent of scholarship recipients during the colonial era).[16] Before the war, most of the few who did came for the certification (*brevet*) necessary to teach in Indochina's growing Franco-indigenous school system, difficult to obtain in the colony (before the war, only possible at the Écoles normales in Gia Định and Hà Nội). "I personally see nothing but advantages," wrote a French official in support of Đoàn Văn Nhiêu, "for this *instituteur* to come to Marseille . . . to productively study the methods and procedures of French instruction."[17] Fewer did so after the war, when it became easier to acquire a brevet in Indochina.

Legal studies, unavailable in the colony until the creation of the École de droit et d'administration in Hà Nội in 1917, also drew some Indochinese to France before the war. "The *licence* in law," fumed Salles, "will make of them politicians."[18] He had evidence in his favor in Phan Văn Trường, who had begun studying law at the Sorbonne while teaching at the École des langues orientales, and who received his *licence* and formed the Đồng Bào Thân Ái in the same year (1912). After his release from prison in 1915, he used his legal training to defend soldiers in military tribunals in the French-occupied Rhineland. It was unsurprising that his supervisor saw "subversive passages of liberal or communist tendency" in his 1922 doctoral thesis on the Gia Long legal code (they were censored, but he still received the degree).[19] But other law students assuaged such anxieties. Đỗ Hữu Trí, son of the influential official Đỗ Hữu Phương and brother of Đỗ Hữu Vị, an officer in the French air force and soon Indochina's most famous martyr of the Great War, was a lawyer at the Paris bar and one of the first Indochinese members of a French masonic lodge.[20] In 1913, Đoàn Vĩnh Thuận became the first Indochinese to receive a French doctorate in law for his thesis "L'Indo-Chine autonome et parlementaire," which helped make him one of the first Indochinese to work in the colonial judiciary.[21]

Some Indochinese also pursued secondary studies in France at a collège, lycée, or private school (*établissement libre*) before the war. Salles estimated about fifty such students in France in 1911, noting that "this movement has been flowing for some time to the lycées of Marseille and Algiers."[22] Most were the children of royals or elite Cochinchinese families. In the 1880s, Indochinese students at the Lycée d'Alger included Bùi Quang Chiêu, Nguyễn Trọng Quản (Trương Vĩnh Ký's son-in-law and the author of *Truyện thầy Lazaro Phiên,* among the first works of modern Vietnamese fiction), and Trần Văn Thông (later the governor of Nam Định and one of Madame Nhu's grandfathers). They also included Nguyễn Văn Cẩm, better known as Kỳ Đồng, a child prodigy revered in his native province of Thái Bình as a reincarnation of the poet Nguyễn Bình Khiêm, whom French officials sent across the world in the vain hope of calming the restive youth. But from early on, colonial officials were leery of French educations without a clear political or economic purpose. Nguyễn Phú Khai, after studying at a lycée in the 1890s, washed out of both engineering school and the École coloniale: "Khai has received an advanced education," a French official wrote, "he will have pretentions, but he will also be without any practical tools and will surely become a déclassé."[23] Such concerns intensified as Indochinese, frustrated by the Comité Paul Bert, left it for a lycée education. Nguyễn Khắc Sư and Nguyễn Khắc Vệ (later minister of justice in the non-communist State of Vietnam before 1954) came to Parangon in 1908; three years later, their father transferred them to a lycée. "I would like for my sons to receive the baccalauréat," he wrote, "otherwise they will be seen as ignorant men limited to a career as mechanics or craftsmen."[24] That same year, Vũ Quang Nhạ and Trần Đình Lượng, Tonkin's lead delegates to the 1900 exposition, also removed their sons from technical study under the Comité's supervision for a baccalauréat course. "Annamite fathers are credulous, ignorant, and vain," fumed Salles; he felt that a lycée would make their sons "pretentious and never satisfied."[25] Official concerns about secondary educations in France soon limited official support, but new demand for this kind of education after the war far exceeded efforts to limit or control it.

In 1923, the director of the Lycée Mignet in Aix-en-Provence wrote to colonial officials about a wave of students, most from Cochinchina, streaming into his school since the war. "The arrival of these young people in the metropole," he wrote, "stems solely from the free will of their families and the appeal of our civilization for an enlightened segment of our Indochinese populations." But like most French officials now did, he perceived "serious disadvantages in this regime of liberal immigration," namely the cultural and political danger of humanistic study and the lures of life in France.[26] Some Indochinese had their own concerns. Nguyễn Văn Vĩnh was one of many who worried about "spoiled brats" (*fils à papa*) who "take the boat to Europe dreaming of a cushy job earning them thousands of piasters a month," and whose families "take on heavy burdens" for French educations that are simply "a pretext to go taste the pleasures of Europe's big cities," and who "will return with new needs that this country cannot satisfy."[27] As reductive as both perspectives were, Indochinese educational sojourns in France in the 1920s did derail for many reasons: finances, insufficient talent or preparation, the temptations of time away from family and supervision, the difficulties of life and study far from home, and their French teachers and peers. Like much else during the 1920s, the Indochinese study boom in France often busted.

"Since my arrival in the town, I had still not thought about studying," recounts Nhất Linh's narrator Lãng Du in "Going to France"; "every day I went to sit on the long benches in the University courtyard waiting for my friends who were sitting their exams, then we went from one coffee shop to another tasting the wines bought by those who had passed their exams. This was a pleasant introduction to my studies in France."[28] The character embodies the many Indochinese who had a decidedly casual attitude towards their studies. Trần Văn Mại had enrolled in Marseille's Lycée Saint Charles on the advice of a passenger on the steamship to France, but he soon moved to Aix because a friend needed a roommate.[29] "I first studied in Montpellier because the climate was nice," Trần Duy Đàm told a Sûreté officer; "after the vacation, I went to a lycée in Chartres because I had read that it was a beautiful city."[30] Upon arrival, many well-intentioned students had no idea how France's school system worked. "Last October," wrote Huỳnh Kim Hữu in 1929, "I met two new arrivals. One asked, 'Do you know if there's an engineering school here? I would like to study for my engineering diploma.' I responded: 'In Marseille, there isn't one . . . but do you have the baccalauréat?' 'No, but I want to become an engineer.' 'Do you have the brevet élémentaire?' 'Not yet.' So I told him that to be admitted to engineering school, one has to pass an advanced mathematics exam for which even those with the baccalauréat prepare for two years if they hope to have success. . . . I have no idea what has happened to this young man, abandoned to his own devices."[31] When Tống Văn Hên arrived in

Marseille in 1929, he found that he could not pay for even one trimester at a lycée, so he borrowed some money from a mutual aid association. When the economic crisis hit, he—like many hundreds of other Indochinese—had to abandon his studies to work (in his case, in a factory).[32]

Many students struggled with academic and disciplinary demands. "I am directing all of my efforts toward study as I await exam day," wrote Trần Văn Nhu to his father in 1929. "If I fail again this year I don't know what I will do."[33] Phạm Viết Cẩn failed the baccalauréat exam *eight* times before giving up and moving on to study law in Aix in 1925; in 1931, he still had not completed the first-year curriculum.[34] Some students could not correct poor habits that plagued them in Indochina: Lê Văn Tiều had been expelled from the Lycée Chasseloup-Laubat in Sài Gòn for failing to finish schoolwork and leaving school without permission; he was expelled from a lycée in Montpellier months later for the same reasons.[35] Struggling (or simply lazy) students at times resorted to cheating; some hatched complex schemes to exploit the spotty nature of personal documentation and interagency communication. In October 1931, Nguyễn Văn Lịnh passed the baccalauréat—he had the practice, for he had also done so that June using his brother's identity papers, sent from Cochinchina.[36] Others were victims of ill treatment. In 1928, Lê Công Nên and his brothers left their lycée because their teacher, "a shark who had been in Indochina," abused them with "unjust reproaches" and "unjustified punishments, accompanied with threats."[37] In 1925, Indochinese students in Montpellier protested when their lycée chose Léon Josselme, the hated head of the CAI, to examine them in Vietnamese for the baccalauréat. "Mr. Josselme detests Annamites," they wrote; "he succeeds in making them all fail even when their compositions are good, so as to break their futures by denying them entrance to university."[38] In sum, many who hoped to escape what they hated about colonial schools were disappointed to find much the same in France. "Compared to my school in Saigon, the education here is not really that different," wrote Tùng Hương; "what a shame to have come so far!"[39]

But for others, a collège or lycée education in France could be transformative. "There are other students," wrote one Henri Là Phương, "who know that piasters don't fall from the sky" and that "their short stay in the metropole demands heavy sacrifices." They "prefer to be alone, spending their time thinking, reflecting, and enriching themselves."[40] "I can see that you do not fully understand instruction in France, a true instruction that is behind the prodigious material development of all of Europe," Trần Văn Hà wrote

FIGURE 5. The executive board of the Association des étudiants indochinois de Bordeaux, 1929. Source: Dossier Bùi Văn Sanh, Box 64, Fonds de la police de l'Indochine puis direction des Services de sécurité du haut commissariat français au Vietnam-Sud (589PO2/SVN), Centre des archives diplomatiques, Nantes, France.

to his father in 1928. Studying in Toulouse "annihilated all of the ideas I had until now, utterly destroyed all my preconceptions."[41] "In class I am neither too high nor too low," wrote Cao Quỳnh An, "but every day, I walk the path of progress. . . . In History, Geography, and even in French I'm not among the Annamites of Saigon, but with the Parisians."[42] Personal fulfillment rarely brought academic stardom, but the "regime of liberal immigration" bemoaned by French officials did vault a talented few into the rarefied strata of France's elite universities. In 1927 the director of the Lycée Mignet had rejected sixteen-year-old Hồ Hữu Tường's request for placement in the lycée's final year: he went instead to a collège in Arles, where he earned the best grades in his class. The next summer, he received the highest score of twenty successful Indochinese baccalauréat candidates and went on to university studies in mathematics in Aix-en-Provence, Lyon, and the Sorbonne. He was not exceptional: the number of Indochinese studying at the University of Paris grew from 45 in 1925 to 203 in 1931, and many more studied at other universities.[43]

The strong piaster did not last forever. "I wanted to prepare my doctorate ... but I have had enough of living a dog's life," wrote Nguyễn Văn Hy in 1932.

> I live day to day ... thanks to the generosity of some friends, but now that we are on vacation they are leaving Paris; who can I count on now? Day after day I await the money that will let me leave. . . . I have sold all of my books to buy food. . . . This bohemian life is weighing on me, and I will end up being crushed.[44]

He was one of hundreds of Indochinese students in France left destitute by the Depression, which devastated Cochinchina's landed and professional classes. Some found menial jobs to try to continue their studies, but most soon returned home. But economic crisis did not stop some of Indochina's most talented students from studying in France's most prestigious universities. Some did so thanks to wealth that survived the Depression; Bùi Quang Chiêu had refused scholarships for his children Louis and Henriette when they began medical study in France in the mid-1920s, which the economic crisis did not interrupt.[45] More were like Phạm Duy Khiêm, the eldest son of an elite family thrown into financial stress by his father's death when he was fifteen. His brilliance earned him scholarships first to Hà Nội's Lycée Albert Sarraut, where he was valedictorian, then to Paris's elite Lycée Louis-le-Grand, and finally to the École normale supérieure in 1931.[46] A third of Indochinese who received state scholarships during the colonial era did so during the 1930s, many of them graduates of an expanded and modernized Université indochinoise, and many (unlike in the 1920s) from Tonkin and Annam.[47]

Scholarships in the 1930s continued to heavily favor technical or applied courses of study. Dozens came via pipelines between Hà Nội's École de médecine and French medical schools. Hồ Đắc Di had come in 1918 for the war but was spared service on the front. During his world-class surgical training in Paris's clinics and hospitals until 1931, he was "dazzled by the refined, intense and captivating life" there at a time when "a veritable revolution was taking place in all realms of thought."[48] In 1928, a medical student penned an open letter to the colony's medical professionals urging them to come to France to "perfect themselves and one day become true scholars for their country."[49] Many who did excelled. In 1927, Trần Quang Đệ placed fourth out of four hundred in the exam for externships in Paris hospitals; in 1935, Phạm Hữu Chí placed sixth.[50] In 1932, Nguyễn Huy Lê finished *first* in the national exam for scholarships for doctoral study in medicine but was denied one because he was not a French citizen (the Ministry of Education and Indochina's administration eventually split the costs).[51] Lê Văn Chỉnh had been shocked to study alongside French women in 1913, but by the 1930s there were two Indochinese women *docteurs de médecine;* Henriette Bùi (1934) and Lê Thị Hoàng (1937). "Whenever I presented myself in the hospitals," Henriette Bùi recalled, "they would ask: 'What's she doing there, that Chinese girl?' And they were surprised to see that I spoke French fluently. It was so rare to see a woman doctor, let alone an Asian one!"[52] Khmer and Lao who studied medicine in France were also unusual; Sonn Mam (Cambodia's first *docteur de médecine,* in 1925, who placed second in the national competition for heads of asylums in 1927) and Norodom Ritharasi (1929) were the only Khmer with doctorates in medicine before 1945; one Laotian, Oudom Souphanouvong (1947), received the degree before 1954.

A small but highly influential group of Indochinese studied scientific and technical fields in France's most elite institutions during the 1930s. Many studied engineering: Hoàng Xuân Hãn at the École polytechnique and the École nationale des ponts et chaussées, Phạm Quang Lễ at polytechnique, and Lê Viết Hương, Trần Hữu Phương, and Võ Qúy Huân at Ponts et chaussées, among others. In 1934, Phạm Tỉnh Quát became the first Indochinese to study mathematics at the École normale supérieure. Lê Văn Thiêm came five years later for the same reason; he received his *licence* in one year (instead of the typical three) and began doctoral study as war broke out. Tạ Quang Bửu earned a *licence* in physics from the Sorbonne and went on to doctoral study at Oxford; fellow students in Paris included Nguy Như Kontum (who would collaborate with the Nobel physicist Frédéric Joliot-Curie), Bửu Hội (great-great grandson of the Minh Mạng emperor and a talented chemist) and Hoàng Thị Nga (the first Indochinese woman to receive a doctorate, in physics, in 1935). Trần Văn Du was the first Indochinese at the École nationale vétérinaire. Most ended up in Paris, but some studied elsewhere: Nguyễn Thúc Hào received a doctorate in mathematics in Marseille; Nguyễn Xiển studied atmospheric science in Toulouse. Their professional and intellectual horizons varied; some sought careers in industry, others in research, and others in teaching. Some prepared for the agrégation (a qualification expected of all secondary and university instructors in France that was unavailable in Indochina) after non-citizens became eligible in 1935: Hoàng Xuân Hãn, Phạm Tỉnh Quát, Nguy Như Kontum, and Lê Văn Thiêm, among others.[53]

Indochinese continued to study law in France after the war because Hà Nội's École supérieure de droit did not offer the *licence* necessary to practice law until 1933 or doctorates until 1941. Some continued to justify French fears about a legal education. By the time Nguyễn An Ninh had received his *licence* from the Sorbonne in 1922, his budding anti-colonialism had made him well-known to the Sûreté. Dương Văn Giáo's 1924 doctoral thesis in law called for colonial political reform.[54] Trịnh Đình Thảo, a lawyer at the Aix court of appeals, organized the politically-charged Congrès des étudiants indochinois in Aix in 1927. Phan Anh was already a member of the French Socialist Party in Tonkin when he began his doctoral studies in law.[55] But most with a French *licence* in law aimed for jobs in the colonial judiciary or administration. All forty-three Indochinese with a doctoral degree in law before 1945 had earned it in France.[56] It was a far more scholarly course of study than legal studies in Indochina. Some of their theses used legal codes to explore precolonial governance, communal property, individual civil rights, and marriage and family law. Others focused on contemporary issues: French legal reforms, the status of Chinese under colonial law, and French naturalization.[57] Phạm Huy Thông, doctor in law, was also the first Indochinese agrégé in the field of history. One Indochinese woman seems to have earned a French law degree before 1945: Bùi Thị Cẩm, a cousin of Henriette Bùi's and later a member of the communist National Assembly, who wrote a thesis on the condition of women in Vietnamese law.[58] The brilliant Au Chhieng had begun doctoral study in Khmer epigraphy before turning to law, but his thesis was rejected in 1941 for its revisionist account of the legal origins of the French protectorate. He returned to the study of classical Cambodia, becoming an influential figure in postwar French Orientalism.[59]

Finally, a small cohort of Indochinese also achieved advanced degrees in the humanities and social sciences, the most illustrious laurels of French scholarly life. In 1932, Nguyễn Mạnh Tường received doctorates in law and literature from the University of Montpellier (he was the first Indochinese doctor in literature). Phạm Duy Khiêm received his agrégation in rhetoric in 1933, the first Indochinese to do so in any field. Close behind him was Trần Đức Thảo who, after the Lycée Sarraut and a year studying law in Hà Nội, received a scholarship to the Lycée Louis-le-Grand to prepare for the exams to the École normale supérieure. He placed third in the national exam in 1939 and first in the agrégation in 1943 in philosophy.[60] Nguyễn Văn Huyên entered the Sorbonne in 1930 as his family's finances were collapsing. Like Phan Văn Trường and Dương Văn Giáo, he supported himself by teaching at the École des langues orientales. In 1934, he became the first Indochinese *doctorat ès lettres* (in ethnology, writing two theses), followed three years later by Hoàng Xuân Nhị (Hoàng Xuân Hãn's brother) in literature. In 1938, Ngô Đình Nhu became the first Indochinese graduate of the École des chartes, France's national school of historical and archival sciences.[61] The few Khmer and Lao who studied at the *grandes écoles* in the interwar era included the royals Souvanna Phouma and Sisavang Vatthana (Laos's last king), as well as the future communist Prince Souphanouvong.

While strolling through Paris, the narrator of Nguyễn Mạnh Tường's 1937 *Pierres de France* stops to contemplate "the austere Sorbonne, built of gray stone and venerable science," and the Collège de France, "a necessary and symbolic anachronism amidst a civilization of Standard Oil and radio waves, a modern ark and a refuge for all souls who preserve their faith in a redemptive humanism."[62] The passage captures the profound sense of fulfillment instilled in these students during their studies at some of the world's great universities. Of course, it required hard work: Nguyễn Khắc Viện recalled the "extreme toil" of his medical exams, especially the oral portion in front of a "terrifying silver-haired and bearded professor" during which "talented students who were not sufficiently self-possessed or prepared broke down in ten minutes and could not finish."[63] "When I arrived in Paris," Trần Đức Thảo remembered, "I decided to study philosophy. . . . My choice at the time reflected only the arrogance and ebullience of youth. . . . I wanted to prove that I had a powerful enough intellect to do so. . . . But the deeper I went into the discipline, the more I realized its value, and I became somebody who learned how to search for truth in a world full of errors and crimes."[64] Fifty years later, he remembered Maurice Merleau-Ponty reading aloud from his doctoral thesis, a synthesis of Husserl, Hegel, and Marx that would transform Thảo's thought, "in the intimacy under the eaves of Cuzin's room" during the early months of the resistance to which François Cuzin would soon sacrifice his life.[65] Phạm Duy Khiêm recalled of his years as a *normalien*:

> It was among my friends that little by little I became aware of who I was: different from all of them. In contact with them, through comparison, I became conscious of who I was, of the ways in which I had less than they, and of what I had in addition to what they had. I heard things about myself during those years, directly and otherwise, that had a clarity and a depth that have never been surpassed. I will add that these judgments bore no dishonor for Annam and our race, far from it. Did they only help me to define myself? They also allowed me to respond in a certain way, to live in a certain way, to feel, to be as I had never been able to before without them.[66]

Trần Đức Thảo's top ranking in the 1943 national exam for the agrégation in philosophy did not prevent him from being classified *hors rang* (unranked) because he was not a citizen, which barred him from a teaching position in France. As this indignity reveals, even the most brilliant Indochinese graduates of France's *grandes écoles* had few opportunities in French intellectual life. They remained marginal even in the École des langues orientales, where they served as assistants (*répétiteurs*) to French scholars when teaching their own language, culture, and history—among them figures like the linguist Trần Văn Giáp and the ethnologist Nguyễn Văn Huyên, *répétiteurs* from 1927–31 and 1931–35 and later major figures in scholarly life in the Democratic Republic of Vietnam. Some were dismissed for their politics despite their credentials and professionalism. In 1912, the director of the École des langues orientales described Phan Văn Trường as "exact in his lessons, receptive to instructions received, devoted to his students" and "intelligent, conscientious, and a good pedagogue," shortly before the minister of colonies forced him from the position during the Đồng Bào Thân Ái affair.[67] In 1927, Lâm Văn Nghị lost the same job for his ties to the political activist Nguyễn Thế Truyền.

Indochinese were also marginal in the learned societies interested in the French empire, which often met at the Hôtel des sociétés savantes on Paris's rue Danton. Indochinese speakers at these gatherings gave little sense of the colony's cultural creativity and ferment: most were figures like Bùi Quang Chiêu and Dương Văn Giáo, whose superficial forays into Indochina's history and culture were meant only to frame their political agendas. Some Indochinese organized a more substantive lecture series in 1929 spanning Indochinese religion, poetry, medicine, music, and theater.[68] A similar series in Lyon in 1930 included lectures on Nguyễn Du, on the condition of Indochinese students in France, and on the question "Must we speak French or Annamite?"[69] Some of these events became political: when Trần Văn Mại spoke about Confucius at a geographical society in Montpellier, "I soon shifted the discussion to politics, and by way of conclusion I discussed an article in the *Quotidien* about the misery of workers on Indochinese plantations."[70] But more often, Indochinese at such events just tried to complicate petrified conceptions of their societies. "I must perhaps apologize for the austerity of this allocution," Phạm Huy Thông said in a speech in Paris in 1944, "for you may well have come to this gathering in search of exoticism or eager for words to cradle your nostalgia."[71]

By the 1930s, Indochinese pursuing advanced degrees in France were producing works that would significantly contribute to scholarly knowledge about the region. But only a few were published in France, and even fewer were published for a non-scholarly audience. They included the journalist Đỗ Đức Hồ's 1938 book *Soviets d'Annam et désarroi des dieux blancs*. It argued that the 1930–31 uprisings in Indochina reflected a fatal destablization of social structures under French rule that had opened the door to Soviet and Chinese communist influence, an argument presaging his later collaboration with Nazi officials.[72] Also published in France was Tào Kim Hải's *L'Indochine française depuis Pigneau de Béhaine* (1939). Catholic and a French citizen, he came to France to study in 1923, married a French woman, received a doctorate in law, and became a journalist. He volunteered for the war in 1939 at the age of thirty-four. He finished his book on the Moselle front; during his unit's breakneck retreat along the Loire in spring 1940, he learned that it had won a gold medal from the Académie française. Despite its accolades, it is mediocre colonial mythology. "France's oeuvre in Indochina is, on the whole, extremely beneficent," he said in an interview. "We Indochinese can surely criticize you for a few things . . . but those are questions of detail that we'll work out between ourselves after we take back Indochina from the Japanese."[73] A staunch Gaullist, he fought for the Free French and served as a French delegate to international conferences in 1945 (an Institute of Pacific Relations conference in Virginia and a UN conference in San Francisco). He remained in the United States after 1945, writing for *The New Yorker, Esquire,* and *Gourmet.*

Trần Đức Thảo is probably the only Indochinese who had a marked influence on French intellectual life before decolonization. The brilliant *normalien* became a leader in Indochinese independence politics in France in 1944–45, in between transporting manuscripts from Leuven to Paris from the archives of Edmund Husserl, whose thought Thảo explored in his 1943 doctoral thesis. In 1946–47, Thảo wrote a series of articles calling for Vietnamese independence in *Les Temps modernes,* a political and cultural journal edited by his former professor Maurice Merleau-Ponty. They, and his 1948 article on Alexander Kojève, reflected his ongoing turn away from existentialism toward a more materialist approach to phenomenology, which led to a break with Jean-Paul Sartre after a series of tense dialogues in 1949–50. In his book *Phenomenology and Dialectical Materialism* (1951) he explored how the "capitalist division of labor disguises not just the similarities between different instantiations of the means of production, but also the unity of human perception and a full phenomenological appreciation of lived experience. Individual ownership encourages individual perception and an idealization of the object that relies on closure, possession, and a denial of real exteriority."[74] Soon after its publication, Trần Đức Thảo left the cafés of the Left Bank for the Việt Bắc revolutionary zone. "The second part of *Phenomenology and Dialectical Materialism*," he later wrote, "resulted in an impasse, a solution to which I hoped to find in the Vietnamese revolution."[75]

Thảo's articles in *Les Temps modernes* were unusual, for few Indochinese journalists found meaningful opportunities in the French press. The few who did wrote almost exclusively about colonial issues: the pro-colonial press featured Đỗ Đức Hồ in *Le Midi colonial*, Tào Kim Hải in *Annales coloniales* (he also wrote occasionally for *Le Petit parisien*, *Paris-soir*, and *La Revue des vivants*) and Hoàng Văn Cơ (grandson of the pro-French *kinh lược* Hoàng Cao Khải) in *Dépêche coloniale*; the latter also commented on Radiodiffusion française and Radio-Paris.[76] Reformist figures in colonial politics used metropolitan newspapers to advance their agendas: Bùi Quang Chiêu wrote editorials in *Le Quotidien* and *Annales coloniales*.[77] So did more radical figures. In the early 1920s, Nguyễn Ái Quốc wrote for *L'Humanité* and *Revue communiste*, while Nguyễn An Ninh wrote for the anarchist *Le Libertaire* and the more moderate *Europe*. Nguyễn Văn Tạo and Cao Văn Chánh wrote for PCF newspapers (usually under a French pseudonym). Tạ Thu Thâu, Huỳnh Văn Phương, Hồ Hữu Tường, and Phan Văn Hùm wrote for the Trotskyist *La Vérité*. And Lê Hiền, an employee of Agence France-Presse, explored the changing landscape of colonial issues under the Popular Front in his articles in *Combat* and *Le Monde illustré*.[78]

But alongside this relatively limited Indochinese involvement in metropolitan newspapers was a rich circulation of texts and journalists that made France part of the colony's vibrant "newspaper village" (*làng báo*). Indochinese newspapers circulated widely in France. Most student associations subscribed to several, and a few well-heeled sojourners had personal subscriptions. The less well-off had access to them too: during the Great War, the Alliance française imported *Trung Bắc Tân Văn* and *Lục Tỉnh Tân Văn*.[79] Indochinese soldiers stationed in interwar France read "brochures and publications provided by the Government General."[80] Colonial newspapers came to France with new arrivals or in letters from home. Postal controls made sensitive newspapers harder to get: Trần Văn Giàu, suffering through Toulouse's frigid 1929 winter in his "big room with no central heating," wrote a friend in Sài Gòn bemoaning how hard it was to obtain *Thần Chung* and *Tiếng*

Dân.[81] But these newspapers made it to France anyway in the masses of letters that censors could never all read, or in the many places on a steamship that police overlooked.

Letters from France reveal regular and impassioned engagement with the colonial press. "I received the newspapers; thank you very much," wrote Đỗ Tất Văn in 1927; "send me copies of *L'Echo annamite* that you've already read, for I would like some news of home."[82] In Paris, Hoàng Quang Giụ closely read *Đông Pháp Thời Báo*'s coverage of colonial causes célèbres. He wrote to its editor Trần Huy Liệu, "we appreciate the precious quality of your newspaper. . . . Your estimable journal's thoughts are those that we and the entire country think and desire. As such, despite the thousands of leagues between us, we call out in a unified voice: 'Long live an independent Annam! Long live the newspaper *Đông Pháp Thời Báo*!'"[83] Others sent critiques. "Newspapers of our country do not constitute an organ (of defense) for the poor classes," wrote one student in Paris; "they remain indifferent to important events" and "only pretend to oppose the government's acts." He pilloried *Đuốc Nhà Nam* for its criticisms of the Soviet Union and *Thần Chung* for not defending those convicted in the Rue Barbier affair.[84] Another wrote from Paris to Huỳnh Thúc Kháng in Huế, flaying *Tiếng Dân* for an article that placed China and Siam at a higher civilizational level than Annam.[85]

Indochinese journalists often sojourned in France seeking copy and professional advancement. In 1922, Phạm Quỳnh and Nguyễn Văn Vĩnh, editors of *Nam Phong* and *Trung Bắc Tân Văn*, visited *Le Journal*, *Le Matin*, and *La Liberté* in between their responsibilities as delegates to the colonial exposition. Phạm Quỳnh marveled at the grandeur of the offices, the champagne offered to guests, and the "collegial" treatment given him as a "junior member" of the newspaper guild.[86] Many established Indochinese journalists followed them to France in the 1920s, including Nguyễn An Ninh, Nguyễn Phú Khai, Cao Văn Chánh, Đào Trinh Nhất, Hoàng Tích Chu, Trịnh Hưng Ngẫu, Cao Triều Phát, Bùi Ái, Bùi Công Trừng, and Nguyễn Khánh Toàn. Some wrote for colonial newspapers from there. Cao Văn Chánh was *Phụ Nữ Tân Văn*'s correspondent in France from 1929 until 1933, reporting under the name Thạch Lan on student life, political activism, the colonial exposition, and other subjects of interest (Parisian brothels among them). And some aspiring journalists tried to break into the colonial newspaper world from France. "I admittedly have not had the honor to meet you," wrote Ngô Quang Huy to *Đông Pháp Thời Báo* in 1928, "but I take a timid step into the land of journalism with the hopes of making known my humble ideas that could be profitable to our compatriots. . . . I plan to send you, every month, an article that I beg you to entitle 'The Humble Ideas of a Little Student in France.' I would be very grateful if you could offer me a small remuneration for my troubles."[87] "When something comes from afar," pitched Nguyễn Văn Sang to the publisher Nguyễn Văn Của, "it always has some value. Articles from afar are thus precious. If you agree to my proposal, I will send you impartial and truthful articles about events in Europe." "My style is not revolutionary or communist," he promised, "my prose is national."[88]

The first Indochinese newspaper in France was *Tin Mới*, first published by the Ministry of War in 1916, which contained mostly games, stories, and cartoons meant to distract from the miserable wartime conditions. In 1921, Nguyễn Phú Khai, who had become an entrepreneur, politician, and editor of the Constitutionalist *Tribune indigène* after studying in France, returned to Paris to found *Tribune annamite* to strengthen the ties between his party and the French left. He convinced Alfred-Ernest Babut, the muckraking Indochinese journalist, to go to France as its editor. Babut was a good choice: he had ties to the French left and, thanks to his friendship with Phan Châu Trinh, to Indochinese radicals in Paris. Nguyễn Minh Quang, another former editor of *Tribune indigène,* worked for the 1922 colonial exposition while circulating *Tribune annamite* in Marseille.[89] But *Tribune annamite,* starved of funds after Nguyễn Phú Khai returned to Sài Gòn, folded in August 1921. A French edition of the Constitutionalist *Tribune indochinoise,* published in 1927, was equally short-lived.

For a time after the failure of *Tribune annamite,* the only organ of Indochinese journalism in France was *Le Paria,* published by the Intercolonial Union, a group of anti-colonial activists with ties to the French Communist Party (PCF). It appeared sporadically between 1922 and 1926; its editorial line reflected the disparate agendas of activists from around the French empire and the PCF's emerging interest in colonial issues. *Le Paria's* two main Indochinese authors were Nguyễn Ái Quốc and Nguyễn Thế Truyền, who had studied chemistry at Parangon a decade earlier and returned to France in 1921 for doctoral studies before entering politics. Despite their close ties to the PCF, they soon recognized *Le Paria's* limits. Nguyễn Thế Truyền tried to popularize it among Indochinese in Paris, but most were indifferent or unable to read it; he often composed impromptu translations to read to workers who did not know French.[90] Before leaving for the Soviet Union in 1923, Nguyễn Ái Quốc began planning for a bilingual newspaper, *Việt Nam Hồn* (The Soul of Vietnam), to appeal more to

Indochinese in France, for "despite having eyes and ears, they do not understand the affairs of the century, beautiful or ugly, good or bad."[91] But it did not appear until January 1926, after Nguyễn Ái Quốc wrote to the PCF Colonial Commission to urge that Nguyễn Thế Truyền more actively counter growing Constitutionalist activity in France.[92]

Việt Nam Hồn sought to focus more squarely on Indochina from the start. In this effort, Nguyễn Thế Truyền scored a coup when Diệp Văn Kỳ agreed to join its editorial board. The law *licencié* from the Sorbonne had strong ties to the colonial newspaper world. His father, the intellectual and interpreter Diệp Văn Cương, had founded *Phan Yên Báo,* an early Cochinchinese quốc ngữ newspaper, in 1898. Diệp Văn Kỳ helped shape *Việt Nam Hồn*'s financial and circulation models and obtained copy from *Tribune indochinoise* and *L'Echo annamite,* as well as some of Bùi Quang Chiêu's speeches, for republication.[93] But the tense accord between the Constitutionalists and more radical activists broke down in 1926, leaving the latter in charge of the newspaper. This produced a potent cross-pollination between *Việt Nam Hồn* and Indochina's burgeoning radical press: it published articles censored from colonial newspapers (many by Phan Văn Trường), and journalists like Đào Trinh Nhất, Hoàng Tích Chu, and Bùi Ái (who had written for *L'Annam* and *Voix libre* in Cochinchina) wrote for *Việt Nam Hồn* when in France. *Việt Nam Hồn* and its various reincarnations (*Phục Quốc, L'Ame annamite, La nation annamite,* and the cheekily-renamed *Hồn Nam Việt*) spread into Indochinese associations and army units in France. But financial and logistical support from the PCF could not surmount police harassment, mismanagement, and political infighting: it folded in June 1927.

Việt Nam Hồn's focus on colonial politics inspired several publications in student circles in France. *L'Annam scolaire,* the first of these, was formed in April 1927 by Trần Văn Ân, a graduate of Chasseloup-Laubat with Constitutionalist ties studying in Aix-en-Provence (he also distributed the French edition of *Tribune indochinoise,* the Constitutionalists' short-lived effort to counter *Việt Nam Hồn*).[94] It had a Vietnamese-language edition (*Việt Nam Học Sanh Báo*). Two others soon followed: *Journal des étudiants annamites* (published in Toulouse by Trần Văn Thạch, also an alum of Chasseloup-Laubat) and *Bulletin de l'association générale des étudiants indochinois* (published in Aix by Trần Văn Đốc). Trần Văn Đốc's *Bulletin* took a moderate line but *Journal des étudiants annamites* and *L'Annam scolaire* were both provocative enough to be banned in Indochina. *L'Annam scolaire* folded in early 1928, leading Trần Văn Ân to return to Sài Gòn for a lifelong career in journalism. Trần Văn Thạch, who had been elected president of the student congress, took *Journal des étudiants annamites* to Paris when he moved there to study in late 1927 (it was replaced in Toulouse by the short-lived *L'Avenir de l'annam* and *L'Annam de demain*). In Paris, he reconnected with Phan Văn Chánh and Huỳnh Văn Phương, friends from Chasseloup-Laubat who had written for *Bulletin de l'association générale des étudiants indochinois* (by then defunct). The last issue of *Journal des étudiants annamites* proclaimed their political awakening: "Will the Annamite race, newly awakened from its lethargic sleep . . . fall again into a sleep from which it will never wake? It will surely do so unless—ah, the ultimate hope!—it can expel, with all its might, the parasites that gnaw at and exhaust it."[95]

In April 1928, the remnants of the *Việt Nam Hồn* group founded another newspaper, *Lao Nông* (Worker and Peasant), under the leadership of Nguyễn Văn Tạo, a PCF militant. The name reflected the Comintern's new line against cooperation with other leftist parties. In December, an anti-PCF faction led by the journalist and Jeune Annam militant Tạ Thu Thâu founded a rival newspaper, *La Résurrection,* which Trần Văn Thạch, Huỳnh Văn Phương, and Phan Văn Chánh joined following the ban of the *Journal des étudiants annamites* in January 1929, but it folded after a few months. *La Résurrection*'s editorial group would later reemerge as the core of *La Lutte.* But its collapse made PCF-affiliated Indochinese newspapers the de facto vanguard of Indochinese leftist journalism in France. *Lao Nông* and its successors (*Vô Sản,* published from 1930 until 1934, and *Ánh Sáng,* published from 1934 until 1936) were printed at *L'Humanité* or by the Confédération générale du travail unitaire (CGTU) and then distributed via PCF-aligned associations and labor unions. The PCF also supported publications for Indochinese workers: *Cri du Marin* and *Bạn Hải Thuyền* for sailors, and *Tiếng Lính Annam* for soldiers.

But PCF involvement limited editorial autonomy. Indochinese communist newspapers in France boasted seasoned journalists; *Vô Sản*'s editors included Nguyễn Văn Luận and Hoàng Quang Giụ, both former editors of *Việt Nam Hồn,* and Cao Văn Chánh, who edited *Tân Thế Kỷ* (New Century) in Sài Gòn before coming to France and edited *Phụ Nữ Tân Văn* after his return to Indochina. But the newspapers they edited could be little more than, in the words of a French official, "PCF watchwords and extracts from various communist works," which turned talented journalists into glorified translators.[96] Coverage of Indochinese issues was sporadic and limited to party-line accounts of the uprisings that erupted in Indochina in 1930–31. This was especially true of *Vô Sản,* which replaced *Lao Nông* after the Yên

Báy uprising; although speculative, it is possible that *Lao Nông*'s abrupt demise stemmed from its enthusiasm for the mutiny, which the Comintern critiqued. In any case, *Vô Sản* left little room for ideological or operational autonomy. In 1932, despite Indochinese involvement with *Vô Sản*, the PCF tasked two Frenchmen with "a few notions of quốc ngữ" to write and edit an issue. The result was "riddled with spelling mistakes" and "unintelligible."[97] Perhaps unsurprisingly, Cao Văn Chánh and Hoàng Quang Giụ broke with the PCF shortly after their work with *Vô Sản*.

The first issue of *Tiên Quân,* the first Trotskyist Indochinese newspaper in France or Indochina, appeared in August 1930. It reassembled *La Résurrection*'s editorial team, who were now engaging with Trotskyism as a solution to the impasse of Stalinism or bourgeois nationalism. *Tiên Quân* was the idea of Tạ Thu Thâu and Huỳnh Văn Phương—both had written for the Trotskyist *La Vérité* since 1929—but they and Phan Văn Chánh were expelled from France in June 1930 for protesting French repression of the Yên Báy uprising (Trần Văn Thạch, the other key figure in *La Résurrection,* had returned to Indochina in January 1929). This left two new figures at the head of the newspaper. One, Phan Văn Hùm, had founded the short-lived *Le Jalon* while a student in Hà Nội, and he wrote for Sài Gòn newspapers before coming to France in 1929.[98] The other, Hồ Hữu Tường, had no journalistic experience before coming to France in 1926; *Tiên Quân* was the beginning of his own lifelong career in journalism. *Tiên Quân* was first written in Brussels, where they had fled to escape the fallout of the Yên Báy protests and to continue Tạ Thu Thâu and Huỳnh Văn Phương's work for *La Vérité.* Hồ Hữu Tường described the "photo-mechanical" process typical of many Indochinese newspapers in France, where few printers could reproduce quốc ngữ; "we handwrote articles in careful calligraphy, which were glued flat for the layout and then photographed, which could then be printed anywhere."[99] *Tiên Quân* grew out of a sectarian split in French communism that had not yet reached Indochina, and as Stalinists and Trotskyists in Indochina cooperated in *La Lutte* (whose principal figures had all known one another in France), the Trotkyist press in France (including *Đuốc Vô Sản,* edited by Phan Văn Hùm in 1932, a revival of *Tiên Quân* in 1934, a French edition of *Tiên Đạo* in 1936, and *Quốc Tế IV* in 1937) would adhere firmly to the French Trotskyist opposition to cooperation with Stalinists and to the Popular Front.

The Comintern's anti-Fascist line and the liberalization of the colonial press after the Popular Front's electoral victory in 1936 revived connections and exchanges between newspapers in France and Indochina. Nghiêm Xuân

Toàn, editor of the PCF newspaper *Ánh Sáng,* became the French correspondent of *Vie indochinoise,* edited by Cao Văn Chánh, who in turn distributed *Ánh Sáng* in Indochina.[100] Nguyễn Văn Trị, head of the PCF-aligned Association d'entraide et culture des indochinois, did the same at *Le Monde,* another of Cao Văn Chánh's newspapers.[101] In France, Indochinese affiliated with the PCF-led Comité de rassemblement des indochinois had close ties to newspapers in Indochina led by activists returned from France; these included *La Lutte* and the Hà Nội-based *Le Travail,* edited by Trịnh Văn Phú, who had also been expelled from France after the Yên Báy protests.[102] In France, the Comité de rassemblement des indochinois published *L'Appel,* edited by Phan Tất Tốn and Daniel Guérin, an anarcho-syndicalist who had witnessed the brutal repression of the Yên Báy uprising.[103] And in 1938, Indochinese sailors in France formed the Committee to Support the Indochinese Democratic Press (Ủy Ban Ủng Hộ Báo Chí Dân Chủ Đông Dương) that promoted "the sale and diffusion in Annamite milieus of extremist newspapers and brochures of Indochinese origin."[104]

The Second World War abruptly cleaved these revived transimperial journalistic ties. With freedom of the press and movement both drastically restricted, Indochinese newspapers in France dwindled. *Công Binh* (War Worker) was an official Vichy organ for Indochinese brought over as soldiers and laborers who were languishing in camps around France. Like *Tin Mới,* its predecessor in the Great War, *Công Binh*'s main goal was to distract, but Vichy officials also hoped to spread the National Revolution to a captive colonial audience. Its editor, Hoàng Văn Cơ, had parlayed his work as a right-wing journalist into a position as head of propaganda for the Service de la main-d'oeuvre indigene, nord-africaine et coloniale (MOI). His journalists, MOI interpreters, did not always share his politics. As Hoàng Khoa Khôi (a future Trotskyist activist) remembered, "I wrote poems. Sometimes we had to translate pro-MOI articles. Since we were all anti-French, I made do with writing trivialities."[105] More interesting was *Nam Việt,* the project of a few Indochinese (including the future communist luminaries Nguyễn Khắc Viện, Hoàng Xuân Nhị, and Lê Văn Thiêm) whose wartime study in Berlin led them toward authoritarian nationalism as a vehicle for anti-colonialism. Published with the help of Henri Legrauclaude, a former editor of *L'Impartial* in Sài Gòn and now assistant to the head of the Vichy press Jean Luchaire, the newspaper explored aspects of right-wing ideology and state-making. After the liberation, the *Nam Việt* group (some of whom had barely dodged arrest in summer of 1944) would suddenly and totally change their editorial line.[106]

As Indochina's new postcolonial states emerged in and after 1945, they would make the printed word part of their diplomacy and state-making projects in France. Alongside this official journalism, and often in opposition to it, was Minh Tân ("Modernization"), the only Indochinese publishing house in France during the colonial era. Hồ Hữu Tường had renounced Trotskyism in 1939, spent most of the war in prison, and took up journalism again in 1945. He came to France with his family in mid-1949, officially as correspondent for *Sài Gòn Mới*, in hopes "of founding a great publishing house to give life to valuable works" and to reprint works that risked being lost or destroyed in the war.[107] In Paris, he connected with the journalist Lê Hiến, the engineer Nguyễn Ngọc Bích, and the artist Hồ Viết Tự (known as Việt Hồ), who had studied photogravure in Germany and Switzerland. From 1950 to 1955, the Minh Tân group published dozens of works: school primers, new editions of modern scientific and linguistic works (notably by Đào Duy Anh and Hoàng Xuân Hãn), fiction, and Trần Đức Thảo's magnum opus *Phenomenology and Dialectical Materialism*. Revenues from sales funded two journals. *Cảo Thơm* (Fragrant Pages), a fine arts journal, was short-lived. *Pacific: Asian Review* (1952–57) advanced, in French and English, what Hồ Hữu Tường described as a "nostalgic utopian" program for a pan-Asian Third Force that hoped to solve Asia's political conflicts through the region's shared "spiritual and moral messages, and all else that constitutes, in all forms, the Asian flower in the garden of humanity."[108] Its authors were not just Indochinese, but Indian, Chinese, Indonesian, and Filipino; when the Ngô Đình Diệm government jailed Hồ Hữu Tường in 1957, *Pacific*'s readers waged a successful campaign urging Albert Camus, that year's recipient of the Nobel Prize in literature, to sign a letter of protest. Like *Le Paria* had decades before, *Pacific* reflected the fleeting internationalist dreams that beckoned to some Indochinese in France.

LITERATURE AND THE ARTS

French sojourns inspired Indochinese writers throughout the colonial era in a range of genres, from embassy reports to poetry. Virtually all of these writings were intended for audiences or markets in Indochina: few of their authors dreamed of or sought literary careers in France itself. The hurdles were formidable: neither French translations of Indochinese literature (themselves quite rare) or influential Indochinese Francophone works like Nguyễn

Phan Long's *Le Roman de madmoiselle Lys* (1921) received any attention in France. But that did not deter a few aspirant writers. One was Vũ Đình Hải, who arrived in France in 1929. He had sniffed success at home, writing plays and coauthoring a dictionary with two French officials. When one of Vũ Đình Hải's coauthor's brothers offered to help him pursue his literary career in Paris, he jumped at the chance. He joined the journalists and writers union and wrote a play, *Dernier éspoir* (The Last Hope), which hit Parisian stages in 1929. It told "of an Annamite, once a rebel, who after a trip to France became an admirer of our country and an ardent partisan of Franco-Annamite collaboration."[109] The play's political platitudes won him plaudits from colonial officials but few literary admirers, and it closed after a few performances. The colonial press had fêted Vũ Đình Hải as "the first dramatic author of Annamite origin to receive the honors of a Parisian premiere" but no crowds awaited him on the docks when he returned a few months later.[110] An Indochinese playwright did eventually break into French theater, when Vi Huyền Đắc, well-known in Indochina, won the Grand diplôme d'honneur from the Académie des jeux floraux de Nice in 1937 for his first play in French, *Éternels regrets.*

The first Indochinese novel to be published in France was *Bà Đầm* (Madame, 1930), a collaboration between Trương Đình Tri and Albert de Teneuille. It is unclear where they wrote it or how it came to be published in France. *Bà Đầm* tells of the marriage of Sao, a law student in France, to Janine, his professor's daughter. Their respective fantasies (Sao's of Westernization, Janine's of racial uplift) wilt after the couple's return to Indochina, as Sao is pulled inexorably back into timeless traditions and Janine succumbs to the racial hierarchies she had hoped to transcend. The union is a casualty, depending on one's reading, of the unbridgeable cultural chasm between East and West or of, as Karl Britto argues, the "hallucinatory realms of the colonial imagination" that produce racial and cultural difference.[111] Ambivalence saturates the novel; its granular portrait of daily life reflects "an ethnographic strain . . . intended to give French readers a deeper insight into Vietnamese cultural practices than could be found in colonialist texts," but it remains suffused with stereotypes of "the ancestor cult, Tet, traditional medicine, opium smoking, rice culture, and funeral customs and attitudes towards death" that "reinforce cultural difference and accumulate to construct an elaborate and equally valid cultural edifice that stands of necessity in opposition to French civilization."[112] As such, although *Bà Đầm* hints at "discursive practices at work behind the construction of these identities," it resolves with the failure of "interculturality," "silenced by the rigid categories of identity imposed by the colonial imagination."[113]

As these works suggest, most of the few Indochinese writers published in France during the colonial era offered either exotic and sentimental portraits of difference, or explorations of the "cultural conflicts and the difficult, even impossible (re)conciliation between two systems of thought" that such differences produced.[114] Trần Văn Tùng, the now largely forgotten recipient of four prizes from the Académie française before 1945, embodied both impulses.[115] He was a journalist at the governor general's press bureau when his *Aventures intellectuelles* (1938), a paean to French men of letters, catapulted him to fame; he, Phạm Quỳnh, and Nguyễn Tiến Lãng (also honored by the Académie française for his 1933 novella *Eurydice*) were Indochina's representatives to the sesquicentennial celebrations of the French Revolution. He stayed in Paris to study at the Sorbonne and hobnobbed with André Gide, Georges Duhamel, and Jean Luchaire. During the occupation, his ties to Luchaire (who headed the collaborationist press) got him work in Vichy newspapers and radio.[116] In France, he published several more works that are little more than banal exoticism and Francophilia. *Rêves d'un campagnard annamite* (1940), published by Mercure de France (then under Duhamel's direction), is a syrupy story of a student's love for the France he encountered in classrooms, books, and encounters in Indochina: "I owe to Indochina the shape of my body, but my conscience, my thought and my future, I owe to France!"[117] *Muses de Paris* (1942) are love poems set in Paris's most clichéd romantic spots. *Bach-Yên, ou la fille a coeur fidèle* (1946) is a predictable tragedy of young love crushed by Confucian values: Van, forbidden to marry the Catholic Bach-Yên, flees to France after her suicide: "Leaving! It is to go to another world, a world wholly apart from the world that shutters, imprisons, and poisons you!" But at the novel's end, years in France have left Van disillusioned, and he now evinces an equally exotic nostalgia for Indochina. He confronts, in the end, interculturality's impossible burden: "I do not want to balance! I want to be! I want to be!"[118]

Makhali Phal (the pen name of the Franco-Khmer writer Nelly-Pierrette Guesde), born in 1908 to a French official and a Khmer mother "of ostensibly royal lineage," came to France in 1916 and never left; she could not speak Khmer.[119] But she found literary success in France as a "native" conduit of colonial mythologies about Cambodia that, thanks to the reconstructions of Angkor at expositions, had broad appeal in France. "This young Parisian of today," read a profile of her, "still feels her Cambodian heart inside her, vibrating with all the pride of her race."[120] Her poetry collections *Cambodge* (1933) and *Chant de paix* (1937) offer "imaginative reconstructions of a national culture" drawing from famous events in Cambodian history.[121] Her most famous work, *La Favorite de dix ans* (1940), is a tragedy about "straddling boundaries and reconciling the irreconcilable."[122] Atman, the young *métis* daughter of the Khmer king, is plagued by racial and cultural dislocation, for which she compensates with a blind filial piety that excuses her father's murder of his lover (a ten-year-old dancing girl at the court) and his incestuous desires for her. In France, where her father sends her in hopes of assuaging his guilt, she is scarred by her convent education and haunted by her memories of Cambodia. She finally agrees to an incestuous marriage to her French uncle so long as they return to Cambodia; there, the king banishes them to the jungle, where Atman hopes to finally reunite with her ancestral origins. After a hallucinatory night of wandering, torn between her desire for and fear of the jungle, she is killed by Djarai sorcerers. Utimately, Atman cannot "maintain a stable identity in any sphere of human relations"; her experience "leads to discovery but not to empowerment or happiness or decolonization."[123] *La Favorite de dix ans* was met with great acclaim, winning the Grand prix international du roman, but Makhali Phal moved away from the experience of *métissage* in later works, retreating to imagined versions of the myths, rites, and poetry of the distant Khmer past.

But Indochinese literary production in France was more complex than the exoticism of these few visible figures. "We could," wrote the critic Jean Desthieux in 1931, "express more of an interest in their native literature . . . for it might reveal to us the spirit of the great Indochinese people, about which we only possess romantic notions."[124] The source of his sentiment was one Đào Văn Phúc, who had come to France to study but had to leave his lycée in Bordeaux when his family's finances soured. He then worked as secretary to a stockbroker in Toulouse and as an usher in a "cinéma chinois" in Paris, where he found inspiration in the capital's streets and sounds. One Indochinese student in the Latin Quarter described him as "a young man of yellow complexion, bare head, hair to his neck, slovenly clothes and ripped shoes, eyes fixed on what was in front of him." Đào Văn Phúc was a regular at the café La Capoulade; he "would say hello to the waiters, order a café au lait and a carafe of water, spread out his papers on the table, and begin to write." One of his stories, "La Paille" (Straw), appeared in 1931 in *Monde,* a communist weekly that had published George Orwell's first article (on censorship in England) in 1928. It recounted "the life of a young Annamese peasant with a generous heart, hunted by servile mandarins, who takes refuge in the forest but is killed by the guardians of a village." News of his literary success spread to Indochina; *Courrier de Saigon* cast him as "one of these philosophical spirits who rejects the rigid boundaries of the classical educations that allow us to conquer only scrolls." But "this Annamese poet and writer . . . who had conquered the attention of France's literary critics!" died shortly thereafter of unknown causes.[125]

Like Đào Văn Phúc, other Indochinese found inspiration in France for more modernist literary experiments. Two decades after his father's futile political campaigns during the 1900 exposition, the Khmer prince Areno Yukanthor arrived in Paris to study at the École des arts décoratifs. After discovering Apollinaire, Baudelaire, Flaubert, and Mallarmé, he began to write poetry. *Le Monde illustré* described *La Cantate angkoréenne* (1923), his collection of symbolist poetry, as of a "rare and absorbing originality."[126] His literary mysticism and his studies with the orientalist Sylvain Levi cultivated in him "an aesthetic system" steeped in a belief in a timeless, essential Khmer culture, as well as a visceral hostility to the French center-left's modernizing colonial agenda. His affinity for Sorelian syndicalism drew him to the right-wing L'Action française and Croix de Feu. In scathing satires written in 1931 and 1935, he subjected his (many) political enemies to "a verbal flurry exposing their contradictions with derision and wit, but one derailed by its profusion of obscure references." He returned abruptly to Indochina in 1938 and became a recluse. Areno's forgotten literary legacy was, perhaps, a casualty of his politics; he was replaced in the French "panthéon of artists" by Makhali Phal, "an insipid writer whose sticky sentimentality Areno attacked mercilessly."[127]

Hoàng Xuân Nhị's literary muse was Ranier Maria Rilke's "cult of the self, solitude, and melancholy."[128] While pursuing a doctorate in literature at the Sorbonne (which he received in 1937), Hoàng Xuân Nhị translated works by Gorky and Myakovsky as well as two Indochinese literary classics (*Chinh Phụ Ngâm* and *Truyện Kiều*) for Mercure de France. He became close to Georges Duhamel, who published and influenced his novel, *Les Cahiers intimes de Heou-Tâm, étudiant d'Extrême-Orient* (1939). As in many of Indochina's modernist novels, Heou-Tâm's rural village is a hell of a remote mandarin father, cruel stepmother, and stultifying Confucian values. Heou-Tâm seeks liberation in France and in a relationship with a Western woman, but it only truly comes when he makes "a pilgrimage into my past" to "embrace one last time all the miseries, all the denials, that make up the richness of my life. I want to persuade myself that my confidence and my joy are strong, that they are not feints or fleeting, but the very essence of my nature . . . If my soul, now, is a symphony, each of its notes is a sob."[129] Heou-Tâm's heroic act of self-reckoning transcends both the weight of "civilization" and the anguish of his interculturality: "I create in myself a better world where harmony flowers . . . it is a world rich with tenderness, and even when life overwhelms me with distrust, it cannot kill this tenderness that I carry in myself like my own homeland."[130] *Heou-Tâm* was the first Indochinese novel published in France to explore core elements of the region's literary modernism: the oppressions of traditional society, intergenerational conflict, and the quest for self-fulfillment.

Some Indochinese Francophone authors who first became famous in the colony had formative literary experiences in France. Phạm Duy Khiêm's first known literary activities came at the École normale supérieure, where he lectured about Vietnamese poetry to classmates, and at the Maison des étudiants de l'Indochine (years later, military service in France offered further inspiration). Nguyễn Mạnh Tường began writing fiction between finishing his two doctoral theses in 1932 and returning to Indochina in 1936. Pierre Đỗ Đình Thạch was a part of French Catholic modernist circles during his studies at the Sorbonne, becoming close to the members of the Décades de Pontigny, a literary collective that gathered for many-day marathons of literary exchange in a Cistercian abbey owned by the writer Paul Desjardins (among them André Gide, whose 1938 book *La Porte étroite* Đỗ Đình Thạch translated into Vietnamese).[131] By the late 1930s, the French sojourns of these and other writers would help give rise to new literary currents, centered in Indochina but transimperial at their core, exploring the possibilities of cross-cultural humanism at a moment suffused by the binaries of colonial collaboration and anti-colonial nationalism.

French sojourns also shaped the lives and works of some of Indochina's most significant modern artists. The first Indochinese painters to travel to France did so to decorate the pavilions and pagodas of the early expositions: although their art was largely decorative, many relished their exposure to French artistic traditions and techniques. Some tried to pursue artistic training in France; a group of Khmer painters petitioned to study at Paris's École des beaux-arts after the 1900 exposition but were denied despite faculty support.[132] But the first Indochinese to study in a French art school had not gone to France to do so. Lê Văn Miến (also known as Lê Huy Miến) was, with Hoàng Trong Phụ and Thân Trọng Huế, one of the first three Indochinese sent to study at the École coloniale in 1889. But in Paris, he fell under the spell of fin de siècle art, immersed himself in museums and galleries, and made friends in the art world; one, the painter and sculptor Jean-Léon Gérôme, helped him to obtain a scholarship to Paris's École des beaux-arts in 1891.[133] Huỳnh Đình Tựu had participated in the Permanent Mission in 1908 and was working as a secretary when a French observer noticed his talent and paid for him to study at Marseille's École des beaux-arts.[134] His return to Indochina was delayed because of the logistical difficulties of safely boxing the dozens of canvases he had painted in France.[135]

The École des beaux-arts indochinois (EBAI), founded in 1925, "offered students what were considered foundational skills in the fine arts—based on a European pedagogical model—while also orienting them to reconsider the sources of their own local aesthetic traditions, including in the decorative arts."[136] Victor Tardieu, the EBAI's founder, sought to forge links between the colonial and metropolitan art worlds by sending artists to France for formal training, and to display and sell their work. The first EBAI student to study in France was the painter Nam Sơn, Tardieu's assistant, who spent 1925 at the École des arts décoratifs in Paris before becoming the first Indochinese instructor at the EBAI.[137] A dozen EBAI students' works were displayed at the 1931 exposition.[138] Though excluded from its Palais des beaux-arts, they were a centerpiece of the Indochina pavillion, and some of the artists themselves (notably the brilliant Lê Phổ) "were responsible for designing and fashioning much of the *mise-en-scène* of their artworks."[139] After the exposition, Tardieu lobbied the Agence économique de l'Indochine (AEI) in Paris to continue promoting these artists, which made their work more visible in France than other Indochinese cultural forms. The AEI entered Indochinese paintings and sculptures into Parisian salons, like the venerable Société des artistes français, and it sent them to expositions in London (1932), Cologne (1933), and Belgium (1935 and 1937).[140]

The artworks themselves, reflecting Tardieu's generally classicist and anti-modernist tendencies, were "recognisable and assimilable in academic circles in France, even if they were framed by a rhetoric of difference and exoticism."[141] They evoked landscapes, gardens, and scenes of family and village life in forms and colors evoking a "sense of stillness, containment, and even privacy," thus echoing "a tendency in interwar French art, in which a number of French artists began to reject the frenetic stylistic experiments of the preceding decades" for "a revival of naturalistic painting and an interest in the artistic forms of the past."[142] This ironically endeared painters like Lê Phổ, Lê Văn Đệ, and Tô Ngọc Vân to xenophobic right-wing art critics, who saw the works as embodying an essential "Frenchness." But when considered in the context of the EBAI and Indochinese traditions, the works contain clear modern elements and techniques reflecting "a synthesising practice" that "allowed for an aesthetic development" but "nonetheless conformed to their new audience's expectations of exoticism."[143]

Many Indochinese artists whose work was exhibited and sold in France never set foot there; others did so only for an exposition. But for some, longer sojourns were at the heart of their artistic development. Lê Văn Đệ stayed in France for seven years after his studies at the École nationale supérieure des beaux-arts. He converted to Catholicism (he was baptized by the Pope in 1936), traveled in Italy and Greece, had his work exhibited around Europe, received numerous commissions for religious art, and won first prize in an art competition at the Catholic World Press Exhibition in Rome in 1936.[144] "Put yourself in the place of a young artist who had only ever seen photographs of the masterpieces of the West," he remembered. "What a joy to see the originals! I remember the first time that I went to the Louvre, I didn't know where to start! I was as excited and undecided as a child among too many toys."[145] Some remained in France as the first generation of an Indochinese artistic diaspora. Vũ Cao Đàm came to France in 1931 to continue studying sculpture and never left. Lê Phổ, Mai Trung Thứ, and Lê Thị Lựu (the first woman to graduate from the EBAI), also stayed in France after the 1937 exposition. The last major figure in this group, Lê Bá Đảng, came to France not to study or for an exhibition, but as a laborer in the Second World War. Captured by the Germans in 1940, he worked in labor camps around France and Germany before escaping and finding his way to Toulouse. There, he befriended an Indochinese student at the École des beaux-arts who helped him secure admission. After graduating first in his class in 1946, he moved to Paris and never left.[146]

Although there was a robust market for Indochinese lacquered objets d'art in interwar France, few practitioners in the medium received recognition in critical circles.[147] Trần Đình Nam was one of hundreds of Indochinese lacquer workers brought to France in 1916 to treat and repair wooden war materials. His highly employable skills allowed him to stay in Paris after the war, where he found work at the Atelier Dunand, France's best-known lacquer workshop. Most of his fellow Indochinese workers had stable but anonymous careers making trays and boxes for the Parisian bourgeoisie, but Trần Đình Nam became well-known, displaying at the 1929 international exposition in Barcelona and winning a bronze medal at the 1931 colonial

FIGURE 6. Hoàng Thị Thế on the set of *La Lettre,* c. 1930. Source: Dossier Hoàng Thị Thế, Box 51, Série XV, Fonds de la Service de liaison avec les originaires des territoires français d'outre-mer, Archives nationales d'outre-mer, Aix-en-Provence, France.

exposition; he also received the Ordre du dragon d'Annam in 1932 and the French Officier d'académie in 1937. Trần Đình Nam returned to Indochina when the Second World War forced Jean Dunand to close his workshop.[148] Bùi Văn Đặng had also come to France in 1916; thereafter, he worked briefly as a domestic before opening his own lacquer studio. By 1927, his work was featured at the Salon d'automne, the pinnacle of a career in French decorative arts. "How," wrote one reviewer, "does Dang Bui achieve the illusion of reality, such perfect grace and expression, with these materials? It is his secret, I can but admire it and acknowledge his mastery."[149]

Much like fine art, Indochinese music and dance had appeared in French expositions since the nineteenth century, especially the wildly popular performances by Khmer dancers in 1906. Early expositions relegated these performers to roles as exotic avatars of Indochinese tradition, but visitors to the 1931 exposition could experience the decidedly modern form of *cải lương*, a Vietnamese folk opera heavily marked by Western dramatic and staging elements. One of the genre's best-known performers, Lê Thị Phỉ (better known by her stage name Cô Năm Phỉ) dramatically entered the exposition grounds by airplane before performing *Sĩ Văn Công Chúa*, a *cải lương* opera based on Wagner's *Tristan and Isolde*. Her performance in Paris "created a sensation."[150] Her time on the scene was fleeting, but other Indochinese performing artists had longer tenures in France's nascent film industry, usually in roles of different or indeterminate Asian ethnicity. Most famous at the time was Hoàng Thị Thế, the jetsetting daughter of the anti-French rebel Đề Thám, whom the director Louis Mercanton cast in his adaptation of Somerset Maugham's play *The Letter* (1930). Hoàng Thị Thế's career soon fizzled; she only appeared in one more film, a bit part in the potboiler *Le Secret de l'émeraude* (1935). One of that film's stars was Phạm Ngọc Thạch (known as Kỳ Duyên), who would appear in over thirty films in France, Italy, and Czechoslovakia. Cécile Nguyễn Ngọc Tuế, known as Foun Sen, appeared in several dozen French films as late as the 1970s, some directed by her husband Léo Joannon.[151] And other Indochinese sojourners dreamed of a career on the silver screen. "I have done some cinema," bragged Cao Quỳnh An to a friend in 1929. "You'll see me on the screen in Saigon probably next year. I play a Japanese officer. And listen to this: I made 150 francs per day and got to embrace stars like Huguette Duflos and Dolly Davis!"[152] His star soon faded despite the promising debut.

FIVE

Labor Sojourners

WHEN FRENCH AUTHORITIES FINALLY CAUGHT up with Nguyễn Văn Hiến in 1922, his labor sojourn in France had taken decidedly unexpected turns. A low-level official of the Public Works office in Indochina, he had come to France in 1913 as the secretary of his French supervisor. But his employer left the country when war broke out, leaving him with 500 francs and his thanks. In 1917, broke, Nguyễn Văn Hiến enlisted as a colonial war laborer. He met a woman and skipped his repatriation, officially making him a deserter. He made do for a time by selling cocaine, but he and a girlfriend eventually scraped up the funds to open "a confectionary store for women" in Marseille. It did well, but the relationship didn't. In February 1922, tipped off by his purchase of a ticket home, military police arrested Nguyễn Văn Hiến hours before his steamship's departure. On his person were nearly 25,000 francs from the store's cash reserves; his "trunk and bicycle," already in the ship's hold, returned to Indochina without him.[1]

Private secretary, war laborer, drug dealer, bourgeois shopkeeper: as Nguyễn Văn Hiến's life shows, Indochinese labor sojourns in France were as varied as the pressures and motivations that had produced them. The nearly one hundred twenty thousand Indochinese who served in the two World Wars bookended other Indochinese labor sojourns in interwar France as foot soldiers of colonial power: metropolitan tours of duty or officer training school for soldiers, artisanal or manual labor at an exposition, and even service as agents in the colonial security services. But other Indochinese labor sojourns in France reflected the colonial economy's new possibilities and perils: from wealthy Indochinese seeking white-collar work or business opportunities to steamship workers, cooks, and domestics seeking relief from precarity and unpredictability. Once in France, unemployment or the lure of a quick franc led many to unexpected labor, from starting a restaurant to smuggling drugs or political documents. Some would find higher wages and better opportunities, while others found only the cruel end of a dream and even more uncertain and exploitative labor than what they had left behind. Though far from home, Indochina's labor sojourners in France remained very much part of the French imperial nation-state's "veritable—and painful—economic revolution" in Indochina.[2]

THE GREAT WAR

When the Great War erupted in the summer of 1914, Indochinese soldiers had been traveling to France for half a century. In 1868, eleven Indochinese who fought for France during its conquest of Cochinchina's western provinces were sent to France to serve prison terms for violating orders.[3] Between 1900 and 1905, fourteen Indochinese soldiers received treatment in Marseille's St. Pierre asylum.[4] Indochinese soldiers, selected "from among the most vigorous, and who spoke a little French," provisioned with new uniforms and months' worth of betel leaf and areca nut, paraded on Paris's Champ de Mars during the 1889 and 1900 expositions.[5] Indochinese also began studying at Saint-Cyr, France's elite military school, before the war. Among them were Đỗ Hữu Vị, who graduated as a lieutenant, served in colonial campaigns in North Africa, and was one of several Indochinese to join France's fledgling air force in 1910. He had returned to Indochina by 1914 but hurried back when war broke out. Wounded in 1915 and unable to fly, he rejoined the infantry. He died at the Battle of the Somme in July 1916.

Đỗ Hữu Vị was one of about five thousand Indochinese who served in combat during the Great War. A handful were elites, often naturalized, some of whom had been in France for years before volunteering; most had humbler origins. Few were new to military service, but their experiences of combat had been limited to campaigns against smugglers, mercenaries, and lingering rebels after the French conquest of Tonkin. Like their fellow French soldiers, they could never have imagined the cataclysm of modern industrial warfare. Just four Indochinese battalions out of nineteen saw combat, and only then after disastrous French losses at the Somme and Verdun; their battalions were divided into smaller units and attached to French divisions.[6] Many French officials believed that, unlike naturally fierce and barbaric West Africans, weak and effeminate Indochinese had little value as fighters.[7] In early 1917, upon taking command of an Indochinese battalion, a French officer named Monroux wrote his superiors explaining why their racial and psychological makeup ("indolent," "timid," and "sensitive") would render them ineffective.[8]

After seeing his soldiers fight during the terrible years of 1917–18, Monroux, like nearly all other French who fought alongside Indochinese, felt very differently. "These men," he later wrote, "made themselves noted by their courage, skill, and tenacity in the face of the most violent bombardments. . . . Indochinese soldiers played a glorious part in our army's operations and their numerous citations testify to their courage and military qualities."[9] Indochinese soldiers experienced just as much of the horrors of the Great War as the French soldiers beside them in the trenches. When they confronted trench warfare, "the gap between traditional representations and lived experience was great enough to produce silence . . . but the war was too different and powerful to stay hidden for long."[10] But there was no Indochinese Barbusse or Remarque; only fragments of their testimonies of combat remain, culled mostly from reports of postal censors.

At first, many soldiers writing home expressed wonder. "The railways pass through mountains," wrote a Khmer war laborer, "the airplanes fly above the clouds, and submarines explore the very bottoms of the seas."[11] Some expressed optimism: "Many are dying, but we will win."[12] But despair soon set in. "With each step," wrote François-Bertrand Can in 1915, "I stumble over a body; as I shuffle over the soft, bloody things that are the inanimate bodies of those who preceded us just yesterday, I feel an indescribable sensation of distress and horror." Shrapnel took one of his arms.[13] On the eastern front, two Indochinese batallions worked to fortify the Greek city of Thessaloniki before moving to reconnaissance and ambush missions in Serbia, Macedonia and Albania.[14] "I saw them fight and die bravely for my country," recalled a French general, "their fine features impassible in the snow of far-off, glacial Albania."[15] "One must go to northern France to fully realize the genius of the twentieth century," wrote Kiều Xuân Quang; "one sees the plains of the countryside upended as far as the eye can see, littered with all sorts of machines. Destroyed houses testify painfully to the struggles and battles of ambition, hatred, and revenge."[16] Almost a third of Indochinese in combat during the war died.[17]

Fifteen of the nineteen Indochinese batallions worked in the war's massive rearguard operations. They built trenches, tunnels, and shelters, and they relandscaped captured territory. They fixed roads, railways, and telegraph

FIGURE 7. Four *tirailleurs indochinois*, Breuil-sur-Verse, May 26, 1917. Source: Fonds des albums Valois-Marne, Service photographique de l'armée, Bibliothèque La contemporaine, Nanterre, France.

lines, and built new ones. They loaded and unloaded trucks and trains bringing munitions and food to the trenches and dead or maimed soldiers back. They protected bridges and railway junctions against sabotage, guarded prisoners of war, cut down trees for lumber, mined coal, and cut stone from quarries. Five thousand, trained at the École pratique des mécaniciens in Sài Gòn, drove supply trucks. Most of the nine thousand who worked in hospitals and infirmaries did menial labor: cleaning, stoking fires, doing laundry, serving food. Those with medical experience gave shots or dressed wounds, although language could be a challenge. One French soldier bemoaned being tended by an Indochinese auxiliary "who did not understand a word of French" and who "guessed everything wrong."[18] But Indochinese had the same problem: the Orientalist scholar Jean Przyluski recalled meeting an Indochinese soldier at a train station, "lost in a crowd of French soldiers," returning to the front after a stay at a hospital. The soldier "did not hide his sadness, and he told me that he had suffered a great deal from spending so many days without anybody to talk to."[19]

About half of the Indochinese who came to France for the war worked in factories and workshops. A handful were skilled workers from the colony's small industrial sector; most were rural farmers thrust into the cauldron of wartime industry. To the French, Indochinese "docility, skillfulness and sobriety" had made them a better fit for war labor, even if their "cunning and dissimulation" tempered expectations.[20] Most endured harsh, often horrendous conditions. The worst work was in arsenals and gunpowder factories, where they worked with unstable gases or corrosive chemicals. "Do not ask to come to France," wrote one worker to a friend, "you will lose your life by the yellow powder [melanite]."[21] Luckier ones made uniforms or boots, and the luckiest worked as farmers—in the case of 115 of them, growing salad on the grounds of the Château de Versailles.[22] Poor working and living conditions, harsh weather, inadequate clothing, and meager food took their toll. Even those who escaped chemical burns or maimed limbs often suffered from pulmonary disease, tuberculosis, or exhaustion. There was some passive resistance; coming late or leaving early, lingering, hiding, or feigning an illness. But like their countrymen fighting on the front, Indochinese workers soon shattered stereotypes. "It is particularly in all work requiring attention and care, precision, skill and ingenuity," wrote one French official, "that the Indochinese workers are most appreciated. All that is mechanical, operation and overseeing of machines, interests them to the highest degree . . . but one must not think that they are incapable of heavy labor."[23] One factory owner spoke for many when saying that "in all realms in which work requires dexterity and care, the Indochinese provide production superior to all other European or exotic laborers."[24] By the end of the war, many factory owners and overseers were lobbying to keep them on in peacetime.

Many Indochinese worked alongside French workers, and circumstances did not favor good relations between the two groups. Many French workers were also new to such brutal work, and most had their right to organize or strike curtailed in the name of national security. Colonial laborers, cheap and disposable, stoked their resentment. Some French did appreciate Indochinese contributions to the war, and they occasionally protested their poor treatment or the unfair distribution of dangerous work. But tensions predominated, especially in 1917, a year of widespread labor action and mutinies among French workers. Indochinese almost never struck, and management depended on them to keep up production. Labor unions and leftist newspapers whipped up resentment; rumors spread that Indochinese serving as auxiliary police had broken up protests in Paris and had shot into a crowd of female workers.[25] One official cited "jealousy toward foreigners who have had some success with local women, and the competition from a rival labor force," as the cause of a brawl between French and Indochinese workers in a factory in Bourges in 1917, one instance of many in a wave of racial violence that swept across France in that year.[26] "For some time now," one Indochinese worker wrote, "the more we work (I mean, the more we persevere in our resolute willingness to serve France whatever the circumstances), the more we are the object of general distrust and the atmosphere of hostility for us grows daily. We toil in obscurity, misunderstood, like pariahs, but endlessly exploitable."[27]

The war stoked many Indochinese political awakenings. By 1918, many expressed open admiration for Germany. One Indochinese sergeant noted that German trenches flew banners reading, "If the French are so powerful, why can't they fight their own battles?" and "Why do the Annamites have to die for France?"[28] Wounded Indochinese and Germans often lay side by side in infirmaries: "It seems necessary," wrote a French official, "to end as soon as possible this promiscuity which I deem not only shocking, but susceptible to have regrettable repercussions on the spirit of those natives in close contact with our enemies."[29] Germany's 1918 offensive, which reached the outskirts of Paris, produced admiring commentary and rumors. A postal censor noted that many Indochinese believed that "the Germans are in all ways superior; their airplanes, faster than ours and silent, rise to unattainable heights and melt onto our planes, leaving our towns and troops defenseless; their cannons are stronger; they have more 'tai' (talent) than all of the allies combined."[30] Rumors spread that the French army had stopped sending Indochinese into battle because of mass defections to Germany.[31] "Stronger and more talented than the Allies," wrote one; "to take one German prisoner the French had to sacrifice ten men!" wrote another; "they had one tenth of the German military skill," wrote a third.[32] "If Heaven fought them," another speculated, "it would lose too."[33] Some Indochinese were assigned to American divisions in 1918; they expressed admiration for the skill and dynamism of France's "saviors."[34] Rumors spread that America would replace France in Indochina after the war.[35]

Diminished and hostile views of France intersected with news of political unrest in Indochina, which spread through recently-arrived Indochinese units and (despite the censors) letters from home. One interpreted the war as part of a prophecy by the scholar and sage Nguyễn Bình Khiêm foreseeing the imminent fall of a dynasty (in this case, the French).[36] Another reflected bitterly on the failed Duy Tân uprising in 1916, describing the French as "silkworms gnawing at mulberry leaves" and criticizing Nguyễn officials for "betraying their king out of personal interest."[37] In late 1917, as French soldiers mutinied, news spread of a mutiny in Thái Nguyên. One letter-writer described it as a "revolution."[38] Rumors spread that Sun Yat-Sen, returned to Guangdong from exile, would lead the rebels to victory.[39] Other rumors suggested that the rebel Đề Thám, whom the French had killed in 1913, had returned and was leading the uprising.[40] Censors noted the names Phan Bội Châu and Phan Châu Trinh in many letters.[41] This kind of sentiment, limited to a minority of Indochinese soldiers and workers even during the war's darkest days, would grow in the electric political atmosphere of 1919.

Mercifully for all, the end finally came. Some Indochinese saw France's victory as a validation of their years of service and sacrifice. "Our protégés," wrote a French official, "were not indifferent in the face of the eruptions of joy, in cities and countryside, on the day of the armistice. Everywhere, without second thought, they seem to have taken part in the rejoicing."[42] "On this day of November 11," wrote one worker, "all of the pain, suffering and misery of the last fifty-two months can be forgotten in the joy of this day of glory and happiness when, for the first time in so long, the human race can breathe peacefully."[43] But others felt only melancholy. "What joy can we express in the face of these celebrations?" wrote one. "It is certain that the happier these people become, the more our sorrows will grow, for they have won the war and we have lost our hope."[44] But the desire to return home was nearly universal. "In their letters," wrote a French official, "the hymn to departure accompanies the hymn of victory.... Some have gone so far as to tell their parents not to write back, believing that they will not have the time to receive more news from Indochina. It will be very difficult to calm this impatience."[45] "What a blessing to return to Indochina to live as a simple *nhà quê*," wrote one, "to again pick up the plow and spend my days free from worry in the Indochinese countryside, that is now my only desire."[46]

But the long-awaited demobilization unfolded slowly. The first repatriations prioritized only Indochinese soldiers who had been in combat, and the massive material demands of reconstruction put steamships in short supply. The demands on the French military were also not over, and enlisted Indochinese were put to work. Ten months after the armistice, about thirteen thousand Indochinese soldiers were still in France.[47] Many were sent to the French-occupied Rhineland to work as drivers, medical auxiliaries, or clerks. The novelty of being in Germany soon faded: in a letter to *Tribune indigène,* one group wrote of being treated like "beggars."[48] Some blamed France for the desperate state of German civilians (whom many Indochinese saw as welcoming and civilized): "The French oppress the Germans," wrote one, "and it is always the ordinary people who pay the consequences."[49] Indochinese soldiers sent to the Levant as part of France's postwar occupation were also unhappy. "I am now in a country they call Syria," one wrote; "the weather is excessively hot, we only leave the trenches at night, and the food is awful.... The Syrians are discontented and resent French domination."[50] In July 1920, nearly two years after the cease-fire, four thousand Indochinese soldiers had still not returned home.[51]

Demobilization was even slower for laborers: in June 1920, nearly nineteen thousand remained in France.[52] The Ministry of Public Works began conscripting them in 1919 to replace the labor of prisoners of war: they rebuilt railways and roads, disassembled unused ordnance, and dug up mass graves for reburial. With victory achieved, French officials had less incentive to maintain their well-being; twelve hundred sent to Belgium were unpaid and unprovisioned, forcing them to scavenge. Rampant inflation ate into their hard-earned savings, and widespread unemployment and strikes, often broken with their labor, worsened relations with French workers. Labor unions called for their exclusion from the workforce. Ultimately, anxiety about the revolutionary political atmosphere accelerated Indochinese demobilization. The strikes of 1919, an official fretted,

> have had an enormous impression upon our protégés, who are very attentive to what is happening around them; it would be wise for the economic interests of our colony to strictly control camps when a strike is announced ... as well as forbidding newspapers in the camps. Without such measures, the natives could soon come to think of work stoppage as a form of protest and especially as a way to gain the upper hand over their employer.[53]

By the end of 1920, virtually all had been sent home.[54]

The return of Indochinese war laborers disappointed Albert Sarraut and other French planners who had hoped to integrate colonial labor into the postwar metropolitan economy. Nevertheless, the military continued to bring several thousand Indochinese to France annually until the early 1930s. Conditions were a world away from the hell of the war: for most, their greatest hardship was that their service in France often meant, ironically, "a negation of their existence as soldier."[55] Most worked as cooks, bakers, tailors, butchers, barbers, cobblers, drivers, porters, carpenters, or gardeners, while officers worked as secretaries or assistants to French officers. Their experience reflected what military planners had hoped to avoid: the systematic exclusion of colonial soldiers and officers from combat training in France. This was partly due to pressure from the Nguyễn court, which lobbied French officials to bar Indochinese noncommissioned officers from the officer school in Fréjus to prevent them from receiving what they saw as an inappropriately high imperial grade.[56] But it also reflected deeply ingrained attitudes within the French military. Indochinese noncombat specialists were often downgraded in France; in one example, medical auxiliaries went from caring for patients in Indochina to sweeping the floor of a clinic in France. In France, most were, in the words of one French military official, "valets of the army."[57]

Such was the experience of Nguyễn Văn Ký, an officer and the son of a fallen soldier in the Great War who came in 1922 for officer training. Nguyễn Văn Ký chafed at the secretarial work that filled his days in France, and for which—thanks to the strength of the Indochinese piaster during the 1920s— he received about half of what he had made in Indochina. Other indignities filled the lives of his fellow soldiers in France. Bound to years-long service terms, they could not return home in the event of a family crisis. The military lodged Indochinese soldiers together and provided culturally-specific leisure, but this often reinforced their separation from French soldiers. Officers particularly resented this segregation, which they felt undermined their authority.[58] French officers had other ways to enforce officially barred racial hierarchies: in one camp, Indochinese soldiers were only assigned to watch duty after midnight—after all personnel were required to have returned to camp—to limit their authority over French soldiers.[59] A few especially bitter soldiers dabbled in anti-colonial politics, but most just waited out their contracts. Nguyễn Văn Ký returned to Indochina in 1926. In a final indignity, his request for repatriation of his father's remains from France was denied.[60]

Very few Indochinese received permission to work in France after demobilization. The few who did were skilled industrial or white-collar workers (mostly secretaries and interpreters) with the active support of an employer. Many quickly found new professions.[61] Trần Lệ Luật came to France in 1916 as a laborer before becoming an interpreter for Indochinese soldiers. He was allowed to stay in France after the war to work as a bookkeeper at the Société des rizières indochinoises de Marseille. But by 1922 he had started importing and selling Asian dry goods.[62] Quách Văn An left his job at a tool factory in Toulouse after a few years; over the next thirty years, he worked in factories that made everything from buttons to soap before returning to Indochina in 1948.[63] Tạ Văn Cẩn, a sergeant-major in the war, left his postwar factory job and worked in a restaurant before starting a photography business that employed, among others, Nguyễn Ái Quốc as a retoucher.[64]

Lacquer was the only industry in interwar France connected to war-era mobilization of Indochinese labor. Indochinese lacquerers in France had been trained in a rich artisanal tradition that adorned everything from votive objects to kitchenware. Because their skills were hard to replicate or replace, lacquer workers were well-represented among the few Indochinese workers allowed to stay in France after the war; in 1929, about one-quarter of the thousand Indochinese in Paris were lacquer workers. Like other interwar urban industries, most lacquer workshops had been pushed to outer arrondissements or near suburbs.[65] On Paris's margins, Indochinese lacquer workers made boxes, platters, and, as the communist daily *L'Humanité* described it, "wonders of art that are the pride of bourgeois salons."[66] When lacquer workers had no work or needed extra money, their skills made it easy for them to moonlight in carpentry or construction. Lacquer workers were among the best-paid Indochinese workers in France; many also had room and board included in their contracts.

Most Indochinese lacquer workers in France worked for a French employer. One of the biggest lacquer companies in interwar France was the Société des lacques indochinoises, which started as a military workshop in Boulogne where seventy-five Indochinese fixed propellers. Simoni, the founder of the company, hired many of them after the war and began recruiting more from Indochina. In 1924 it was the only factory in France that lacquered propellers, and it drew clients from as far away as Japan.[67] The famous Swiss lacquer artist Jean Dunand, whose specialty was objets d'art, also recruited Indochinese lacquer workers; by 1930 he employed seventeen in his workshop in the thirteenth arrondissement.[68] But Indochinese-owned lacquer workshops also existed in France. Đinh Văn Phụng began his own lacquer business after the war; by 1930, he employed several people and owned a workshop in Boulogne worth 150,000 francs.[69] Võ Thành Long, a former interpreter in the Great War, invested a decade of savings in a lacquer business, "Veritable lacque d'Annam," that made him wealthy. Thái Văn Huyền's lacquer business had clients in Germany, where he often traveled.[70] His workshop taught French workers the trade, which some Indochinese criticized.[71] The threat of competition led some lacquer workers and their investors to form a guild. But the Syndicat des lacquers indochinois could do little to stave off the Depression, which forced many lacquer workers to leave the profession for menial work as taxi drivers or restaurant workers.

The war also integrated Indochinese into the colonial security services. Indochinese agents of the Contrôle général des tirailleurs et travailleurs indochinois in France (CGI) extended into France a security apparatus that had employed Nguyễn officials for recruitment and mobilization efforts in the colony. All had impeccable records. Phạm Gia Thụy and Vũ Huy Trức had been to France with the Permanent Mission; Lê Quang Liêm was a rising star in the Cochinchina administration who had organized charity events to support the war effort and wrote a play, *The Nation before the Family*, urging enlistment.[72] During visits to Indochinese battalions and work units, the officials "inspected their living quarters, tested their food, listened to their complaints, reported on their activities and abuses against them, promoted their interests, and recommended changes to higher authorities," as well as heading postal controls that, by early 1918, contended with three hundred thousand letters a month (they only managed to read about forty thousand).[73] These men were "the inner lining of the French administration. . . . There was no reason to worry that these mandarins would awaken new political ideas among their countrymen."[74] But they had a sincere, if paternalistic interest in the welfare of the soldiers and workers, at times expressing anguish or anger at their compatriots' miserable condition.

As the French confronted the political efflorescence around the "Revendications du peuple Annamite" in 1919, it became evident that a wartime surveillance regime based on the widely accepted authority of imperial officials and army officers was now inadequate. Nguyễn Văn Ái, an interpreter and sergeant-major during the war, was quickly unmasked as an informant after attending meetings of the Intercolonial Union. "If

Annamites in France and in our country learn of your mean and devious actions," Phan Châu Trinh berated him in a withering letter, "they will all want to spit in your face, for you are of those without any conscience who will do anything to your compatriots if you personally benefit from it."[75]

Infiltrating small, tightly-knit communities and semi-illicit political networks required a different kind of agent, and French officials quickly abandoned the idea of importing them from Indochina and set about recruiting them locally. In 1930, Phan Văn Dung recounted the experience in a letter home:

> The head of the Sûreté asked me to visit him in his office. . . . Over the course of the interview, I came to realize that he was trying to prevent me from returning to Indochina. I requested that he write to the minister of colonies for help with my repatriation, since I had no place to stay in France and not enough food and clothing. He refused to answer my questions about this and tried changing the subject. Eventually, he tried to pay me to become an agent among the Annamite students.[76]

The imperial nation-state's metropolitan surveillance regime approached Indochinese who wanted a quick way up or needed a quick way out. Those arrested for drugs, theft, or assault might agree in hopes of a lighter sentence. Some did so to pay overdue tuition and hotel bills. Informing could also forestall repatriation after the loss of a job or a change in legal status. But some did it to get ahead: Phạm Văn Mạch's informing got him scholarships for his children in colonial schools.[77] Tống Việt Triêm, the head of Dunkerque's Foyer indochinois, reported on suspicious activities to convince French officials that his organization was worthy of financial support.[78] Most such arrangements were situational, but some Indochinese worked as full-time employees, complete with a monthly wage and administrative alias. The pay could be good: Trần Văn Hy's 1929 contract with the CAI paid him 10,000 francs plus 2000 francs in an expense account, about what a skilled lacquer worker earned at the time and about four times the wages of a cook or domestic.[79] But many still felt disposable. "We carefully carry out the delicate work entrusted to us, risking our lives, and neither haggling over our hardships nor sparing our suffering," wrote Nguyễn Văn Nuôi in a letter of resignation. "We had hopes that the government would recognize our loyalty and devotion by assuring us a minimum guarantee of our future. Alas! What an illusion. Day laborers (*journaliers*) we were, and day laborers we will always be."[80]

Work for the security services was a peculiar mix of dreary and dangerous. It often required creating intrigue out of thin air; informants learned to infuse their reports with words and tones that validated bureaucratic paranoia, and to use salacious gossip to fill frequent lulls in political activism.[81] But their work had real consequences, and many informants offered known or ex post facto information to try to avoid exposure or doing too much damage to others. Even rumors of being a *lính kín* (police spy) could mean personal catastrophe. In 1928, Trần Lệ Luật found his Asian dry goods business threatened by a boycott on the grounds, probably false, that his financial success was thanks to informing.[82] Similar accusations left Hoàng Thị Thế, daughter of the anti-colonial icon Đề Thám, shunned in the Latin Quarter.[83] Bùi Ái's roommate kicked him out after Nguyễn Thế Truyền accused him of informing, forcing him to sleep in metro stations until he found another room.[84] Even those who remained incognito endured other strains on their lives. One informant's wife complained to her husband's French minder that their lives had become consumed by "the dregs of Indochina, rude gamblers whom he despises"—his work forced him to pay café bills for dubious characters while listening to their "absurd political discussions that are, for him, a nightmare."[85]

The universal and colonial expositions brought hundreds of Indochinese workers of all kinds to France for months to help bring French visitors to Indochina for a day. Indochina's first appearance at an exposition, an "Oriental" pavilion (also representing North Africa and Siam) at the 1878 universal exposition, was French-built. But in 1889, Indochinese stonemasons and carpenters built pavilions and pagodas on the Esplanade des Invalides, Indochinese painters decorated their interiors, and Indochinese soldiers stood guard at opening and closing ceremonies. One innovation in 1889 was "native villages" featuring people, in the words of one visitor, "living and working and amusing themselves as they and their kinfolk do in their country. . . . They have brought with them the materials for their huts, their tools, and everything necessary for them to reproduce in the capital of the civilized world the everyday life of Africa, the Pacific, and the Far East."[86] More came to France to work at these phantasmagorias as they expanded: they included skilled artisans (metalwork, silk, lace, ivory, wood, ceramics, jewelry), musicians and dancers, theater troupes, painters, sculptors, cooks, rickshaw pullers, carpenters, tailors, and gardeners. Nearly a thousand Indochinese worked for months at the 1931 Exposition internationale coloniale in the Bois de Vincennes. Expositions could also provide temporary employment for some Indochinese already in France. Phạm Văn Hồ kept his job in a chemical factory after the war, but he broke his contract and used a false identity to find work at the 1922 exposition; when this was revealed, he dodged a repatriation order and vanished.[87] Many who had never pulled a rickshaw or sold soup in Indochina found themselves doing so at an exposition in France.

Indochinese experiences of expositions are difficult to capture. Some skilled artisans found exposure and lucrative sales, but others lost reliable income at home due to a failed European venture. Fine and performing artists may have felt pride at the thousands of visitors who enjoyed their work; in 1889 these included Claude Débussy, whose fascination with the region's classical drama (hát bội) marked his composing.[88] But some found performing to be a slog. In 1931, a troupe working under the cải lương director Nguyễn Ngọc Cương protested a relentless and poorly compensated performance calendar in Paris's cabarets and dancehalls during their official nights off.[89] As for those working in recreated restaurants, workshops, and villages, it is hard to know whether they felt objectified, or just bemused and bored, while pretending to live and work "normally" for gawking visitors. Material conditions could elicit protest. Indochinese workers at the 1900 universal exposition protested lost pay and bad food.[90] In 1922, Phạm Quỳnh wrote that "lodging reserved for Annamites is unattractive, and the food leaves much to be desired," noting that delegates and others who could afford it paid for private lodging.[91] French officials sometimes responded to calls for better conditions; at the 1907 colonial exposition in Nogent-sur-Marne, Indochinese workers even requested and received instruction in French.[92] It is perhaps telling that militants protesting the 1931 colonial exposition criticized not only its French organizers, but the many Indochinese who "collaborated" with it.[93]

Expositions mobilized the labor and bodies of Indochinese workers in the service of the imperial nation-state, but they were largely left to themselves once their workday was done. In fact, exposition officials in 1931 removed many restrictions on movement written into contracts for fear they would hurt recruitment.[94] Some stayed close to their dormitories and dining halls. But others enjoyed their surroundings; for some, tourism was even part of their compensation. In 1931, Cochinchinese gardes indigènes and theater troupes had bus tours in their contracts; they visited "the capital's most important public monuments as well as nearby historic castles" and "the department store Printemps where they admired the merchandise and made select purchases."[95] Indochinese exposition workers did other things in their time off. Phạm Văn Lựu, a delegate to the 1906 exposition, gave lectures to geographical societies.[96] For Nguyễn Xuân Bái, working in an infirmary at the 1922 exposition helped him gain admission to the Faculté de médecine de Paris.[97] French officials also noted more troublesome activities after hours. In 1906, one noted that the "well known tendencies for indiscipline" among Indochinese tirailleurs "found in a city as populated and rambunctious as Marseille a very friendly terrain."[98] In 1931, two Indochinese cooks "worked as prostitutes in the bowels of the exposition; sometimes they snuck out of the grounds ... at late hours with Annamite or European men."[99] Every exposition brought from Indochina people like Nguyễn Tân Bửu, who in 1922 "abandoned himself to the basest excesses, deserting work and staying out all night with shady women, often in the most drunken states."[100] And for Nguyễn Thị Khang, a reporter at *Phụ Nữ Tân Văn* with revolutionary dreams, selling embroidery at the 1931 exposition was cover for her failed attempt to get to Moscow.[101]

LABOR SOJOURNERS BEYOND AND BELOW THE IMPERIAL NATION-STATE

"You know well, father, that in this world, it is very hard to access high office," wrote Phan Văn Thiết shortly after receiving his *licence* in law in Montpellier. "You know that Dương Văn Giáo, Hồ Đắc Điểm, Trịnh Đình Thảo, etc. have bent over backward to be magistrates, but to no avail."[102] Indochinese graduates of elite French schools were well aware of the colony's notorious glass ceiling that even top credentials could not break, and some sought professional careers in France instead. Nguyễn Thanh Kiết had fought in the Great War, received a degree in law, and was a French citizen, but still failed to become a deputy judge in Indochina, so he joined the appeals court in Montpellier.[103] He was one of several dozen Indochinese lawyers who practiced law in interwar France. In 1934, Bùi Quang Chiêu (whose son and daughter had French medical degrees) noted about a dozen Indochinese doctors in France, in hospitals and private practice. One, he noted, "became appreciated by a clientele that was naturally suspicious of a 'Chinese doctor' whose professional qualifications did not go unquestioned."[104] This may have been Nguyễn Văn Nghị, whose practice mixing Eastern and Western medicine helped popularize acupuncture in France. Hoàng Xuân Mãn had an optometry practice in Paris. Some graduates of the *grandes écoles* worked in France; Phạm Quang Lễ, graduate of the École polytechnique, taught at the École nationale supérieure de l'aéronautique, while Võ Qúy Huân, a graduate of the École nationale des ponts et chaussées, worked as an engineer for a shipping firm and an airplane manufacturer. Of course, glass ceilings existed in France too: nationality barred Trần Đức Thảo and the other Indochinese success stories of the agrégation examinations from career paths open to French citizens with the same qualifications. And in 1930 Phan Văn Hùm, who had left the Sorbonne for a job teaching Vietnamese at a lycée in Toulouse, taught one class before he was fired due to his political activism.[105]

Indochinese also went to France for business. During the interwar era, many exposition delegates were landowners and entrepreneurs cultivating French networks and markets for their enterprises. The Comité annamite de Cochinchine of the 1931 exposition sent among its delegates Nguyễn Văn Của, the rice magnate and publisher.[106] Trần Mạnh Nhẫn, editor of the commercial journal *Nông Công Thương*, went to Paris's 1937 exposition of arts and techniques to explore exporting Indochinese meat and produce to France, as well as importing water filters, hearing aids, eyeglasses, electric lamps, and other objects for Indochina's growing middle class. He was looking forward to upcoming expositions in Italy (1941) and Japan (1945) (that the war would prevent): "If Cochinchina's business and industry leaders could participate in these diverse expositions," he wrote, "their fields of activity and their bodies of knowledge would be greatly broadened. To arrive at this goal, our compatriots must organize and equip themselves as rapidly as possible, so as to put on a good face at these events of great distinction."[107] Many other Indochinese entrepreneurs came apart from expositions. Nguyễn Như Chuyên went to Rouen, Le Havre, and Bordeaux in 1912 "to enter into relations with importers and businessmen to whom I presented various proposals related to Indochinese items," including "embroideries, inlays, copper and pewter crafts, wicker, rattan, and fans."[108] Nguyễn Bá Chính, the founder of the Hợp Lợi ceramics works, went to France in 1921 to buy equipment and observe production techniques.[109] And the owners of the Société franco-annamite des textiles sent employees to France to study dyeing and fabric.[110]

One of the first Indochinese entrepreneurs in France was Nguyễn Đình Khánh, known as Khánh Ký. He was one of the first professional Indochinese photographers, with studios in Hà Nội and Nam Định. In 1909 he went to France to further study photography and decided to open a studio in Paris. In 1913, he photographed Raymond Poincaré, president of the Republic. A friend of Phan Châu Trinh's, by 1919 he was living at 6 Villa des Gobelins

FIGURE 8. Bar-restaurant "Franco-Annam," Paris, 1945. Source: François Trieu personal collection.

and financially supporting its residents. After the war, he formed an import-export business with offices in Frankfurt and Mainz but overextended himself and had to return to Indochina in 1921.[111] Other Indochinese in France opened restaurants, the dream of many Indochinese cooks working in French homes. Sai Văn Hóa worked as a domestic and a cook before opening a restaurant at 22 rue St. Martin in Paris in 1931. It became the unofficial restaurant of the Association mutuelle des indochinois, and drew "sixty-odd" of its members daily. After the meals, patrons would "move to the reunion hall in the basement of the building" to "reminisce about stories from home and comment on news brought by recently-arrived comrades from Indochina."[112]

But competition was stiff in Paris, where French cafés and Chinese restaurants still drew most Indochinese business. There were only two Indochinese restaurants on the Right Bank listed in the city's main business directory before 1932, and it was not until 1936 that one was able to compete with the Latin Quarter's popular Chinese restaurants.[113] But not all were listed. In 1932, Jacques Thiên, unable to afford the rent for a restaurant in the Latin Quarter, decided to run one out of his apartment. *Au noir* restaurants were popular for gambling, drug deals, or subversive talk; militants used Jacques Thiên's restaurant to "gather without being in public, so they could do their work for the Parti annamite de l'indépendance without any bother."[114] Indochinese restaurants fared better in port cities. In the 1930s, there were a few in Marseille, as well as Le Havre's "Restaurant Intercoloniale" run by Đặng Văn Thư, a former sailor, which also served to distribute drugs and illicit political tracts, so its success may not have had much to do with food. Shadowy or legit, a restaurant was a risky venture. In 1917, Lý Văn Thủy opened a restaurant in Bordeaux with "an exclusively American and Annamite clientele." Business was good until he was implicated in an opium ring, which forced him to close.[115] Nguyễn Văn Đức got a job on a ship in 1915, married a French woman, had six children, and saved for twenty-three years to open a restaurant in Le Havre. Two years later, a German bomb destroyed it.[116]

Some ingredients in these restaurants and kitchens came from the shelves of Indochinese-owned groceries. One was Trân Lệ Luật's dry goods store on rue Geoffrey Saint-Hilaire, a block from the Paris Mosque, which he opened after a stint selling Indochinese tea at the 1922 colonial exposition. By 1927, it was sucessful enough for him to invest in a restaurant organized by members of the Association des cuisiniers annamites et domestiques des maisons bourgeoises, in hopes that the restaurant would support his business. The Depression forced Trân Lệ Luật first to drive a taxi at night to make up for falling revenue, and then to close his shop altogether for a job managing Sai Văn Hóa's restaurant.[117] A year later, a former cook named Hà Vân Hợi bought the "Marchand de vins" restaurant and hotel building on the place Maubert, with "ten-odd furnished rooms, a bar-restaurant, and a small shop," where he sold dry goods, imported silks, linens, and embroideries.[118]

But such petit bourgeois enterprises were a world away from most Indochinese laboring in France outside of the imperial nation-state's structures. "Sailor" (*marin*) was a category spanning the wide range of work that Indochinese did on steamships: maintaining machinery, repairing wood in hulls and gangways, cooking food or baking bread, sweeping decks, cleaning the cabins and staterooms, doing laundry, and even cutting hair. In 1929, Nguyễn Văn Ngốc, a journalist for *Thần Chung*, took a job on a steamship to ease his wanderlust and found himself washing the ship's hundreds of portholes. In few days he was "tired as a water buffalo with its throat cut," but the work, and the calls to "hurry up!" and "keep moving," were endless.[119] "Work on the ship is exhausting," he wrote, "and the sailors' situation is pitiful. . . . If they have no work they have to create some; any idling, and everyone sees it. Don't say that you're tired or in pain, just work!"[120] Đào Trinh Nhất saw much the same: "At 4:30 or 5 in the morning you already see them wiping and sweeping everywhere, and they don't rest until 8 or 9 at night."[121] Overworked and underfed, they could rarely even get off the ship to see the cities they passed through. "They live," wrote Nguyễn Văn Ngốc, "in the world of the ship, not the world outside."[122]

An irregular legal status made many sailors even more vulnerable. Many could not satisfy a 1922 decree requiring them to obtain the *livret de marin* required of French steamship workers; those already employed were issued temporary work permits but had to regularize their status when they next returned to Indochina. But some could not obtain the documents necessary for the *livret*, while others worried that being fingerprinted and photographed would reveal a closely-kept secret. Many falsified their identities or worked *au noir*. This left them vulnerable to employer abuse, who knew that few would lodge a complaint. One reported that when he asked for overtime pay, the ship's captain "ripped a box out of my hands and beat my head with it so violently that blood went everywhere."[123] An irregular legal status also made it hard to keep work. In 1925, officials in Le Havre noted fifty Indochinese "with no resources in this port" because "their uncertain identity prevented them from obtaining new engagements."[124] In 1932 there were several hundred Indochinese sailors without work in Marseille.[125] Some scraped up work as stevedores as they looked for work on any ship that would hire them. Their precarity made them cosmopolitan: from Marseille or Le Havre, they found work on ships serving dozens of global ports, where some started new lives. Pham Van Thu began working the Far East line of Messageries maritimes in 1917 but soon shifted to its South America line. He married in Buenos Aires, had a family, and worked as a cook before the Depression forced him back to the seas. He was still working the Bordeaux–Buenos Aires line in 1946.[126] Lê Văn Tư trained as a mechanic in the colony and took a job on a ship seeking factory work in France. He found a job making tractors but lost it during the Depression, and stowed away on a ship to Buenos Aires where he worked for years in factories; by 1935, he was working in a garage in Dakar.[127]

Sailors were often isolated from other Indochinese in France. Marseille, Le Havre, and Dunkerque attracted almost no students, and most other Indochinese laborers gravitated to Paris. Sailors were thus far from movements to unify cooks, domestics, mechanics, lacquer workers, photo retouchers, and other Indochinese laborers into workers' associations and to link them to student associations and anti-colonial groups. Indochinese sailors in Marseille were unmoved by the organizing efforts of Indochinese student activists in nearby bourgeois Aix-en-Provence in the 1920s; in Dunkerque, they shunned the Foyer indochinois, a collaboration between a local Indochinese businessman and CAI officials aiming to keep an eye on the city's floating Indochinese population. Before the Depression, Indochinese sailors also had poor relations with French maritime unions, which were largely indifferent to their situation if not hostile to them. They relied on one another. The Ái Hữu Thủy Thủ Hội (Shiphands Friendship Association), with chapters in Hải Phòng and Marseille, was an unofficial union that pressured employers for better pay and working conditions.[128] In Le Havre, the Đông Dương Hải Thuyền Liên Hiệp Hội (Union of Indochinese Sailors) helped sick or unemployed members. But in the 1930s, the PCF's turn to organizing colonial workers brought more of them into the PCF's Syndicat unitaire des marins.

Like sailors, Indochinese domestic servants in France labored wholly outside of the imperial nation-state's official initiatives. The first of them came with the nineteenth-century embassies. Richard Cortambert, one of Trương Vĩnh Ký's French interlocutors in 1863, noted "rooms where coolies slept in corners like dogs in kennels" as he visited the embassy's hotel on the rue Byron.[129] Formal embassy reports do not shed light on their experiences. They were likely discouraged or prevented from leaving the hotel; language and lack of money would have limited such forays anyway. They likely spent most of their time washing clothes or helping hotel staff prepare meals. Domestic servants with the Permanent Mission do appear sporadically in official reports. Of the three who served Annam's participants in 1907, one, "attached to his master's service in a special way," returned to Indochina when the latter took ill. Another "was an excellent man, but a little old and insufficiently educated in modes of European service," and the last was in fact a low-level imperial official who had passed as a domestic to come to France. "Once his goal had been achieved," wrote the delegation's frustrated minder, "he did everything possible to avoid the responsibilities of his job," claiming climatic and dietary alienation while sneaking out to join other officials on field trips. "One could say of him," wrote the French official, "that he wanted to become a mandarin in order to scrupulously avoid working at all."[130]

Nearly all Indochinese domestics in interwar France worked for a French family. Some had worked for their employers in Indochina for years; others were hired as part of a French official's last-minute preparations before departure. Once in France, employers had far greater control over Indochinese domestic servants. Many withheld much, sometimes even all, compensation until the end of the term of service, whether or not a contract allowed it. Some employers did this to protect their investment (paying a domestic's steamship passage was expensive), but others abused it. In one egregious case, Vũ Văn Tụ was cheated out of years of pay when his employer died and greedy inheritors did not honor his contract.[131] Underpaying and overworking were common: Vũ Thị Tý's contract stipulated a salary of 15 piasters a month working for two people, but she received only 12 piasters while working for a family of five.[132] Some suffered negligence or outright brutality. Some protested to authorities about excessive work, insufficient food, and inadequate lodging (including closets, bathrooms, automobiles, and garden sheds). Some employers lodged their own protests when domestics took extra days off, stole family heirlooms, came home drunk, made lewd advances to their daughters, or (in one case) lost shopping money at the racetrack and tried borrowing it back with the employer's jewelry as collateral.[133] But such instances of abuse and conflict are more visible in archives than the affective ties of years of domestic intimacy. In 1944, a French engineer wrote colonial officials seeking his longtime Indochinese domestic servant, requisitioned by a German general in 1940. He feared rumors of repatriation were true but was overjoyed to find him still in France.[134] Some ended up elsewhere in Europe. The great scholar of Southeast Asia Benedict Anderson's first words were in Vietnamese, learned from the family's beloved Indochinese domestic servant who traveled with them from Kunming to Ireland when his father was on leave. She was barred entry to the United States in 1941 and forced to return to Indochina; Anderson's mother tried but failed to find traces of her after the war.[135]

The networks and relationships that shaped the lives of Indochinese domestics in France outside the home varied considerably based on geography and gender. In Paris, domestics were often men seeking temporary work; in most cases, they found it in homes that had no past ties to Indochina (including, famously, with Gertrude Stein and Alice B. Toklas, an experience given life in Monique Truong's novel *The Book of Salt*). Nguyễn Tắt Du was typical: he came to France to study in 1924 but drifted away from his studies, finding work in Paris as a cook in private homes, as a dishwasher, and as a janitor.[136] Those who lived with employers were clustered in bourgeois neighborhoods in the seventh or sixteenth arrondissements, but in Paris they were more likely to live outside of the home, usually with other Indochinese. This facilitated mutual aid through groups like the Association des cuisiniers annamites et domestiques des maisons bourgeoises, founded in Paris in 1922. Its dues aided sick, disabled, or unemployed members, and funded their meetings (usually in restaurants, but occasionally in homes when well-heeled employers were on vacation). Its 450 members in the late 1920s represented most Indochinese domestics in the capital.[137] It first drew scrutiny for "troubles with the vice squad and the fact of the occasionally dissolute lives of its members."[138] In the mid-1920s, it forged an alliance with the anti-colonial Parti annamite de l'indépendance (PAI) but it soon dissolved, a casualty of purported misuse of funds and the arrogance of PAI leaders. The association disbanded in 1930, but it illustrates the professional and social ties among Indochinese domestic servants in Paris.

But few such ties shaped the lives of domestic servants in smaller cities or villages, where they may have been the only Indochinese residents. Loneliness and isolation must have been common even in good conditions; in situations of neglect or abuse, these domestics truly were "subalterns among the subalterns."[139] Hoàng Kim Tuyết was twenty-four when she came to the tiny coastal town of Loguivy-de-la-Mer as the domestic servant of one Dr. Laime. The treatment she outlined in a letter to the minister of colonies was enslavement: work from early morning until night, little food, lodging in a garden shed, and two hours off a week, when she was forbidden to leave the property.[140] Trần Văn Minh came to France in 1926 with his employer in Indochina, a factory owner in Hà Nội. Months later, the employer and his wife committed suicide, leaving him at the mercy of his original employer's mother-in-law, who worked him to the bone but paid him nothing. When he took refuge at the Association mutuelle des indochinois in Paris, his belongings were stolen.[141] But some stories had happy endings. In 1922, Nguyễn Thị Sanh came to Nîmes to work in the home of a military officer. Seven years later, she left an abusive situation to work for a former Resident Superior of Tonkin in Paris. Faring no better there, she gave notice, at which point her angry employer tried to force her repatriation by taking her identity papers and sending them to officials in Marseille. "I will not be forced to return to

Indochina," she wrote to the minister of colonies. "I have the right to be in possession of my identity papers. . . . I know how to employ legal, even judicial means to return them to my possession, and these men cannot think themselves allowed to do anything like in Indochina, where they have the power of life and death over ignorant natives. In France, I am a woman. I deserve help and protection."[142] By 1943, Nguyễn Thị Sanh was a *commerçante* living in the bourgeois sixth arrondissement.

Entrepreneurialism, more visible among petit bourgeois restaurant owners or grocers, was also common among more marginal Indochinese. Many monetized their mobility through brisk sidelines importing goods and exploiting exchange rates. During the Great War, demand for Indochinese tobacco (*thuốc lào*) far exceeded official imports, and many Indochinese had bundles sent from home to resell in France. One enterprising soldier imported 100 kilos of dried fish, 30 kilos of dried pepper, 100 kilos of "Chinese sausages," 10 kilos of ginger, and 10 kilos of tea for resale.[143] Another soldier asked a friend in Tonkin to send him "encrusted platters, silks, etc." and sold them to French colleagues or in town during his leave.[144] During the French occupation of the Rhineland, some Indochinese did a brisk business buying consumer goods in marks and reselling them at a profit.[145] Sailors bought silks, ceramics, needlework, and even exotic birds in Asian ports to resell in France.[146] Some recruited friends or family at home to invest in these ventures.[147] One told Đào Trinh Nhất that the extra income from such sidelines made the brutal work and low pay of ship's work worth it.[148]

Many such entrepreneurs crossed the borders of legality. Scams and cons of all kinds were common among Indochinese sojourners. In 1922, a *métis* named Henri Vally came to the colonial exposition in Marseille pretending to represent an Indochinese textile enterprise; he not only conned a few would-be investors, he seduced one of their daughters and tried to kill her when she discovered the scam.[149] Another *métis*, Khanard Dumont, got tired of his low wages at a Renault factory and opened a dentist's office in Paris – without any dental training whatsoever – until complaints led him to flee.[150] Phạm Văn Man deserted the army in Marseille in 1939 and began "living by his wits, regularly duping people in the Indochinese milieu by not paying back loans and stealing the belongings of others. He passes himself off as an aviation officer and to give that impression. . . . He wears an aviator's hat with the winged coat of arms, but without the tassels."[151] Many destitute students in France wrote wealthy Indochinese to ask for assistance, but one group of seventeen threatened to wage a slander campaign against a retired official in

Trà Vinh if he did not send them funds. "Money can cause happiness, and it can also cause unhappiness," they wrote; "we will leave it to you to decide which."[152]

Many Indochinese made a living by trafficking narcotics. Indochinese soldiers and workers in France during the Great War were a captive market for opium, which was illegal in France. This led to a wave of smuggling, often in tea tins.[153] Opium networks expanded with steamship lines after the war. Indochinese sailors had intimate knowledge of customs and police procedure, had contacts in the bustling and seedy corners of port cities, and were often badly paid—a recipe for smuggling. Most of their contacts on shore dealt when unemployed or to support their own drug habits, but some had long, prolific careers. The best example is Đặng Văn Thư, proprietor of the long-standing "Restaurant Intercoloniale" in Le Havre. Đặng Văn Thư became a sailor after serving six months in prison in Indochina in 1917 for counterfeiting. He soon began trafficking in opium, at times buying as much as 50,000 French francs of it in Indochina to sell in France. He founded his restaurant with the proceeds, and for a time he used drug money to support anti-colonial groups. Philippe Moi's work as a domestic, cook, lacquer worker, and maître d' in Paris gave him cover to sell opium and cocaine to clients like "an attaché of the President of the Republic and a baroness living in the quartier de l'Étoile."[154] But drug dealing in the lucrative French market could be risky. One sailor named Phạm Văn Đặng was drawn into opium trafficking by Corsican associates of Paul Mariani, an inspector of police in Dunkerque. The investigation after his arrest revealed a range of Mariani's illegalities, and Phạm Văn Đặng's sudden death during the investigation provoked widespread speculation, as far as Indochina, that the Corsican mafia had poisoned him.[155] Policing reveals the breadth of Indochinese drug trafficking in this era. In 1929, Đào Nhật Vinh did jail time in New York for smuggling cocaine.[156] In 1932, Nguyễn Đức Trát was arrested in Madagascar with forty kilos of opium.[157] Nguyễn Đoàn Chược spent six months in an Istanbul jail for opium smuggling.[158] And Phạm Văn Khánh, the manager of the Air France bar-restaurant in Bamako, was expelled from Mali in 1941 for narcotics trafficking.[159]

Indochinese also smuggled weapons and ammunition from France to Indochina. In 1930, a 100-franc pistol could sell for 600 francs in Sài Gòn.[160] Such margins led to some large-scale trafficking efforts, like the 310 pistols and over 31,000 bullets seized on the *Athos II* in Sài Gòn in 1933.[161] Some anti-colonial organizations tried to smuggle weapons to Indochina from Europe, but it often went badly. In February 1930, agents of the Việt Nam Quốc Dân Đảng arranged for part of a German arms shipment to China to be unloaded off Tonkin's coast but could not find a ship captain willing to repeat the experiment. A year later they went to Berlin to try to make a deal directly but were swindled when the manufacturer delivered bricks instead.[162] In 1931, French officials foiled Nguyễn Văn Tạo's plot to send an ICP agent from France to Indochina with 30 pistols.[163] But traffickers continued to smuggle small shipments of pistols that could be easily hidden and resold in Indochina.

In March 1930, the newspaper *L'Ami du peuple* described "a deluge of tracts in the Annamite language, printed . . . in Moscow and Paris, brought by the bundle to Asia by the Annamite boys of Messageries maritimes, [and] found in the most remote hamlets."[164] PCF-produced documents were "transported either in boxes or tubes, hermetically sealed, then hidden in the coal cellars or immersed in water tanks."[165] Indochinese, French, and Chinese workers on steamships began smuggling communist communications and tracts from France to Indochina in the 1920s. It was risky: in the 1935 "Deschamps Affair," the Sûreté ensnared dozens of communist agents in Indochina (including Trần Văn Giàu, head of the ICP's Cochinchina branch) after the arrests of sailors working as PCF liaisons.[166] Many of these sailors were militants themselves. In 1930, Nguyễn Văn Thuận was arrested in Chợ Lớn with typesets and communist tracts printed in France. He had worked on steamships since 1920 and as a liaison between the PCF and communist networks in Cochinchina since 1927. In Marseille, he recruited Indochinese to join the PCF and to subscribe to the PCF's Indochinese newspapers; in Sài Gòn, he distributed illicit tracts he had smuggled and formed communist cells.[167] But others were like Bùi Văn Tô, arrested in 1927 in Sài Gòn with eight hundred copies of Jacques Doriot's speech to Indochinese revolutionary youth in Canton. He had bounced from job to job before finding work on a ship, had no known political involvement, and became an occasional informant after his release from prison. Though possibly spurred by a spasm of idealism, his profile suggests more opportunistic motives for undertaking a risky, one-time job that likely paid well.[168]

INDOCHINESE IN FRANCE'S SECOND WORLD WAR

After receiving the requisite identity papers, physical examinations, vaccinations, and haircuts in dirty, disease-ridden transit camps in Hải Phòng,

Tourane, and Sài Gòn, and then spending a month to six weeks at sea, the second generation of Indochinese to join a world war arrived in Marseille in early 1940. Roughly seven thousand Indochinese tirailleurs joined the ten divisions of colonial troops making up 9 percent of the French army on the eve of war. First stationed in southern garrison towns like Carcassonne and Fréjus, they were deployed along the Maginot line as the German army mobilized. The twenty thousand Indochinese *ouvriers non spécialisés* (ONS) directed by the Service de la main-d'oeuvre indigène, nord-africaine et coloniale (MOI), organized in companies of two to three hundred men, were sent around France to factories, arsenals, airfields, and shipyards. From their arrival to the sudden end of France's war, their letters home were much like those written during the last war, expressing interest in the novelty of their surroundings, awe at the scope of the war effort, and adaptation to the demands of wartime industry. Relatively few complained about their housing and food; the poor salaries were a greater concern, but this did not prevent many ONS from leaving their barracks during off hours for the cafés, cinemas, and cabarets of nearby towns.[169]

On May 10, the 52nd demi-brigade, a mixed colonial unit stationed along the Meuse, was pummeled by the German 8th Panzer division and heavy artillery bombardments. Equipped with outdated Hotchkiss rifles and hopelessly outgunned, they surrendered after five days with almost half the brigade killed or injured.[170] A memorial honors the 18 Indochinese soldiers who fought to defend the town of Beaune and were executed after the Germans took it. Vichy authorities calculated that 4439 colonial soldiers died and 11504 were presumed dead at the June 22 armistice.[171] Others fled into the countryside. "I am living in a stable," wrote Phạm Duy Khiêm; "manure, humidity, flies. I know that it's nothing. But it is a painful place to endure the misery of France, and to wait in anguish."[172] Indochinese were spared the massacres of some West African soldiers in the temporary internment camps of the northeast, as well as in Holland and Germany, the result of vicious propaganda urging "revenge" for their role in the French occupation of the Rhineland.[173] The Vichy regime, worried about maintaining authority in the French empire, negotiated the return of colonial POWs to France, where they were housed in German-run camps (*frontstalags*) in the occupied zone and put to work. They harvested crops, cut timber, and rebuilt roads, airfields, and coastal fortifications. Their importance to Germany's war effort made their conditions, if harsh, generally livable for much of the war; they were paid and allowed to leave their camps, and they experienced surprisingly little German racism or abuse. But conditions worsened later. Some were sent to Germany after the Normandy invasion; some died under Allied bombing.[174]

Most of the ONS were already in southern France during the German invasion. Those further north, in most cases, found their workplaces summarily closed, with their overseers disappeared into the mass of millions fleeing the Wehrmacht. Before long they too headed south, subsisting on the charity of the Red Cross and the kindness of local populations. Most were soon caught by German troops and sent to camps in the Vichy "free zone," where other ONS—their factories ground to a halt—were awaiting what they hoped would be a rapid repatriation. From November 1940 to July 1941, 4437 of them left Marseille on steamships for Indochina.[175] Some (Phạm Duy Khiêm among them) made it back, but blockades and submarine warfare forced others to turn around. Some ended up stranded in Algiers, Oran, Port Said, Lattakia, or other Mediterranean ports. The British captured 448 outside of Durban, most of whom were sent to Madagascar.[176] Many waited out the war in these places, working for the military or in local industries, living in warehouses or vehicle hangars, and thinking of home. Some never saw it again. In 1943, a French official "saw, in the pious gesture of the Annamites of Oran toward their nineteen dead over the past two years, beautiful qualities of solidarity and mutual aid." The dead had been buried in scattered parts of the city cemetery, but their friends disinterred and reburied them together under tombs "framed in stone, with a marble plaque with their name, their village of origin, the date of their death, sometimes a small cross. The tombs are well kept by the Annamites themselves, who visit them each Sunday."[177]

The chaos of defeat and demobilization brought some Indochinese into the Free French forces early in the war. Among the earliest were sailors working on ships that fled to England after the defeat; French officials estimated about 150 of them in 1941.[178] Others trickled into England from around the world. Trần Phúc Chiêu joined the Free French navy in Buenos Aires in 1940. By mid-1941 he was working for the Free French information services in London, teaching Vietnamese at the School of Oriental Languages, and married to an English woman.[179] British operations in the Mediterranean and North Africa in 1941 led more Indochinese to join the Free French. Five hundred in Syria volunteered instead of being repatriated to Indochina, as did dozens on the *Saint-Loubert Bié*, captured by the British as it rounded the Cape of Good Hope. They served in North Africa and Italy before landing in Provence during the Liberation.[180] Indochinese also deserted Vichy regiments to fight with the Free French. Nguyễn Hữu An fought in Tunisia and at the battle of Bir Hakeim, winning the Croix de Guerre.[181] Lê Văn Bê deserted Vichy forces in Tunisia in mid-1943 and fought up the line—Algeria, Naples, Toulon, Alsace—until the liberation.[182] Some, especially those who declined repatriation, were surely fighting for a cause they believed in; for others, it was simply a better bet than becoming a prisoner of war.

Most Indochinese would not have this choice until later in the war: three-quarters of the twenty thousand ONS in France remained marooned in makeshift camps after the armistice. For a time, there was nothing to do. But Vichy soon re-mobilized them, either directly or by leasing them to private employers. The period before the German occupation of the Vichy zone was, in the "bucolic words" of an MOI official, a "sylvan period" of a "return to the soil" that saw the largest Indochinese involvement in France's rural economy during the colonial era. ONS built and repaired roads, dug and cleared canals, cut forests, hauled timber, burned wood for charcoal, mined salt, and helped with harvests. Alongside Spanish and Italian workers, the 25th company of ONS helped revive the Camargue rice industry, an episode whose symbolic "return" of Indochinese to their "natural" conditions held an outsized place in Vichy propaganda and in contemporary popular memory of the ONS in France.[183] Like Albert Sarraut had twenty years before, Vichy officials hoped that this labor would serve as the foundation for a postwar *mise en valeur* in Indochina, and that the returning ONS would be the "vanguards of French colonialism and carriers of the National Revolution."[184] The German army also mobilized ONS after occupying Vichy France in November 1942; despite an exemption from the Service de travail obligatoire (STO), which sent over half a million French citizens to Germany as war laborers, nearly half of them ended up working for Germany's war effort.[185] Some returned to the chemical and munitions factories where they had worked before France's defeat to make weapons for Germany. About two thousand worked for Todt, the German industrial conglomerate, building bunkers and naval bases along France's western and northern coasts.[186] And much of what agricultural workers harvested was siphoned off to feed German soldiers.

Because the MOI leased Indochinese labor in short-term contracts to employers from Todt to rural French communes, ONS carried out a broad range of work during the war. Many were effectively migrant workers, moving from place to place every few months or even weeks, often far from their base camps; a unit could be mining salt or picking chestnuts one month, and building a German submarine base the next. Some work was tolerable, other work terrible. Many remembered happily their work in small French towns at harvest time, where they were often treated well and lodged with families, but they despised other rural work, especially clearing forests and hauling timber, for the toll it took on their bodies. Factory work, if never easy, also varied; as Indochinese had a generation before, the ONS reviled chemical and munitions factories but were happier making textiles.[187] But most ONS discontent related less to the work itself than to their housing and food, which were worse than during the Great War and declined steadily over time. The MOI, administered by the Ministry of Labor, was funded mostly through ONS labor: three-quarters of their wages went to feed, house, clothe, and heal them. The MOI rarely found enough work for the ONS to cover their costs, and as ONS sat idling in the camps, MOI budgets shrank and their living conditions suffered.[188] Corruption was also rife: MOI officials and camp guards stole food, clothing, and supplies meant for the ONS to sell on the black market. Hunger, cold, and fatigue suffused their days. One remembered, "I have only memories of hunger, cold, and misery."[189] By 1943, some began deserting. Most went north, seeking *au noir* work or the preferable legal status of Originaires des territoires français d'outre-mer, outside of MOI oversight, to work legally and obtain ration cards.[190] Some ended up working in Germany; a few actually walked there.[191]

ONS suffering was more complex than simple colonial exploitation; their living conditions were about the same as European refugee war laborers in France, and possibly even better than some parts of French society.[192] But their acute material deprivation, the chronic exploitation of their labor, and the increasingly carceral regime they lived under soon gave rise to acts of resistance. Before 1944, these were often individual: feigning injury or illness, or violent acts against officers and supervisors. But there were collective acts. Most typical were demands for more food and better clothing, but some ONS also engaged in work stoppages. The first seem to have been in spring 1940, when ONS working at munitions factories in Angoulême and Saint-Fons went on strike. In January 1941, Hoàng Khoa Khôi, an MOI interpreter and later a Trotskyist militant, led interpreters and Indochinese officers in a strike in Vénissieux. Sporadic strikes continued throughout the war: their leaders often went to prison, but the inability to repatriate the ONS, and the need for their labor, led most participants to be simply reassigned to other units, if punished at all. Collective acts like these, essentially absent among Indochinese workers during the Great War, "were not the result of a modernity acquired by these workers through contact with metropolitan France . . . but the extension of a claims process already extant in interwar Indochina," especially experience gained in the colony-wide strikes of 1936–37.[193] By mid-1944, as the German occupation began to crumble, the ONS were organizing their camps into into proto-unions, electing delegates, and making contact with French labor unions and workers associations, often through PCF militants reemerging after years of evasion and resistance. In the euphoria of the liberation, their demands were simple: "We demand, in all realms, the same rights as French workers."[194] Even in 1944, national independence was still a remote idea, or a distant dream, for many Indochinese laborers in France.

SIX

Daily Life

DƯƠNG VĂN MÙI'S DEATH IN PARIS in 1930 did not go unnoticed. He had served as treasurer of the Indochinese section of France's Union fédérale des étudiants, whose members were among the two hundred people who attended his funeral. Other Indochinese came from Montpellier, Bordeaux, Nice, and Lyon to pay their respects; they brought flowers and took pictures of the sad occasion to send to his family. After the ceremony, "a young French woman following the coffin fainted" and had to be helped out.[1] But the sailor Bùi Văn Khóat, who died alone in Marseille's Hôpital Dieu in 1938, received no such adieux. His wife and child in Kiến An heard news of his death not from his friends, but in a terse telegram from the Ministry of Colonies. Aside from the fact of his death, it informed them that to take possession of his life savings of 4301 francs and his meager personal effects, they would have to pay the hospital bill of 6272 francs. Barring any other arrangements, his body would be buried in a common grave.[2]

This chapter shows how, in life as in death, the socio-cultural differences and disparities of colonial society shaped Indochinese sojourns in France far more than any common status or experience as "colonial subjects." These sojourns did begin with the shared experience of, in Jennifer Boittin's words, "dislocation—a movement from one space to another."[3] The new contexts of daily life in France—where they lived, how they dressed, and what they ate—also reinforced feelings of departure that had grown as the steamship crossed the oceans, as did the sites and forms of leisure that shaped their lives outside of study or work, from solemn libraries and museums to raucous cafés and dance halls. But as novel and as different as the metropole was, the daily lives of Indochinese sojourners in France remained deeply rooted in the colonial society they had come from. Occupational and mutual aid associations, and the transplanted cultural practices they facilitated, reinforced ethno-racial distinctions between Indochinese and other parts of French society and reinforced socio-cultural distinctions and divisions among them. Racism, language, forms of labor, and residency patterns limited social and affective ties to both white French and to people from other parts of the empire, while epistolary networks preserved ties to family and friends at home. Many Indochinese sojourners had imagined that going to France would be to leave one nation for another, but their daily lives in France, in Gary Wilder's words, "provided them with concrete experience that they belonged to a broad imperial system that disrupted provincial definitions of nation and colony."[4]

THE BARE NECESSITIES

Indochinese who came to France before the Great War lived under close supervision. Embassies and envoys from Indochina's imperial states stayed in hotels or private homes during their carefully managed visits. Students, most of them children of royals or imperial officials, often lodged with former colonial officials, who kept their families abreast of their activities and well-being; others lodged at school. Nguyễn Thế Truyền, son of an imperial official in Thái Bình, came to study in France in 1911 at the urging of an official named Charles Dupuy (a friend of his father's), who placed him at Parangon. He lived there during the school year and with Dupuy during vacations.[5] As more Indochinese began studying in France, officials urged parents to house their children at a collège or lycée or (failing this) in a French home. This could go poorly: the head of one school in Paris overcharged a student's family for room and board (even when he was in the hospital),[6] and some families fell prey to French "correspondants" who did not provide what they had promised in the newspaper advertisements they took out in Indochina. "I am not allowed to go out at all," wrote one student; "I am always locked in my room.... Mr. Cartray insults me and calls me *gamin* and *voyou*."[7] Some offloaded their charges in cheap hotels and pocketed a healthy profit.[8] Initiatives by old Indochina hands, like a missionary-run dormitory, A. R. Fontaine's Foyer vaquelin in Paris, or Paul Monet's Foyer des étudiants annamites in Toulon, had little appeal. Anti-colonial activists protested the opening of the Cité universitaire's Maison des étudiants de l'Indochine in 1930; for most of the next decade, it housed more French students with connections to the colony than it did Indochinese themselves.[9]

Most Indochinese in interwar France lived in places outside of all official or familial *in loco parentis*. But this could make lodging tricky to secure. Indochinese mutual aid societies gave new arrivals a place to sleep or store their things for a few days, domestics often lived with the families who employed them, and some lacquer workers lived in dormitories attached to their workshops; one included "laundry, central heating, and electricity, as well as winter and work clothes. . . . For bed, they have one or two mattresses, and one or three wool blankets, depending on the season."[10] Some found roommates on a steamship, at school, at work, in a café, or at a political meeting. In the 1920s, many political activists crashed at Nguyễn Thế Truyền's apartment at 23 rue du Sommerard, "a sixth-floor garret with a mattress on the floor, a folding table and chairs, a piano, pots and pans next to the chimney, and an overloaded little bookshelf."[11] Class shaped residency patterns: in Paris, students clustered in the fifth arrondissement while workers lived with their employers in posh quarters of the Right Bank or in the peripheral working-class areas.[12] Sailors and dockworkers in Marseille lived around the port, while students lived off the elegant boulevard La Canebière—or, more often, avoided the city entirely for the nearby bourgeois town of Aix-en-Provence. Many students lived in modest hotels or rooming houses, which were flexible and cheap. Bùi Ái's room had a twin bed "whose springs are so old and loose that it resembles a hammock when lying down in it . . . a dresser, two stuffed chairs, a sofa of faded red velour, and an ordinary wooden table and two chairs. Add a sink with running water, and you have an image of my Parisian home."[13] When things got tight, some skipped out on bills and hotel-hopped, sleeping under friends' beds. As Bùi Ái wrote, "In the morning, the guest had to get up and dress very early, not to leave, but to sit in a chair like a morning visitor. If ever the owner entered, he could do nothing but greet you with 'Bonjour monsieur! What brings you here so early?'"[14]

Mobility and precarity made housing arrangements fluid and diverse. Trương Văn Vĩnh left Nam Định for France in 1930. After a brief stay in Marseille, he lived in Paris for two years in (at least) the following places: a hotel with a friend who had come with him from Marseille, on rue Vaugirard with a student after his friend moved in with a "woman of dubious morals," in a rooming house with a friend from Hải Phòng who he bumped into in the Luxembourg Gardens, and in a hotel room with a Chinese opium dealer he met playing billiards. He moved back to Marseille in 1932 and lived in the basement of the restaurant where he worked, and then moved to a rooming house with a former butcher on a steamship after the two met applying for a job at Messageries maritimes. Then he went back to Paris, where he lived first with the restauranter and drug trafficker Đặng Văn Thư, then in a wealthy home in the eighth arrondissement where he worked as a domestic, and finally at a hotel after losing his job where, broke and desperate, he attempted suicide.[15] Itineraries like these could cut across the class and geographic lines that often shaped residency patterns. In June 1930, fifteen Indochinese living at 10 rue Vaugirard in Paris included lacquer workers and mechanics; students in science, law, and medicine; an optician; and one of their French girlfriends. They came from Hà Nội, Sài Gòn, Cần Thơ, and smaller cities and towns from around Tonkin, Annam, and Cochinchina.[16]

In France, Indochinese dressed differently—even in the warmer south, new clothes were necessary. This was easy for the wealthy, but for poor laborers finding new clothes could be a matter of real concern. Some abusive employers did not provide the clothing stipulated in many employment contracts. "I have been in Loguivy for more than five months," wrote Hoàng Kim Tuyết, a domestic, "and my employers have not bought me pants, a dress, or a coat. . . . When I protested, they gave me rags and told me to make clothes out of them."[17] In 1931, Nguyễn Văn Tôn, an unemployed lacquer worker, agreed to become a paid informant. "I'll get straight to the point," he told his supervisor. "I need a coat for the upcoming winter. . . . My own has long taken its retirement. . . . I am envious of Mahatma Gandhi, whom the heavens have graced with countless qualities. He travels to the land of Shakespeare . . . and not only does he not wear a coat or vest, he dispenses with a shirt."[18]

But new clothes were not only functional: they were a way to adapt, outwardly and psychologically, to new surroundings. "Desiring to dress *à l'européenne* upon my departure," wrote a Nguyễn official in 1908, "I have the honor of respectfully submitting this present request to obtain an advance on the stipend allotted me."[19] Bùi Thanh Vân hedged his bets, packing his turban and silk robe with his Western-style clothes; "total weight, thirty kilos, about the same as a soldier's equipment . . . at least I shall be warm and dressed adequately to stroll alongside courteous Parisians."[20] Phạm Quỳnh bought his first suit in Sài Gòn before going to France in 1922. He struggled with neckties early in the journey but eventually mastered them. "When I arrived in Marseille," he exulted, "I seemed as if I had been wearing Western clothes for years!" "If only that were all there was to it," he concluded, "one could become civilized just by spending a few hundred."[21] But dressing *à l'européenne* was not always enough. Bùi Ái's suit could not cut the *mistral* winds in 1927, and its light beige color marked him as a new arrival from the

FIGURE 9. Phí Thị Hợi, Paris, c. 1935. Source: François Trieu personal collection.

tropics, a target for hawkers, cab drivers, and con men. "It is useless to bring clothes with you, even the fanciest and best tailored of them," he wrote. "You will have to get rid of them in France to avoid the scornful comments of gawkers who take pleasure in insulting inappropriately dressed Asians as 'dirty Chinese.'"[22]

Indochinese also ate differently in France. Many cities had Indochinese or Chinese restaurants; those who cooked for themselves could buy foodstuffs at Asian grocers (Lê Văn Đức's 1931 guidebook gave tips on where to buy *nước mắm* in Paris and Marseille) and cook together in the kitchens of student or worker associations.[23] Some associations had their own restaurants, and the

Foyer indochinois in Dunkerque even organized public demonstrations of how to cook with rice.[24] But many had to get creative. "We received the rice that papa sent," wrote Lê Văn Ri from tiny Oloron-Sainte-Marie in the Basses-Pyrénées in 1935. "I'll write again when it runs out. And send us a few bottles of fish sauce."[25] Bùi Ái and seven friends were among the many who could not afford restaurants or association fees, so they scratched up 3 francs a day to cook on a hot plate in one of their rooms: "First we had to buy enough rice to get us through the day. With the money that was left over, we bought either fish or cabbage with a few salted pork feet or a lamb head. Add to that a few 'Kubs,' a sort of condensed broth, which replaces the *nước mắm*. . . ." The members of the student association in "Going to France" make the same substitution, and are preparing a commemorative statue of the waiter who first discovered it.[26] After their modest meal, the group splurged for a pack of cigarettes and strolled along the Boulevard Saint-Michel, "watching people eat, drink, laugh, and hug."[27] In his travel account, Phan Văn Hùm included one doctor's recommended diet for "cold climates" with a grim calculation of how much it cost to eat even a bit of of bread, cabbage, cauliflower, and a rare scrap of meat or fish.[28] Most got used to French foodways. "Breakfast," wrote Tùng Hương, "was a long piece of baguette and a cup of coffee with milk, more nutritious than canned milk. . . . Lunch is celery soup and beef or pork. Supper is white or green beans with macaroni." He delighted in the "bread with sugar and chocolate" and the melons, "sweeter and sharper than at home . . . what a strange fruit! Grapes are also delicious—three francs a kilo."[29]

Housing, clothing, and food were all radically different in wartime. After soldiers and workers left transit camps, "home" was a range of repurposed, often rankly inadequate spaces. In the Great War, the luckiest had barracks with heat, plumbing, and decent bedding. In 1940, Nguyen Van Thanh's barracks had "an athletic field, dormitories with wooden beds, mattresses, sleeping bags, clean blankets, and a large common room with tables and benches. A building with toilets, sinks, and showers was on the other side of the field. It was paradise compared to other places we had stayed."[30] But in both wars, most experienced far worse. In the Great War, most barracks were overcrowded; coal and wood often ran out, bedding was insufficient, leaky roofs and broken windows went unfixed, and lice, rats, and other pests proliferated.[31] And conditions were often worse in the next war. Indochinese working as leased labor for private employers often lived in barns, stables, factories, hangers, warehouses, tents, or makeshift shanties that they built themselves. Beds were piles of straw or planks, there was often no bedding, and their water frequently came from streams. As Nguyễn Liên remembered, "we suffered tremendously . . . sleeping one day in a cowshed, another in a stable, and doing all kinds of work. I was a strong and robust soldier and I adapted to circumstances, but such conditions explain why I fell sick." He spent eighteen months in a hospital in Bordeaux with sepsis.[32] One of seven Indochinese who came to France in 1939–40 had died by 1946, most from contagious disease.[33]

Most soldiers and workers in the wars received clothes upon arrival. "They gave us what was necessary," wrote an ONS in 1939: "2 work suits, 3 wool and 3 cotton blankets, a wool suit for Sunday, a sweater, 2 flannel shirts, 2 underpants, 1 béret, socks, suspenders, and handkerchiefs."[34] But hard labor in factories and fields soon ravaged clothes, and when replacements came (if they did), they were torn, had holes, were mismatched, or worse. "It is impossible to wear the clothes provided by the administration," one worker wrote in 1917. "They are clothes taken from the dead on the battlefield and then disinfected. Some are still stained with blood."[35] In both wars, Indochinese were forced to make shoes from pleated straw, scraps of wood, and pilfered pieces of leather.[36] But they also made real sacrifices to dress for occasional evenings out at a café or cabaret. "Indochinese have a reputation for spending," wrote a French overseer in the Great War; "soon after their arrival, they spend a great deal on a new suit, a trunk, a watch, and other objects far from indispensable for factory workers." Another official referred to them as "the young dandies of our war factories."[37] Some borrowed or rented a suit to pose for a formal portrait to send home.[38] But not all adapted seamlessly to new sartorial norms. In Toulouse in 1917, hundreds of workers protested that required short haircuts would make them look like criminals.[39]

Soldiers and war laborers were largely dependent on what food the military or factory owners provided. Soldiers stationed in interwar France often had noodles and rice for their meals (often prepared by an Indochinese cook); some had "little gardens where they can grow things outside work hours: lettuce, tomatoes, onions, etc., of which Annamites are very fond."[40] Many were stationed near the coast in Fréjus or Carcassonne, which meant fresh fish. During the Great War, the French military substituted rice for part of the daily bread rations, provided tea instead of coffee, and imported fish sauce, pickled vegetables, dried fish, bamboo, and tobacco (*thuốc lào*) from Indochina. But war inevitably exposed Indochinese to "the great alimentary classics of the military at the time: beef with tomatoes or macaroni *au gratin*, for example."[41] Those Indochinese who worked for American battalions in 1917–18 got used to other new items: canned salmon and sliced sandwich bread.[42] Results were mixed; officials noted Indochinese fondness for tomatoes and loathing of horse meat. "Wine is never allotted to the Annamites," wrote a military official in 1925, "and there are no grounds to reconsider this policy."[43] But such rules did little. Phạm Duy Khiêm had studied in France for years, but if we are to believe his autobiographical novel, his first glass of wine came during his service in 1940 as he fled south to escape the German army. "An isolated house on the edge of the road," he wrote, "I asked for a glass of water; the woman takes me to the cellar and pours me white wine. I never drink wine but I don't have courage to refuse ... at the moment, an indescribable pleasure: it churns inside me, like a cat, and warms me up. But afterward...."[44] In 1917–18, rationing and interrupted imports from Indochina caused discontent, as did an ill-fated attempt to substitute Chinese soy sauce for *nước mắm*.[45] But this paled next to the abject misery of most ONS in the next war, for whom, as Lê Hữu Thọ wrote, "eating became an obsession."[46] Rations meant for two weeks often only lasted a few days, after which many ONS were on their own. This meant foraging, with meager and often risky results—some got sick or died from eating poisonous mushrooms.[47] It also forced many to pilfer fruits, vegetables, and animals from nearby homes or farms, which poisoned their relations with local populations who saw the desparate act of eating a dog or cat (frequently against personal belief or taste) as a sign of an essential Asian barbarism.[48]

LEISURE

Leisure, like the basic conditions and circumstances of daily life, also varied greatly between Indochinese of different backgrounds and circumstances. One example of this were celebrations of the lunar new year (Tết), often the largest gatherings of the year; they occasionally attracted Lao and Khmer for whom the holiday was foreign. Most celebrated Tết in restaurants or in the meeting halls of student and worker associations. Some festivities crossed class lines, others did not (although non-Indochinese guests were often there), and they usually took place before Tết because of the French holiday calendar.[49] One scandalized attendee at a Tết ball in Bordeaux in 1929 saw the event as "truly shameful! They think only of abandoning themselves to pleasure ... embracing each other, men and women, without distinction, to rush into the crowd and jump like a band of monkeys, and when they leave the hall at 3 or 4 in the morning each couple goes straight to a hotel or a solitary place.... Our ancestors did not behave in this way."[50] But in Paris's rationed, fearful atmosphere in 1942, Tết celebrations were sober and subdued.[51] In the throes of the winter of 1918, military officials preserved Tết as a day for Indochinese to rest and receive medals for meritorious service.[52] Vichy officials, obsessed with folklore, tried to create appealing Tết festivities. In 1946, soldiers and workers awaiting repatriation refused the Ministry of Colony's gift of firecrackers, used in celebrations to ward off evil spirits, because the noise "painfully evokes the bombs and cannons of General Leclerc's expeditionary corps" then wresting back control of Cochinchina.[53]

Tết celebrations were, in fact, one of the few sites of leisure where Indochinese of all backgrounds interacted. For some wealthy Indochinese landowners, merchants, or officials, their entire purpose of being in France was leisure. Nguyễn Ngọc Xuân's account of his trip in France in 1920 was one of the first Indochinese tourist accounts of France; he followed the itinerary of wealthy tourists the world over, from Marseille to Paris's major sights (the Louvre, the Opéra, the Jardin des plantes, a show at the Folies bergères) with plenty of time set aside to shop at the *grands magasins*.[54] Like many delegates to an exposition, Trần Bá Vinh spent more time on tourism than on official duties: aside from Paris's sites and shops, he visited the Indochinese Great War memorial at Nogent-sur-Marne, stopped by the Association mutuelle des indochinois, and even called on Bảo Đại (he was out).[55] In 1921, Bùi Thanh Vân was one of the first tourists from Indochina to record impressions of French rural life. "I was eager to see the countryside," he wrote of the overnight train from Marseille into the Puy-de-Dôme. When "the dawn finally tore down the last veils of night" he beheld "a new, joyous landscape: fields of wheat, grapevines, potatoes, lettuce, squash, melons, and corn; trees with apples, pears and apricots; rolling hills, pine trees, fir trees, and more."[56] Most Indochinese tourists traveled in France for a few months, but some vacations took unexpected turns. Nguyen Tan Hon took a French vacation in the summer of 1939, but the outbreak of war prevented him from returning home. In 1941, he was still in France, studying physical education.[57]

Some tourists went elsewhere in Europe. Nguyễn Văn Vĩnh bought a printing press and specialized ink for *Trung Bắc Tân Văn* in Frankfurt, met with publishers in Berlin and Leipzig, and went on to Vienna and Prague just for fun.[58] Lê Văn Đức wrote popular accounts of his travels in Belgium, England, Germany, and Italy. Catholics made pilgrimages to Rome, while the nephew of the Cao Đài leader Lê Văn Trung visited the pope of the German Gnostic Church.[59] Nguyễn Văn Hoành, son of a wealthy merchant, visited England, Germany, Switzerland, Italy, Denmark, Sweden, Norway, and Romania during his school vacation in 1934.[60] Nguyễn Văn Trường took the long way home from Paris to Hà Nội, visiting London, the United States, and Haiti before crossing the Pacific.[61] Nguyễn Thị Anh went to Switzerland, Germany, and England during her school vacation.[62] Meng Ly, a Laotian student, traveled to the United Kingdom with his football team.[63] For some, such travels reinforced a sense of cultural inferiority that many elite Indochinese felt at the time: "We poor rubes have enough to worry about with our own trivialities," wrote Lê Văn Đức, "and we are not equipped to speculate on the great powers and their great men."[64] But Tạ Thu Thâu's 1929 trip to Germany intensified his political awakening. "I will never forget this active and industrious youth, so different from the youth of France," he wrote. "Germany lost the war and its youth has no fear of saying to the old generation 'you have nothing left to do, you led us to catastrophe, get lost.'"[65]

For those who thought of French sojourns as a form of self-cultivation, the line between study and leisure was blurry. When Phạm Quỳnh traveled to the 1922 colonial exposition, he filled his free time with a relentless itinerary of museums, historic sights, lectures, meetings with men of letters and politicians, and studious strolls. "Here," he wrote, "ambling in the streets is not just a pleasure, it is a form of study for the traveler. . . . After you return home and recall a street corner, a store window, a face, or a voice, such things evoke the soul of the places you have seen just as much as its sights and splendors."[66] Đào Trinh Nhất wrote that "it is impossible to guess how many bookstores there are in Paris, much like it is impossible to guess how many opium dens or Fontaine liquor stores there are in Saigon and Cholon."[67] A young Hồ Chí Minh spent happy hours at some of Paris's great libraries.[68] "These hours that trickle away along the Seine," wrote Tạ Quang Bửu, "we want to live them to the fullest, to follow them freely. . . . Where to go on this beautiful Sunday? I was young, I had just arrived in Paris. I decided to go see *La Joconde*." But it was only years later, after "suffering from hunger, cold and love" and reading Edmond Rostand and Paul Valéry, that he fully realized the painting's genius, and by extension his own "inferiority, impotence, and infirmity."[69] "I have learned a lot at the lycée," wrote Cao Quỳnh An, "but I've learned more from gatherings and conversations outside of it. Brother Doc's house is our salon, where we read books of all kinds; on Thursdays and Sundays, many of us gather to discuss philosophy or the events of the day." "What a change and what a blessing," he exulted, "when I look back to my past as a spoiled youth, to see myself now as a Parisian student."[70] "I rarely go to cafés," wrote Lê Phát Trung, "but I spend too much on books, which are expensive because they are printed on clean, elegant paper. I never miss an artistic exposition and I wander around in museums. That, in sum, is my existence."[71] "I am leaving for Strasbourg in three days," wrote Nguyễn Văn Hiệp, "where I will take advantage of these two months of vacation to read for my general culture and self-improvement."[72]

Most elite leisure was rarely this high-minded. For the wealthiest, France's pleasures were their oyster. "Tennis, baths, long walks, excursions by car. . . . It's a prince's life and all we could ask for is your presence among us," wrote Louis Bùi to his father, Bùi Quang Chiêu, from his and his sister's seaside vacation in 1927. "I'm not sure what all this will cost," he admitted, "the maid costs 250 francs a month. . . . Life is a little more expensive than in Paris, then there's the rented piano for Henriette at 100 francs and a tent to sit outside at 100 francs. Aside from these fixed costs are the incidentals that are impossible to predict. Oh, and there is also the car bought for the season."[73] In 1922, Nguyễn Văn Vĩnh bought a car but had trouble navigating Paris's narrow streets, so he asked Albert Sarraut to drive him to the war memorial at Nogent-Sur-Marne. On the way, a policeman stopped them for driving on a pedestrian-only street: "I am the minister of colonies," an indignant Sarraut huffed to the unmoved officer.[74] Trần Quang Huy brought his own car with him when he came to France in 1931.[75] Some surely drove their own cars to the Union Sportif Annamite's tennis tournament in Toulouse in 1929, which despite the hefty registration fee (including access to "a table well stocked with fruit syrups and ice") drew players from as far away as Bordeaux.[76] More ordinary students whiled away hours in cafés, at the local Indochinese mutual aid associations, or in parks doing not much at all. Some were more ambitious. During a vacation from medical school in 1938, Nguyễn Khắc Viện rode a bicycle from Paris to the Pyrenees and back—two thousand kilometers. He rode in the mornings and spent afternoons sightseeing. "By bike," he wrote, "one can contemplate the fields, mountains, and beautiful scenery, meet many parts of society, and better understand the society and culture of a foreign country." He noted that as in Indochina, most farmers still used beasts of burden and plows. He recreated parts of his trip decades later, when many places had changed beyond recognition.[77]

Wealthy or not, many sought the good life. "After walking out of the Sorbonne, Minh hurried to his room at the pension Matignon," reads the first line of Lương Việt Hùng's novel *Đời du học* (The Life of Study Abroad); the rest of the novel follows Minh as he wanders around his many Parisian haunts, never making it back to class.[78] "Our students are barflys (*piliers de café*)," wrote Nguyễn Văn Bạch from Aix-en-Provence in 1927. "They spend their time chatting and shooting pool. The French have renamed the Café des Deux Garçons, the headquarters of our compatriots, the 'Université des Deux Garçons.'"[79] "These *fils à papa*," wrote Trịnh Hưng Ngẫu, "crazily waste their parents' money, dress in the latest fashions, have nothing at all in their minds, understand nothing of what they see, and eventually return home empty-handed. At this rate, how will our nation advance on the path of progress?"[80] Leisure was more likely than politics to get somebody sent home. "Just two weeks after entering the lycée," Trần Vân Đốc wrote to a friend whose son he was hosting in Paris, "he started going to a cabaret in the Latin Quarter" and "began coming home scandalously late.... He was a sorry sight when he came to see me each morning."[81] Lương Dân Nguyên (grandson of Lương Văn Can, one of the founders of the Đông Kinh Nghĩa Thục) was, to his principal, "a lazy student, smitten with the good life, far more attentive to his elegant and varied wardrobe than to his studies. He spends a lot, all of it borrowed, and now he owes thousands of francs."[82] "How can we admire France and Paris," wrote Bùi Quang Tấn, "if we sleep all day and spend our nights in clubs, unholy rooms where you see horrors and prostitutes prancing about, or in discreet little cinemas where they show obscenities to excite spectators, rather than in the great theaters or cinemas that show immortal plays and films in which education and civilization reaches their highest degree?"[83] Hundreds of profligate students borrowed money without any way to pay it back, left a city to avoid paying tuition or rent, stole from an association, lied to their parents, and even used money sent for their return home for one last night out. The award for the most ingenious ruse goes to a student who asked a friend to mail postcards in his handwriting from each stop on the steamship voyage back to Indochina to make French officials believe that he had actually gone home.[84]

France's high culture, vacations, and fancy nightlife were another planet for more ordinary Indochinese, who spent their free time in cafés and restaurants near where they lived and worked, where their associations also often met. Indochinese workers in Paris frequented the Café Hoche in the eighth arrondissement or the Café de l'Europe in the seventeenth. But French owners were more apt to call the police over gambling or arguments.[85] Paris's Chinese restaurants offered familiar food and discreet owners: before the

FIGURE 10. An Indochinese New Year's party, Marseille, 1928. Source: Dossier Trần Vĩnh Hiến, Box 29, Fonds de la police de l'Indochine puis direction des Services de sécurité du haut commissariat français au Vietnam-Sud (589PO2/SVN), Centre des archives diplomatiques, Nantes, France.

Great War, Indochinese in Paris often gathered at a Chinese restaurant on rue Cardinal Lemoine, where "students of diverse Asian nationalities" mixed with "soldiers in uniform" and the *filles galantes* of the Latin Quarter."[86] In conversations during the hours whiled away in cafés and restaurants, "money, business, scandals, drugs, and women played as large a role as politics."[87]

Indochinese soldiers and war laborers had some leisure time near where they were stationed, but most remained within the confines of their barracks or work camps. French officials tried to forestall their boredom. "Many factories," wrote the official Phạm Gia Thụy in 1917, "place at their dispositions a house furnished in the Annamite style with chairs and tables, mats to nap, musical instruments, and even theatrical costumes. They contain French and Annamite newspapers as well as letter paper and quills. Workers gather there during their resting hours and days off to chat a bit, smoke, drink tea, read the news, write home, or play guitar or flute, all things that give them the sense of their native soil and mitigate their nostalgia."[88] Many cities also had "Maisons indochinoises" like these for soldiers and workers on leave during the Great War. They offered classes, organized by the Alliance française, to learn to read and write French and quốc ngữ (Phan Văn Trường taught some of them after his release from jail in 1915). It was the first formal instruction for many of the twenty-five thousand who participated.[89] During the Second World War, reflecting the regime's obsession with tradition and cultivating the body, Vichy officials provided traditional theatrical costumes and musical instruments for leisure, even as food and clothing were in critically short supply.[90]

Ordinary Indochinese were also prone to temptations in their down time. Gambling was endemic in work camps and barracks during the wars, and many sailors and domestic servants also spent the first hours of their paydays in secret gambling halls. In Marseille, Chinese restaurants hosted games like *đố chữ, chẵm chữ, phán thán* and *sóc đĩa* behind guarded doors; Europeans could watch but not play.[91] The back room of a bar on Paris's rue Débarcadère was an Indochinese casino from 10:00 p.m. until dawn; the owner also lent money at the ruinous rate of 10 percent per week.[92] Trần Lệ Luật supplemented the income from his thriving dry goods business by hosting gambling at his apartment; on a good night he could make 500 to 600 francs, about a month's salary for a skilled lacquer worker in the city.[93] In 1926, lacquer workers hosted marathon card games in the pagoda at the memorial to Indochinese Great War dead at Nogent-sur-Marne.[94] As always in gambling, there were some winners and more losers. "My compatriots play cards with a frenzy," wrote Lê Văn Khi, "and they all owe me money, some as much as fifty piasters.... When they get paid, they simply pay their debts." "Two workers," he noted, "fought each other over cards. One was killed and the other convicted and deported."[95]

At a Chinese restaurant on the rue Torte in Marseille, gamblers could also buy "opium wrapped in transparent paper, for 5 francs a packet."[96] Many Indochinese turned to drugs like opium and heroin to numb the despair of menial work, debt, and unemployment. Phạm Văn Quất began using and selling opium after losing his job washing ships docked in Marseille.[97] Đinh Thị Triệu came to France in 1938 to work for her former employer in Sài Gòn but quit because of abuse; a year later, unemployed, she was arrested in Marseille with opium.[98] Like class solidarity or romantic love, drugs crossed racial lines: in 1938, Marseille police arrested Nguyễn Văn Ba and his companion, Elise Stein, for heroin possession.[99] And for friends and family in Indochina, an arrest for drugs was often the first (and sometimes the last) news of loved ones long since departed. Nguyễn Đức Chàng left in 1924 to work on a steamship; a decade later, he was arrested with two Chinese sailors for smoking opium. Sûreté officials in Indochina dug into his background to see if he was connected to broader smuggling networks; when they interviewed his family, it was the first they had heard of him since his departure.[100] In 1932, a lacquer worker named Nguyễn Văn Tháp was arrested with opium. Facing jail and an unpayable fine, he hung himself in his boarding house in Paris. He left two notes: one for his friends and family, whom he had not seen for a decade, and one for the police commissioner in his arrondissement, an old Indochina hand, with whom he had often sat and reminisced about the place they had both left long ago.[101]

RELATIONSHIPS

When Bùi Ái ate his first restaurant meal in France, he "experienced a certain pride in ordering a European woman around. It is puerile on my part, I admit. But honestly, who among you doesn't feel pleasantly tickled to be served for the first time in his life by a French servant who, if fortune allowed her to come to Indochina, would become 'Madame.'" Imagine his surprise when a few hours later, while window shopping, he felt a tap on his shoulder and turned to face "two damsels—French of course—as gracious as possible, talking to me in a way that knocked me over. 'Oh! My coco from Peking! Why stay here? Come with us, my sweetie.'" Stupefied, he scurried away. A few days later, as he caught a train to Toulon, he was astonished when French people helped him carry his luggage and buy food so that he didn't overpay.[102] Bùi Ái's discombobulated first few days in France capture the shock, and liberation, that many Indochinese felt at unexpected deviations from the colonial social and sexual order. But this soon gave way to more complex friendships and romantic relationships in France, whether with French people or with sojourners from other colonies, that remained irreducibly bound to the hierarchies and differences of empire.

"My compatriots still live in darkness and in the shadow of devils," wrote Cao Quỳnh An to his father from Paris. "In contact with such people . . . we inevitably end up with a darkened face and heart. That explains my close relationships with foreigners and French. . . . With them, I don't have these kinds of worries. *Au contraire.*"[103] The lives of well-known figures reveal the strong friendships with French people that shaped some Indochinese sojourns. One of Phan Châu Trinh's closest friends, Captain Jules Roux, had fought to commute his death sentence in Indochina and remained an unwavering advocate and interlocutor in Paris.[104] The journalist Léon Werth offered Nguyễn An Ninh financial and emotional support during his difficult stay in Paris in 1925; Ninh described him as "the first European to give me the confidence in mankind that is the foundation of international solidarity."[105] Phạm Duy Khiêm's closest friends at the Lycée Louis-le-Grand and the École normale were Georges Pompidou and Léopold Sédar Senghor, both future heads of state. In 1943, home from war, he remembered his *camarades* on the rue d'Ulm as "opposed spirits" tied to one another by "the same honesty, ardor to understand, and desire to think truthfully."[106]

Such deep friendships, however, were relatively rare. For some students, the sting of familiar insults from some classmates prevented friendship with others. "Patriotism bears many fruits but it also has serious consequences," wrote Dương Văn Quản. "Annamites work hard for the future, but the hatred in their hearts is often too visible. Some entirely refuse to have amicable relations with their French *camarades*."[107] Requesting naturalization, a process "grounded in essentially cultural criteria" and often futile, was a stark reminder of difference.[108] Ngam Mouth served in the army for years in France and Algeria and was working as an orderly in Marseille's Hôpital des Marins when he requested naturalization in 1930; three years later, his dossier had not even been acknowledged.[109] Housing, social spaces like cafés or restaurants, and associational life all worked against close relationships with white French. Language often did too: while most Indochinese elites were fluent in French, many laborers spoke just enough to get by in basic interactions. For most, in short, cultural barriers persisted during their French sojourns. Tùng Hương recalled the isolation he and two Indochinese friends felt during the Christmas holiday in 1929, surrounded by people immersed in activities that meant little to them. They tried to get into the spirit of things by going to mass and eating their version of Christmas dinner—a chicken porridge (*cháo*). They were not necessarily unhappy, but the holiday was a cultural veil that they had a hard time peering through. "We barely speak to anybody," he wrote, "and nobody seems very interested in speaking to us."[110]

Dreams of anti-colonial solidarity with people from other parts of the empire also often encountered more complex realities. In the Great War, Indochinese relations "were excellent with Malagasys, occasionally tense with North Africans, and often violent with the Senegalese," culminating in a 1918 clash near Pau that killed three Senegalese and sixteen Indochinese. French officials noted that Indochinese "had not escaped German propaganda representing Senegalese as 'barbarous ogres.'" If exceptional, the incident reflects "mutual incomprehension, language barriers and prejudices that existed between these gathered communities."[111] In Paris, Indochinese "clustered within a few specific addresses or streets, which by and large remained the same throughout the 1920s and 1930s."[112] Apart from the fleeting Intercolonial Union, there was not a single student, worker, or mutual aid association in interwar France that meaningfully linked people from across the empire. Efforts to cross these lines were rare and could end badly: a 1933 joint ball between Indochinese and black migrants spiraled into mutual accusations of financial chicanery.[113] An Indochinese informant noted in 1930 that an oft-frequented Chinese restaurant in the Latin Quarter "was becoming a negro restaurant. . . . Since there are too many blacks, Annamite students are urging their classmates not to eat there."[114] In his critique of the 1931 exposition, Phan Tư Nghĩa railed against the French, "who have always viewed us with contempt as negroes and inferior beings."[115] One exposition worker was thankful that the event had properly introduced Indochina to French people, who before had "thought we were the same as black-skinned people in Africa or red-skinned people in America!"[116] Marriage between Indochinese and other colonial populations in France was also very rare. Only two examples of this emerged in thousands of biographical dossiers: Trần Thọ and Nguyễn Giáp, who met their wives, Marguerite Beyrouti and Habibé El Assis, while serving with Free French forces in Lebanon, and were married in Paris in 1945.[117]

Indochinese sojourners in France were almost all young men, and many experienced sexual encounters with white French women. Miscegenation-obsessed French officials did all in their power to learn about and prevent these encounters; their bureaucratic interventions reveal relationships ranging from assignations to lifelong ties, from adoration to neglect and abuse. For some soldiers and workers in the Great War, the French women they wrote home about were a fantasy. Some sent home pictures of "girlfriends" that they had picked up in abandoned homes on the front. A photography studio in Perpignan did a brisk business taking pictures of Indochinese with one of its employees; "it is always the same young woman," noted a censor, "posing arm in arm with these noble warriors."[118] More explicit pictures were everywhere and immensely popular as souvenirs. By December 1918, censors had counted nearly ten thousand photographs of French women—from formal portraits to pornography—sent to Indochina, and that was only a fraction of them.[119] But the letters mailed with these pictures made clear the inevitable results of Indochinese working alongside French women in factories and socializing with them in towns drained of French men. There were many fleeting, purely transactional encounters. "In our country," wrote a soldier, "the women of this race are very hard to approach, but us being here, two francs is enough for us to have fun with them."[120] "I do not flinch at spending money to woo some of these women," wrote one factory worker; "I'm here, and it would be silly not to give myself this satisfaction."[121] There were so many assignations in the wheat fields of a farm abutting the Indochinese barracks in Bergerac that the farmer protested his crop was being damaged.[122] By 1917, a postal censor noted that "the Indochinese repertoire has furnished some new terms for a comparative anatomy that is not at all flattering to French women."[123]

Sex, of course, could lead to children: "Annamites," noted a censor, "will leave indelible traces of their passage in France."[124] In 1940, an Indochinese worker wrote that he had met some "*demoiselles métisses* sown in the last war."[125] Many Indochinese probably had no idea that they had become fathers in France. Some who did abandoned or came to a mutual arrangement with the mother: a Sergeant Minh was surely not alone in paying 100 francs to the waitress at his usual café to "make disappear the '*gosse qui pousse*.'"[126] Children who did not "disappear" could be an unwelcome surprise for French men returning home. In 1918, Jean Michel sent a "souvenir of my bastard" to Lê Văn Muốn. "It seems, my dear sir," he wrote, "that we make little Annamites in France, much like the French make little Frenchmen in Indochina."[127] A French official observed that Indochinese stationed in the Rhineland "find easy success with German women," which he worried "would give rise to sentiments of pity among the Annamites for our so-called oppression of Germany."[128]

Some relationships became serious, if at times for instrumental reasons. "I plan to obtain naturalization by marrying a Frenchwoman," wrote one Indochinese, "which will permit me to set myself up in a job [here] later." "She has a lot of money," wrote another to his parents.[129] For others, a pregnancy birthed feelings of obligation. "You will never guess my news," wrote one sergeant-major to a friend: "Marie-Louise, *agrégée des lettres,* is pregnant! . . . I desire with all my heart the possibility of our union, I contemplate with horror any situation that would ruin the reputation of an honest young woman."[130] When repatriation threatened to separate Phạm Công Phược from his pregnant girlfriend, her father protested, begging officials to let him remain "so that the the child will not be a pariah and that my daughter, now my only reason to exist, will not be forced to expatriate."[131] And of course, many Indochinese men and French women simply fell in love. "Mother," wrote a worker, "I wish to tell you that I have been living for some months with a young French woman whom I hope to marry. She is virtuous and conducts herself beautifully."[132] "Do not worry," wrote a worker to his girl-friend, "I will one day be by your side to give you my heart and my name!"[133] "I love him with all of my soul," a French woman wrote about her *beau indochinois*; "I will never be happy without tying my fate to his. His intelligence, his gentle character, and his loyalty have drawn me to him. I reserve all my affection for him."[134] Many French families felt the same way. "Because he is always kind and well-mannered and we love him like our own son," wrote one woman's parents, "we would be happy to have him as part our family after demobilization."[135] "A year after arriving in France," wrote a worker, "I have come to know a girl and her parents. They care for me deeply. I eat at their home, they take me for drives in the country. . . . When we are kept to the barracks, they ask my commander for permission to take me out. I am happy."[136]

French officials, however, were far from happy. "The lure of sex continues and even crescendos," wrote one horrified postal censor. "We spend our nights reliving intimate scenes, painful to read, repulsive to write about!"[137] Interracial encounters stoked official anxieties about racial contamination, the erosion of French bourgeois femininity, and the transgression of colonial hierarchies. Officials feared that Indochinese relations with white women would not only racially empower them, it would instill "a hatred of the French among native women, whose photographs they have seen in their husbands' hands."[138] French officials could do little about passing encounters in cafés or cabarets (or wheat fields, for that matter), but they tried hard to sabotage relationships that risked becoming permanent, usually by discrediting the husband-to-be by showing that he was already married in Indochina or digging for other dirt. The prefect of the Var, the minister of colonies, and the governor general all collaborated to end Nguyễn Văn Khánh's engagement by telling his fiancée that he had come to France under a false name and had lied about his sterling employment record at the Toulon arsenal.[139] Another engagement ended "following the visit to Toulouse of a missionary interpreter . . . who depicted to the Rousse family the precarious social situation of the parents of Nguyễn Văn Côn" and warned the worker that marrying a French woman might prevent him from ever going back to Tonkin.[140] When such sabotage failed, however, French officials often relented and let

Indochinese remain in France after demobilization.[141] This reflected their greatest fear: that French women would follow their lovers to the colony, where conditions "were insufficient to allow a European woman to live decently" and where legal polygamy might even make them "wives of second rank."[142] But other than the return of mixed couples to the colony, which they never stopped trying to prevent, French officials came to shrug at mixed relationships by the 1930s.

Cultural barriers remained as official ones waned. Despite a few prominent mixed marriages in France (Nguyễn Thế Truyền and Dương Văn Giáo), many more relationships ended because of the pressures of difference. Lydie Corbière declined Nguyễn Thế Phu's proposal of marriage "because first, and above all, we do not have the same religion" and "we are not of the same race. I know very well that this is less of a concern these days, especially in a big city like Toulouse, but I fear that we have been raised in such different ways that we would eventually clash and offend one another and that this would result in our disunion. Rest assured, my dear sir, that I recognize your personal qualities and beg your pardon."[143] "I have women friends," wrote Cao Quỳnh An; "well you might imagine how difficult it is, given that my relations with them must be appropriate."[144] The end of a relationship could be devastating. Before taking his own life in 1924, Hà Minh Thương wrote to a lost love: "I loved you from the moment I first met you, dear Dolly, a love without hope, but not any less true or profound. . . . Goodbye Dodo, be happy and honest, and I will watch over you for eternity."[145] In 1928, Do Huu Trinh "became crazed with love for a young white woman he had conquered," reported *Tribune indochinoise*, but his "modest allowance . . . could not satisfy the young woman" and she left him. He shot himself in his classroom at the Lycée Henri IV.[146]

But elite Indochinese had their own reservations about interracial relationships. Most knew how rare and stigmatized such relationships were in the colony, a common theme in much Indochinese modernist literature of the era.[147] For others, these relationships violated their nationalist pride. "Everybody thinks I'm going to marry a French woman," wrote Nguyễn Văn Trụ, "but I cannot forget the outrageous acts that the French have committed toward our country, our race, and despite my generous nature I cannot forgive them."[148] One Indochinese sergeant imagined his encounter with a prostitute as a kind of political revenge. "I made her suck my cock to my satisfaction," he gloated. "Afterward I told her, 'I'm forcing the *mère patrie de la métropole* to suck Annamite cock to know what it's like. It's my own form of vengeance toward these despicable people."[149] For others, class—not race—was the barrier. "French women who marry Annamites are low class," wrote a student; "it is scandalous to see them honored as 'Ba Dam' (madame) in Indochina."[150] "When we are united at the lips it becomes serious," wrote another. "From there comes the danger of returning to Cochinchina accompanied by a French woman ... and who are the French wives of Annamites with diplomas from the great universities of France? They're mostly secretaries, waitresses in cafés, daughters of laborers ... and they are ugly, much uglier than our cute Cochinchinese."[151]

Cultural barriers to long-term relationships often led privileged Indochinese to seek casual ones, easily found in cafés and cabarets and on boulevards. "Your parents make great sacrifices to pay for your expensive educations in France," Bùi Quang Chiêu hectored a group of students in Paris in 1926, "and many among you spend your time in cafés and with 'femmes de boulevards' whom you support with money that your parents send to you with difficulty."[152] Ngô Quang Huy boasted to a friend of the evenings he spent in 1929 with one "Melle Charlotte ... first at Pékin, or at the Café de la Sorbonne." But after learning of her profession, he asked his friend to "burn this letter after you read it.... If it falls into the wrong hands, it might make people think that in France we only know prostitutes. I'm worried to be thought about in this way because I plan to return to Indochina to become a judge!"[153] When the fifty-five-year-old Sai Văn Hóa's eighteen-year-old French mistress grew tired of him, he tried to woo her back with jewelry and lingerie.[154] Casual relationships could cause financial problems and domestic tensions. "Will he blame me for not permitting him all liberties?" wrote Tạ Thu Thâu after evicting a roommate from their apartment. "In my opinion, we are free to do what we like, but if being free means going to cafés, amusing one's self with prostitutes, and always having a *fille publique* in one's arms, I don't claim this kind of liberty and I don't accept it in another."[155]

Most Indochinese men who had longer-term relationships with French women were laborers, who tended to stay longer in France and had more pressing need for cohabitation. Many family histories reveal ties and commitments that survived in desperate circumstances. Trần Văn Nghĩa came to France in 1916 and stayed to work as an accountant for his wartime employer. By 1931, he and his French wife had eight children, he had been unemployed for fifteen months, and they were desperate to return to the colony to live with his parents, but the minister of colonies denied passports for the family.[156] Nguyễn Văn Ba came to France to fight in the Great War; in 1917, he married Marie Forestier. Their first child, born in 1918, kept him in France, where he worked as a cook on a steamship. In 1933, fifty years old and with five children, Nguyễn Văn Ba lost his job because he did not have the required *livret de marin* and could not afford to go to Indochina to obtain it. "Please let me tell you about him," his wife wrote to the minister of colonies. "He is a good father who works hard to feed his children without asking anything of anybody. . . . Please do something, it will be for the poor children."[157]

There are also many examples of fragile, even brutal relationships lived across racial lines in the margins of French society. Lục Văn Sau wooed a married woman until she divorced her husband, then sold off many of her personal belongings to pay his debts.[158] Vũ Văn Trang, a domestic, fell in love with a prostitute and quit his job to be with her, working as a security guard in her brothel.[159] Nguyễn Thị Nhân, also a domestic, had a relationship with her employer that broke up his marriage. When he left her months later, she turned to prostitution.[160] Đình Văn Miến married two different French women, had children with both of them, and was twice cited for abandoning his family.[161] "He is a *gambler,* a *liar,* and *brutal,*" wrote a woman of Nguyễn Văn Phan, "and he gives me nothing despite having fathered my two children. . . . He is already married in Tonkin with a fifteen-year-old daughter." At times she would beg for food from her child's school cafeteria only to come home to find money missing. When their children's godfather (also Indochinese) forced Nguyễn Văn Phan to leave the home, he threatened to kill them.[162] Émilie Bedonet divorced Huỳnh Nhiên because he was abusive; when the court ordered him to pay a hundred francs a month in child support, he fled to Indochina.[163] Lý Văn Thủy, a failed restauranter and opium addict, had a French wife who danced in a cabaret to support him and their children even after he served a month in jail for beating her.[164] But domestic violence, of course, knew no class boundaries. In 1927, Đặng Vân Thanh, a chemical engineer, married Christiane Lagarde, an eighteen-year-old secretary fourteen years his junior. Months later she left him for another man. Distraught and high on ether, he shot her dead and turned himself in to the police. The affair, a minor sensation in the Paris press, reveals how male privilege in France could occasionally extend to colonial subjects. "If the man was serious and industrious," read one article, "the little *Bordelaise* was fickle and often abandoned the marital home." "Mme Thanh lived the high life and was always demanding more money," read another; "she was coquetteish and ignored all entreaties."[165] In June 1929, Đặng Vân Thanh was acquitted. "What will you do to me," her mother cried in the courtroom, "when I will have taken my vengeance?"[166] When Lê Văn Huế shot and killed his French wife after an argument, he tried to shoot himself and, when that failed, he jumped out of his hospital window. He received only five years in prison.[167]

FAMILY MATTERS

Paul Thái died at L'Hôpital de la Conception in Marseille on January 13, 1933 at the age of fifty-nine. He had been born in Gia Định. His father was a policeman, and his mother sold vegetables at the market. In 1905, he found work on a steamship. He eventually settled in Marseille and worked in a restaurant, at the desk of a cheap hotel, and as a night watchman on the docks. He returned to Gia Định only once, in 1924, to see his widowed mother.[168] These fleeting traces of Paul Thái's life are a reminder that virtually all Indochinese, from wealthy students to poor laborers, left behind their parents, spouses, children, or extended families, and that ties to them persisted in France. For wealthy sojourners, letters, telegrams, and occasional returns home were normal; poorer migrants like Paul Thái could press a note into the palm of a friend traveling home when postage was too expensive, or hear news of home when an acquaintance from Indochina walked onto Marseille's docks. We do not know how Paul Thái knew to go see his mother for the last time, or what it was like to go home after so long. But the archives are rich with traces of family matters that bound Indochinese in France to loved ones at home, and how this shaped their daily lives.

Many sojourners traveled to France with a powerful sense of obligation to the family they left behind. "My dear father," wrote Hồ Tá Khanh in 1926, "you have sacrificed so much for my education. If I succeed in life it is thanks to you.... My way of living is wholly different from the ordinary. And it is you, father, you taught me to live like this."[169] "I hope to have some success at the end of the year," wrote Nguyễn Văn Lai, "just to please my parents. That will be reward enough."[170] Tran Van Cui, oldest of eleven children, requested free passage home to help his indebted and sick parents—but only after the baccalauréat exam. "I should have returned immediately, but once home what could I do to help? For I have no diploma and I need one to get a job."[171] Some were haunted by fear of failure, especially when families had disapproved of their departure. "Why do you not leave that worthless society which you know is full of imbeciles?" wrote Phan Cao Ly to Phan Văn Trường in 1923. "You could leave your worldly life to live in the mountains or forest.... You would simply follow in the footsteps of the hermits and exiles of antiquity, especially those of great China."[172] Many felt a duty to advise younger siblings, especially sisters, from afar. "I love you and want to see you happy," wrote Nguyễn Thới Lai. "I am always thinking of your future. I will work here not only for our parents, but for you."[173] "As the oldest child of the family," wrote Nguyễn Văn Kim to his parents, "I am responsible for my brothers and sisters as well as the honor of the family. I thus ask you to allow me to express my opinion about sister Dang's upcoming marriage" (he disapproved).[174]

Soldiers and workers often had more pressing obligations. Many had gone to France in the hope of better supporting wives, children, and other relatives at home, who awaited news not of scholarly success, but of badly needed remittances. These were sometimes regular and predictable: during the Great War, soldiers' families received 3 piasters monthly; civil workers had a part of their salaries withheld and sent home.[175] During the next war, wives of soldiers and workers received 3 piasters a month and .3 piasters for each child (raised to 4 and .4 in June 1942 because of inflation). While less than the salary of many working poor in Indochina, it was crucial at a time of widespread deprivation.[176] In 1931, married exposition workers could send part of their salaries directly home; some sent as much as two-thirds.[177] Soldiers and workers in the Great War, whose finances military officials closely tracked, offer a rare quantitative glimpse at remittances. From June to November 1918, 4,573 Indochinese workers at munitions factories in St. Médard and Bergerac saved 174,036 francs and sent nearly 88 percent of it home.[178] But few sent home nearly as much, especially when the Indochinese piaster's value exploded after the Great War at a time when workers earning French francs faced the devaluation of their backbreaking work. And some employers withheld parts of salaries to ensure that Indochinese stayed in their jobs, which limited how much they could send home.

Emotional distance and poor earnings gave some sojourners an overwhelming sense of obligation. "To what end," wrote Nguyễn Duy Kiêm in 1926, "should I continue to live in a strange home with strangers, far from family and those dear to me? . . . Every time I receive a letter from home, a ray of joy passes in front of my eyes, and through a veil I see, far off, our house, my little sisters running and playing."[179] "My silence may trouble you, please forgive me," wrote Nguyễn Văn Lai to his uncle; "to push myself in my work, I must leave my beloved to the side, but far from forgetting them, I think of them constantly. My spirit works, my thoughts fly off to a little corner of the Orient where lies my home, my family."[180] Nguyễn Thị Hoa, a domestic, attempted suicide and was sent to live in an orphanage in Bordeaux in 1931. "The poor girl," said the nun watching over her, "had *le mal du pays* and was dying of sorrow at the thought of never seeing her family or her country again."[181] Phạm Văn Nhân remembered the suicide of a fellow laborer in winter 1942: "he hung himself in a shack. We don't know why he decided to do it. But many were thinking about their families in Vietnam and had no news of them."[182] And sometimes, news from Indochina underscored how sojourns left some families vulnerable. After Trịnh Đao Thiêm left for France in 1940, the mayor (*lý trưởng*) in his village "came often to court my wife. . . . After many refusals, he threatened to destroy her shop and expel her from the village."[183] Many Indochinese in France protested to colonial officials that a *lý trưởng* had stolen an indemnity or a remittance, unfairly reassessed or confiscated their land, raised their taxes, or harrassed or intimidated their families.[184]

Such feelings of loss and anxiety went in both directions. "When my mother and my wife come to see you," wrote Nguyễn Văn Ất to a friend in Sài Gòn, "please reassure them about my situation. For no reason, they have gone and consulted a medium. And whenever that happens, evil spirits are always at work. My wife has written me countless letters . . . accusing me of sleeping with prostitutes . . . [and] my mother believes that I will be arbitrarily thrown into prison and harmed."[185] "For some time," wrote Trịnh Thế Qúy about her husband, "I have heard rumors that he is neglecting his studies and has surrendered himself to harmful pleasures."[186] Hundreds of parents of students in France, hoping for news of academic success, instead received alarming requests to send more and more money, followed by stern letters from officials or creditors filled with tales of carelessness and excess. In 1926, Nghiêm Xuân Hoàng wrote to French officials that his son's "conduct and discipline ceased to live up to the important financial sacrifices that I made for his education" and that he had fallen prey to "delinquent friends and café habits." "I have ordered him many times to return to Tonkin and each time have sent him enough money for the journey home, but I have not received any news of him since October 30, 1925, and I have no idea where he currently is."[187] But many were furious when family tried to direct their lives from across the sea. "When I write you to say that school is too hard for me, you reply that I just don't want to work," wrote Lê Văn Dẩu to his uncle in 1924. "You say you are just giving me advice, but I say no, you still take me for a child and an imbecile."[188]

Love and marriage were chronic sources of conflict between sojourners and their families. Diệp Văn Vàng's parents, wealthy landowners in Mỹ Thọ, cut him off after learning about his marriage in Paris to a Tonkinese woman "who came to France to study sewing and haberdashery."[189] Many were even more upset when their child's beau was European. "You have told me of your plan to marry a European," Nguyễn Văn Phương wrote to his nephew, "but think again about it to avoid difficulties later.... If you marry a European, how will you ever come back to the countryside?"[190] In 1938, Nguyễn Khoa Kỳ, the minister of the economy at the Nguyễn court, sent money to repatriate his son after learning about his German girlfriend: the couple used the money to fund a trip to the Balearec Islands.[191] Đỗ Đình Đắc, a municipal official in Hà Nội, jumped on a ship in 1931 after learning of his son's plan to marry a maid working in his Parisian hotel. He finally tracked them down in Caen thanks to French officials, who had intervened to deny the maid the passport she hoped to use to go to Indochina.[192] Suzanne Oliver and Lương Văn Thành had been married for years when he returned to Sài Gòn in 1924 to see his family. When he got sick, his parents ignored Suzanne's requests to send him back to France or to let her visit.[193] In 1936, *Tribune indochinoise* reported on "the pitiable case of a poor Frenchwoman" who traveled to Sài Gòn with her husband but was shunned by her father-in-law, who offered her nothing but a hundred francs and a third-class ticket back to France.[194]

Unexpected news of romance or marriage in France was especially hard when there were already spouses and children in Indochina. Some sojourners heard this unwelcome news while in France: in 1939, Nguyễn Tuấn heard not only that his wife had had an affair, but that she was in jail for abandoning the resulting baby, leaving their ten-year-old son at risk.[195] But some built new lives in France and never saw their families again. Nguyễn Thị Lương, married since she was thirteen, came to France in 1928 for a teaching certification. One of her last letters to her husband was to ask for her birth certificate, necessary for her to get remarried in France.[196] But more often, spouses in Indochina heard such news second hand, or were left to interpret a deafening silence. "How could you be so cruel to forget me?" wrote one soldier's wife. "The heavens have condemned me to misery.... I wish you and your *madame française* good health."[197] And some sojourners left behind spouses and children in France when they returned to Indochina. "My love," wrote one French woman, "do you not sometimes feel like I am with you ... now and forever until the day I will blessedly finally see you again.... When will it be?"[198] In 1934, Nguyễn Xuân Lâm returned to Indochina from France, leaving behind a wife and children aged four, three, and eighteen months. Thirteen years later, a French official noted that "he desires to return to France to rejoin his wife and children."[199]

But remarriage was only one of many forces that could fray, or permanently break, the ties between sojourners and their families at home. The most irrevocable, of course, was death. Some families could afford to repatriate the bodies of their loved ones from France to bury them in ancentral land. "If your mother wants to have the body sent home I can arrange it for her," wrote Nguyễn Thế Phu to family in Nam Định in June 1928 after his cousin's suicide, "or I'll bring you to France so you can visit your brother's grave and buy a plot for his tomb."[200] Poorer families had to live with condolences sent from countrymen in France or a perfunctory official telegram. Often, these came with the crushing news that an illness had wiped out their loved one's meager but crucial savings. Some families waited years for news of a death: for one family in Bình Định, it was not until 1935, after dozens of inquiries, that colonial officials confirmed that their son had died in the Great War and not abandoned them.[201] And many never received any news at all. Some sojourners had given false personal details to authorities that made it impossible for their families to learn of their fates. In 1925, colonial officials tried to inform the family of Nguyễn Văn Liên that he was in an asylum in Paris, but they discovered that he had invented his personal details, rendering himself person-less.[202] And in many cases, the archives simply give no answers. Phạm Gia Nghi went to France to study in 1925. Twelve years later, his mother wrote the governor general about him. "I have had some news here and there," she worried, "but I don't know what he is doing now. . . . I am getting older, and so is my son (he is now in his thirties), and I am very anxious about him. Has he gotten married in France and started a family? Where is he in his studies? Will he come back?"[203] After inquiries, French officials reported that Phạm Gia Nghi, living in Lyon, refused to communicate with his mother. Why did he break off ties? One hopes that his mother may one day have seen her son again or at least had some news of his new life, but we will never know.

SEVEN

Political Sojourners from Peace to War

AS THE PARIS PEACE CONFERENCE ended in 1919, the atmosphere was subdued at Paris's 6 Villa des Gobelins. The great powers had ignored the "Revendications du peuple annamite" and there were few francs and little food to go around. Phan Văn Trường was often away defending soldiers in military courts, Phan Châu Trinh was scratching out a living retouching photographs, he and Nguyễn Ái Quốc were struggling with health problems, and the police kept a close eye on all of them. But postwar Paris's political winds breathed new life into the group. In December 1920, a festering schism in the Section française de l'Internationale ouvrière (SFIO) erupted when a faction calling itself the Section française de l'Internationale communiste proclaimed allegiance to Moscow and the Third International at its congress in Tours. Nguyễn Ái Quốc gave a speech calling for support for France's colonial subjects that received "a warm response from the hall, where cries of 'Down with the colonial sharks!' could be heard among the applause."[1] 1921 brought more hardship—a long hospitalization for Nguyễn Ái Quốc and the death of Phan Châu Trinh's son—but also more inspiration from the capital's libraries, radical bookshops, left-wing press, and constellation of union, socialist, anarchist, and émigré political meetings. And the new year also brought new faces into the circle: Nguyễn An Ninh and Nguyễn Thế Truyền, both interested far more in politics than in studying at the Sorbonne. But despite their shared cause, the group—later dubbed "the Five Dragons" (nhóm Ngũ Long)—also had spirited, often intense arguments, regularly noted by police informants keeping an eye on 6 Villa des Gobelins, that presaged the divergent political paths they would soon follow.[2]

This chapter explores the hundreds of Indochinese political sojourners who followed the Five Dragons to interwar France, making it a theater of colonial politics defined, as Gary Wilder argues of West Africans, "not only by their participation in metropolitan civil society but by their marginalization within it." Metropolitan France's distinct political culture and legal regime inarguably gave Indochinese "a greater degree of political freedom" than in the colonies, which allowed them to pursue—or discover—politics in "student organizations, mutual aid societies, workers' cooperatives, trade unions, sports clubs, and literary groups . . . nourished by periodicals, manifestos, posters, essays, poetry readings, political meetings, public addresses, cultural salons, and popular entertainment." Indochinese political sojourners thus "'practiced citizenship in the imperial metropolis" by "behaving according to the protocols of republican citizenship and preparing for a citizenship to come." Nevertheless, the metropole was not a state of exception to the empire: Indochinese political sojourners in interwar France faced racial and socioeconomic marginality, and the surveillance and repression of a security and intelligence apparatus seeking "to mediate metropolitan and colonial governmentality by infiltrating immigrant civil society." "Exercising civic virtue without enjoying full civil rights," Wilder concludes, "they were at once part of the French *cité* and apart from it."[3] During the interwar era, some Indochinese sought to transcend this double bind by pursuing more far-reaching forms of anti-colonial activism in France, efforts that would intersect with and transform the other realms of Indochina's revolutionary underground.

THE AFTERMATHS OF 1919

The epicenter of the Five Dragons' political activity shifted when Nguyễn Ái Quốc joined the Intercolonial Union in October 1921. Phan Châu Trinh and Phan Văn Trường had long been inspired by world political events, but Nguyễn Ái Quốc's peregrinations had made his horizons even more global. He had ties to Korean, Irish, and Chinese radicals who had made their own appeals in 1919 and he frequented Paris's Chinese political circles after the peace conference, where he may have met future communist luminaries Zhou Enlai and Deng Xiao Ping.[4] The Intercolonial Union united anti-colonial activists from around the French empire who hoped that the Third International would more actively support their causes than the Socialists. Its activists moved in the same meetings, bookstores, and union halls, and lived in the same neighborhoods.[5] Although they had taken the lead in form-

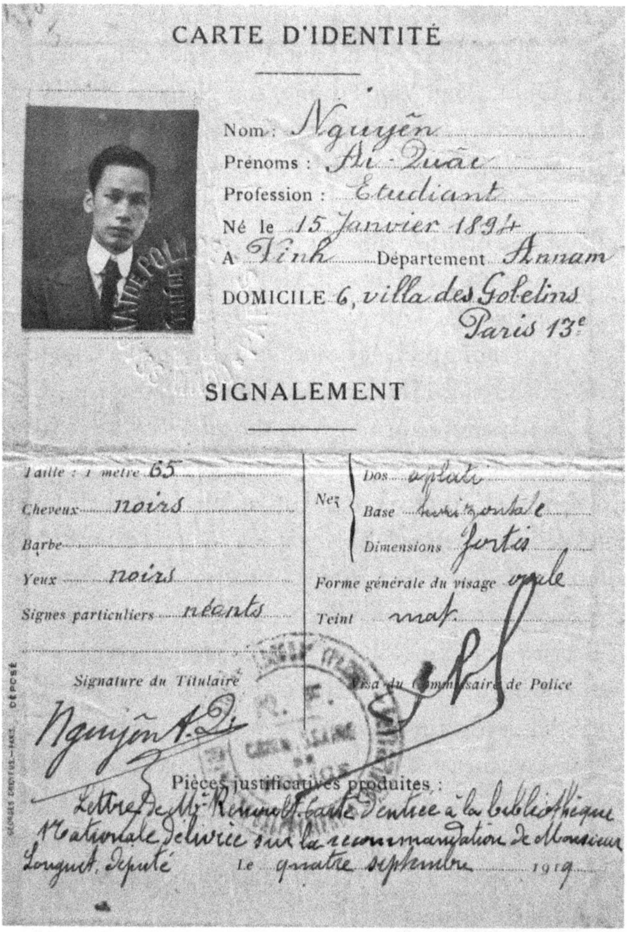

CARTE D'IDENTITÉ

Nom : Nguyễn
Prénoms : Ai Quâc
Profession : Etudiant
Né le 15 Janvier 1894
A Vinh Département Annam
DOMICILE 6, villa des Gobelins
Paris 13e

SIGNALEMENT

Taille : 1 mètre 65
Cheveux noirs
Barbe
Yeux noirs
Signes particuliers néants
Nez — Dos aplati
Base horizontale
Dimensions fortes
Forme générale du visage ovale
Teint mat

Signature du Titulaire
Nguyễn A. Q.
Visa du Commissaire de Police

Pièces justificatives produites : Lettre de Mr Renoult. Carte d'entrée à la bibliothèque Nationale délivrée sur la recommandation de Monsieur Longuet, député
Le quatre septembre 1919

FIGURE 11. Nguyễn Ái Quốc's French identity card, issued September 4, 1919. Source: Dossier 59497, Box 1W1142, Archives de la Préfecture de Police, Paris.

ing the Intercolonial Union, the group was never "independent" from what would soon be rebaptized the Parti communiste-Section française de l'Internationale communiste (PCF); it was in fact an effort to achieve a greater voice in a new political party whose Comité d'études coloniales (renamed the Section coloniale in 1924) was dominated by white French.[6] As a Sûreté official wrote, "communists in Paris ... like to present the Intercolonial Union as independent, even as they borrow its members to fill the sub-commissions of their own party's colonial commission."[7] At its meetings and in its newspaper *Le Paria,* the group worked to heed the Third International's call to build a "global anti-imperialist comradery."[8]

Nguyễn Ái Quốc, Phan Văn Trường, and Nguyễn Thế Truyền worked hard to spread the Intercolonial Union's influence. This mainly involved expanding the reach of *Le Paria,* which by 1923 was circulating in Indochina.[9] Nguyễn Ái Quốc also attended socialist, anarchist, and trade union meetings, as well as those of other émigré groups; in June 1922, he even joined a Masonic lodge. Alongside *Le Paria,* he also wrote for the radical newspapers *Le Journal du peuple, La Voix ouvrière, L'Humanité, Le Libertaire,* and *Clarté* (Phan Văn Trường probably continued to help him with his French).[10] Nguyễn An Ninh attended Intercolonial Union meetings in 1922 while finishing his law *licence;* after returning from the colony in late 1922 for doctoral study (soon abandoned), he also proofread and edited *Le Paria.*[11] Phan Châu Trinh also attended Intercolonial Union meetings before moving to Marseille in late 1921 to retouch photos at the colonial exposition. Although he collaborated with Nguyễn Ái Quốc in the 1922 campaign against Khải Định, increasingly bitter debates reflected the old friends' diverging political outlooks. "Because of our disagreements you have called me a 'conservative and backwards scholar,'" Phan Châu Trinh wrote to his former disciple in February 1922, while assuring him that he was "not the least bit angry about the label." "I am an exhausted horse who can no longer gallop," he continued, and "you are a fiery stallion." He urged Nguyễn Ái Quốc to return to Indochina "to awaken the people, so that our compatriots will engage in combat against the occupiers."[12] But he himself soon turned toward a very different brand of colonial politics.

In the early 1920s, with Albert Sarraut's support, the Constitutionalist Party led reforms in Cochinchina's Colonial Council and performed well in elections, and its newspapers *Tribune indigène* and *L'Écho annamite* dominated Sài Gòn journalism. In Tonkin, Phạm Quỳnh's *Nam Phong* (Southern Wind) and Nguyễn Văn Vĩnh's *Trung Bắc Tân Văn* (News of the Center and North), underwritten by Sarraut, explored the possibilities of Franco-Vietnamese collaboration. The Constitutionalists' reformist agenda spread in France in 1922 through two vehicles. The first was the Association mutuelle des indochinois, an initiative of the Ministry of Colonies in 1920. Two of its members led Constitutionalist campaigns in France: Dương Văn Giáo, the former war interpreter, law student, and assistant at the École des langues orientales, and Trần Văn Khá, an employee in the Ministry of War. The other was the 1922 colonial exposition, most of whose Indochinese delegates were Sarraut's allies or Constitutionalists. With Nguyễn Văn Vĩnh and Phạm Quỳnh, they included the rice and rubber entrepreneur Trương Văn Bến; Cao Triều Phát, who had joined the leftist League of the Rights of Man while an interpreter during the Great War and wrote for *Tribune indigène;* the veteran journalist Lương Khắc Ninh; and Nguyễn Khắc Vệ, who had received his doctorate in law in 1921. The winds of Indochinese reformist politics swirled through France in 1922.

The spread of Indochinese reformist activism in France pulled Phan Châu Trinh back to the Republicanism at the heart of his prewar politics. In 1922, as he campaigned against Khải Định with Nguyễn Ái Quốc in Marseille, he also worked closely with the Constitutionalist Nguyễn Minh Quang and with the city's chapter of the League of the Rights of Man.[13] At a meeting with Nguyễn Văn Vĩnh and Phạm Quỳnh, he outlined a plan for a colonial Chamber of Deputies modeled on the French one.[14] After his return to Paris in 1923, despite attending a few Intercolonial Union meetings, he spent far more time in reformist circles. His closest political ally in 1924 was Trần Văn Khá, soon to be ousted from leadership of the Association mutuelle des indochinois by more radical activists; the two founded the reformist Union Franco-Indochinoise (Hội Liên Hiệp Pháp-Đông Dương).[15] At a meeting of the League of the Rights of Man in March 1925 that was his final public appearance in France before his return to Indochina in March 1925, he proclaimed that "for us to live and grow in Asia, we need the support that only France can provide. For its part, France needs our collaboration to maintain its prestige in Asia. Together all is possible but divided nothing is."[16]

Phan Văn Trường and Nguyễn An Ninh had mostly bitter epitaphs for Phan Châu Trinh when he died in March 1926.[17] Nguyễn An Ninh had left France in 1922 after two years of immersion in the Latin Quarter's student circles, overseas travel (Belgium, Austria, Germany, and Italy in 1922), and writing for left-wing newspapers (*L'Europe* and *Le Libertaire*).[18] Phan Văn Trường left France in late 1923. Although both were committed anticolonial activists, their politics did not always align with the Intercolonial Union's global horizons. In Indochina, as Phan Văn Trường "played the constitutional game to advance ideas that ultimately represented a radical rejection of the established political order," Ninh explored a range of political mediums, from anarchism to popular religion.[19] They collaborated on two newspapers—*La Cloche fêlée* and *L'Annam*—which became the most influential oppositional newspapers in Indochina before 1925. With Phan Châu Trinh, they were the greatest influences on the wave of more radical politics that surged in the colony in 1925–26. As many younger activists followed in their footsteps to France, many would experience the same kinds of ambivalence between reformist republicanism and radicalism, nationalism and internationalism.

One night in June 1923, Nguyễn Ái Quốc left his Paris apartment and shook his French minders, who had no further trace of him until his name appeared in Soviet newspapers that fall. The circumstances of his departure are murky; PCF or Soviet agents may have tapped him as a promising candidate for training, he may have gone seeking support for the Intercolonial Union, or he may simply have been trying to return to Indochina. Phan Văn Trường and Nguyễn Thế Truyền believed he was on vacation and postponed an issue of *Le Paria* as they awaited his return. As time passed, Phan Châu Trinh accused a known Indochinese informant of involvement in his disappearance. Although rumors swirled about his return, apart from a brief trip in 1927 he would not return to France until 1946, as the head of state of an independent Vietnam.[20] Nguyễn Ái Quốc's politics were far from fully formed when he left for Moscow, but his decision to go there reflected the decisive influence of the PCF on his budding internationalist vision of anticolonial revolution. He was the first of dozens of Indochinese for whom France would become a point of entry into transnational communist networks during the interwar era.

By late 1923, Nguyễn Thế Truyền was the only one of the Five Dragons left in Paris. The dispersal of his political allies came at an explosive moment in colonial politics. As the promise of Sarraut's reformism faded, young Indochinese political activists mobilized around a series of high-profile issues and events to express their grievances. Restrictive laws on speech and print, abusive colonial monopolies, and toothless political institutions all became targets of journalists and activists hoping to mobilize discontent into formal opposition. Constitutionalist activists—officially sanctioned, better organized, and with deeper pockets—were initially the most visible and vocal in this new political opposition. But more militant political voices soon responded to the disappointment of the Socialist governor general Alexandre Varenne's brief term, the arrests and trials of Phan Bội Châu and Nguyễn An Ninh, and Phan Châu Trinh's death in March 1926; the latter's funeral set off a wave of demonstrations, strikes, and oppositional journalism. In Paris, Nguyễn Thế Truyền quickly became the hub of a vibrant and fractious French theater of Indochinese politics, as the small core of Intercolonial Union activists gave way to a larger and more diverse community of political sojourners.

REPUBLICANISM, RADICALISM,
AND INTERNATIONALISM IN THE ERA
OF THE UNITED FRONT

When the leading Constitutionalist Bùi Quang Chiêu traveled to France in mid-1925, he did so as an exile of sorts. After the governor of Cochinchina transferred him to Phnom Penh as a reprisal for his increasingly truculent political activities, he received permission to spend a year in France, where he hoped—like Nguyễn and Khmer officials had a generation before—to find more sympathetic French interlocutors.[21] Thanks to the advance work of Constitutionalist activists in Paris (Nguyễn Phú Khai, Trân Văn Khá, and Dương Văn Giáo), Bùi Quang Chiêu barnstormed around learned societies, masonic lodges, and political clubs giving lectures; he published articles and pamphlets; and he met with officials, politicians, and journalists. Apart from a brief return to Indochina in mid-1926, Bùi Quang Chiêu remained in France for about a year and a half. In October 1925, the Constitutionalist party gained official status under French law, which allowed Bùi Quang Chiêu to legally establish it in Cochinchina.[22] From mid-1925 into 1926, Constitutionalists dominated Indochinese politics in France.

The Constitutionalist challenge added to what was already a difficult situation for the remnants of the Intercolonial Union's Indochinese networks. The exuberance of the group's beginnings had faded in the face of tensions over ethno-national priorities, ideological differences, and the PCF's persistent reluctance to give it meaningful operational autonomy.[23] Bùi Quang Chiêu's relations with Nguyễn Thế Truyền were initially cordial—the two appeared at meetings together and praised each other publicly into early 1926—but the niceties soon faded. Shortly after his arrival, Bùi Quang Chiêu drew an ideological line in the sand by refusing an invitation to join the Intercolonial Union.[24] Also in 1925, Nguyễn Ái Quốc wrote from Canton urging the Comintern's French delegation to have Nguyễn Thế Truyền "enter the newly organized Constitutionalist group in Paris, in order to infiltrate it."[25] But Indochinese opposition to Constitutionalism in France ultimately took a different form. In early 1926, Indochinese activists led by Nguyễn Thế Truyền began speaking of a new political party: the Parti annamite de l'indépendance (PAI, or Việt Nam Độc Lập Đảng), which acquired a belated and fleeting legal status in June 1927.[26] Until its dissolution in 1929, the PAI reflected the potent and combustible intersection of anti-colonial radicalism and the Comintern's growing focus on colonial issues.

The PAI began its life as the Indochinese section of the Intercolonial Union, formed along with other national groups in late 1925 as an effort to resolve its internal tensions. Thanks to both Nguyễn Ái Quốc and Jacques Doriot (the head of the PCF's Colonial Commission), the Comintern was well aware of these tensions; Nguyễn Ái Quốc had tried to address them before leaving Paris in late 1923 with an aborted effort to revive the Đồng Bào Thân Ái and to form *Việt Nam Hồn*. In Moscow, as the Intercolonial Union's representative, he urged the Comintern to focus more on colonial issues before departing for Canton as a Comintern operative in late 1924. He kept in touch with Nguyễn Thế Truyền in 1925, requesting news and offering advice about Indochinese politics in France.[27] Nguyễn Thế Truyền wrote the preface to Nguyễn Ái Quốc's 1926 pamphlet *Le procès de la colonisation française*, published by the PCF's Librarie de travail. Nguyễn Ái Quốc probably helped direct Nguyễn Thế Truyền's push in 1925 to form an Indochinese section of the Intercolonial Union, which paralleled his own appeals to Moscow to recognize the Indochinese group he was organizing in southern China. When the Intercolonial Union collapsed in 1926, its Indochinese section became the PAI; other "national" organizations like the Comité de défense de la race nègre and Étoile nord-africaine emerged from the wreckage. The groups reflected a real desire among colonial activists in France for more autonomy within the PCF. But they were also sanctioned, and encouraged, by the Comintern, who saw them as having more potential than the Intercolonial Union for a revolutionary united front in the colonial empires; PCF support for the PAI would have been unthinkable without Moscow's approval.[28] The PCF subsidized the PAI's newspapers, offered logistical support, and supported its leaders with monthly stipends. Even if some PAI activists had no meaningful ties to the PCF (or even little interest in communism), the two parties remained deeply intertwined.

The PAI soon became the main arena for new variants of Indochinese radicalism that, thanks to student sojourns, had spread like wildfire in France. Nguyễn Thế Truyền had stayed in contact with Nguyễn An Ninh and Phan Văn Trường after they returned to Indochina. Ninh traveled again to France in early 1925, where he wrote anti-colonial tracts, courted figures on the French left, and surely tried to persuade Phan Châu Trinh to support the new political movements in the colony during the hours they spent together (including on a steamship home in July). He remained close to PCF-aligned Indochinese even if he did not share their enthusiasm for communism, perhaps due to the palpable dysfunction he had seen at the Intercolonial Union.[29]

Ninh's long-standing ties to Nguyễn Thế Truyền facilitated a powerful cross-pollination between colony and metropole during the mid-1920s. PAI newspapers and like-minded ones in Indochina (*La Cloche fêlée, L'Annam, Jeune Annam,* and *Đông Pháp Thời Báo*) published one another's articles, and radical journalists came to France and worked in PAI newspapers. Most (including Đào Trinh Nhất, Hoàng Tích Chu, Bùi Ái, Bùi Công Trừng, Trịnh Hưng Ngẫu and Huỳnh Văn Phương) came out of Jeune Annam networks in Cochinchina, but a few (notably Nguyễn Văn Ngọc) came from Phúc Việt circles in Annam and Tonkin. Nguyễn Thế Nghiệp, a relative of Nguyễn Thế Truyền's, was involved in the Nam Đồng Thư Xã publishing house in Hà Nội, out of which would emerge the Việt Nam Quốc Dân Đảng (Vietnam Nationalist Party, modeled after the KMT—hereafter VNQDĐ), and several other members of his family were PAI activists.[30] The PAI even identified Bùi Công Trừng and Nguyễn Văn Ngọc as the party's "delegates" from Jeune Annam and Phúc Việt in public appeals to the United Nations in 1926 and the Ministry of Colonies in 1927. The PAI, though a co-creation of the PCF, helped to extend a range of Indochinese radical political networks into France—just like Cường Để had attempted before the war and the Constitutionalists were doing at the same time.

Indochinese radicalism and internationalism were a potentially combustible mix. But as Nguyễn Thế Truyền built the PAI, he, unlike his West African or North African comrades from the now-moribund Intercolonial Union, had a clear, Comintern-sanctioned model to follow: the united front between Chinese communists and the nationalist Kuomintang, developed by the Comintern since 1921 and formalized in 1924.[31] As Daniel Hémery writes, "Comintern interest in Indochina grew as a function of its perspectives on the revolution of 1924–27: it saw Indochina above all as a Chinese hinterland."[32] In 1925, Nguyễn Ái Quốc described a nascent Indochinese revolutionary network in south China (the Việt Nam Thanh Niên Cách Mạng Đồng Chí Hội, or Thanh Niên) as "The Komintang [*sic*] of Indochina," and Nguyễn Thế Truyền imagined the PAI in the same way—indeed, the men probably thought of the two parties as branches of a single Indochinese revolutionary organization.[33] Before creating the PAI, Nguyễn Thế Truyền was the Intercolonial Union liaison to Chinese groups in Paris; he distributed their tracts in Indochinese associations and recruited people to attend their meetings.[34] In turn, leaders of the European Kuomintang's branch in Paris helped Nguyễn Thế Truyền organize the PAI (the dominance of leftists and communists in the European KMT likely helped to make the alliance palatable for the PCF).[35] Far from Asia and closely watched, Indochinese and Chinese activists in France could do little more than hold joint meetings and distribute each other's tracts. But their optimism was undimmed. "Follow heroic China!" trumpeted a PAI newspaper in February 1926; other articles praised Indochinese participation in the KMT and its army.[36] The PAI's March 1927 memo to the minister of colonies urged France to withdraw from Indochina to improve its relations with Chiang Kai-Shek, whose rise threatened French interests in Asia.[37] PAI activists, a Sûreté agent wrote, "hope to see a Chinese invasion of Indochina; they do not fear it, for they believe that even if the Chinese stay in the country, Indochinese autonomy would be guaranteed by the decentralized model established in the Soviet Union. A Bolshevized China, even one that spilled over its borders, would simply be a federation of sister republics where, like in Russia, minority groups would enjoy equality with the dominant race."[38]

As the PAI shifted from the PCF's colonial organs to the Comintern-sanctioned Chinese united front, it also pivoted toward Moscow's growing European networks. The League Against Imperialism, led by the German communist Willi Münzenberg, was formed in 1926 to draw anti-colonial activists in Europe toward the Comintern. It appealed to a broad swath of activists, many of whom had no meaningful ties to any communist party.[39] The League's first major event was the International Congress Against Imperialism, held in Brussels in February 1927. Three of the six Indochinese there (Bùi Công Trừng, Trần Văn Chỉ, and Hoàng Quang Giụ) were PAI activists with close PCF ties (Nguyễn Thế Truyền's visibility made him too risky a choice).[40] The other three, led by Dương Văn Giáo, were Constitutionalists who had continued working with the PAI after Bùi Quang Chiêu had broken with it. Trần Văn Chỉ was the first Indochinese representative to the League's French section, formed soon after the congress—the first of many French branches of Comintern organizations that would mobilize Indochinese in France.

The PAI and the PCF also began recruiting Indochinese activists to go to Moscow. After Nguyễn Thế Truyền left France, the PAI's efforts in this realm shifted to Hoàng Quang Giụ, who had been to Moscow in 1925.[41] The covert travel across Europe was difficult. Trần Vĩnh Hiến described it as "a road through a forest full of panthers and tigers. You have a good chance of missing them, but if by misfortune you don't, they will tear you into pieces and devour you. . . . At home, to escape to China, you don't need any papers. Here, you must produce all sorts of them."[42] At each stop (the principal transit points were Brussels or Liège in Belgium; Hamburg or Berlin in Germany;

and Warsaw), Comintern agents met the travelers, ushered them to hotels or safe houses, gave them new identity papers and money, kept them a step ahead of local police or French agents, and verified their bona fides. Three Indochinese going to Moscow reportedly met Nguyễn Ái Quốc in Berlin in March 1928; he asked "where they came from ... who sent them to Moscow ... if they had a letter of support from the PCF ... and who paid for the trip."[43] From 1929 to 1931, Nghiêm Xuân Toàn, in Berlin working for the League Against Imperialism, did this work.[44] Indochinese who went through Hamburg had help from the owner of an Indochinese restaurant there.[45] These European networks remained crucial pipelines to Moscow even as more Indochinese began traveling there directly from Asia during the 1930s.

The PAI's blend of colonial radicalism and communist internationalism proved potent but unstable. By late 1926, the PAI had used bruising electoral campaigns (often accompanied by fights in cafés and meeting halls) to wrest away control of most Indochinese student associations from the Constitutionalists, even though a few remained moderate (the Bordeaux Association mutuelle des indochinois controversially invited the emperor Bảo Đại to their Tết gala in 1931).[46] The PAI gave rebuttals at Constitutionalist meetings and organized a busy slate of their own. In 1927, Nguyễn Thế Truyền spoke in Paris, Le Havre, Toulouse, Montpellier, Aix-en-Provence, and Bordeaux; he assailed colonial taxation, monopolies, land seizures, and limits on speech and association.[47] That August, PAI activists organized a hostile reception at Marseille's docks for the đốc phủ sứ of Mỹ Thọ Nguyễn Văn Vịnh, who had served as an agent of the CAI during the Great War and was returning to France as a representative of agricultural concerns. He was beaten as he walked off the gangplank: the Association mutuelle des indo-chinois in Aix displayed his bloody hat as a trophy.[48] In September, Nguyễn An Ninh again returned to PAI circles. After his release from prison in late 1926, he had witnessed the rapid rise of Thanh Niên and the millenarian Cao Đài sect in Cochinchina and had begun to think more seriously about the problem of political organization; he likely came to France to explore ties between the PAI and Jeune Annam, many of whose activists were now study-ing in France and active in the PAI.[49] "After my arrest," he wrote to Léon Werth before leaving for France, "I saw that little Ninh was quite far from Lenin, that Lenin had mastered the complex exigencies of the twentieth century, while little Ninh remained engaged in pure sentimentality."[50] He and Nguyễn Thế Truyền presented the PAI's agenda at the Congrès des étu-diants indochinois in Aix-en-Provence in September 1927, organized by the lawyer and Constitutionalist activist Trịnh Đình Thảo. On the heels of the congress, in a nod to French revolutionary history, the PAI staged a "Bal des victimes" "to benefit the victims of the white terror in Indochina."[51] By late 1927, Constitutionalism's followers in France had either faded away or been radicalized (most notably Dương Văn Giáo, once the party's face in France).

Despite this success, the PAI faced serious challenges. Money was always short despite PCF subsidies, the Sûreté regularly harassed its activists and seized its tracts and newspapers, and it was riven by bitter internal debates about ideology and tactics.[52] But it was events in mid-1927 that threw the PAI into real turmoil. That April, KMT forces devastated Chinese communist networks, leading Moscow to abandon the united front. This further complicated relations among various Indochinese revolutionary groups in south China and the colony. In September 1927, Moscow sent Nguyễn Ái Quốc to Paris to work with the PCF to organize Indochinese. But French police repression and ideological battles following purges in Moscow had left the PCF in chaos and with little time for colonial affairs.[53] Some PAI leaders fled Paris, and rumors of spies abounded (Nguyễn Văn Ngọc, a militant since 1925, was forced from the party and lost his position on the PCF's Commission coloniale because of such rumors).[54] Nguyễn Thế Truyền tried to adjust to the circumstances. In June, he filed for legal recognition of the PAI and penned an elliptical manifesto casting the party as "neither separatist, nor communist, nor even nationalist in the European sense of the word."[55] He resigned from the PCF's Commission coloniale in October.[56] The Sûreté saw this as a purely tactical move to protect the PAI "by removing it of all communist elements, partly to attract as many Indochinese as possible, and partly to lighten the anti-communist surveillance currently ensnaring many Annamites."[57] But sailing the communist world's stormy seas had clearly taken a toll on Nguyễn Thế Truyền, especially as a new line against cross-class political alliances emerged in Moscow. Bùi Ái recalled that Nguyễn Thế Truyền "could not tolerate it when PCF 'proles' commented on and critiqued his political activity."[58] But the new line gained steam among some PAI activists, some of whom had been to Moscow. In 1928, Trần Vĩnh Hiến, whom Nguyễn Thế Truyền had sent to the Soviet Union in 1926, wrote his father that "in Paris and the provinces . . . we work closely with the C.S. [cộng sản]; our party's purpose and program is different from the Parti annamite de l'indépendance. . . . Truyền has made mistakes. . . . How can a revolution benefit the rich bourgeois while neglecting the proletariat?"[59]

On December 7, 1927, Nguyễn An Ninh and Nguyễn Thế Truyền (the latter with his French wife and three children) boarded the Chantilly for Sài

Gòn.[60] Ninh, who had been in France for just three months, was likely discouraged by the repression and political sectarianism he had witnessed.[61] Nguyễn Thế Truyền, who had lived largely in France since his adolescence, was leaving because his frayed relations with the PCF and many PAI activists had dimmed his political star. But he had not abandoned hope for a united front for Indochina, which remained the Comintern's policy until mid-1929. Upon his return, he would try, with little success, to coordinate revolutionary groups in Indochina and south China. Before leaving, the men arranged for two younger activists to take over the PAI. One, Nguyễn Văn Luận (known as Như Phong), had been a PAI militant since coming from Hà Nội to study in 1925.[62] The other, Tạ Thu Thâu, was a teacher and an associate of Nguyễn An Ninh's in Jeune Annam who traveled with him to France in August.[63] Tạ Thu Thâu was a logical choice; he was influential in radical circles in Indochina and had studied at the Lycée Chasseloup-Laubat in Sài Gòn with several of the leading Indochinese activists in France.

The two men set about rebuilding a PAI in tatters after Nguyễn Thế Truyền's departure. Tạ Thu Thâu soon built ties to Trần Văn Thạch, Phan Văn Chánh, and Huỳnh Văn Phương, the leaders of the *Journal des étudiants annamites* in Paris, as well as Lê Bá Cang and Hồ Tá Khanh (a medical student in Marseille); all had studied together at Chasseloup-Laubat. Tạ Thu Thâu probably also urged Nguyễn Khánh Toàn, his coeditor in the short-lived Sài Gòn newspaper *Nha-Quê*, to come to France in 1928. Other new PAI activists came out of student radical circles, notably Hồ Văn Ngà, the top-ranked entering student in his class at the École centrale de Paris.[64] The new party leadership created a newspaper (*La Résurrection*) and associations (the Société d'enseignment mutuel des annamites in Paris and the Comité de réception des étudiants annamites in Paris and Marseille) to attract support.[65] Nguyễn Văn Luận and Tạ Thu Thâu hoped that Nguyễn An Ninh and Nguyễn Thế Truyền would help them build ties to colonial political networks. But after many letters went unanswered, they tried to do it themselves.[66] Nguyễn Văn Luận wrote repeatedly to Diệp Văn Kỳ at *Đông Pháp Thời Báo* in 1928, sending PAI tracts and requesting articles for *La Résurrection*.[67] In early 1929, Phan Văn Trường returned to France to contest a judgment against him in colonial courts; he was in touch with PAI leaders before going to jail in August. A few months later, Nguyễn Ngọc Phong, a VNQDĐ militant, wrote to Nguyễn Văn Luận, perhaps at Nguyễn Thế Truyền's urging, asking the PAI to take up the party's cause in the French press and among the French left.[68]

From 1928 until the party's dissolution in mid-1929, PAI leaders struggled to reconcile nationalism and communism after the collapse of the united front. Unlike Nguyễn Thế Truyền, Tạ Thu Thâu had been profoundly influenced by Social Darwinist ideas, which cast the world as a zero-sum competition between nations for global survival. Anti-colonialism was thus for him, above all, "a racial struggle." "If this state of affairs continues," he wrote in *La Résurrection,*

> there will remain in the land of Annam but a decayed race, a people that will never arise from its fall.... Time is on the side of our oppressors, who are consolidating and reinforcing their economic and political enterprises in our poor country.... In twenty more years, things will have changed so much that any effort at national liberation would be suicide. For Annam will have lost its soul.

Tạ Thu Thâu believed that revolutionary nationalism must seek the liberation of the proletariat; his engagement with Marxism led him to attend communist trade union meetings and the second International Congress Against Imperialism in Frankfurt in July 1929. But as PAI leader, he remained "suspicious of all forms of dependence and jealous of its political autonomy"; he declined an invitation to travel to Moscow in 1928 with other PAI militants. "It is hard to see," he wrote in *La Résurrection,*

> that on the side of the Parti annamite de l'indépendance ... are a few compatriots who believe that foreign involvement is crucial to the *interior* organization of a revolutionary party. Let us not believe that we want to act in isolation. We understand as well as anybody that in this century of airplanes and railways, each nation is a link in the global chain. But in the first steps of the internal organization of a revolutionary party, we will not tolerate the interference of present or future imperialisms, who ignore completely our country and people.[69]

In February 1930, colonial repression of a mutiny of Vietnamese soldiers at the garrison at Yên Báy led by the VNQDĐ set off the largest wave of Indochinese political protest in France before 1945. Just after the mutiny, six were arrested protesting emperor Bảo Đại's inauguration of the Cité Universitaire's Maison des étudiants de l'Indochine. After the French executed the leaders of the Yên Báy uprising, thirteen more Indochinese activists were arrested following demonstrations in front of the Élysée Palace and the Mur des fédérés, where the communards had made their last stand in 1871.[70]

Eighteen of the nineteen arrested that spring were repatriated; one (Nguyễn Văn Tạo) went to prison in France. But what appeared as nationalist efflorescence belied the deep divides that had grown in Indochinese politics in France over the Comintern's new policy of extreme leftism, set forth at its Sixth Congress in 1928. On January 9, 1929, Indochinese supporters of the PCF attacked the literature student Đỗ Đình Thạch while he spoke on Franco-Vietnamese cooperation at Paris's Café Turquetti. The melee led to arrests and a vicious feud within the PAI; its pro-PCF factions berated the party leadership for its lack of direct action, while other activists accused the PCF of starting the brawl to provoke a French crackdown on the PAI.[71] And indeed, in March 1929 the tribunal de la Seine revoked the PAI's statutes despite Tạ Thu Thâu's brilliant defense of the party at the proceedings. Anti-PCF figures within the PAI tried to regroup with a takeover of the Association générale des étudiants indochinois in April, but it too was quickly banned.[72] In April 1930, Tạ Thu Thâu and Huỳnh Văn Phương wrote an article, "After Yên Báy: What To Do," arguing "that the Vietnamese bourgeoisie was fundamentally dependent on colonial capitalism, and that it was thus bound to collude with it against fellow Vietnamese."[73] Their search for an anti-bourgeois, anti-Comintern politics would give rise to new sectarian divides that would define Indochinese politics in France until the Popular Front.

LEFTIST SECTARIANISM IN THE ERA OF THE SIXTH COMINTERN CONGRESS

In November 1927, Tạ Thu Thâu wrote from Paris to his friend Nguyễn Huỳnh Điểu, the director of the Bảo Tồn printing house in Sài Gòn: "I have an Annamite for a neighbor, M. Dương Bạch Mai, a graduate of the commercial school of Hanoi, who is now working at the Comptoir nationale d'escompte in Paris. M. Mai traveled to France clandestinely in 1925, hoping to work while pursuing his studies. Sadly, consumed by the need to support himself, he has no time for school." Tạ Thu Thâu proposed that Nguyễn Huỳnh Điểu pay for Dương Bạch Mai to take a course in typography and binding, after which he would return to Sài Gòn to work for Bảo Tồn. "I will vouch for M. Mai," wrote Tạ Thu Thâu; "I would only recommend him if I were sure."[74] But the friends and neighbors soon became political enemies. As Tạ Thu Thâu's relations with the PCF frayed, Dương Bạch Mai remained loyal to the party: on April 22, 1928, he and about a hundred other Indochinese supporters of the PCF gathered in a hangar in Saint-Denis and voted against an attempted takeover of the PAI in favor of forming an Indochinese section of the PCF.[75] Three months later, he was in Moscow.[76]

Despite the end of the Chinese united front and new barriers to alliances with the non-communist left, some Indochinese in France continued to believe in pursuing revolution through an alliance with the PCF, which was briefly formally responsible for developing communism in Indochina after the collapse of the Comintern's organization in China.[77] The PCF was far from an ideal partner at that time. Uncertainty, infighting, purges, and crackdowns from a succession of right-wing French governments left it with little time for colonial affairs: it cared mostly about how best to wield the French empire as a cudgel in the party's domestic electoral wars.[78] Although the PCF's Section coloniale did create positions for representatives from the colonies after the Sixth Congress, its anemic efforts toward colonial populations in France drew sharp rebukes from the Comintern in late 1931.[79] The growth of an Indochinese presence within the PCF between 1928 and 1932 was thus due mostly to a few core Indochinese militants who remained committed to the party despite its disinterest in colonial issues.

The most important of these was Nguyễn Văn Tạo, unquestionably the most influential Indochinese communist in France during this period. Expelled from Chasseloup-Laubat in 1926, he traveled clandestinely to France and, after briefly studying in Aix, began working in a lacquer workshop in Paris. On the strength of his militancy, his lack of ties to the PAI, and his bona fides as a worker, he became the Indochinese representative to the PCF's Section coloniale and leader of the new Section indochinoise in 1928. Until his expulsion from France in August 1931 for spearheading protests against the colonial exposition, Nguyễn Văn Tạo created Indochinese sections of Comintern front groups (League Against Imperialism and International Red Aid) and communist-leaning French groups (the Federal Union of Students) and he led the PCF's quốc ngữ newspaper *Lao Nông,* first published in May 1928. He, Nguyễn Thế Vinh (Nguyễn Thế Truyền's cousin), and a sailor named Trần Thiên Ban were Indochina's three representatives to the Sixth Congress in Moscow. A few other militants seconded Nguyễn Văn Tạo in Paris. Hoàng Quang Giụ had gravitated from the PAI to the PCF in 1928; his newspaper experience made him an important figure in *Lao Nông.* During Nguyễn Văn Tạo's nine-month incarceration after the protests at the Élysée Palace and the Mur des fédérés, Hoàng Quang Giụ filled in as

Indochinese representative at the Section coloniale.[80] Cao Văn Chánh, a prominent leftist journalist in Sài Gòn, had come to France in mid-1929. Drawn to Marxism during his studies at the Sorbonne, he joined the PCF in 1930.[81] He and Nguyễn Văn Tạo wrote regularly (under pseudonyms) about Indochina for *L'Humanité, Rouge midi,* and other PCF newspapers. He and Hoàng Quang Giụ were also the key figures in *Vô Sản,* the PCF's successor to *Lao Nông,* published from 1930 until 1934.

Toulouse was another hotbed of Indochinese communist activism in France. The city's most important Indochinese militant was Trần Văn Giàu, a former student of Tạ Thu Thâu's at Chasseloup-Laubat who had come to France in late 1928. Tạ Thu Thâu seems to have hoped to use their relationship to build the PAI in Toulouse, but the PCF was a stronger influence on the Indochinese radicals in the city, whose activism exploded after Yên Báy. In 1930, they invited PCF militants to speak at the Indochinese student association and formed a "Committee of Struggle." In 1931, with Nguyễn Văn Tạo's assistance, they began forming local Indochinese sections of PCF organizations.[82] Phan Tư Nghĩa, who had come to France from Hà Nội when he was fifteen, led the Committe of Struggle after Trần Văn Giàu's expulsion from France; after Nguyễn Văn Tạo's expulsion a year later, he and other militants from Toulouse moved to Paris to help fill the leadership void.[83] Several other Indochinese were initiated into communism in Toulouse, notably Nguyễn Văn Dựt and Đỗ Đình Thiện, who had studied in Moscow. When the latter returned to Indochina in 1932, he wrote a letter to his PCF comradres in Toulouse: "No form of repression nor political corruption can take away my focus on the struggle of the proletariat for liberation for which I live and am prepared to die if necessary!"[84]

Indochinese communist activity also grew in Marseille after 1928. Despite its importance in French leftist politics, the city's small Indochinese student population made it an afterthought for the Intercolonial Union and the PAI. But as the PAI collapsed, some Indochinese in Marseille and the nearby university town of Aix-en-Provence turned to the PCF. The most important was Hồ Tá Khanh, who had come to Marseille to study after being expelled from Chasseloup-Laubat in April 1926. Expulsion only intensified his political commitment. "It is no longer time to act only in hiding," he wrote a friend in August 1928; "let us obey our duty and defy the inhumans who smother the voice of our conscience."[85] He took over the Comité de réception des étudiants annamites in Marseille, a PAI group co-opted by the PCF in 1928. As in Toulouse, the lull in Indochinese political activism after the PAI's decline ended abruptly after Yên Báy. By mid-1930, there was an Indochinese section of the PCF in the city, likely organized by Nguyễn Khánh Toàn, another graduate of Chasseloup-Laubat who had studied in the Soviet Union, and who was briefly active in Marseille after Yên Báy before returning to Moscow for much of the 1930s.[86] By the early 1930s, Marseille's Indochinese PCF section controlled the local Comité de réception and the Association mutuelle des indochinois.[87]

The Indochinese communist political culture that emerged in interwar France was distinct from the Stalinist world of Moscow's University of the Toilers of the East or the covert networks linking Indochina and southern China. To be sure, the PCF's fraught relationship with the French state, and the precarious circumstances of its Indochinese members, made harassment and repression everyday realities: party gatherings drew informants, newspapers were censored, and activists were followed. By 1930, Indochinese PCF sections had formed secret committees (cơ quan bí mật) to "watch over Annamites belonging to these organizations, to denounce them if they betray them, and to implement any decisions taken against them."[88] Nevertheless, Indochinese communist political culture in France was also a world of public rallies and meetings, associations, political journalism, and electoral campaigns. At a 1934 celebration of the newspaper L'Humanité, for instance, Indochinese communists organized a booth in a public square in the suburbs of Paris adorned with a banner reading "Tie [Governor General Eugène] Robin to the post: Down with Fascism in Indochina!" Interested passers-by could pick up newspaper clippings, tracts, or drawings—or listen to thunderous speeches—laying bare the truth about "Indochina under the boot of imperialism."[89] The deeply republican qualities of this world of communist militancy, a strategy and style that its leading militants would bring back with them to Indochina, would strongly influence the wave of short-lived legal communist activity in the colony after the Popular Front victory in 1936.

The relationship between the PCF's Indochinese sections and early communist activity in Indochina remains obscure. Most news about growing Indochinese communist networks in Asia reached France via the PCF's Section coloniale and the back-and-forth of activists. Communist tracts and pamphlets printed in France traveled to Indochina via networks among sailors first developed by Nguyễn Ái Quốc and expanded by the PAI. In September 1928, the Comintern returned Indochina to the direction of the Middle Eastern Section of its Eastern Secretariat: the PCF and its Indochinese sections do not seem to have played any role in forming the

Comintern-sanctioned Indochinese Communist Party (ICP) in October 1930. But 1931 saw tentative efforts to develop ties between the ICP and the PCF's Indochinese sections. In February 1931, Nguyễn Văn Tạo proposed a "bureau de liaison" to streamline communication between France and the colony.[90] After the Franco-British dismantling of the ICP's apparatus in 1931 (including Nguyễn Ái Quốc's arrest in Hong Kong) made communication between Moscow and Indochina almost impossible, the Comintern sought to reestablish these ties via the PCF.[91] To this end, Ngô Gia Tự, head of the ICP's Provisional Executive Committee in Cochinchina, sent his brother to Marseille to liaise with the PCF's Indochinese sections.[92] The ICP also sent Nguyễn Văn Khánh to France to reorganize maritime contacts with the PCF.[93] French sources from 1931 reveal a proposal to make the PCF's Indochinese section in Paris a branch of the ICP.[94] A similar plan emerged in 1935, when Trần Văn Điện, who had studied in Moscow, was sent from Indochina to France to explore forming an ICP branch in Marseille.[95] Although such plans never came to fruition, the PCF remained critical in mounting a political defense of the ICP in the mid-1930s, as well as in helping form a number of influential Indochinese communist militants.

For all this activity, the years following the Sixth Congress were often dispiriting and divisive. The principal problem remained, as during the united front, the PCF's tepid commitment to colonial affairs. At the Sixth Congress in 1928, two of three Indochinese delegates (Nguyễn Thế Vinh and Trần Thiên Ban) were expelled for criticizing the PCF's Colonial Commission and Nguyễn Văn Tạo's pliant attitude toward it.[96] But two years later, Nguyễn Văn Tạo's own patience with the PCF had worn thin. "During this last period," he wrote in December 1930, "our colonial efforts have been entirely defective. As critical events unfold in French imperialism's various colonies, we have proven unworthy of the task of supporting our oppressed brothers' struggle and exposing colonial brigandage and assassination with all of our energy."[97] Franco-Indochinese relations in the PCF remained deeply hierarchical. At Nguyễn Văn Phải's first PCF meeting after coming back from Moscow, he was dismayed to see that "only the French received tasks to accomplish; the Annamites were only there to listen." "The work among the French and among the Indochinese in the metropole," he noted, "is so different that going to meetings is a waste of my time."[98] Indochinese, as we have seen, had little influence over the PCF's quốc ngữ newspapers. The new class line also disfavored some of the PCF's most committed Indochinese communist militants. In late 1931, Hoàng Quang Giụ, editor of *Vô Sản*, was refused permission to go to Moscow because he was not a worker.[99] A year earlier, four Indochinese in Moscow (including Dương Bạch Mai) had to return to France for the same reason.[100] Many were disillusioned. After his return to France in 1932, Nguyễn Văn Quang "strongly criticized the Soviet administration and the proletarian dictatorship under which, in practice, workers only enjoy very restricted freedoms. Agriculture, industry and commerce, he says, are entirely in the hands of the state, to whom farmers must give half of their harvest at the end of the year, and workers, who earn barely enough to live, give part of their salaries every month to feed the propaganda machine."[101]

For all its shortcomings, the PCF seemed the only viable home for Indochinese leftists in France after the PAI's collapse. But that soon changed. The mutiny at Yên Báy in February 1930 devastated the VNQDĐ; as the French tracked down its militants, some sought to rebuild the party partly in France, where it had no presence before 1930. One VNQDĐ activist arrived a month after the mutiny, and others followed him.[102] In December 1930, one Lý Nghị went to Marseille to develop VNQDĐ networks.[103] Indochinese students in Paris also went to Marseille, Toulouse, and Bordeaux to try to build a French chapter of the party, although it is unclear whether this was a party-led initiative.[104] From a prison cell in Indochina, the VNQDĐ militant Bửu Đình contacted anti-PCF activists in France to urge them to support the VNQDĐ.[105] After Yên Báy, Tạ Thu Thâu organized a mobilization culminating in the protests at the Elysée Palace and the Mur des fédérés. Indochinese PCF militants sought to channel the enthusiasm of the moment; just after the mutiny, Nguyễn Văn Tạo claimed in public meetings that communists had led the uprising, a claim echoed in the communist newspaper *Lao Nông*.[106] Nguyễn Văn Tạo and Trần Văn Giàu also helped Tạ Thu Thâu organize the protests. But despite enthusiasm on both sides, the cooperation was largely part of an effort to lay claim to this seismic political event: Indochinese PCF militants and their opponents nearly brawled the night before the Elysée protests.[107] But Indochinese communist enthusiasm for Yên Báy butted against the PCF's official view of it as a premature, bourgeois-led uprising.[108] By Yên Báy's first anniversary, Indochinese PCF militants were criticizing the VNQDĐ.[109] Nguyễn Văn Tạo also reportedly tipped off the Sûreté about the identity of VNQDĐ militants in Marseille.[110]

Though the VNQDĐ's tentative efforts to rebuild itself in France soon faded, another source of Indochinese opposition to the PCF soon emerged. Clashes between Stalinists and Trotskyists, if still remote in Asia, had set off

FIGURE 12. Arrest photographs of Trần Văn Giàu and Tạ Thu Thâu after Elysée Palace protests, May 22, 1930. Source: Dossier 74971, Box 1W1390 and Dossier 19954, Box 1W0626, Archives de la Préfecture de Police, Paris.

a civil war in French communism, as some PCF militants joined the new Opposition de gauche and its newspapers *Contre le courant, La Lutte des classes,* and *La Vérité*.[111] Ideologically, the Left Opposition seemed a natural home for PAI activists who were hostile to the Comintern. After the PAI's dissolution in March 1929, Tạ Thu Thâu, Trần Văn Thạch, Huỳnh Văn Phương, and Phan Văn Chánh formed an Indochinese chapter of Left Opposition (Đông Dương Cộng Sản Đối Lập Tả Phái), which grew out of Tạ Thu Thâu's contacts with the *Contre le courant* group in 1929.[112] The Trotskyist-leaning group soon added two more figures. Phan Văn Hùm had studied at Chasseloup-Laubat and at the School of Public Works in Hà Nội before taking a job with the Public Works bureau in Huế; he lost his job for supporting Phan Bội Châu and student strikers, and then moved to Sài Gòn and grew close to Nguyễn An Ninh. He was arrested in September 1928 and spent eight months in prison, during which he wrote his iconic memoir *Ngồi Tù Khám Lớn* (Sitting in the Big Jail). He went to France in August 1929 to study at the Sorbonne.[113] Phan Văn Hùm had not seriously engaged with Marxism to that point. "Since meeting M. Tạ Thu Thâu in France," he wrote in 1932, "he explained to me several aspects of Marxism of which I was unaware. I was happy to receive his explanations, though my lack of instruction meant that it was not the work of a moment. My French was inadequate to fully understand the doctrine that is the basis of today's Soviet Union. Moreover, given my age, I was a bit slow to comprehend."[114] Shortly after arriving in Paris, he plunged into Tạ Thu Thâu's activism around Yên Báy.

The other key new figure in the nascent Indochinese Trotskyist movement in France was Hồ Hữu Tường, who after being expelled from Chasseloup-Laubat in 1926 continued his studies in Arles, Aix-en-Provence, Marseille, Lyon, and at the Sorbonne, where he arrived in April 1930. "Before July 1929," he wrote, "I was in no way a revolutionary, and even less a Marxist. During the hours of revolutionary effervescence, I experienced some juvenile enthusiasm.... I knew many revolutionaries, but I was but a sympathizer."[115] That changed after meeting Tạ Thu Thâu and Phan Văn Hùm that summer in Marseille, which led him to buy Trotsky's complete works from a bookseller (eager to sell them because of the harassment they brought him from PCF partisans). He spent his vacation reading about the rift in Soviet politics, which evoked wars between rival factions in the Chinese classic *Fengsheng Yanyi*, which he had devoured as a boy. When he went to Paris in April 1930 for the Sorbonne's entrance exam in physics, Tạ Thu Thâu met him at the Gare de Lyon. Hồ Hữu Tường soon forgot his studies; he moved in with Tạ Thu Thâu, Phan Văn Chánh, and Huỳnh Văn Phương and began organizing around Yên Báy.[116]

The May 1930 protests at the Elysée Palace and the Mur des fédérés, masterminded by Tạ Thu Thâu, helped thrust Indochina into French politics. For years, groups on the French left would invoke Yên Báy at meetings, in editorials, and in the Chamber of Deputies as a symbol of what had gone wrong with the *mission civilisatrice*. But the protests came at a significant cost for the small Indochinese Trotskyist circle; Tạ Thu Thâu, Huỳnh Văn Phương, and Phan Văn Chánh were among the eighteen Indochinese deported in their aftermath (Trần Văn Thạch had returned in 1929). Months later, about fifteen participants in the protest remained in Switzerland, where they had fled to avoid expulsion.[117] With the help of French Trotskyist militants Raymond Molinier and Gérard Rosenthal (later Trotsky's lawyer), Phan Văn Hùm and Hồ Hữu Tường evaded the police, traveling by train to Brussels disguised as an Indian prince and his Japanese secretary.[118] Until their return in July, they wrote for the Trotskyist *La Vérité* and continued plans for their own newspaper, *Tiền Quân* (Vanguard), first published in Paris that August. It appeared in bleak circumstances; only a few Indochinese were drawn to Trotskyist ideas, French Trotskyists ignored them, and their first attempt at a manifesto, "Resolutions of Indochinese Trotskyists" sent to Trotsky in late 1930, came back "with pages of criticism from 'the old man.'"[119] Hồ Hữu Tường returned to Indochina in January 1931, and Phan Văn Hùm moved to Toulouse to teach Vietnamese at a lycée but lost his job when the school learned of his political activities. After spending a few months as a gadfly in PCF circles in Toulouse and Marseille, he returned to Paris to continue his studies.

Despite inauspicious beginnings, an Indochinese Trotskyist group with about forty militants existed in Paris in 1932. Its main activists had all left the PCF: Trần Văn Sĩ (identified as the group's head in French police reports), Lê Văn Rớt, Nguyễn Văn Nam, and Nguyễn Văn Lịnh.[120] This initial core siphoned others from the PCF: Hoàng Quang Giụ (former editor of Vô Sản), Bùi Đông (once the Indochinese representative of the PCF's Section coloniale), Nguyễn Văn Tư (who had studied in Moscow in 1930–31), and Trần Thiên Ban (one of two Indochinese delegates expelled from the Sixth Congress in 1928 for criticizing the PCF). In July 1932 they started a newspaper, Đuốc Vô Sản (Torch of the Proletariat), to replace the defunct Tiền Quân. The rival Indochinese communist factions soon began to joust. In August, an unnamed "Annamite from Berlin" defended Trotsky at the Comintern-sponsored World Congress Against War in Amsterdam, which led to fights and expulsions from the meeting.[121] Phan Văn Hùm sparred with Stalin's supporters at the Association d'entraide et culture des indochinois, a PCF-controlled mutual aid and debating society; in October 1932, Nguyễn Văn Lịnh was permanently barred from its meetings for distributing Trotskyist tracts.[122] Trotskyists and other leftist critics of the PCF began to meet in a new association, the Cercle d'études sociales des indochinois. When Tạ Thu Thâu was arrested in Sài Gòn in August 1932, the Paris Trotskyist group pilloried the PCF for not supporting his cause; the League Against Imperialism's Indochinese section then ripped Trotskyists as counterrevolutionaries.[123]

Well into 1932, the PCF's Indochinese militants had navigated the rise of opposition groups and the general indifference or hostility of most Indochinese to the party's ultra-leftist line largely on their own. But that year, the PCF's approach to colonial issues changed in crucial ways. The PCF's electoral fortunes had fallen precipitously low in 1932, a casualty of its thorough Bolshevization.[124] As a new leadership led by Maurice Thorez reassessed the party's strategy, its leaders responded to the Comintern's call for closer focus on colonial issues. Lucien Midol offered a mea culpa at the seventh congress in March 1932: "On the whole, our party has failed to grasp the importance for the proletariat of the collapse of France's colonial empire and revolutionary development in the colonies. It has not understood that the collapse of the French empire would be a decisive factor in a revolutionary solution to this crisis."[125] The speech's author was the new head of the PCF's Section coloniale, André Ferrat, who had helped engineer the purge of Henri Lozeray and Pierre Celor for letting it fall into disarray.[126] The Yên Báy mutiny, strikes by rubber workers in the Mekong Delta, and the Nghệ-Tĩnh Soviet uprising offered striking evidence of Indochina's revolutionary potential, and the PCF began to pay closer attention. In 1931 the party began campaigns for prisoner amnesty, in 1933 it sent a "workers' delegation of inquiry" to Indochina to expose colonial abuses, and it began to pay more attention to Indochinese laborers in France.[127] This would soon give these laborers a space to pursue politics outside of the insular, largely elite circles that had dominated Indochinese political activism in France before the 1930s.

WORKERS AND POLITICS

In May 1920, a French official noted that in their letters home, Indochinese soldiers and workers still in France were increasingly focusing less on the problems of life in wartime and more on "*việc đời*—that is to say, worldly affairs, political affairs."[128] France's effervescent political atmosphere in 1919 had indeed stoked the politics of Indochinese soldiers and workers. The "Revendications du peuple annamite" circulated widely in their camps and were found in letters sent to Indochina.[129] Translations of Cường Để's articles in the Chinese newspaper *Tsein Tsin* also circulated, and the names Phan Châu Trinh and Nguyễn Ái Quốc "were known in almost every company."[130] "The blind theories of socialism," one French official worried, "have certainly penetrated our natives, particularly those who have worked side by side with the French worker."[131] Some certainly felt solidarity. "In Marseille," remembered one sailor, "it was a revolutionary atmosphere. It was the end of 1919. All were talking about the Black Sea Mutiny, as if it had happened yesterday. I was dazzled by stories of French sailors hoisting the red flag to salute the proletarian revolution, and putting their commanders and officers in irons in the hold."[132] (Tôn Đức Thắng's participation in the Black Sea Mutiny, a staple of party history, is mythology.)[133] But unions and other labor organizations worried about colonial workers taking jobs from demobilized soldiers and corrupting France's social fabric; unions like the Conféderation générale du travail (CGT) opposed their presence in France.[134] As the utopian possibilities of 1919 receded, the political activities of Indochinese workers in France retreated into émigré associations.

Cross-class political interactions in these associations were complex and often tense. Meaningful cooperation did exist. Some of the hundreds of Indochinese workers who stayed in France after the war were part of political circles at 6 Villa des Gobelins and the Intercolonial Union, thanks largely to Nguyễn Ái Quốc, who "assiduously cultivated links with . . . sailors and other manual workers."[135] The PAI leaned on worker activism and financial support. Đặng Văn Thư used profits from drug trafficking to support the party, and his restaurant in Le Havre was a site for its meetings and distribution of its newspapers.[136] In 1926, the cook Võ Văn Toàn and the grocer Trần Lệ Luật planned a similar venture but it never materialized.[137] Nguyễn Thế Truyền and Tạ Thu Thâu spent hours organizing Indochinese "lacquerers, cooks, clerks, photograph retouchers, and mechanics," urging them to contribute some of their wages to the PAI.[138] Some were enthusiastic, like an Indochinese sergeant stationed near Toulouse who, after learning of the PAI during a leave in Paris, read *Việt Nam Hồn* aloud in his barracks.[139] Cross-class alliances were crucial in associational elections, like the one in 1926 that placed radicals at the head of the Association mutuelle des indochinois in Paris.[140] At the PAI's 1929 Tết ball, a mixed crowd heard dozens of soldiers sing patriotic songs. "Our home is destroyed, our homeland conquered," they sang; "what a misfortune for our ancestors, who are unable to rest peacefully."[141]

But socio-cultural difference also bred political tensions between students and workers. For most Indochinese workers, "*việc đời*" meant something quite far from the Intercolonial Union's global anti-imperialism, even when the PAI repackaged it in nationalist language. Indochinese workers in Paris often avoided the Association mutuelle des indochinois because they did not want to be forced to speak French.[142] In 1922, a group of them created their own mutual aid society. Intercolonial Union militants sought an alliance with the association to rival the moderate AMI. But tensions soon flared; the militant Trần Tiến Nam "spoke in highly disparaging terms of his working class compatriots," who cut off cooperation.[143] Nguyễn Thế Truyền, a Sûreté agent noted, "has a hard time reaching his compatriots . . . thanks to his haughty character."[144] In 1928, a cook railed against PAI activists who "solicited money on the pretext of leading the struggle for Indochinese independence" that "went instead to feed a lazy bunch of people who live without doing anything."[145] When leaders of workers' associations proposed diverting funds to the PAI, most of the rank and file strenuously objected.[146] One cook protested that he had lent the party "large sums of money for propaganda needs and for the well-being of Indochina, but he was never paid back and nobody speaks of it anymore."[147]

To elites, worker indifference or hostility signified political apathy. But Indochinese workers organized politically around other priorities. In the early 1920s, Indochinese worker associations in France had focused mostly on mutual aid. But beginning in 1928, they began to advance their members' rights in their workplaces. As the PAI was collapsing, a group of lacquer workers in Paris formed the Syndicat des lacquers indochinois—the first Indochinese workers group in France resembling a union, not an association or mutual aid society. Their main goal was not national independence or revolution, but to protect their labor by preventing their employers from teaching lacquer techniques to French workers.[148] In Marseille, the Comité de défense des travailleurs annamites (created in December 1927) also began defending the wages and working conditions of Indochinese across occupational lines. As one of its tracts read,

> All men have the right to desire a better life and the duty to live as free men. To achieve this, come with us and support the society that will make us stronger by uniting us in fraternity. Europeans are organized into unions, who defend them in all cases. But we are dispersed, that is why we are miserable and defenseless in the face of injustice! Now it is our turn for us to see clearly. . . . Join your *comité de défense* that awaits you to become stronger and to support you when bad times descend upon you.[149]

In 1928, some Indochinese sailors objected to Chinese working on French ships, arguing that French firms had a moral obligation to hire Indochinese: "How many of us died as soldiers in the field of battle, and how many sailors drowned in the oceans?"[150] A year later, with nothing changed, some Indochinese sailors on the *Ville d'Amiens* went on strike; they were fired and jailed in Le Havre.[151]

Indochinese political activists tried to harness this growing labor militancy, but initial efforts went badly. In 1928, Trần Lệ Luật failed to link the lacquer workers union to the PAI.[152] In 1929, Đặng Văn Thư failed to form a general Indochinese workers' association in Paris under PCF control.[153] Also in 1929, Trần Văn Thọ, president of the Comité de défense des travailleurs annamites, tried to subsume the group into an PCF organization, which "raised powerful emotions among Indochinese sailors."[154] But putschist tactics soon gave way to more sustained efforts. In March 1930, the Moscow-trained militant Nguyễn

Khánh Toàn, in Marseille to organize an Indochinese section of the PCF there, successfully (purportedly at Nguyễn Ái Quốc's urging) transformed the Comité de défense des travailleurs annamites into the Đông Dương Lao Động Tương Tế Hội (Indochinese Workers' Mutual Aid Association) and placed it under PCF direction.[155] In May 1929, the PCF's Central Committee called for a "serious and methodical" effort to harness Indochinese labor activism in Marseille, including a campaign "to bring unions most connected to Indochinese laborers (sailors, cooks, etc.) . . . to defend them against exploitation and imperialist repression."[156] In March 1930, PCF militants Bùi Đức Kiên and Nguyễn Văn Tư—both of whom had studied in Moscow—formed the newspaper *Bạn Hải Thuyền* (Sailors' Friend), the first Indochinese newspaper in France specifically for workers. Its first issue included an article about the PCF-controlled Confédération générale du travail unitaire (CGTU), which Indochinese would join in growing numbers during the next decade.[157] In November, the PCF newspaper *Rouge midi* published a "call to colonial sailors," proclaiming that the "Syndicat unitaire des marins calls all of them without distinction of race or color to reinforce its ranks and to form a unified front to achieve their goals." It also invited them to join the PCF-allied Club international des marins in Marseille.[158] That month, police agents found quốc ngữ tracts at the club calling on Indochinese to join the CGTU and Secours rouge international.[159] The PCF next turned to organizing soldiers, which the PAI had also tried. In October 1931, the PCF activist Đỗ Đình Thiện, recently returned from Moscow, was arrested for distributing tracts among members of the 52nd Indochinese batallion: he had hidden them "in a loaf of bread, whose soft inside was hollowed out with the crust replaced as a sort of lid."[160] They included copies of another PCF Indochinese newspaper, *Tiếng Lính Annam* (Voice of Annamese Soldiers). "It seems," noted a Sûreté official in late 1931, "that closer ties between Annamites and the various organs of the Third International in France is the order of the day."[161]

The PCF's ties to Indochinese labor activism grew further after the party, in a reversal of the past hostility of French organized labor, responded to Comintern pressure and affirmed its support for colonial workers at its Seventh Congress in March 1932. The Depression had left many Indochinese workers in France in desperate straits, and a PCF-led campaign against the 1931 colonial exposition (which got Nguyễn Văn Tạo expelled from France) made PCF-led organizations like the League Against Imperialism, Secours rouge international, and the CGTU more visible to Indochinese in France.[162] In May 1932, Đặng Đình Thọ and Trần Phương Đơn went to Hamburg for the Congress of the Comintern-controlled Internationale des marins et dockers.[163] In that same month, the Club international des marins hosted a wildly successful recreation of the Yên Báy mutiny.[164] That October, Indochinese and French sailors on the steamship *L'Angkor* struck over pay cuts.[165] Also in October, Cao Văn Chánh began organizing a union of Indochinese domestics in Paris.[166] By September 1933, the CGTU had an Indochinese section, led by the Moscow-trained militant Trần Quốc Mại.[167] So did the Syndicat unitaire des marins, which helped smuggle communist documents between France and Indochina during the 1930s. And eight Indochinese workers were among the first students at the PCF's Université ouvrière (Workers' University) when it opened in Paris in 1933, in hopes of replicating the kind of instruction that communist activists received in Moscow.[168]

For the Comintern and the PCF, the goal of mobilizing colonial workers in France was to intensify revolutionary anti-colonial activity in France and to link it to communist movements around the French empire. In this respect, it was a failure. The fate of the Comité d'entraide et culture des indochinois illustrates this. The group tried to bridge cross-class political divisions: its activities spanned "causeries on scientific, philosophical, literary and artistic questions" to free medical care and legal advocacy.[169] But it rapidly divided along class lines. The Paris chapter became a political debating club, hosting discussions of the Paris Commune, the Abyssinian crisis, and the Tây Sơn uprising.[170] Meanwhile, student members of the Marseille chapter reproached the worker majority for "thinking only about their personal interests, without worrying about those of the collective." When the students quit, the group became a de facto workers association.[171] But the efforts of the PCF and its Indochinese militants had, by the 1930s, helped transform Indochinese worker activism in France. In trade unionism, they would find a form of political action that had been largely absent from elite-led organizations like the Intercolonial Union and PAI, one that would continue to shape their politics as they navigated the currents of the Popular Front, the Second World War, and decolonization.

FROM POPULAR FRONT TO WAR

On March 26, 1934, six years after he had left France, Nguyễn Thế Truyền descended the gangplank of the *Aramis* onto Marseille's docks. Five days later, he wrote to his wife from Paris.

My dear Mad, just after returning to Paris, I saw the old neighborhood where we spent so many difficult but joyful years together. I passed by the Pont Sully and took the tramway from the Gare de Lyon to the Jardin des Plantes, where we so often stopped on our way to pick up Kit Kit at Moisenay. I saw the Panthéon, the Bibliothèque Saint-Geneviève and the Chinese restaurants. . . . Cafés are more comfortable now, they all play concerts on the radio. I'm listening to a Milanese singer as I write these lines.

Like his nostalgia for Paris, Nguyễn Thế Truyền's political commitments had not dimmed during his six years in Indochina. "If we are unhappy," he wrote to his wife, "it is because it is so hard to live well while remaining honest and proud, in these times and in a colony like Indochina where all barbaries, debasements, and ignominies flourish! But those colonial lackeys have gotten nothing from me save a hatred intense enough to withstand anything without debasing myself." He promised to return in a few months, but he would not see his family again until early 1940, with France on the brink of war.[172]

"The traitor Nguyễn Thế Truyền has returned to France," proclaimed the PCF newspaper *Vô Sản*. "Here is an agitator for the cause of Indochinese feudalism and for landlords. . . . He is in cahoots with the police, spies, and fascists. No, Indochinese workers see clearly. They will not allow themselves to be duped by a vulgar traitor and will receive him like he deserves."[173] The article reveals the anxiety of the PCF's Indochinese sections in 1934. They were without effective leadership: Nguyễn Văn Tạo had been expelled from France in 1931 and Cao Văn Chánh had returned to Indochina in 1933, leaving the unremarkable Trần Quốc Mại as the PCF's leading Indochinese militant. Lack of autonomy from the PCF and Moscow's strict class line had stoked dissent. The Trotskyist-led Cercle des études sociales des indochinois was becoming a hub of Indochinese anti-Stalinism. And the Fédération des peuples colonisés, formed in March 1935, was fostering a rapprochement between the Socialist SFIO and leftist colonial elites calling for "a 'humanitarian' colonial policy centered on the idea of an eventual free association of peoples in which each could realize its full development."[174] Nguyễn Thế Truyền, hoping to capitalize on these new fault lines, plunged back into his political organizing.[175]

The changing political landscape that Nguyễn Thế Truyền encountered upon his return was due largely to the rise of fascism and Moscow's easing relations with "bourgeois" European states, which led it to resurrect a policy of tactical alliances with the non-communist left. Despite the chaos this created in the PCF (which had just expelled Jacques Doriot, an early advocate of

Indochinese revolutionary groups at the Comintern, for supporting a united front), its leadership gamely sought ties to other groups on the French left.[176] This included the Fédération des peuples colonisés and other noncommunist groups attempting to mobilize colonial subjects, for the PCF had cause to worry that fascism might appeal to them too; North Africans "enlisting in far-right shock groups such as the Solidarité Française and the Jeunesses Patriotes rose sharply in spring 1934."[177] The leaders of the PCF's Section coloniale, a Sûreté official wrote, "feel that this campaign of 'fascist militarization' must be resisted at all costs, by demonstrating to the natives that national parties will be of no help, that to the contrary, only the communist party is capable of helping to defend them against their exploiters."[178]

As the PCF reconsidered alliances with other leftist groups, communist militants in Indochina revived a strategy of public legal activism—in both the colony and in France—as part of their political strategy. This began in 1933 when, bludgeoned by Sûreté repression, Stalinist and Trotskyist activists in Cochinchina decided to pursue a united front for electoral politics, labor organizing and in the press (through their group's eponymous newspaper, *La Lutte*). La Lutte's central figures (Nguyễn An Ninh, Tạ Thu Thâu, Huỳnh Văn Phương, Phan Văn Hùm, Trần Văn Thạch, Nguyễn Văn Tạo, and Dương Bạch Mai) had all cut their political teeth in France, and their apprenticeships in Republican strategies and styles of communist activism would transform colonial political life. As Daniel Hémery notes, the alliance between Stalinists and Trotskyists in Cochinchina in 1933 "had only an experimental character and was only the result of a private initiative"; it received tepid support from the ICP and waned after French authorities invalidated election results and banned its newspapers.[179] However, a wave of political trials in Indochina in 1933 outraged the PCF, which formed a Committee of Amnesty and sent a delegation to Indochina in early 1934 to investigate working conditions there. La Lutte's leaders, who knew most members of the PCF delegation, helped guide the inquiry. La Lutte's revival in late 1934 likely only happened after Moscow learned more about the alliance that summer (via the PCF's report about the delegation) and authorized ICP involvement.[180] Following the Popular Front victory in 1936, La Lutte became the driving force in Indochinese anti-colonialism's legal front, notably in its campaigns for an "Indochinese Congress" and as a model for other leftist electoral campaigns and newspapers (notably *Le Travail* in Hà Nội).

PCF Indochinese sections sought to use La Lutte's success to revive their waning political fortunes. PCF and ICP activists working on steamships linked La Lutte's ICP faction to Paris's Association d'entraide et culture, an Indochinese PCF front organization. In November 1934, the group replaced *Vô Sản* with *Ánh Sáng* (Light), whose editorial line mirrored *La Lutte*'s; its editors Nghiêm Xuân Toàn and Nguyễn Đình Tịnh drew from copies of *La Lutte* sent from Indochina (*Ánh Sáng,* in turn, circulated in Indochina).[181] The Comité de rassemblement des indochinois, founded in July 1936, was modeled both on La Lutte and on the Rassemblement populaire, a leftist coalition in France. The PCF controlled the Comité (its head, Nguyễn Đình Tịnh, was editor of *Ánh Sáng* and president of the Association d'entraide et culture), but the Popular Front's big tent made it an eclectic political forum. Some members, like the former editor of *Vô Sản* Hoàng Quang Giụ, had left or been expelled from the PCF. The Comité also included figures like the journalist Lê Hiến and the lawyer Phan Tất Tốn, associates of the anarcho-syndicalist Daniel Guérin (who directed the Comité's newspaper *L'Appel*).[182] Some activists of the Fédération des peuples colonisés also joined when their own group folded, even Nguyễn Thế Truyền, who reportedly joined the SFIO in 1936.[183] But despite the breadth of its membership, the Comité remained essentially a PCF effort to use an anti-fascist front to resurrect the political fortunes of its Indochinese sections. *L'Humanité,* the Comité d'amnistie, Secours rouge internationale, and other PCF organs publicized La Lutte, while the party's lawyers went to Indochina to defend La Lutte against legal attacks from the colonial administration.[184]

PCF support gave La Lutte's ICP faction a faith in the Popular Front that their Indochinese comrades in France did not all share: in a letter to *La Lutte, Ánh Sáng*'s editors noted its "great reservation as to the possibilities of the Popular Front when it will have not only to win at the ballot box, but to govern. We know that compromises at the heart of the Front with groups whose reactionary character we underestimate—bourgeois Radicals—are incompatible with effective solutions to social questions."[185] La Lutte's ICP faction experienced similar doubts after Dương Bạch Mai's failed trip to Paris in December 1936 to convince the minister of colonies, Marius Moutet, to end repression of the Indochinese Congress movement. Indochinese anti-Stalinist leftists in France, more aware of compromises and backsliding seeping into the Popular Front's colonial policy, did not hesitate to mock Dương Bạch Mai's quixotic diplomacy: Lê Hiến skewered his self-serving account of his tête-à-tête with Moutet, noting that "although he recognized that dining with a minister is a rare event for an Annamite, it is far from a revolutionary act."[186] Subsequent months confirmed the barb: as the Popular Front frayed, colonial officials arrested La Lutte's activists, broke strikes, and closed news-papers, forcing its leadership back into clandestine activity. In France, Indochinese PCF militants left the Comité de rassemblement des indochi-nois as their party's relations with the Popular Front government soured: its non-Stalinist members joined the Rassemblement colonial, a new cross-colonial group that continued to hold out hope in the Popular Front.

Trotskyist involvement in La Lutte reflected Tạ Thu Thâu's belief in the tactical utility of an alliance with Stalinists, and international Trotskyism's institutional weakness gave him "total freedom of action" to pursue it.[187] He worked to build support for La Lutte in the French press and among anti-Stalinist factions in the Comité de rassemblement des indochinois.[188] But French Trotskyists were implacably opposed to the Popular Front and to any cooperation with Stalinists, and many of their Indochinese comrades—in the colony and France alike—followed their lead. In 1932, Phan Văn Hùm founded a Trotskyist newspaper in Paris, *Đuốc Vô Sản,* which echoed the editorial line of *Tháng Mười (October),* published in Indochina by a Trotskyist faction led by Hồ Hữu Tường, Lư Sanh Hạnh, and Ngô Văn Xuyết that opposed Tạ Thu Thâu's cooperation with Stalinists (it folded after Phan Văn Hum returned to Indochina in 1933). Trân Văn Sĩ and Nguyễn Văn Lịnh, the two main Trotskyists in France, criticized La Lutte in the Trotskyist-led Cercle des études sociales des indochinois in Paris and in a French edition of the so-called "Octoberist" group's newspaper, *Tiên Đạo.* In early 1936, the Indochinese chapter of Left Opposition in France proclaimed its support for a Fourth International.[189] After the Popular Front victory in 1936, the Indochinese Trotskyist newspapers in France, *Quân Chúng* and *Quốc Tế IV,* again echoed Hồ Hữu Tường in *Le Militant* (formed in September 1936 to oppose La Lutte) in excoriating the PCF's role in a nonrevolutionary political alliance. Indochinese Trotskyists in France also criticized Moscow's show trials and its repression of the non-Stalinist left in the Spanish civil war—topics that the Stalinist-Trotskyist *modus vivendi* left off limits in La Lutte.[190] Some Indochinese Trotskyists in France were even involved in the Spanish Civil War, raising funds, smuggling weapons, and going there to fight: Stalinist militias executed six of them in September 1936.[191] Most leading Trotskyists in France returned to Indochina in the late 1930s. By 1939, the few still in France had aligned with the Parti socialiste ouvrier et paysan (PSOP), a dissident SFIO faction influenced by Daniel Guérin's evolving anarcho-Trotskyism.[192]

When the Popular Front took power, most Indochinese workers in France saw anti-colonialism as a far more remote cause than wages or working conditions. Membership in trade unions in France, which had grown during the Depression, exploded after the Popular Front victory in April 1936 and the reunification of the CGT and the PCF-controlled CGTU later that fall.[193] Labor activism was intense among Indochinese sailors and dockers, who had been joining the Syndicat unitaire des marins for years. "Following the new parliament's election," wrote some Indochinese sailors in Marseille in December 1936, "we ask all Annamite sailors to help us establish our demands and to ask the Popular Front government to lighten the weight of our misery."[194] Colonial subjects working on steamships won a huge victory in 1937 when the CGT agreed to recognize their unions.[195] Emboldened leaders of associations like the Ái Hữu Thủy Thủ Hội (Sailor Friendship Association) "enjoined their comrades ... to express their demands about salary, food, lodging, overtime, etc."[196] The CGTU's Indochinese group, which had organized cooks and servants for years, also saw its membership rise in the Syndicat des cuisiniers.[197] The Popular Front ultimately did not bridge gaps between Indochinese workers and elite-led groups like the Fédération des peuples colonisés or the Comité de rassemblement des indochinois. But it did create, for a fleeting moment, ties between Indochinese worker organizations in the colony and France. As a workers' movement rose in Indochina in 1936 and 1937, colonial workers' associations sought to forge ties to metropolitan organizations. In 1939, for example, the Amicale des navigateurs cochinchinois in Sài Gòn asked the CGT-affiliated Association générale des indochinois in Le Havre for help when facing dissolution (the CGT's appeal to the minister of colonies went for naught).[198] The Popular Front thus helped cement trade unionism as a form of identification and action among Indochinese laborers in France, with lasting consequences for their politics during the era of revolution and decolonization.

EIGHT

Political Sojourners from War
to Decolonization

AS THE GERMAN ARMY PLUNGED into France in May 1940, the Third Republic's government and military collapsed, and millions took to the roads. "We had lost all point of reference," one wrote; "all our habits and all the rules of life were floating."[1] Nguyễn Khắc Viện was seeing patients at the Hôpital Trousseau when a colleague urged him to leave Paris to avoid being conscripted or killed when the Germans arrived. As he recalled:

> I invited Hoàng Xuân Nhị and Phạm Quang Lễ to come with me. We walked gradually south, carrying camping equipment and sleeping on the side of the road. The road was full of people and vehicles: ten million French people from the northern and eastern departments were going south, cars, horses, cows, and peasants, some pushing their cows down the road. A scene of total panic, no organization! Occasionally German planes flew by, which prompted no response, but cries that the German army was approaching caused crowds to scatter in panic. Not a shot was fired from the ground into the air.[2]

The three friends made it to the Haute-Vienne, where they stayed for a week before making their way back to Paris. Nguyễn Khắc Viện went back to his old job in a new world.

This chapter explores how what Marc Bloch called the "Strange Defeat" transformed Indochinese politics in France. The occupation not only ruptured the sojourns that had closely bound the metropolitan and colonial theaters of Indochinese politics, it created radically new conditions that reshaped the political orientations and alliances of Indochinese in France. In the early part of the occupation, German economic and military dynamism led some to engage with European fascism as a vehicle for anti-colonial liberation. But as the French resistance to the Nazis grew, others would turn to

Gaullism's vision for a revitalized and reformed republican empire, or to the PCF's resurgent trade unions and mass organizations. After the liberation, disparate Indochinese political forces in France—spanning Trotskyists to royalists—came together in a fleeting nationwide political coalition that had few ties or parallels to wartime politics in Indochina. But as the tensions surrounding the colony's future erupted into a revolution and another war, the extension of the region's postcolonial regimes into France would reorient the French world of Indochinese politics toward the possibilities and perils of an imminent decolonization.

FROM WAR TO LIBERATION

The Vichy regime, in Eric Jennings's words, "cloned itself overseas . . . by introducing to the empire Pétain's cherished themes of authenticity, tradition, and folklore."[3] In France as in the colony, some Indochinese supported Vichy and worked to build its legitimacy. Like many of Vichy's French functionaries, they collaborated not out of fear or force, but out of a belief in the regime's vision of national and imperial renewal. Hoàng Văn Cơ, a descendant of the pro-French imperial official Hoàng Cao Khải, had come to France to study business but became a journalist for right-wing newspapers and a commentator on colonial questions for Radiodiffusion française and Radio-Paris. He became head of Vichy's Ministry of Information's Section coloniale despite his wife being Jewish.[4] Cao Văn Sen, a French citizen, had volunteered for the Great War; in 1939, now fifty years old and a successful engineer, he volunteered again and became deputy commander of the Third Foreign Regiment, and then joined the Ministry of Information's Section coloniale to observe and report on the conditions of the thousands of Indochinese laborers languishing in camps. One remembered him as "rarely removing his military beret with its four silver braids even when dressed as a civilian."[5] The writer Đỗ Đình Thạch, who also voluteered for war in 1939, also worked for the Section coloniale. Trần Văn Hy, who had volunteered in 1914 and worked for colonial intelligence services for two decades, later served in the fascist paramilitary *milice,* which would earn him five years in jail.[6]

These men saw Vichy as a stronger, more vital engine for the empire-ordered world they believed in. But other Indochinese saw right-wing European nationalism as an ideological model for a post-imperial world. Such influences stretched deep into the interwar era. In 1922, Phạm Quỳnh found time in his busy schedule to attend meetings of the right-wing L' Action française; "he did not hide his sympathy for the doctrine of Charles Maurras."[7] On Ngô Quốc Quyển's trip to France, he had met "two Italian fascists who conversed intimately with me. I asked them about Mussolini. . . ."[8] "Annam's soul is still errant," wrote Hinh Thái Thông in 1927; "the nation is still asleep, but when it awakens, it will do so suddenly like Germany in 1816," now "the great nation of our times." "Work hard to perfect yourself," he urged his friend; "Benito Mussolini, son of a blacksmith, abandoned a teaching position to work as a porter in Switzerland. He lived through hardship and built a powerful Italy."[9] Nguyễn Hữu Thư's 1927 trip to Perugia to study the Italian wheat industry awakened his own interest in Mussolini.[10] In Paris, "Indochina's need for a man like Hitler in Germany" was fodder for café talk in 1932.[11]

For some, this engagement hardened into meaningful commitments. For the journalist Đỗ Đức Hồ, the communist-led Nghệ-Tĩnh uprising in 1930–31 signified a collapse of Indochina's social order and the threat of Soviet and Chinese domination; in *The Annam Soviets and the Disorder of the White Gods,* published in France in 1938, he extolled Maurice Barrès's rural idyllism and Maurras's integral nationalism. Nguyễn Thượng Khoa, son of the imperial official Nguyễn Thượng Hiền (exiled from Indochina for accepting German support for anticolonial activities during the Great War), was drawn to Nazism while studying film in Berlin. In 1937, he sent a manifesto to Nazi officials urging them to offer "moral participation and material assistance" to "an immediate revolution across our territory." He claimed the existence of a secret Indochinese National-Socialist party with twenty thousand members.[12] Although this was pure fantasy, the ideas of the modern European right were spreading in political circles at the Université indochinoise; several people who studied there before pursuing advanced degrees in France in the late 1930s (like Nguyễn Khắc Viện and the engineer Lê Văn Thiêm) would be active in right-wing political circles in Paris during the war. And in some cases, like the brilliant literature student Hoàng Xuân Nhị, a long-standing love of German culture (in his case, of Rilke) pulled him towards pro-Nazi politics as war loomed.[13]

After Japan occupied French Indochina in September 1940 and promised its liberation, Đỗ Đức Hồ—whose admiration for Japan descended to an ugly denial of its crimes in Nanjing in his book—set out to build a pro-Japanese Indochinese political network in France. His "Party of Independence" and its newspaper *Đại Đông* (The Great East) withered after Japanese officials showed no interest. But Indochinese engagement with German authorities in France was more consequential. By the time the Germans occupied Vichy France in

November 1942, the terrible conditions in ONS camps had stoked desertions. Many who made their way to Paris ended up at the mutual aid society L'Amicale annamite (11 rue Jean Beauvais) seeking lodging, work, ration cards, or false identity papers. Vichy limited German mobilization of colonial workers out of fear that it might erode the regime's authority among colonial subjects. But German officials, desperate for labor, offered Amicale leaders a fee *au noir* for each ONS it recruited to work for Germany. By mid-1943, Amicale chapters in Lyon, Bordeaux, Grenoble, Toulouse, Marseille, and Montpellier began helping ONS desert and work for Germany. Also in 1943, German agents (with help from Pierre Fauquenot, a former newspaper editor in Indochina jailed for working with Japanese intelligence agents but freed during the German invasion) recruited Indochinese to continue their studies in Berlin. These men (Trần Văn Du, Hoàng Xuân Nhị, Nguyễn Khắc Viện, Lê Văn Thiêm, Lê Viết Hương, Nguyễn Hoán, Phan Thuyết, and perhaps others) followed Phạm Quang Lễ, an engineer whom German officials had recruited in 1942 from the École nationale supérieure de l'aéronautique to work in the German aeronautical industry.

These Indochinese were among hundreds of anti-colonial activists from around the British and French empires who went to Berlin in hopes of forming a "nationalist international against empire."[14] After returning to Paris in March 1944, some of these students joined some leaders of the Amicale (notably Trần Hữu Phương and Hoàng Xuân Mãn) in a newspaper, *Nam Việt*, whose pro-Axis editorial line advanced a right-wing vision for Indochina's racial and cultural renewal. In its pages, Nguyễn Khắc Viện blamed parliamentary systems and class-based ideologies for Europe's division and radicalization: "99 percent" of Europeans, he argued, preferred command economies and authoritarian regimes to market economies and representative government.[15] The engineer Võ Qúy Huân criticized modern life's "materialist civilization" (*văn minh vật chất*), urging workers and students to join in "collective action and struggle to allow the race (*nòi giống*) to live prosperously, vigorously, and gloriously together."[16] *Nam Việt* envisioned a modernized authoritarian state, led by scientific and technical experts, as an engine for racial renewal. Võ Qúy Huân argued for a *kinh tế liên kết* (a translation of *économie associée*, a term used by French economists to describe the Nazi economy) linking the "action of labor" and "the action of capital."[17] Lê Viết Hương called for state economic and political management to reach harmony and cooperation among classes, what Nguyễn Khắc Viện believed the "revolutions" in Germany and Italy had achieved.[18]

The *Nam Việt* group made no effort to politically organize the ONS, but its ideas spread among them anyway. Many ONS favored an Axis victory, and pro-Japanese sentiment was rife in the camps.[19] Some even tried to fight for Germany. In 1944, some of the roughly one hundred ONS serving in the paramilitary organization Nationalsozialistisches Kraftfahrkorps (National Socialist Motor Corps) approached Đỗ Đức Hồ with a plan to form a Wehrmacht battalion and, later, the core of independent Vietnam's national army. He was soon in charge of hundreds of ONS volunteers stationed near Paris. But when German officials made it clear that they expected Đỗ Đức Hồ to fight alongside them, he got cold feet and stalled, and volunteers trickled off into the *milice*. In August, he agreed to go to the ONS camps to recruit more volunteers, but the trains had stopped running. His German contact gave him a final order to prepare ONS interned in a camp near the German border for combat. As a French official noted, "Out of fear of reprisals Đỗ Đức Hồ did not dare to openly refuse, but M. Vestrick never saw him again."[20]

The small core of Indochinese Trotskyists still in France also began mobilizing when war broke out. In January 1941, the interpreter Hoàng Khoa Khôi spent three months in prison for leading a hunger strike among ONS in Vénissieux; after his release, a friend found him a job in Paris writing for *Công Binh Tạp Chí,* Vichy's propaganda sheet for the ONS. He soon met Hoàng Đôn Trí (a former student of Tạ Thu Thâu's) and Nguyễn Được, engineering students at the Ecole centrale and leaders of an Indochinese "Bolshevik-Leninist" group based in Suresnes. In 1943, through Amicale networks, Indochinese Trotskyist activists established ties to Indochinese militants in the south; they were soon circulating tracts and recruiting militants in ONS camps. This extremely dangerous activism, coming at a time when forms of solidarity and mutual aid among ONS "were transforming into more durable structures of action as a result of the struggle against the MOI hierarchy," would give Trotskyist leaders enormous prestige among the ONS as the Vichy regime crumbled in 1944.[21]

On October 22, 1941, Nazi soldiers executed twenty-seven political prisoners in Chateaubriand. One of them was Huỳnh Khương An, a teacher at a lycée in Versailles and a PCF militant for years, who had been arrested for spreading Soviet propaganda and sheltering German communists hiding in Paris. Today, Huỳnh Khương An has been apotheosized by the PCF and has streets named after him in Vietnam.[22] But his martyrdom belies how weak PCF influence on Indochinese in France really was when the war began. In

1937, the party had chosen anti-fascism over anti-colonialism: "against fascism," Maurice Thorez proclaimed, "the interests of colonial people is in their union with the people of France."[23] Purges in Moscow, Soviet opportunism in the Spanish Civil War, and the shock of the 1939 nonaggression pact had further alienated many Indochinese PCF activists. But the PCF's leadership in the anti-German resistance helped it regain and extend its influence among Indochinese. Many of the roughly seven hundred ONS deserters between mid-1943 and April 1944 went to areas controlled by the FTP (Francs-tireurs et partisans, the PCF's resistance arm).[24] Some were believers; some, more simply, sought basic needs and physical safety. But the PCF-led maquis helped many to "rediscover a dignity that had been utterly abused in MOI camps." Indochinese in FTP units wore the same uniforms as French fighters, and occasionally even led them.[25] PCF influence on Indochinese workers would grow further after liberation, as the party consolidated its control over trade unions and began pursuing a national political program to build a "new people's democracy."

As with the PCF, some Indochinese who joined the Free French movement led by Charles de Gaulle did so by circumstance. But many also rallied to its cause in hopes that if the Republic survived, it would pursue a more just and humane vision for its empire. The Duy Tân emperor, exiled to Réunion in 1916, as Prince Nguyễn Phúc Vĩnh San had proclaimed his love for France and requested, futilely, naturalization and permission to live in Paris. After the liberation of Réunion in late 1942, he volunteered for the Free French naval forces as a radio officer and then joined the army, rising to lieutenant colonel by September 1944.[26] The journalist and writer Tào Kim Hải was serving as an army officer when he was captured in June 1940; after his release from a German camp, he joined the Free French. In 1945, as a French delegate to international conferences on postwar affairs, he would work to resurrect the Fourth Republic's empire.[27] A fellow delegate at these conferences was Sisowath Youtevong, a member of the Khmer royal family who received a doctorate in mathematics in Montpellier, soon to become the leader of a republican political movement in Cambodia after the war.[28] Nguyễn Tấn Trịnh, who joined the army in 1939 after graduating from Saint-Cyr, led a Free French parachutist battalion in 1944. After the liberation, he remained in the French army until November 1945, when he resigned to protest the arrest of Indochinese political activists.[29] Nguyễn Hữu Bích, a lawyer in Marseille, worked during the war with Max Juvénal, an influential figure in the Gaullist resistance.[30]

Francophile elites were not the only ones drawn to the Free French. In the summer of 1944, ONS escaped their camps by the hundreds to join Gaullist or Giraudist units.[31] Most died, during or after the war, unrecognized. But not all. In 2014, ninety-seven-year-old Phạm Văn Kiêm received the Légion d'honneur for his service in the resistance. Orphaned at five, he was a domestic in Huế when he volunteered in 1939. He never forgot his employer's reaction: "You? Going to war? You're going to get yourself killed." His response: "If I have to die, it'll be that way. I'll die for France. And you can keep your beautiful life in my country." Captured in 1940, he survived internment in Normandy and backbreaking labor in the Jura forests before fleeing to Paris, where he worked as a cook before joining the resistance. After the liberation he joined the army as a sergeant but left the military when France went to war in Indochina. He spent most of the rest of his life in Sevran, outside of Paris, serving food to schoolchildren in the *cantine*.[32]

FROM LIBERATION TO REVOLUTION

When Allied troops entered Paris in August 1944, *Nam Việt* shuttered its doors. Đỗ Đức Hồ, who had led Indochinese volunteers for the Wehrmacht, did not escape justice: arrested by the FFI, he would spend years in prison. The provisional French government considered charges against other pro-Axis Indochinese but decided against it. "Such action," wrote a French official, "could risk . . . alienating people who . . . may not all be irreducibly hostile."[33] ONS took justice into their own hands that summer, branding as "collaborators" Indochinese who had worked for Vichy. Violent acts and ad hoc tribunals sprouted in ONS camps. As one accused described it, "the victims were tied to chairs, a Tribunal was constituted, a parody of judgment took place, and its three leaders violently pronounced the condemnation."[34] One force in these acts of retributive justice was the "Battalion of Vietnam," a resistance unit formed in summer 1944. Its leader Trần Ngọc Diệp, who went by the nom de guerre "Captain Sài Gòn," had joined the French army in 1939, and then worked in a garage in Nîmes until joining the resistance in 1944. Indochinese Trotskyist militants also intensified their activities among the ONS that summer, organizing protests and strikes calling for better wages and living conditions and for rapid repatriation. In January 1945 in *Công Bình Tạp Chí*—the Vichy propaganda sheet now repurposed by Indochinese political activists as a liberationist newspaper—one ONS aptly

FIGURE 13. Plenary Session, Congrès des Indochinois de France, Avignon, December 15, 1944. Source: Hoàng Xuân Mai personal collection.

evoked the optimism and uncertainty of the moment: "After the war, we will return home. When we get there, we will begin building a different life—one more meaningful and more productive for ourselves, our families, and our society. But in what way will we build it?"[35]

On September 15, 1944, three weeks after the German surrender in Paris, Indochinese political activists met at L'Amicale annamite at 11 rue Jean Beauvais to consider that question. The meeting led to "the election of a general delegation ... to represent the Indochinese colony to French authorities."[36] The delegation toured ONS camps, urging them to elect delegates to an upcoming political assembly. In December, Indochinese political activists gathered in Avignon and founded the Délégation générale des indochinois (DGI), the first nationwide Indochinese political organization in France. They elected forty delegates: fifteen from the Paris Amicale (who made up the DGI's central committee), one from each of its six provincial chapters, fifteen from the ONS, and three from Trần Ngọc Diệp's "Battalion du Vietnam." In its founding manifesto, the self-identified "provisional government of Indochina" called on "authorities to help Indochinese workers obtain the same rights as French workers" and "for the establishment of a democratic regime in Indochina." "Only a government responsible to representatives elected by universal suffrage," it affirmed, "can assure the essential liberties for which allied armies are fighting." "The Delegation," it concluded, "will speak in the name of all of Indochina."[37]

The political affiliations of the DGI leadership reflected the war's transformative effects on Indochinese politics in France. There was, of course, no room for Indochinese who had worked for Vichy: Hoàng Văn Cơ and Cao Văn Sen barely escaped harsh sentences handed down by ONS tribunals.[38] But some of the DGI leadership had close ties to the French provisional government. They included two descendants of the Minh Mạng emperor: Bửu Hội, a chemist, had served in the military in 1939, spent the war at the Centre nationale de recherches scientifiques in Paris, and became a professor at the École polytechnique after liberation, while Bửu Dưỡng, a chaplain for the ONS, had turned against Vichy in 1944.[39] This faction also included the doctors Lê Tấn Vĩnh and Lê Đình Thi and the engineers Nguyễn Đắc Lộ and Phạm Quang Lễ: the latter bore no trace of pro-Axis politics despite two years working as an aeronautical engineer in Germany. Four anti-Vichy, pro-Axis figures (Hoàng Xuân Mãn, Võ Quý Huân, Lê Viết Hương, and Trần Hữu Phương) were also elected to the central committee. Trotskyists had no friends in the provisional government but deep support among the ONS, who elected the militants Hoàng Đôn Trí, Nguyễn Được, and Bùi Thạnh. The only central committee member without a clear political affiliation was Trần Đức Thảo, the brilliant *normalien*. He had been in France since 1936 without any known involvement in politics, whether on the Left during the Popular Front or, despite his deep interest in German philosophy, with the *Nam Việt* group (although some sources claim he accepted a scholarship to study in Berlin but decided not to go).[40] One of his teachers, Jean Cavaillès, a socialist and resistance leader, was executed by the Germans in April 1944. He seems to have been drawn into the Amicale via Indochinese Trotskyists, but their influence on him was fleeting. His brilliance and passion were on full display in Avignon—he was principal author of the DGI's manifesto—and resulted in his election as a DGI delegate.[41]

As 1945 dawned, the DGI began holding meetings, organizing the ONS, publishing tracts and newspapers (including reviving the Vichyist *Công Bình* and the pro-Axis *Nam Việt* with new editorial lines), and appealing to French authorities. Its leadership hoped that a shared experience of resistance and liberation would bring real change, or a peaceful end, to colonial rule. "We can truthfully say that the moons that have passed have been memorable," wrote the DGI leadership to Charles de Gaulle during Tết in 1945.

We witnessed the liberation of France, and we will someday recount to our compatriots in Indochina the degree of joy felt by a people rediscovering its liberty and independence. The fact of a great nation that, through the force of resistance, breaks the chains of occupation, is moving in and of itself. But France's liberation signifies more; it seems to be the harbinger of other liberations that will bring greater good and more liberty to people. The liberation's true lesson is that no nation can be free if it oppresses another.[42]

"Many of us," remembered the priest Cao Văn Luận, "fervently praised General de Gaulle as a wise and lucid man, and believed that as someone who had suffered the indignity of losing his country and then fought to liberate it, he would surely sympathize with the Vietnamese people's desires for independence."[43]

Years later, the physician Phạm Hữu Điệc recalled the fleeting optimism of that spring. "After France tragically retreated, capitulated to Germany and signed the armistice, I could only think of living day by day. . . . What misery and misfortune I endured," he remembered. "After the liberation, we felt joy and hope. . . . During the occupation, most French people suffered in the same way that we did, for we were all part of the same tragic situation. Thus we hoped that the liberation would be for all of us, and not just for France itself."[44] The powerful influence of the American army in France (some ONS deserters had worked for it) gave DGI leaders optimism about Franklin Roosevelt's trusteeship plan. "We must encourage the United States to intervene as quickly and officially as possible in Indochina," said its Montpellier delegate, "to, through their influence, achieve independence or, in the worst case, international oversight."[45] Moreover, before the August Revolution recast the question of independence along nationalist lines, the DGI was still thinking in Indochinese terms. "Indochina, a land of ancient civilization, has long since reached political maturation," read one resolution from April 1945. "Annamites, who form three-quarters of the population, must form a democratic federation with Cambodians and Laotians, whose own interests must be defended by diplomatic representation guaranteed by international authority. The Indochinese people wait with impatience for the Allied powers to bring them democracy and true liberty."[46]

The DGI's fragile political coalition soon began to fray. In December 1944, Cao Văn Luận was shocked when a shabbily-dressed man appeared at his door and introduced himself as the Duy Tân emperor. At the Amicale weeks later, now dressed in full military garb, he outlined a plan for a restored

Nguyễn monarchy within a French union. "Having never sullied myself with political intrigue," he wrote, "I could serve as a legitimate emperor, separated from the throne by circumstances, and now brought back to it."[47] Duy Tân's campaign divided the Ministry of Colonies and moderate voices in the DGI, some of whom moved toward a nascent royalist group, the Parti autonomiste indochinois.[48] Although Duy Tân died in a plane crash as he returned to Indochina in late 1945, divisions between royalists and republicans would persist. Meanwhile, the ONS were growing angry that elites controlled the DGI while they paid its bills. As an ONS put it, "this movement began in the camps before moving outward. There were only four or five students, what could they do? We, the workers, began this movement."[49] But as 1945 unfolded, independence displaced workers' rights as the DGI's main concern. Trotskyist militants flayed the DGI leadership (whose moderate elements had tried to bar them from the Avignon Congress) for failing to defend ONS syndicalist rights or advocating for their repatriation.[50] But the feeble French Trotskyist party, reunified in 1944 after years of sectarian division and struggling to overcome the hostility of the police and the PCF, had no time for colonial issues. Any such efforts were left to the tiny Indochinese Trotskyist group, seconded by a few French supporters (notably Daniel Guérin and Claude Bernard, better known by his nom de guerre "Raoul"). The Trotskyists' hard-earned influence in the ONS camps began to fade over the course of 1945.[51]

"We were promised so much," lamented a group of ONS in November 1944; "new salaries, professional training, reforms . . . but while we're cradled with beautiful promises, we're also subjected to indignations without measure. What do you expect? That's colonial politics, that's racial politics. During the last few months, with the help of a few enlightened Frenchmen, we have reclaimed a few basic rights . . . which even foreigners in France enjoy, but refused to us since our arrival."[52] The "few enlightened Frenchmen" here were PCF activists, whose influence among the ONS exploded after liberation. The PCF "emerged from the occupation as, by almost any objective test, the strongest political force in France," taking control of trade unions and dominating the first postwar election.[53] In the summer of 1944, the CGT pressured French authorities to let the ONS compete on the French labor market and to join labor unions.[54] "It is certain," wrote a French official in June, "that their urban sojourns and factory work have greatly influenced the spirits of some workers . . . who have now acquired communist doctrine."[55] CGT leaders attended the DGI's founding congress, where one ONS proclaimed, "We will need the CGT. Syndicalism is necessary, and it will help us when we return to Indochina."[56] One French official was only slightly exaggerating when he wrote, in early 1946, that "all of the Indochinese workers are affiliated with the CGT."[57] But, as one of many ONS resolutions from that summer shows, their concerns were often far from the DGI's growing focus on Indochina's political independence. One critiqued French officials who "hampered our effort to join the CGT from the earliest days of the liberation"; who, "following Indochinese worker participation in May Day celebrations in Lyon, punished and refused to recognize our union delegates"; and who "prevented Indochinese from continuing to work in Berliet factories in order to cut their ties with French workers."[58]

The French provisional government quickly disappointed the DGI leadership. Clouds had been on the horizon since the Brazzaville Conference in January 1944, when de Gaulle promised colonial reforms but rejected full independence. Two weeks before the Avignon Congress, eight Indochinese activists were arrested in Toulouse.[59] But the big blow came in March 1945, weeks after the Japanese had founded independent regimes in Indochina in a desperate attempt to stave off an allied invasion. On March 24, the French provisional government affirmed that Indochina would remain part of a French Union. "The declaration," wrote the DGI leadership, "announces the reestablishment of an absolutely unacceptable regime of authority that is against France's most basic interests. Indochina refuses Japanese domination, which represents the most acute form of fascist imperialism, but it is critical that its liberation does not place it again under the odious yoke of colonialism."[60] The DGI proposed a federal Indochina governed by an elected parliament that preserved autonomy for its three constituent nations, but this fell on deaf ears.[61] In April, French authorities appealed in ONS camps for volunteers for an expeditionary corps preparing to return to Indochina. In the "Camp Phạm Quỳnh" in Marseille, 150 responded to the appeal; after a DGI mobilization against it, just three showed up to be formally enlisted.[62]

In mid-August, the communist-led Việt Minh seized power in Hà Nội. Hồ Chí Minh proclaimed the Democratic Republic of Vietnam on September 2. The news set off "a week of unceasing celebration and speeches" in the Camp Phạm Quỳnh, which the ONS now renamed the "Camp Việt Nam," replacing its *tricolore* with the DRV's red flag with a yellow star.[63] The September 13 issue of the "revolutionary organ" *Công Nông* (Worker and Peasant), one of many such newspapers to sprout in France that fall, cast the Việt Minh as "defenders of equality" and of a "democratic and independent Việt Nam."[64] Students and professionals began to form patriotic associations supporting the DRV.[65] In the DGI, Bửu Hội's moderate faction was ambivalent about the Việt Minh seizure of power while Trotskyists decried it as a Stalinist coup. But other DGI leaders—Hoàng Xuân Mãn, Hoàng Xuân Nhị, Võ Qúy Huân, Trần Hữu Phương, and especially Trần Đức Thảo—raced to build support for the DRV, speaking at ONS camps and organizing demonstrations in Paris (including direct appeals to the Soviet, American, and English embassies). Trần Đức Thảo and fifty-one other Indochinese were arrested on September 21.[66] "We admired the French people's nationalism during the enemy occupation," protested dozens of Indochinese in an open letter; "we request that you observe reciprocity and that the nationalism of the Annamite people, whose legitimacy you Mr. President have recognized, be treated with respect."[67] French authorities dissolved the DGI on October 19; its leadership appealed to the United Nations and continued to hold meetings. Nearly three thousand people came to one on November 13 at Paris's Salle Wagram.[68] "The Việt Minh," one speaker argued, "is a resistance movement born in 1941 out of the struggle against Japanese oppression and Vichy treason. For four years, its sabotage and intelligence contributed to the success of Allied operations in the Pacific. What would you say if today the government of the Liberation called on the Germans to muzzle the liberation's own partisans?"[69] On December 2, the DGI central committee founded the Việt Kiều Liên Minh (League of Overseas Vietnamese) and formally affirmed the group's support for the DRV.

Political unrest in the ONS camps quickly escalated. ONS around France carried out hunger strikes on October 18 to protest the mass arrests in Paris, resulting in hundreds more arrests.[70] More protests and arrests followed the DGI's dissolution. French authority largely vanished in ONS camps that fall, as one visitor to the former "Camp Phạm Quỳnh" noted:

> Foreigners encounter serious difficulties when attempting to enter the Camp Phạm Quỳnh. Surrounded, he is asked the following questions: What are you doing? What do you want? What are you bringing in with you? Etc. In the camps, there is a committee to screen new arrivals, and anybody working for the French administration is dragged immediately in front of judges who claim the authority to bestow the following punishments: torture, beatings, lashes, or disappearance. . . . The political sections are very well organized; a cadre is always present at the main gate, and theatrical productions spread anti-French politics.[71]

But unlike the DGI's Indochinese vision in 1944, *national* independence was now the order of the day. Committees organized ONS by their province, district, and even village of origin to prepare them to help build "Vietnam" upon their return, and issued certificates for ONS to prove their political bona fides to DRV officials.[72] As French forces returned to Cochinchina that fall, political cadres in the camps urged the ONS to enlist and then desert with their weapons to the Việt Minh side.[73] Rumors of "sabotage by timorous or loyalist elements of the Indochinese colony" swept through the camps; suspects were either placed under surveillance or in a camp prison "where nationalists hold them in secret until their return to Indochina. There, they will be dealt with."[74] Indochinese soldiers formed a General Assembly of Annamite Soldiers, formally affiliated with the Việt Kiều Liên Minh, which urged its members to reject orders from French officers and only engage in activities preparing them for service in an independent Vietnamese army.[75] By late 1945, the situation was so tense that most of the thousands of Indochinese in the military in France were confined to their barracks and stripped of their weapons.[76] Political violence spread in military units that fall: dozens met fates like sergeant Lê Văn Yên, who was beaten with a hammer and thrown into the Seine.[77]

Before mid-1946, the pro-DRV movement in France operated in near-total isolation from the nascent DRV state. Its only real support base was the PCF: "Indochinese workers," noted one French official, "wear both PCF and Việt Minh insignias. It doesn't seem like there exists in their spirit any distinction between the two."[78] But the PCF's official line remained support for a democratized French Union, not colonial independence. "Stay with us in the French Union," beseeched one speaker at the party's tenth congress in 1946; "nothing will be strong enough to prevent French workers and republicans from allying with your democratic and national forces to form a true, fraternal, and progressive Union."[79] An "exacerbated nationalism," warned another French PCF activist, risked causing the revolutionary government to "fall back under the yoke of local tyrants, kings, and mandarins."[80] "The PCF's attitude," one Indochinese retorted, is "increasingly incomprehensible. Realpolitik should not repress a certain revolutionary exigency for which I search in vain."[81] In *Les Temps modernes,* Trần Đức Thảo argued that dialogue between the DRV and France was pointless: "Opposition is anterior to discourse, it is in the very sources of existence, from which all possible meaning is determined.... Absolute awareness [*conscience absolue*] can only be fully developed through independence and integration into the international community." The journal's editorial board (including Maurice Merleau-Ponty, one of his former professors) appended a note underscoring that his views were not their own.[82]

France, however, quickly became one of the principal sites of the kind of dialogue and diplomacy that Trần Đức Thảo dismissed. On April 25, 1946, a "friendship delegation" from the DRV arrived in Paris. Hundreds of supporters met the delegation at the airport, waving flags and bearing flowers. The priest Cao Văn Luận was among them. "Trembling with excitement and curiosity," he noted that "the French government had not sent anybody important or organized any ceremonies."[83] This absence of protocol reflected the DRV's precarious position. A month earlier, diplomatically isolated and militarily vulnerable, Hồ Chí Minh had signed an agreement recognizing Vietnamese independence within an Indochinese Federation and a French Union and allowing French forces to remain in DRV territory for five years. Another delegation, including Hồ Chí Minh, was soon expected for talks in Fontainebleau. DRV leaders hoped that diplomatic negotiations in France might garner support from sympathetic metropolitan officials, the PCF, and French public opinion. They also hoped to channel the political enthusiasm of Indochinese in France. "We must closely follow the opinions of our overseas compatriots," wrote the doctor and delegate Nguyễn Tấn Di Trọng, "for a majority are deeply dissatisfied with the preliminary agreement. We are an official delegation ... and we must behave as such." The DRV delegation "engaged with groups of all political tendencies," including the Việt Kiều Liên Minh, Indochinese CGT sections, ONS committees, patriotic associations, and even Indochinese working at the Ministry of Colonies. This left the DRV delegates well aware not only of the political diversity among Indochinese in France, but also of the doubts that many of them felt about the revolutionary government. "We need," Nguyễn Tấn Di Trọng wrote, "a committee to support Vietnamese independence with our own representative directing its political line."[84] On May 29, the DRV delegation replaced the Việt Kiều Liên Minh with a new organization, the Việt Kiều Liên Hiệp (Coalition of Overseas Vietnamese); although Liên Minh leaders remained on the central committee, the DRV official Trần Ngọc Danh took the reins.

THE DRV IN FRANCE

When the DRV's delegation to the Fontainebleau conference arrived in Paris, it was a return for many of its members: Nguyễn Tường Tam, Hoàng Xuân Hãn, Dương Bạch Mai, Phạm Ngọc Thạch, and Bùi Công Trừng had spent formative years in France as students and activists. So too, of course, had Hồ Chí Minh, officially an "honored guest" accompanying the delegation. His arrival at the airport, wrote Cao Văn Luận, "was the first time in my life that I had the honor of seeing a Vietnamese head of state received with proper diplomatic rituals, and the first time I heard Vietnam's national anthem. Many around me in the crowd were openly weeping. Even a few in the crowd living in France since 1918 who had almost forgotten how to speak Vietnamese could not help but be moved."[85] The talks ended inconclusively on September 10, doomed by the French High Commission's creation of the Republic of Cochinchina (which the delegates learned about on their way to France). As the two sides hammered away, Hồ wooed French politicians, journalists, and intellectuals, some of whom he had known since the 1920s. He also met with Indochinese political activists, students, and workers, profoundly moving many of them.[86] "From that afternoon," wrote the future National Liberation Front activist (and later anti-communist dissident) Trương Như Tảng, "I was Ho Chi Minh's fervent partisan. I had been won by his simplicity, his charm, his familiarity. His culture and burning patriotism offered me a model that I could follow in my own life.... Although I knew nothing of his past, his politics, or his actions, the force of Ho's personality had by itself created a turning point in my life."[87]

After the DRV delegation returned home, the regime continued its public relations campaigns through its new permanent delegation. Housed in a hotel at 10 rue Sainte-Anne, the delegation had a thin legal standing and little influence in Franco-Vietnamese diplomacy. But over the next several years, it extended the revolutionary state's presence and influence in France. After fighting between France and the DRV broke out in December 1946, the delegation's weekly bulletin offered one of the most detailed (though highly partisan) available news sources in France about events in Indochina; it received its information from direct communications with Hà Nội (initially via Morse code) and from the DRV's Bangkok bureau.[88] The delegation held press conferences, lectures, and cultural events, and it reached out to politicians, journalists, and intellectuals. It also founded a French branch of the Hội Cứu Quốc (National Salvation Association), a DRV front organization whose Central Committee (led by Phan Nhuận, a lawyer at the Paris bar who also translated many of Hồ Chí Minh's writings into French) used propaganda and DRV financial support to transform the patriotic associations that had spread in 1945 into Cứu Quốc chapters.[89] By 1948, the delegation had ties to journalists, intellectuals, and political organizations around Europe and in the United States (its American supporters in the 1940s

FIGURE 14. Phạm Văn Đồng's visit to the Camp Việt Nam, Mazargues, May 1946. Source: Joël Pham personal collection.

included the novelist Pearl Buck, the socialist activist Norman Thomas, director of the ACLU Roger Baldwin, and Asia scholars Harold Isaacs and Ellen Hammer).[90] It organized the travel of pro-DRV activists to student, worker, and youth congresses in Europe either affiliated with or sympathetic to the Soviet Union. It even bought a restaurant in Paris, "Hoành Sơn," run by the former sailor Nguyễn Viết Ty (Hồ Chí Minh's personal chef during his time in Paris), for some of its gatherings and events.[91]

Before Chinese and Soviet aid began to flow in 1950, the DRV delegation in France was an important part of the revolutionary state's bricolage of efforts to wage war. Delegates at Fontainebleau brought home technical manuals and textbooks, radio and audio-visual equipment, microscopes, and microfilms.[92] The DRV's French financial networks, cloaked in personal bank accounts, facilitated a traffic in piasters from Indochina exchanged at a fixed (artificially high) rate for a nearly 80 percent profit; this only ended after a public scandal in 1952.[93] The delegation oversaw the Société vietnamienne d'expansion culturelle, industrielle et technique, which bought and manufactured (at a laboratory in the Parisian suburbs) chemicals and pharmaceuticals and funneled them into DRV networks in Indochina. Nguyễn Văn Thoại, its principal chemist, came to France in 1933, earned a doctorate in chemistry, and worked as a researcher in Marseille and then at the Collège de France before being recruited to the DRV by his friend and fellow scientist Hoàng Xuân Mãn.[94] After studying film and radio in France, Thái Thúc Nha returned to Sài Gòn and opened Alpha Radio to import radio, photographic, and film equipment from France, which he redirected to southern resistance forces.[95] Trương Quảng Thụy, a member of the DRV delegation, went from Paris to Czechoslovakia in 1946 to negotiate an arms buy.[96]

The DRV delegation soon garnered broad support among Indochinese in France. Trần Đức Thảo, Hoàng Xuân Mãn, Hoàng Xuân Nhị, Võ Quý Huân and other leaders of the former Việt Kiều Liên Minh became important figures in the delegation, though under the authority of imported militants (Trần Ngọc Danh, Hoàng Minh Giám, and Dương Bạch Mai) unquestionably loyal to the DRV. Bửu Hội, head of the DGI's moderate faction, also rallied to the delegation for years. So did people who had played no role in the DGI. Phạm Huy Thông had come to France in 1938 and received a doctorate in law in 1942; he was not politically active before 1945. But by mid-1946, his Liên Minh activism led him to be chosen as Hồ Chí Minh's personal secretary for the Fontainebleau conference.[97] Nguyễn Văn Chí, thanks to his resistance activities and his marriage to Françoise Corrèze (then editor of *L'Humanité*), became a crucial liaison between the DRV delegation and leftist intellectuals like Louis Aragon and Jean Rous.[98] The respected artists Vũ Cao Đàm, Lê Phổ, Lê Bá Đảng, Lê Thị Lựu, and Mai Trung Thứ prominently supported the delegation in the 1940s: Mai Trung Thứ filmed some of Hồ Chí Minh's activities in 1946, Vũ Cao Đàm cast a bust of Hồ, and Hồ gave the resistance hero Raymond Aubrac one of Vũ Cao Đàm's canvases for his birthday.[99] Equally crucial were teachers, doctors, lawyers, and other Indochinese elites in France whose support helped the DRV maintain a moderate nationalist image. There were hundreds of people like Lê Văn Cưu, a gastrointestinal specialist and leader of mutual aid and cultural associations in Paris, or Trần Văn Khương, graduate of the École libre des sciences politiques and doctor of law, who were both indefatigable supporters of the DRV during the war.[100]

The delegation also extended the DRV's influence over Indochinese soldiers and workers in France, whose enthusiasm for independence only stoked their anger at miserable conditions in their camps and the glacial pace of their repatriation. Hồ Chí Minh visited the ONS during his tours around France in 1946. One interned at the recently-renamed "Camp Việt Nam" in Mazargues remembered that "all of the ONS in the camp came to see him. . . . Together, we expressed confidence in the revolution, opposition to colonialism, and condemnation of the war. Hồ Chí Minh assured us that with the solidarity of the entire nation, we would win."[101] By 1947, the DRV's partisans dominated the representative bodies that had emerged in the camps during the liberation. They formed Cứu Quốc chapters to spread pro-DRV propaganda and to raise money for the delegation; the ONS contributed nearly 5 million francs between April and June 1947.[102] Political violence in camps spiked as DRV propaganda became increasingly sectarian; tribunals that had once convicted Indochinese who had collaborated with Vichy now convicted the DRV's opponents. In January 1947, three soldiers executed after conviction by secret tribunals were among dozens tortured or killed in acts of political violence since the summer of 1945.[103] By mid-1947, opponents of the DRV in the Camp Việt Nam were under siege, leading French authorities to transfer some to a military barracks in Tarascon.[104] They did not extend the same courtesy to the Trotskyists, who fought to protect their hard-earned influence among the ONS. Tensions in the camp between DRV partisans and Trotskyists exploded on the night of May 15, 1948: "Savage scenes of carnage in the Indochinese camp" was how one newspaper described the clashes that left six dead and over sixty wounded.[105]

Despite its successes, the DRV delegation in Paris also keenly felt the many challenges facing the regime in the first half of the war. Its heavy-handed methods caused tension with some supporters; workers and soldiers especially resented its efforts to control their organizations and squeeze francs out of them.[106] In 1950, a pen war broke out between the editors of the ONS journal Tiếng Thợ (The Voice of the Workers) and Nguyễn Khắc Viện, who brushed off their critiques as tepid revolutionary commitment.[107] The delegation also experienced constant French harrassment, most notably the arrests of Dương Bạch Mai in 1947 and Trần Ngọc Danh in 1948. Marie-Louise Jacquier-Cachin, the daughter of one of the PCF's founders, adroitly defended them in court, and the PCF defended the DRV more forcefully after the party's ejection from government in 1947. But PCF influence, a source of tension for Indochinese communists in France since the 1920s, also caused rifts in the DRV delegation; Phạm Huy Thông was forced from his leadership of the Việt Kiều Liên Hiệp because of perceived French communist influence over him.[108] The delegation sought to improve the DRV's tenuous standing in the communist world: in 1947, it facilitated Phạm Ngọc Thạch's fruitless trip to France to appeal to the PCF and Soviet diplomats for more support. By 1949, Soviet snubs had helped give rise to an Indochinese Titoist faction in France, some of whose members joined a student and workers' brigade to Yugoslavia in 1950 (it included, among others, Saloth Sar, the future Pol Pot).[109] When the delegation dissolved in August 1949, it was due not to the French but to Trần Ngọc Danh himself, who fled to Prague and sent missives to the PCF, the CCP, and Moscow blaming the DRV's precarious position on Hồ Chí Minh's "opportunist and nationalist line."[110]

After its dissolution, the delegation continued operating as a French chapter of the Vietnam National Alliance (Hội Liên Hiệp Quốc Dân Việt Nam, better known as Liên Việt), a DRV front formed in 1946 to exert control over autonomous or competing organizations. But aside from Phạm Huy Thông and Hoàng Xuân Mãn, most of the Liên Việt leadership after 1950 was new. It included some experienced political activists like Nguyễn Khắc Viện, who returned to Paris in 1950 after years of recovery from tuberculosis in a sanatorium, where he had been recruited to the PCF by François Furet, later a famous historian and fervent anti-communist. After Phạm Huy Thông's 1953 expulsion from France, Nguyễn Khắc Viện became the lead DRV activist in France until his own expulsion a decade later. But most Liên Việt activists were part of a postwar wave of students and professionals from Indochina's urban centers to France. Lý Vĩnh Khuông (pen name Khuông Việt) was a journalist and SFIO member in Sài Gòn who went to France in 1948 as a newspaper correspondant and stayed there until 1955.[111] Trịnh Trọng Thực, who received his electrical engineering degree in Paris in 1950, led pro-DRV associations until being expelled in 1953.[112] There were more women among this group than before the war. Mai Thị Trình went to France in 1947; "I went to so many fascinating meetings and conversations about politics," she wrote, "that convinced me of the importance of the resistance movement and made me pity my poor mother and siblings living through so much hardship."[113] Phương Thị Tiệp advanced the DRV's cause at women's congresses in Hungary, Italy, and England.[114] And Nguyễn Thị Bình joined the PCF, which her father—Nguyễn An Ninh—never did.[115]

French officials banned the Liên Việt in late 1950, but the DRV's agents and supporters continued their political activity through friendship and cultural associations that were harder to ban entirely. The Vietnamese Cultural Association in France (Văn Hóa Liên Hiệp Việt Nam Tại Pháp), led by pro-DRV activists, coordinated with Vietnamese student, women's, and Catholic associations around France. There were also some pro-DRV worker associations, but by 1950 most ONS had been repatriated; the few still in France were mostly officers or interpreters, often married to French women, and working in factories, petty trades, or (less often) white-collar professions. As their lives became more French, so did their activism. "I protested the war in Việt Nam alongside French workers," Nguyen Van Thanh wrote, "but I kept my distance from Vietnamese organizations."[116] Although Chinese and Soviet support made the DRV's French networks less critical, the regime maintained them for propaganda and intelligence purposes (as it would continue to do after 1954).[117] At a moment when the DRV was implementing radical socioeconomic and cultural policies, the regime's image in France remained largely moderate and nationalist, sustained by sojourners from elite, urban milieus in Indochina whose support for the DRV stemmed largely from their opposition to the French-backed Vietnamese state. DRV officials in Hà Nội welcomed their support, but they remained uneasy about a vibrant but diverse milieu that they could not fully control. "They are mostly bourgeois," wrote a DRV official; "their attitudes are not firm or decided, and their individualism remains very strong."[118] Many who returned to the DRV from France in the 1950s would experience this suspicion firsthand.

REPUBLICAN VIETNAM IN FRANCE

Just as it was for the DRV, France was a crucial theater of noncommunist Vietnamese state-building projects during decolonization. In late April 1946, Nguyễn Văn Xuân arrived in Paris as member of an "information mission" from the consultative council of the Republic of Cochinchina, sent as a foil to the DRV's own "friendship delegation," which had arrived in France a few weeks earlier. By all measures, he embodied what the French had hoped for Indochina. Born in 1892, he became the first Indochinese to graduate from the École polytechnique. He volunteered for war in 1914; by the armistice, he was a lieutenant colonel and recipient of the Croix de guerre and the Légion d'honneur. He married a French woman, joined the Freemasons, and served in Indochina until the next war when, now a colonel, he returned to France to work in the military division of the Ministry of Colonies.[119] But Nguyễn Văn Xuân was also a member of the French Socialist Party; he supported the French High Commission's plan for an autonomous Republic of Cochinchina because he "believed that this 'new France' would implement liberal change," and he hoped metropolitan officials would be more moderate than the settler interests that controlled the new republic.[120] But the delegation's members were soon discouraged. "Ignored," wrote one of their supporters, "they wandered like beggars.... Their situation in France pained us, and we appealed to the authorities to give them an automobile and a security detail. We are ashamed for them."[121] That summer, the High Commissioner Thierry d'Argenlieu and his allies advanced a hardline separatist agenda for Cochinchina and sidelined advocates of negotiation. In November, the president of the Republic of Cochinchina, Nguyễn Văn Thinh, who had received a medical degree in France and served in the Great War, committed suicide in despair.

In November 1946, as the DRV expanded its activities in France, the government of Cochinchina proposed forming an "Official and Permanent Delegation of Cochinchina in France." Like the DRV's delegation, it was created to appeal to Indochinese as much as to the French: its goals were "to group Cochinchinese regardless of class in one organization to protect them from anti-French Vietnamese propaganda," "to provide assistance to Cochinchinese students, workers and soldiers in France," and to wage "a methodical, scientific and psychological anti-Vietnamese propaganda campaign" in hopes of "devietnamizing their compatriots."[122] The "delegation" was largely just a communication channel between pro-separatist forces in Cochinchina and their allies in France: figures like René Clogne, a chemist turned pharmaceutical entrepreneur in Indochina, and a "Mme Radigue," a métis who had once owned an opium den in Sài Gòn. They worked to control information from Cochinchina and to discredit the political campaigns in France of their rivals, like Nguyễn Văn Xuân or the publisher Nguyễn Phú Khai, both members of delegations to France in 1947. "It is dreadful to see," Xuân wrote, "how little the interests of France and Indochina matter to some.... Those in high circles are utterly resigned to those who seek to destroy all possible dialogue by sowing division."[123] Even the Republic of Cochinchina's few supporters in France found the regime's efforts tepid. In June 1947, Nguyễn Trung Trinh, later minister of the economy in the Republic of Vietnam, attended a tea in support of the new republic. After enduring jeers from pro-DRV protesters outside, he was dismayed to find that "the speaker was pathetic! His arguments were worthless.... His idiotic references and comic diversions only helped lay bare the poverty of his spirit." "France," he concluded, "was wrong to proclaim this autonomous government, which has only hindered peace by its brazen provocations."[124] In July

1946, hundreds of "Vietnamese of southern origin" in France, from engineers and doctors to hairdressers and metalworkers, petitioned the French goverment "to disavow publicly this rank political maneuver by a clique of colonialists that will only serve to sow discord and erode Franco-Vietnamese friendship."[125]

By mid-1947, with war now raging, the hopes of the French and many noncommunist Vietnamese turned to Bảo Đại, who had served as an adviser to the DRV government before a self-exile to Hong Kong in mid-1946 and a final break from the DRV. French engagement with Bảo Đại was a victory for opponents of negotiations with the DRV, who hoped to enlist the former emperor as the titular head of a unified Vietnamese state within a French Union—a postwar version of his role as a colonial emperor. But Bảo Đại also appealed to many of the DRV's Vietnamese opponents, whether they supported a unifed Vietnam in the French Union or total independence. In early 1947, a coalition of Vietnamese nationalist groups—from moderate opponents of settler interests in Cochinchina to more militant nationalist parties ejected from the DRV government—joined a political front led by Bảo Đại.[126] In early 1948, with French agreement, they formed the Việt Nam Quốc Gia Liên Hiệp (Rassemblement national vietnamien), a framework for a noncommunist state that, unlike the Republic of Cochinchina, would place Indochina's three Vietnamese regions under Bảo Đại's authority.

As this "Bảo Đại solution" emerged, the former emperor became the next in a long line of Indochinese political figures to travel to France seeking political support. In December 1947, after fruitless negotiations with the French High Commission about Vietnam's status in the French Union, he went to France for the first time since his return to Huế in 1932. In Cannes and in Paris, he and his advisers lobbied French officials and the press on the territorial integrity of a noncommunist Vietnam with autonomy within the French Union.[127] They also called for a permanent delegation in France for the nascent noncommunist state, "to follow, guide and aid its elites during their studies in France; to make Vietnam known to French of the metropole," and to "inform, guide, and advise importers, exporters and industrialists of France and Vietnam to further develop commercial exchange between the two countries."[128] The High Commissioner saw another motive behind the request: "for its advocates, the Office of Vietnam prefigures, in fact and without any doubt, the future embassy of Vietnam in France." It had been founded "to cast the state's representation as a foreign diplomatic one whose relations with France are governed by international law."[129]

Nguyễn Văn Xuân dispatched allies from Sài Gòn to head the provisional government's French office. Hoàng Văn Cơ, the former Vichy official, had resigned from the French Ministry of Information in October 1945 to start a newspaper, *Cờ Tự Lập* (The Flag of Independence), criticizing the French-controlled Republic of Cochinchina. He became a strong supporter of Nguyễn Văn Xuân during the general's travels in France and went with him to Sài Gòn to head his cabinet after he became president of the Republic of Cochinchina in October 1947.[130] His second was Trần Văn Ân, whose activity in the Indochinese press in France during the 1920s had kicked off his long career in journalism. He was an ally of the Trotskyist faction of La Lutte in the 1930s, was active in pro-Japanese circles during the war, and helped found the Việt Nam Dân Chủ Xã Hội Đảng, a socialist political party allied with the Hòa Hảo, in 1946. This led to a role in the Republic of Cochinchina under Lê Văn Hoạch, during which he became an ally of Nguyễn Văn Xuân.[131] When Trần Văn Ân went to France in mid-1948, he was, despite being minister of information, in real danger of being arrested by French authorities for his role in a failed effort to form a neutral zone to rally anti-communist forces.[132]

In March 1949, Bảo Đại signed an accord that created the Associated State of Vietnam (ASV), formally established in June. The nascent noncommunist state faced an uphill battle. The maneuvers of the new high commissioner, Léon Pignon, gave France broad authority over the ASV, and the Chinese communist seizure of power led France's Atlantic allies to accept its control over this new, second "Vietnam." Pignon's diplomatic coup left ASV officials little room to negotiate with metropolitan officials over their autonomy within the French Union, and the French public—at first largely apathetic about the war—was growing more supportive of the DRV. Rivalries within the ASV did not help. Soon after the formation of the Office of Vietnam in fall 1948, Bảo Đại began developing his own French political base to counter the "Xuânists" who controlled the ASV's Paris office. In September 1948, the lawyer Bửu Lộc (Bảo Đại's uncle) formed an office to serve as his nephew's French "cabinet" in hopes of "smothering the Paris delegation, which it persists in viewing as a 'Xuânist' organ."[133] In March 1949, it published a bulletin, "modeled exactly on that of Ho Chi Minh's agency," to counter the Office of Vietnam's pro-Xuân *L'Horizon vietnamien*. Bửu Lộc and the lawyers Nguyễn Đắc Khê and Nguyễn Quốc Định (the latter a professor in Toulouse and later Bảo Đại's minister of foreign affairs), also began drafting the ASV's constitution without communicating with the ASV's

French office.[134] Tensions grew that spring; a brawl even broke out at an ASV banquet in May.[135] But by June, the Office of Vietnam and Bảo Đại's cabinet merged into a single delegation, housed in a forty-room building on the Avenue de Villiers.[136]

On July 21, 1949, the new ASV delegation hosted a banquet at the chic Hôtel Crillon, its facade adorned with the *tricolore* and the flags of the French Union's three new Indochinese states, where the delegation's head celebrated "this new family of people and nations."[137] But until the end of the war, the ASV's French delegation, its representatives in the French Union assembly, and its regular envoys to Paris continued to challenge the French High Commission by "contacting, or seeking to influence, all French or foreign officials susceptible to help them."[138] From Paris, ASV officials sought to build more direct ties to foreign governments; its delegation, like the DRV's, was a hub for ASV participation in conferences and expositions around the world. In September 1951, over four hundred people attended a reception in Paris after the ASV's participation in the San Francisco conference that finalized peace terms with Japan. The ASV president Trần Văn Hữu glowed in describing "the warm welcome he received from President Truman" and "the sympathy Vietnam received from the world's noncommunist nations." "It is interesting to note," said a French observer, "that whether by accident or by design, not one of the orators mentioned France in their speeches."[139] Bửu Lộc's campaign in Paris for parity in bilateral relations resulted in the Vietnamese High Commission in France, a proto-embassy, in 1952.[140] That same year, ASV officials in France initiated discreet contacts with Phạm Huy Thông and Nguyên Khắc Viện to discuss possible political solutions.[141] Just like they were for the DRV, the ASV's networks in France were a crucial part of the noncommunist state's effort to achieve political independence and international legitimacy.

ASV officials worked hard to win back the hearts and minds of Vietnamese in France from the DRV. In 1949, the lawyer Vũ Quốc Thúc assessed the situation from his position at the ASV delegation. "Here, it's like feeling one's way in the dark; I want to improve the situation but don't have the means." The ASV, he felt, needed to develop print and media organs and a robust associational network in France to advance its cause.[142] Its delegation created newspapers (notably *Gió Việt* and *Tổ Quốc*); organized press conferences, Tết celebrations, receptions for students, art expositions, and concerts; lobbied French journalists; and formed cultural, student, and women's associations. Visiting delegations brought the ASV's officials and exemplary citizens to

France. These ranged from Bảo Đại and his family (who spent much time at their villa in Cannes) to a team of ping-pong stars who, "for purposes of propaganda, crisscrossed Belgium, Holland, Switzerland, Italy, and Austria" after a trip to France in 1950.[143] "Since the beginning of the month," wrote a French official in early 1950, "many Indochinese have presented themselves at Bảo Đại's cabinet . . . to affirm their support. This state of affairs seriously concerns Việt Minh leaders in Paris, as seen in the wave of threats addressed to the Vietnamese community in France."[144] In April 1950, a DRV agent assassinated the wealthy rice merchant Nguyễn Văn Tấn at his villa in Perreux—a major provisioner for the French and ASV armies, he had fled to France after attempts on his life.[145] Rumors also swirled about a DRV plan to kidnap Bảo Đại's son and hold him for ransom.[146]

Despite the DRV's efforts, the nationalist state built a diverse constituency in France. The remnants of the Duy Tân movement, devastated by the former emperor's untimely death, were assuaged by the possibility of a Bảo Đại-ruled Vietnam. The ASV also peeled away Bửu Hội and other moderates in the former DGI. By 1950, most Vietnamese Catholics in France also opposed the DRV: Trương Công Cửu, who had defended the DRV in the influential journal *Témoignages chrétiennes* before 1949, now took up Bảo Đại's cause in its pages.[147] Like the DRV, the ASV delegation received support from artistic and literary figures. The ASV's Union nationale des intellectuelles et artistes du Viet-Nam included the painters Nguyễn Sao and Vũ Gia as well as the writer Trần Văn Tùng, who set aside his fiction to write several books advancing the ASV cause while serving as its representative in the French Union assembly. The rising literary star Phạm Văn Ký also circulated in ASV circles in the early 1950s before souring on the regime.[148] More and more educated professionals also joined ASV circles as the DRV's politics radicalized. ASV networks in France also grew through regular diplomatic, military, commercial, educational, and medical exchanges between France and ASV-controlled regions during the war: hundreds of officials of the new ASV state came to France for formations in the ministries of finance, public works, and foreign affairs, as well as in the military.[149]

As the ASV's structures extended into France, so did the networks of the regime's diverse and vocal noncommunist opposition. They included disaffected former ASV insiders like Hoàng Văn Cơ, Trần Văn Ân, and other allies of Nguyễn Văn Xuân. They also included Nguyễn Bảo Toàn, an ally of Trần Văn Ân's and an influential anti-communist politician who broke with Bảo Đại during the Provisional Central Government.[150] In October 1949, after Bảo Đại's allies took over the ASV delegation, this group formed the Parti socialiste unioniste vietnamien in Paris. Its focus was "industrial, agricultural, and commercial questions relating to society, especially those touching on Vietnam's internal affairs and its relations to the French Union and to the world." It hoped to gain influence among Vietnamese workers in France, who despite their dissatisfaction with the DRV had shown little interest in its rival; its headquarters was a Vietnamese workers' association, and its central committee included a metalworker, a foreman, an electrician, and a typographer.[151] Its activities intensified when Nguyễn Văn Xuân came to France to continue his political activities after being forced out of the ASV. In June 1950, he laid a wreath and spoke at a memorial to Indochinese soldiers executed by German soldiers for defending the town of Beaune, leading a French official to observe that "the general does not remotely consider his political career to be over."[152] In late 1950, the party was renamed the "Parti républicain vietnamien" to reassure American officials that it was not too far to the left.[153] In early 1951, Nguyễn Văn Xuân's former minister of information, Nguyên Văn Trí, was arrested at the Swiss border with copies of a party manifesto that he hoped to present to UN officials in Geneva.[154] Thereafter, some of these anti-Bảo Đại forces would gravitate toward the networks of another of Bảo Đại's long-standing opponents: Ngô Đình Diệm, whose brother Luyện had begun building up the family's own French political networks in 1948.[155]

Bảo Đại's opponents in France also included the anti-Stalinist Vietnamese left. Most were Trotskyist militants who had fled to France to avoid Stalinist assassination. Lư Sanh Hạnh, Ngô Văn Xuyết, and Nguyễn Văn Nam arrived in France early 1948. The first two joined the fervent but fading anti-DRV campaigns of France's Indochinese Trotskyist group; Lư Sanh Hạnh left France in 1954 but Ngô Văn Xuyết would remain a core member (with Đặng Văn Long, Hoàng Khoa Khôi, Hoàng Đôn Trí, and Nguyễn Được) of the Vietnamese group of the French Trotskyist party, a force in diaspora politics for decades. Nguyễn Văn Nam drifted away from Trotskyism, spending much of 1949 and 1950 bicycling around war-torn Europe and then working at a factory and as a bookkeeper while writing a doctoral thesis about immigration in England.[156] Hồ Hữu Tường, who had renounced Trotsksyism a decade before, also returned to France with his family in 1949. In Paris, he collaborated with Nguyễn Ngọc Bích (Henriette Bùi's longtime romantic partner), exiled to France in 1946 for his role in participation in the southern resistance, whose gradual disillusion with the DRV culminated with his expulsion from the regime's French organ in 1952 for "deviationism."[157]

In January 1948, a group of Khmer students in Paris, among them several future leaders of the Khmer Rouge, wrote to the minister of overseas France to protest that the writer Trần Văn Tùng, "in his book *Annam* . . . consecrated entirely to his country, chose to publish pictures of the temples and statues of our holy city of Angkor, without mentioning that this oeuvre and heritage of our ancestors belongs to Cambodia." "In the face of such claims," they continued, "we suffer the same painful reaction as a French person would feel if a writer included pictures of Paris in a book devoted to Germany."[158] In the colonial era, Khmer and Lao had been far more ambivalent about "Indochina" than many Vietnamese.[159] Nevertheless, the letter reflected a newly powerful nationalism not in evidence among the few Khmer and Lao who had been politically active in France before 1945. "Indochina" had clearly meant something to the Laotian Thao Nhouy Abhay, almost expelled from France in 1931 for signing a petition protesting the repression after Yên Báy.[160] It did too to Prince Norodom Yukanthor, who in 1916 had sought an alliance with Cường Để and in 1925 had campaigned with Bùi Quang Chiêu in France calling for a reform agenda for Indochina.[161] Sơn Ngọc Thành, the most prominent Khmer nationalist during the 1940s and 1950s, had been part of Indochinese political circles while studying in Montpellier and Paris from 1925 to 1933.[162] Perhaps the most "Indochinese" of them all was the Lao "Red Prince" Souphanouvong, who had studied in Hà Nội's Lycée Sarraut before continuing his education at the Lycée Saint-Louis and Ponts et chaussées in Paris, where he was first drawn to radical politics. After his studies, he worked as an engineer in Tonkin and Annam and married a Vietnamese woman.[163]

Much like during the colonial era, Lao political networks had only a faint presence in France during the First Indochina War. The Lao Student Association, the first explicitly Lao association in France, was formed only in 1949; three years later it had only thirty members.[164] Drawn from royal and elite families, these students of law, medicine, and political administration, to a man (there were no women members) supported the Lao monarchy; as their Sûreté biographical notices all read, "his presence has never been noted in Indochinese nationalist milieus in the Parisian region."[165] The group's founder, Oudom Souphanouvong, was the only Laotian to earn a French medical degree before independence (with regrets to the fictional Dr. Siri Paiboun).[166] The only visit of a Lao head of state to France during the war was

Sisavang Vong's four-day trip to Paris in 1949, fifty years after his studies at the École coloniale, for the formation of the Associated States of Indochina.[167] Laos, unlike Vietnam and Cambodia, never had a permanent delegation in France; its European diplomacy was largely in the hands of Ouroth Souphanouvong (who earned a law degree in France in 1933), its representative at a few postwar conferences in Europe.[168] And Lao communist networks emerging in the early 1950s had essentially no presence in France; they were likely not much more than two of Prince Souphanouvong's cousins, students in Strasbourg, whom the Sûreté reported had "close relations with the PCF and attended weekly meetings of a Marxist study group," as well as having ties to pro-DRV Vietnamese.[169]

Khmer sojourners in France after 1945, however, would have enormous legacies for their new nation. The Fraternité Khmer, the first explicitly Khmer association in France, was founded in fall 1945. Its leaders were among the first in a wave of Khmer elites coming to study in France after the war: French officials counted 120 of them in 1945.[170] The Fraternité Khmer's founder, Sisowath Youtevong, had received his doctorate in physics in Montpellier in 1941 and become active in the SFIO in 1944; in 1945 he wrote a book with Léopold Sédar Senghor about the future of the French empire. The group's other leaders had French university degrees: Chhean Vam (philosophy), Thonn Ouk (history), and Nginn Karet (geography).[171] France's small Khmer community had closely followed the tumultuous events in their country in 1945: a Japanese coup in March placing the young King Sihanouk at the head of an independent state, followed by an anti-royalist coup led by the foreign minister Sơn Ngọc Thành. On October 15, returning French forces arrested Sơn Ngọc Thành and sent him to Sài Gòn for a trial. The leaders of the Fraternité Khmer returned to Cambodia in 1946 and helped to form the Parti démocrate, the main legal opposition to the monarchy; the party soon began sending Khmer students to study in France. The new leaders of the Fraternité Khmer included Thiounn Thieunn, Thiounn Thioum, and Thiounn Mumm, whose grandfather had studied at the École coloniale and became palace minister; Thiounn Mumm would be the first Cambodian graduate of the École polytechnique. Ea Sichau (École des hautes études commerciales), Touch Kim (École de chimie appliquée), Mau Say (Faculté des lettres), and Keng Vannsak (Faculté des lettres et philosophie, who also invented the Khmer typewriter in 1952), were other prominent members.[172]

These budding anti-royalist Khmer activists were immersed in a range of political milieus in France. One of the most influential was one coming to be known as "Vietnamese." Many Khmer students who had been inspired by the August Revolution lived at the Maison des étudiants de l'Indochine and ate at the restaurants of Indochinese mutual aid associations dominated by Vietnamese (some of them front organizations of the DRV's Paris delegation). Their activism began to reflect these influences; the Sûreté noted that the DRV delegation "assured liaisons between Vietnamese and Cambodians and provided directives for its [the Fraternité Khmer's] anti-French activities," and that it was "at the urging of their Marxist Vietnamese comrades" that Khmer activists "chose to abandon their association to form a new, specifically student association," the Association des étudiants khmers (AEK) in December 1947.[173] The new AEK continued to have close ties to pro-DRV groups, attending their demonstrations and diffusing their tracts. The spread of violence in Cambodia at first reinforced this, by exposing the limits of the Parti démocrate's parliamentary tactics and forging ties between the DRV and factions of the Khmer Issarak armed resistance, news of which came to France via a pipeline of Khmer students coming to Paris (and, perhaps, from the DRV delegation).

But like in Indochina, Khmer-Vietnamese ties in France soon showed signs of strain. Although some of the early Khmer political activists in France later became Marxists (most notably Thiounn Mumm), before 1951 most were avowed nationalists, several of whom were deeply engaged in recovering what they saw as a lost national essence. Keng Vannsak, for example, "tried to uncover pre-Buddhist, pre-Sanskrit layers of Cambodian vocabulary and culture" in his philological work.[174] Their enthusiasm for the DRV began to fade as they chafed at Cambodia's irrelevance in France's Indochinese political circles. "The French press uses 'Vietnam' and 'Indochina' as though they are interchangeable," the AEK's bulletin *Khemara Nisut* (which circulated in Cambodia) bemoaned in 1949; Mey Mann "recalled trying to explain to a group of French students at a holiday camp one summer that Cambodians formed a separate nation, with their own culture and traditions which were nothing to do with Vietnam's."[175] In 1949, the AEK stopped celebrating the Khmer New Year at the Indochina Pavilion because "it was built in the Vietnamese style" and, as one activist said, "the national problem is instinctively linked to the cultural problem."[176] One important influence on these activists was Sơn Ngọc Thành, convicted of "high treason" in 1947 and sentenced to twenty years hard labor but sent instead to exile at a "lax *résidence surveillée* at Poitiers, where he studied at the *Faculté de droit*" and "traveled freely to Paris once a month."[177] Thiounn Mumm, one of many Khmer to visit Sơn Ngọc Thành in Poitiers, remembered seeing editions of the works of Marx and Lenin on his shelves with the pages still uncut.[178] As the 1950s dawned, political debates among Khmer in France remained squarely nationalist—political versus armed struggle, or how an alliance with the DRV would affect the cause of Cambodian independence.

Cambodia's entry into the Associated States of Indochina in 1949 made France a site for the diplomatic agenda and state-building projects of a regime increasingly under the control of King Sihanouk, who owed his crown to Vichy and his political power after 1945 to d'Argenlieu and Pignon. The officials of this French-aligned Khmer state, just like some officials of the Khmer monarchy had done during the colonial era, came to France for formations in administration, military, finance, or industry. Neal Phleng studied medicine in Paris before the war; in 1949, as minister of public health, he returned to Europe for conferences on world health issues.[179] Srey Saman had studied at the École de cavalerie in Saumur as a young officer in the Cambodian army; in 1951, now a lieutenant colonel, he returned to France for training at the École d'état-major.[180] Dozens, perhaps hundreds of officials of the Sihanouk regime had similar trajectories. The French hoped, just as they had in the colonial era, that metropolitan sojourns would help solidify the new Cambodia's relationship with France. However, Sihanouk's representatives in France clashed with their French partners over everything from the political contacts of the Cambodian officials in Paris to the style of the Maison du Cambodge (built in 1950 at the Cité universitaire).[181] In 1953, Sihanouk went again to France to kick off a full-fledged diplomatic offensive in the high council of the French Union in Paris and the press; by the end of the year, facing a deteriorating war effort, France gave in.

The Sihanouk regime found some supporters in AEK circles in France. Some had been partisans of the Parti démocrate: they included Vann Molyvann, a student at the École nationale supérieure des beaux-arts who later became perhaps the greatest Khmer modern architect, as well as Duoc Rasy, later a prominent jurist. Sihanouk's supporters met in associations like the Amicale des cambodgiens de France (1950) or the Communauté khmer d'outre-mer (1953).[182] They faced off against Khmer students hostile to the monarchy. When Sihanouk came to France in 1949 to inaugurate the Associated States, he invited AEK leaders to the festivities at the Hôtel Crillon, where a student, "tipsy thanks to the libations on offer, said loudly that everybody thought badly of Sihanouk, impugning his dandy life as unbecoming of a king. His friends calmed him, fearful for their scholarships."[183] But when Sihanouk stripped power away from the Cambodian parliament in 1952 and early 1953, the AEK pilloried him with demonstrations and broadsides in its bulletin (widely read in Cambodia); an open letter in its final issue proclaimed, "We will judge Sihanouk in the public square." Furious, the king sent his adviser Penn Nouth to Paris to discipline the AEK's leaders, but they received him not as "son excellence" but as "monsieur," and soon employed harsher words like "traitor." The Sihanouk regime then revoked the scholarships of many members of the AEK leadership and pressured the French to dissolve the group, which they did in early 1953.[184]

Many of Sihanouk's opponents in the AEK remained supporters of either the fading Parti démocrate or of Sơn Ngọc Thành and the Khmer Issarak. But communism was spreading in their ranks. Ieng Sary, who came to Paris in 1950, embodied the rise of radical leftist politics in Cambodia after 1945. A disciple of Sisowath Youtevong and member of a socialist faction of the Parti démocrate, he had led a strike at the Lycée Sisowath in which students discarded school uniforms for red kerchiefs; he is said to have first encountered *The Communist Manifesto* among a pile of books his mentor brought back from France.[185] Many critical figures in Khmer communism—Khieu Samphan, Hou Youn, Son Sen, Rath Samoeun, Hu Nim, Sien An, and the sisters Khieu Thirith and Khieu Ponnary—studied in Paris between 1949 and 1952. They had varying histories of leftist activism before arriving, but all were aware of growing Vietnamese communist influence on the armed resistance to Sihanouk. The DRV had supported Khmer Issarak factions since 1948; in 1950, to counter the creation of the Associated States of Indochina and growing defections to the Sihanouk regime, it spearheaded the formation of the Khmer national front and a resistance government, followed in mid-1951 by the Khmer People's Revolutionary Party, led by Sơn Ngọc Minh, a Khmer-Vietnamese Buddhist lay preacher who joined the ICP in 1945. In late 1950, a Khmer political study group began to meet in Keng Vannsak's apartment in Paris. Although the group "eschewed political labels" and "did not claim to be either Left or Right," it was split between Sơn Ngọc Thành's partisans and supporters of an alliance with the DRV.[186] The latter faction soon developed ties to the PCF, which helped Thiounn Mumm, Thiounn Prasith, Sien An, Rath Samoeun, Hou Youn, and Ieng Sary go to the "World Youth Festival for Peace" in Berlin in August 1951, led by the World Federation of Democratic Youth, a pro-Soviet group. There, the activists "learned from Viet Minh delegates about Cambodian participation in the struggle against France" and they "returned excitedly to Paris with brochures that included photographs of Sơn Ngọc Minh and a sample of the Issarak five-towered flag."[187]

By 1952, the pro-communist faction dominated the AEK, now under the leadership of Hou Youn. As he strengthened the association's ties to the PCF and anti-colonial organizations, Thiounn Mumm oversaw the transformation of Keng Vannsak's political study group into the Cercle d'études marxistes khmer, organized in secret cells along the model of a revolutionary party. The group read Marx, Lenin, and Mao and engaged in criticism and self-criticism sessions, and some of its members joined the PCF. One was Saloth Sar, previously a student at a mediocre technical school in the provincial town of Kompong Cham, and thus an unlikely recipient of the scholarship that had brought him to study at the École française de radio-électricité. Sar was a regular but marginal presence in Khmer political circles in Paris after his arrival in late 1949; he was among Sơn Ngọc Thành's supporters in Keng Vannsak's political study group and seems only to have turned toward communism in late 1951, after the AEK's political center of gravity had shifted in that direction. His limited education and poor French made him an outlier among brilliant cosmopolitans like Keng Vannsak and Thiounn Mumm. After 1975, as Pol Pot, he would rule over a revolutionary regime whose core traits were autarchy and radical xenophobia, particularly toward Vietnam. But in Paris in the early 1950s, Sar and his fellow future Khmers Rouges, whatever their misgivings about Vietnamese influence (often exaggerated in ex post facto accounts of their early political lives), remained fervent internationalists, awash in the utopian culture of the postwar revolutionary left, who hoped to, in the language of the AEK program of action for 1953, "establish the Khmer people's strong and entirely equal bonds with the Soviet Union and other popular and new democracies, in particular the People's Republic of China and the Democratic Republic of Vietnam."[188] In June 1954, as the Geneva conference drew to a close, the AEK bulletin *Reaksmei* offered its full-throated support of Indochinese revolutionary unity, hailing Sơn Ngọc Minh's "free Cambodia" for having "liberated a million inhabitants" and affirming "no imperialist objectives on the part of democratic Vietnam" in its direction of Khmer resistance forces.[189] As these Khmer communists returned to Cambodia during the 1950s, their revolutionary dreams still had a distinctly Indochinese ring.

NINE

Returns

"THE OTHER NIGHT, IN MY DEEPEST SLEEP, I had a fantastic dream. It was dark, dark inside my head, when suddenly images appeared and I saw myself, I don't know how, walking through the exit of the Messageries maritimes in Saigon." Making his way down the street, the dreamer feels two hands on his shoulders, and he turns to face an unfamiliar old man. "What do you want," the dreamer asks, irritated. "Don't you recognize me?" says the old man; "I am Luu Van Phu, your old classmate." "You are mocking me, sir. My school friend Luu Van Phu died in 1920." "I'm not dead, my friend, and I'm fifty years old like you." "You're crazy," the dreamer says; "I'm only twenty-two." "Ha!" the old man replies; "look in the mirror and tell me if you have the face of a young man." "What year is it?" asks the dreamer, now shocked. "Today is June 17, 1955," the old man replies. "We have not seen each other for thirty-five years. Remember that two years after school ended, you left for France." "I stayed for eighteen months," says the dreamer. "It was twenty-nine years, my friend," replies the old man.

The old man explains that during those twenty-nine years, despite three failed uprisings against French rule, the illegal Workers Party had gained strength and was now on the verge of another uprising. The population, now widely literate, was boycotting French and Chinese goods and denouncing colonial injustice and abuse. "All he revealed to me in this conversation," the dreamer thinks, "confused my ideas to a point that I entirely lost my already tenuous sense of reality. What paths had he and I taken? I didn't know." The two wander the streets, stopping into several political rallies in enormous meeting halls, packed with humbly-dressed crowds. In a thunderous culmination, one speaker predicts that "the workers will rally to us . . . and all parts of society will join against our common and intractable enemy who has made us suffer for nearly a century." "Let's go," says the old man, "we've heard the essentials. . . . Another time, my friend, we'll walk together like today. But now let's go home, it's late." And then the old man pushes the dreamer so hard that he wakes up.

The dreamer was Trần Văn Thạch; the bed in which he awoke was in Toulouse in 1927, where he had been studying psychology and sociology for a little over a year. He would spend three more years in France, earning degrees in Toulouse and at the Sorbonne, forming a newspaper (*Journal des étudiants annamites*), and being elected president of the Congrès des étudiants indochinois and of the Association générale des étudiants indochinois. But he eventually went home. His degrees had broadened his professional prospects, and he hoped to pursue his journalistic and literary ambitions in Indochina's burgeoning press. His wife and son were with him in France, and they felt far from family. And he had experienced a political awakening that, although forged in French radical-socialist milieus, remained irreducibly oriented toward Indochina. In early 1930, as he had in his dream three years earlier, Trần Văn Thạch walked through the door of Messageries maritimes in Sài Gòn—home forever, and forever changed.[1]

Like Trần Văn Thạch, nearly all Indochinese sojourners in France went home. By the end of 1920, only two hundred war workers and interpreters—out of nearly one hundred thousand who had served in the Great War—were still in France on legal labor contracts (some remained illegally, but not many and not for long).[2] The war also produced only two hundred and fifty legally recognized marriages between Indochinese men and French women in France.[3] Of the nearly eight thousand people classified as "Asian subjects" in France in 1931, fewer than one hundred were naturalized.[4] The Depression sharply reduced Indochinese sojourns to France, and most who were there returned before the start of the Second World War: in 1941, the Paris police estimated there were only two hundred Indochinese in the capital.[5] Although the Second World War and the First Indochina War brought new waves of sojourners, few even in this final wave stayed in France; in 1954, only a quarter of the roughly eight thousand Vietnamese in France were naturalized.[6] France's communities of Indochinese origin date almost entirely from post-colonial migrations that began with decolonization in 1954 and intensified after 1975. In short, of the perhaps two hundred thousand Indochinese who sojourned in France during the colonial era, virtually all returned home.

Powerful forces pushed them back. During the interwar era, metropolitan France's migration regime "developed systemic means to enforce distinctions between citizens, nationals, and foreigners," it watched over colonial subjects more closely than virtually any other population in France, and it was relatively effective at enforcing its prescribed limits on Indochinese sojourns.[7] Any personal crisis that drew bureaucratic scrutiny—unemployment, lost or expired identity papers, expulsion from school, homelessness—could also end a sojourn prematurely. So could arrest. Despite a few political expulsions, expulsion for things like theft or assault was far more common, even if repatriations were often delayed as metropolitan and colonial officials fought over who had to pay the steamship fare. Whatever the circumstances of a sojourn's bureaucratic end, it could be painful. "Pain crossed my heart, and involuntary tears spilled out of my eyes," Nguyễn Mạnh Tường wrote about awaiting a steamship in Marseille. "How could I leave France? I left it nevertheless, but I was not obeying my own desire."[8]

Personal situations, ambitions, and desires to return were often equally powerful. "Could you not consent to letting me stay in France?" a laborer in the Great War wrote to his father; "I could make my life here."[9] His father refused, making him one of many whose obligations to parents, siblings, spouses, children, and friends pulled them home. But many others wanted or simply expected to return. As diverse as sojourners were, most imagined their time in France as temporary and saw a return to Indochina as the natural order of things. "So, today we leave France," wrote Phạm Quỳnh on August 11, 1922. "However attached one might become to a foreign land, the sadness one feels when it's time to leave is never equal to the sadness of leaving one's home. From this point, each day is one day closer to the home the soul yearns for and awaits."[10] And many felt an acute desire to leave. Most of the soldiers and laborers in the Great War shared the hopes of the one who wrote of his desire "to return home to Indochina to live as a simple *nha-que* ... to once again pass happy days, free of worries in our Indochinese countryside, from this day forward this is my one and only desire."[11] Most soldiers and laborers in the next war felt the same way. "I wanted to leave," one remembered. "Stay for what? With whom?"[12]

"For five years," wrote the journalist Phan Văn Gia, "I was often hungry, cold, and homesick for my family. As the days and months sped by, I studied so I could return home." But when it was finally time to leave, melancholy gripped him. "In a place like Paris," he wrote, "the longer you're there, the more attached you become; the better you know it, the more difficult it is to forget." He thought of the freedom of walking about unknown and unremarked, stopping at a café or a bookstore here and there, and the small

FIGURE 15. Banquet honoring Phan Châu Trinh before his return to Indochina, Paris, May 1925. Source: Véronique Baverstock personal collection.

kindnesses that had lightened hard days. Friends came to bid him goodbye at the train; as they waved, "their mouths smiled, but their hearts were filled with pity." As Paris's lights faded into the night and his fellow passengers slept, he felt alone. "I remembered this; thought about that. What was I doing at this time yesterday? Thinking about the past made me sad; thinking about the future did too." Unlike his wealthier friends, he could not just "start a newspaper, create a business or build a factory" in Indochina; his family needed his help, and he feared his situation would be difficult. On the steamship, Phan Văn Gia was reminded of colonial life's petty brutalities. He was ejected from the first-class deck for sitting there without a proper ticket; a white passenger shoved him out of a spot along the ship's rail as he tried to catch a glimpse of Singapore. When the ship reached Sài Gòn, despite having the necessary paperwork, the police detained him and five others for questioning. A fight broke out when a Sûreté agent shoved aside one of the passengers' mothers as they were being dragged to the station; the six were arrested, detained for days, and later sentenced to jail or fines. "Our compatriots who have traveled in the metropole for a long time," wrote the journalist Nguyễn Văn Bá, "are used to the agreeable regimen of liberty, equality and fraternity. Their mistake was to have been unable, upon returning to their country, to suddenly change their mentality!"[13]

Few experienced such dramatic return voyages; most actually had little to say about a trip that was often less novel the second time. Phạm Quỳnh offered only a few desultory remarks about the weather during the journey home in his travelogue; Tùng Hương skipped it entirely. Their narratives both end with a celebratory meal with friends or family on hand to greet them at the port before setting off for home. But the effects of sojourns in France were immediately palpable. Many were suffused by nostalgia for the life they had left. "I am miserable here and my deepest desire is to return to Paris," wrote the Khmer prince Sisowath Watchayavong in 1920; "the people and things here disgust me . . . in this savage country all is sad and dreary."[14] "I will never overcome my sadness at having left Paris," wrote Nguyễn Xuân Bái; "I'm here with my compatriots but their mentality is so different that I feel completely out of place."[15] Habits had changed. Some families were shocked by their loved ones' new interpersonal norms (handshakes or even hugs) and casual, often irreverent forms of speech.[16] Nguyễn Văn Vĩnh was one of many who, after returning, never abandoned his Western suits and leather shoes.[17] Nguyễn Tường Tam's friends ribbed him for now only liking music when it was accompanied by a clarinet.[18] Nguyễn Vỹ wrote about the returned daughter of a court minister in Huế who rejected rice for bread and chopsticks for a knife and fork.[19] Many who had spoken no French when they left now spoke it a bit, or a lot. Many had also learned to read: French officials estimated that 20 percent of Indochinese in France during the Great War learned basic reading and writing in quốc ngữ during their service.[20] And all had stories to tell; about rollicking cafés and cabarets on broad boulevards, assignations and star-crossed lovers, shared garrets in Latin Quarter hotels, triumphs and failures in school, mangled landscapes and bodies. These *retours de France*, visible even in elite urban milieus, were more so in rural areas, where, as Tonkin's Resident Superior said of returnees from the Great War, "on all occasions, whether festivals, ritual feasts, or gatherings at the communal hall, they do not miss a chance to tell their neighbors what they saw in France."

"Doubtless," the Resident Superior continued, "the effect of this is hard to establish: it remains in the shadows, working slowly in a manner only detectable in certain circumstances."[21] This final chapter explores how Indochinese sojourns in France, from the conquest era until decolonization, shaped both sojourners themselves and the societies they returned to. Doing so, as the Resident Superior noted, presents thorny challenges of causality: hard to disentangle from other factors within the frame of an individual life, and far more so on a broader scale. But this chapter nevertheless argues that the French sojourns explored in this book were a critical force in the making and remaking of colonial society over time. Indeed, it is difficult and at times impossible to fully understand many aspects of Indochina's modern history without French sojourns: conquest-era diplomacy; the intersections and tensions between early colonial rule and Indochinese reformism; new forms and ideas about education; the emergence and development of journalism and modernist literature and the arts; new regimes and repertoires of labor; and the transformation of political life, among others. Indeed, the new habits that family and friends first noticed were but the most visible signs of deeper transformations. As the days and weeks became months and years, Indochinese marked indelibly by their French sojourns would in turn indelibly mark their own societies after coming home.

FROM CONTACT TO CONQUEST

When Mighê Văn Phụng finally returned to Tonkin in 1703, sixteen years after he had left, it was the end of a journey "from partisan Jesuit catechist to defender of the apostolic mission." Well aware of the new realities of ecclesiastical politics after his years away, the former Jesuit novice—one of the first two people we know of from the future Indochina to set foot in France—affirmed the sole authority of the apostolic missionaries in his church, in which he now held the status of "teacher catechist" (thầy giảng).[22] When they returned to Tonkin in 1787, the catechists John Thiều and Paul Cuyền had also "gained valuable experience of the European world and, more importantly, had returned as ordained priests." They too had shifted their allegiance from the Jesuits to the MEP.[23] The Bishop d'Adran's efforts to spiritually conquer Prince Nguyễn Phúc Cảnh after their return to Cochinchina did not bear similar fruit: though Nguyễn annals state that he at first "refused to kneel in front of the ancestral altar and painted crosses across the faces of Buddha statues," he drifted away from Catholicism before his sudden death in 1801 at the age of twenty-two.[24]

Indochina's formal creation in 1887 ended a generation of efforts by the Nguyễn dynasty to use embassies and envoys to France to stave off colonial rule. Minh Mạng had died before his embassy to Europe returned in 1841, and his successors were less receptive to the reformist ideas their envoys brought back from France. Phạm Phú Thứ's formal report of the 1863 embassy was the most detailed and insightful account of a western country ever produced by a Nguyễn official; Tự Đức promoted him, and the report shaped the emperor's decision two years later to send Nguyễn Trường Tộ to France to purchase equipment and books and hire French advisers.[25] But the French invasion of western Cochinchina in 1867 ended that mission prematurely and emboldened anti-reformist voices in the court; after Nguyễn Trường Tộ's return, the materials he brought back were put in storage and plans to open a school for studying Western machinery were shelved. Nguyễn Trường Tộ continued to send petitions for reform to the court until his death in 1871, but to no avail.[26] When the 1878 embassy report "noted more enthusiasm than acceptable for European technical achievement and customs in the report on aspects of European institutions and culture," Nguyễn Tăng Doãn's rank was downgraded and Nguyễn Thành Ý was removed from service.[27] Nguyễn Hữu Thơ, also part of that embassy, remained in service as a customs inspector but he retired shortly thereafter to Đà Nẵng, where he opened a private school to teach French.[28]

The Nguyễn court's formal diplomacy in France fared poorly. In 1867, the shock of the French invasion of western Cochinchina led Phan Thanh Giản, head of the 1863 embassy, to take his own life. "Our pain was profound and unconsolable, our blood mixed with tears streaming from our eyes," his two sons wrote from exile in Toulon to explain why they joined the anti-French resistance in 1867.[29] Nguyễn Tăng Doãn died two years after his reprimand from Tự Đức, and Nguyễn Trọng Hiệp retired soon after the 1894 embassy returned. "Always sure of the generous sentiment animating the representatives of France toward my country, I would have liked to continue to be useful," he wrote to Governor General Paul Doumer; "but *Hélas!* I am old and worn out, and I no longer feel capable of any effort!"[30] The Khmer and Lao monarchies, more receptive to a French protectorate as a bulwark against its larger neighbors, had made no such diplomatic efforts; neither of the two members of the Khmer royal family who waged quixotic campaigns in Paris for colonial reform ever returned to Cambodia. After sojourns in Belgium and Singapore, Prince Yukanthor lived in exile in Siam from 1913 until his death in 1934. And Duong Chakr, exiled from Paris to Djelfa in the Algerian Sahara (his wife declined to accompany him), died there in 1897 "of the combined effects of climate, boredom, and alcoholism."[31]

As French sojourns during the conquest era marked the twilight of some careers in imperial service, they helped give rise to others. "Having seen Europe, he knows most of its nations well," wrote the Đồng Khánh emperor in an 1886 homage to Trương Vĩnh Ký. "He knows their languages and their writings; he possesses their manners and their cultures."[32] After returning from the 1863 embassy, the young interpreter worked closely with French officials as editor of the official bulletin *Gia Định Báo,* instructor at the Collège des interprètes, director of the Collège des stagiaires, envoy to Tonkin in 1876, and advisor and intermediary to Đồng Khánh as the French consolidated their control over the Huế court. He held this critical position thanks partly to a friendship with the French Resident General Paul Bert that had begun twenty-three years before during his visit to Paris. Tôn Thọ Tường's star also rose after his return; he worked as a district chief in Vĩnh Long and later for French consular officials in Tonkin before his death in 1877. He is remembered today for defending the colonial regime in a poetic exchange with the scholar and poet Phan Văn Trị.[33] Two similarly influential figures in early protectorate rule in Cambodia had studied at the École cambodgienne in the 1880s: Peich Ponn, later a minister of education and war, and Oknya Keth, later president of the Khmer Council of Administration.[34] The École coloniale, the Permanent Mission, and colonial scholarships to French schools set off hundreds of other, more ordinary careers in the colonial and protectorate bureaucracies.

But far from all Indochinese imperial officials who sojourned in France returned as loyal subalterns. Phạm Phú Thứ's time in France helped shape a reform program he advanced in the service of the Nguyễn dynasty: during the 1870s, he implemented bureaucratic, agricultural, and commercial reforms; wrote and translated studies of law, the natural and physical sciences, navigation, and mining; and opened a French school in Hải Dương.[35] After Tự Đức downgraded his rank, Nguyễn Thành Ý returned to France to study at a technical school in Toulon, bringing a group of students with him. He rejoined the Nguyễn administration as the consul to French Cochinchina, then as the governor of Bình Định. In 1881, Tự Đức tapped him and Nguyễn Trọng Hiệp to lead another embassy to quell the diplomatic crisis with France, but Rivière's invasion in early 1882 rendered it moot.[36] One recent study cites Phạm Phú Thứ, Nguyễn Thành Ý, and Nguyễn Trường Tộ—whose sojourns to France helped to shape their visions of reform—as three of the four principal predecessors of the modernization movement (*phong trào Duy Tân*) in official and literati circles in Annam and Tonkin at the turn of the century.[37]

The influence of French sojourns on Indochinese reformism only intensified after the consolidation of protectorate rule. Thân Trọng Huế returned to Huế in 1895 after seven years at the École coloniale. His reform proposals (notably to abolish the triennial exams) ran him afoul of other officials in the Nguyễn administration in Annam, and he left to direct the Trường Hậu bổ in Hà Nội and for other posts in Tonkin's administration. Phan Khôi remembered that Thân Trọng Huế brought voluminous journals to Tonkin, one for each of his years in France, in which he had written his observations and passages from books he had read.[38] These may have been among the modernist texts that Phan Châu Trinh borrowed from Thân Trọng Huế during their many exchanges in Huế in 1903–04. "He was so fascinated by them," Huỳnh Thúc Kháng wrote, "he would even neglect eating and sleeping, and from that point on his ideas were completely renewed."[39] Hoàng Trọng Phu, who studied at the École coloniale with Thân Trọng Huế, would work to "undo the hostile prejudices to artisanal and commercial professions" among Nguyễn officials by instituting classes in commerce at the Trường Hậu bổ and promoting light industry as governor of Hà Đông.[40] Both became leaders in the reformist Société d'enseignement mutuel du Tonkin (Hội Trí Tri) and the Association pour la formation intellectuelle et morale des annamites (Hội Khai Trí Tiến Đức), which they cofounded in 1919. Both groups, if politically quiescent, were critical intermediaries in the transmission of modernist thought to Indochina. After returning from the 1889 embassy, Miên Triện "closed his doors and wrote for years," producing ten volumes. Decades later, his daughter, the journalist and social reformer Đạm Phương, let Phạm Quỳnh read them. He begged to publish them "for people to learn of the reformist ideas of one of our great Confucian scholars," but they remained in the family's possession.[41]

Returnees from France entered, and shaped, the fertile and combustible debates over colonial modernization and reform between 1905 and 1908. After the Permanent Mission, Trần Tấn Bình and Nguyễn Năng Quốc gave conferences to hundreds of people around Tonkin at meetings of the Société d'enseignement mutuel, outlining a program of economic modernization grounded in rural industry, scientific agriculture, banking and credit, and expanded education.[42] Tonkin's Resident Superior found the conferences "violent," reporting that Nguyễn Năng Quốc expressed "ill will and opposition" at Colonial Council meetings.[43] Both men joined the Tonkin Free School (Đông Kinh Nghĩa Thục). So too did Nguyễn Văn Vĩnh, who had returned from the 1906 exposition having "decided once and for all that he would have to play a leading role in the modernisation of Vietnamese culture and society."[44] Trần Trọng Kim returned from the École coloniale and Melun's École normale des instituteurs to teach at the Trường Hậu bổ and the Lycée du Protectorat; he soon became one of the colony's most influential pedagogical reformers. In 1907, Thân Trọng Huế, Nguyễn Văn Vĩnh, and Trần Trọng Kim helped found Tonkin's Du Học Bảo Trợ Hội (Society for the Encouragement of Overseas Study, soon renamed the Society for the Encouragement of Study in France to distance it from the Đông Du movement). It lasted for three decades and supported the study of dozens of Tonkin's elites in interwar France.

Though far fewer, the sojourns of Khmer elites in early twentieth-century France had similar effects. After returning from the École cambodgienne in Paris, Oknya Keth founded the Franco-Khmer Mutual Education Society in 1905 before returning to France with the Permanent Mission. The society (modeled after the Société d'enseignement mutuel de Tonkin, which he learned about from the Tonkinese with whom he traveled to France) became a hub for a parallel, if more modest effort by Khmer officials to introduce Western ideas and techniques into the protectorate economy and administration.[45] Son Diep and Thiounn Sambath, two of the society's most important patrons, had been to France for the 1900 exposition (Son Diep) and for King Sisowath's visit (both men); their sojourns helped them rise to the top of the protectorate administration, where they oversaw "the emergence of a secular literati tied not to kings or individuals but to the state administration."[46]

As colonial officials had hoped, some Indochinese royals who sojourned in France became useful political partners. Prince Sisavang Vong, among the only Lao students at the École coloniale when he studied there in 1901–02, became king three years after his return; his reign was notable for its near-total harmony with French authorities. The Khmer prince Sisowath Monivong had stayed to study at the Saint-Maixent military academy after traveling with his father to the 1906 exposition. He served briefly in the French army before returning to Cambodia and rising in its military ranks. He helped recruit Khmer soldiers and workers for the Great War and reportedly "preferred to be addressed by his army rank rather than his royal title" after becoming king in 1927.[47] Two of his sons studied at Saint-Cyr and volunteered when war broke out in 1939, but upon Monivong's death in 1941, the French passed over his preferred son Monireth for Norodom Sihanouk, a young prince from a rival royal line whom Governor General Jean Decoux saw as more dynamic and more pliable—a fateful decision for modern Cambodia.[48] Bảo Đại, whisked off to France after his ascension in 1926, returned only in 1932, when the French hoped choreographed tours and appearances they planned for him might help quell political unrest. But Bảo Đại, plagued by "internal destablization born of years of colonial instrumentalization," turned to a passive resistance to French manipulation that evolved into a vision of royal nationalism with no French partners.[49] The same could be said of the Lao prince Phetsarath Ratanavongsa, who studied at the École coloniale and at Paris's elite Lycées Lavoisier and Louis-le-Grand before returning to a career in protectorate administration. His modernist vision for the kingdom and his later opposition to French rule made him perhaps the most important figure in the rise of Lao political nationalism.[50] In the end, years in France did not make these Indochinese royals—both critical figures in the region's decolonization—into the allies the French had hoped for.

THE *RETOURS DE FRANCE* AND INDOCHINESE INTELLECTUAL LIFE

When hundreds of Indochinese students began streaming to France after the Great War, the expectations they embodied were weighty indeed. "From our end of the Empire," wrote Đào Đăng Vỹ, "we palpitated with hope, we awaited the prodigies. A new dawn would rise with the return of the young saviors!" "Their return," he continued, "was rather dreary." Đào Đăng Vỹ was one of many who, by the early 1930s, saw the ubiquitously known *retours de France* as avatars of colonialism's disappointments. "It seems like for some," he wrote, "simply having 'returned from France' constitutes for them a profession" of performative personal habits, condescending attitudes, and self-satisfied stories "about what they saw . . . or hadn't seen at all. But that doesn't matter, for you are uninitiated, and you don't know any better!"[51] Nguyễn Văn Vĩnh bemoaned the sacrifices made on behalf of youth who returned "with new needs that this country cannot satisfy, with lifestyles that make our country's simple life seem boring and insipid and our habits seem ridiculous."[52] Cao Văn Chánh mocked French degree holders, recounting his encounters with "doctors in literature who don't know literature, doctors in law who are ignorant of the law."[53] "Why did these people go play at study?" asked an anguished observer. "Why didn't they understand their duty to the nation? Why couldn't they establish themselves and build our future, despite the privilege of having studied in the heart of civilization?"[54]

Few of the *retours de France*, however, had seen themselves as a vanguard of national renewal when they left. In 1931, the Cochinchina administration collected data about students from the region who had studied in France since 1920. Eighty percent originated from outside of greater Sài Gòn. Of those who had returned to Cochinchina by 1931, 71 percent were classified as "landowners or in families," with 9 percent classified as "functionaries." In short, the wave of students from Cochinchina who studied in France during the 1920s mostly came from and returned to provincial landholding and white-collar milieus; most seem to have pursued an education in France to enter or rise in colonial administration, or for motivations unrelated either to a profession or to the cultural and political movements of the time (described either as for personal experience or for social climbing, depending on the observers' degree of cynicism).[55] These educational sojourns, as important as they may have been personally, did little to transform colonial life.

Some of the *retours de France*, however, had not gone to France casually on the back of a booming piaster, but via scholarships from the colonial administration or an overseas study association, which only top students in elite schools could hope to win. Their success in France became a source of cultural pride: newspapers regularly trumpeted their grades or admissions to an elite university, and their triumphs stood out among the feckless and wayward returnees. "Three such prodigies," *Tribune indochinoise* wrote of Hoàng Xuân Hãn, Phạm Duy Khiêm, and Ngô Đình Nhu, "deserve utmost praise, and we must not miss a chance to say that they are true examples for their fellow countrymen."[56] As *Phụ Nữ Tân Văn* wrote of Nguyễn Mạnh Tường's two doctoral theses, "it is certain that all feel a collective emotion, that if a youthful race can harness its intelligence and study hard, then it can accomplish all under heaven."[57] The uproar surrounding Phạm Duy Khiêm's decision to volunteer for the Second World War, which provoked reactions from pride to incredulity to condemnation, only makes sense in the context of the academic success in France that had made his life a contested parable. French officials knew how important these returnees were. "I consider it of the highest importance that they receive a welcome appropriate to their education and achievements," wrote the governor general. "If abandoned, many would be lost, whereas with direction, they could become precious collaborators."[58] Many took positions in the French or Nguyễn administrations or taught in secondary schools for which they were vastly overqualified.[59] But some achieved a renown in colonial intellectual and scholarly life that made them prominent figures in the postcolonial era.

Among humanists and social scientists, none was more influential than Nguyễn Văn Huyên, who returned with two doctorates from the Sorbonne in 1935 and later became the first full Indochinese member of the École française d'Extrême-Orient. During the decade before the 1945 August Revolution, his immensely important work in history, religion, folklore, and other fields, grounded in a "research program that mobilized written, oral, and epigraphic sources for the study of local traditions," made him the first Indochinese scholar of this stature to argue for the autonomy and dynamism of a society he saw oriented as much toward Southeast Asia as China, core assumptions of postcolonial national histories in the region.[60] He and Trần Văn Giáp (a fellow assistant at the École des langues orientales in Paris) were also crucial in curriculum reforms to develop Asian humanities in colonial schools in the early 1940s.[61] Dozens of other Indochinese who received advanced degrees in France before 1945 wrote studies of aspects of precolonial economy and society that would become part of the "colonial corpus" that later Vietnamese scholars would use heavily for empirical material and data.[62] Ngô Đình Nhu, the first Indochinese graduate of France's national school of archival science in 1938, returned to a position in the Service des archives et bibliothèques de l'Indochine, becoming its deputy director after the March 1945 Japanese coup and, briefly, its director after the August Revolution. His work as an archivist, understandably overshadowed by his political career, was critical in organization and preservation projects for precolonial and colonial documentation.[63]

Although few French-trained humanists and social scientists held such prominent official positions before the revolution, many remained extremely influential in these fields. At *Thanh Nghị,* arguably the most influential Indochinese journal of the late colonial era, scholars trained in France (the lawyers Phan Anh, Nguyễn Mạnh Tường, Vũ Văn Hiến, and Nguyễn Ngọc Minh; the geographer Nguyễn Thiệu Lâu; the polymath Hoàng Xuân Hãn; as well as Nguyễn Văn Huyên and Trần Văn Giáp) were the journal's main figures on historical, socioeconomic and political questions. Of the twenty-three authors of more than ten articles in *Thanh Nghị,* six had earned advanced degrees in France.[64] Graduates of French universities filled the ranks of teachers at the colony's elite schools: Nguyễn Văn Huyên (history at the Lycée du Protectorat), Nguyễn Mạnh Tường (French literature at Protectorat), Phạm Duy Khiêm (French and classical languages at the Lycée Albert Sarraut), Lê Thành Ý (French and Vietnamese at Sarraut), Nguyễn Thiệu Lâu (geography at the Lycée Khải Định), Nguyễn Huy Bảo (philosophy at Khải Định), and Lê Văn Kim (law at the Université indochinoise) were among the many who joined Bùi Kỷ and Trần Trọng Kim, who had distinguished careers at Hà Nội's École de pédagogie after returning from France. Nearly all Indochinese who practiced law during the colonial era were trained in France, as the *licence* was not available in the colony until 1933 and the doctorate (required to argue in French appeals courts) not available until 1951.

Returnees from France were especially prominent in scientific and technical fields in the late colonial era, especially in medicine and public health: of the 252 Indochinese who held a doctorate in medicine before 1945, nearly half (112 out of 252) had earned it in France.[65] They returned to important roles in an expanding and professionalizing colonial medical sector. A French doctorate made many leading specialists in their fields in Indochina by the late 1930s: Nguyễn Xuân Nguyên (mycosis), Hoàng Tích Trí (epidemiology), Đặng Vũ Hỷ (venereal disease), Trần Quang Đệ (anatomy), Phạm Bá Viên (urology), Nguyễn Văn Hương (typhus), and Hoàng Gia Hợp (anesthesiology), among others. Sonn Mam, one of only two Khmer with a French doctorate in medicine before decolonization and one of the only Indochinese to study psychiatry in France, directed the Biên Hòa asylum from 1930–39 before becoming director of Cambodia's first asylum in Ta Khmau.[66] Until the first doctoral recipients from the Université indochinoise in the late 1930s, returnees from France were virtually the only Indochinese who researched at the colony's Pasteur Institutes and published in medical journals. Indochinese with French medical degrees were also among the few who met the strict requirements for opening a private medical practice or medical laboratory. Some became important conduits of medical knowledge to the public. In 1923, Trần Văn Đôn founded *Khoa Học Tạp Chí* (Scientific Review); the coeditor of its medical section was Nguyễn Văn Thinh, who had opened a private practice after returning from France. Trần Văn Đôn wrote widely about medicine and public health in interwar journals, including over sixty articles in *Phụ Nữ Tân Văn* alone. Nguyễn Văn Luyện, another returnee in private practice, published manuals on hygiene and founded *Bảo An Y Báo* (Medical Review) to explain the science of medicine and public health to broader audiences.[67]

Indochinese trained in France also produced and popularized scientific and technical knowledge. A second *Khoa Học Tạp Chí*, published in Hà Nội from 1931–40 by the agronomist Nguyễn Công Tiểu, was arguably colonial Indochina's most influential scientific journal. Many of its core contributors had French degrees: Hoàng Xuân Hãn, Nguỵ Như Kontum (physical sciences, who like Hoàng Xuân Hãn also contributed to *Thanh Nghị*), Nguyễn Xiển (atmospheric science), Đặng Phúc Thông (engineering), and Nguyễn Văn Luyện (medicine). Hoàng Xuân Hãn's 1942 *Scientific Vocabulary* (*Danh từ khoa học*) would be republished for decades. "It is clear," wrote Cù Huy Cận, head of the DRV's Ministry of Agriculture in 1945, "that the journal *Khoa Học* and especially *Danh từ khọa học* prepared us to teach scientific fundamentals and technique at the university level after independence."[68] Returnees from France also filled many of the most prestigious teaching positions in scientific and technical fields then available to Indochinese: among them were Vũ Văn An (chemistry at the Lycée du Protectorat), Phạm Tỉnh Quát (mathematics at the Lycée Pétrus Ký), Phạm Đình Ái (physical sciences at the Lycée Khải Định), Nguyễn Dương Đôn and Nguyễn Thúc Hào (both mathematics at Khải Định), Tạ Quang Bửu (mathematics and English at the Lycée Providence in Huế), Ngụy Như Kontum and Nguyễn Xiển (both physical sciences at the Lycée du Protectorat).[69]

But for all their prominence and influence, late colonial life also limited, at times even demeaned, these intellectuals. "What we dream of," one *retour de France* told Đào Đăng Vỹ, "is French intellectual life. What we want more than anything is that intellectual community that is lacking here. Here, there is no ambiance, not enough liberty. The material is insufficient, life is not comfortable enough for us to give ourselves to our studies."[70] Most returned to an economic crisis; the French administration and private industry were cutting positions, which only intensified the racial glass ceilings in hiring and salaries. In one famous example of many, Hoàng Xuân Hãn was limited by law to a mediocre position in the Department of Public Works despite his degree from France's top engineering school; even an intervention by the emperor Bảo Đại was for naught.[71] It was only during the Second World War that Indochinese were allowed to teach at Hà Nội's medical school; Hồ Đắc Di, its only full professor before the revolution, was also the only Indochinese surgeon with full privileges in a colonial hospital. After he had returned from France, "my dreams about 'saving humanity' and 'helping society' were utterly shattered," he remembered; "Vietnamese doctors were simply lackeys, no more, no less."[72] Henriette Bùi, who returned in 1935 to become chief physician at a maternity hospital in Sài Gòn, never forgot criticisms of her in the French press or the fact that she earned ten times less than a French colleague with a lower degree.[73] Many Indochinese with French doctorates in law were blocked from entering the colonial judiciary despite (really, because of) their elite degrees. Some turned to legal activism: Phan Văn Trường, Lê

Văn Kim, Huỳnh Văn Chính, Trịnh Đình Thảo, Dương Văn Giáo, and Vương Quang Nhường defended political activists in some of the colonial era's most high-profile trials.[74] Nguyễn Hữu Thọ, later a president of communist Vietnam, was Lê Văn Kim's assistant during the late 1930s before opening his own practice.[75] For figures like these, the 1945 revolution seemed to offer not only independence but "a historic opportunity to fully pursue their vocation," a desire that would mesh seamlessly with the desperate need for expertise in Indochina's postcolonial regimes.[76]

LITERATURE AND THE ARTS

"On this trip to France," Phạm Quỳnh had written on the eve of his departure in 1922, "I intend to observe all interesting things, and when I return, I will compile them into a book to benefit my fellow citizens. But it will be a long time before I return; as such, I will keep a journal during the trip and will write in it every day." Though "all of its contents would be accurate," he felt that the journal "would contain no literary reflections; just materials I will use to write my book after I've returned."[77] But even before his steamship reached France, he had reconsidered: he sent the journal's first entries home for publication in *Nam Phong*. Unwilling to be outdone, his fellow traveler and rival editor Nguyễn Văn Vĩnh did the same for his readers in *Trung Bắc Tân Văn*. Their accounts, particularly Phạm Quỳnh's, became some of the most influential works of modern Indochinese travel literature (*du ký* in Vietnamese, *nirās* in Khmer), one of several genres of Indochinese literature and art indelibly shaped by French sojourns.

Phạm Quỳnh was far from the first Indochinese to chronicle a French sojourn; official accounts of Nguyễn embassies to France reflect a "tradition of accounts of official missions to China . . . prepared for the emperor which aims to 'inform,' in as objective a manner as possible—thus its composition as an extremely scrupulous daily chronicle—on official greetings, protocol, receptions, audiences," while the accounts of two Khmer embassies to France before the Great War reflect the influence of nineteenth-century Thai diplomatic accounts.[78] Despite classical conventions and forms—Tang-era regulated verse (*Đường luật*) in classical Chinese, *pad bāky prambīr* in Khmer—they were innovative: Nguyễn accounts included neologisms for technical, administrative, and geographic terms that remained in use for decades.[79] By the late nineteenth century, these accounts began to reflect some of the literary and commercial qualities typical of modern travel literature. Trương Minh Ký's account of his French sojourns, the first *du ký* written in quốc ngữ, reflected a quotidian sensibility and "a lyrical sense of self and bold personality."[80] These texts, serialized in *Gia Định Báo* and published as books, were also the first *du ký* with something resembling a modern reading public. Perhaps reflecting their appeal, accounts of travel in France by Nguyễn Trọng Hiệp (head of the 1894 embassy) and Son Diep (the Khmer delegate to the 1900 exposition) were published in 1897 and 1901, followed in 1916 by a quốc ngữ translation of Tôn Thọ Tường's account of the 1863 embassy.[81]

Interwar accounts of French sojourns used "the prerogative of the traveler" to advance competing claims about the colonial condition.[82] Wealthy, Francophile sojourners whose *du ký* dominated the genre in the 1920s (Phạm Quỳnh, Nguyễn Văn Vĩnh, Bùi Thanh Vân, and Lê Văn Đức) cast travel to France as a process of self-actualization and enrichment through encounters with monuments, institutions, and cultivated interlocutors. Their comparisons (the Sorbonne is like Hà Nội's Temple of Literature, Versailles is like Huế's imperial city) lay bare their desire for civilizational belonging, even as nagging feelings of inferiority and self-deprecation lace their narratives. "What a shame," wrote Phan Khôi in a blistering review of Trần Bá Vinh's account of the 1931 exposition, "that authors of these accounts so often avoid things or are dishonest.... Reading this, I found no useful ideas whatsoever."[83] Reflecting the rise of realism (*hiện thực*) and reportage (*phóng sự*) in Indochinese literature and journalism, *du ký* emerged in the 1930s that stressed the alienation and anomie of French sojourns, often as political critique. Nhất Linh's *Đi Tây*, the most famous of them (probably a parody of Phạm Quỳnh's 1922 text), echoed other accounts of poor, bitter students in France from the decade like Tùng Hương's journal, serialized in *Nam Phong* in 1932.[84] These texts satirized discourses about civilizational difference to critique "colonial underdevelopment."[85] Some did so by exoticizing the ordinary and humble realms of French society (Nguyễn Công Tiễu and Nguyễn Tiến Lãng's portraits of rural France) while others described French slums, alcoholism, and disease to challenge claims about essential difference (Đào Trinh Nhất, writing under the pen name Phạm Vân Anh).[86] In *De Hanoi à La Courtine* (1941), a fictionalized account of his war service, Phạm Duy Khiêm used France's bleak, unsparing wartime landscape to justify his choice to volunteer for a war he saw as "above and beyond ordinary quarrels."[87]

French sojourns also shaped Indochinese Francophone literature. Some of the genre's most prominent figures had returned to Indochina in the late

1930s, and their returns had been hard. Phạm Duy Khiêm returned in 1935: "separated from the intellectual life he loved and the friends he had made . . . life in an extended family all living under one roof, the petty jealousies, the disagreements about money, the constant visitors and the gossip were unbearable."[88] "First glimpse of the homeland: black rocks under a grey sky," wrote Nguyễn Mạnh Tường in 1936; his two collections of autobiographical fiction and essays published in Hà Nội in 1937 laid bare the anomie he felt after his return.[89] In France, he wrote, Indochinese youth had "tasted all that human genius can bring to life on earth: art, elegance, spirit" and "thus learned to love, and to know true happiness and suffering." "Returned to Indochinese soil," he went on, "it encounters the deception of unsuspected realities. Its vitality is sapped by a skillfully conducted politics of denigration."[90] The Catholic modernist Pierre Đỗ Đình Thạch "had hoped to find a more stable material situation" when he returned to Indochina in 1934, only to find that "the colonial climate of the time prevented him from realizing his wish."[91]

These writers sought refuge in the networks of two new literary journals, published in the unlikely cities of Vinh and Nha Trang. *Nouvelle revue indochinoise,* modeled after *Nouvelle revue française,* brought together French literary observers of Indochina and, in the words of its co-founder Christiane Fourier (a teacher and writer), "Annamites seeking to express the 'crisis of growth' of their generation" in French. "Language is the exterior form of thought, not thought itself," she wrote; "through this form we want to discover an original spirit, an intact soul."[92] Raoul Serène, co-founder of *Les Cahiers de la jeunesse,* was a scientist working at Indochina's Oceanographic Institute; his literary interests grew from his ties to Paris's Catholic literary and intellectual circles. *Cahiers,* modeled after the personalist journal *Ordre nouveau,* sought "the elaboration of a new order, based on human values . . . concerned with man's entirety, not only the homo economicus and homo politicus of our ideologies." Its editors saw it as "the organ of a team and group of French and Annamites unified by a shared sense of work to accomplish and goodness to conquer. . . . We are with those who love life and believe in it, with those who have in their heart the desire not only to preserve but extend certain human values."[93] The journals were genuinely cross-cultural. *Nouvelle revue*'s cofounder was Nguyễn Đức Giang, a former student of Fourier's who became a teacher in Vinh. *Cahiers*'s coeditor was Cung Giữ Nguyên, who had graduated from the Quốc Học and become a teacher in Nha Trang before losing his job in 1930 for political reasons. He then became a journalist and writer; after 1933, probably due to his conversion to

Catholicism, he began writing in French.[94] Both journals published many well-known French observers of Indochina (Roland Dorgelès, André Baudrit, René Crayssac, Albert de Pouvourville, Raphael Barquissau, and Louis Malleret, among others), but they were most significant as a crucible for the final colonial-era generation of Indochinese Francophone writers.

Indochinese sojourns in France helped shape these journals' colonial humanism. Nguyễn Mạnh Tường and Phạm Duy Khiêm wrote reviews, essays, and fiction for *Nouvelle revue,* including excerpts of some of their first works (the former's 1937 *Sourires et larmes d'une jeunesse,* the latter's 1942 *Légendes des terres sereines*). Pierre Đỗ Đình Thạch, who very likely had known Raoul Serène in Paris's Catholic intellectual circles, wrote essays for *Cahiers,* which also underwrote the publication of his masterwork, the long poem *Le Grand tranquille* (1937). It also published essays on cultural exchange by Nguyễn Huy Bảo, Phạm Quang Bách, Tạ Quang Bửu, Nguyễn Thúc Hào, and other French returnees in Huế intellectual life. *Nouvelle revue* and *Cahiers* also published Indochinese still in France, like the journalist Tào Kim Hải, and even a article by the former Duy Tân emperor, then desperately trying to leave his exile in Réunion for Paris. The journals were also a home for Francophone writers who had not yet been to France but would end up there during the First Indochina War, often for good. Some, like Nguyễn Tiến Lãng, were already well known. But for Trần Văn Tùng, then an anonymous functionary, appearing in *Nouvelle revue* led to his discovery and celebration by French audiences. The most significant was Phạm Văn Ký, who studied at the Lycée du Protectorat before becoming a journalist, editing *L'Impartial* and *Gazette de Hué.* He wrote two novels (one serialized, the other lost) before his breakthrough with *Une voix sur la voie* (1935), a collection of poems heavily influenced by Mallarmé that received a colonial literary prize. He published in *Nouvelle revue* and *Cahiers* before leaving for Paris in 1939 for good to study literature at the Sorbonne and religion (with Marcel Mauss) at the Institut des hautes études chinoises.[95]

French sojourns also marked modern theater and performing arts in Indochina. In a letter to his friend Phạm Duy Tốn from the 1906 colonial exposition, Nguyễn Văn Vĩnh "shared the excitement of seeing El Cid on stage. He explained the impact that seeing this play live on stage had for him, insisting that it was vastly more effective than just reading it."[96] Soon after retuning, he produced the first Vietnamese translations of French drama; the first performance of modern spoken theater in Indochina (April 20, 1920) was his version of Molière's *Malade imaginaire.*[97] One of the genre's most popular works in interwar Indochina was Nam Xương's *The Frenchman from Annam*, a satire about an Indochinese student who returns from France thinking that he is European.[98] Nguyễn Ngọc Cương, who learned to love French theater and popular songs while a student in Paris, became one of the most influential figures in Cochinchina's reform theater (*cải lương*), directing productions and introducing the genre to audiences in Annam and Tonkin and (during the 1931 and 1937 expositions) in France. His biggest star during those tours was Năm Phỉ, whose enthusiastic reception in Paris generated breathless press coverage in Indochina and helped to convince critics of *cải lương*'s artistic value—the trip itself became the subject of a *cải lương* production.[99] Indochinese film "stars" in France, though limited to one-dimensional roles as "oriental" characters, were celebrated in Indochina as vanguards of a modern cultural form. As *Đuốc Nhà Nam* wrote of Foun Sen, "there is not a person in Annam not applauding in the face of a Vietnamese woman with such talent."[100] Hoàng Thị Thế's parentage made her even more compelling: some newspapers speculated that she would leave Paris for the greener pastures of Hollywood.[101] But others blamed her for cultivating the myth, widespread in the French press, that she was the daughter of the last emperor of China. "One would imagine being in a fairy tale," *L'Annam nouveau* sneered, "if a few regrettable realities were not there to remind you of life on earth."[102]

Indochinese fine arts also bore powerful traces of French sojourns. Lê Văn Miến had left for France in 1888 as one of the first three Indochinese students at the École coloniale, destined for a career in imperial administration. But he returned with beaux-arts training and became the first Indochinese to paint portraits in a Western neoclassical style. Though his subjects included the Thành Thái emperor, he could not support himself through art and became a teacher of French and art at the Quốc Học (where he taught the future Hồ Chí Minh), and later the director of the Quốc Tử Giám (Imperial Academy) in Huế.[103] Huỳnh Đình Tựu, who studied at Marseille's École des beaux-arts thanks to a chance encounter with a French patron, became the first Indochinese director of the colony's first French fine arts school, founded in Gia Định in 1913, where he taught some in the next generation of Indochina's modern artists who studied and exhibited in France. Like Năm Phỉ and Foun Sen, fine artists who went to France were celebrated as Indochinese cultural ambassadors. "We must enthusiastically support our country's talented artists," proclaimed *Đuốc Nhà Nam* in 1931, "to make their worth known to the country and world alike."[104] Even those who would spend the rest of their lives in France (Vũ Cao Đàm, Lê Phổ, Mai Trung Thứ,

Lê Thị Lựu, and Lê Bá Đảng) have been claimed as part of the Vietnamese "national" canon. But those who returned more immediately infuenced art in the region. Lê Văn Đệ returned to Indochina in 1938 after spending much of the 1930s in France. He became a leading figure in Hà Nội's Foyer de l'art annamite, which valorized Indochinese artists in the face of the dismissive attitudes of the EBAI's new French director.[105] In 1945, soon after helping design the stage where Hồ Chí Minh declared Vietnamese independence, he moved to Sài Gòn.[106] In 1954, he became the first director of the Republic of Vietnam's National School of Art (Trường Quốc gia Cao đẳng Mỹ thuật); he also designed the new country's flag.

JOURNALISM

It was at the 1906 colonial exposition in Marseille that Nguyễn Văn Vĩnh discovered "the modern printing press, the newspaper and their potential firepower on the cultural front."[107] As he recalled thirty years later, "Every day, I watched that scene of activity with hungry eyes—the humming presses, reporters dashing off to gather news. I became infatuated with the newspaper business. All day I came over to learn, asking this and that, and the editor [of *Le Petit Marseillais*] explained everything to me very kindly."[108] In 1907 he cofounded *Đăng Cổ Tùng Báo,* whose "unsparing auto-critique of Vietnamese culture . . . focus on economic development and on raising educational levels" and "the question of women's rights" made journalism part of Tonkin's reformist milieus.[109] Although it soon closed, Nguyễn Văn Vĩnh was just getting started. In 1911, Albert Sarraut recruited him as part of a project to use the vernacular press to create support for colonial reforms. Sarraut underwrote two journals—*Đông Dương Tạp Chí* (1913–19) and *Trung Bắc Tân Văn* (1915–45, Tonkin's first daily newspaper)—and turned them over to Nguyễn Văn Vĩnh. The journals became a platform for the ambitious editor to advance a broad cultural agenda, aligned with but not reducible to colonial reforms, centered on promoting quốc ngữ, translating and popularizing modern thought for the public, and finding solutions to social problems. Other returnees from France in Tonkin's modernist circles, Trần Trọng Kim and Thân Trọng Huề among them, wrote for both journals.

Nguyễn Văn Vĩnh's French sojourn was just the first of many to shape Indochinese journalism. In Cochinchina, Sarraut tapped Nguyễn Phú Khai and Bùi Quang Chiêu (whose educations in France made them seem more trustworthy) to lead the government-backed *Tribune indigène*.[110] But return-ees from France soon became leaders in Sài Gòn's oppositional journalism. After Nguyễn An Ninh's return, he drew on "editorial forms and techniques used by two popular anticonformist contemporary French papers: *L'Oeuvre* and *Le Canard enchaîné*" in founding *La Cloche fêlée*, the epicenter of oppo-sitional journalism in Sài Gòn in the early 1920s.[111] Phan Văn Trường, who also first wrote for newspapers in France, was one of *La Cloche fêlée*'s main contributors after his return in 1923. When it shuttered in 1926, Phan Văn Trường recast it as *L'Annam;* it published articles from Indochinese in France and reprinted articles from *L'Humanité*.[112] Diệp Văn Kỳ's entry into journal-ism was with *Việt Nam Hồn* during his legal studies in France; after return-ing, he bought a stake in *Đông Pháp Thời Báo* (Indochina Times) and set out to make it "a national mass-circulation paper worthy of its Parisian models—*grands journaux d'information.*"[113] After it closed in 1928, Diệp Văn Kỳ founded *Thần Chung* (1929–30). Some of the most prominent journalists in his newspapers had written for Indochinese newspapers in France, including Bùi Công Trừng, Đào Trinh Nhất, Trịnh Hưng Ngẫu, Hoàng Tích Chu, and Phan Văn Hùm. In 1928, Nguyễn Phan Long started the first Constitutionalist newspaper in quốc ngữ, *Đuốc Nhà Nam* (Flame of the South), to broaden the party's reach. Its editors also first cut their journalistic teeth in France: Dương Văn Giáo as a contributor to *Việt Nam Hồn* and editor of a French edition of *Tribune indochinoise,* and Trần Văn Ân as founder of the student journal *L'Annam scolaire.*

French sojourns also shaped the new journalism in Hà Nội. Hoàng Tích Chu's "efforts to introduce modern journalism into Tonkin grew out of an intense admiration for the French press," particularly the Parisian *Quotidien*'s lucidity and elegance, that grew during his time in France. "When we return home," he had told Đào Trinh Nhất, "we must strive to revolutionize our prose in this way."[114] He got his chance as editor of *Hà Thành Ngọ Báo,* which he and Đỗ Vân (who studied printing in France) helped make "the first quốc ngữ daily in Tonkin to follow journalistic practices and maintain production qualities consistent with metropolitan standards," including "a spare and straightforward style that quickly became somewhat of a standard for the northern Vietnamese press" and a Western-style layout "with narrow, vertical rectangular columns beneath eye-catching headlines."[115] A few years later, Nguyễn Tường Tam returned to Hà Nội and founded a satirical journal modeled after *Le Rire,* which he had read avidly in France.[116] He and some collaborators took over a moribund journal, *Phong Hóa* (Customs) and founded a publishing house. The nascent literary collective styled itself the Self-Reliant Literary Group (Tự Lực Văn Đoàn). Until 1940, *Phong Hóa* and the group's other journal, *Ngày Nay* (These Days) became a home for seminal modernist literature and poetry, as well as "foundational contributions to divergent intellectual and cultural fields such as fashion, applied design, architecture, theater, and political reporting."[117]

Indochinese newspapers published in France were also part of the colony's newspaper world. *Le Paria* may or may not have first come to Indochina in Nguyễn An Ninh's luggage, as his daughter claimed, but it did circulate there: in early 1924 Nguyễn Thế Truyền requested three to five hundred copies to send to the colony.[118] There is little evidence of *Le Paria*'s influence in Indochina, but there is more for *Việt Nam Hồn* and its later incarnations. In summer 1926, the Sûreté found thousands of copies in steamship mail deliveries, in packages of five hundred.[119] In just two months in late 1927, the Sûreté in Indochina confiscated over two thousand copies of *La Nation annamite*.[120] Many more came in individual letters. "*Việt Nam Hồn,*" wrote a student in Lyon to his brother, "has a character that newspapers in our own country do not have, because we students are brave and express ourselves freely, without fearing anybody."[121] Indochina's radical newspapers republished articles from *Việt Nam Hồn* while moderate ones like *L'Echo annamite* and *Đông Pháp Thời Báo* ran concerned editorials about its influence.[122] Though these may have been overstated, *Việt Nam Hồn* did circulate among some future political luminaries. In Sài Gòn, Jeune Annam activists read it with *La Cloche fêlée* and *Tiếng Dân*.[123] And budding communist activists Ngô Đức Trì and Tôn Quang Phiệt read it at the Collège de Vinh.[124]

The French realms of Indochina's "newspaper village" also helped revive the colonial radical press in the mid-1930s. *La Lutte*'s leadership first cut their teeth as political journalists in France. Trần Văn Thạch's career as an editor began with the *Journal des étudiants annamites* in Aix-en-Provence, which Huỳnh Văn Phương and Phan Văn Chánh wrote for; thereafter, all three joined *La Résurrection*, Tạ Thu Thâu's first editorship. Hồ Hữu Tường's decades as a journalist began in France as coeditor (with Phan Văn Hùm) of the Trotkyist *Tiền Quân*. Nguyễn Văn Tạo's first editorship was of *Lao Nông*, the PCF's quốc ngữ newspaper. *La Lutte* was without a doubt, in Daniel Hémery's words, "formed in the school of nationalist and communist journalism in France."[125] After falling out with Tạ Thu Thâu, Huỳnh Văn Phương cofounded *Le Travail* in Hà Nội, modeled after *La Lutte*.[126] Nguyễn Văn Tiến and Trịnh Văn Phú, *Le Travail*'s publisher and editor, had entered journalism in Paris working under Nguyễn Văn Tạo at *Lao Động*.[127] Vũ Liên, also involved with *Le Travail*, had helped run the PCF's quốc ngữ newspapers for sailors (*Bạn Hải Thuyền*) and students (*Tân Học Sinh*) in France; he later became a major figure in the Popular Front-era press in Hà Nội, writing for or editing *Công Dân, Nông Công Thương*, and *Phụ Nữ Thời Đàm*, and helping lead a campaign to form a press union for Tonkin.[128] French sojourns also shaped the nascent vernacular press in Cambodia and Laos. Two of the three founders of *Nagarravata*, the first newspaper in Khmer, had formative experiences in France: Sơn Ngọc Thành studying law, and Pach Chhoeun as a translator during the Great War. So too did two of the three leaders of *Lao Nhay*, the first newspaper in Lao: Somchine Nginn (at the École coloniale) and Thao Nhouy Abhay (who studied art in Paris).[129]

WAR AND WORK

In the aftermath of the Great War, monuments honoring Indochinese who had died in France began to dot the colonial landscape, extending outside of Hà Nội, Sài Gòn, and Phnom Penh into provincial cities. Most were commissioned by Souvenir indochinois, an association that had purchased a village hall (*dinh*) brought to Marseille for the 1906 colonial exposition, and later refashioned it as a war memorial in the Jardin colonial in Nogent-sur-Marne near Paris. Memorials built in Indochina echoed its hybrid pastiche of temple, pagoda, and stele forms mixed with French elements; they listed French and Indochinese war dead on the same memorial, but separately. Souvenir indochinois was not solely an official initiative; most of its members were Indochinese, and it received donations not only from elites eager to curry favor, but also from ordinary people whose small gifts, a real sacrifice, reflected the meaning and solace they found in the memorials. Some even supported memorials in France; in May 1920, the town of Carency in the Pas-de-Calais gratefully thanked the people of Cần Thơ for their support.[130] But the memorials' solemnity and fixity belied the war's unfolding legacies and divisions: they drew criticism for cultural artificiality and political triumphalism, and virtually none would survive the wars that would later ravage Indochina.

The experiences of the nearly one hundred thousand Great War returnees mirrored the complexities of these memorials. Đỗ Hữu Vị, the son of a prominent Cochinchinese family who had died at the Somme, returned home a colonial martyr, his remains solemnly paraded from the docks to the family burial plot in Chợ Lớn.[131] Streets were named after him in Sài Gòn and even in Casablanca. Phạm Quỳnh eulogized him as "a trace of a living union— even more alive since his death thanks to the indelible souvenirs he left in our spirits and our hearts."[132] For some elites who returned alive, the war experience only intensified their patriotic ardor for Indochina. "Goodbye to the military life I so loved," wrote François-Bertrand Can in 1916; "goodbye to the elegant infantry uniform I was so proud to wear; goodbye also to my dear comrades with whom I shared joys and sorrows for so long, and to whom I was so close."[133] Some rose in the colonial military (Nguyễn Văn Xuân, a general in the French army by 1947, and Sisowath Monivong before his ascension as king); some who served as inspectors and interpreters returned to careers as establishment political figures on Cochinchina's Colonial Council (Lê Quang Liêm, Nguyễn Văn Thinh, Trân Văn Khá) or in the Nguyễn imperial administration (Hồ Đắc Khải, Nguyễn Văn Hiển). During the war, popular literature also celebrated the patriotism and sacrifices of ordinary Indochinese who had served.[134] The war undoubtedly improved some lives. Some laborers used new competencies to work in manufacturing, shipping, mining, and public works.[135] Some used money they had saved to buy land in their villages. And some now served as intermediaries with officials, or as brokers in transactions or disputes, because of their time abroad, their knowledge of French, and their honorific imperial military titles.[136]

Just as often, however, these "retours de France . . . posed more problems for colonial society than had been raised by their recruitment."[137] By mid-1920, the celebrations organized for the first returnees had given way to official and popular indifference. Few benefited from official hiring initiatives or accepted the offer of land concessions in harsh upland regions, pensions and tax exemptions were cut or eliminated, and many nonspecialized laborers returned reluctantly to their villages after failing to find work in cities. For those with more modest savings, the postwar spike in the value of the piaster often prevented them from buying land or helping their families. Moreover, the lasting effects of time in France—new professional competencies, experience of salaried work and a monetary economy, and different ideas about personal rights and freedoms—caused tensions in a rural society that, unlike France's, was largely unchanged by the war. Some who wore their uniforms or western suits were accused of disrupting social order by "playing French."[138] Returnees, now less apt to accept indignities and petty abuses from local officials, often found themselves punished with false accusations or retributive acts. French officials attributed crime, violence, and suicide among returnees to the cultural and psychological uprooting of time in France.[139] By the late 1920s, popular literature about the war began to evoke the hardships of their service and separation.[140] In Huỳnh Thị Bảo Hòa's 1927 novel *The Belle of the West* (*Tây phương mỹ nhơn*), Tuấn Ngọc and his brother volunteer to escape the cul-de-sac of rural life and endure abusive overseers in transit camps, the taxing journey to France, the bruising labor of munitions factories, and the horrors of the trenches. They also find meaning in their sacrifices, their friendships, and (in Tuấn Ngọc's case) in love with a French woman. In Indochina, where he is forced to return without his family, Tuấn Ngọc endures professional disappointment and abuses at the hands of authorities. When his wife eventually arrives, authorities do everything they can to keep them apart, and then force the mixed family to go back to France. Ultimately, in the novel as in many lives, "volunteering was a promise of a better life that remained a dream."[141]

In interwar Indochina, political radicals would cast the mobilization and recruitment of soldiers and workers as a form of colonial exploitation. Although the war did not make all Indochinese who served into anti-colonial activists, its political ripples were significant. In rural Annam and Tonkin, clashes between war returnees and Nguyễn officials "brought an opening to the outside into a deeply hierarchical society, where traditional relations of domination and dependence were becoming more and more tense."[142] The future president of Vietnam Tôn Đức Thắng did not, as official histories claim, participate in the Black Sea mutinies supporting the Russian Revolution, but his service in Toulon, "a stronghold of radical socialism, labor activism, and proletarian self-assertion," helped make him a leader in Sài Gòn's labor activism (heading illicit unions) and a critical intermediary between the PCF and communist networks in south China.[143] For those who remained in military service, "the differences they observed between France and the colony . . . led to dissatisfactions" that worried military officials.[144] Of the 101 soldiers tried by the first criminal commission after the 1930 mutiny at Yên Báy, 17 had served in France.[145] Great War returnees also participated in the Nghệ-Tĩnh uprisings in 1930–31; "the most rebellious villages," one French official claimed, "are those where we note the presence of soldiers returned from France."[146]

Sojourns for professional formation, the most elite form of labor sojourns in peacetime, became part of the emergence of a native capitalist class. In 1895, a young Bạch Thái Bưởi went to Bordeaux to introduce Indochinese goods at an exposition; his obituary marked that year as "the decisive date of his life; the sight of this immense activity had an effect on him that he would feel for the rest of his life."[147] A decade later, he had built a business empire that would dominate commercial shipping in the region.[148] For delegates to expositions like the rice magnates Nguyễn Văn Của or Trương Văn Bền, French sojourns created or strengthened ties to French importers. A 1943 compendium of Indochinese notables, the most detailed portrait of the late colonial elite, lists dozens of figures who studied agriculture, engineering, or commerce in France before becoming owners of plantations, factories, or enterprises.[149] Other entrepreneurs had similar trajectories. After returning to Indochina, Khánh Ký became the colony's most prominent photographer, opening studios in four cities (and in Guangzhou) before the Depression destroyed his business.[150] Phạm Tá had studied Neapolitan fashion in Paris before opening a tailor shop in Hà Nội in 1928; he returned to France to study chemical dyeing and then opened a dye factory in Hà Nội.[151]

Indochinese sailors, domestics, exposition workers, or other marginal laborers in France appear fleetingly in archives and virtually always become invisible after leaving France. As such, it is usually impossible to trace their fortunes upon their returns to Indochina, except when a later labor sojourn in France brought their experiences in Indochina back into their French immigration dossiers. Those cases include figures like Phung Văn Mớt, who left his village in 1921 to work as a rickshaw puller in Hải Phòng, was hired there to work as a domestic in France, returned to his village in 1926 to grow rice and start a family, and then returned to France in 1931 (as rice prices were crashing) for more domestic work.[152] Nguyễn Văn Vương had been a primary school teacher in Tonkin before working as an on-ship secretary for Messageries maritimes; after being fired for using opium, he found work as an overseer on a Michelin plantation in Cochinchina.[153] Cases like these show how labor sojourns in France were part of a landscape of Indochinese economic precarity that spanned the colony, other parts of Asia, around the French empire, and elsewhere around the globe. Indochinese who worked in interwar France became restauranters in Argentina, machinists in the United States, pedicurists in Holland, mechanics in Senegal, and drug traffickers in Istanbul; their experiences echo those of soldiers and laborers during the world wars, who surely had never dreamed of seeing the Balkans, Syria, England, Algeria, Italy, or many other places those wars took them. Fleeting glimpses into the human sides of these far-flung labor sojourns speak volumes. "I have passed two years on the oceans, far from my wife and children," wrote a sailor to a friend working at the treasury in Huế, "but the honor of working freely on the oceans more than makes up for the difficulty and fatigue of the work. So, what is growing in your garden? How is your family's health? There you are, in the same situation as a bird in a cage or a fish in a vase . . . to each their own. I'm just joking, don't be angry!" He closed: "In the middle of the night's silence, I think of my friend Vinh and I write him this note. This proves that Dong hasn't forgotten Vinh, even if Vinh has forgotten Dong. The Sahara desert is a witness to my sentiment."[154]

Soldiers and workers in the Second World War returned to a war of decolonization. A few had served as officers in the French army. Major Nguyễn Văn Hinh, son of the Great War veteran and ranking colonel Nguyễn Văn Tâm, had been stationed in Germany and Algeria after 1945 before returning to Indochina in 1948, soon rising to chief of staff of the State of Vietnam's fledgling army. His military career, cut short by his opposition to Ngô Đình Diệm, continued in France, where he rose to the rank of general. Trần Văn Đôn and his brother-in-law Lê Văn Kim, both Free French officers, became leaders in the ASV's army and later spearheaded the military coup that toppled Ngô Đình Diệm's regime in 1963. Trần Xuân Quang, a German prisoner of war for four years, became a major in the ARVN.[155] But virtually all who returned were ordinary laborers whose repatriations, delayed in the chaos and penury of the end of the war, had been put off further out of fear that they would join the anti-French resistance. Most only returned between 1948–50, nearly a decade after their departures. They disembarked in the southern ports of Vũng Tàu, Nha Trang, or Đà Nẵng, far from their homes and with any transportation further north irregular and uncertain. Quarantines, security concerns, and bureaucratic dysfunction stranded many in transit camps, and the French military often recruited or just requisitioned some for more labor. But many were too sick to work; tuberculosis, injuries, and psychological trauma were common. Healthy returnees, a priori "dangerous" in the context of the independence war, were often labeled politically suspect. Those lucky enough to catch a ship to Hải Phòng did not have as far to go; those who didn't might walk for weeks, through war zones, before getting home.[156]

And their homecomings were not easy. In French-controlled areas, many returnees were scrutinized and subject to police and military harassment. Some expressed political attitudes that were unwelcome in French-controlled areas: "In France," one remembered, "we had participated in protests demanding raises, we belonged to unions, it was very poorly seen here."[157] Some who protested to obtain back pay or other compensation for their poor treatment were arrested or (in a few cases) killed for their trouble. Others, whether out of political conviction or just the location of their village, returned to DRV-controlled areas. Some were militants with the right bona fides; Hoàng Tuân Nha had been expelled from France in 1948 and imprisoned in Huế for his activism before reaching Interzone IV in 1949, where he joined the DRV's propaganda bureau and later worked for the newspaper *Nhân Dân*.[158] But those without such credentials had more difficult returns to DRV-controlled areas. Many were criticized for having worked for France, some even accused of espionage. Many destroyed precious souvenirs of their sojourns—papers, letters, and photographs—to ease suspicions. Some were fortunate to find their families intact, but others found parents had passed away, siblings and friends had moved, and wives had remarried. As one recalled: "We were totally lost: no work, and given our age, we could not easily remake our lives. Moreover, our country was at war and our life was becoming even more difficult."[159] Some with technical skills returned to cities, but "for the peasants, there was no choice: the rice fields remained the only horizon for survival. Most of them thus suffered through an experience that robbed them of much of their youth without any benefit or personal compensation."[160]

FRENCH SOJOURNS AND THE POLITICS OF REVOLUTION AND DECOLONIZATION

In the summer of 1945, three Indochinese returnees from France helped to lead three seizures of power in what would become the nations of Vietnam, Cambodia, and Laos. Nguyễn Tất Thành had left for France in 1911 a budding critic of French rule and returned in 1941 as the seasoned communist Hồ Chí Minh: on August 21, he entered Hà Nội at the head of a revolutionary coalition that declared the Democratic Republic of Vietnam on September 2. Twelve days earlier, Sơn Ngọc Thành, who had become Cambodia's most prominent anti-colonial figure after returning from his legal studies in France, had become prime minister after a coup in Phnom Penh against the French-backed regime led by the young king Norodom Sihanouk. And in September in Laos, Prime Minister Prince Phetsarath Ratanavongsa, an École coloniale graduate, declared the unification of Indochina's Lao provinces and joined the Lao Issara, a nationalist group that proclaimed independence and deposed the pro-French king. The French reacted swiftly, ejecting the nascent Vietnamese revolutionary regime in

Cochinchina in September, arresting and jailing Sơn Ngọc Thành in October, and forcing the Lao Issara into exile in Thailand in early 1946.

French sojourns had not only transformed the lives of these three individuals; they had also helped forge a colonial Indochinese political culture whose plural and fractious character shaped 1945's aftermaths. Christopher Goscha casts modern Vietnamese history as a conflict between republican and authoritarian communist political projects.[161] The DRV's Declaration of Independence is steeped in French republicanism's language of "popular sovereignty, universal suffrage, multiparty politics, free elections, and an independent national assembly and judiciary" that had transformed the region's politics during the colonial era.[162] Phan Châu Trinh's exile in France in 1911 was the first of many Indochinese sojourns in France to shape Vietnamese republicanism. What some sojourners experienced in France—elite educations, the opportunity to represent Indochina at an exposition, service and sacrifice in war, a vibrant print sphere, associational life, multiparty politics, or the Third Republic's material and cultural power—birthed or intensified their faith in French republicanism's universalist, emancipatory promises, and thus their belief that moderate reform could solve the problems of empire. French sojourns deeply shaped major forms of Vietnamese reformist republicanism during the 1920s: Constitutionalism (Bùi Quang Chiêu, Nguyễn Phú Khai, Trần Văn Khá, Lê Quang Liêm, Diệp Văn Kỳ, Vương Quang Nhường) and cultural renovation and modernization (Nguyễn Văn Vĩnh, Phạm Quỳnh). Returnees from France also helped shaped further-reaching variants of reformist republicanism in the Popular Front era: the "cosmopolitan nationalism" of the Self-Reliant Literary Group (Nguyễn Tường Tam), noncommunist figures in SFIO branches in Cochinchina (Nguyễn Hữu Thọ, Cao Văn Chánh) and Tonkin (Phạm Hữu Chương, Lê Thăng), Sài Gòn's Parti démocrate indochinois (Nguyễn Văn Thinh, Đỗ Hữu Thinh, Trịnh Đình Thảo, Dương Văn Giáo, Trần Văn Đôn), and left-wing Social Catholic circles in Tonkin (Nguyễn Mạnh Hà).

French sojourns were equally important in shaping more radical visions of Vietnamese republicanism in Vietnam's Declaration of Independence, whose very existence categorically rejected the possibility of colonial reform. In "France in Indochina," which he wrote in Paris in 1925, Nguyễn An Ninh scorned the "Gallicized Vietnamese Youth," dazzled by the "ideas of democracy, a critical mind, a strength and a faith" he discovered in France, who "attempts to reconcile colonial interests with Vietnamese aspirations."[163] French sojourns had offered him and Phan Văn Trường elite educations, introduced them to political journalism, and immersed them in oppositional political milieus more robust and vibrant than those in Indochina. But their sojourns also underscored that France offered no refuge from the surveillance, censorship, and (in Phan Văn Trường's case) incarceration that often followed direct challenges to colonialism. The sojourns of hundreds of youth who followed in Ninh's and Trường's footsteps extended the colony's radical republican milieus to France, and they helped reshape colonial politics. The later trajectories of nineteen activists arrested in May 1930 for protesting the repression of the Yên Báy mutiny in front of the Élysée Palace and the Mur des fédérés, an apt symbolic culmination of this French realm of Vietnamese radical politics, reflects its diverse aftermaths: they included future Stalinist luminaries (Trần Văn Giàu, Nguyễn Văn Tạo, Dương Bạch Mai), Trotskyists (Tạ Thu Thâu, Huỳnh Văn Phương, Phan Văn Chánh), noncommunist leftists (Hồ Văn Ngà, Lê Bá Cang, Lê Văn Thử), and a candidate in the Republic of Vietnam's 1967 presidential election (Trần Văn Chiêu).[164]

Indochinese political milieus in France also helped make Vietnamese communism. The PCF was the only political force in France to articulate a sustained anti-colonial critique and to offer (or channel from Moscow) material support for anti-colonial activists. Nguyễn Ái Quốc was the first of many Vietnamese to get to Moscow via France: twenty-six out of twenty-eight who spent time in Moscow between 1925 and the Sixth Comintern Congress in 1928 got there from France, while one of the other two (the future party chair Trần Phú) returned to the colony via France.[165] And communist activism in France was formative for many Vietnamese Stalinists: Trần Văn Giàu, Nguyễn Văn Tạo, Dương Bạch Mai, Bùi Công Trừng, Phan Tư Nghĩa, Nguyễn Khánh Toàn, Phạm Văn Điều, and Đỗ Đình Thiện, among others. But it was also in France where Vietnamese communist anti-Stalinism first emerged in the early 1930s, as alienated activists left the PCF for the French Trotskyist oppostion or the PCF's United Front faction. By 1936, the Comintern was blaming the PCF for having allowed "certain Annamite communist intellectuals to be drawn to the 'Party's internal factions.'"[166]

French connections helped shape Vietnamese communism. The PCF's "permanent campaign against repression in Indochina" through amnesty committees, political delegations, and clandestine networks was critical in saving the nascent ICP after its near-stillbirth in the early 1930s.[167] And during the Popular Front, the fleeting but critical alliances between ICP and Trotskyist militants—born in political networks forged in France—became the epicenter of a movement that resurrected the revolutionary left in colonial politics. The newspapers, electoral campaigns, strikes, and popular action committees of French returnees in La Lutte and Le Travail "took on the appearance of an open political struggle modeled on those of the great European communist parties" that "managed not only to turn Vietnamese opinion . . . to their advantage but also to impose a new style of revolutionary action."[168] But the figures who collaborated in La Lutte and Le Travail had also bitterly clashed in France, and they continued to take cues from "the advanced observation post that was Vietnamese immigration in France," notably French Trotskyist disavowal of the Popular Front and the breakup of the Comité de rassemblement des Indochinois (La Lutte and Le Travail's metropolitan equivalent).[169] The PCF also enforced the Comintern's decision in mid-1937 to pressure the ICP to abandon the alliances, which some of its activists were reluctant to do.[170] France was, in real ways, a crucible of the ideological fault lines that would erupt in political violence in Vietnam during and after 1945.

As the Japanese withdrew from Indochina in March 1945, seven of the nine "men of talent and virtue" whom the prime minister, Trần Trọng Kim, chose to head ministries of the new Empire of Vietnam had earned advanced degrees in France; that summer, they "started rolling back decades of colonial rule by nationalizing education, culture, and the civil service."[171] As this first independent Vietnamese state gave way to two others, French returnees played an equally important role in their construction. In October 1945, the DRV named a commission to guide its education system along "democratic, national, and scientific" principles; about 80 percent held degrees from France.[172] Some became influential figures in DRV higher education: Nguyễn Văn Huyên (minister of higher education and architect of the National University), Nguy Như Kontum (minister of secondary education and rector of Hà Nội General University), Tạ Quang Bửu (rector of Hà Nội's University of Science and Technology and minister of higher education), Nguyễn Thúc Hào (director of Hà Nội's University of Science, vice-rector of the University of Pedagogy and principal of Vinh Pedagogical University), and Phạm Huy Thông (rector of Hà Nội's University of Education and director of the Institute of Archaeology for two decades), to name a few. Dozens with French degrees filled professorial ranks. Returnees were weakest in the humanities and social sciences, for they were suspected of "having kept from their stay in the West liberal convictions and inclinations to free speech."[173] For some, this proved untrue: Hoàng Xuân Nhị (literature), Trần Văn Giáp (history), Nguyễn Khánh Toàn (literature), Hồ Đắc Điểm (law), and Phạm

Văn Bạch (law) were influential in their fields in the DRV for decades. Trần Văn Giàu (history) and Nguyễn Khắc Viện (psychology and history) became two of the DRV's top ideological propagandists. But for Trần Đức Thảo and Nguyễn Mạnh Tường, two of the DRV's most brilliant humanists, commitment to free thought and debate proved fatal, as the regime crushed their intellectual and personal lives during the Nhân Văn-Giai Phẩm affair. Each returned to France one final time; Thảo died in Paris in 1993.[174]

Scientists and technical experts trained in France offered critical expertise to the nascent DRV state in its early years. Hồ Đắc Di became chief of Hà Nội's main hospital and dean of the medical school in 1945. He was one of many French medical school graduates to help lead the DRV's medical service, born under the fire of war: they included Hoàng Tích Trí (the first minister of health and principal immunologist), Phạm Ngọc Thạch (chief of the Party health services and Hoàng Tích Trí's succcessor as minister of health), Trương Gia Thọ (director of medical services in Interzone 5), Trương Công Quyền (head of the military's pharmaceutical school), Nguyễn Văn Hưởng (head of the party's medical networks in the south during the First Indochina War), and Phạm Khắc Quảng (author of an influential medical textbook), among others.[175] Engineers, some recruited by Hồ Chí Minh during the Fontainebleau conference, became leaders in the Ministry of Industry (Lê Viết Hương and Võ Quý Huân), Public Works (Đặng Phúc Thông), and the armament industry (Phạm Quang Lễ, better known by his revolutionary name Trần Đại Nghĩa, whose expertise allowed the DRV to produce heavy weaponry before Chinese and Soviet aid began in 1949).[176] Nguyễn Xiển was the DRV's national director of meteorology from the beginning of war with France in 1946 until unification thirty years later.[177] Others, less directly involved in the war effort, were pillars of the physical and life sciences, like Lê Văn Thiêm, the DRV's most prominent mathematician. These are but the best-known of dozens of returnees whose expertise helped shape the DRV regime's transition from a "colonial graft" into a revolutionary regime. Much like Vietnamese communism had some of its roots in French sojourns, so too did the state the Vietnamese communists built.

Vietnamese republicanism seemed doomed early after the revolution, as it became clear that the Republic of Cochinchina created by the French in 1946 was just a vehicle for colonial reconquest. Nguyễn Văn Thinh, the Great War veteran and graduate of a French medical school who was its first president, took his own life in protest, leaving a note that beseeched "you my friends, the intellectuals of center, south, and north," to build a meaningful opposition to communism, warning of "the dangers of a menacing red dictatorship."[178] Like they did in the DRV, returnees from France helped shape the noncommunist Vietnamese state that emerged over the next decade. They included seven of its first nine heads of state (Nguyễn Văn Thinh, Lê Văn Hoạch, Nguyễn Văn Xuân, Bảo Đại, Trần Văn Hữu, Nguyễn Văn Tâm, and Bửu Lộc) and a appreciable part (between a quarter and a third) of the members of the fourteen cabinets during the history of the Republic of Cochinchina and the State of Vietnam (1946–55).[179] They also included foundational figures in noncommunist jurisprudence (Nguyễn Khắc Vệ, Trần Văn Tỵ), education (Vương Quang Nhường, Phạm Đình Ái, Nguyễn Dương Đôn, Nguyễn Thanh Giưng), medicine (Hoàng Gia Hợp, Trần Quang Đệ), public works (Lê Quang Huy), and international affairs (Trần Văn Chương, Trần Văn Khá). Many noncommunist army officers were formed in France during and after the First Indochina War (including the future head of state Nguyễn Văn Thiệu). Dozens of less-prominent figures in the political and military establishment of republican Vietnam also spent time in France.

But French sojourns were equally important to republican Vietnam's vibrant culture of political opposition to a state that often strayed far from its republican principles. The United National Front, the main opposition to the communist-led Việt Minh in Sài Gòn in 1945, grew out of political alliances forged in France during the 1920s: Hồ Văn Ngà, Lê Bá Cang, Trần Văn Ân, and the Trotskyists.[180] Trần Văn Ân survived the Stalinist destruction of this movement and continued opposing French-backed regimes through his political activism and journalism, as would Hồ Hữu Tường—both fled to France during the war, returned, and served prison terms under Ngô Đình Diệm. Nguyễn Thế Truyền, perhaps the most influential Vietnamese political activist in interwar France, reemerged as an opposition politician and journalist in Sài Gòn after 1945, and he advocated for neutralization and nonalignment before his death in 1969.[181] At least four of the eighteen signatories of the 1960 Caravelle Manifesto opposing Ngô Đình Diệm's government (Phan Khắc Sửu, Trần Văn Đỗ, Phạm Hữu Chương, Hồ Văn Vui) had studied in France. Some such figures remained anti-communist, but for other returnees, opposition politics led to communism. Phạm Ngọc Thuần left Sài Gòn for the maquis after the French tortured and killed Thái Văn Lung, a fellow French-trained lawyer and friend.[182] Nguyễn Hữu Thọ joined the party after becoming involved in Sài Gòn's French cultural marxist circle.[183] Lưu Văn Lang, a 1904 graduate of Arts et manufactures, became a prominent critic of the Diệm regime, an advocate of reunification, and a supporter of the NLF. Trịnh Đình Thảo, active with Nguyễn Hữu Thọ and Lưu Văn Lang in the anti-Diệm Peace Movement, was jailed for political activism before joining the NLF.[184] Perhaps republican Vietnam's greatest act of political opposition was Nguyễn Tường Tam's 1963 suicide, which "helped create a new understanding of legitimacy among politicians and citizens: the RVN's ideal government had to oppose both communism . . . and dictatorship."[185] When republican Vietnam collapsed in 1975, many of the returnees who had shaped its political life would again leave for one final journey to France.

Although far fewer Khmer and Lao elites studied in France during the colonial era, those who did played an equally important role in their countries' politics during decolonization. In Laos, five of the twelve ministers of the first Lao Issara government, declared in October 1945, were returnees from France. Although Prince Phetsarath died shortly after returning from exile in Thailand in 1957, the others faced off in a political struggle that would erupt into civil war. The artist and poet Thao Nhouy Abhay and his brother Kou (a graduate of Parangon) led several ministries in the 1950s and remained loyal to the monarchy until their deaths. They were soon joined by most of the few Lao who studied in France during the war and who returned to high-ranking official posts, like Oudom Souphanouvong (minister of health) and Khamphan Phanya (minister of foreign affairs and ambassador to France and to the United States). But Souvanna Phouma became leader of the neutralist political faction, serving as prime minister several times during the civil war; he and Phetsarath may be the two most republican figures in Lao political history. Khoun Sisoumang, who studied in France during the mid-1950s, returned to become a prominent neutralist journalist until his assassination in 1963. And the "Red Prince" Souphanouvong was a principal architect of the Lao revolutionary government largely under DRV control, first as its representative in parliamentary politics and later in the resistance government. In 1975, the king and Sciences politiques graduate Sisavang Vatthana was sent to die in a reeducation camp, as the "Red Prince" and Ponts et chaussées graduate Souphanouvong became the first head of state of revolutionary Laos.[186]

The Parti démocrate, the first political party in Cambodian history, was in many ways born in the French home of Sisowath Youtevong, doctor of physics, member of the SFIO, and founder of the Fraternité Khmer. After the French arrested Sơn Ngọc Thành in October 1945, Youtevong sent Chhean Vam home to Phnom Penh to join a nascent opposition to Sihanouk's modus vivendi with France.[187] When Youtevong himself returned in early 1946, he brought "a suitcase full of 'progressive' works," including a copy of *The Communist Manifesto* that would introduce several future leaders of the Khmer Rouge to Marxism.[188] The Parti démocrate he cofounded in 1946 used electoral campaigns, political journalism, and mass public events to build a national organization that represented a revolution in Cambodian politics, which unlike Vietnam had been only glancingly touched by republican political culture before 1945. Its ranks were filled with French returnees: Thonn Ouk, Huy Kanthoul, Son Voeunsai, Pach Chhoeun, Sam Nhean, and others. "When we came back," one remembered, "we had the prestige of greater learning, so much so that we were considered leaders. Our stay abroad had opened our minds, and we had information that was not available to our compatriots."[189] From the beginning, party leaders sought to strengthen their coalition by sending the most promising young elites they mobilized— hundreds during the First Indochina War—to France via party or state scholarships. Despite its inexperience and problems with corruption, the Parti démocrate was the most powerful force in Khmer politics for many years after 1945; its platform of "obtaining the country's independence through dialogue with Paris, and bringing about a democratic evolution of the regime" dominated elections well into the 1950s.[190] But it could not withstand Sihanouk's own political revolution, which used the monarchy's traditional appeal, French support, and alliances with opposing parties to destroy the Parti démocrate through extraconstitutional power plays, censorship, and violence before wresting independence from France. In the 1955 elections, the last before the party's dissolution, it was crushed by Sangkum, Sihanouk's mass organization, whose tactics and style owed much to the Parti démocrate's revolution in Khmer politics.

In 1952, Saloth Sar wrote a blistering critique from France of Sihanouk's dissolution of the National Assembly, in which he eulogized Youtevong for having "abandoned the monarchists to inculcate democracy among the Khmer people."[191] The future Pol Pot, along with Ieng Sary, Khieu Samphan, Son Sen, Thiounn Mumm, and virtually all of the future leaders of the revolutionary Khmer Rouge regime, had known little about communism when they set out for France as students and supporters of the Parti démocrate: "Their sentiments of anticolonial and antimonarchical revolt were born before their arrival in France, but ... it was in Paris that the hard core of Cambodian communists and 'progressists' learned the foundations of democratic centralism, autocritique, anti-intellectualism, and economic theories and revolutionary lessons of Lenin, Stalin, Hồ Chí Minh and Mao, as well as the bloody but politically justified purges of the French Revolution and the Russian and Chinese Soviet Republics."[192] They learned much from the PCF of the 1950s, a party recently ejected from government, actively persecuted by the police, profoundly Stalinist, fervently opposed to the wars in Indochina and Korea, and committed to national economic and cultural autarchy in the face of massive American influence. But their politicization transcended the PCF, which many Khmer students found "too moderate, too legalistic, too parliamentary" and blamed for prioritizing Vietnam's cause and for not contending with the Maoist thought electrifying the popular organizations, festivals, protests, and study circles that made up their political milieu in France.[193] "The theoretical baggage that they brought with them from France would not be lost," either in their brief flirtation with public and legal political organization after returning to Cambodia or "in the midst of Vietnamese and Maoist slogans and techniques for combat and popular organization" that they would learn in the maquis.[194] "In France," Khieu Samphan remembered years later, "workers and students were extremely politicized and dynamic. We were almost led to believe that a great revolution was going to take place."[195] French sojourns did not make the Khmer Rouge revolution inevitable, but they were at the very heart of its uniquely radical character and destructive consequences.

Coda

FINAL VOYAGES

ON OCTOBER 5, 1863, PHẠM PHÚ THỨ, preoccupied with the diplomatic crisis that had brought him to Paris, found time to meet with Nguyễn Thị Liên, who now went by Magdalene Sen. She had left Huế in 1826 with her husband Phillipe Vannier and most of their children after he and Jean-Baptiste Chaigneau had resigned their posts as advisers to the Nguyễn court following Minh Mạng's accession. Nguyễn Thị Liên was now a widow of seventy-five, but after thirty-seven years in France she had not forgotten her origins. "When she saw her countrymen," Phạm Phú Thứ wrote,

> she became very emotional and burst into tears. . . . When he was alive, her husband promised her that they would return together to Annam. But he died suddenly. Because of her advanced age, and because her children discourage it, she doubts she will ever return. . . . That an embassy from our country has come to France and received her is a source of great joy and happiness for her.[1]

She died in Lorient in 1878 without ever returning to what would soon become French Indochina. Chaigneau and Vannier's children never returned either, but of mixed heritages and younger, they had fewer difficulties becoming part of a new society. They married into bourgeois families, and had respectable, sometimes prominent careers: teacher, navy purser, preceptor, commissioner at the Ministry of Finance, and secretary-general of Rennes. In a novelistic irony, her grandson Emile was serving as a French naval officer in Cochinchina at the time of her encounter with Phạm Phú Thứ.[2]

Like Chaigneau's and Vannier's families, other sojourners who came to France during the colonial era never left. Although many could remain in

France for years with an irregular or unresolved legal status, virtually none could remain for good without being naturalized. Of those who did, those with French paternity enjoyed, in the words of a French official, "a claim to the status of French citizen greatly superior to what individuals of pure race and equal qualifications could claim."[3] One was Nguyễn Văn Hiến, whose French father abandoned his mother, who left him in the care of the Société de protection des enfants métis abandonnées franco-indochinois in Nam Định. In 1924 the society sent him to Cherbourg to work as a lathe operator. He resumed relations with his father, took his name, became a French citizen, and joined the army; he never returned to Indochina.[4] Others came from the rarefied realms of colonial society whom French officials deemed worthy of citizenship. Nguyễn Văn Truyết, son of a landowner in Cochinchina, was already a citizen when he came to France to study; he received a doctorate in law in 1924 and opened a practice in Montpellier, offering pro bono advice to Indochinese students on their naturalization requests.[5] Others became French through marriage. Vũ Xuân Đào met Marie Coquelet while working in a factory in Saint-Auban during the Great War; when his repatriation order came in 1920, they had a two-year-old daughter. His wife, herself an orphan, pleaded that he be allowed to remain to take care of his family. French authorities relented, and Vũ Xuân Đào became a French citizen in October 1924.[6]

But few Indochinese—perhaps several hundred at most—had settled in France for good before the First Indochina War, the watershed between colonial sojourns and postcolonial migrations to France. Educational and professional qualifications made it easier for elites to go there permanently during the war. Hoàng Thị Nga, the first Indochinese woman with a French doctorate in the sciences, served in the Ministries of Education in the Empire of Vietnam and the DRV before coming to France in 1946. She spent the rest of her life as a largely anonymous researcher for the French CNRS.[7] The doctor Hồ Tá Khanh, minister of the economy of the Empire of Vietnam, declined positions in both the DRV and the Republic of Cochinchina and returned to his hometown of Phan Thiết; he returned to France in 1949 and worked as a pediatrician there and in Réunion for the rest of his life. Hoàng Xuân Hãn, his friend and fellow former minister in the Empire of Vietnam, came to France in 1951 and stayed there, writing and building European library holdings on Vietnam. One of his best students, Tạ Trọng Hiệp, also came in 1951 to study at the Sorbonne and the École pratique des hautes études and later became a pillar of French Southeast Asian studies.[8] Lê Thành Khôi, another of the hundreds to resume their educational sojourns in France after 1945, stayed in France for a career in law and economics; his histories of Vietnam were influential in the West for decades.[9] And the journalist and ethnologist Nguyễn Tiến Lãng came in 1952 and worked for Empress Nam Phương and the French Ministry of Education until his death in 1976. These well-known figures were among hundreds from the region's intellectual and professional classes to move permanently to France during the First Indochina War; thousands more would join them in later decades.

In 1953, Nguyễn Tiến Lãng wrote from Paris of "a school of Indochinese literary expression in French."[10] Just as he had, most of this school's brightest lights had come to France permanently by the 1950s. Their choice reflected the "progressive separation between this group of Francophone writers and the Vietnamese literary space, especially after 1945, for reasons related both to historical context and to the writers themselves."[11] Trần Văn Tùng, fêted from his arrival in 1939, never found reason to leave. Pierre Đỗ Đình Thạch, when his war service ended, returned to journalism and criticism in the French Catholic intellectual circles that had shaped him in the 1920s. Phạm Văn Ký was a rising literary star when he left Indochina in 1939 to study literature at the Sorbonne and religion at the Institut des hautes études chinoises with Marcel Mauss. He scratched out a living teaching during the war but found literary success with *Frères de sang* (1947) that culminated with the highest honor for fiction from the Académie française for *Perdre la demeure* (1961). Phạm Duy Khiêm had returned to Hà Nội after the war and retreated from public life when war broke out; in 1954 he became High Commissioner to Paris of the State of Vietnam. He remained in France for the rest of his life, finding literary success with his autobiographical novel *Nam et Sylvie* (1957). These writers joined the painters Lê Phổ, Mai Trung Thứ, Lê Thị Lựu, and Lê Bá Đảng, who had all come to France permanently in the late 1930s, in France's growing Indochinese literary and artistic diaspora. Many of their explorations of interculturality echo the figure of the narrator in Phạm Văn Ký's *Frères de sang,* who exists "at a crossing of cultures and traditions, carrying within himself the ailments and joys of forced contact whose consequences are both pleasurable and painful, a rupture of identity that gives rise to cultural questioning rather than essentialist reaffirmation."[12] *Frères de sang* and *Nam et Sylvie* use the failures of returns home and of intercultural relationships to explore the feeling of existential displacement after empire. Both authors died in France largely forgotten, Phạm Duy Khiêm by his own hand. Other traumas, of course, shaped later generations of this literary and artistic diaspora ("We are from Nowhere," Linda Lê writes in *Calomnies,* a literary exploration of her refugee experience).[13] But eventually, so too would the generative, even playful qualities of interculturality, and even the possibility of transcending it altogether.

As war intensified, France became a site of permanent political exile. Hoàng Xuân Hãn had left in 1951 to avoid arrest for his visible support for the DRV while teaching in Hà Nội.[14] So did Nguyễn Mạnh Hà, a Catholic and the DRV's first minister of the economy, whose criticisms of the French and contacts with DRV leaders led to his exile to France in 1951 (ironically, his marriage to the daughter of the communist deputy Georges Marrane may have spared him a worse fate). Nguyễn Tiến Lãng came after spending eight years in DRV captivity. Trotskyists Ngô Văn Xuyết, Lư Sanh Hạnh, and Nguyễn Văn Nam escaped Stalinist assassination for constant harassment and threat of arrest in French-controlled areas: they went to France in 1948 after a Sûreté raid of Sài Gòn's Tìm Học bookstore, a Trotskyist meeting place and letter drop.[15] They would remain there for the rest of their lives, lonely torchbearers of a movement that had been at the heart of late colonial politics. The end of empire in Indochina would not mark an end to political exile in France. In 1955, Bảo Đại left Indochina for good after Ngô Đình Diệm forced him from power. Dozens, perhaps even hundreds, of political figures would follow him to France from then until the 1990s, after falling afoul of one of the former Indochina's new regimes.

Many others came permanently to France to escape the war's intractable and devastating violence. The imperial official Phạm Gia Thụy had come to France in 1906 as a delegate of the Permanent Mission and during the Great War as an overseer of soldiers and laborers; in 1952 he came as a refugee, with what remained of his wealth converted into gold and diamonds and hidden in cookie tins.[16] Some who came during the First Indochina War had deep resources: Nguyễn Viết Cảnh, after studying in France, built a successful pharmaceutical business in Indochina. As a hedge to the war's instabilities, he bought a villa in Biarritz, moved his family there in 1950, and began transferring his wealth to France, 5000 francs at a time (the most allowed in one money order).[17] Hundreds of other elites did something similar. But most of the thirty thousand "repatriates" who came to France as Indochina collapsed were "the marginal and the marginalized of colonial society, who despite their French citizenship had neither wealth ... nor prestigious symbolic capital." Most were the Vietnamese, Khmer, or Lao spouses and children of French *colons* or soldiers, or the adult offspring of interracial relationships. Many were already refugees before leaving Indochina, fleeing a war zone for a French-controlled city before their journey to France. Many only became legally French through hasty procedures just before or sometimes during the journey. When they arrived, a few had personal networks to help them adapt. But for many, "home" was the Centres d'acceuil des rapatriés d'Indochine, soon renamed Centres d'acceuil des français d'Indochine (Cafi), hastily refashioned out of army barracks, labor camps, or even prisons that "paid no regard to the physical or psychological condition of the repatriates or their isolation from the rest of the French population." Their sudden, often traumatic departures from Indochina only added to their hardship. Most had left behind parents, siblings, and friends without knowing when, or if, they would ever see them again. Lost loved ones would remain "a source of nostalgia and anguish (especially during the hostilities of the American war) as well as a very close tie to their country of origin," whether through the slow and painful process of renewing ties or simply in the realm of memory.[18]

"Maman, c'est ça la France?" asked a child as buses of repatriates arrived at the Cafi in Sainte-Livrade-sur-Lot in 1956.[19] The child could be forgiven the question, for in many ways the camps replicated the colonial society they had left behind. Their administrative and medical personnel often "had experience in the colonies as soldiers or civilian functionaries, with a preference for those who had lived in Indochina." Camp schools sought, in the words of one Cafi director, "to make our little Eurasians into good, honest French people." The "paternalism inherent in the camp structure," coupled with the terrible conditions, led to tension between residents and administrators. The curiosity of the local population soon turned to hostility, "characterized by a lack of understanding of cultural differences, and irritation with repatriates' habits," reflected in civic isolation, economic marginalization, and episodes of violence. As months stretched into years, some Cafi evolved from "welcome centers" into permanent neighborhoods, whose visible reminders of cultural difference were branded as signs of a "failed integration." Such attitudes would gradually give way to a superficially more celebratory view of the Cafi as sites of French "multiculturalism" that nevertheless papered over the histories of their residents—testimonies to the ineradicable distances and margins marking the lives of many non-white French. In the early 2000s, a project to tear down many of the original Cafi structures created a controversy that gave voice to some of these silenced histories and illuminated—for neither the first time nor the last—the inescapably present and ongoing legacies of empire in contemporary France.[20]

During the controversy, one former Cafi resident recalled:

France, we had dreamt of it. What was there more desirable than France? Over there in Indochina, all that was beautiful, clean, enviable, rich, and powerful was called France. It manifested itself in the white villas and the gardens with armies of domestics, the broad avenues with the cafés, fancy storefronts and automobile traffic. France was the luminous whiteness of suits, of uniforms, of ballgowns, tablecloths, sheets, garlands, plaster virgins in the churches, marriages and communions, villas and steamships. All this white pushed back the dirty gray sky of the monsoon, the low muddy horizon over the rice paddies, the smoke-filled servant quarters, the obscure peasant huts, the dirty waters of the arroyos, the heavy and sticky earth trampled by the water buffaloes, the earth-colored clothes of the peasants, the black tunics of the literati, the lacquered teeth of the women. . . . Yes, France was all the immaculate white that shined in the sun and illuminated everything around it.
 The whiteness of colonization.
 France, everybody wanted to go there, of course. It was a mirage that we dreamt to see one day, from the third-class deck, when the Provencal coast emerged over a violet morning sea, made real by an outstretched hand pointing to its fine line: 'La France!'[21]

In 2009, the scholar Dominique Rolland recorded the stories of some of the thousands of Indochinese who, in those barren camps, first truly began the fraught and often incomplete journey toward becoming French. "France, for those in the camps," she concluded, "would be fifty-two years of gray."[22]

NOTES

INTRODUCTION

1. Greg and Monique Lockhart, "Broken Journey: Nhất Linh's 'Going to France,'" *East Asian History* 8 (December 1994): 98.

2. Ibid., 79.

3. Quoted in Nhật Tịnh, *Chân dung Nhất Linh* (Sài Gòn: Đại Nam, 1971), 33.

4. Ibid., 30.

5. Ibid.

6. Nguyễn Tường Bách, *Việt Nam, những ngày lịch sử* (Montréal: Nhóm Nghiên Cứu Sử Địa, 1981), 49.

7. Nguyễn Thị Thế, *Hồi ký gia đình Nguyễn Tường* (Santa Ana, CA: Văn Hóa Ngày Nay, 1996), 105.

8. Tư Can to Phạm Chi Mẫn, February 25, 1930, Dossier Tư Can, SLOTFOM XV.113, ANOM.

9. Lockhart, "Broken Journey," 80.

10. Ibid., 87.

11. A 1931 compendium of contemporary Vietnamese word usage and colloquialisms translates "lãng du" as "Chơi hờ hễnh: Promenade sans but." See Tây Dương, *Petit Passe-Partout de la Presse Sino-Annamite/Hán Việt Khan Tiểu Linh Dược* (Hà Nội: Imprimerie Trung Hòa Thiện Bản, 1931), 237. As Greg Lockhart points out, Nhất Linh took the phrase from Thế Lữ's poem "Giây phút chạnh lòng," which he dedicated to Nhất Linh. Lockhart translates the term as "wanderer."

12. Lockhart, "Broken Journey," 133.

13. Nguyễn Tường Bách, *Việt Nam, những ngày lịch sử,* 49.

14. Martina Thucchi Nguyen, *On Our Own Strength: The Self-Reliant Literary Group and Cosmopolitan Nationalism in Late Colonial Vietnam* (Honolulu: University of Hawai'i Press, 2020), 120.

15. Ibid., 204.

16. Gary Wilder, *The French Imperial Nation-State: Negritude and Colonial Humanism between the Two World Wars* (Chicago: University of Chicago Press, 2005), 9, 26, 80.

17. Ibid., 5.

18. Ibid., 27–28.

19. Ibid., 25–26, 28.

20. Ibid., 5; Pierre Brocheux and Daniel Hémery, *Indochina: An Ambiguous Colonization* (Berkeley: University of California Press, 2011).

21. The best-known sojourns outside of colonial Indochina were anti-colonial networks that extended into Siam, Japan, southern China, and the USSR. Only two hundred Indochinese went to Japan as part of the Đông Du movement between 1905 and 1909. Perhaps one hundred spent time in the USSR between the mid-20s and the late 1930s: with the exception of Hồ Chí Minh, they did not include any of the region's most important communist figures during the Cold War: Lê Duẩn, Trường Chinh, Lê Đức Thọ, or Võ Nguyên Giáp in Vietnam, or any of the Khmer Rouge or Pathet Lao leadership. It is more difficult to quantify the political radicals who moved between the colony and radical networks in Siam and southern China, but they were likely no more than two thousand for the entire colonial era. The largest quantified labor migration outside of colonial-era Indochina to somewhere other than France was of about two thousand Tonkinese miners and their families to New Caledonia, although more may ultimately have gone to China for work during the colonial era whether voluntarily or by force. On Đông Du, see Vinh Sinh, *Phan Bội Châu and the Đông Du Movement* (New Haven: Council on Southeast Asian Studies, Yale Center for International and Area Studies, 1988). On Indochinese in the USSR, see Tuong Vu, *Vietnam's Communist Revolution: The Power and Limits of Ideology* (New York: Cambridge University Press, 2017). On Indochinese networks in Siam and southern China, see Christopher Goscha, *Thailand and the Southeast Asian Networks of the Vietnamese Revolution, 1885–1954* (London: Routledge, 1999). On Vietnamese in New Caledonia, see Jean Vanmai, *Centenaire de la présence vietnamienne en Nouvelle-Calédonie* (Nouméa: Points d'histoire, 1991). On trafficking between Indochina and China, see Michelene Lessard, *Human Trafficking in Colonial Vietnam* (London: Routledge, 2015).

22. Sukanya Banerjee, "Transimperial," *Victorian Literature and Culture* 46.3–4 (Fall/Winter 2018), 926.

23. Antoinette Burton, *At the Heart of the Empire: Indians and the Colonial Encounter in Victorian Britain* (Berkeley: University of California Press, 1998), 1, 8, 10.

24. Pascal Blanchard, Sandrine Lemaire, Nicolas Bancel, and Dominic Thomas, eds., *Colonial Cultures in France since the Revolution* (Bloomington: Indiana University Press, 2013).

25. An influential example is Paul Silverstein, *Algeria in France: Transpolitics, Race, and Nation* (Bloomington: Indiana University Press, 2004).

26. Rudolf Mrazek, "Tan Malaka: A Political Personality's Structure of Experience," *Indonesia* 14 (October 1972): 1–48.

27. Scott McConnell, *Leftward Journey: The Education of Vietnamese Students in France, 1919–1939* (New Brunswick: Transaction Publishers, 1989), xvi.

28. Benedict Anderson, *Under Three Flags: Anarchism and the Anti-Colonial Imagination* (London: Verso, 2005).

29. Sunil Amrith, *Crossing the Bay of Bengal: The Fury of Nature and the Fortunes of Migrants* (Cambridge: Harvard University Press, 2015); Su Lin Lewis, *Cities in Motion: Urban Life and Cosmopolitanism in Southeast Asia, 1920–1940* (Cambridge: Cambridge University Press, 2016); Ronit Ricci, *Banishment and Belonging: Exile and Diaspora in Sarandib, Lanka and Ceylon* (Cambridge: Cambridge University Press, 2019); Takashi Shiraishi, *An Age in Motion: Popular Radicalism in Java, 1912–1926* (Ithaca, NY: Cornell University Press, 1990).

30. Michel Espagne, "Écrire une histoire vietnamienne de la France?" in Michel Espagne, Nguyen Ba Cuong, and Nguyen Thi Hanh, eds., *Hanoi-Paris: Un nouvel espace des sciences humaines* (Paris: KIME, 2020), 73. One of the only works of Vietnamese scholarship to consider French sojourns beyond biographical frameworks is Trần Tứ Nghĩa, *Một thế kỷ của phong trào người Việt ở Pháp hướng về đất nước* (Thành Phố Hồ Chí Minh: Nhà Xuất Bản Trẻ, 2010).

31. Marc Matera, *Black London: The Imperial Metropolis and Decolonization in the Twentieth Century* (Berkeley: University of California Press, 2015); David Motadel, "The Global Authoritarian Moment and the Revolt Against Empire," *The American Historical Review* 124.3 (June 2019): 843–77.

32. Michael Goebel, *Anti-Imperial Metropolis: Interwar Paris and the Seeds of Third World Nationalism* (New York: Cambridge University Press, 2015), 3, 6, 291.

33. Matthias Middell, "Transregional Studies: A New Approach to Global Processes," in *The Routledge Handbook of Transregional Studies,* ed. Matthias Middell (London: Routledge, 2018), 11.

34. Wilder, *The French Imperial Nation-State,* 8.

35. Espagne, "Écrire une histoire vietnamienne de la France?," 73.

36. Ellen Rooney, interview with Gayatri Chakravorty Spivak, "In a Word: Interview," in *Outside in the Teaching Machine* (New York: Routledge, 2008).

37. Christopher Goscha, *Going Indochinese: Contesting Concepts of Space and Place in French Indochina* (Copenhagen: NIAS Press, 2012).

38. Maureen Lynch, "Sojourners," in *The Encyclopedia of Global Human Migration,* ed. Immanuel Ness (Blackwell Publishing, 2013), published online, February 4, 2013.

39. The classic analysis of the concept is Wang Gungwu, "Sojourning: The Chinese Experience in Southeast Asia," in *Sojourners and Settlers: Histories of Southeast Asia and the Chinese,* ed. Anthony Reid (Honolulu: University of Hawai'i Press, 1996), 1–14.

40. Early studies on political figures include McConnell, *Leftward Journey;* Daniel Hémery, "Du patriotisme au marxisme: l'immigration vietnamienne en France de 1926 à 1930," *Le mouvement sociale* 90 (January-March 1975), 3–54; Thu Trang-Gaspard, *Hồ Chí Minh à Paris, 1917–1923* (Paris: L'Harmattan, 1992) and *Những hoạt động của Phan Châu Trinh tại Pháp, 1911–1925* (Thành Phố Hồ Chí

Minh: Nhà Xuất Bản Văn Nghệ Thành Phố Hồ Chí Minh, 2000); Đặng Văn Long, *Người Việt ở Pháp, 1940–1954* (Paris: Tủ Sách Nghiên Cứu, 1997); and Sacha Sher, *L'Essor de l'Angkar: des rêves de grands soirs de sorbonnards, à la victoire des maquisards* (Texte issu et remanié de la première partie de Thèse de doctorat, Sociologie politique, L'Université de Paris X, 2003). More recent socio-cultural and literary studies include Mireille Le Van Ho, *Des Vietnamiens dans la Grande Guerre: 50000 recrues dans les usines françaises* (Paris: Vendémiaire, 2014); Kimloan Vu-Hill, *Coolies into Rebels: Impact of World War I on French Indochina* (Paris: Les Indes Savantes, 2011); Liêm-Khê Luguern, "Les 'Travailleurs Indochinois': étude socio-historique d'une immigration coloniale (1939–1954)" (PhD diss., Ecole des hautes études en sciences sociales, 2014); Solène Granier, *Domestiques indochinois* (Paris: Vendémiaire, 2014); Giang-Huong Nguyen, *La Littérature vietnamienne francophone (1913–1986)* (Paris: Classiques Garnier, 2018); and Nguyễn Hữu Sơn's many articles and compilations about Vietnamese travel literature in France. Recent memoirs and memory projects include Nguyen Van Thanh, *Saigon-Marseille allez simple: un fils de mandarin dans les camps de travailleurs en France* (Bordeaux: Elytis, 2012); Pierre Daum, *Immigrés de force: les travailleurs indochinois en France (1939–1952)* (Paris: Solin, 2009); Ngô Văn, *In the Crossfire: Adventures of a Vietnamese Revolutionary* (Edinburgh: AK Press, 2010); Châu Tran, *Trần Văn Thạch (1905–1945): Une plume contre l'oppression* (Paris: Les Indes Savantes, 2020); and a number of online resources that have collected oral histories, personal documents, and photographs.

41. Durba Ghosh, "Another Set of Imperial Turns?," *The American Historical Review* 117.3 (June 2012): 792.

42. Claire Anderson, *Subaltern Lives: Biographies of Colonialism in the Indian Ocean World* (Cambridge: Cambridge University Press, 2012), 1, 6.

43. Haydon Cherry, *Down and Out in Saigon: Stories of the Poor in a Colonial City* (New Haven: Yale University Press, 2019).

44. Anderson, *Subaltern Lives*, 6.

45. Ibid., 7.

46. Saër Maty Bâ, "Culture and migration, a critical assessment," *The Encyclopedia of Global Human Migration* (Blackwell Publishing, 2013), published online, February 4, 2013.

CHAPTER I. TO THE DOCKS

1. Lê Văn Đức, *Tây hành lược ký* (Qui Nhơn: Imprimerie de Qui Nhơn, 1923), 5.

2. Phạm Quỳnh, *Pháp du hành trình nhật ký,* in *Phạm Quỳnh: tuyển tập du ký,* ed. Nguyễn Hữu Sơn (Hà Nội: Nhà Xuất Bản Tri Thức, 2012), 177.

3. Đặng Văn Long, *Les travailleurs réquis* (Paris: Bibliothêque Nghiên Cứu, 2004), 39.

4. "Sa đà du tử" [Phan Văn Hùm], "Người Á sang Âu," *Thần Chung,* October 2, 1929.

5. Wilder, *The French Imperial Nation-State*, 3.

6. Lockhart, "Broken Journey," 108.

7. Nhung Tuyet Tran, "Confession, Cosmopolitanism, and Catholic Moralizing in Early Modern Vietnam," unpublished manuscript provided to me by the author.

8. George E. Dutton, *A Vietnamese Moses: Philiphê Bỉnh and the Geographies of Early Modern Vietnamese Catholicism* (Berkeley: University of California Press, 2017), 39–40.

9. Wynn Wilcox, *Allegories of the Vietnamese Past* (New Haven: Yale Southeast Asia Monograph Series, 2011), chapter 2.

10. André Salles, *Un mandarin Breton au service du roi de Cochinchine* (Rennes: Les Portes du Large, 2006).

11. Quốc sử quán triều Nguyễn, *Đại Nam Thực Lục* (Hà Nội: Nhà Xuất Bản Giáo Dục, 2007), vol. V, 588–589.

12. Jenny Huangfu Day, *Qing Travelers to the Far West: Diplomacy and the Information Order in Late Imperial China* (Cambridge: Cambridge University Press, 2018), 2–3.

13. R. Stanley Thomson, "France in Cochinchina: The Question of Retrocession, 1862–1865," *Far Eastern Quarterly* 6.4 (August 1947): 364–78. On changing Vietnamese historical interpretations of Phan Thanh Giản, see *Thế kỷ XXI nhìn về nhân vật lịch sử Phan Thanh Giản* (Thành Phố Hồ Chí Minh: Nhà Xuất Bản Hồng Đức, 2013).

14. GGI to MC, January 30, 1894, IC AF 20, ANOM.

15. GGI to MC, September 26, 1894, GGI 22180, ANOM.

16. Mark McLeod, "Nguyen Truong To: A Catholic Reformer at Emperor Tu-Duc's Court," *Journal of Southeast Asian Studies* 25.2 (September 1994): 313–30.

17. Nguyễn Thế Anh, *Monarchie et fait colonial au Viêt-Nam (1875–1925): Le crépuscule d'un ordre traditionnel* (Paris: L'Harmattan, 1992), 33.

18. Nguyễn Trọng Hiệp to GGI, February 28, 1899, GGI 6033, ANOM.

19. Nguyễn Bá Thế, *Tôn Thọ Tường (1826–1877)* (Sài Gòn: Tủ Sách "Những Mảnh Gương" Tân Việt, 1957).

20. H. Peyssonnaux and Bùi Văn Cung, "Le traité de 1874: journal du secrétaire de l'ambassade annamite," *Bulletin des amis du vieux Hué* 7.3 (July-September 1920): 365–84.

21. GOUCOCH to Chefs de province, October 1905, IB.24/145 (2), TTLT II.

22. Emmanuel Poisson, *Mandarins et subalternes au nord du Viêt Nam: Une bureaucratie à l'épreuve (1820–1918)* (Paris: Maisonneuve & Larose, 2004), 135.

23. Marie Aberdam, "Élites cambodgiennes en situation coloniale, essai d'histoire sociale des réseaux de pouvoir dans l'administration cambodgienne sous le protectorat français (1860–1953)" (PhD diss., Université Paris I Panthéon Sorbonne, 2019), 799–803.

24. Poisson, *Mandarins et subalternes*, 184.

25. Okna Veang Thiounn, *Voyage en France du roi Sisowath: en l'année du cheval, huitième de la décade correspondant à l'année occidentale 1906, royaume du Cambodge*, trans. Olivier De Bernon (Paris: Mercure, 2005), iv.

26. Amiral gouverneur to Préfet maritime de Toulon, December 1, 1873, IC AF 22, ANOM.

27. GGI to MC, February 19, 1922, Dossier Phạm Quỳnh, SLOTFOM XV.78, ANOM. Phạm Quỳnh's talks were later published as *Quelques conférences à Paris, mai-juillet 1922* (Hà Nội: Imprimerie Tonkinoise, 1923).

28. Phạm Quỳnh, "Thuật chuyện du lịch ở Paris," in Nguyễn Hữu Sơn, *Phạm Quỳnh: tuyển tập du ký*, 422–423.

29. "Renseignements provenant de l'agent Jolin," April 18, 1922, Dossier Nguyễn Văn Vĩnh, SLOTFOM XV.21, ANOM.

30. Brett M. Reilly, "The Origins of the Vietnamese Civil War and the State of Vietnam" (PhD diss., University of Wisconsin-Madison, 2018), 27.

31. Penny Edwards, *Cambodge: The Cultivation of a Nation* (Honolulu: University of Hawai'i Press, 2007), 7–8.

32. Peter Van der Veer, "Colonial Cosmopolitanism," in *Conceiving Cosmopolitanism: Theory, Context, and Practice*, ed. Steven Vertovec and Robin Cohen (New York: Oxford University Press, 2002), 167.

33. Brocheux and Hémery, *Indochina,* 217.

34. MAE to MC, September 12, 1863, 8MD/28, MAE.

35. GOUCOCH to MC, July 11, 1871, IC AF 316, ANOM.

36. GOUCOCH to Administrateurs de province, October 1905, GOUCOCH IB.24/145(2), TTLT II.

37. P. Edwards, *Cambodge,* 74.

38. "Rapport sur l'École coloniale adressé au Conseil d'administration par M. Aymonier, Directeur," July 15, 1889, SL 4019, TTLT II.

39. Pierre Pasquier to RST, January 16, 1907, IC AF 27, ANOM.

40. Fourès to GGI, October 5, 1906, IC AF 27, ANOM.

41. Tim Doling, "Dinner with 'Tong Doc' Do Huu Phuong": https://www.historicvietnam.com/dinner-with-the-tong-doc.

42. Trần Đại Học to Inspecteur des affaires civiles de Cochinchine, January 10, 1900, GOUCOCH IA.3/092 (2), TTLT II.

43. Đại học Quốc gia Hà Nội, Trường đại học Khoa học Xã hội và Nhân văn, *Tân thư và xã hội Việt Nam cuối thế kỷ XIX đầu thế kỷ XX* (Hà Nội: Nhà Xuất Bản Chính Trị Quốc Gia, 1997).

44. Poisson, *Mandarins et subalternes,* 96–99.

45. Nguyễn Phương Ngọc, "La Société d'enseignement mutuel du Tonkin (Hội Trí Tri, 1892–1946), une autre version de l'action moderniste," in *Vietnam: le moment moderniste,* ed. Gilles de Gantès and Nguyễn Phương Ngọc (Aix en Provence: Publications de l'Université de Provence, 2009), 223–38.

46. Đỗ Văn Tâm to Comité de patronage des étudiants indochinois, August 20, 1907, IC NF 278, ANOM.

47. "Pupilles du comité Paul Bert, 1910," 9PA4, ANOM.

48. GGI to MC, December 1923, GGI 51536, ANOM.

49. "Note au sujet des jeunes Annamites qui vont faire leurs études en France," October 16, 1911, GGI 51537, ANOM.

50. Nguyễn Văn Sang to "chère Chính," March 5, 1928, Dossier Nguyễn Văn Sang, SLOTFOM XV.79, ANOM.

51. Trần Văn Hà to "cher Papa," April 14, 1928, Dossier Trần Văn Hà, SLOTFOM XV.103, ANOM.

52. Lưu Thực Tự to his family, April 3, 1930, Dossier Lưu Thực Tự, SLOTFOM XV.132, ANOM.

53. "Rapport de mission de Monsieur Thalamas, Directeur général de l'instruction publique en Indochine," undated, IC AF 2226, ANOM.

54. Đào Đăng Vỹ, L'Annam qui nait (Huế: Imprimerie du Mirador, 1938), 216.

55. "Rapport de mission de Monsieur Thalamas, Directeur général de l'instruction publique en Indochine," undated, IC AF 2226, ANOM.

56. AGEFOM 244/330, ANOM.

57. Hoang Van Tuan, "L'Université de Hanoi (1906–1945). Un outil de renouvellement des élites et de la culture vietnamiennes?," Outre-mers 394–395.1 (2017): 61–84.

58. Trần Văn Tùng, Rêves d'un campagnard annamite (Paris: Mercure de France, 1940), 187.

59. Nguyễn Mạnh Tường, Pierres de France (Hà Nội: Éditions de la Revue indochinoise, 1937), 14.

60. Hoàng Xuân Nhị, Les Cahiers intimes de Heou-Tam, étudiant d'Extrême-Orient (Paris: Mercure de France, 1939), 15, 19.

61. Hà Vũ Trọng, "Vũ Cao Đàm—nghệ thuật từ Đông sang Tây," Tạp Chí Mỹ Thuật, June 2019.

62. On Nguyễn Ngọc Cương, see Vương Hồng Sển, Hồi ký: 50 năm mê hát, 50 năm cải lương (Thành Phố Hồ Chí Minh: Nhà Xuất Bản Trẻ, 2010).

63. Dossier Đỗ Tất Văn, SLOTFOM XV.32, ANOM.

64. Philippe Peycam, The Birth of Vietnamese Political Journalism: Saigon, 1916–1930 (New York: Columbia University Press, 2012), 267n10.

65. Cao Văn Chánh, "Đáp Tàu André Lebon," serialized in Phụ Nữ Tân Văn in the second half of 1929.

66. Nguyễn Văn Sang to "chère Chính," March 5, 1928, Dossier Nguyễn Văn Sang, SLOTFOM XV.79, ANOM.

67. His account of the trip is Du lịch Âu Châu, hội chợ Marseille, đấu xảo quốc tế Paris, ed. Nguyễn Hữu Sơn (Hà Nội: Nhà Xuất Bản Tri Thức, 2017).

68. Lê Hữu Xứng to Chef du bureau de l'immigration indigène, June 8, 1939, SLOTFOM III.13, ANOM.

69. Eric Guerassimoff, Andrew Hardy, Nguyễn Phương Ngọc, and Emmanuel Poisson, eds., Les migrations impériales au Vietnam: Travail et colonisations dans l'Asie-Pacifique français, XIXe-XXe siècles (Paris: Hémisphères Éditions, 2020), 20.

70. Ibid., 11.

71. See Richard Fogarty, Race and War in France: Colonial Subjects in the French Army, 1914–1918 (Baltimore: Johns Hopkins University Press, 2008), chapter 1.

72. Albert Sarraut, La mise en valeur des colonies françaises (Paris: Payot, 1923), 100.

73. Cited in Le Van Ho, *Des Vietnamiens dans la Grande Guerre,* 30.

74. Ibid., chapter 1.

75. François-Bertrand Can, *Carnet de route d'un petit marsouin cochinchinois* (Sài Gòn: Imprimerie Albert Portail, 1918), 8.

76. Le Van Ho, *Des Vietnamiens dans la Grande Guerre,* 42–44.

77. Vu-Hill, *Coolies into Rebels,* 41–43.

78. Ibid., 46.

79. Multiple signatories to GGI, March 7, 1916, RST 21307, TTLT I.

80. Quoted in Le Van Ho, *Des Vietnamiens dans la Grande Guerre,* 53.

81. Ibid., 55.

82. Ibid., chapter 1.

83. Ibid., 104.

84. Général Peltier to MC, October 8, 1925, SLOTFOM III.22, ANOM.

85. Dossier Nguyễn Văn Ký, SLOTFOM XV.22, ANOM.

86. Luguern, "Les 'Travailleurs Indochinois,'" 277.

87. Ibid., 283.

88. Ibid., 316, 399.

89. Ibid., 950.

90. "Chị Lê Hoàng Yến đi lính!," *Tiếng Dân,* October 21, 1939.

91. GGI to Phạm Duy Khiêm, September 28, 1939, GGI 1169, TTLT I.

92. Julia Emerson, "Phạm Duy Khiêm: A Man Apart," *Moussons: Recherches en sciences humaines sur l'Asie du Sud-Est* 24 (2014), note 19.

93. Liêm-Khê Luguern, "Les réquisitions pour les Guerres mondiales en Europe révélatrices des dynamiques socio-spatiales de l'Indochine coloniale," in Guerassimoff, Hardy, Nguyễn, and Poisson, *Les migrations impériales au Vietnam,* 160–61.

94. Luguern, "Les 'Travailleurs Indochinois,'" 292.

95. Đốc phủ sứ to Procureur de la république, November 8, 1939, IIA.45/196(3), TTLT II.

96. Herman Lebovics, *True France: The Wars over Cultural Identity, 1900–1945* (Ithaca, NY: Cornell University Press, 1992), 55–56.

97. "Các nhà mĩ nghệ ta với cuộc đấu xảo mĩ nghệ ở Paris sang năm," *Trung Bắc Tân Văn,* December 20, 1924.

98. GGI 1677, ANOM.

99. Dana Hale, *Races on Display: French Representations of Colonized Peoples, 1886–1940* (Bloomington: Indiana University Press, 2008), 148.

100. Commissaire général de l'exposition de 1907 to GGI, September 12, 1907, GGI 1682, ANOM.

101. Commissaire général de l'exposition de 1931 to GGI, July 15, 1930, GOUCOCH VI.A.6/191 (1), TTLT II.

102. Phạm Văn Đào to Délégué du CAI, December 9, 1936, SLOFTOM IV.2, ANOM.

103. Inspecteur des affaires politiques to RST, June 21, 1937, RST NF 4522, ANOM.

104. Dossier Nguyễn Văn Hiện, SLOTFOM XV.112, ANOM.

105. Solène Granier, *Domestiques indochinois*, 84, 88.

106. Ibid., 9.

107. Brocheux and Hémery, *Indochina*, 282.

108. Wilder, *The French Imperial Nation-State*, 23.

109. "Note sur le Comité Paul Bert," undated, 9PA4, ANOM.

110. Nguyễn Văn Sang to "chère Chính," March 3, 1928, Dossier Nguyễn Văn Sang, SLOTFOM XV.79, ANOM.

111. Hồ Hữu Tường, "Un fétu de paille dans la tourmente," unpublished memoir in the possession of Hue-Tam Ho Tai, 47.

112. Cited in Julie Pham, "Revolution, Communism, and History in the Thought of Trần Văn Giàu" (PhD diss., University of Cambridge, 2008), 55.

113. Nguyễn An Ninh to Nguyễn Văn Bá, September 8, 1927, Dossier Nguyễn An Ninh, SLOTFOM XV.28, ANOM.

114. Nguyễn Tấn Di Trọng, unpublished journal of the Democratic Republic of Vietnam's friendship delegation to France, April-September 1946, QH 603, TTLT III.

115. "A/s de Tran Ngoc Danh, Le Van Truong et d'autres détenues," February 10, 1948, BA 2153, APPP.

116. Julia Clancy-Smith, *Mediterraneans: North Africa and Europe in an Age of Migration, c. 1800–1900* (Berkeley: University of California Press, 2011), 9.

117. Bùi Quang Tấn to Bùi Quang Chiêu, November 16, 1927, Dossier Bùi Quang Tấn, SLOTFOM XV.101, ANOM.

118. Lê Hữu Thọ, *Itinéraire d'un petit mandarin* (Paris: L'Harmattan, 1997), 21.

119. Lý Bình Kiệt to Lương Văn Mới, October 17, 1928, Dossier Lý Bình Kiệt, SLOTFOM XV.98, ANOM.

120. Dossier Trương Văn Vĩnh, SLOTFOM XV.109, ANOM.

121. See, for example, IC NF 1687, ANOM.

122. Hiển Vương, *Minh ơi! Tôi muốn đi coi cuộc đấu xảo Paris* (Sài Gòn: Đức Lưu Phương, 1931).

123. Lê Văn Đức, *Cách đi Tây* (Sài Gòn: Đức Lưu Phương, 1931).

124. "Note de l'agent DeVilliers," July 28, 1922, Dossier Nguyễn Văn Vĩnh, SLOTFOM XV.21, ANOM.

125. Nguyen Van Thanh, *Saigon-Marseille, allez simple*, 31.

126. Phan Tấn Lựu to MC, June 26, 1938, Dossier Phan Tấn Lựu, SLOTFOM XV.31, ANOM.

127. "Fiche de renseignements—Bùi Thị Trâm," undated, Dossier Bùi Thị Trâm, SLOTFOM XV.90, ANOM.

128. Directeur du SAMI to GGI, November 23, 1928, Dossier Nguyễn Văn Khuê, SLOTFOM XV.65, ANOM.

129. GGI to RSA, June 19, 1922, GGI 51303, ANOM.

130. Dossier Nguyễn Đào Thành, SLOTFOM XV.43, ANOM.

131. Dossier Phạm Hữu Điệc, SLOFTOM XV.125, ANOM.

132. Dossier Phạm Viết Cẩn, SLOTFOM XV.41, ANOM.

1. Trần Lý to Trần Kim Xương, August 9, 1929, Dossier Trần Lý, SLOTFOM XV.106, ANOM.

2. Trần Bá Vinh, *Pháp du ký sự* (Vinh: Châu Tinh, 1932), 2, 4.

3. Bùi Ái, "Aventures et voyages," *Gazette de Hué,* March 22, 1935. Although he is known by Bùi Ái, a French police documentaion system suggests his given name was Nguyen Doan Ai (diacritics unknown).

4. Lê Văn Đức, *Tây hành lược ký,* 6.

5. Lockhart, "Broken Journey," 98–99.

6. Tùng Hương, "Trên đường nam Pháp," in *Du ký Việt Nam: tạp chí Nam Phong,* ed. Nguyễn Hữu Sơn (Thành Phố Hồ Chí Minh: Nhà Xuất Bản Trẻ, 2007), 2:304.

7. Lê Hữu Thọ, *Itinéraire d'un petit mandarin,* 26.

8. Nguyen Van Thanh, *Saigon-Marseille, allez simple,* 103.

9. Anderson, *Under Three Flags,* 3.

10. Paul Bois, *Le grand siècle des Messageries maritimes* (Marseille: Chambre de commerce et d'industrie Marseille-Provence, 1992). On the expansion of air travel in Indochina, see Gregory Seltzer, "The Hopes and the Realities of Aviation in French Indochina, 1919–1940" (PhD diss., University of Kentucky, 2017).

11. Charles Fawell, "In-Between Empires: Steaming the Trans-Suez Highways of French Imperialism (1830–1930)" (PhD diss., University of Chicago, 2021), 6.

12. Cao Văn Chánh, "Đáp Tàu André Lebon," *Phu Nữ Tân Văn,* September 12, 1929.

13. Bùi Ái, "Aventures et voyages," *Gazette de Hué,* April 12, 1935.

14. Nguyễn Văn Vĩnh, "Bản quán chủ nhiệm đi Marseille," *Trung Bắc Tân Văn,* April 29, 1922.

15. Phạm Phú Thứ, *Nhật ký đi Tây,* trans. Quang Uyên (Đà Nẵng: Nhà Xuất Bản Đà Nẵng, 1999), 62. When translating passages from this source, I also made reference to a French translation: "L'ambassade de Phan Thanh Giản (1863–1864)," trans. Nguyễn Đình Hòe, Ngô Đình Diệm, and Trần Xuân Toạn, *Bulletin des amis du vieux Hué* 2 (1919): 161–216 and 4 (1921): 147–87, 243–81. The French translation, however, is only of the first two-thirds of the text.

16. Lê Văn Đức, *Tây hành lược ký,* 24.

17. Cao Văn Chánh, "Đáp Tàu André Lebon," *Phu Nữ Tân Văn,* September 12, 1929.

18. Paul Fourès to MC, September 24, 1908, IC AF 27, ANOM.

19. Bùi Ái, "Aventures et voyages," *Gazette de Hué,* April 12, 1935.

20. Bùi Ái, "Aventures et voyages," *Gazette de Hué,* April 26, 1935.

21. Bùi Ái, "Aventures et voyages," *Gazette de Hué,* March 29, 1935.

22. Georges Grandjean, "Les Messageries maritimes," *Tribune indigène,* September 11, 1924.

23. "Correspondances diverses," undated, L 19/8/12, MM 12, CCIMP.

24. Trần Văn Lâm to Nguyễn An Ninh, October 25, 1926, Dossier Nguyễn An Ninh, SLOTFOM XV.14, ANOM.

25. Vu-Hill, *Coolies into Rebels*, 62.

26. Ibid., 369.

27. See Luguern, "Les 'Travailleurs Indochinois,'" 361–82; Vu-Hill, *Coolies into Rebels*, 58–64.

28. "Rapport général de voyage n. 2 (Marseille à Haiphong et retour)," February 24, 1931, L 18/9/13, MM 13, CCIMP.

29. Bùi Ái, "Aventures et voyages," *Gazette de Hué*, April 26, 1935.

30. Trần Văn Thạch, "Souvenir de traversée ou entretien avec un commandant français," *Journal des étudiants annamites*, October 15, 1928.

31. Luguern, "Les 'Travailleurs Indochinois,'" 368.

32. Nguyen Van Thanh, *Saigon-Marseille, allez simple*, 104.

33. Bùi Ái, "Aventures et voyages," *Gazette de Hué*, March 22, 1935.

34. Can, *Carnet de route*, 8.

35. Bùi Ái, "Aventures et voyages," *Gazette de Hué*, April 5, 1935.

36. Bùi Thanh Vân, *La France: relations de voyage* (Hué: Imprimerie Đắc Lập, 1923), 29.

37. Lê Hữu Thọ, *Itinéraire d'un petit mandarin*, 27.

38. Lê Văn Đức, *Tây hành lược ký*, 32.

39. Nguyễn Văn Vĩnh, "Bản quán chủ nhiệm đi Marseille," *Trung Bắc Tân Văn*, April 29, 1922.

40. Bùi Ái, "Aventures et voyages," *Gazette de Hué*, March 22, 1935.

41. Trịnh Hưng Ngẫu, "Impressions de voyage III, de Colombo à Aden," *Tribune indochinoise*, November 14, 1927.

42. Trịnh Hưng Ngẫu, "Impressions de voyage V, de Djibouti à Suez," *Tribune indochinoise*, December 9, 1927.

43. "Rapport general du voyage n. 7 (Marseille à Haiphong et retour)," July 17, 1930, L 18/9/117, MM 117, CCIMP.

44. Bùi Thanh Vân, *Le tour du monde par un Annamite* (Hué: Bùi Huy Tín, 1929), 19.

45. Phạm Quỳnh, *Pháp du hành trình nhật ký*, 189.

46. Bùi Ái, "Aventures et voyages," *Gazette de Hué*, April 26, 1935.

47. Bùi Ái, "Aventures et voyages," *Gazette de Hué*, May 24, 1935.

48. Phạm Quỳnh, *Pháp du hành trình nhật ký*, 177, 189.

49. Vương Văn Mui to "Hai Viet," November 22, 1927, Dossier Vương Văn Mui, SLOTFOM XV.101, ANOM.

50. Serialized in *Đuốc Nhà Nam* in 1932.

51. Lê Văn Đức, *Tây hành lược ký*, 21.

52. Cao Văn Chánh, "Đáp tàu André Lebon," *Phụ Nữ Tân Văn*, September 12, 1929.

53. "Sa đà du tử" [Phan Văn Hùm], "Người Á sang Âu," *Thần Chung*, October 1–2, 1929.

54. Written under the name Phạm Vân Anh and serialized as "Sang Tây (du ký của một thiếu nữ)" and "Mười tháng ở Pháp" in *Phụ Nữ Tân Văn* from May 1929 to July 1930.

55. Cao Văn Chánh, "Đáp tàu André Lebon," *Phụ Nữ Tân Văn,* August 8, 1929.

56. Lockhart, "Broken Journey," 102.

57. Bùi Ái, "Aventures et voyages," *Gazette de Hué,* May 3, 1935.

58. Lockhart, "Broken Journey," 102.

59. Bùi Thanh Vân, *La France,* 29.

60. Consul de France à Kobe et Osaka to Ambassadeur de France au Japon, December 31, 1928, 29 CPCOM/24, MAE.

61. Phan Văn Gia, "Paris—Khám Lớn Saigon," *Thần Chung,* February 28, 1929.

62. Phạm Vân Anh [Đào Trinh Nhất], "Sang Tây (du ký của một thiếu nữ)," *Phụ Nữ Tân Văn,* May 16, 1929.

63. Nguyễn Hiến to "Mme Khanh," February 7, 1929, Dossier Nguyễn Võ Hiến, SLOTFOM XV.52, ANOM.

64. "Rapport général du voyage n. 5 (Marseille à Haiphong et retour)," May 23, 1927, L 19/8/12 (MM 12), CCIMP.

65. Nguyễn Thị Liên to MC, March 23, 1926, Dossier Nguyễn Thị Liên, SLOTFOM XV.34, ANOM.

66. Goebel, *Anti-Imperial Metropolis,* 69; "Rapport de Durand," July 18, 1929, Dossier Bùi Đức Kiên, SLOTFOM XV.97, ANOM.

67. Nguyễn Văn Vĩnh, "Bản quán chủ nhiệm đi Marseille," *Trung Bắc Tân Văn,* April 3, 1922.

68. Phạm Vân Anh [Đào Trinh Nhất], "Sang Tây (du ký của một thiếu nữ)," *Phụ Nữ Tân Văn,* June 13, 1929.

69. Okna Veang Thiounn, *Voyage en France du roi Sisowath,* 21.

70. Lê Văn Đức, *Tây hành lược ký,* 15.

71. Bùi Thanh Vân, *La France,* 44.

72. Cited in Ching Selao, *Le roman vietnamien francophone: orientalisme, occidentalisme et hybridité* (Montréal: Presses de l'Université de Montréal, 2011), 75.

73. Nguyễn Công Tiểu, *Du lịch Âu Châu,* 21.

74. Tùng Hương, "Trên đường Nam Pháp," in Nguyễn Hữu Sơn, *Du ký Việt Nam: tạp chí Nam Phong,* 2:307.

75. Trịnh Hưng Ngẫu, "Impressions de voyage II," *Tribune indochinoise,* November 4, 1927.

76. "Sa đà du tử" [Phan Văn Hùm], "Người Á sang Âu," *Thần Chung,* October 19, 1929.

77. Bùi Thanh Vân, *La France,* 20; Cao Văn Chánh, "Đáp tàu André Lebon," *Phụ Nữ Tân Văn,* October 3, 1929.

78. Trần Bá Vinh, *Pháp du ký sự,* 4.

79. Lê Văn Đức, *Tây hành lược ký,* 10.

80. Bùi Thanh Vân, *La France,* 24.

81. Trần Bá Vinh, *Pháp du ký sự,* 8.

82. Can, *Carnet de route*, 17.

83. "Linh Ve," "Impressions de voyage," *L'Echo annamite*, April 18, 1928.

84. Cao Văn Chánh, "Đáp tàu André Lebon," *Phụ Nữ Tân Văn*, August 22, 1929.

85. "Sa đà du tử" [Phan Văn Hùm], "Người Á sang Âu," *Thần Chung*, October 3, 1929.

86. Phạm Quỳnh, *Pháp du hành trình nhật ký*, 178–79.

87. Bùi Thanh Vân, *La France*, 21.

88. Ibid., 25.

89. Phạm Quỳnh, *Pháp du hành trình nhật ký*, 187.

90. Cao Văn Chánh, "Đáp tàu André Lebon," *Phụ Nữ Tân Văn*, October 3, 1929.

91. Bùi Ái, "Aventures et voyages," *Gazette de Hué*, April 26, 1935.

92. Nguyễn Công Tiễu, *Du lịch Âu Châu*, 38.

93. Can, *Carnet de route*, 16.

94. Phạm Quỳnh, *Pháp du hành trình nhật ký*, 196.

95. Bùi Thanh Vân, *La France*, 24.

96. Bùi Ái, "Aventures et voyages," *Gazette de Hué*, June 7, 1935.

97. Lê Hữu Thọ, *Itinéraire d'un petit mandarin*, 28.

98. Bùi Ái, "Aventures et voyages," *Gazette de Hué*, June 14, 1935.

99. Okna Veang Thiounn, *Voyage en France du roi Sisowath*, 103.

100. Luguern, "Les 'Travailleurs Indochinois,'" 420–21.

101. Citied in Ibid., 204.

102. Phan Văn Trường, *Une histoire de conspirateurs annamites à Paris, ou la vérité en Indochine* (Paris: Editions l'Insomniaque, 2003), 78.

103. Quoted in Patrice Morlat, "La surveillance des Indochinois à Marseille après la Première Guerre mondiale (1917–1935)," in *Une vie pour le Viêt Nam: Mélanges en l'honneur de Charles Fourniau*, ed. Alain Ruscio (Paris: Les Indes Savantes, 2016), 254.

104. Ibid., 251.

105. "Note sur le Service d'assistance morale et intellectuelle des indochinois en France," August 29, 1931, GGI 51530, ANOM.

106. See Dossier Vu Van Hien, SLOTFOM XV.124, ANOM. His case is also discussed in Granier, *Domestiques indochinois*, 161–62.

107. Directeur du SAMI to Nguyen Khanh Lieu, October 9, 1930, GGI 2229, TTLT I.

108. "Note sur le Service d'assistance morale et intellectuelle des indochinois en France," August 29, 1931, GGI 51530, ANOM.

109. Ngô Quốc Quyền to Bùi Ái, September 21, 1927, Dossier Ngô Quốc Quyền, SLOTFOM XV.85, ANOM.

110. Cao Văn Chánh, "Hai mươi bốn giờ của tôi ở đất Pháp," *Phụ Nữ Tân Văn*, October 10, 1929.

111. Trương Mỹ Sáo to Huỳnh Văn Ngọc, September 4, 1929, Dossier Trương Mỹ Sáo, SLOTFOM XV.55, ANOM.

112. Phan Văn Thiết to "mon cher Hai," November 30, 1927, Dossier Phan Văn Thiết, SLOTFOM XV.86, ANOM.

113. See Dossier Lê Văn Tiểu, SLOTFOM XV.12, ANOM.

114. "Déclarations de Trần Văn Mại faites à la Direction de la Sûreté générale du 4 novembre au 10 décembre 1935," Dossier Trần Văn Mại, SLOTFOM XV.40, ANOM.

115. Bùi Ái, "Aventures et voyages," *Gazette de Hué,* August 16, 1935.

116. Phạm Vân Anh [Đào Trinh Nhất], "Sang Tây (du ký của một thiếu nữ)," *Phụ Nữ Tân Văn,* October 17, 1929.

117. Nguyễn Tiến Lăng, "Paris: la grande ville," *Gazette de Hué,* November 11, 1939.

118. Lê Văn Huê to Đặng Văn Cương, July 20, 1929, Dossier Đặng Văn Cương, carton 14, 589PO2, CADN.

119. Phan Tư Nghĩa to Phạn Xuân Mai, May 25, 1927, Dossier Phan Tư Nghĩa, SLOTFOM XV.78, ANOM.

120. Hoàng Văn Tấn to his father, cited in GGI to MC, December 12, 1926, Dossier Hoàng Văn Tấn, SLOTFOM XV.17, ANOM.

121. Nguyễn Văn Chừng to "bien cher Phuc," January 29, 1928, Dossier Nguyễn Văn Chừng, SLOTFOM XV.75, ANOM.

122. Lý Binh Huệ to "Binh-Hoa-Ly," *Journal des étudiants annamites,* May 15, 1927.

123. Phạm Quỳnh, *Pháp du hành trinh nhật ký,* 280.

124. Phạm Thông Thảo to "Cher cousin Luân," January 30, 1928, Dossier Phạm Thông Thảo, SLOTFOM XV.99, ANOM.

125. Trinh Dinh Khai, *Décolonisation du Viêt Nam: un avocat témoigne* (Paris: L'Harmattan, 1994), 17.

126. Hồ Hữu Tường to Lê Kê Hưng, September 6, 1927, Dossier Hồ Hữu Tường, SLOTFOM XV.84, ANOM.

127. Trần Xuân Hồ to Trần Tiến Nam, February 14, 1921, Dossier Trần Xuân Hồ, SLOTFOM XV.5, ANOM.

128. Đặng Văn Long, *Les travailleurs réquis,* 50.

129. Nguyễn Văn Ngàn to Trần Văn Ngân, September 29, 1927, Dossier Nguyễn Văn Ngàn, SLOTFOM XV.87, ANOM.

130. "Impressions d'un ouvrier qui revient de France," *L'Avenir du Tonkin,* May 27, 1917.

131. Lieu Sanh Tran to his parents, June 2, 1927, Dossier Lieu Sanh Tran, SLOTFOM XV.74, ANOM.

132. Phạm Chí Phụng to Phan Thị Nhiều, June 24, 1947, CONSPOL 107, ANOM.

133. Lê Quang Ngọc, "Orient et Occident," conference at the Foyer des étudiants orientaux de Marseille, December 1934, Dossier Lê Quang Ngọc, SLOTFOM XV.109, ANOM.

134. Ngô Quốc Quyền to Bùi Ái, September 21, 1927, Dossier Ngô Quốc Quyền, SLOTFOM XV.85, ANOM.

135. Lê Văn Đắc to Ứng Văn Vỹ, August 30, 1920, Dosser Lê Văn Đắc, SLOTFOM XV.49, ANOM.

136. Bùi Thanh Vân, *La France*, 66, 68.

137. Luguern, "Les 'Travailleurs indochinois,'" 423.

CHAPTER 3. FROM CONTACT TO CONQUEST

1. Translated from a French translation in Tạ Trọng Hiệp, "Le journal de l'ambassade de Phan Thanh Giản en France (4 juillet 1863–18 avril 1864)," in *Récits de voyages asiatiques: Genres, mentalités, conception de l'espace*, ed. Claudine Salmon (Paris: Presses de l'École Française d'Extrême-Orient, Études thématiques, n. 5, 1996), 359.

2. This history, which has been closely studied, is well-summarized in Brocheux and Hémery, *Indochina*, chapter 1.

3. Tran, "Confession, Cosmopolitanism, and Catholic Moralizing in Early Modern Vietnam," 2.

4. Jonathan Spence, *The Question of Hu* (New York: Vintage, 1989), 119.

5. J. P. Daughton, "Recasting Pigneau de Béhaine," in *Việt Nam: Borderless Histories*, Nhung Tuyet Tran and Anthony Reid (Madison: University of Wisconsin Press, 2006), 293.

6. Robert Hopkins Miller, *The United States and Vietnam, 1787–1941* (Washington, DC: National Defense University Press, 1990), xv.

7. Frédéric Mantienne, *Pierre Pigneaux: Évêque d'Adran et mandarin de Cochinchine (1741–1799)* (Paris: Les Indes Savantes, 2012), 91.

8. R. P. Delvaux, "L'Ambassade de Minh-Mang à Louis-Philippe," *Bulletin des amis du vieux Hué* 15.4 (October-December 1928): 257–64.

9. Tạ Trọng Hiệp, "Le journal de l'ambassade de Phan Thanh Giản en France," 356.

10. "Journal de l'ambassade envoyée en France et en Espagne par S.M. Tự Đức (Août 1877 à Septembre 1878)," *Bulletin des amis du vieux Hué* 7.4 (October-November 1920): 407–43.

11. Unidentified official to Président de la république, April 18, 1894, IC AF 20, ANOM.

12. Nguyễn Trọng Hiệp, "Paris, capital de la France" (Hà Nội: F. H. Schneider, 1897), XXXIII.

13. "Rapport des hauts mandarins envoyés a l'exposition de 1900," RST 56850, TTLT I.

14. David Harvey, *Paris, Capital of Modernity* (London: Routledge, 2006), 95, 310.

15. Walter Benjamin, "Paris, The Capital of the Nineteenth Century," in *Walter Benjamin: Selected Writings*, vol. 3 (1935–38), ed. Howard Eiland and Michael W. Jennings (Cambridge: Belknap, 2002), 42.

16. Ibid., 36.

17. Nguyễn Thu Hoài, "Lần đầu tiên Việt Nam tham dự đấu xảo tại Pháp năm 1877," *Xưa & Nay* 406 (June 2012): 9–12. Although the envoys departed for France in 1877, the exposition was in 1878.

18. "Rapport des hauts mandarins envoyés a l'exposition de 1900," RST 56850, TTLT I.

19. Harvey, *Paris, Capital of Modernity,* 246.

20. Phạm Phú Thứ, *Nhật ký đi Tây,* 142.

21. Nguyễn Trọng Hiệp, "Paris, capital de la France," II.

22. Ibid., VI.

23. Vanessa Schwartz, *Spectacular Realities: Early Mass Culture in Fin-De-Siècle Paris* (Berkeley: University of California Press, 1998), 12.

24. Phạm Phú Thứ, *Nhật ký đi Tây,* 179.

25. Cited in Khing Hoc Dy, "Le voyage de l'envoyé cambodgien Son Diêp à Paris en 1900," in Salmon, *Récits de voyages asiatiques,* 378.

26. Benjamin, "Paris: The Capital of the Nineteenth Century," 43–44.

27. Nguyễn Trọng Hiệp, "Paris, capital de la France," XXXVI.

28. IC AF 22, ANOM.

29. Zeynep Celik, *Displaying the Orient: Architecture of Islam at Nineteenth-Century World's Fairs* (Berkeley: University of California Press, 1992), 69.

30. Jean Réville, "L'Histoire des religions à l'exposition universelle de 1889," *Revue de l'histoire des religions* 20 (1889): 97.

31. Nguyễn Trọng Hiệp, "Paris, capital de la France," IX.

32. Cited in Chun-shu Chang and Shelly Hsueh-lun Chang, *Redefining History: Ghosts, Spirits, and Human Society in P'u Sung-ling's World, 1640–1715* (Ann Arbor: University of Michigan Press, 1998), 138.

33. Directeur des affaires politiques to Délégué du CAI à Marseille, August 31, 1926, Dossier Nguyễn Sĩ Giác, SLOTFOM XV.39, ANOM.

34. Benjamin, "Paris, The Capital of the Nineteenth Century," 43–44.

35. The full poems are in Nguyễn Văn Kinh, *Nam Âm* (Sài Gòn: Nhà In Xưa Nay, 1925), 80–81.

36. Whether or not Trương Vĩnh Ký wrote an account of his time in France is unclear. The most thorough bibliography of his works makes no mention of such an account: see Anne Madelin, "Pétrus J.-B. Trương Vĩnh Ký (1837–1898), un lettré Cochinchinois entre deux cultures" (MA thesis, Université Paris VII, 1995). Neither does P. J. Honey in his translation of Trương Vĩnh Ký's report of his trip to Tonkin in 1876: see Trương Vĩnh Ký, *Voyage to Tonking in the Year Ất Hợi,* trans. P. J. Honey (London: School of Oriental and African Studies, 1982). Honey had personal connections to Trương Vĩnh Ký's family in Sài Gòn, and he lists a number of unpublished manuscripts in the family's possession before 1975. Some sources claim the existence of two texts by Trương Vĩnh Ký about his trip to France. One is a text written in Spanish and published in an unnamed Spanish newspaper, titled "Alguna reflexions de su viaje por Europe," supposedly published in French in November 1863 in a newspaper titled "Paris." The other is a Vietnamese narrative of his trip, *Nhựt trình đi sứ Lang-Sa;* the author referencing it notes that this source

exists "according to oral tradition" (*tương truyền*): see Nguyễn Vy Khanh, "Trương Vĩnh Ký va chuyến Âu-du 1863–1864," *Nghiên Cứu Lịch Sử*, March 2015: https://nghiencuulichsu.com/2015/08/03/truong-vinh-ky-va-chuyen-au%E2%80%90du-1863%E2%80%90901864. I have found no trace of either text. Nguyễn Văn Trấn, *Trương Vĩnh Ký (con người và sự thật)* (Thành Phố Hồ Chí Minh: Ban Khoa Học Xã Hội Thành Ủy, 1993), 25, quotes an unspecified account of Trương Vĩnh Ký's time in France, but he provides no reference. The best assessment of the biographical evidence on Trương Vĩnh Ký is Nguyễn Đình Đầu, *Pétrus Ký, nỗi oan thế kỷ* (Hà Nội: Nhã Nam, 2017).

37. Richard Cortambert, *Impressions d'un japonais en France; suivies des Impressions des annamites en Europe* (Paris: Achille Fauré, 1864), 204.

38. McLeod, "Nguyen Truong To," 317.

39. Trương Bá Cần, *Nguyễn Trường Tộ: con người và di thảo* (Thành Phố Hồ Chí Minh: Nhà Xuất Bản Thành Phố Hồ Chí Minh, 2002), 49–53; the full text of his report is on 259–328.

40. Portions of the unpublished manuscript (*Nhựt trình đi sứ định đi hòa ước thương ước, năm qui dậu*) related to the 1873 Franco-Nguyễn negotiations were published in translation in *Bulletin des amis du vieux Hué* in 1920, but the full text has apparently been lost.

41. Trương Minh Ký, *Như tây nhựt trình* (Sài Gòn: Rey & Curiol, 1889), lines 1611–1612, 1840.

42. Ibid., line 61.

43. Trương Minh Ký, *Chư quấc thại hội* (Sài Gòn: Rey & Curiol, 1889), cited in Nguyễn Hữu Sơn, "Du ký của người Việt Nam."

44. Prefect of Collège des Frerès Maristes de Seyne to MC, August 25, 1869, IC AF 316.

45. For biographical information on these students, see Aberdam, "Élites cambodgiennes en situation coloniale," 303–7.

46. *Revue pédagogique* XII.1 (Janvier-Juin 1888), 255.

47. P. Edwards, *Cambodge*, 75.

48. "Rapport du conseil colonial, November 24, 1888," SL 4019, TTLT II.

49. Luguern, "Les 'Travailleurs Indochinois,'" 255.

50. On Trần Trọng Kim's time in France, see Hà Vinh, "Trần Trọng Kim trong góc khuất của lịch sử," *Tạp Chí Xưa & Nay* 212 (May 2004): 11–13.

51. Poisson, *Mandarins et subalternes*, 186. On intellectual and scholarly currents at the Quốc Học, see *Đặc san kỷ niệm 105 năm Trường Quốc học Huế (1896–2001)* (Huế: Sở Văn Hóa Thông Tin Thừa Thiên—Huế, 2001).

52. Fourès to GGI, September 26, 1907, GGI 2559, ANOM.

53. "Rapport de la Mission Indo-Chinoise (Section Cambodgienne) adressé à monsieur le Résident Supérieur de la République Francaise au Cambodge par l'Okhna Phinit Vohar Keth, 1er Secrétaire du Conseil des Ministres," December 30, 1906, GGI 2559, ANOM.

54. Fourès to GGI, December 31, 1907, GGI 2560, ANOM.

55. Fourès to GGI, September 26, 1907, GGI 2559, ANOM.

56. Fourès to GGI, September 16, 1906, IC AF 27, ANOM.

57. GGI to MC, February 19, 1909, GGI 2562, ANOM.

58. Trần Tấn Bình, "Conférence du 6 mars 1907 à Nam Định," *Bulletin de l'École française d'Extrême-Orient,* January-June 1907, 156.

59. "Rapport mensuel du 22 juin au 22 juillet 1906," GGI 2558, ANOM.

60. Members of Permanent Mission to MC, November 26, 1907, IC AF 27, ANOM.

61. Nguyễn Trọng Hiệp, "Paris: capital de la France," XXIV.

62. Nguyễn Huy Tương, "Pensées d'un Annamite sur la France et sur son pays," unpublished manuscript from 1909, GGI 20422, ANOM.

63. Trần Tấn Bình, "Conférence du 6 mars 1907 à Nam Định," 166.

64. Letter from participant in Permanent Mission to "Monsieur le Directeur," September 22, 1906, GGI 2558, ANOM.

65. Fourès to MC, September 24, 1908, IC AF 27, ANOM.

66. Tonkin participants in the Permanent Mission of Indochinese Mandarins to GGI, August 1908, IC AF 27, ANOM.

67. MC to Chef de service coloniale à Marseille, undated, IC AF 27, ANOM.

68. Pasquier to RST, January 16, 1907, IC AF 27, ANOM.

69. Christopher Goscha, "Bao Dai et Sihanouk: la fabrique indochinoise des rois coloniaux," in *La Colonisation des corps: de l'Indochine au Viet Nam,* ed. François Guillemot and Agathe Larcher-Goscha (Paris: Vendémiaire, 2014), 129.

70. Pierre Lamant, *L'Affaire Yukanthor: une autopsie d'un scandal colonial* (Paris: L'Harmattan, 1989), 105.

71. Robert Aldrich, "Colonial Kings in the Metropole: The Visits to France of King Sisowath (1906) and Emperor Khai Dinh (1922)," in *Royals on Tour: Politics, Pageantry and Colonialism,* ed. Robert Aldrich and Cindy McCreedy (Manchester: Manchester University Press, 2018), 130.

72. Okna Veang Thiounn, *Voyage du roi Sisowath en France,* xi.

73. "Note au sujet du voyage du roi Khai-Dinh en France," September 30, 1921, SLOTFOM III.125, ANOM.

74. Nguyễn Thế Anh, *Monarchie et fait colonial au Viêt-Nam,* 19.

75. Ibid., 237.

76. "Note de l'agent Jolin du 9 Septembre 1922," Dossier Nguyễn Hữu Giai, SLOTFOM XV.31, ANOM.

77. The most detailed account of his daily activities is Nguyễn Cao Tiêu, *Ngự giá như Tây ký* (Huế: Đắc Lập, 1922).

78. Phan Châu Trinh, "L'Empereur d'Annam en France," undated, SLOTFOM III.125, ANOM.

79. Nguyễn Thế Anh, *Monarchie et fait coloniale au Viêt-Nam,* 245.

80. Goscha, "Bao Dai et Sihanouk," 135–36.

81. Ibid., 139–41.

82. Account by Pierre Guesde of Prince Souphanouvong's time in France, undated, SLOTFOM I.6, ANOM.

83. Phan Tấn Quế to his parents, March 27, 1927, Dossier Phan Tấn Quế, SLOTFOM XV.79, ANOM.

84. Bửu Thập to Bửu Trác, June 9, 1923, Dossier Bửu Thập, SLOTFOM XV.28, ANOM.

85. "Paris ou Pnom-Penh?," unidentified newspaper article, Dossier Norodom Norindeth, SLOTFOM XV.9, ANOM.

86. Undated note, Dossier Norodom Ritharasi, SLOTFOM XV.10, ANOM.

87. The complete text of Phan Châu Trinh's letter is in *Phan Châu Trinh and His Political Writings*, ed. Vinh Sinh (Ithaca, NY: Cornell University Southeast Asia Program Publications, 2009), 87–102.

88. Trang-Gaspard, *Hồ Chí Minh à Paris*, 199.

89. Christopher Goscha, "Aux origines du républicanisme vietnamien: circulations mondiales et connexions coloniales," *Vingtième siècle: revue d'histoire* 131.3 (July-September 2016): 26.

90. Nguyễn Phan Quang and Phan Văn Hoàng, *Luật sư Phan Văn Trường* (Thành Phố Hồ Chí Minh: Nhà Xuất Bản Thành Phố Hồ Chí Minh, 1995), chapters 1–2.

91. "Extrait du procès-verbal de la séance du 29 Mars 1912," GGI 2563, ANOM.

92. Ibid.; Pierre Brocheux, "Phan Van Truong, 1876–1933. Acteur d'une histoire partagée," *Moussons: Recherches en sciences humaines sur l'Asie du Sud-Est* 24 (2014): 19–32.

93. "Extrait du procès-verbal de la séance du 29 Mars 1912," GGI 2563, ANOM.

94. Sophie Quinn-Judge, *Ho Chi Minh: The Missing Years, 1919–1941* (Berkeley: University of California Press, 2002), 15.

95. A dossier on this episode is GGI 2573, ANOM.

96. The most detailed account of this episode is in Trần Mỹ-Vân, *A Vietnamese Royal Exile in Japan: Prince Cường Để (1882–1951)* (New York: Routledge, 2005), 88–89.

97. Quinn-Judge, *Ho Chi Minh*, 14.

98. Phan Văn Trường, *Une histoire de conspirateurs annamites à Paris*, 124–25.

99. Ibid., 128.

100. Vinh Sinh, *Phan Châu Trinh and His Political Writings*, 34.

101. Phan Văn Trường, *Une histoire des conspirateurs annamites à Paris*, 160–82.

102. Quinn-Judge, *Ho Chi Minh*, 24.

103. Ibid., 12.

104. The full petition is in François Guillemot, *Viêt-Nam, fractures d'une nation: une histoire contemporaine de 1858 à nos jours* (Paris: La Découverte, 2018).

105. Goscha, "Aux origines du républicanisme vietnamien."

106. Vinh Sinh, *Phan Châu Trinh and His Political Writings*, 88.

107. The observation and source quotations on this point are from Goscha, *Going Indochinese*, 53–54.

1. "Note sur le Comité Paul Bert," August 20, 1907, IC NF 278, ANOM.

2. Phan Văn Trường, *Une histoire de conspirateurs annamites à Paris,* 80.

3. The letter is quoted in Salles to "mon cher ami" (a member of the Alliance française), November 23, 1912, Dossier Phan Văn Trường, SLOTFOM XV.3, ANOM.

4. Brocheux and Hémery, *Indochina,* 89.

5. Peter Zinoman, "Provincial Cosmopolitanism: Vũ Trọng Phụng's Literary Engagements," in *Traveling Nation-Makers: Transnational Flows and Movements in the Making of Modern Southeast Asia,* ed. Caroline Hau and Kasian Tejapira (Singapore and Kyoto: Kyoto University Press, 2011), 127.

6. RST to GGI, July 27, 1915, GGI 51537, ANOM.

7. Brochure describing the school's course of study, RST 21404, TTLT I.

8. Directeur de l'École pratique d'enseignement colonial to MC, July 9, 1910, GGI 2563, ANOM.

9. "Note sur le Comité Paul Bert," August 20, 1907, IC NF 278.

10. "Arrêté modifiant l'organisation de la Mission permanente indochinoise en France (31 October 1908)," 9PA4, ANOM.

11. Trịnh Văn Thảo, *L'école française en Indochine* (Paris: Karthala, 1995), 276.

12. Lê Văn Chỉnh, *Voyage médico-chirurgical en France: Paris—Amiens—Berck* (Extrait des archives provinciales de chirurgie, n.d.), 7.

13. Lê Văn Chỉnh to RST, May 27, 1911, IC NF 275(1), ANOM.

14. Claire Trần Thị Liên, "Nguyễn Xuân Mai (1890–1929). Itinéraire d'un médecin indochinois engagé pendant la Première Guerre mondiale," in *Entrer en guerre,* ed. Hélène Baty-Delalande and Carine Trévisan (Paris: Herrman, 2016), 297–316.

15. "Conclusions adoptées par le Comité Paul Bert dans sa séance du 25 Octobre 1912," IC NF 278, ANOM.

16. Trịnh Văn Thảo, *L'école française en Indochine,* 276.

17. Ernest Outrey to GOUCOCH, November 27, 1905, GOUCOCH IB.24/145(2), TTLT II.

18. "Conclusions adoptées par le Comité Paul Bert dans sa séance du 25 Octobre 1912," IC NF 278, ANOM.

19. "Renseignements envoyées aux gouverneur général de l'Indochine," April 4, 1922, SLOTFOM I.27, ANOM.

20. Jacques Dalloz, "Les Vietnamiens dans la franc-maçonnerie coloniale," *Revue française d'histoire d'outre-mer* 85.320 (1998), 104.

21. Nguyễn Phương Ngọc, *À l'origine de l'anthropologie au Vietnam: Recherche sur les auteurs de la première moitié du XXe siècle* (Marseille: Presses universitaires de Provence, 2012), 103.

22. "Note sur le Comité Paul Bert," July 5, 1911, 9PA4, ANOM.

23. Unspecified author to MC, November 19, 1907, IC AF 315, ANOM.

24. Nguyễn Khắc Kiệm to Salles, February 28, 1911, 9PA4, ANOM.

25. Salles to MC, August 1, 1911, 9PA4, ANOM.

26. Proviseur du Lycée Mignet to Monsieur l'inspecteur d'académie, January 10, 1923, GGI 51536, ANOM.

27. Nguyễn Văn Vĩnh, "Nos étudiants en France," *L'Annam nouveau,* February 11, 1932.

28. Lockhart, "Broken Journey," 121.

29. Dossier Trần Văn Mại, SLOTFOM XV.40, ANOM.

30. "Procès verbal" (Paul Pujol interrogation of Trần Duy Đẩm), September 5, 1939, Dossier Trần Duy Đẩm, SLOTFOM XV.73, ANOM.

31. Huỳnh Kim Hữu to Trần Văn Kẹm, May 22, 1929, Dossier Huỳnh Kim Hữu, SLOTFOM XV.127, ANOM.

32. Dossier Tống Văn Hên, SLOTFOM XV.54, ANOM.

33. Trần Văn Nhu to his father, April 8, 1929, Dossier Trần Văn Nhu, SLOT-FOM XV.52, ANOM.

34. Dossier Phạm Viết Cẩn, SLOTFOM XV.41, ANOM.

35. Dossier Lê Văn Tiểu, SLOTFOM XV.12, ANOM.

36. Dossier Nguyễn Văn Lịnh, SLOTFOM XV.137, ANOM.

37. Lê Công Nên to his uncle, March 18, 1928, Dossier Lê Công Nên, SLOT-FOM XV.104, ANOM.

38. "Note du 17 décembre 1925," SLOTFOM III.25, ANOM.

39. Tùng Hương, "Trên đường Nam Pháp," in Nguyễn Hữu Sơn, *Du ký Việt Nam: tạp chí Nam Phong,* 2:311.

40. Henri Là Phương, "Ceux qui étudient," unpublished submission to *Progrès annamite,* Dossier Henri Là Phương, SLOTFOM XV.9, ANOM.

41. Trần Văn Hà to his father, April 14, 1928, Dossier Trần Văn Hà, SLOT-FOM XV.103, ANOM.

42. Cao Quỳnh An to his father, February 2, 1927, Dossier Cao Quỳnh An, SLOTFOM XV.80, ANOM.

43. McConnell, *Leftward Journey,* 52–53.

44. Nguyễn Văn Hy to Nguyễn Tin, July 18, 1932, Dossier Nguyễn Văn Hy, SLOTFOM XV.123, ANOM.

45. Claire Trần Thị Liên, "Henriette Bui: The Narrative of Vietnam's First Woman Doctor," in *Viêt-Nam Exposé: French Scholarship on Twentieth-Century Vietnamese Society,* ed. Gisèle Bousquet and Pierre Brocheux (Ann Arbor: University of Michigan, 2002), 278–312.

46. Emerson, "Phạm Duy Khiêm," 107–26.

47. During the 1930s, 34 percent of official scholarship recipients were identified as from Tonkin, 15 percent from Annam, and 20 percent from Cochinchina. Of the remaining 31 percent, 24 percent were from an unidentified part of Vietnam, and 7 percent from Cambodia or Laos. See Trịnh Văn Thảo, *L'école française en Indochine,* 272.

48. Hồ Đắc Di, "Những năm học y khoa tại Pháp (1918–1931)," in *Hồ Đắc Di: nhà y học triết nhân* (Hà Nội: Nhà Xuất Bản Chính Trị Quốc Gia Sự Thật, 2014), 193.

49. "Lettre de France aux médecins auxiliaires de l'Indochine," *Tribune indochinoise,* October 8, 1928.

50. "A propos d'un succès," *Bulletin de l'association générale des étudiants indochinois,* December 1927-January 1928, 24–33.

51. IC NF 1852, ANOM.

52. Claire Trần Thị Liên, "Henriette Bui," 287.

53. See Trịnh Văn Thảo, *Les compagnons de route de Ho Chi Minh: histoire d'un engagement intellectuelle au Viêt-Nam* (Paris: Karthala, 2004), 77–83.

54. Dương Văn Giáo, *L'Indochine pendant la guerre 1914–1918: contribution à l'étude de la colonisation indochinoise* (Paris: J. Budry, 1925).

55. Nguyễn Sơn Dương, "Luật sư Phan Anh: kẻ sĩ từ tâm," *Báo Đại Đoàn Kết,* May 23, 2019.

56. Nguyễn Phương Ngọc, *À l'origine de l'anthropologie au Vietnam,* 102.

57. Ibid., 104.

58. Bùi Thị Cẩm, *Étude sur la condition privée de la femme en droit Annamite* (Paris: Domat-Montchrestien, 1940).

59. Grégory Mikaelian, "The Gru of Parnassus: Au Chhieng among the Titans," *UDAYA, Journal of Khmer Studies* 15 (2020): 127–82.

60. On his early life, see Daniel Hémery, "Itinéraire I: Premier exil," in *L'itinéraire de Tran Duc Thao: Phénoménologie et transfert culturel*, ed. Jocelyn Benoist and Michel Espagne (Paris: Armand Colin, 2013).

61. Biographical information for many of these figures is in Trịnh Văn Thảo, *Les compagnons de route de Hô Chi Minh,* chapter 2.

62. Nguyễn Mạnh Tường, *Pierres de France,* 27.

63. Nguyễn Khắc Viện, *Tự truyện* (Hà Nội: Nhà Xuất Bản Khoa Học Xã Hội, 2007), 53.

64. Tri Vũ and Phan Nhọc Khuê, *Trần Đức Thảo: những lời trăng trối* (Arlington, VA: Tổ Hợp Xuất Bản Miền Đông Hoa Kỳ, 2014), 83.

65. Quoted in Hémery, "Itinéraire I: Premier exil," 52.

66. Cited in Emerson, "Phạm Duy Khiệm."

67. Directeur de l'Ecole des langues orientales vivantes to MC, November 8, 1912, SLOTFOM XV.3, ANOM.

68. Documents on this lecture series are in SLOTFOM III.16, ANOM.

69. "Note de la direction de la Sûreté générale indochinoise relative au cochinchinois Le Van Ngon et à l'association des étudiants annamites à Lyon," August 26, 1930, SLOTFOM III.32, ANOM.

70. "Déclarations de Trần Văn Mại faites à la Direction de la Sûreté générale du 4 novembre au 10 décembre 1935," Dossier Trần Văn Mại, SLOTFOM XV.40, ANOM.

71. Phạm Huy Thông, "Le Tet et le problème des traditions annamites," speech at the Foyer d'étudiants de la France d'outre-mer, February 6, 1944, *Bulletin de la France d'outre-mer* 6, February 1944.

72. Đỗ Đức Hồ, *Soviets d'Annam et désarroi des dieux blancs* (Paris: Imprimerie de France, 1938).

73. Undated interview (likely mid-1944) of Tào Kim Hải by an official at the Ministry of Colonies, Dossier Tào Kim Hải, SLOTFOM XV.109, ANOM.

74. Tim Herrick, "'A book which is no longer discussed today': Tran Duc Thao, Jacques Derrida, and Maurice Merleau-Ponty," *Journal of the History of Ideas* 66.1 (January 2005): 118.

75. Hémery, "Itinéraire I: Premier exil," 61.

76. "Note," February 4, 1950, Dossier Hoàng Văn Cơ, SLOTFOM XV.82, ANOM.

77. McConnell, *Leftward Journey,* 57.

78. Biographical note (undated), Dossier Lê Hiến, SLOTFOM XV.153, ANOM.

79. IC NF 229, ANOM.

80. Général Peltier to MC, October 8, 1925, SLOTFOM III.22, ANOM.

81. Trần Văn Giàu to Huỳnh Văn Diệp, January 28, 1929, Dossier Trần Văn Giàu, SLOTFOM XV.110, ANOM.

82. Đỗ Tất Văn to Nguyễn Kim Đính, August 17, 1927, Dossier Đỗ Tất Văn, SLOTFOM XV.32, ANOM.

83. Hoàng Quang Giụ to Trần Huy Liệu, May 29, 1926, SPCE 381, ANOM.

84. Unnamed to Thu Cúc, Dossier Thu Cúc, SLOTFOM XV.150, ANOM.

85. Vũ Liên to Huỳnh Thúc Kháng, April 5, 1930, Dossier Vũ Liên, SLOTFOM XV.50, ANOM.

86. Phạm Quỳnh, *Pháp du hành trình nhật ký,* 318–19.

87. Ngô Quang Huy to Editor of *Đông Pháp Thời Báo,* January 24, 1928, Dossier Ngô Quang Huy, SLOTFOM XV.79, ANOM.

88. Nguyễn Văn Sang to Nguyễn Văn Của, May 1, 1929, Dossier Nguyễn Văn Sang, SLOTFOM XV.79, ANOM.

89. Dossier Nguyễn Minh Quang, SLOTFOM XV.12, ANOM.

90. "Rapport de Désiré," December 3, 1925, SLOTFOM III.1, ANOM.

91. Subscription call for *Việt Nam Hồn,* May 15, 1923, SLOTFOM III.86, ANOM.

92. Quinn-Judge, *Ho Chi Minh,* 59.

93. On Diệp Văn Kỳ's role in *Việt Nam Hồn,* see SLOTFOM XV.15, ANOM.

94. "Transmission d'un journal," August 20, 1927, SLOTFOM V.36, ANOM.

95. Trần Văn Thạch, "Propagande colonialiste," *Journal des étudiants annamites,* January 15, 1929.

96. "Entrevue de l'agent Thomas du 30 janvier 1932," SLOTFOM V.24, ANOM.

97. "Entrevue de l'agent Thomas du 15 février 1932," SLOTFOM V.24, ANOM.

98. Trần Ngươn Phiêu, *Phan Văn Hùm: thân thế và sự nghiệp* (Amarillo, TX: Hải Mã: 2003), chapter 1.

99. Hồ Hữu Tường, "Un fétu de paille dans la tourmente," 69.

100. "Note de la direction de la Sûreté générale indochinoise concernant Nghiem Xuan Toan et la revue hebdomadaire 'La vie indochinoise,'" January 3, 1936, Dossier Nghiêm Xuân Toàn, SLOTFOM XV.115, ANOM; "Note sur l'association d'entraide et culture des indochinois de Paris," undated, SLOTFOM V.33, ANOM.

101. See SLOTFOM V.21, ANOM.

102. "Note de la direction de la Sûreté générale indochinoise au sujet de plus-ieures lettres et tracts envoyés de Marseille par le Comité de rassemblement des indochinois au journal 'Le Travail' de Hanoi," December 23, 1936, SLOTFOM III.119, ANOM.

103. Daniel Guérin, *Autobiographie de jeunesse* (Paris: Pierre Belfond, 1972), 223–29.

104. GGI to MC, March 15, 1939, SLOTFOM V.38–39, ANOM.

105. Cited in Luguern, "Les 'Travailleurs Indochinois,'" 642.

106. Charles Keith, "Vietnamese Collaborationism in Vichy France," *Journal of Asian Studies* 76.4 (November 2017): 987–1008.

107. Hồ Hữu Tường, *41 năm làm báo* (Hà Nội: Nhà Xuất Bản Hội Nhà Văn, 2017), 188.

108. Hồ Hữu Tường, "Un fétu de paille dans la tourmente," 279.

109. "Note de Guillaume," January 23, 1930, Dossier Vũ Đình Hải, SLOTFOM XV.138, ANOM.

110. "Un Annamite auteur dramatique français: 'Dernier éspoir' par Vu-dinh-Hai," *L'Echo annamite,* November 29, 1929.

111. Karl Britto, *Disorientation: France, Vietnam, and the Ambivalence of Inter-culturality* (Hong Kong: Hong Kong University Press, 2004), 105.

112. Ibid., 103; Jack Yeager, *The Vietnamese Novel in French* (Hanover: University Press of New Hampshire, 1987), 72.

113. Britto, *Disorientation,* 107.

114. Nguyen, *La Littérature vietnamienne francophone,* 73.

115. The 1939 Prix de la langue française for *Aventures intellectuelles,* the 1941 Prix Verrière for *Rêves d'un campagnard annamite,* the 1943 Prix d'académie for *Muses de Paris,* and the 1945 Prix Lange for *Le coeur de diamant,* which he won again in 1952 for *Le Viêt-Nam et sa civilisation.*

116. Biographical information is in Dossier Trần Văn Tùng, SLOTFOM XV.159, ANOM.

117. Cited in Britto, *Disorientation,* 28.

118. A good discussion of the novel is in Selao, *Le roman vietnamien francophone,* chapter III; the quote is from page 143.

119. Richard Serrano, *Against the Postcolonial: 'Francophone' Writers at the Ends of French Empire* (Lanham, MD: Lexington Books, 2005), 108.

120. Léon-Gontran Damas, *Poètes d'expression française, 1900–1945* (Paris: Seuil, 1947).

121. Serrano, *Against the Postcolonial,* 118.

122. Ibid., 119.

123. Ibid., 120.

124. Jean Desthieux, "Les provinces lointaines du parler français," *L'Homme libre,* August 29–30, 1931.

125. "A propos d'un poète annamite mort en France," *L'Annam nouveau,* September 27, 1934.

126. "Bibliographie," *Le Monde illustré*, November 3, 1923.

127. Grégory Mikaelian, "L'aristocratie khmère à l'école des humanités françaises, *Bulletin de l'association d'échanges de formation pour les études khmères* 19 (2014).

128. Nguyen, *La Littérature vietnamienne francophone*, 96.

129. Hoàng Xuân Nhị, *Les cahiers intimes de Heou-Tâm, étudiant d'Extrême-Orient*, 28.

130. Quoted in Nguyen, *La Littérature vietnamienne francophone*, 99.

131. Nguyen Huy Bao, "Un poète chrétien vietnamien," in *Indochine: Reflets littéraires*, ed. Bernard Hue (Rennes: Presses universitaires de Rennes, 1992), 35–41.

132. Albert Gauttard to MC, May 26, 1900, IC AF 241, ANOM.

133. Nguyễn Khắc Phê, *Hoa sĩ Lê Văn Miến: cuộc đời và sự nghiệp giáo dục* (Hà Nội: Nhà Xuất Bản Giáo Dục, 1997).

134. Uyên Huy, "Kỷ niệm 100 năm thành lập trường vẽ Gia Định—trường đại học mỹ thuật Thành Phố Hồ Chí Minh (1913–2013)," *Tạp Chí Mỹ Thuật*, November 2013.

135. Huỳnh Đình Tựu to Directeur du Groupe d'enseignement indochinois, August 10, 1912, IC NF 279, ANOM.

136. Phoebe Scott, "Vietnamese Art in Paris in the 30s-40s," *Southeast of Now: Directions in Contemporary and Modern Art in Asia* 3.2 (October 2019): 191.

137. Nadine André-Pallois, *L'Indochine: un lieu d'échange culturel? Les peintres français et indochinois (fin XIXe-XXe siècle)* (Paris: Presses de l'École française d'Extrême-Orient, 1997), 224.

138. Ibid., 221.

139. Scott, "Vietnamese Art in Paris," 195.

140. André-Pallois, *L'Indochine: un lieu d'échange culturel?*, 222.

141. Scott, "Vietnamese Art in Paris," 202.

142. Ibid., 198, 203.

143. Ibid., 218.

144. Scott, "Vietnamese Art in Paris," 208, 231.

145. "Un peintre annamite catholique: M. Le Van De," *Tribune indochinoise*, June 10, 1938.

146. A good summary of the Indochinese painters who settled in France is Bùi Như Hương, "Một số họa sĩ Việt Nam sống và làm việc tại nước ngoài," in *Mỹ thuật Việt Nam hiện đại*, ed. Nguyễn Lương Tiểu Bạch (Hà Nội: Trường Đại học Mỹ thuật Hà Nội, 2005), 339–50. On Lê Bá Đăng's wartime experiences see Luguern, "Les 'Travailleurs Indochoinois,'" 972–77.

147. See Lisa Bixenstine Safford, "Art at the Crossroads: Lacquer Painting in French Vietnam," *Transcultural Studies* 6.1 (2015): 126–70.

148. MC to GGI, November 6, 1939, Dossier Nguyễn Thị Liên, SLOTFOM XV.139, ANOM.

149. Cieslas Mysykowski, "Le Salon d'Automne," *Revue du vrai et du beau*, January 25, 1928.

150. Jason Gibbs, "Spoken Theater, La Scène Tonkinoise, and the First Modern Vietnamese Songs," *Asian Music* 31.2 (Spring-Summer 2000): 6.

151. Dossier Cécile Nguyễn Ngọc Tuế, SLOTFOM XV.143, ANOM.

152. Cao Quỳnh An to Nguyễn Văn Thân, October 31, 1928, Dossier Cao Quỳnh An, SLOTFOM XV.80, ANOM.

CHAPTER 5. LABOR SOJOURNERS

1. Dossier Nguyễn Văn Hiến, SLOTFOM XV.18, ANOM.

2. Brocheux and Hémery, *Indochina,* 116.

3. Henri Eckert, "Les militaires indochinois au service de la France (1859–1939)" (PhD diss., Université de Paris IV, 1998), 448.

4. Claire Edington, *Beyond the Asylum: Mental Illness in French Colonial Vietnam* (Ithaca, NY: Cornell University Press, 2019), 35.

5. Eckert, "Les militaires indochinois," 449.

6. Vu-Hill, *Coolies into Rebels,* 72.

7. Fogarty, *Race and War in France,* 43–47.

8. Monroux, "Le tirailleur annamite," January 1917, SLOTFOM X.4, ANOM.

9. Monroux, "Les indochinois en France," undated, SLOTFOM X.4, ANOM.

10. Eckert, "Les militaires indochinois," 590–91.

11. "Contrôle postal indochinois, août 1918," IC NF 227, ANOM.

12. Eckert, "Les militaires indochinois," 554.

13. Can, *Carnet de route,* 20–21.

14. Vu-Hill, *Coolies into Rebels,* 81–83.

15. Eckert, "Les militaires indochinois," 758.

16. Kiều Xuân Quang to "bien cher Phong," January 12, 1920, Dossier Kiều Xuân Quang, SLOTFOM XV.6, ANOM.

17. Le Van Ho, *Des Vietnamiens dans la Grande Guerre,* 189.

18. Eckert, "Les militaires indochinois," 554.

19. Jean Przyluski, "Note sur l'utilisation des infirmiers indochinois," March 14, 1918, SLOTFOM X.5, ANOM.

20. Le Van Ho, *Des Vietnamiens dans la Grande Guerre,* 88.

21. Ibid., 113.

22. "Le Trianon cultivé par les annamites et les tonkinois," *Tribune indochinoise,* October 29, 1917.

23. Pierre Guesde, "Rapport d'ensemble sur le contrôle générale des tirailleurs et travailleurs indochinois en France," July 1, 1919, SLOTFOM X.4, ANOM.

24. Le Van Ho, *Des Vietnamiens dans la Grande Guerre,* 106.

25. See Jean-François Jagielski, "Entre fiction et réalité, la rumeur des Annamites massacrant les Parisiennes," in *Obéir/désobéir: les mutinéries de 1917 en perspective,* ed. André Loez and Nicolas Mariot (Paris: Editions La Découverte, 2008), 139–50.

26. "Rapport de M. Przyluski," July 23, 1917, SLOTFOM III.139, ANOM. On the phenomenon in general, see Tyler Stovall, "The Color Line behind the Lines:

Racial Violence in France during the Great War," *The American Historical Review* 103.3 (June 1998): 737–69.

27. "Contrôle postal indochinois, décembre 1917," SLOTFOM I.8, ANOM.

28. Vu-Hill, *Coolies Into Rebels,* 76.

29. MC to Président du conseil, Ministre de la guerre, May 7, 1918, SLOTFOM X.5, ANOM.

30. "Contrôle postal indochinois, avril 1918," IC NF 245, ANOM.

31. "Contrôle postal indochinois, mars 1918," SLOTFOM I.8, ANOM.

32. "Contrôle postal indochinois, juin 1918," IC NF 227, ANOM; Vu-Hill, *Coolies Into Rebels,* 80, 89.

33. Vu-Hill, *Coolies into Rebels,* 88.

34. Ibid., 89–91.

35. "Contrôle postal indochinois, avril 1918," IC NF 245, ANOM.

36. "Contrôle postal indochinois, mai 1918," IC NF 245, ANOM.

37. Cited in Mireille Favre, "Un milieu porteur de modernisation: travailleurs et tirailleurs vietnamiens en France pendant la première guerre mondiale" (Thèse pour l'obtention du diplôme d'archiviste-paléographe, École nationale des chartes, 1986), 492.

38. "Contrôle postal indochinois, juin 1918," IC NF 245, ANOM.

39. "Contrôle postal indochinois, mai 1918," IC NF 245, ANOM.

40. "Contrôle postal indochinois, janvier 1918," IC NF 227, ANOM; "Contrôle postal indochinois, mai 1917," SLOTFOM I.8, ANOM.

41. "Contrôle postal indochinois, juin 1918," SLOTFOM I.8, ANOM.

42. "Contrôle postal indochinois, novembre 1918," SLOTFOM I.8, ANOM.

43. Ibid.

44. Quoted in Léon Josselme to RST, July 1, 1921, Dossier Huỳnh Tân Quang, SLOTFOM XV.26, ANOM.

45. "Contrôle postal indochinois, novembre 1918," SLOTFOM I.8, ANOM.

46. "Contrôle postal indochinois, mai 1918," IC NF 245, ANOM.

47. Vu-Hill, *Coolies into Rebels,* 116.

48. Unsigned letter to director of *Tribune indigène,* August 5, 1924, SLOTFOM III.22, ANOM.

49. "Contrôle postal indochinois, juin 1923," SLOTFOM I.8, ANOM.

50. Letter attached to memo from GGI to MC, March 11, 1921, SLOTFOM III.22, ANOM.

51. Vu-Hill, *Coolies into Rebels,* 116.

52. Ibid.

53. Quoted in Le Van Ho, *Des Vietnamiens dans la Grande guerre,* 172.

54. Ibid., 169–75.

55. Eckert, "Les militaires indochinois," 190.

56. Unspecified official to GGI, December 26, 1923, SLOTFOM XI.1, ANOM.

57. Eckert, "Les militaires indochinois," 186.

58. Commandant supérieur des Troupes du groupe indochinois to GGI, October 4, 1923, SLOTFOM I.10, ANOM.

59. "Rapport du Capitaine Le Baron du Service de contrôle des militaires indochinois en France et dans le bassin Méditerranéen à la suite des visites faites en février 1928, aux détachements stationnés dans le gouvernement militaire de Paris," March 13, 1928, SLOTFOM III.22, ANOM.

60. Nguyễn Văn Ký to GOUCOCH, November 12, 1926, GOUCOCH V/10.04.07, TTLT II.

61. Vu-Hill, *Coolies into Rebels,* 116.

62. Le Van Ho, *Des Vietnamiens dans la Grande Guerre,* 184–85.

63. Dossier Quách Văn An, SLOTFOM XV.23, ANOM.

64. Dossier Tạ Văn Cẩn, SLOTFOM XV.40, ANOM.

65. "A.s. de la colonie indochinoise de Paris," December 1929, SLOTFOM III.32, ANOM.

66. "El Djazairi," "La société des lacques indochinoises," *L'Humanité,* September 4, 1924.

67. "Renseignements sur la situation des ouvriers indochinois employées par la société des lacques," undated, SLOTFOM I.10, ANOM.

68. Goebel, *Anti-Imperial Metropolis,* 37.

69. Dossier Đinh Văn Phụng, SLOTFOM XV.36, ANOM.

70. Dossier Thái Văn Huỳnh, SLOTFOM XV.44, ANOM.

71. "Rapport de Durand," April 10, 1929, ANOM.

72. "État des services de M Le Quang Liem dit Bay, Phu de 1ère class du gouvernement de la Cochinchine, Contrôleur des tirailleurs et travailleurs indochinois en France," undated, SLOTFOM I.6, ANOM.

73. Vu-Hill, *Coolies into Rebels,* 67; Guesde to GGI, June 28, 1918, IC NF 225, ANOM.

74. Le Van Ho, *Des Vietnamiens dans la Grande Guerre,* 85.

75. The letter is in Dossier Nguyễn Văn Ái, SLOTFOM XV.19, ANOM.

76. Phạm Văn Dung to Phan Kim Chung, January 24, 1930, Dossier Phan Văn Dung, SLOTFOM XV.137, ANOM.

77. Dossier Phạm Văn Mạch, SLOTFOM XV.9, ANOM.

78. SLOTFOM III.34, ANOM.

79. A copy of his contract is in SLOTFOM I.7, ANOM.

80. Nguyễn Văn Nuôi to Léon Josselme, April 16, 1926, Dossier Nguyễn Văn Nuôi, SLOTFOM XV.9, ANOM.

81. Jennifer Boittin, *Colonial Metropolis: The Urban Grounds of Anti-Imperialism and Feminism in Interwar Paris* (Lincoln: University of Nebraska Press, 2010), 67.

82. Unmarked report, July 12, 1928, SLOTFOM III.1, ANOM.

83. Charles Keith, "The Curious Case of Hoàng Thị Thế," *Journal of Vietnamese Studies* 8.3 (2013): 98.

84. Bùi Ái, "Aventures et voyages," *Gazette de Hué,* December 27, 1935.

85. "Madame Durand" to "Monsieur," March 7, 1929, dossier Võ Thành Long, SLOTFOM XV.17, ANOM.

86. Quoted in Paul Greenhalgh, *Ephemeral Vistas: The Expositions Universelles, Great Exhibitions and World's Fairs, 1851–1939* (Manchester: Manchester University Press, 1988), 88.

87. Dossier Phạm Văn Hổ, SLOTFOM XV.48, ANOM.

88. Annegret Fauser, *Musical Encounters at the 1889 Paris World's Fair* (Rochester: University of Rochester Press, 2005), 183–95, 200–3.

89. Undated letter to "monsieur Cương," SLOTFOM III.5, ANOM.

90. Hale, *Races on Display*, 81.

91. "Note de l'agent Jolin," December 21, 1922, Dossier Phạm Quỳnh, SLOTFOM XV.78, ANOM.

92. MC to GGI, September 12, 1907, GGI 1682, ANOM.

93. "Note pour le ministre," April 14, 1931, SLOTFOM III.5, ANOM.

94. Délégué de la Cochinchine à l'exposition to Délégué général de l'exposition, November 27, 1930, GOUCOCH VI.A.6/191, TTLT II.

95. "Note sur la tenue de la garde civile locale et de la troupe théâtrale de Cochinchine pendant leur séjour à l'exposition coloniale," undated, GOUCOCH VI.A.5/063(4–7), TTLT II.

96. Report by Phan Văn Lựu about his visit to the 1906 exposition, July 20, 1906, IB.24/145 (2), TTLT II.

97. See Dossier Nguyễn Xuân Bái, SLOTFOM XV.59, ANOM.

98. Ernest Outrey to Commissaire générale de l'Indochine à l'exposition de Marseille, August 27, 1905, GGI 1681, ANOM.

99. "Rapport de Désiré," June 15, 1931, SLOTFOM III.5, ANOM.

100. Commissaire général de l'Indochine to MC, November 17, 1921, SLOTFOM XV.41, ANOM.

101. Dossier Nguyễn Thị Khang, SLOTFOM XV.64, ANOM.

102. Phan Văn Thiết to his father, August 14, 1928, Dossier Phan Văn Thiết, SLOTFOM XV.86, ANOM.

103. Dossier Nguyễn Thanh Kiết, SLOTFOM XV.25, ANOM.

104. Bùi Quang Chiêu, "Les Annamites en France," *Tribune indochinoise,* October 22, 1934.

105. "Rapport de Roseau," November 24, 1930, Dossier Phan Văn Hùm, SLOTFOM XV.80, ANOM.

106. GOUCOCH VI.A.5/033(2–4), TTLT II.

107. "Rapport de M. Trần Mạnh Nhẫn sur sa visite à l'exposition internationale de Paris de 1937," GOUCOCH III.59/N53(2), TTLT II.

108. Nguyễn Như Chuyên to RST, March 11, 1913, RST 79868, TTLT I.

109. GGI 2401, TTLT I.

110. Ibid.

111. "Note au sujet du Tonkinois KHANH KY," undated, Dossier Khánh Ký, SLOTFOM XV.3, ANOM.

112. "Note sur la propagande revolutionnaire intéressant les pays d'outre-mer" [hereafter "NPRPOM"], October 31, 1931, SLOTFOM III.149, ANOM.

113. Erica Peters, "Resistance, Rivalries, and Restaurants: Vietnamese Workers in Interwar France," *Journal of Vietnamese Studies* 2.1 (2007): 122.

114. "Rapport de Durand," April 7, 1932, SLOTFOM II.8.

115. "Note de Désiré," May 31, 1924, Dossier Lý Văn Thủy, SLOTFOM XV.24, ANOM.

116. Nguyễn Văn Đức to Secrétaire d'état aux colonies à Vichy, February 24, 1942, SLOTFOM III.99, ANOM.

117. "Rapport de Vincent," June 10, 1930, Dossier Trần Lệ Luật, SLOTFOM XV.40, ANOM.

118. "Rapport de Désiré," March 14, 1932, Dossier Hà Vân Hợi, SLOTFOM XV.82, ANOM.

119. "Saigon—Thượng Hãi—Hoành Tân: nhựt ký của người bồi tàu," *Thần Chung,* May 3, 1929.

120. "Saigon—Thượng Hãi—Hoành Tân: nhựt ký của người bồi tàu," *Thần Chung,* October 23, 1929.

121. Phạm Vân Anh [Đào Trinh Nhất], "Sang Tây (du ký của một thiếu nữ)," *Phụ Nữ Tân Văn,* May 30, 1929.

122. "Saigon—Thượng Hãi—Hoành Tân: nhựt ký của người bồi tàu," *Thần Chung,* October 23, 1929.

123. Nguyễn Bùi Sữa to Délégué du Service de contrôle des indigènes à Marseille, July 25, 1936, dossier Nguyễn Bùi Sữa, SLOTFOM XV.48, ANOM.

124. Sous-secrétaire d'état des ports de la marine marchande et des pêches to MC, February 4, 1925, SLOTFOM VI.8, ANOM.

125. "Note pour la Direction des affaires politiques, Service de contrôle et d'assistance en France des indigènes des colonies françaises," September 7, 1932, SLOTFOM VI.8, ANOM.

126. Dossier Pham Van Thu, SLOTFOM XV.82, ANOM.

127. Dossier Lê Văn Tư, SLOTFOM XV.46, ANOM.

128. Chef du bureau de l'immigration indigène to Directeur des affaires politiques aux ministère des colonies, February 11, 1939, SLOTFOM III.20, ANOM.

129. Cortambert, *Impressions d'un japonais en France; suivies des impressions des Annamites en Europe,* 180.

130. Directeur de la Mission permanente des mandarins indochinois en France to GGI, December 31, 1907, GGI 2560, ANOM.

131. Dossier Vũ Văn Tụ, SLOTFOM XV.50, ANOM.

132. Vũ Thị Tý to Chef du bureau de l'immigration indigène, November 4, 1938, Dossier Vũ Thị Tý, SLOTFOM XV.128, ANOM.

133. "Rapport de Durand," May 3, 1930, Dossier Bùi Văn Huỳnh, SLOTFOM XV.142, ANOM.

134. Dossier Trần Tư, SLOTFOM XV.66, ANOM.

135. Benedict Anderson, *A Life Beyond Boundaries: A Memoir* (London: Verso, 2016), 23–24.

136. Dossier Nguyễn Tắt Du, SLOTFOM XV.9, ANOM.

137. Granier, *Domestiques indochinois,* 131.

138. Ibid., 130.

139. Ibid., 14.

140. Hoàng Kim Tuyết to MC, December 4, 1938, SLOTFOM IV.11, ANOM.

141. Dossier Trân Văn Minh, SLOTFOM XV.26, ANOM.

142. Nguyễn Thị Sanh to MC, January 4, 1928, Dossier Nguyễn Thị Sanh, SLOTFOM XV.36, ANOM.

143. "Contrôle postal indochinois, octobre 1917," SLOTFOM I.8, ANOM.

144. "Rapport du Capitaine Le Baron du Service du contrôle des militaires indochinois en France et dans le bassin Méditerranéen à la suite des visites faites en février 1928," March 13, 1928, SLOTFOM III.22, ANOM.

145. Daniel Brückenhaus, *Policing Transnational Protest: Liberal Imperialism and the Surveillance of Anticolonialists in Europe, 1905–1945* (New York: Oxford University Press, 2017), 94.

146. MC to Ministre de la marine, July 27, 1933, SLOTFOM VI.3, ANOM.

147. "Rapport de l'agent Durand," April 25, 1929, SLOTFOM XV.95, ANOM.

148. Phạm Vân Anh [Đào Trinh Nhất], "Sang Tây (du ký của một thiếu nữ)," *Phụ Nữ Tân Văn,* May 30, 1929.

149. Dossier Henri Vally, SLOTFOM XV.36, ANOM.

150. "Rapport de l'agent Durand," undated, Dossier Khanard Dumont, SLOTFOM XV.46, ANOM.

151. Inspecteur général de la police to Inspecteur générale de la Sûreté, April 17, 1941, Dossier Phạm Văn Man, SLOTFOM XV.158, ANOM.

152. Seventeen unnamed students to Huỳnh Kỳ, October 31, 1927, Dossier Nguyễn Văn Sang, SLOTFOM XV.79, ANOM.

153. Vu-Hill, *Coolies into Rebels,* 75.

154. "Note de l'agent Désiré," May 24, 1924, Dossier Trân Văn Lưu, SLOTFOM XV.36, ANOM.

155. No author, "Một người Việt Nam buôn thuốc phiện bị Mariani hại," *Đuốc Nhà Nam,* November 4–5, 1934.

156. Dossier Đào Nhật Vinh, SLOTFOM XV.83, ANOM.

157. Dossier Nguyễn Đức Trát, SLOTFOM XV.146, ANOM.

158. Dossier Nguyễn Đoàn Chược, SLOTFOM XV.66, ANOM.

159. Dossier Phạm Văn Khánh, SLOTFOM XV.91, ANOM.

160. Commissaire spécial to Directeur de la Sûreté, November 22, 1930, SLOTFOM IV.5, ANOM.

161. "Note pour monsieur le Directeur des services civiles en Indochine," July 27, 1933, SLOTFOM IV.5, ANOM.

162. Undated note, SLOTFOM IV.5, ANOM.

163. Délégué du CAI to Directeur des affaires politiques, February 9, 1931, SLOTFOM IV.5, ANOM.

164. Cited in Didier de Fautereau, "Le Nationalisme Vietnamien: contribution des marins vietnamien au nationalisme vietnamien (période entre deux

guerres)" (Mémoire pour le Diplôme d'Etudes Supérieures de Science Politique, 1975), 37.

165. MC to GGI, December 26, 1930, SLOTFOM V.24, ANOM.

166. On the Deschamps affair, see Pham, "Revolution, Communism, and History in the Thought of Trần Văn Giàu," chapter 2.

167. Dossier Nguyễn Văn Thuận, SLOTFOM XV.54, ANOM.

168. Dossier Bùi Văn Tô, SLOTFOM XV.140, ANOM.

169. Luguern, "Les 'Travailleurs Indochinois,'" 490–503.

170. Eric Deroo and Antoine Champeaux, "Panorama des troupes coloniales françaises dans les deux guerres mondiales," *Revue historique des armées* 271 (2013): 8.

171. Martin Thomas, "The Vichy Government and French Colonial Prisoners of War, 1940–1944," *French Colonial Studies* 25.4 (Fall 2002): 663.

172. Phạm Duy Khiêm, "De La Courtine à Vichy," 25, RST NF 2697, ANOM.

173. See Raffael Scheck, *Hitler's African Victims: The German Army Massacres of Black French Soldiers in 1940* (Cambridge: Cambridge University Press, 2006).

174. See Raffael Scheck, *French Colonial Soldiers in German Captivity during World War II* (New York: Cambridge University Press, 2014).

175. Luguern, "Les 'Travailleurs Indochinois,'" 513.

176. Ibid., 514.

177. "Note pour monsieur le Directeur des affaires politiques," December 4, 1943, IC NF 1098, ANOM.

178. "Note de renseignements N5294/5," November 7, 1941, SLOTFOM III.52, ANOM.

179. Dossier Trần Phúc Chiêu, SLOTOM XV.77, ANOM.

180. Maurice Rives, "Les tirailleurs indochinois au Levant et dans les Forces Françaises Libres," *Bulletin de l'A.N.A.I* (July-August-September 1992): 4–7.

181. Dossier Nguyễn Hữu An, SLOTFOM XV.160, ANOM.

182. Dossier Lê Văn Bê, SLOTFOM XV.162, ANOM.

183. Luguern, "Les 'Travailleurs Indochinois,'" 521–24.

184. David Smith, "'French Like the Others': Colonial Migrants in Wartime France, 1939–1947" (PhD diss., University of Toronto, 2013), 198.

185. Luguern, "Les 'Travailleurs Indochinois,'" 531.

186. Rémy Desquesnes, "L'Organisation Todt en France (1940–1944)," *Histoire, économie et société* 11.3 (3e trimestre 1992): 535–50.

187. Luguern, "Les 'Travailleurs Indochinois,'" 538–47.

188. Ibid., 507.

189. Ibid., 574.

190. Keith, "Vietnamese Collaboration in Vichy France," 995–96.

191. Đặng Văn Long, *Người Việt ở Pháp,* 48.

192. Luguern, "Les 'Travailleurs Indochinois,'" 537.

193. Ibid., 469, 642–70.

194. Ibid., 744.

1. "Note de Guillaume," February 11, 1930, Dossier Nguyễn Văn Mũi, SLOTFOM XV.123, ANOM. Interagency communication surrounding his death established that his family name was Dương rather than Nguyễn.

2. GGI to RST, June 23, 1938, GGI 306, TTLT I.

3. Jennifer Boittin, "'Among Them Complicit? Life and Politics in France's Black Communities, 1919–1939," in *Africa in Europe: Studies in Transnational Practice in the Long Twentieth Century*, eds. Eve Rosenhaft and Robbie Aitken (Liverpool: Liverpool University Press, 2013), 61.

4. Wilder, *The French Imperial Nation-State*, 28.

5. Đặng Hữu Thụ, *Thân thế và sự nghiệp nhà cách mạng Nguyễn Thế Truyền* (Paris: Melun, 1993), chapter 1.

6. Dossier Phạm Di, SLOTFOM XV.23, ANOM.

7. Trần Văn Đức to Trần Văn Sanh, December 23, 1930, Dossier Trần Văn Đức, SLOTFOM XV.123, ANOM.

8. Dossier Trương Văn Huấn, SLOTFOM XV.4, ANOM.

9. Sara Legrandjacques, "Des colonisés à la cité: la Maison des étudiants indochinois à la Cité universitaire de Paris, 1927–1939," *Revue d'Histoire/Zeitschrift für Geschichte*, submitted on June 5, 2018: https://hal.science/hal-01808163/document.

10. "Renseignements sur la situation des ouvriers indochinois employés par la Société des laques, 33 Rue de Silly à Boulogne (Seine)," undated, SLOTFOM I.10, ANOM.

11. "Déclarations de Nguyễn Thế Vinh recueillies par la direction de la Sûreté générale indochinoise," August 1931, SLOTFOM III.44, ANOM.

12. Goebel, *Anti-Imperial Metropolis*, 39–44.

13. Bùi Ái, "Aventures et voyages," *Gazette de Hué*, August 30, 1935.

14. Bùi Ái, "Aventures et voyages," *Gazette de Hué*, December 27, 1935.

15. "Déclarations receuillies auprès du Tonkinois Trung Van Vinh," July 4, 1934, Dossier Ngô Quang Thấu, SLOTFOM XV.106, ANOM.

16. "Liste des Annamites habitant au 10 rue de Vaugirard," SLOTFOM II.12, ANOM.

17. Hoàng Kim Tuyết to MC, December 4, 1935, SLOTFOM IV.11, ANOM.

18. Nguyễn Văn Tôn to Monsieur du Couchet, September 12, 1931, SLOTFOM II.9, ANOM.

19. Nguyễn Thừa Đặt to RST, April 22, 1908, RST NF 1693, ANOM.

20. Bùi Thanh Vân, *La France: relations de voyage*, 53.

21. Phạm Quỳnh, *Pháp du hành trình nhật ký*, 235–36.

22. Bùi Ái, "Aventures et voyages," *Gazette de Hué*, May 10, 1935.

23. Lê Văn Đức, *Cách đi Tây* (Sài Gòn: Đức Lưu Phương, 1931).

24. SLOTFOM III.134, ANOM.

25. Lê Văn Ri to Trần Thị Nhân, November 7, 1932, Dossier Lê Văn Ri, SLOTFOM XV.34, ANOM.

26. Lockhart, "Broken Journey," 116.

27. Bùi Ái, "Aventures et voyages," *Gazette de Hué,* December 13, 1935.

28. "Sa đà du tử" [Phan Văn Hùm], "Sống ở Paris," *Thần Chung,* January 17, 1930.

29. Tùng Hương, "Trên đường Nam Pháp," in Nguyễn Hữu Sơn, *Du ký Việt Nam: tạp chí Nam Phong,* 2:314.

30. Luguern, "Les 'Travailleurs Indochinois,'" 554.

31. Le Van Ho, *Des Vietnamiens dans la Grande Guerre,* chapter 2.

32. Luguern, "Les 'Travailleurs Indochinois,'" 567.

33. Ibid., 1024.

34. Ibid., 549.

35. Cited in Le Van Ho, *Des Vietnamiens dans la Grande Guerre,* 74.

36. Luguern, "Les 'Travailleurs Indochinois,'" 571.

37. "Rapport trimestriel," January 25, 1918, SLOTFOM III.139, ANOM; "Contrôle postal indochinois, mars 1917," SLOTFOM I.8, ANOM.

38. Luguern, "Les 'Travailleurs Indochinois,'" 550–53.

39. Vu-Hill, *Coolies into Rebels,* 105–6.

40. "Rapport du Capitaine Le Baron du Service du contrôle des militaires indochinois en France," May 9, 1920, SLOTFOM III.22, ANOM.

41. Eckert, "Les militaires indochinois," 509.

42. Contrôleur des contingents indochinois au XIVè et XVè régions to MC, June 15, 1918, IC NF 245, ANOM.

43. Contrôleur des troupes indochinoises to MC, October 8, 1925, SLOTFOM III.22, ANOM.

44. Phạm Duy Khiêm, "De La Courtine à Vichy (Mai-Juillet 1940)," 43, IC NF 2697, ANOM.

45. Eckert, "Les militaires indochinois," 506.

46. Luguern, "Les 'Travailleurs Indochinois,'" 573.

47. Ibid., 575–76.

48. Ibid., 577–80.

49. Peters, "Resistance, Rivalries, and Restaurants," 118.

50. Phạm Thông Thảo to Nguyễn Hữu Lủy, Dossier Phạm Thông Thảo, SLOTFOM XV.99, ANOM.

51. "Đồng bào Việt Nam ăn Tết ở Paris," *Tràng An Báo,* February 20, 1942.

52. "Contrôle postal indochinois, février 1918," IC AF 227, ANOM.

53. Travailleurs indochinois de la 63ème compagnie to MC, February 4, 1946.

54. Nguyễn Ngọc Xuân, *Pháp du hành trình* (Hải Phòng: Văn Minh, 1923).

55. Trần Bá Vinh, *Pháp du ký sự.*

56. Bùi Thanh Vân, *La France: relations de voyage,* 66, 68.

57. Dossier Nguyen Tan Hon, SLOTFOM XV.156, ANOM.

58. "Renseignements," August 10, 1922, Dossier Nguyễn Văn Vĩnh, SLOTFOM XV.21, ANOM.

59. "Note de la direction de la Sûreté générale indochinoise concernant l'activité caodaiste en France," May 15, 1933, SLOTFOM IV.12, ANOM.

60. Ministre de l'intérieur to MC, June 12, 1934, Dossier Nguyễn Văn Hoành, SLOTFOM XV.66, ANOM.

61. Dossier Nguyễn Văn Trường, SLOTFOM XV.45, ANOM.

62. Dossier Nguyễn Thị Anh, SLOTFOM XV.95, ANOM.

63. Dossier Meng Ly, SLOTFOM XV.30, ANOM.

64. Lê Văn Đức, *A travers l'Allemagne, la Belgique et l'Angleterre: Impressions de voyage d'un annamite* (Qui Nhơn: Imprimerie de Qui Nhơn, 1924), 46.

65. Tạ Thu Thâu to Trịnh Hưng Ngẫu, January 27, 1930, Dossier Tạ Thu Thâu, SLOTFOM XV.86, ANOM.

66. Phạm Quỳnh, *Pháp du hành trình nhật ký*, 239.

67. Phạm Vân Anh [Đào Trinh Nhất], "Mười Tháng ở Pháp," *Phụ Nữ Tân Văn*, December 19, 1929.

68. Denis Gazquez, "Révolution, culture, et bibliothèques: Hô Chi Minh à Paris, 1917–1923," in Ruscio, *Une vie pour le Viêt Nam*, 231–44.

69. Tạ Quang Bửu, "La Joconde," *Bulletin de la société d'encouragement aux études occidentales*, December 1934.

70. Cao Quỳnh An to his father, February 2, 1927, Dossier Cao Quỳnh An, SLOTFOM XV.80, ANOM.

71. Lê Phát Trung to "mon cher Joseph," January 23, 1927, Dossier Lê Phát Trung, SLOTFOM XV.4, ANOM.

72. Nguyễn Văn Hiệp to Nguyễn Văn Tung, July 30, 1929, Dossier Nguyễn Văn Hiệp, SLOTFOM XV.94, ANOM.

73. Louis Bùi to Bùi Quang Chiêu, July 25, 1927, Dossier Louis Bùi, SLOTFOM XV.23, ANOM.

74. Phạm Quỳnh, "Thuật chuyện du lịch ở Paris," in Nguyễn Hữu Sơn, *Du ký Việt Nam: tạp chí Nam Phong*, 1:323.

75. Dossier Trần Quang Huy, SLOTFOM XV.43, ANOM.

76. "Un grand tournoi de tennis à Toulouse," *Tribune indochinoise*, December 27, 1929.

77. Nguyễn Khắc Viện, *Tự truyện*, 54–55.

78. Lương Việt Hùng, *Đời du học* (Chợ Lớn: Lương Việt Hùng, 193?).

79. Nguyễn Văn Bạch to "bien cher Anh," undated, Dossier Nguyễn Văn Bạch, SLOTFOM XV.86, ANOM.

80. Trịnh Hưng Ngẫu to Nguyễn Lệ Hóa, May 29, 1928, Dossier Trịnh Hưng Ngẫu, SLOTFOM XV.31, ANOM.

81. Trần Văn Đốc to Cao Quỳnh Cư, August 12, 1927, Dossier Trần Văn Đốc, SLOTFOM XV.47, ANOM.

82. Principal of unnamed lycée in Bordeaux to Directeur du CAI, January 31, 1933, Dossier Lương Dân Nguyên, SLOTFOM XV.152, ANOM.

83. Bùi Quang Tấn to Bùi Quang Chiêu, November 14, 1927, Dossier Bùi Quang Tấn, SLOTFOM XV.101, ANOM.

84. Directeur du SAMI to Direction du cabinet et des affaires politiques, Services des affaires indigènes, April 18, 1929, GGI 2228, TTLT I.

85. Peters, "Resistance, Rivalries, and Restaurants," 127.

86. Préfet de police to MC, August 8, 1911, GGI 2563, ANOM.

87. Peters, "Resistance, Rivalries, and Restaurants," 117.

88. "Note du RST," January 30, 1917, RST 20828, TTLT I.

89. Vu-Hill, *Coolies into Rebels,* 101.

90. Luguern, "Les 'Travailleurs Indochinois,'" 616.

91. Letter from a group of Indochinese to Directeur du CAI, June 11, 1934, SLOTFOM IV.11, ANOM.

92. "Note de l'agent Désiré," undated, SLOTFOM III.1, ANOM.

93. "Rapport de Durand," November 20, 1929, SLOTFOM II.8, ANOM.

94. "Note de l'agent Désiré," March 2, 1926, SLOTFOM III.1, ANOM.

95. Lê Văn Khi to "Mme Chương," March 2, 1940, SLOTFOM III.109.

96. Group of Indochinese to Directeur du CAI, June 11, 1934, SLOTFOM IV.11, ANOM.

97. Dossier Phạm Văn Quất, SLOTFOM XV.63, ANOM.

98. Dossier Đinh Thi Triệu, SLOTFOM XV.120, ANOM.

99. Dossier Nguyễn Văn Ba, SLOTFOM XV.144, ANOM.

100. Dossier Nguyễn Đức Chàng, SLOTFOM XV.110, ANOM.

101. Dossier Nguyễn Văn Tháp, SLOTFOM XV.125, ANOM.

102. Bùi Ái, "Aventures et voyages," *Gazette de Hué,* July 5, 1935.

103. Cao Quỳnh An to Cao Quỳnh Cư, February 16, 1927, Dossier Cao Quỳnh An, SLOTFOM XV.80, ANOM.

104. The most detailed account of their friendship, based in now-lost personal letters, is Nguyễn Thiều Dũng, "Jules Roux: người bạn thiết nghĩa của nhà cách mạng Phan Châu Trinh," *Bách Khoa* 406 (1974): 39–48.

105. Nguyễn An Ninh to Léon Werth, March 18, 1939, Papiers Léon Werth, 1LW198, Archives Municipales, Issoudun.

106. Phạm Duy Khiêm, "Quelques souvenirs sur Normale Supérieure," *Indochine: hébdomadaire illustré,* December 30, 1943.

107. Dương Văn Quản to "ông Chính," August 6, 1928, Dossier Dương Văn Quản, SLOTFOM XV.105, ANOM.

108. Goebel, *Anti-Imperial Metropolis,* 65.

109. Dossier Ngam Mouth, SLOTFOM XV.21, ANOM.

110. Tùng Hương, "Trên đường Nam Pháp," in Nguyễn Hữu Sơn, *Du ký Việt Nam: tạp chí Nam Phong,* 2:319.

111. Le Van Ho, *Des Vietnamiens dans la Grande Guerre,* 77, 79.

112. Goebel, *Anti-Imperial Metropolis,* 44.

113. Ibid., 76.

114. "Rapport de Vincent," March 4, 1930, SLOTFOM II.9, ANOM.

115. "Rapport de Roseau," May 3, 1931, SLOTFOM III.5, ANOM.

116. Châu Du Tử, "Một người phụ nữ Việt Nam ở Paris về," *Phụ Nữ Tân Văn*, January 21, 1932.

117. Dossier Trần Tho, SLOTFOM XV.164, ANOM.

118. "Contrôle postal indochinois, octobre 1918," IC NF 227, ANOM.

119. Fogarty, *Race and War in France*, 220.

120. Ibid., 209.

121. Le Van Ho, *Des Vietnamiens dans la Grande Guerre*, 145.

122. Contrôleur des contigents coloniaux des 12è et 18è régions to MC, August 25, 1918, IC NF 243, ANOM.

123. Fogarty, *Race and War in France*, 208–9.

124. "Contrôle postal indochinois, juin 1919," IC NF 227, ANOM.

125. Lê Văn Khi to Trần Đình Nhà, March 21, 1940, SLOTFOM III.109, ANOM.

126. "Contrôle postal indochinois, janvier 1918," IC NF 227, ANOM.

127. "Contrôle postal indochinois, avril 1918," IC NF 248, ANOM.

128. "Rapport du Contrôleur général des troupes indochinoises au sujet de la situation materielle et morale des détachements annamites de l'armée du Rhin," n.d., SLOTFOM I.10, ANOM.

129. Both sources cited in Fogarty, *Race and War in France*, 208.

130. "Contrôle postal indochinois, mars 1918," IC NF 227, ANOM.

131. Moraux-Godart to Ministre de la guerre, June 14, 1920, Dossier Phạm Công Phước, SLOTFOM XV.11, ANOM.

132. "Contrôle postal indochinois, juin 1917," SLOTFOM I.8, ANOM.

133. "Contrôle postal indochinois, novembre 1918," SLOTFOM I.8, ANOM.

134. M.Y. Meinen to Ministre de la guerre, April 29, 1920, SLOTFOM VI.7, ANOM.

135. Alphonse Litvogel to MC, July 23, 1921, SLOTFOM VI.7, ANOM.

136. "Contrôle postal indochinois, avril 1919," SLOTFOM I.8, ANOM.

137. Ibid.

138. RST to GGI, April 12, 1920, SLOTFOM III.22, ANOM.

139. Dossier Nguyễn Văn Khánh, SLOTFOM XV.5, ANOM.

140. Résident Supérieur à Ninh Bình to RST, June 4, 1917, SLOTFOM VI.7, ANOM.

141. "Instruction confidentielle pour la libération en France à titre exceptionnel des militaires et travailleurs indigènes des colonies outre que l'Algérie, la Tunisie et le Maroc, qui demandent à rester dans la métropole," undated, SLOTFOM I.8, ANOM.

142. Ministre de la justice to Monsieur le Procureur général, February 2, 1917, SLOTFOM VI.7, ANOM.

143. Lydie Corbière to Nguyễn Thế Phu, March 15, 1929, Dossier Nguyễn Thế Phu, SLOTFOM XV.22, ANOM.

144. Cao Quỳnh An to Nguyễn Văn Thân, November 21, 1927, Dossier Cao Quỳnh An, SLOTFOM XV.80, ANOM.

145. "Note de Désiré," October 25, 1924, Dossier Hà Minh Thương, SLOTFOM XV.28, ANOM.

146. Jacques Danlor, "Un désespoir d'amour coute la vie à un jeune lycéen annamite du Lycée Henri IV," *Tribune indochinoise,* March 26, 1928.

147. Alphonse Litvogel to MC, July 23, 1921, SLOTFOM VI.7, ANOM.

148. Nguyễn Văn Trụ to his sister, May 3, 1927, Dossier Nguyễn Văn Trụ, SLOTFOM XV.79, ANOM.

149. Lê Văn Đốc to unknown recipient, January 10, 1926, SLOTFOM XI.1, ANOM.

150. Nguyễn Văn Ấn to Tăng Cung Chương, April 16, 1929, Dossier Nguyễn Văn Ấn, SLOTFOM XV.124, ANOM.

151. Unknown to Lê Thị Ba, May 25, 1927, SLOTFOM III.28, ANOM.

152. "Note de l'agent Désiré," January 20, 1926, SLOTFOM III.I, ANOM.

153. Ngô Quang Huy to Nguyễn Văn Trụ, April 10, 1929, Dossier Ngô Quang Huy, SLOTFOM XV.79, ANOM.

154. "Note de Désiré," November 3, 1927, SLOTFOM II.17, ANOM.

155. Tạ Thu Thâu to Nguyễn Văn Hóa, January 26, 1929, Dossier Nguyễn Văn Thơm, SLOTFOM XV.109, ANOM.

156. GGI 2236, TTLT I.

157. Madame Nguyễn Văn Ba to MC, April 13, 1933, Dossier Nguyễn Văn Ba, SLOTFOM XV.40, ANOM.

158. Dossier Lục Văn Sau, SLOTFOM XV.43, ANOM.

159. Dossier Vũ Văn Trang, SLOTFOM XV.39, ANOM.

160. Dossier Nguyễn Thị Nhân, SLOTFOM XV.48, ANOM.

161. Dossier Đình Văn Miển, SLOTFOM XV.57, ANOM.

162. H.L. Leclerc to MC, April 1, 1935, Dossier Nguyễn Văn Pham, SLOTFOM XV.20, ANOM.

163. Dossier Huỳnh Nhiên, SLOTFOM XV.50, ANOM.

164. Dossier Lý Văn Thủy, SLOTFOM XV.24, ANOM.

165. "Le désespoir de l'annamite," *La Liberté,* September 2, 1927; "Délaissé, un Japonais croyait avoir regagné le coeur de sa femme," *Le Matin,* September 2, 1927. The second article obviously misidentifies his nationality.

166. "Un ingénieur annamite qui tua sa femme est acquitté," *Le Matin,* June 15, 1929.

167. Dossier Lê Văn Huế, SLOTFOM XV.53, ANOM.

168. Dossier Paul Thái, SLOTFOM XV.52, ANOM.

169. Hồ Tá Khanh to his father, April 2, 1926, Dossier Hồ Tá Khanh, SLOTFOM XV.69, ANOM.

170. Nguyễn Văn Lai to "Messieurs Dao et Kiet," November 22, 1928, Dossier Nguyễn Văn Lai, SLOTFOM XV.99, ANOM.

171. Tran Van Cui to MC, April 1, 1931, GGI 2229, TTLT I.

172. Phan Cao Ly to Phan Văn Trường, January 6, 1923, RST NF 7023, ANOM.

173. Nguyễn Thới Lai to his sister, July 3, 1928, Dossier Nguyễn Thới Lai, SLOTFOM XV.99, ANOM.

174. Nguyễn Văn Kim to his parents, July 26, 1927, Dossier Nguyễn Văn Kim, SLOTFOM XV.84, ANOM.

175. Vu-Hill, *Coolies into Rebels*, 42–43.

176. Luguern, "Les 'Travailleurs Indochinois,'" 311–12.

177. GOUCOCH VIA.6/191 (1), TTLT II.

178. "Rapport d'ensemble concernant le 2ème semestre de 1918," IC NF 225, ANOM.

179. Nguyễn Duy Kiêm to his brother, March 20, 1926, Dossier Nguyễn Duy Kiêm, SLOTFOM XV.77, ANOM.

180. Nguyễn Văn Lai to his uncle, November 29, 1928, Dossier Nguyễn Văn Lai, SLOTFOM XV.99, ANOM.

181. Directeur du SAMI to GGI, July 31, 1931, GGI 1253, TTLT I.

182. Luguern, "Les 'Travailleurs Indochinois,'" 601.

183. Trịnh Đao Thiêm to "monsieur le général," March 25, 1940, SLOTFOM VI.4, ANOM.

184. Many such cases are documented in SLOTFOM IV.4, ANOM.

185. Nguyễn Văn Ất to Đinh Văn Lực, February 20, 1929, Dossier Nguyễn Văn Ất, SLOTFOM XV.98, ANOM.

186. Trịnh Thế Qúy to the Directeur du CAI, January 11, 1940, Dossier Trịnh Thế Qúy, SLOTFOM XV.117, ANOM.

187. Nghiêm Xuân Hoàng to Directeur du CAI, February 27, 1926, Dossier Nghiêm Xuân Toàn, SLOTFOM XV.115, ANOM.

188. Lê Văn Dậu to Quách Văn Giáo, January 13, 1924, Dossier Lê Văn Dậu, SLOTFOM XV.24, ANOM.

189. Diệp Văn Vàng to his parents, April 4, 1930, Dossier Diệp Văn Vàng, SLOTFOM XV.74, ANOM.

190. Nguyễn Văn Phương to Nguyễn Văn Quyển, January 17, 1931, Dossier Phan Chấn Thế, SLOTFOM XV.62, ANOM.

191. Dossier Nguyễn Khoa Thi, SLOTFOM XV.106, ANOM.

192. Dossier Vũ Đỗ Tân, SLOTFOM XV.51, ANOM.

193. Dossier Lương Văn Thành, SLOTFOM XV.25, ANOM.

194. "Le cas pitoyable d'une pauvre française," *Tribune indochinoise*, July 27, 1936.

195. Nguyễn Tuấn to Chef de bureau, Délégue du ministère des colonies, December 6, 1939, SLOTFOM IV.2, ANOM.

196. Dossier Nguyễn Thị Lương, SLOTFOM XV.112, ANOM.

197. Unknown author to "mon cher Nghĩa," March 2, 1919, SLOTFOM VI.7, ANOM.

198. Marthe Oddo to Ưng Du, March 15, 1923, Dossier Ưng Du, SLOTFOM XV.9, ANOM.

199. "Fiche de renseignements," undated, Dossier Nguyễn Xuân Lâm, SLOTFOM XV.50, ANOM.

200. Nguyễn Thế Phu to Nguyễn Thế Tập, July 3, 1928, Dossier Nguyễn Thế Rục, SLOTFOM XV.99, ANOM.

201. "Man Luc" to MC, April 30, 1936, SLOTFOM VI.2, ANOM.

202. Dossier Nguyễn Văn Liên, SLOTFOM XV.25, ANOM.

203. Nguyen Thi Ty to GGI, December 25, 1937, GGI 283, TTLT I.

CHAPTER 7. POLITICAL SOJOURNERS
FROM PEACE TO WAR

1. Quinn-Judge, *Ho Chi Minh*, 32.

2. The first person to use the phrase appears to have been Hồ Hữu Tường in his 1972 memoir *41 năm làm báo*.

3. Wilder, *The French Imperial Nation-State*, 150, 157–58, 160.

4. Quinn-Judge, *Ho Chi Minh*, 36.

5. Goebel, *Anti-Imperial Metropolis*, 189–90.

6. Goebel's claim that the Intercolonial Union was initially "independent" is incorrect. The predecessor of the Intercolonial Union was the "Groupe socialiste des originaires des colonies," created just after the Tours Congress and replaced by the Comité d'études coloniales in early 1921. The Intercolonial Union was created months later.

7. NPRPOM, March 31, 1925, SLOTFOM III.144, ANOM.

8. Goebel, *Anti-Imperial Metropolis*, 191.

9. Trang-Gaspard, *Hồ Chí Minh à Paris*, 214–215; Peycam, *The Birth of Vietnamese Political Journalism*, 118.

10. Ibid., 157–79.

11. Hue-Tam Ho Tai, *Radicalism and the Origins of the Vietnamese Revolution* (Cambridge: Harvard University Press, 1992), 76.

12. Quinn-Judge, *Ho Chi Minh*, 38.

13. Trang Thu, *Những hoạt động của Phan Châu Trinh tại Pháp, 1911–1925* (Paris: Đông Nam Á, 1983), chapter 8.

14. "Rapport de l'agent Jolin à monsieur le Résident Supérieur Guesde," May 22, 1922, Dossier Nguyễn Văn Vĩnh, SLOTFOM XV.21, ANOM.

15. Nguyễn Phan Quang and Phan Văn Hoàng, *Luật sư Phan Văn Trường*, 60.

16. Thu Trang-Gaspard, "Contribution à l'étude de la vie et de l'oeuvre de Phan Châu Trinh (1872–1926) (PhD diss., Université de Paris VII, 1978), 117.

17. Nguyễn Phan Quang and Phan Văn Hoàng, *Luật sư Phan Văn Trường*, 61–62.

18. Ibid., 76.

19. Peycam, *The Birth of Vietnamese Political Journalism*, 192.

20. Quinn-Judge, *Ho Chi Minh*, 40.

21. Ibid., 132.

22. Hémery, "Du patriotisme au marxisme," 14–15.

23. Goebel, *Anti-Imperial Metropolis*, 194.

24. Ho Tai, *Radicalism*, 149.

25. Quinn-Judge, *Ho Chi Minh*, 59.

26. Several historians mistakenly identify June 1927 as the actual foundation of the party. See Goebel, *Anti-Imperial Metropolis*, 198; Quinn-Judge, *Ho Chi Minh*, 118–19.

27. He wrote to Nguyễn Thế Truyền in April 1925 asking him "to keep him informed on the communist movement in France and its possessions" (NPRPOM, April 20, 1925, SPCE 380, ANOM).

28. Quinn-Judge suggests that Nguyễn Thế Truyền was simply following the Comintern's call for the formation of national revolutionary parties (*Ho Chi Minh*, 117).

29. Ho Tai, *Radicalism*, 289–90n73.

30. Đặng Hữu Thụ, *Thân thế và sự nghiệp nhà cách mạng Nguyễn Thế Truyền*, 141–54.

31. See Quinn-Judge, *Ho Chi Minh*, chapter 2.

32. Hémery, "Du patriotisme au marxisme," 19–20.

33. Quinn-Judge, *Ho Chi Minh*, 79.

34. "Note de l'agent Désiré," April 9, 1925, SPCE 380, ANOM.

35. Goebel, *Anti-Imperial Metropolis*, 139. On the European Kuomintang, see Marilyn Levine and Chen San-Ching, "Communist-Leftist Control of the European Branch of the Guomindang, 1923–1927," *Modern China* 22.1 (January 1996): 62–92.

36. "Theo gương nước Tầu," *Việt Nam Hồn*, February 1926; "Tình hình người Việt Nam ở Tầu" and "Đồng bào trong quân ngũ," *Hồn Nam Việt*, March 1927.

37. Truong Buu Lam, *Colonialism Experienced: Vietnamese Writings on Colonialism, 1900–1931* (Ann Arbor: University of Michigan Press, 2000), 239–47.

38. NPRPOM, March 31, 1927, SLOTFOM III.144, ANOM.

39. Brückenhaus, *Policing Transnational Protest*, chapter 5.

40. Goebel, *Anti-Imperial Metropolis*, 201.

41. "Annexe 1 au rapport de mission du 27 septembre 1930," SLOTFOM I.10, ANOM.

42. Trần Vĩnh Hiến to Trần Vĩnh Hoài, June 1, 1927, Dossier Trần Vĩnh Hiến, SLOTFOM XV.26, ANOM.

43. "Déclarations de Théologien en Avril 1932 par la Direction de la Sûreté générale," Dossier Nguyễn Thế Thạch, SLOTFOM XV.43, ANOM.

44. "Rapport de l'agent Jacques," October 10, 1932, SLOTFOM III.58, ANOM.

45. Délégue du CAI to Directeur des affaires politiques, ministère des colonies, August 21, 1929, SLOTFOM III.141, ANOM.

46. RST NF 6830, ANOM.

47. Detailed accounts of these speeches are in Đặng Hữu Thụ, *Thân thế và sự nghiệp nhà cách mạng Nguyễn Thế Truyền*, chapter VIII.

48. Documents on the affair are in SLOTFOM III.12, ANOM. On the hat, see Directeur du CAI to Directeur des affaires politiques, ministère des colonies, August 11, 1927, SPCE 380, ANOM.

49. Ho Tai, *Radicalism*, 188. Some scholars claim that Nguyễn An Ninh had come into contact with Thanh Niên activists while in prison and was working for the party when he left for France in 1927. See Quinn-Judge, *Ho Chi Minh*, 105.

50. NPRPOM, June 30, 1927, SLOTFOM III.145, ANOM.

51. A poster for the event is in SLOTFOM II.17, ANOM.

52. See, for example, "Note du 7 Mai 1926," SPCE 380, ANOM.

53. Quinn-Judge, *Ho Chi Minh*, 106–15.

54. NPRPOM, June 30, 1927, SLOTFOM III.145, ANOM.

55. Quoted in Ho Tai, *Radicalism*, 234.

56. "CAI envoi n.2438," October 25, 1927, SPCE 380, ANOM.

57. NPRPOM, July 31, 1927, SLOTFOM III.144, ANOM.

58. "Déclarations de Bui Ai, dit MAIZEN, receuillies au moi de juin 1932," Dossier Bùi Ái, SLOTFOM XV.16, ANOM.

59. Trần Vĩnh Hiến to his father, April 3, 1928, Dossier Trần Vĩnh Hiến, SLOTFOM XV.26, ANOM.

60. Đặng Hữu Thụ, *Thân thế và sự nghiệp nhà cách mạng Nguyễn Thế Truyền*, 273.

61. Ho Tai, *Radicalism*, chapter 6.

62. Dossier Nguyễn Văn Luận, SLOTFOM XV.24, ANOM.

63. A contemporary source affirming this is "Déclarations de Bui Ai, dit MAIZEN, receuillies au moi de juin 1932," Dossier Bùi Ái, SLOTFOM XV.16, ANOM.

64. Trịnh Văn Thảo, *L'école française en Indochine*, 291–92.

65. "A.s. de la colonie indochinoise de Paris," December 1929, SLOTFOM III.32, ANOM.

66. The letters are in Dossier Nguyễn Văn Luận, SLOTFOM XV.24, ANOM.

67. Nguyễn Văn Luận to Diệp Văn Kỳ, March 8, 1928, Dossier Nguyễn Văn Luận, SLOTFOM XV.24, ANOM.

68. Nguyễn Ngọc Phong to Nguyễn Văn Luận, July 19, 1929, Dossier Nguyễn Văn Luận, SLOTFOM XV.24, ANOM.

69. Cited in Daniel Hémery, "Ta Thu Thau: l'itinéraire politique d'un révolutionnaire vietnamien pendant les années 1930," in *Histoire de l'Asie du Sud-Est: révoltes, réformes, révolutions*, ed. Pierre Brocheux (Lille: Presses universitaires de Lille, 1981), 193–222.

70. McConnell, *Leftward Journey*, 131–36.

71. See NPRPOM, January 31, February 28, and March 31, 1929, SLOTFOM III.148B, ANOM.

72. Goebel mistakenly describes this as a "communist" takeover (*Anti-Imperial Metropolis*, 140).

73. Ho Tai, *Radicalism*, 239.

74. Tạ Thu Thâu to Nguyễn Huỳnh Điểu, November 25, 1927, Dossier Tạ Thu Thâu, SLOTFOM XV.86, ANOM.

75. Daniel Hémery, *Révolutionnaires vietnamiens et pouvoir colonial en indochine: communistes, trotskystes, nationalistes à Saigon, 1932–1937* (Paris: François Maspero, 1975), 39.

76. "Interrogatoire," October 31, 1931, Dossier Dương Bạch Mai, SLOTFOM XV.88, ANOM.

77. Quinn-Judge, *Ho Chi Minh,* 116.

78. Thomas Schweitzer, "The French Communist Party and the Colonial Question, 1928–1939" (PhD diss., University of Wisconsin-Madison, 1968), chapter 3.

79. MC to GGI, January 20, 1932, SLOTFOM III.31, ANOM.

80. Dossier Hoàng Quang Giụ, SLOTFOM XV.17, ANOM.

81. Peycam, *The Birth of Vietnamese Political Journalism,* 201–2.

82. See Pham, "Revolution, Communism, and History in the Thought of Trần Văn Giàu," chapter 2.

83. A key source on Toulouse politics in 1931 is "Declarations de Tran Van Minh faites à la direction de la Sûreté générale du 29 juin au 16 juillet 1935," Dossier Trần Văn Minh, SLOTFOM XV.129, ANOM.

84. Đỗ Đình Thiện to Toulouse branch of the PCF, February 2, 1932, Dossier Đỗ Đình Thiện, SLOTFOM XV.79, ANOM.

85. Hồ Tá Khanh to Đỗ Dư Anh, August 1, 1928, Dossier Hồ Tá Khanh, SLOTFOM XV.69, ANOM.

86. For his and Hồ Tá Khanh's activities in early 1930, see SLOTFOM III.1, ANOM.

87. Délégué du CAI to Directeur des affaires politiques, ministère des colonies, July 26, 1930.

88. NPRPOM, April 30, 1930, SLOTFOM III.150–151, ANOM.

89. "Activité du groupe communiste annamite de Paris: Fête annuelle du journal 'L'Humanité,'" September 7, 1934, SLOTFOM III.113, ANOM.

90. Délégué du CAI to Directeur des affaires politiques, ministère des colonies, February 7, 1931, SLOTFOM III.6, ANOM.

91. MC to GGI, January 20, 1932, SLOTFOM III.31, ANOM.

92. MC to GGI, December 24, 1931, SLOTFOM III.20, ANOM.

93. MC to GGI, May 24, 1932, SLOTFOM III.20, ANOM.

94. Délégué du CAI to Directeur des affaires politiques, ministère des colonies, November 7, 1931, SLOTFOM III.113, ANOM.

95. Délégué du CAI to Directeur des affaires politiques, ministère des colonies, August 12, 1935, Dossier Trần Văn Điện, SLOTFOM XV.59, ANOM.

96. Quinn-Judge, *Ho Chi Minh,* 125.

97. Cited in Claude Liauzu, *Aux origines des tiers-mondismes; colonisés et anticolonialistes en France (1919–1939)* (Paris: L'Harmattan, 1982), 22n29.

98. "Déclarations de Nguyen Van Phai dit Goubin receuillies en Juin 1932 par la direction de la Sûreté indochinoise," 15–16, Dossier Nguyễn Văn Phải, SLOTFOM XV.123, ANOM.

99. "Entrevue de l'agent 'Thomas' du 2 Octobre 1932," Dossier Hoàng Quang Giụ, SLOTFOM XV.17, ANOM.

100. "Déclarations de 'Théologien' [Nguyễn Thế Thạch] recueillies en avril 1932 par la direction de la Sûreté générale," Dossier Nguyễn Thế Thạch, SLOTFOM XV.43, ANOM.

101. Délégué du CAI to Directeur des affaires politiques, ministère des colonies, November 5, 1932, Dossier Nguyễn Văn Quang, SLOTFOM XV.144, ANOM.

102. Délégué du CAI to Directeur des affaires politiques, ministère des colonies, February 16, 1931, Dossier Chú Hỷ, SLOTFOM XV.113, ANOM.

103. Délégué du CAI to Directeur des affaires politiques, ministère des colonies, February 4, 1931, Dossier Lý Nghị, SLOTFOM XV.133, ANOM.

104. NPRPOM, January 31, 1931, SLOTFOM III.150–151, ANOM.

105. NPRPOM, December 31, 1930, SLOTFOM III.150–151, ANOM.

106. McConnell, *Leftward Journey,* 133.

107. Ibid., 134.

108. Schweitzer, "The French Communist Party and the Colonial Question," chapter VI.

109. Délégué du CAI to Directeur des affaires politiques, ministère des colonies, February 3, 1931, SLOTFOM III.6, ANOM.

110. Délégué du CAI to Directeur des affaires politiques, ministère des colonies, February 16, 1931, Dossier Đào Nguyên Định, SLOTFOM XV.10, ANOM.

111. See Frédéric Charpier, *L'Histoire de l'extrême gauche Trotskiste de 1929 à nos jours* (Paris: Editions1, 2002).

112. Ho Tai, *Radicalism,* 238–39.

113. See Trần Ngươn Phiêu, *Phan Văn Hùm: thân thế và sự nghiệp,* chapter 1.

114. "Journal d'un errant," translated excerpts of unpublished manuscript reportedly sent to Phan Văn Hòa in 1932, Dossier Phan Văn Hùm, SLOTFOM XV.84, ANOM.

115. Hồ Hữu Tường, "Un fétu de paille dans la tourmente," 65.

116. Ibid., chapter 2.

117. "Rapport de Durand," September 3, 1930, Dossier Vũ Gia, SLOTFOM XV.93, ANOM.

118. Hồ Hữu Tường, "Un fétu de paille dans la tourmente," 74.

119. Ibid., 79.

120. MC to GGI, October 8, 1932, Dossier Lê Văn Rớt, SLOTFOM XV.55, ANOM.

121. "Agent Thomas, entrevue du 5 septembre 1932," SLOTFOM III.127, ANOM.

122. "Note de renseignements—Le groupe Trotskyist indochinois de Paris et l'Association d'entraide et de culture—incident Nguyen Van Linh," October 29, 1932, SLOTFOM V.41, ANOM.

123. "Note de renseignements," September 25, 1932, Dossier Phan Tư Nghĩa, SLOTFOM XV.142, ANOM.

124. See Edward Mortimer, *The Rise of the French Communist Party, 1920–1947* (Boston: Faber & Faber, 1984), chapter 4.

125. NPRPOM, March 31, 1932, SLOTFOM III.149, ANOM.

126. On Ferrat, see Céline Marangé, "André Ferrat et la création du parti communiste Algérien (1931–1936)," *histoire@politique* 29.2 (2016): 190–219.

127. Schweitzer, "The French Communist Party and the Colonial Question," 157–62.

128. "Contrôle générale des troupes indochinoises, rapport de mai 1920," June 1, 1920, SLOTFOM I.8, ANOM.

129. "Contrôle postal des indochinois, juillet 1919," IC NF 227, ANOM.

130. Le Van Ho, *Des Vietnamiens dans la Grande Guerre*, 181.

131. "Contrôle postal des indochinois, mai 1919," SLOTFOM I.8, ANOM.

132. Quoted in de Fautereau, "Le Nationalisme vietnamien," 5–6.

133. Christoph Giebel, *Imagined Ancestries of Vietnamese Communism: Tôn Đức Thắng and the Politics of History and Memory* (Seattle: University of Washington Press, 2004).

134. Tyler Stovall, *Paris and the Spirit of 1919: Consumer Struggles, Transnationalism, and Revolution* (Cambridge: Cambridge University Press, 2012), 131.

135. Ho Tai, *Radicalism*, 69.

136. On Đặng Văn Thư's activities on behalf of the PAI, see Dossier Đặng Văn Thư, SLOTFOM XV.15, ANOM.

137. Peters, "Resistance, Rivalries, and Restaurants," 123–24.

138. Ibid., 117.

139. "Note de renseignements," undated, SLOTFOM III.22, ANOM.

140. Peters, "Resistance, Rivalries, and Restaurants," 125.

141. "Se sacrifier pour la patrie," lyrics of songs sung at PAI Tết celebration, February 9, 1929, SLOTFOM III.23, ANOM.

142. Peters, "Resistance, Rivalries, and Restaurants," 125.

143. "Note sur les associations indochinois à Paris," June 14, 1923, SLOTFOM III.40, ANOM.

144. Trang-Gaspard, *Hồ Chí Minh à Paris*, 223.

145. "Note," November 23, 1928, SLOTFOM III.1, ANOM.

146. Peters, "Resistance, Rivalries, and Restaurants," 125–26.

147. "Note," January 14, 1927, SLOTFOM III.1, ANOM.

148. "Rapport de l'agent Durand," April 10, 1929, SLOTFOM II.8, ANOM.

149. Annex to letter from Délégue du CAI to MC, January 11, 1928, SLOTFOM III.4, ANOM.

150. Group of Indochinese sailors to GGI, January 17, 1928, GOUCOCH IB. 30/034(9), TTLT II.

151. "Note," February 4, 1929, SLOTFOM IV.9, ANOM.

152. "Note Durand: tentative d'un syndicat des lacquers par Tran Le Luat," undated, SLOTFOM II.8, ANOM.

153. NPRPOM, January 31, 1929, SLOTFOM III.148B, ANOM.

154. NPRPOM, September 30, 1929, SLOTFOM III.148B, ANOM.

155. Délégué du CAI to Directeur des affaires politiques, ministère des colonies, March 20, 1930, SLOTFOM III.1, ANOM.

156. Comité central du PCF to Region Marseillaise, May 21, 1929, SLOTFOM III.7, ANOM.

157. "Note de Guillaume," March 11, 1930, SLOTFOM V.25–26, ANOM.

158. "Appel aux marins coloniaux," *Rouge midi*, November 8, 1930.

159. MC to GGI, November 18, 1930, SLOTFOM III.7, ANOM.

160. Untitled document, October 7, 1931, Dossier Đỗ Đình Thiện, SLOTFOM XV.79, ANOM.

161. MC to GGI, November 18, 1930, SLOTFOM III.7, ANOM.

162. Goebel, *Anti-Imperial Metropolis,* 212.

163. NPRPOM, April 30, 1932, SLOTFOM III.149, ANOM.

164. NPRPOM, May 31, 1932, SLOTFOM III.149, ANOM.

165. Délégué du CAI to Directeur des affaires politiques, ministère des colonies, October 11, 1932, SLOTFOM III.126, ANOM.

166. "Agent Thomas, entrevue du 12 October 1932," SLOTFOM III.18, ANOM.

167. NPRPOM, September 30, 1933, SLOTFOM III.147, ANOM.

168. NPRPOM, October 31, 1934, SLOTFOM III.147, ANOM.

169. NPRPOM, June 30, 1932, SLOTFOM III.149, ANOM.

170. SLOTFOM III.58, ANOM.

171. NPRPOM, April 30, 1933, SLOTFOM III.147, ANOM.

172. Nguyễn Thế Truyền to Madeleine Latour, March 31, 1934, Dossier Nguyễn Thế Phú, SLOTFOM XV.22, ANOM.

173. "Tên phản bội Nguyễn Thế Truyền đã sang Pháp!," *Vô Sản,* June 1934.

174. James E. Genova, "The Empire Within: The Colonial Popular Front in France, 1934–1938," *Alternatives: Global, Local, Political* 26.2 (April-June 2001): 175–209, 189.

175. Đặng Hữu Thụ, *Thân thế và sự nghiệp nhà cách mạng Nguyễn Thế Truyền,* 314–15.

176. Mortimer, *The Rise of the French Communist Party,* chapter 6.

177. Goebel, *Anti-Imperial Metropolis,* 272.

178. NPRPOM, June 30, 1934, SLOTFOM III.147, ANOM.

179. Hémery, *Révolutionnaires vietnamiens et pouvoir colonial,* 59.

180. Ibid., 62.

181. Ibid., 139.

182. Dossier Lê Hiến, SLOTFOM XV.153, ANOM; Dossier Phan Tất Tốn, SLOTFOM XV.76, ANOM.

183. Chef local des services de police to Directeur des affaires politiques de la Sûreté générale, January 23, 1937, SPCE 380, ANOM.

184. Hémery, *Révolutionnaires vietnamiens et pouvoir colonial,* 142.

185. Ibid., 144–45.

186. "Le réunion de vendredi soir," undated, 28 PA 2, ANOM.

187. Hémery, *Révolutionnaires vietnamiens et pouvoir colonial,* 142.

188. "Note de la direction de la Sûreté générale indochinoise au sujet du communiste Ta Thu Thau qui serait en relations avec M. Alfred Colin, domicilié 10, rue Mozart à Antony (Seine)," February 20, 1936, Dossier Tạ Thu Thâu, SLOTFOM XV.86, ANOM. See also Trần Văn Thạch to Nguyễn Thế Truyền, September 22, 1937, SPCE 380, ANOM.

189. "Note," June 19, 1936, SLOTFOM III.129, ANOM.

190. Some issues of the newspapers are in SLOTFOM XV.41 (*Quốc Tế IV*) and SLOTFOM XV.33 (*Quần Chúng*), ANOM.

191. "Bulletin de renseignements no. 29," January 18, 1937, SLOTFOM III.22, ANOM.

192. "Note," February 20, 1939, SLOTFOM III.119, ANOM.

193. Mortimer, *The Rise of the French Communist Party*, 240–47.

194. French translation of tract circulated among Indochinese sailors in Marseille, December 1936, SLOTFOM V.36, ANOM.

195. "Note au sujet de l'organisation syndicale des marins indochinois," September 7, 1937, SLOTFOM V.25–26, ANOM.

196. Chef du bureau de l'immigration indigène to Directeur des affaires politiques, ministère des colonies, February 11, 1939, SLOTFOM III.20, ANOM.

197. "Activité du Syndicat des cuisiniers auprès des Annamites," February 21, 1935, SLOTFOM III.31, ANOM.

198. IC NF 1851, ANOM.

CHAPTER 8. POLITICAL SOJOURNERS FROM
WAR TO DECOLONIZATION

1. Julian Jackson, *France: The Dark Years, 1940–1944* (New York: Oxford University Press, 2001), 120.

2. Nguyễn Khắc Viện, "Những năm ở Pháp," *Tạp Chí Sông Hương,* November 6, 2015: http://www.tapchisonghuong.com.vn/hue/p0/c107/n21535/Nhung-nam-o-Phap.html.

3. Eric Jennings, *Vichy in the Tropics: Pétain's National Revolution in Madagascar, Guadeloupe, and Indochina, 1940–1944* (Stanford, CA: Stanford University Press, 2001), 2–3.

4. "Note," February 4, 1950, Dossier Hoàng Văn Cơ, SLOTFOM XV.82, ANOM.

5. Cited in Luguern, "Les 'Travailleurs Indochinois,'" 474.

6. "Notice, Tran Van Hy," March 14, 1952, Dossier Trần Văn Hy, SLOTFOM XV.9, ANOM.

7. Pierre Brocheux, "Visions et representations de l'Occident européen chez les voyageurs vietnamiens, 1864–1954," in Ruscio, *Une vie pour le Viêt Nam*, 219.

8. Ngô Quốc Quyền to Ngô Đình Mẫn, September 14, 1927, Dossier Ngô Quốc Quyền, SLOTFOM XV.85, ANOM.

9. Hinh Thái Thông to Võ Thành Vinh, July 15, 1927, Dossier Hinh Thái Thông, SLOTFOM XV.80, ANOM.

10. Délégué du CAI to Directeur des affaires politiques, ministère des colonies, September 20, 1927, Dossier Nguyễn Hữu Thư, SLOTFOM XV.31, ANOM.

11. "Rapport de Durand," April 13, 1932, SLOTFOM II.8, ANOM.

12. The manifesto and biographical documentation are in Dossier Nguyễn Thượng Khoa, SLOTFOM XV.39, ANOM.

13. Keith, "Vietnamese Collaborationism in Vichy France."

14. Motadel, "The Global Authoritarian Movement and the Revolt Against Empire," 843–77.

15. Nguyễn Khắc Viện, "Vì Đâu?," *Nam Việt* 5 and 6 (July and August, 1944).

16. Võ Qúy Huân, "An nhàn," *Nam Việt* 1 (March 1944).

17. Võ Qúy Huân, "Công và của," *Nam Viet* 3 (May 1944).

18. Nguyễn Khắc Viện, "Học giả," *Nam Việt* 4 (June 1944).

19. Đặng Văn Long, *Người Việt ở Pháp, 1940–1954*, 40.

20. "Renseignement," undated, Dossier Đỗ Đức Hồ, SLOTFOM XV.28, ANOM.

21. Trịnh Văn Thảo, *Les compagnons de route de Hô Chi Minh*, 243. See also Benjamin Stora, "Les travailleurs indochinois en France pendant la seconde guerre mondiale," *Les Cahiers de CERMTRI* 28 (April 1983): 19–29.

22. Alain Ruscio, "Huynh Khuong An au Panthéon . . .," *L'Humanité*, May 28, 2015.

23. Alain Ruscio, *Les communistes et l'Algérie: des origins à la guerre d'indépendance, 1920–1962* (Paris: La Découverte, 2019), chapter 4.

24. Luguern, "Les 'Travailleurs Indochinois,'" 537, 671–74.

25. Ibid., 672.

26. See Nguyen Phuoc Bao Vang, *Duy Tan, empereur d'Annam 1900–1945: Exilé à l'île de la Réunion ou Le destin tragique du prince Vinh San* (Sainte-Marie: Azalées, 2000).

27. "Renseignements concernant André-Marie Tao Kim Hai," undated, Dossier Tào Kim Hải, SLOTFOM XV.109, ANOM.

28. David Chandler, *The Tragedy of Cambodian History* (New Haven: Yale University Press, 1991), 30.

29. "Interview du colonel Nguyễn Tấn Trịnh," *Tiếng Gọi*, November 21, 1948.

30. Dossier Nguyễn Hữu Bích, SLOTFOM XV.104, ANOM.

31. Maurice Rives, "Les indochinois de l'opération Dragoon," *Bulletin de l'A.N.A.I* (January-February-March 2004): 4–9.

32. Guy Scaggion, *Kiem Phan-Van, L'évadé des annexes* (Bordeaux: Les Dossiers d'Acquitaine, 2004).

33. "Note pour monsieur le ministre," September 27, 1945, SLOTFOM XIV.4, ANOM.

34. Cited in Luguern, "Les 'Travailleurs Indochinois,'" 674.

35. Thanh Cao, "Tương lai của chúng ta," *Công Binh Tạp Chí*, January 1945.

36. "Du comportement politique actuel des indochinois en France," December 12, 1944, IC NF 1583, ANOM.

37. "Manifeste du congrès national des Indochinois à Avignon," IC NF 1562, ANOM. On the formation of the DGI, see IC NF 1562 and Luguern, "Les 'Travailleurs Indochinois,'" 743–68.

38. Lê Hữu Thọ, *Itinéraire d'un petit mandarin*, 156; "Note," September 16, 1948, Dossier Phạm Ngọc Tiên, SLOTFOM XV.174, ANOM.

39. "Notice de renseignements concernant Buu Hoi," June 1946, HCI 222/647, ANOM; IC NF 1586, ANOM.

40. "Notice de renseignements concernant Tran Duc Thao," undated, Dossier Trần Đức Thảo, SLOTFOM XV.234–236, ANOM.

41. Hémery, "Itinéraire I: Premier exil," 56–57.

42. DGI representatives to Charles de Gaulle, February 15, 1945, IC NF 1587, ANOM.

43. Cao Văn Luận, *Bên giòng lịch sử* (Sài Gòn: Trí Dũng, 1972), 26.

44. Phạm Hữu Điệc to Trần Văn Hại, January 20, 1947, HCI CONSPOL 107, ANOM.

45. "Compte rendu de mission," February 20, 1945, IC NF 1587, ANOM.

46. "Résolution de la Délégation générale des indochinois, approuvée par l'Assemblée générale des indochinois de Paris du 8 avril 1945," IC NF 1587, ANOM.

47. "Memorandum sur le statut futur de l'Indochine établi par le commandant Vinh San," September 25, 1945, Dossier Duy Tân, SLOTFOM XV.7, ANOM. On Duy Tân's arrival and activities in Paris in early 1945 see Cao Văn Luận, *Bên giòng lịch sử*, 30–47.

48. Its principal figures appear to have been the former Vichy administrators Hoàng Văn Cơ and Cao Văn Sen, as well as the medical doctor Nguyễn Văn Tùng.

49. Cited in Luguern, "Les 'Travailleurs Indochinois,'" 748.

50. "Du comportement politique actuel des indochinois en France," December 12, 1944, IC NF 1583, ANOM.

51. Claude Bernard's history of the group from 1943–1947 is in *The Revolution Defamed: A Documentary History of Vietnamese Trotskyism*, ed. Al Richardson (London: Socialist Platform Ltd., 2003), 168–75.

52. Group of ONS to J. N. Taponier, November 15, 1944, IC NF 1585, ANOM.

53. Mortimer, *The Rise of the French Communist Party*, 333.

54. Tobias Rettig, "From Subaltern to Free Worker: Exit, Voice, and Loyalty among Indochina's Subaltern Labor Camp Diaspora in Metropolitan France, 1939–1944," *Journal of Vietnamese Studies* 7.3 (2012): 35.

55. "Note pour monsieur le Directeur du cabinet du secrétariat d'état aux colonies," July 8, 1944, IC NF 1583, ANOM.

56. "Rapport sur le congrès tenu par les annamites le 15, 16, 17 décembre 1944," IC NF 1562, ANOM.

57. "Rapport de Mr. GOUPY, administrateur-adjoint des services civiles de l'Indochine, sur sa mission en France au sujet des travailleurs indochinois stationnées dans la métropole," April 18, 1946, HCI CS 3, ANOM.

58. "Résolution de la comité indochinois à Moulins," June 3, 1945, IC NF 979, ANOM.

59. "L'Agitation parmi les indochinois de France," undated, IC NF 1562, ANOM.

60. "Résolution de la Délégation générale des indochinois, approuvée par l'Assemblée générale des indochinois de Paris du 8 avril 1945," IC NF 1333.

61. "Sur le problème politique en Indochine," *Nam Việt*, August 1945.

62. "Note," May 3, 1945, SLOTFOM XIV.4, ANOM.

63. "Rapport particulier," September 10, 1945, SLOTFOM XIV.4, ANOM.

64. "Các thông tin," *Công Nông*, September 13, 1945, SLOTFOM XIV.6, ANOM.

65. "Activité revolutionnaire indochinois à Aix-en-Provence," September 25, 1945, SLOTFOM XIV.4, ANOM.

66. "Note relative au movement autonomiste indochinois en France," September 26, 1945, SLOTFOM XIV.4, ANOM.

67. Indochinese intellectuals and professionals to Charles de Gaulle, October 11, 1945, IC NF 1577, ANOM.

68. "Note sur le meeting du 13 Novembre 1945 à la Salle Wagram au sujet de l'Indochine," 174QO/22, MAE.

69. "Bulletin de renseignements, activités annamites," December 21, 1945, HCI CONSPOL 166, ANOM.

70. On these hunger strikes, see letters to Charles de Gaulle in IC NF 978, ANOM.

71. "5ème rapport au sujet de l'activité des indochinois à Marseille," undated, SLOTFOM XIV.4, ANOM.

72. Luguern, "Les 'Travailleurs Indochinois,'" 768–71.

73. "Note," October 24, 1945, SLOTFOM XIV.4, ANOM.

74. "L'organisation secrète des nationalistes indochinois," October 27, 1945, SLOTFOM XIV.4, ANOM.

75. "Assemblée générale des militaires annamites (tenue à Paris, le 9 et 10 Mars 1946)," HCI CS 3, ANOM.

76. Résident Supérieur to MC, December 12, 1945, IC NF 2709, ANOM.

77. "Note relative au movement autonomiste annamite en France," November 8, 1945, SLOTFOM XIV.4, ANOM.

78. "Rapport de Mr. Goupy, administrateur adjoint des services civiles de l'Indochine, sur sa mission en France au sujet des travailleurs indochinois stationnés dans la métropole," April 18, 1946, HCI CONSPOL 166, ANOM.

79. Ruscio, *Les communistes français et la guerre d'Indochine, 1944–1954* (Paris: L'Harmattan, 1985), 46.

80. "Compte rendu de la réunion du 12 Février 1946 (Hôtel des sociétés savantes)," SLOTFOM XIV.3, ANOM.

81. Unidentified author to Président de la CGT, February 18, 1945, IC NF 2704, ANOM.

82. Jérôme Melançon, "Anticolonialisme et dissidence: Tran Duc Thao et *Les Temps modernes*," in Benoist and Espagne, *L'Itinéraire de Tran Duc Thao,* 207.

83. Cao Văn Luận, *Bên giòng lịch sử,* 59.

84. Nguyễn Tấn Di Trọng, unpublished journal of the Democratic Republic of Vietnam's friendship delegation to France, April-September 1946, QH 603, TTLT III.

85. Cao Văn Luận, *Bên giòng lịch sử,* 71.

86. On Hồ's interactions with Indochinese in France, see "Nhật ký hành trình của Hồ chủ tịch. Bốn tháng sang Pháp" in *Hồ Chí Minh toàn tập* (Hà Nội: Nhà Xuất Bản Chính Trị Quốc Gia, 2000), vol. 4.

87. Trương Như Tảng, *A Vietcong Memoir* (New York: Harcourt, Brace, and Jovanovich, 1985), 16.

88. "Báo cáo về cộng tác ngoại giao và tuyên truyền ở Pháp," undated, PTT 1714, TTLT III.

89. "Note relative au movement autonomiste indochinois en France," June 4, 1947, SLOTFOM XIV.5, ANOM.

90. "Correspondants à l'étranger de la délégation de la rue de Vaugirard," November 21, 1948, SLOTFOM XIV.5, ANOM.

91. "Note sur Nguyen Viet Ty," June 23, 1947, Dossier Nguyễn Viết Tý, SLOT-FOM XV.41, ANOM.

92. See BTC 9387, TTLT III.

93. On the scandal, see Jacques Despuech, *L'Affaire des piastres* (Paris: Deux Rives, 1953). On DRV piaster-smuggling networks, see SLOTFOM XIV.10.

94. "A.s. de la Société vietnamienne d'expansion culturelle, industrielle, et technique, dite: SOVINA," August 5, 1949, Dossier Nguyễn Văn Thoại, SLOTFOM XV.77, ANOM.

95. "Note de renseignements sur le nommé THAI THUC THUAN et la maison Alpha Radio," January 1952, Dossier Thaí Thúc Thuần, SLOTFOM XV.185, ANOM.

96. "Truong Quang Thuy dit Claude Thuy," January 21, 1947, Dossier Trương Quảng Thụy, SLOTFOM XV.85, ANOM.

97. Christopher Goscha, *Historical Dictionary of the Indochina War (1945–1954): An International and Interdisciplinary Approach* (Honolulu: University of Hawai'i Press, 2012), 370.

98. "Note de renseignements sur monsieur Nguyen-Van-Chi," March 3, 1956, Dossier Nguyễn Văn Chỉ, SLOTFOM XV.105, ANOM.

99. Raymond Aubrac, *Ou la mémoire s'attarde* (Paris: Odile Jacob, 1996), 186.

100. "A.s. de Le Van Cuu, attitude au point de vue politique et nationale," November 18, 1953, Dossier Lê Văn Cửu, SLOTFOM XV.57, ANOM; Nguyễn Quang Trị, "Luật sử Trần Văn Khương: Tấm gương yêu nước, vượt khó," *Đồng Khởi: tiếng nói của đảng bộ và nhân dân tỉnh Bến Tre,* January 25, 2019, https://baodongkhoi.vn/luat-su-tran-van-khuong-tam-guong-yeu-nuoc-vuot-kho-25012019-a56789.html.

101. Quoted in Daum, *Immigrés de force,* 159.

102. "Note relative au mouvement Viet-Minh en France (pour le mois de juillet 1947)," July 30, 1947, SLOTFOM XIV.5, ANOM.

103. "Liste des militaires indochinois blessés ou tués par leur compatriotes en France," April 1947, SLOTFOM XIV.5, ANOM.

104. "Note relative au mouvement Viet-Minh en France (pour le mois de juillet 1947)," July 30, 1947, SLOTFOM XIV.5, ANOM.

105. A detailed account of the clashes is in Daum, *Immigrés de force,* chapter 16.

106. "Note sur les associations de salut national vietnamien," March 1948, SLOTFOM XIV.5, ANOM.

107. See "Trả lời một ông 'trí thức tiểu tư sản,'" *Tiếng Thợ,* May 15, 1950.

108. "Scission probable des éléments vietminhs en France," June 15, 1950, UNCAT 3, MAE.

109. "Note au sujet: voyage d'étudiants en Yougoslavie," September 23, 1950, UNCAT 2, MAE; Philip Short, *Pol Pot: The History of a Nightmare* (London: John Murray, 2004), 50.

110. Quinn-Judge, *Ho Chi Minh,* 254.

111. Lê Minh Quốc, "Khuông Việt: Nhà báo Việt Nam đầu tiên được cấp thẻ nhà báo của Liên hiệp quốc," https://leminhquoc.vn/hoi-hoa/tu-lieu-le-minh-quoc/1692-khuong-viet-nha-bao-viet-nam-dau-tien-duoc-cap-the-nha-bao-cua-liep-hiep-quoc.html.

112. Trinh Trong Thuc, "Note sur son attitude et point de vue politique," June 19, 1953, Dossier Trịnh Trọng Thực, SLOTFOM XV.175, ANOM.

113. Mai Thị Trình, *Những năm tháng không quên* (Hà Nội: Nhà Xuất Bản Thông Tấn, 2018), 35, 37.

114. "Dao Van Chau née Phuong Thi Tiep," undated, Dossier Đào Văn Châu, SLOTFOM XV.136, ANOM.

115. Her account of the infamous "Affaire des Généraux" is "Giở lại hồ sơ vụ án Revers-Mast," in *Mùa thu rồi: ngày hăm ba* (Hà Nội: Nhà Xuất Bản Chính Trị Quốc Gia, 1996), 3:401–12.

116. Quoted in Luguern, "Les 'Travailleurs Indochinois,'" 803.

117. See "Tóm tắt vài đặc điểm và để nghị của phong trào Việt kiểu," January 5, 1956, NKV 88, TTLT III.

118. "Tình hình tổ chức Việt kiểu ở Pháp," July 1956, NKV 88, TTLT III.

119. Biographical details are in "Le colonel Nguyen Van Xuan vue par un de ses compatriotes," October 7, 1946, HCI CONSPOL 11, ANOM.

120. Christopher Goscha, *Vietnam: A New History* (New York: Basic Books, 2016), 218.

121. Đoàn Hữu Giam to Đoàn Hữu Chung, August 26, 1946, HCI CONSPOL 134, ANOM.

122. "Création en France d'une délégation officieuse et permanente cochinchinoise," November 25, 1946, HCI CONSPOL 11, ANOM.

123. Nguyễn Văn Xuân to Lê Văn Hoạch, December 17, 1946, HCI CONSPOL 11, ANOM.

124. Nguyễn Trung Trinh to Nguyễn Hữu Hậu, n.d (intercepted letter received at cabinet du conseiller politique on June 27, 1947), HCI CONSPOL 11, ANOM.

125. The petition is in IC NF 980, ANOM.

126. See Ninh Xuân Thao, "L'État du Viêt-Nam et ses rapports avec la France (1949–1955): Une autre voie pour l'indépendance du Viêt-Nam" (PhD diss., Université Bordeaux-Montaigne, 2019), 185.

127. Ibid., 213–25.

128. "Note au sujet de la création d'un 'Office du Viet-Nam à Paris,'" undated, IC NF 1304, ANOM.

129. Haut-commissaire de France pour l'Indochine to Ministre de la France Outre-Mer, September 25, 1948, IC NF 1304, ANOM.

130. "Note sur Hoang Van Co," February 16, 1947, HCI CONSPOL 166, ANOM.

131. Goscha, *Historical Dictionary of the Indochina War,* 461.

132. Reilly, "The Origins of the Vietnamese Civil War and the State of Vietnam," 225.

133. "Note sur la délégation du gouvernement du Viet-Nam à Paris," August 16, 1949, SLOTFOM XIV.14, ANOM.

134. "Note," March 16, 1949, and "Note relatif au retour de BAO-DAI," March 20, 1949, Dossier Bảo Đại, SLOTFOM XV.75, ANOM.

135. "Note," May 30, 1949, Dossier Hoàng Văn Cơ, SLOTFOM XV.82, ANOM.

136. "Note," June 9, 1949, Dossier Bảo Đại, SLOTFOM XV.75, ANOM.

137. "Allocution prononcée par son excellence Pham Van Binh, Hôtel Crillon, July 21, 1949," HCI 524, ANOM.

138. "Les activités secretès du Prince BUU-LOC," September 12, 1951, HCI SPCE 46, ANOM.

139. "Réception organisée par le Cabinet impérial en l'honneur du Président TRAN VAN HUU, le 22 Septembre," September 25, 1951, HCI SPCE 46, ANOM.

140. Documents on the formation of the Vietnamese High Commission are in HCI SPCE 46, ANOM.

141. "Activité politique des milieux vietnamiens en France, janvier 1952," HCI SPCE 46, ANOM.

142. Vũ Quốc Thúc to Trần Quang Tuyền, November 8, 1949, HCI SPCE 46, ANOM.

143. "Activité des vietnamiens de Paris durant la période du Ier au 31 janvier," February 1, 1950, UNCAT 2, MAE.

144. Ibid.

145. Dossier Nguyễn Văn Tấn, SLOTFOM XV.166, ANOM.

146. "Situation des vietnamiens en France," March 27, 1950, UNCAT 1, MAE.

147. Dossier Trương Công Cửu, SLOTFOM XV.157, ANOM.

148. "Note relative au movement Viet-Minh en France pour le moi de juillet 1949," July 30, 1949, SLOTFOM XIV.5, ANOM.

149. BDDL 124 and BDDL 201, TTLT I.

150. For a detailed account of Nguyễn Bảo Toàn's activities during the First Indochina War, see "Notice: Nguyen Bao Toan," October 30, 1953, Dossier Nguyễn Bảo Toàn, SLOTFOM XV.171, ANOM.

151. "A.s. du Parti socialiste unioniste vietnamien," December 7, 1949, UNCAT 1, MAE.

152. "Lettre de France no. 38," June 21, 1950, HCI SPCE 73, ANOM.

153. "Phan Huy Dan," December 1954, Dossier Phan Huy Đán, SLOTFOM XV.177, ANOM.

154. "Note pour monsieur l'administrateur Varet, Directeur des affaires politiques," February 6, 1951, SLOTFOM XIV.41, ANOM.

155. See Dossier Ngô Đình Luyện, SLOTFOM XV.138, ANOM.

156. "Renseignements sur le nommé Nguyen Van Nam," October 22, 1953, Dossier Nguyễn Văn Nam, SLOTFOM XV.109, ANOM; Ngô Văn, *In the Crossfire,* 173.

157. "Nguyen Ngoc Bich," March 1953, Dossier Nguyễn Ngọc Bích, SLOTFOM XV.105, ANOM.

158. Khmer students to Ministre de la France Oute Mer, January 25, 1948, Dossier Trần Văn Tùng, SLOTFOM XV.159, ANOM.

159. Goscha, *Going Indochinese,* chapter 4.

160. RST to GGI, December 30, 1931, GGI 51507, ANOM.

161. Résident Supérieur à Phnom Penh to GOUCOCH, April 4, 1916, Dossier Areno Yukanthor, carton 99, 589PO2, CADN; NPRPOM, December 31, 1925, SLOTFOM III.144, ANOM.

162. "Extrait du registre des passeports 264/2," May 18, 1925, Dossier Sơn Ngọc Thành, carton 72, 589PO2, CADN.

163. Geoffrey Gunn, *Theravadins, Colonialists and Commissares in Laos* (Bangkok: White Lotus Press, 1998), 99; Goscha, *Historical Dictionary of the Indochina War,* 435–36.

164. "A.s. de l'association dite 'Association des étudiants lao en France' et ses dirigeants," December 9, 1952, SLOTFOM XIV.41, ANOM.

165. The notices are in SLOTFOM XIV.41, ANOM.

166. Conseiller à la Santé publique to Haut commissaire de France, August 6, 1948, HCI 524, ANOM.

167. HCI 524, ANOM.

168. "M. Roger Ouroth Souphanouvong," October 1952, HCI 524.

169. Ministre de l'intérieur to Ministre d'état chargé avec les relations avec les états associés, March 18, 1952, SLOTFOM XV.234–236, ANOM.

170. "Les étudiants cambodgiens en France," February 19, 1955, SLOTFOM XIV.41, ANOM.

171. Marie-Alexandrine Martin, *Cambodia: A Shattered Society* (Berkeley: University of California Press, 1994), 50.

172. Sher, *L'Essor de l'Angkar,* 34.

173. "Les étudiants cambodgiens en France," February 19, 1955, SLOTFOM XIV.41, ANOM. Although numerous sources claim that the AEK was formed in 1946, they are likely referring to activities carried out under the auspices of the Fraternité Khmer.

174. Chandler, *The Tragedy of Cambodian History,* 53.

175. Short, *Pol Pot,* 57–58.

176. P. Edwards, *Cambodge,* 250.

177. Goscha, *Historical Dictionary of the Indochina War,* 431; "Les étudiants cambodgiens en France," February 19, 1955, SLOTFOM XIV.41, ANOM.

178. Chandler, *The Tragedy of Cambodian History,* 325n17.

179. "S.E. Neal Phleng," March 1954, SLOTFOM XIV.42, ANOM.

180. "Commandant Srey Saman," July 1954, SLOTFOM XIV.42, ANOM.

181. Documents on these conflicts are in HCI SPCE 100, ANOM.

182. Martin, *Cambodia: A Shattered Society,* 98.

183. Sher, *L'Essor de l'Angkar,* 39.

184. Ibid., 42–43.

185. Short, *Pol Pot,* 38.

186. Ibid., 59.

187. Chandler, *The Tragedy of Cambodian History,* 55.

188. "Les étudiants cambodgiens en France," February 19, 1955, SLOTFOM XIV.41, ANOM.

189. Sher, *L'Essor de l'Angkar,* 51.

CHAPTER 9. RETURNS

1. Trần Văn Thạch, "Un rêve singulier," *Journal des étudiants annamites,* December 15, 1927, reprinted in Tran, *Trần Văn Thạch (1905–1945),* 135–40.

2. Le Van Ho, *Des Vietnamiens dans la Grande Guerre,* 182.

3. Vu-Hill, *Coolies into Rebels,* 111.

4. Goebel, *Anti-Imperial Metropolis,* 64.

5. "Note," January 23. 1941, BA 2153, APPP.

6. Ida Simon-Barouh, "Les Viêtnamiens en France," *Hommes et Migrations* 1219 (May-June 1999): 71.

7. Clifford Rosenberg, *Policing Paris: The Origins of Modern Immigration Control between the Wars* (Ithaca, NY: Cornell University Press, 2006), 4–5.

8. Nguyễn Mạnh Tường, *Pierres de France,* 17.

9. "Contrôle postal indochinois, février 1918," IC NF 227, ANOM.

10. Phạm Quỳnh, *Pháp du hành trình nhật ký,* 411–12.

11. "Contrôle postal indochinois, mai 1918," IC NF 245, ANOM.

12. Luguern, "Les 'Travailleurs Indochinois,'" 788.

13. Phan Văn Gia's account of his journey home is "Paris—Khám Lớn Saigon," serialized in *Thần Chung* from February 27 to March 7, 1929. His account of the clash with the police was censored; another account is Nguyễn Văn Ba, "Un grave incident à l'arivée de 'L'Athos II,'" *L'Echo annamite,* December 12, 1928.

14. Sisowath Watchayavong to "mon cher délégué," October 12, 1920, Dossier Sisowath Watchayavong, SLOTFOM XV.6, ANOM.

15. Nguyễn Xuân Bái to Nguyen Cong Khanh, October 22, 1930, Dossier Nguyễn Xuân Bái, carton 4, 589PO2, CADN.

16. Đào Đăng Vỹ, *L'Annam qui nait,* 233.

17. Cindy Nguyen, "Reading and Misreading: The Social Life of Libraries and Colonial Control in Vietnam, 1865–1958" (PhD diss., University of California-Berkeley, 2019), 128.

18. Đinh Hùng, *Đốt là hương cũ* (Sài Gòn: Lửa Thiêng, 1971), 64.

19. Nguyễn Thanh Trừng, *Vision de la femme dans la littérature du Sud-Vietnam (de 1858 à 1945)* (Paris: L'Harmattan, 2012), 96.

20. "Note sur la spécialisation des ouvriers Indochinois en France," undated, IC NF 220, ANOM. The figure is based on the roughly twenty-five thousand soldiers and workers that French authorities surveyed.

21. RST to GGI, April 12, 1930, SLOTFOM III.22, ANOM.

22. Tran, "Confession, Cosmopolitanism, and Catholic Moralizing in Early Modern Vietnam," 4.

23. Dutton, *A Vietnamese Moses,* 40–41.

24. Trần Mỹ-Vân, *A Vietnamese Royal Exile in Japan,* 15–16.

25. Tạ Trọng Hiệp, "Le journal de l'ambassade de Phan Thanh Giản en France," 360.

26. McLeod, "Nguyen Truong To," 317.

27. Nguyễn Thế Anh, *Monarchie et fait colonial au Việt-Nam,* 33.

28. H. Peyssonnaux and Bùi Văn Cung, "Le traité de 1874: journal du secrétaire de l'ambassade annamite," 366.

29. Phan Liêm and Phan Tôn to Préfet maritime de Toulon, February 18, 1874, IC AF 22, ANOM.

30. Nguyễn Trọng Hiệp to Paul Doumer, April 9, 1897, GGI 9601, ANOM.

31. Lorraine Paterson, "Prisoners from Indochina in the Nineteenth-Century French Colonial World," in *Exile in Colonial Asia: Kings, Convicts, Commemoration,* ed. Ronit Ricci (Honolulu: University of Hawai'i Press, 2016), 225.

32. *Hommage de la Société des études indochinoises à sa majesté Bảo Đại* (Sài Gòn: Imprimerie C. Ardin, 1932), 30.

33. Thái Bạch, *Cuộc bút chiến giữa Phan Văn Trị—Tôn Thọ Tường* (Sài Gòn: Sống Mới, 1957).

34. P. Edwards, *Cambodge,* 74.

35. See Thái Nhân Hoà, ed., *Phạm Phú Thứ với tư tưởng canh tân* (Thành Phố Hồ Chí Minh: Hội Khoa học Lịch sử Thành Phố Hồ Chí Minh, 1995).

36. Nguyễn Thế Long, *Bang giao Đại Việt triều Nguyễn* (Hà Nội: Nhà Xuất Bản Văn Hóa Thông Tin, 2005), 207–208.

37. Nguyễn Q. Thắng, *Phong trào Duy Tân: các khuôn mặt tiêu biểu* (Hà Nội: Nhà Xuất Bản Văn Hóa Thông Tin, 2006).

38. Phan Khôi, "Con bò của ông Tổng đốc," *Đông Pháp Thời Báo,* December 13, 1928.

39. Quoted in Vinh Sinh, *Phan Châu Trinh and His Political Writings,* 13.

40. Poisson, *Mandarins et subalternes au nord du Việt Nam,* 183, 188.

41. Phạm Quỳnh, "Mười ngày ở Huế," in Nguyễn Hữu Sơn, *Du ký Việt Nam: tạp chí Nam Phong, 1917–1934,* 1:70–71.

42. Poisson, *Mandarins et subalternes au nord du Việt Nam,* 187.

43. RST to GGI, April 1, 1908, GGI 2560, ANOM.

44. Christopher Goscha, "The Modern Barbarian: Nguyen Van Vinh and the Complexity of Colonial Modernity in Vietnam," *European Journal of East Asian Studies* 3.1 (2004): 8.

45. GGI to MC, June 14, 1907, IC AF 27, ANOM; P. Edwards, *Cambodge,* 85, 285.

46. P. Edwards, *Cambodge,* 92.

47. John Tully, *France on the Mekong: A History of the Protectorate in Cambodia, 1863–1953* (Lanham, MD: University Press of America, 2002), 199.

48. Goscha, "Bao Dai et Sihanouk," 163–64.

49. Ibid., 155.

50. Søren Ivarsson and Christopher Goscha, "Prince Phetsarath (1890–1957): Nationalism and Royalty in the Making of Modern Laos," *Journal of Southeast Asian Studies* 38.1 (February 2007): 55–81.

51. Đào Đăng Vỹ, *L'Annam qui nait*, 223–24.

52. Nguyễn Văn Vĩnh, "Nos enfants en France," *L'Annam nouveau*, February 11, 1932.

53. Thạch Lan, "Người Annam đi ngoại quốc học gì?," *Phụ Nữ Tân Văn*, January 16, 1930.

54. Nguyễn Kỳ Phụ, "Có ai chịu qua Paris giúp nước?," *Đuốc Nhà Nam*, January 18, 1933.

55. The survey is in GOUCOCH 1A.11/266(1), TTLT II.

56. J.K., "Trois jeunes annamites honorent notre enseignement supérieur," *Tribune indochinoise*, November 27, 1935.

57. "Một người Việt Nam, mới 22 tuổi, mà đã đậu cả tân sĩ luật và tân sĩ văn chương," *Phụ Nữ Tân Văn*, August 11, 1932.

58. GGI to Administrateurs chefs de province, March 12, 1927, GOUCOCH IIA.45/194 (7), TTLT II.

59. Linh Nam, "Les 'retours de France' et le mandarinat," *Gazette de Hué*, May 17, 1935.

60. Nguyễn Phương Ngọc, *À l'origine de l'anthropologie au Vietnam*, 179, 184.

61. Ibid., 152.

62. Patricia Pelley, *Postcolonial Vietnam: New Histories of the National Past* (Durham: Duke University Press, 2002), 33.

63. Đào Thị Diến, "Ngô Đình Nhu, nhà lưu trữ Việt Nam thời kỳ 1938–1946," *Tạp Chí Nghiên Cứu và Phát Triển* 6–7 (2013): 238–43.

64. Philippe LeFailler and Nguyễn Phương Ngọc, eds., *Mục lục phân tích Tạp chí Thanh Nghị* (Hà Nội: École française d'Extrême-Orient, 2009), 17.

65. Nguyễn Phương Ngọc, *À l'origine de l'anthropologie au Vietnam*, 102.

66. Michel Caire, "Sonn Mam": http://psychiatrie.histoire.free.fr/pers/bio/sonn.htm.

67. Laurence Monnais-Rousselot, "Le Dr. Nguyễn Văn Luyện et ses confrères: La médecine privée dans le Việt Nam colonial," *Moussons: Recherche en sciences humaines sur l'Asie du Sud-Est* 15 (2010): 75–95.

68. Hữu Ngọc and Nguyễn Đức Hiền, eds., *La Sơn Yên Hồ Hoàng Xuân Hãn (1908–1996)* (Hà Nội: Nhà Xuất Bản Giáo Dục, 1996), 1:73.

69. For biographies of faculty at the Lycée du Protectorat, see *Thầy trò Trường Bưởi—Chu Văn An (Hồi ký nhiều tác giả)* (Hà Nội: Nhà Xuất Bản Giáo Dục, 1998).

70. Đào Đăng Vỹ, *L'Annam qui nait*, 247.

71. MC to GGI, August 27, 1932, Dossier Hoàng Xuân Hãn, SLOTFOM XV.134, ANOM.

72. Various authors, *Hồ Đắc Di, Nhà y học triết nhân*, 176.

73. Claire Trần Thị Liên, "Henriette Bui: the Narrative of Vietnam's First Woman Doctor," 291, 293.

74. Hémery, *Révolutionnaires vietnamiens et pouvoir colonial,* 191.

75. Nguyễn Hùng, *Nam bộ những nhân vật một thời vang bóng* (Hà Nội: Công An Nhân Dân, 2003), 158.

76. Trịnh Văn Thảo, *Les compagnons de route de Hồ Chí Minh,* 73.

77. Phạm Quỳnh, *Pháp du hành trinh nhật ký,* 171.

78. Tạ Trọng Hiệp, "Le journal de l'ambassade de Phan Thanh Giản en France," 340; Frédéric Maurel, "A Khmer *Nirat,* 'Travel in France during the World Exhibition of 1900': Influences from the Thai?," *South East Asia Research* 10.1 (2002): 99–112.

79. Tạ Trọng Hiệp, "Le journal de l'ambassade de Phan Thanh Giản en France," 341–42; Nguyễn Kim Oanh, "Giới thiệu tác phẩm *Như Tây Ký* của Nguỵ Khắc Đản," *Thông Báo Hán Nôm Học* (2002): 427–33.

80. Trần Thị Tú Nhi, "Đóng góp của Trương Minh Ký với thể tài du ký quốc ngữ giai đoạn giao thời," *Nghiên Cứu Văn Học* 8 (2014): 38–51.

81. *Tây phù nhụt ký* (Sài Gòn: Huỳnh Kìm Danh, 1916).

82. Duy Lap Nguyen, "Tourism and the Irony of Colonial Underdevelopment in Nhất Linh's 'Going to the West,'" *Studies in Travel Writing* 22.4 (2018): 372. The best survey of interwar Vietnamese travelogues is Christopher Goscha, "Recits de voyage viêtnamiens et prise de conscience indochinoise (c. 1920–1945)," in Salmon, *Récits de voyages des asiatiques,* 253–79.

83. Phan Khôi, "Pháp du ký sự của Trần Bá Vinh," *Phụ Nữ Tân Văn,* November 17, 1932.

84. The argument about the parody is Greg Lockhart's.

85. Nguyen, "Tourism and the Irony of Colonial Underdevelopment," 386.

86. Nguyễn Công Tiễu, "Một làng bên Pháp," *Khoa Học Tạp Chí,* April 1, 1938; Nguyễn Tiến Lãng, *La France que j'ai vue* (Huế: Imprimerie Đắc Lập, 1940); Phạm Vân Anh [Đào Trinh Nhất], "Sang Tây" and "Mười tháng ở Pháp," serialized in *Phụ Nữ Tân Văn* in 1929 and 1930.

87. Phạm Duy Khiêm, *De Hanoi à La Courtine (Septembre 1939–juin 1940), lettres de Nam Liên recueillies par Pham Duy Khiem* (Hà Nội: Lê Thăng, 1941), 13.

88. Emerson, "Phạm Duy Khiêm: A Man Apart."

89. Quoted in Selao, *Le roman vietnamien francophone,* 79.

90. Nguyễn Mạnh Tường, *Sourires et larmes d'une jeunesse* (Hà Nội: Éditions de la Revue indochinoise, 1937), 105.

91. Nguyễn Huy Bảo, "Un poète chrétien vietnamien de langue française: Do Dinh Thach alias Pierre Do Dinh," in Hue, *Indochine,* 36.

92. Christiane Fournier, "Un appel aux jeunes écrivains Annamites," *Nouvelle revue indochinoise,* August 1938.

93. The journal's manifesto was printed on the inside cover of each issue.

94. Alain Guillemin, "Cung Giu Nguyen où l'homme des deux rives," *Moussons: Recherches en sciences sociales sur l'Asie du Sud-Est* 24 (2014): https://doi.org/10.4000/moussons.3008.

95. Giang-Huong Nguyen, "À la découverte d'un écrivain oublié: Phạm Văn Ký (1910–1992)," *Continents manuscrits* 6 (2016): https://journals.openedition.org/coma/662.

96. Goscha, "Modern Barbarian," 8.

97. Gibbs, "Spoken Theater, La Scène Tonkinoise, and the First Modern Vietnamese Songs," 2.

98. On this play, see Wynn Wilcox, "Women, Westernization, and the Origins of Modern Vietnamese Theater," *Journal of Southeast Asian Studies* 37.2 (June 2006): 205–24.

99. Gibbs, "Spoken Theater, La Scène Tonkinoise, and the First Modern Vietnamese Songs," 6; Ngô Vĩnh Khang, *Cô Năm Phỉ Đi Tây* (Sài Gòn: Xưa Nay, 1935).

100. "Một cô gái Việt Nam làm đào hát bóng ở Pháp rất được hoan nghinh," *Đuốc Nhà Nam,* April 2, 1936.

101. "Cô Hoàng Thị Thế qua Mỹ chăng?," *Đuốc Nhà Nam,* January 26, 1931.

102. "La première fête des écrivains sportifs," *L'Annam nouveau,* August 7, 1932.

103. Nguyễn Khắc Phê, *Hoa sĩ Lê Văn Miến.*

104. H.N., "Người Âu-châu vẫn dễ mất thưởng-thức mỹ-thuật ta," *Đuốc Nhà Nam,* August 1, 1931.

105. Nora Taylor, *Painters in Hanoi: An Ethnography of Vietnamese Art* (Honolulu: University of Hawai'i Press, 2004), 34.

106. Xuân Vũ, *Dấu chân xuôi ngược, tập 1* (Houston: Văn Hóa, 1999), 431.

107. Goscha, "Modern Barbarian," 8.

108. Cited in Nguyen, "Reading and Misreading," 128.

109. Phạm Xuân Thạch, "De Đông Kinh Nghĩa Thục au Đăng cổ tùng báo; Nguyễn Văn Vĩnh, le début d'un cheminement intellectuel," in de Gantès and Nguyễn, *Vietnam: le moment moderniste,* 239–48.

110. Peycam, *The Birth of Vietnamese Political Journalism,* 64.

111. Ibid., 127.

112. Ho Tai, *Radicalism,* 162.

113. Peycam, *The Birth of Vietnamese Political Journalism,* 166–67.

114. Vũ Trọng Phụng, *Dumb Luck,* ed., Peter Zinoman, trans. Nguyễn Nguyệt Cầm and Peter Zinoman (Ann Arbor: University of Michigan Press, 2002), 28n62.

115. Ibid., 16.

116. Nhật Tịnh, *Chân dung Nhất Linh,* 33.

117. Nguyen, *On Our Own Strength,* 5.

118. Nguyễn Thị Minh, *Nguyễn An Ninh: "Tôi chỉ làm con gió thôi"* (Thành Phố Hồ Chí Minh: Nhà Xuất Bản Trẻ, 2001), 70; "Note de Désiré," February 27, 1924, SPCE 380, ANOM.

119. Trang-Gaspard, *Hồ Chí Minh à Paris,* 228.

120. "Expédition en Indochine d'écrits de propagande antifrançaise," November 9, 1927 and December 12, 1927, SLOTFOM V.36, ANOM.

121. Huỳnh Công Dương to his brother, January 31, 1927, Dossier Huỳnh Công Dương, SLOTFOM XV.78, ANOM.

122. "Le 'Viêt-Nam Hon' en Annam," *L'Echo annamite,* September 3, 1926; "Cùng các ngài gởi mua báo 'Việt Nam Hồn,'" *Đông Pháp Thời Báo,* March 12, 1926.

123. Hémery, "Ta Thu Thau," 202.

124. "Declarations de Ngo Duc Tri, mai-juin 1931," Dossier Ngô Đức Trì, SLOTFOM XV.7, ANOM.

125. Daniel Hémery, "À Saigon dans les années trente, un journal militant: *La Lutte* (1933–1937)," in Tran, *Trần Văn Thạch*, 315.

126. Hémery, *Révolutionnaires vietnamiens et pouvoir colonial*, 415; Peter Zinoman, *Vietnamese Colonial Republican: The Political Vision of Vũ Trọng Phụng* (Berkeley: University of California Press, 2013), 126–27.

127. Dossier Nguyễn Văn Tiến, SLOTFOM XV.63, ANOM; Dossier Trịnh Văn Phú, SLOTFOM XV.77, ANOM.

128. On Vũ Liên's activites in communist newspapers in France, see SLOTFOM V.25–26, ANOM. On the journalists' association, see *Lịch sử báo chí Việt Nam, 1865–1945*, ed. Đỗ Quang Hưng, Nguyễn Thành, and Dương Trung Quốc (Hà Nội: Nhà Xuất Bản Đại Học Quốc Gia Hà Nội, 2000), 142–48.

129. On *Nagaravatta*, see P. Edwards, *Cambodge*, chapter 9; on *Lao Nhay*, see Chairat Polmuk, "Invoking the Past: The Cultural Politics of Lao Literature, 1941–1975" (MA thesis, Cornell University, 2014).

130. IIB 55/063, TTLT II.

131. "Rapatriement de la dépouille mortelle de l'héroique capitaine aviateur Do Huu Vi," *Tribune indigène*, April 22, 1920.

132. Phạm Quỳnh, *Le capitaine Do-Huu-Vi—héros franco-annamite* (Huế: Đắc Lập, 1937), 8.

133. Can, *Carnet de route d'un petit marsouin cochinchinois*, 55.

134. Đặng Lễ Nghi, *Thơ tuồng lính tập đi Tây* (Sài Gòn: Imprimerie de l'Union, 1915); Đặng Văn Chiếu, *Vè lính tập và thợ đi Tây* (Sài Gòn: Imprimerie de l'Union, 1915).

135. Vu-Hill, *Coolies into Rebels*, 139.

136. Le Van Ho, *Des Vietnamiens dans la Grande Guerre*, 210.

137. Ibid., 193.

138. Ibid., 211.

139. Vu-Hill, *Coolies into Rebels*, 143.

140. See, for example, Hà Chí Hiển, *Thơ Âu-châu chiến cuộc tự thuật* (Sài Gòn: Xưa Nay, 1930) and Cử Hoành Sơn, *Thơ đi Tây* (Sài Gòn: Xưa Nay, 1934).

141. Nguyễn Phương Ngọc, "Les sources littéraires pour l'étude de l'engagement: le cas du roman en vietnamien *Tây phương mỹ nhơn* (1927)," in Guerassimoff, Hardy, Nguyễn, and Poisson, *Les migrations impériales au Vietnam*, 350.

142. Le Van Ho, *Des Vietnamiens dans la Grande Guerre*, 214.

143. Giebel, *Imagined Ancestries of Vietnamese Communism*, 24.

144. Eckert, "Les militaires Indochinois," 617.

145. GGI to MC, May 28, 1930; Tobias Rettig, "Contested Loyalties: Vietnamese Soldiers in the Service of France, 1927–1939" (PhD diss., University of London, 2005), 129.

146. Cited in Le Van Ho, *Des Vietnamiens dans la grande guerre*, 220.

147. "Bach Thai Buoi," *L'Annam nouveau*, July 29, 1932.

148. See Lê Minh Quốc, *Bạch Thái Bưởi: khẳng định doanh thài nước Việt* (Hà Nội: Nhà Xuất Bản Trẻ, 2007).

149. Gouvernment général de l'Indochine, *Souverains et notabilités d'Indochine* (Hà Nội: Éditions du gouvernement général de l'Indochine, 1943).

150. Nguyễn Đức Hiệp, "Photography in Vietnam from the End of the Nineteenth Century to the Start of the Twentieth," trans. Ellen Takata, *In Translation* 4.2 (Spring 2014).

151. Dossier Phạm Tá, SLOTFOM XV.72, ANOM.

152. Dossier Phung Văn Mớt, SLOTFOM XV.112, ANOM.

153. Dossier Nguyễn Văn Vương, SLOTFOM XV.104, ANOM.

154. Dossier "Đông," SLOTFOM XV.150, ANOM.

155. Dossier Trần Xuân Quang, SLOTFOM XV.162, ANOM.

156. Luguern, "Les 'Travailleurs Indochinois,'" 833–60.

157. Ibid., 862.

158. Trịnh Văn Thảo, *Les compagnons de route de Hô Chi Minh*, 65.

159. Cited in Luguern, "Les 'Travailleurs Indochinois,'" 873.

160. Ibid., 875.

161. Goscha, *Vietnam: A New History*.

162. Ibid., 448–49.

163. Nguyễn An Ninh, "France in Indochina," in Truong Buu Lam, *Colonialism Experienced*, 194.

164. Lê Văn Thử, *Mười chín sinh viên Việt Nam bị trục xuất* (Sài Gòn: Nam Việt, 1949).

165. "Liste des Indochinois ayant fait un séjour en Russie ou suivant actuellement les cours d'une école de propagande communiste de Moscou," undated (from 1931), SLOTFOM III.44, ANOM.

166. "Note," June 22, 1936, 28 PA 2, ANOM.

167. Brocheux and Hémery, *Indochina*, 326.

168. Ibid., 326–27.

169. Hémery, *Révolutionnaires vietnamiens et pouvoir colonial*, 409.

170. Ibid., 415; Zinoman, *Vietnamese Colonial Republican*, 126–28.

171. Goscha, *Vietnam: A New History*, 191.

172. Nguyễn Phương Ngọc, *À l'origine de l'anthropologie au Vietnam*, 199–201.

173. Trịnh Văn Thảo, *Les compagnons de route de Hô Chi Minh*, 88.

174. Christopher Goscha, *Vietnam: Un état né de la guerre (1945–1954)* (Paris: Armand Colin, 2011), chapter 5. See also Bộ y tế, *Sư lược lịch sử y tế Việt Nam, tập 1 (Từ tháng 8 năm 1945 đến 10 năm 1954)* (Hà Nội: Nhà Xuất Bản Y Học, 1995).

175. For biographical details of major figures in DRV higher education, see Đại học quốc gia Hà Nội, *100 Chân dung một thế kỷ Đại học quốc gia Hà Nội* (Hà Nội: Nhà Xuất Bản Đại Học Quốc Gia Hà Nội, 2006).

176. Goscha, *Vietnam: Un état né de la guerre*, 100–1.

177. Trịnh Văn Thảo, *Les compagnons de route de Hô Chi Minh*, 82.

178. Quoted in Brett Reilly, "Saigon's Hidden Presidential Palace and Forgotten President: The Republic of Cochinchina and Nguyễn Văn Thinh," *New Mandala*, 14 June 2019.

179. For a full list of these cabinets, see appendices to Ninh Xuân Thao, "L'État du Viêt-Nam et ses rapports avec la France (1949–1955)."

180. Reilly, "The Origins of the Vietnamese Civil War and the State of Vietnam," 160.

181. Đặng Hữu Thụ, *Thân thế và sự nghiệp nhà cách mạng Nguyễn Thế Truyền,* chapter XIV.

182. Goscha, *Historical Dictionary of the Indochina War,* 373.

183. Ibid., 323.

184. Trinh Dinh Khai, *Décolonisation du Viêt Nam.*

185. Nu-Anh Tran, "'Let History Render Judgment on My Life': The Suicide of Nhất Linh (Nguyễn Tường Tam) and the Making of a Martyr in the Republic of Vietnam," *Journal of Vietnamese Studies* 15.3 (Fall 2020): 86–87.

186. Biographical sketches for the figures in this paragraph are in the appendices of Jean Deuve, *Le royaume du Laos, 1949–1965* (Paris: École française d'Extrême-Orient, 1984).

187. Martin, *Cambodia: A Shattered Society,* 51.

188. Short, *Pol Pot,* 38.

189. Martin, *Cambodia: A Shattered Society,* 54.

190. Ibid., 52.

191. Sher, *L'Essor de l'Angkar,* 53.

192. Ibid., 339.

193. Ibid., 123.

194. Ibid., 13.

195. Ibid., 32.

CODA

1. Phạm Phú Thứ, *Nhật ký đi Tây,* 172–73.

2. Salles, *Un mandarin Breton au service du roi de Cochinchine.*

3. Emmanuelle Saada, *Empire's Children: Race, Filiation, and Citizenship in the French Colonies* (Chicago: University of Chicago Press, 2012), 118.

4. Dossier Jean Trebaol, SLOTFOM XV.108, ANOM.

5. Dossier Nguyễn Văn Truyết, SLOTFOM XV.25, ANOM.

6. "Les étrangers pendant la 1ère guerre mondiale," *Archi'classe* 30 (May 2016): 25–30.

7. Dossier Hoàng Thị Nga, SLOTFOM XV.106, ANOM.

8. See Nguyễn Q. Thắng, *Các tác giả người Việt viết tiếng Pháp,* 434–41.

9. Ibid., 369–90.

10. Quoted in Pham Van Quang, *L'Institution de la littérature vietnamienne francophone* (Paris: Publibook, 2013), 30.

11. Nguyen, *La Littérature vietnamienne francophone,* 73–74.

12. Selao, *Le roman vietnamien francophone,* 167.

13. Ibid., 197.

14. Thụy Khuê, *Nói chuyện với Hoàng Xuân Hãn và Tạ Trọng Hiệp* (Westminster, CA: Văn Nghệ, 2002), 101–3.

15. Ngô Văn, *In the Crossfire,* 148–49.

16. Pierre-André Bizien and Dung Pham Tran, *Histoire d'une grande famille vietnamienne: Madame Kiến et les siens de Hà Nội à la France, 1885–2018* (Paris: L'Harmattan, 2022), 48.

17. Dossier Nguyễn Viết Cảnh, SLOTFOM XV.70, ANOM.

18. Trịnh Văn Thảo, "Le retour des rapatriés d'Indochine. L'expérience des centres d'accueil (1954–1960)," in *Marseille et le choc des décolonisations,* ed. Jean-Jacques Jordi and Emile Temime (Marseille: Edisud, 1996), 29.

19. Dominique Rolland, *Petit Viêt-Nams* (Bordeaux: Elytis, 2009), 6.

20. Kathryn Edwards, *Contesting Indochina: French Remembrance between Decolonization and Cold War* (Berkeley: University of California Press, 2016), 125, 126, 132.

21. Rolland, *Petit Viêt-Nams,* 6–7.

22. Ibid., 7.

SOURCES AND BIBLIOGRAPHY

ARCHIVAL SOURCES

France

Archives nationales d'outre-mer, Aix-en-Provence [ANOM]
Fonds ministériels
Agence économique de la France d'outre-mer [AGEFOM]
Conseiller aux affaires sociales [CONSSOC]
Conseiller politique [CONSPOL]
Direction des affaires militaires [AFFMIL]
Direction des affaires politiques, 1920–1954 [AFFPOL]
Haut commissariat de France pour l'Indochine [HCI]
Indochine ancien fonds [IC AF]
Indochine nouveau fonds [IC NF]
Service de liaison avec les originaires des territoires français d'outre-mer [SLOTFOM]
Service de protection du corps éxpeditionnaire [SPCE]
Fonds territoriaux
Gouvernement général de l'Indochine [GGI]
Résidence supérieure au Tonkin, ancien fonds [RSF AF]
Résidence supérieure au Tonkin, nouveau fonds [RST NF]
Papiers d'agents [PA]
Other
Ecole coloniale [EC]

Centre des archives diplomatiques, La Courneuve [MAE]
Asie-Océanie après 1944 [AO]
Correspondence politique et commerciale, 1897–1918 [CPC]
Correspondence politique et commerciale, 1918–1940 [CPC]

États associés [EA]
Mémoires et documents Asie [MDA]
Uncatalogued documentation related to Indochina [UNCAT]

Centre des archives diplomatiques, Nantes [CADN]
589PO2: Police de l'Indochine puis direction des services de Sécurité du haut-commissariat français au Vietnam-Sud

Archives nationales de France, Section contemporaine [AN]
F7: Police générale

Archives de la Préfecture de police de Paris [APPP]
BA: Affaires générales
GA: Renseignements généraux

Archives de la Chambre de commerce et de l'industrie de Marseille-Provence [CCIMP]
Fonds des Messageries maritimes [MM]

Archives départementales de l'Indre, Issodun
Papiers Léon Werth

Vietnam

Trung Tâm Lưu Trữ Quốc Gia I (Vietnam National Archives, center I), Hà Nội [TTLT I]
Gouvernement général de l'Indochine [GGI]
Résidence supérieure au Tonkin [RST]
Cabinet de Bảo Đại (Đà Lạt) [BDDL]

Trung Tâm Lưu Trữ Quốc Gia II (Vietnam National Archives, center II), Hồ Chí Minh City [TTLT II]
Gouvernement de Cochinchine [GOUCOCH]
Services locaux de la Cochinchine [SL]

Trung Tâm Lưu Trữ Quốc Gia III (Vietnam National Archives, center III), Hà Nội [TTLT III]
Bộ Tài Chính [BTC]
Nhà văn hóa, Bác sỹ Nguyễn Khắc Viện [NKV]
Phông Phủ Thủ Tướng [PTT]
Quốc Hội [QH]
Thống Kê Tài Liệu Khối Sưu Tầm [TKTLKST]

Published Bulletins, Journals, and Newspapers

VIETNAMESE
Ánh Sáng
Bạn Hải Thuyền
Công Bình Tạp Chí
Đông Pháp Thời Báo
Đuốc Nhà Nam
Gió Việt
Hà Thành Ngọ Báo
Hồn Nam Việt
Lao Nông
Nam Việt
Phụ Nữ Tân Văn
Phục Quốc
Quốc Tế IV
Thần Chung
Tiền Quân
Tiếng Dân
Tiếng Lính Annam
Tổ Quốc
Tràng An Báo
Trung Bắc Tân Văn
Việt Nam Hồn
Vô Sản

FRENCH
L'Annam de demain
L'Annam nouveau
L'Annam scolaire
L'Avenir de l'Annam
L'Avenir du Tonkin
Bulletin des amis du vieux Hué
Bulletin de l'association générale des étudiants indochinois
L'Echo annamite
Gazette de Hué
L'Humanité
Journal des étudiants annamites
La Lutte
La Nation annamite
Le Progrès annamite
La Résurrection
Tribune indigène
Tribune indochinoise

VIETNAMESE

Bộ y tế. *Sơ lược lịch sử y tế Việt Nam, tập 1 (Từ tháng 8 năm 1945 đến tháng 10 năm 1954)* [A Historical Outline of Vietnamese Medicine, volume 1 (From August 1945 until October 1954)]. Hà Nội: Nhà Xuất Bản Y Học, 1995.

Bùi Như Hương. "Một số họa sĩ Việt Nam sống và làm việc tại nước ngoài" [Some Vietnamese Painters Living and Working Overseas]. In *Mỹ thuật Việt Nam hiện đại* [Modern Vietnamese Art], edited by Nguyễn Lương Tiểu Bạch, 339–50. Hà Nội: Trường Đại học Mỹ thuật Hà Nội, 2005.

Cao Văn Luận. *Bên giòng lịch sử* [Alongside the Course of History]. Sài Gòn: Trí Dũng, 1972.

Đặc san kỷ niệm 105 năm Trường Quốc học Huế (1896–2001) [A Special Commemoration of 105 Years of the Quốc Học Academy in Huế (1896–2001)]. Huế: Sở Văn Hóa Thông Tin Thừa Thiên—Huế, 2001.

Đại học quốc gia Hà Nội. *100 Chân dung một thế kỷ Đại học quốc gia Hà Nội* [100 Portraits of a Century of the National University in Hà Nội]. Hà Nội: Nhà Xuất Bản Đại Học Quốc Gia Hà Nội, 2006.

———. *Tân thư và xã hội Việt Nam cuối thế kỷ XIX đầu thế kỷ XX* [The New Books and Vietnamese Society at the End of the Nineteenth Century and the Beginning of the Twentieth Century]. Hà Nội: Nhà Xuất Bản Chính Trị Quốc Gia, 1997.

Đặng Hữu Thụ. *Thân thế và sự nghiệp nhà cách mạng Nguyễn Thế Truyền* [The Life and Career of the Revolutionary Nguyễn Thế Truyền]. Paris: Melun, 1993.

Đặng Lễ Nghi. *Thơ tuồng lính tập đi Tây* [Poems of Soldiers in France]. Sài Gòn: Imprimerie de l'Union, 1915.

Đặng Văn Chiểu. *Vè lính tập và thợ đi Tây* [On Soldiers and Workers in France]. Sài Gòn: Imprimerie de l'Union, 1915.

Đặng Văn Long, *Người Việt ở Pháp, 1940–1954* [Vietnamese in France, 1940–1954]. Paris: Tủ Sách Nghiên Cứu, 1997.

Đào Thị Diến. "Ngô Đình Nhu, nhà lưu trữ Việt Nam thời kỳ 1938–1946" [Ngô Đình Nhu, a Vietnamese Archivist during the Period 1938–1946]. *Tạp Chí Nghiên Cứu và Phát Triển* 6–7 (2013): 238–43.

Đỗ Quang Hưng, Nguyễn Thành, and Dương Trung Quốc, eds. *Lịch sử báo chí Việt Nam, 1865–1945* [A History of Vietnamese Newspapers, 1865–1945]. Hà Nội: Nhà Xuất Bản Đại Học Quốc Gia Hà Nội, 2000.

Hà Vinh. "Trần Trọng Kim trong góc khuất của lịch sử" [Trần Trọng Kim in a Hidden Corner of History]. *Tạp Chí Xưa & Nay* 212 (May 2004): 11–13.

Hà Vũ Trọng. "Vũ Cao Đàm—nghệ thuật từ Đông sang Tây" [Vũ Cao Đàm: Art from East to West]. *Tạp Chí Mỹ Thuật*. June 2019.

Hiến Vương. *Minh ơi! Tôi muốn đi coi cuộc đấu xảo Paris* [Minh! I Want to Go to the Paris Exposition]. Sài Gòn: Đức Lưu Phương, 1931.

Hồ Chí Minh. "Nhật ký hành trình của Hồ chủ tịch. Bốn tháng sang Pháp" [Chairman Hồ's Travel Journal: Four Months in France]. In *Hồ Chí Minh toàn tập*, vol. 4. Hà Nội: Nhà Xuất Bản Chính Trị Quốc Gia, 2000.

Hồ Đắc Di. "Những năm học y khoa tại Pháp (1918–1931)" [My Years Studying Medicine in France]. In *Hồ Đắc Di: Nhà y học triết nhân* [Hồ Đắc Di: Doctor and Philosopher]. Hà Nội: Nhà Xuất Bản Chính Trị Quốc Gia Sự Thật, 2014.

Hồ Hữu Tường. *41 năm làm báo* [41 Years in Journalism]. Hà Nội: Nhà Xuất Bản Hội Nhà Văn, 2017.

Hữu Ngọc and Nguyễn Đức Hiền, eds. *La Sơn Yên Hồ Hoàng Xuân Hãn (1908–1996)*. 3 vols. Hà Nội: Nhà Xuất Bản Giáo Dục, 1996.

LeFailler, Philippe, and Nguyễn Phương Ngọc, eds. *Mục lục phân tích Tạp chí Thanh Nghị* [Analytical Index of the Journal *Thanh Nghị*]. Hà Nội: Ecole française d'Extrême-Orient, 2009.

Lê Văn Đức. *Cách đi Tây* [How to Go West]. Sài Gòn: Đức Lưu Phương, 1931.

———. *Tây hành lược ký* [An Account of a Journey to the West]. Qui Nhơn: Imprimerie de Qui Nhơn, 1923.

Lê Văn Thử. *Mười chín sinh viên Việt Nam bị trục xuất* [Nineteen Expelled Vietnamese Students]. Sài Gòn: Nam Việt, 1949.

Lương Việt Hùng. *Đời du học* [The Life of Study Abroad]. Chợ Lớn: Lương Việt Hùng, 193?.

Mai Thị Trình. *Những năm tháng không quên* [Unforgettable Months and Years]. Hà Nội: Nhà Xuất Bản Thông Tấn, 2018.

Nguyễn Bá Thế. *Tôn Thọ Tường (1826–1877)*. Saigon: Tủ Sách "Những Mảnh Gương" Tân Việt, 1957.

Nguyễn Cao Tiêu. *Ngự giá như Tây ký* [An Account of His Excellency's Journey to the West]. Huế: Đắc Lập, 1922.

Nguyễn Công Tiễu. *Du lịch Âu Châu, hội chợ Marseille, đấu xảo quốc tế Paris* [Tourism in Europe, a Conference in Marseille, and the International Exposition in Paris]. Edited by Nguyễn Hữu Sơn. Hà Nội: Nhà Xuất Bản Tri Thức, 2017.

Nguyễn Đình Đầu. *Pétrus Ký, nỗi oan thế kỷ* [Pétrus Ký: A Century of Injustice]. Hà Nội: Nhã Nam, 2017.

Nguyễn Hùng. *Nam bộ những nhân vật một thời vang bóng* [Southern Figures from a Golden Era]. Hà Nội: Công An Nhân Dân, 2003.

Nguyễn Hữu Sơn. "Du ký của người Việt Nam viết về nước Pháp và mối quan hệ Việt-Pháp giai đoạn cuối thế kỷ XIX—nửa đầu thế kỷ XX" [Vietnamese Travelogues about France and Franco-Vietnamese Relations from the Late Nineteenth Century to the Mid-Twentieth Century]. Hà Nội: Kỷ Yếu Hội Nghị—Hội Thảo Đại Học Quốc Gia Hà Nội, 2008.

———, ed. *Du ký Việt Nam, Nam: tạp chí Nam Phong* [Vietnamese Travel Writings from the Journal *Southern Wind*]. 3 vols. Thành Phố Hồ Chí Minh: Nhà Xuất Bản Trẻ, 2007.

———, ed. *Phạm Quỳnh: tuyển tập du ký* [Phạm Quỳnh: Selected Travel Writings]. Hà Nội: Nhà Xuất Bản Tri Thức, 2012.

Nguyễn Khắc Phê. *Hoa sĩ Lê Văn Miến: cuộc đời và sự nghiệp giáo dục* [The Painter Lê Văn Miến: Life and Educational Career]. Hà Nội: Nhà Xuất Bản Giáo Dục, 1997.

Nguyễn Khắc Viện. *Tự truyện* [Personal Stories]. Hà Nội: Nhà Xuất Bản Khoa Học Xã Hội, 2007.

Nguyễn Kim Oanh. "Giới thiệu tác phẩm *Như Tây Ký* của Ngụy Khắc Đản" [Introducing Ngụy Khắc Đản's work *Như Tây Ký*]. *Thông báo Hán Nôm học* (2002): 427–33.

Nguyễn Ngọc Xuân. *Pháp du hành trình* [A Journey to France]. Hải Phòng: Văn Minh, 1923.

Nguyễn Phan Quang and Phan Văn Hoàng. *Luật sư Phan Văn Trường* [The Lawyer Phan Văn Trường]. Thành Phố Hồ Chí Minh: Nhà Xuất Bản Thành Phố Hồ Chí Minh, 1995.

Nguyễn Q. Thắng. *Các tác giả người Việt viết tiếng Pháp* [Vietnamese Authors Writing in French]. Thành Phố Hồ Chí Minh: Nhà Xuất Bản Thành Phố Hồ Chí Minh, 2017.

———. *Phong trào Duy Tân: các khuôn mặt tiêu biểu* [The Duy Tân Movement: The Faces of its Participants]. Hà Nội: Nhà Xuất Bản Văn Hóa Thông Tin, 2006.

Nguyễn Thế Long. *Bang giao Đại Việt triều Nguyễn* [Đại Việt's Foreign Relations under the Nguyễn Court]. Hà Nội: Nhà Xuất Bản Văn Hóa Thông Tin, 2005.

Nguyễn Thị Minh. *Nguyễn An Ninh: "Tôi chỉ làm cơn gió thổi"* [Nguyễn An Ninh: "I Only Made the Wind Blow"]. Thành Phố Hồ Chí Minh: Nhà Xuất Bản Trẻ, 2001.

Nguyễn Thị Thế. *Hồi ký gia đình Nguyễn Tường* [Memoir of the Nguyễn Tường Family]. Santa Ana, CA: Văn Hóa Ngày Nay, 1996.

Nguyễn Thiếu Dũng. "Jules Roux: người bạn thiết nghĩa của nhà cách mạng Phan Châu Trinh" [Jules Roux: An Intimate Friend of the Revolutionary Phan Châu Trinh]. *Bách Khoa* 406 (1974): 39–48.

Nguyễn Thu Hoài. "Lần đầu tiên Việt Nam tham dự đấu xảo tại Pháp năm 1877" [Vietnam's First Participation in a French Exposition in 1877]. *Tạp Chí Xưa & Nay* 406 (June 2012): 9–12.

Nguyễn Tường Bách. *Việt Nam, những ngày lịch sử* [Vietnam: Historical Days]. Montréal: Nhóm Nghiên Cứu Sử Địa, 1981.

Nhật Tịnh. *Chân dung Nhất Linh* [Portrait of Nhất Linh]. Sài Gòn: Đại Nam, 1971.

Phạm Phú Thứ. *Nhật ký đi Tây* [Journal of a Trip to the West]. Translated by Quang Uyên. Đà Nẵng: Nhà Xuất Bản Đà Nẵng, 1999.

Phạm Quỳnh. *Pháp du hành trình nhật ký* [A Journal of a Journey to France]. In *Phạm Quỳnh: tuyển tập du ký*, edited by Nguyễn Hữu Sơn. Hà Nội: Nhà Xuất Bản Tri Thức, 2012.

Quốc sử quán triều Nguyễn. *Đại Nam Thực Lục* [The Veritable Records of the Great South]. Hà Nội: Nhà Xuất Bản Giáo Dục, 2007.

Thái Bạch. *Cuộc bút chiến giữa Phan Văn Trị—Tôn Thọ Tường* [The Pen War between Phan Văn Trị and Tôn Thọ Tường]. Sài Gòn: Sống Mới, 1957.

Thái Nhân Hoà, ed. *Phạm Phú Thứ với tư tưởng canh tân* [Phạm Phú Thứ and Reformist Thought]. Thành Phố Hồ Chí Minh: Hội Khoa Học Lịch Sử Thành Phố Hồ Chí Minh, 1995.

Thầy trò Trường Bưởi—Chu Văn An (Hồi ký nhiều tác giả) [Teachers of the Bưởi—Chu Văn An School (Memoirs of Many Authors)]. Hà Nội: Nhà Xuất Bản Giáo Dục, 1998.

Thế kỷ XXI nhìn về nhân vật lịch sử Phan Thanh Giản [The Twenty-First Century Looks at the Historical Figure Phan Thanh Giản]. Thành Phố Hồ Chí Minh: Nhà Xuất Bản Hồng Đức, 2013.

Thụy Khuê. *Nói chuyện với Hoàng Xuân Hãn và Tạ Trọng Hiệp* [Talking with Hoàng Xuân Hãn and Tạ Trọng Hiệp]. Westminster, CA: Văn Nghệ, 2002.

Trần Bá Vinh. *Pháp du ký sự* [An Account of a Trip to France]. Vinh: Châu Tinh, 1932.

Trần Ngươn Phiêu. *Phan Văn Hùm: thân thế và sự nghiệp* [Phan Văn Hùm: His Life and Career]. Amarillo, TX: Hải Mã: 2003.

Trần Thị Tú Nhi. "Đóng góp của Trương Minh Ký với thể tài du ký quốc ngữ giai đoạn giao thời" [Trương Minh Ký's Contributions to Quốc Ngữ Travelogues in a Transitional Era]. *Nghiên Cứu Văn Học* 8 (2014): 38–51.

Trần Tứ Nghĩa. *Một thế kỷ của phong trào người Việt ở Pháp hướng về đất nước* [A Century of Vietnamese Movements in France towards the Nation]. Thành Phố Hồ Chí Minh: Nhà Xuất Bản Trẻ, 2010.

Trang Thu. *Những hoạt động của Phan Châu Trinh tại Pháp, 1911–1925* [Phan Châu Trịnh's Activities in France, 1911–1925]. Thành Phố Hồ Chí Minh: Nhà Xuất Bản Văn Nghệ Thành Phố Hồ Chí Minh, 2000.

Tri Vũ and Phan Nhọc Khuê. *Trần Đức Thảo: những lời trăng trối* [Trần Đức Thảo: His Final Words]. Arlington, VA: Tổ Hợp Xuất Bản Miền Đông Hoa Kỳ, 2014.

Trương Bá Cần. *Nguyễn Trường Tộ: con người và di thảo* [Nguyễn Trường Tộ: The Person and his Works]. Thành Phố Hồ Chí Minh: Nhà Xuất Bản Thành Phố Hồ Chí Minh, 2002.

Trương Minh Ký. *Chư quấc thại hội* [The Universal Exposition]. Sài Gòn: Rey & Curiol, 1889.

———. *Như tây nhựt trình* [An Account of a Trip to the West]. Sài Gòn: Rey & Curiol, 1889.

Uyên Huy. "Kỷ niệm 100 năm thành lập trường vẽ Gia Định—trường đại học mỹ thuật Thành Phố Hồ Chí Minh (1913–2013)" [Commemorating the Centennial of the Gia Định Art School—Arts University of Hồ Chí Minh City (1913–2013)]. *Tạp Chí Mỹ Thuật*. November 2013.

WESTERN LANGUAGES

Aberdam, Marie. "Élites cambodgiennes en situation coloniale, essai d'histoire sociale des réseaux de pouvoir dans l'administration cambodgienne sous le protectorat français (1860–1953). PhD dissertation, Université Paris I Panthéon Sorbonne, 2019.

Aldrich, Robert. "Colonial Kings in the Metropole: The Visits to France of King Sisowath (1906) and Emperor Khai Dinh (1922)." In *Royals on Tour: Politics, Pageantry and Colonialism*, edited by Robert Aldrich and Cindy McCreedy. Manchester: Manchester University Press, 2018.

Amrith, Sunil. *Crossing the Bay of Bengal: The Fury of Nature and the Fortunes of Migrants*. Cambridge, MA: Harvard University Press, 2015.

Anderson, Benedict. *Under Three Flags: Anarchism and the Anti-Colonial Imagination*. London: Verso, 2005.

Anderson, Claire. *Subaltern Lives: Biographies of Colonialism in the Indian Ocean World.* Cambridge, UK: Cambridge University Press, 2012.

André-Pallois, Nadine. *L'Indochine: un lieu d'échange culturel? Les peintres français et indochinois (fin XIXe-XXe siècle).* Paris: École française d'Extrême-Orient, 1997.

Banerjee, Sukanya. "Transimperial." *Victorian Literary Studies* 46.3–4 (2018): 925–28.

Benjamin, Walter. "Paris, The Capital of the Nineteenth Century." In *Walter Benjamin: Selected Writings,* vol. 3 (1935–38), edited by Howard Eiland and Michael W. Jennings, 32–49. Cambridge, MA: Belknap, 2002.

Benoist, Jocelyn, and Michel Espagne, eds. *L'itinéraire de Tran Duc Thao: Phénoménologie et transfert culturel.* Paris: Armand Colin, 2013.

Bizien, Pierre-André, and Dung Pham Tran. *Histoire d'une grande famille vietnamienne: Madame Kiến et les siens de Hà Nội à la France, 1885–2018.* Paris: L'Harmattan, 2022.

Blanchard, Pascal, Sandrine Lemaire, Nicolas Bancel, and Dominic Thomas, eds. *Colonial Cultures in France since the Revolution.* Bloomington: Indiana University Press, 2013.

Bois, Paul. *Le grand siècle des Messageries maritimes.* Marseille: Chambre de commerce et d'industrie Marseille-Provence, 1992.

Boittin, Jennifer. "'Among Them Complicit? Life and Politics in France's Black Communities, 1919–1939." In *Africa in Europe: Studies in Transnational Practice in the Long Twentieth Century,* edited by Eve Rosenhaft and Robbie Aitken, 55–75. Liverpool: Liverpool University Press, 2013.

———. *Colonial Metropolis: The Urban Grounds of Anti-Imperialism and Feminism in Interwar Paris.* Lincoln: University of Nebraska Press, 2010.

Britto, Karl. *Disorientation: France, Vietnam, and the Ambivalence of Interculturality.* Hong Kong: Hong Kong University Press, 2004.

Brocheux, Pierre. "Phan Văn Trường, 1876–1933. Acteur d'une histoire partagée." *Moussons: Recherches en sciences humaines sur l'Asie du Sud-Est* 24 (2014): 19–32.

———. "Visions et représentations de l'Occident européen chez les voyageurs vietnamiens, 1864–1954." In *Une vie pour le Viêt Nam: Mélanges en l'honneur de Charles Fourniau,* edited by Alain Ruscio, 211–22. Paris: Les Indes Savantes, 2016.

Brocheux, Pierre, and Daniel Hémery. *Indochina: An Ambiguous Colonization, 1858–1954.* Berkeley: University of California Press, 2011.

Brückenhaus, Daniel. *Policing Transnational Protest: Liberal Imperialism and the Surveillance of Anticolonialists in Europe, 1905–1945.* New York: Oxford University Press, 2017.

Bùi Thanh Vân. *La France: relations de voyage.* Huế: Imprimerie Đắc Lập, 1923.

———. *Le Tour du monde par un Annamite.* Huế: Bùi Huy Tín, 1929.

Burton, Antoinette. *At the Heart of the Empire: Indians and the Colonial Encounter in Victorian Britain.* Berkeley: University of California Press, 1998.

Can, François-Bertrand. *Carnet de route d'un petit marsouin cochinchinois.* Sài Gòn: Imprimerie Albert Portail, 1918.

Chandler, David. *The Tragedy of Cambodian History.* New Haven: Yale University Press, 1991.

Charpier, Frédéric. *L'Histoire de l'extrême gauche Trotskiste de 1929 à nos jours.* Paris: Editions1, 2002.

Cherry, Haydon. *Down and Out in Saigon: Stories of the Poor in a Colonial City.* New Haven: Yale University Press, 2019.

Clancy-Smith, Julia. *Mediterraneans: North Africa and Europe in an Age of Migration, c. 1800–1900.* Berkeley: University of California Press, 2011.

Cortambert, Richard. *Impressions d'un japonais en France; suivies des Impressions des annamites en Europe.* Paris: Achille Fauré, 1864.

Dalloz, Jacques. "Les Vietnamiens dans la franc-maçonnerie colonial." *Revue française d'histoire d'outre-mer* 85.320 (1998): 103–18.

Daughton, J. P. "Recasting Pigneau de Béhaine." In *Việt Nam: Borderless Histories*, edited by Nhung Tuyet Tran and Anthony Reid, 290–322. Madison: University of Wisconsin Press, 2006.

Daum, Pierre. *Immigrés de force: les travailleurs indochinois en France (1939–1952).* Paris: Solin, 2009.

Day, Jenny Huangfu. *Qing Travelers to the Far West: Diplomacy and the Information Order in Late Imperial China.* Cambridge, UK: Cambridge University Press, 2018.

Delvaux, R. P. "L'Ambassade de Minh-Mang à Louis-Philippe." *Bulletin des amis du vieux Hué* 15, no. 4 (October-December 1928): 257–64.

Deroo, Eric, and Antoine Champeaux. "Panorama des troupes coloniales françaises dans les deux guerres mondiales." *Revue historique des armées* 271 (2013): 72–88.

Despuech, Jacques. *L'Affaire des piastres.* Paris: Deux Rives, 1953.

Desquesnes, Rémy. "L'Organisation Todt en France (1940–1944)." *Histoire, économie et société* 11, no. 3 (3e trimestre 1992): 535–50.

Deuve, Jean. *Le royaume du Laos, 1949–1965.* Paris: École française d'Extrême-Orient, 1984.

Dutton, George E. *A Vietnamese Moses: Philiphê Binh and the Geographies of Early Modern Vietnamese Catholicism.* Berkeley: University of California Press, 2017.

Dương Văn Giáo. *L'Indochine pendant la guerre 1914–1918: contribution à l'étude de la colonisation indochinoise.* Paris: J. Budry, 1925.

Đào Đăng Vỹ. *L'Annam qui nait.* Huế: Imprimerie du Mirador, 1938.

Đặng Văn Long. *Les travailleurs réquis.* Paris: Bibliothêque Nghiên Cứu, 2004.

Đỗ Đức Hồ. *Soviets d'Annam et désarroi des dieux blancs.* Paris: Imprimerie de France, 1938.

Eckert, Henri. "Les militaires indochinois au service de la France (1859–1939)." PhD dissertation, Université de Paris IV, 1998.

Edington, Claire. *Beyond the Asylum: Mental Illness in French Colonial Vietnam.* Ithaca, NY: Cornell University Press, 2019.

Edwards, Kathryn. *Contesting Indochina: French Remembrance between Decolonization and Cold War.* Berkeley: University of California Press, 2016.

Edwards, Penny. *Cambodge: The Cultivation of a Nation, 1860–1945.* Honolulu: University of Hawai'i Press, 2007.

Emerson, Julia. "Phạm Duy Khiêm: A Man Apart." *Moussons: Recherches en sciences humaines sur l'Asie du Sud-Est* 24 (2014): 107–26.

Espagne, Michel. "Écrire une histoire vietnamienne de la France?" In *Hanoi-Paris: Un nouvel espace des sciences humaines*, edited by Michel Espagne, Nguyen Ba Cuong, and Nguyen Thi Hanh, 71–89. Paris: KIME, 2020.

Fautereau, Didier de. "Le Nationalisme vietnamien: contribution des marins vietnamiens au nationalisme vietnamien (période entre deux guerres)." Paris: Mémoire pour le Diplôme d'Etudes Supérieures de Science Politique, 1975.

Fawell, Charles. "In-Between Empires: Steaming the Trans-Suez Highways of French Imperialism (1830–1930)." PhD dissertation, University of Chicago, 2021.

Fogarty, Richard. *Race and War in France: Colonial Subjects in the French Army, 1914–1918*. Baltimore: Johns Hopkins University Press, 2008.

Gantès, Gilles de, and Nguyễn Phương Ngọc, eds. *Vietnam: le moment moderniste*. Aix-en-Provence: Publications de l'Université de Provence, 2009.

Gazquez, Denis. "Révolution, culture et bibliothèques: Hồ Chi Minh à Paris, 1917–1923." In *Une vie pour le Viêt Nam: Mélanges en honneur de Charles Fourniau*, edited by Alain Ruscio, 231–44. Paris: Les Indes Savantes, 2016.

Genova, James E. "The Empire Within: The Colonial Popular Front in France, 1934–1938." *Alternatives: Global, Local, Political* 26, no. 2 (April–June 2001): 175–209.

Gibbs, Jason. "Spoken Theater, La Scène Tonkinoise, and the First Modern Vietnamese Songs." *Asian Music* 31, no. 2 (Spring-Summer 2000): 1–33.

Giebel, Christoph. *Imagined Ancestries of Vietnamese Communism: Tôn Đức Thắng and the Politics of History and Memory*. Seattle: University of Washington Press, 2004.

Goebel, Michael. *Anti-Imperial Metropolis: Interwar Paris and the Seeds of Third World Nationalism*. New York: Cambridge University Press, 2015.

Goscha, Christopher. "Aux origines du républicanisme vietnamien: circulations mondiales et connexions coloniales." *Vingtième siècle: revue d'histoire* 131, no. 3 (July-September 2016): 17–35.

———. "Bao Dai et Sihanouk: la fabrique indochinoise des rois coloniaux." In *La Colonisation des corps: de l'Indochine au Viet Nam*, edited by François Guillemot and Agathe Larcher-Goscha, 127–75. Paris: Vendémiaire, 2014.

———. *Going Indochinese: Contesting Concepts of Space and Place in French Indochina*. Copenhagen: NIAS Press, 2012.

———. *Historical Dictionary of the Indochina War (1945–1954): An International and Interdisciplinary Approach*. Honolulu: University of Hawai'i Press, 2012.

———. "Recits de voyage viêtnamiens et prise de conscience indochinoise (c. 1920–1945)." In *Récits de voyages des asiatiques: genres, mentalités, conceptions de l'espace*, edited by Claudine Salmon, 253–279. Paris: École française d'Extrême-Orient, Études thématiques, n. 5, 1996.

———. *Thailand and the Southeast Asian Networks of the Vietnamese Revolution, 1885–1954*. London: Routledge, 1999.

———. "The Modern Barbarian: Nguyen Van Vinh and the Complexity of Colonial Modernity in Vietnam." *European Journal of East Asian Studies* 3, no. 1 (2004): 135–69.

———. *Vietnam: A New History*. New York: Basic Books, 2016.

———. *Vietnam: Un état né de la guerre (1945–1954)*. Paris: Armand Colin, 2011.

Gouvernement général de l'Indochine. *Souverains et notabilités d'Indochine*. Hà Nội: Éditions du gouvernement général de l'Indochine, 1943.

Granier, Solène. *Domestiques indochinois*. Paris: Vendémiaire, 2014.

Greenhalgh, Paul. *Ephemeral Vistas: The Expositions Universelles, Great Exhibitions and World's Fairs, 1851–1939*. Manchester: Manchester University Press, 1988.

Guerassimoff, Eric, Andrew Hardy, Nguyễn Phương Ngọc, and Emmanuel Poisson, eds. *Les migrations impériales au Vietnam: Travail et colonisations dans l'Asie-Pacifique français, XIXe-XXe siècles*. Paris: Hémisphères Éditions, 2020.

Guillemin, Alain. "Cung Giu Nguyen où l'homme des deux rives." *Moussons: Recherches en sciences sociales sur l'Asie du Sud-Est* 24 (2014): doi.org/10.4000/moussons.3008.

Guillemot, François. *Viêt-Nam, fractures d'une nation: une histoire contemporaine de 1858 à nos jours*. Paris: La Découverte, 2018.

Hale, Dana. *Races on Display: French Representations of Colonized Peoples, 1886–1940*. Bloomington: Indiana University Press, 2008.

Harvey, David. *Paris, Capital of Modernity*. London: Routledge, 2006.

Hémery, Daniel. "Du patriotisme au marxisme: l'immigration vietnamienne en France de 1926 à 1930." *Le mouvement sociale* 90 (January-March 1975): 3–54.

———. *Révolutionnaires vietnamiens et pouvoir colonial en indochine: communistes, trotskystes, nationalistes à Saigon, 1932–1937*. Paris: François Maspero, 1975.

———. "Ta Thu Thau: l'itinéraire politique d'un révolutionnaire vietnamien pendant les années 1930." In *L'Histoire de l'Asie du sud-est: révoltes, réformes, révolutions*, edited by Pierre Brocheux, 193–222. Lille: Presses Universitaires de Lille, 1981.

Herrick, Tim. "'A book which is no longer discussed today': Tran Duc Thao, Jacques Derrida, and Maurice Merleau-Ponty." *Journal of the History of Ideas* 66, no. 1 (January 2005): 113–31.

Ho Tai, Hue-Tam. *Radicalism and the Origins of the Vietnamese Revolution*. Cambridge, MA: Harvard University Press, 1992.

Hoang Van Tuan. "L'Université de Hanoi (1906–1945). Un outil de renouvellement des élites et de la culture vietnamiennes?" *Outre-mers* 394–395, no. 1 (2017): 61–84.

Hoàng Xuân Nhị. *Les Cahiers intimes de Heou-Tam, étudiant d'Extrême-Orient*. Paris: Mercure de France, 1939.

Hue, Bernard, ed. *Indochine: Reflets littéraires*. Rennes: Presses universitaires de Rennes, 1992.

Ivarsson, Søren, and Christopher Goscha. "Prince Phetsarath (1890–1957): Nationalism and Royalty in the Making of Modern Laos." *Journal of Southeast Asian Studies* 38, no. 1 (February 2007): 55–81.

Jackson, Julian. *France: The Dark Years, 1940–1944*. New York: Oxford University Press, 2001.

Jagielski, Jean-François. "Entre fiction et réalité, la rumeur des Annamites massacrant les Parisiennes." In *Obéir/désobéir: les mutinéries de 1917 en perspective*, edited by André Loez and Nicolas Mariot, 139–50. Paris: Editions La Découverte, 2008.

Jennings, Eric. *Vichy in the Tropics*. Stanford, CA: Stanford University Press, 2000.

"Journal de l'ambassade envoyée en France et en Espagne par S.M. Tự Đức (Août 1877 à Septembre 1878)." *Bulletin des amis du vieux Hué* 7, no.4 (October-November 1920): 407–43.

Keith, Charles. *Catholic Vietnam: A Church from Empire to Nation*. Berkeley: University of California Press, 2012.

———. "The Curious Case of Hoàng Thị Thế." *Journal of Vietnamese Studies* 8, no. 3 (November 2013): 71–119.

———. "Vietnamese Collaborationism in Vichy France." *Journal of Asian Studies* 76, no. 4 (November 2017): 987–1008.

Khing Hoc Dy. "Le voyage de l'envoyé cambodgien Son Diệp à Paris en 1900." In *Récits de voyages asiatiques: Genres, mentalités, conception de l'espace*, edited by Claudine Salmon, 367–83. Paris: École française d'Extrême-Orient, Études thématiques, n. 5, 1996.

Lamant, Pierre. *L'Affaire Yukanthor: une autopsie d'un scandal colonial*. Paris: L'Harmattan, 1989.

Le Van Ho, Mireille. *Des Vietnamiens dans la Grande Guerre: 50000 recrues dans les usines françaises*. Paris: Vendémiaire, 2014.

Lê Hữu Thọ. *Itinéraire d'un petit mandarin*. Paris: L'Harmattan, 1997.

Lê Văn Chỉnh. *Voyage médico-chirurgical en France: Paris—Amiens—Berck*. Extrait des archives provinciales de chirurgie, n.d.

Lê Văn Đức. *A travers l'Allemagne, la Belgique et l'Angleterre: impressions de voyage d'un annamite*. Qui Nhơn: Imprimerie de Qui Nhơn, 1924.

Lebovics, Herman. *True France: The Wars over Cultural Identity, 1900–1945*. Ithaca, NY: Cornell University Press, 1992.

Legrandjacques, Sara. "Des colonisés à la cité: la Maison des étudiants indochinois à la Cité universitaire de Paris, 1927–1939." *Revue d'Histoire/Zeitschrift für Geschichte*. Online: submitted on June 5, 2018: https://hal.science/hal-01808163/document.

Lessard, Michelene. *Human Trafficking in Colonial Vietnam*. London: Routledge, 2015.

Levine, Marilyn, and Chen San-Ching. "Communist-Leftist Control of the European Branch of the Guomindang, 1923–1927." *Modern China* 22, no. 1 (January 1996): 62–92.

Lewis, Su Lin. *Cities in Motion: Urban Life and Cosmopolitanism in Southeast Asia, 1920–1940*. Cambridge, UK: Cambridge University Press, 2016.

Liauzu, Claude. *Aux origines des tiers-mondismes; colonisés et anticolonialistes en France (1919–1939)*. Paris: L'Harmattan, 1982.

Lockhart, Greg, and Monique Lockhart. "Broken Journey: Nhất Linh's 'Going to France.'" *East Asian History* 8 (December 1994): 73–134.

Luguern, Liêm-Khê. "Les 'Travailleurs Indochinois': étude socio-historique d'une immigration coloniale (1939–1954)." PhD dissertation, Ecole des hautes études en sciences sociales, 2014.

Mantienne, Frédéric. *Pierre Pigneaux, Évêque d'Adran et mandarin de Cochinchine (1741–1799)*. Paris: Les Indes Savantes, 2012.

Martin, Marie-Alexandrine. *Cambodia: A Shattered Society*. Berkeley: University of California Press, 1994.

Matera, Marc. *Black London: The Imperial Metropolis and Decolonization in the Twentieth Century*. Berkeley: University of California Press, 2015.

Maurel, Frédéric. "A Khmer *Nirat*, 'Travel in France during the World Exhibition of 1900': Influences from the Thai?" *South East Asia Research* 10, no. 1 (2002): 99–112.

McConnell, Scott. *Leftward Journey: The Education of Vietnamese Students in France, 1919–1939*. New Brunswick: Transaction Publishers, 1989.

McLeod, Mark. "Nguyen Truong To: A Catholic Reformer at Emperor Tu Duc's Court." *Journal of Southeast Asian Studies* 25, no. 2 (June 1994): 313–31.

Middell, Matthias. "Transregional Studies: A New Approach to Global Processes." In *The Routledge Handbook of Transregional Studies,* edited by Matthias Middell, 1–16. London: Routledge, 2018.

Mikaelian, Grégory. "L'aristocratie khmère à l'école des humanités françaises." *Bulletin de l'association d'échanges et de formation pour les études khmères* 19 (2014): www.aefek.fr/baefek19.html.

———. "The Gru of Parnassus: Au Chhieng among the Titans." *UDAYA, Journal of Khmer Studies* 15 (2020): 127–82.

Monnais-Rousselot, Laurence. "Le Dr. Nguyễn Văn Luyện et ses confrères: La médecine privée dans le Việt Nam colonial." *Moussons: Recherche en sciences humaines sur l'Asie du Sud-Est* 15 (2010): 75–95.

Morlat, Patrice. "La surveillance des Indochinois à Marseille après la Première Guerre mondiale (1917–1935)." In *Une vie pour le Viêt Nam: Mélanges en l'honneur de Charles Fourniau,* edited by Alain Ruscio, 245–94. Paris: Les Indes Savantes, 2016.

Mortimer, Edward. *The Rise of the French Communist Party, 1920–1947*. Boston: Faber & Faber, 1984.

Motadel, David. "The Global Authoritarian Movement and the Revolt Against Empire." *The American Historical Review* 124, no. 3 (2019): 843–77.

Mrazek, Rudolf. "Tan Malaka: A Political Personality's Structure of Experience." *Indonesia* 14 (October 1972): 1–48.

Ngô Văn. *In the Crossfire: Adventures of a Vietnamese Revolutionary*. Edinburgh: AK Press, 2010.

Nguyen, Cindy. "Reading and Misreading: The Social Life of Libraries and Colonial Control in Vietnam, 1865–1958." PhD dissertation, University of California-Berkeley, 2019.

Nguyen, Duy Lap. "Tourism and the irony of colonial underdevelopment in Nhất Linh's 'Going to the West.'" *Studies in Travel Writing* 22.4 (2018): 371–88.

Nguyen, Giang-Huong. "À la découverte d'un écrivain oublié: Phạm Văn Ký (1910–1992)." *Continents manuscrits* 6 (2016): https://journals.openedition.org/coma/662.

———. *La Littérature vietnamienne francophone.* Paris: Classiques Garnier, 2018.

Nguyen, Martina Thucchi. *On Our Own Strength: The Self-Reliant Literary Group and Cosmopolitan Nationalism in Late Colonial Vietnam.* Honolulu: University of Hawai'i Press, 2020.

Nguyen Phuoc Bao Vang. *Duy Tan, empereur d'Annam 1900–1945: Exilé à l'île de la Réunion ou Le destin tragique du prince Vinh San.* Sainte-Marie: Azalées, 2000.

Nguyen Van Thanh. *Saigon-Marseille, allez simple: un fils de mandarin dans les camps de travailleurs en France.* Lyon: Elytis, 2012.

Nguyễn Đức Hiệp. "Photography in Vietnam from the End of the Nineteenth Century to the Start of the Twentieth." Translated by Ellen Takata. *In Translation* 4, no. 2 (Spring 2014): http://hdl.handle.net/2027/spo.7977573.0004.204.

Nguyễn Mạnh Tường. *Pierres de France.* Hà Nội: Éditions de la Revue indochinoise, 1937.

———. *Sourires et larmes d'une jeunesse.* Hà Nội: Éditions de la Revue indochinoise, 1937.

Nguyễn Phương Ngọc. *À l'origine de l'anthropologie au Vietnam: recherche sur les auteurs de la première moitié de XXe siècle.* Aix-en-Provence: Presses universitaires de Provence, 2012.

Nguyễn Thanh Trừng. *Vision de la femme dans la littérature du Sud-Vietnam (de 1858 à 1945).* Paris: L'Harmattan, 2012.

Nguyễn Thế Anh. *Monarchie et fait colonial au Viêt-Nam (1875–1925): Le crepuscule d'un ordre traditionnel.* Paris: l'Harmattan, 1992.

Nguyễn Tiến Lãng. *La France que j'ai vue.* Huế: Imprimerie Đắc Lập, 1940.

Nguyễn Trọng Hiệp. "Paris, capital de la France." Hà Nội: F. H. Schneider, 1897.

Ninh Xuân Thao. "L'État du Viêt-Nam et ses rapports avec la France (1949–1955): Une autre voie pour l'indépendance du Viêt-Nam." PhD dissertation, Université Bordeaux Montaigne, 2019.

Owen, Nicholas. "The Soft Heart of the British Empire: Indian Revolutionaries in Edwardian London." *Past and Present* 220, no. 1 (August 2013): 143–84.

Paterson, Lorraine. "Prisoners from Indochina in the Nineteenth-Century French Colonial World." In *Exile in Colonial Asia: Kings, Convicts, Commemoration*, edited by Ronit Ricci, 220–47. Honolulu: University of Hawai'i Press, 2016.

Pelley, Patricia. *Postcolonial Vietnam: New Histories of the National Past.* Durham: Duke University Press, 2002.

Peters, Erica. "Resistance, Rivalries, and Restaurants: Vietnamese Workers in Interwar France." *Journal of Vietnamese Studies* 2, no. 1 (2007): 109–43.

Peycam, Philippe. *The Birth of Vietnamese Political Journalism: Saigon, 1916–1930.* New York: Columbia University Press, 2012.

Peyssonnaux, Jean-Henri-Eugène, and Bùi Văn Cung. "Le traité de 1874: journal du secrétaire de l'ambassade annamite." *Bulletin des amis du vieux Hué* 7, no. 3 (July-September 1920): 365–84.

Pham, Julie. "Revolution, Communism, and History in the Thought of Trần Văn Giàu." PhD dissertation, University of Cambridge, 2008.

Phạm Phú Thứ. "L'ambassade de Phan Thanh Giản (1863–1864)." Translated by Nguyễn Đình Hoè, Ngô Đình Diệm, and Trần Xuân Toạn. In *Bulletin des amis du vieux Hué* vol. 2 (1919): 161–216 and vol. 4 (1921): 147–187, 243–281.

Pham Van Quang. *L'Institution de la littérature vietnamienne francophone.* Paris: Publibook, 2013.

Phạm Duy Khiêm. *De Hanoi à La Courtine (Septembre 1939-juin 1940), lettres de Nam Liên recueillies par Pham Duy Khiem.* Hà Nội: Lê Thăng, 1941.

Phạm Quỳnh. *Le capitaine Do-Huu-Vi—héros franco-annamite.* Huế: Đắc Lập, 1937.

———. *Quelques conférences à Paris, mai-juillet 1922.* Hà Nội: Imprimerie Tonkinoise, 1923.

Phan Văn Trường. *Une histoire de conspirateurs annamites à Paris, ou la vérité en Indochine.* Paris: Editions l'Insomniaque, 2003.

Poisson, Emmanuel. *Mandarins et subalternes au nord du Việt Nam: Une bureaucratie à l'épreuve, 1820–1918.* Paris: Maisonneuve et Larose, 2004.

Polmuk, Chairat. "Invoking the Past: The Cultural Politics of Lao Literature, 1941–1975." MA thesis, Cornell University, 2014.

Quinn-Judge, Sophie. *Ho Chi Minh: The Missing Years, 1919–1941.* Berkeley: University of California Press, 2002.

Reid, Anthony, ed. *Sojourners and Settlers: Histories of Southeast Asia and the Chinese.* Honolulu: University of Hawai'i Press, 1996.

Reilly, Brett. "Saigon's Hidden Presidential Palace and Forgotten President: The Republic of Cochinchina and Nguyễn Văn Thinh." *New Mandala,* June 14, 2019: https://www.newmandala.org/saigons-hidden-presidential-palace-and-forgotten-president-the-republic-of-cochinchina-and-nguyen-van-thinh.

———. "The Origins of the Vietnamese Civil War and the State of Vietnam." PhD dissertation, University of Wisconsin-Madison, 2018.

Rettig, Tobias. "Contested Loyalties: Vietnamese Soldiers in the Service of France, 1927–1939." PhD dissertation, University of London, 2005.

———. "From Subaltern to Free Worker: Exit, Voice, and Loyalty among Indochina's Subaltern Labor Camp Diaspora in Metropolitan France, 1939–1944." *Journal of Vietnamese Studies* 7, no. 3 (2012): 7–54.

Ricci, Ronit. *Banishment and Belonging: Exile and Diaspora in Sarandib, Lanka and Ceylon.* Cambridge, UK: Cambridge University Press, 2019.

Richardson, Al, ed. *The Revolution Defamed: A Documentary History of Vietnamese Trotskyism.* London: Socialist Platform Ltd., 2003.

Rives, Maurice. "Les indochinois de l'opération Dragoon." *Bulletin de l'A.N.A.I* (January-February-March 2004): 4–9.

———. "Les tirailleurs indochinois au Levant et dans les Forces Françaises Libres." *Bulletin de l'A.N.A.I* (July-August-September 1992): 4–7.

Rolland, Dominique. *Petit Việt-Nams.* Bordeaux: Elytis, 2009.

Rosenberg, Clifford. *Policing Paris: The Origins of Modern Immigration Control between the Wars.* Ithaca, NY: Cornell University Press, 2006.

Ruscio, Alain. *Les communistes et l'Algérie: des origins à la guerre d'indépendance, 1920–1962*. Paris: La Découverte, 2019.

———. *Les communistes français et la guerre d'Indochine, 1944–1954*. Paris: L'Harmattan, 1985.

Saada, Emmanuelle. *Empire's Children: Race, Filiation, and Citizenship in the French Colonies*. Chicago: University of Chicago Press, 2012.

Safford, Lisa Bixenstine. "Art at the Crossroads: Lacquer Painting in French Vietnam." *Transcultural Studies* 6, no. 1 (2015): 126–70.

Salles, André. *Un mandarin breton au service du roi de Cochinchine*. Rennes: Les Portes du Large, 2006.

Scheck, Raffael. *French Colonial Soldiers in German Captivity during World War II*. New York: Cambridge University Press, 2014.

———. *Hitler's African Victims: The German Army Massacres of Black French Soldiers in 1940*. Cambridge, UK: Cambridge University Press, 2006.

Schwartz, Vanessa. *Spectacular Realities: Early Mass Culture in Fin-De-Siècle Paris*. Berkeley: University of California Press, 1998.

Schweitzer, Thomas. "The French Communist Party and the Colonial Question, 1928–1939." PhD dissertation, University of Wisconsin-Madison, 1968.

Scott, Phoebe. "Vietnamese Art in Paris in the 30s-40s." *Southeast of Now: Directions in Contemporary and Modern Art in Asia* 3, no. 2 (October 2019): 187–240.

Selao, Ching. *Le roman vietnamien francophone: orientalisme, occidentalisme et hybridité*. Montréal: Presses de l'Université de Montréal, 2011.

Seltzer, Gregory. "The Hopes and the Realities of Aviation in French Indochina, 1919–1940." PhD dissertation, University of Kentucky, 2017.

Serrano, Richard. *Against the Postcolonial: 'Francophone' Writers at the Ends of French Empire*. Lanham, MD: Lexington Books, 2005.

Sher, Sacha. *L'Essor de l'Angkar: des rêves de grands soirs de sorbonnards, à la victoire des maquisards*. Texte issu et remanié de la première partie de Thèse de doctorat, Sociologie politique, Université de Paris X, 2003.

Shiraishi, Takashi. *An Age in Motion: Popular Radicalism in Java, 1912–1926*. Ithaca, NY: Cornell University Press, 1990.

Short, Philip. *Pol Pot: The History of a Nightmare*. London: John Murray, 2004.

Silverstein, Paul. *Algeria in France: Transpolitics, Race, and Nation*. Bloomington: Indiana University Press, 2004.

Simon-Barouh, Ida. "Les Viêtnamiens en France." *Hommes et Migrations* 1219 (May-June 1999): 69–89.

Smith, David. "'French Like the Others': Colonial Migrants in Wartime France, 1939–1947." PhD dissertation, University of Toronto, 2013.

Stora, Benjamin. "Les travailleurs indochinois en France pendant la seconde guerre mondiale." *Les Cahiers de CERMTRI* 28 (April 1983): 19–29.

Stovall, Tyler. *Paris and the Spirit of 1919: Consumer Struggles, Transnationalism, and Revolution*. Cambridge, UK: Cambridge University Press, 2012.

———. "The Color Line behind the Lines: Racial Violence in France during the Great War." *The American Historical Review* 103, no. 3 (June 1998): 737–69.

Tạ Trọng Hiệp. "Le journal de l'ambassade de Phan Thanh Giản en France (4 juillet 1863–18 avril 1864)." In *Récits de voyages asiatiques: Genres, mentalités, conception de l'espace*, edited by Claudine Salmon, 335–63. Paris: École française d'Extrême-Orient, Études thématiques, n. 5, 1996.

Taylor, Nora. *Painters in Hanoi: An Ethnography of Vietnamese Art*. Honolulu: University of Hawai'i Press, 2004.

Thiounn, Okna Veang. *Voyage en France du roi Sisowath: en l'année du cheval, huitième de la décade correspondant à l'année occidentale 1906, royaume du Cambodge*. Translated by Olivier De Bernon. Paris: Mercure, 2005.

Thomas, Martin. "The Vichy Government and French Colonial Prisoners of War, 1940–1944." *French Colonial Studies* 25, no. 4 (Fall 2002): 657–92.

Thomson, R. Stanley. "France in Cochinchina: The Question of Retrocession, 1862–1865." *Far Eastern Quarterly* 6, no. 4 (August 1947): 364–78.

Tran, Châu. *Trần Văn Thạch (1905–1945): Une plume contre l'oppression*. Paris: Les Indes Savantes, 2020.

Tran, Nhung Tuyet. "Confession, Cosmopolitanism, and Catholic Moralizing in Early Modern Vietnam." Unpublished manuscript.

Trần Mỹ-Vân. *A Vietnamese Royal Exile in Japan: Prince Cường Để (1882–1951)*. London: Routledge, 2005.

Trần Tấn Bình. "Conférence du 6 mars 1907 à Nam Định." *Bulletin de l'École française d'Extrême-Orient* (January-June 1907): 155–66.

Trần Thị Liên, Claire. "Henriette Bui: The Narrative of Vietnam's First Woman Doctor." In *Việt-Nam Exposé: French Scholarship on Twentieth-Century Vietnamese Society*, edited by Gisèle Bousquet and Pierre Brocheux, 278–312. Ann Arbor: University of Michigan, 2002.

———. "Nguyễn Xuân Mai (1890–1929). Itinéraire d'un médecin indochinois pendant la Première Guerre mondiale." In *Entrer en guerre*, edited by Hélène Baty-Delalande and Carine Trévisan, 297–316. Paris: Herrman, 2016.

Trần Văn Tùng. *Rêves d'un campagnard annamite*. Paris: Mercure de France, 1940.

Trang-Gaspard, Thu. "Contribution à l'étude de la vie et de l'oeuvre de Phan Châu Trinh (1872–1926). PhD dissertation, Université de Paris VII, 1978.

———. *Hồ Chí Minh à Paris, 1917–1923*. Paris: L'Harmattan, 1992.

Trinh Dinh Khai. *Décolonisation du Viêt Nam: un avocat témoigne*. Paris: L'Harmattan, 1994.

Trịnh Văn Thảo. *L'école française en Indochine*. Paris: Karthala, 1995.

———. "Le retour des rapatriés d'Indochine. L'expérience des centres d'accueil (1954–1960)." In *Marseille et le choc des décolonisations*, edited by Jean-Jacques Jordi and Emile Temime, 29–38. Marseille: Edisud, 1996.

———. *Les compagnons de route de Ho Chi Minh: histoire d'un engagement intellectuelle au Viêt-Nam*. Paris: Karthala, 2004.

Trương Như Tảng. *A Vietcong Memoir*. New York: Harcourt, Brace and Jovanovich, 1985.

Tully, John. *France on the Mekong: A History of the Protectorate in Cambodia, 1863–1953*. Lanham, MD: University Press of America, 2002.

Van der Veer, Peter. "Colonial Cosmopolitanism." In *Conceiving Cosmopolitanism: Theory, Context, and Practice*, edited by Steven Vertovec and Robin Cohen, 165–79. New York: Oxford University Press, 2002.

Vanmai, Jean. *Centenaire de la présence vietnamienne en Nouvelle-Calédonie*. Nouméa: Points d'histoire, 1991.

Vinh Sinh. *Phan Bội Châu and the Đông Du Movement*. New Haven: Council on Southeast Asian Studies, Yale Center for International and Area Studies, 1988.

———, ed. *Phan Châu Trinh and His Political Writings*. Ithaca, NY: Cornell University Southeast Asia Program Publications, 2009.

Vu, Tuong. *Vietnam's Communist Revolution: The Power and Limits of Ideology*. New York: Cambridge University Press, 2017.

Vũ Trọng Phụng. *Dumb Luck*. Edited by Peter Zinoman. Translated by Nguyễn Nguyệt Cầm and Peter Zinoman. Ann Arbor: University of Michigan Press, 2002.

Vu-Hill, Kimloan. *Coolies into Rebels: Impact of World War I on French Indochina*. Paris: Les Indes Savantes, 2011.

Wilcox, Wynn. *Allegories of the Vietnamese Past*. New Haven: Yale Southeast Asia Monograph Series, 2011.

Wilder, Gary. *The French Imperial Nation-State: Negritude and Colonial Humanism between the Two World Wars*. Chicago: University of Chicago Press, 2005.

Yeager, Jack. *The Vietnamese Novel in French*. Hanover: University Press of New Hampshire, 1987.

Zinoman, Peter. "Provincial Cosmopolitanism: Vũ Trọng Phụng's Literary Engagements." In *Traveling Nation-Makers: Transnational Flows and Movements in the Making of Modern Southeast Asia*, edited by Caroline Hau and Kasian Tejapira, 126–52. Singapore and Kyoto: Kyoto University Press, 2011.

———. *Vietnamese Colonial Republican: The Political Vision of Vũ Trọng Phụng*. Berkeley: University of California Press, 2013.

Founded in 1893,
UNIVERSITY OF CALIFORNIA PRESS
publishes bold, progressive books and journals
on topics in the arts, humanities, social sciences,
and natural sciences—with a focus on social
justice issues—that inspire thought and action
among readers worldwide.

The UC PRESS FOUNDATION
raises funds to uphold the press's vital role
as an independent, nonprofit publisher, and
receives philanthropic support from a wide
range of individuals and institutions—and from
committed readers like you. To learn more, visit
ucpress.edu/supportus.